GIRL GENIUS

A Gaslamp Fantasy
with
ADVENTURE, ROMANCE & MAD SCIENCE

OMNIBUS EDITION VOLUME ONE

BEETLEBURG CLANK • AIRSHIP CITY • MONSTER ENGINE

STORY BY PHIL & KAJA FOGLIO
•
ART BY PHIL FOGLIO
WITH BRIAN SNŌDDY, MARK McNABB & LAURIE E. SMITH
•
COVER COLORS BY CHEYENNE WRIGHT

AIRSHIP
ENTERTAINMENT

Wash...

READ MORE COMICS ONLINE AT:

WWW.GIRL GENIUS.NET

MONDAY · WEDNESDAY · FRIDAY

ALSO AVAILABLE IN
DELUXE EDITION GRAPHIC NOVELS

GIRL GENIUS VOLUME ONE:
AGATHA HETERODYNE AND THE BEETLEBURG CLANK

GIRL GENIUS VOLUME TWO:
AGATHA HETERODYNE AND THE AIRSHIP CITY

GIRL GENIUS VOLUME THREE:
AGATHA HETERODYNE AND THE MONSTER ENGINE

GIRL GENIUS VOLUME FOUR:
AGATHA HETERODYNE AND THE CIRCUS OF DREAMS

GIRL GENIUS VOLUME FIVE:
AGATHA HETERODYNE AND THE CLOCKWORK PRINCESS

Girl Genius® is published by:
Airship Entertainment™, a happy part of Studio Foglio, LLC
2400 NW 80th St #129 Seattle WA 98117-4449, USA

Girl Genius is a registered trademark of Studio Foglio, LLC. Girl Genius, the Girl Genius logos, Studio Foglio and the Studio Foglio logo, Airship Entertainment, Airship Books & Comics & the Airship logo, the Jägermonsters, Mr. Tock, the Heterodyne trilobite badge, the Jägermonsters' monster badge, the Wulfenbach badge, the Spark, Agatha Heterodyne, the Heterodyne Boys, Transylvania Polygnostic, the Transylvania Polygnostic University arms, the Secret Cypher Society, Krosp, Castle Wulfenbach, Castle Heterodyne and all the Girl Genius characters are © & ™ 2000 Studio Foglio.

All material ©2001–2006 Studio Foglio. All rights reserved. No part of this book may be reproduced in any form (including electronic) without permission in writing from the publisher except for brief passages in connection with a review.

This is a work of fiction and any resemblance herein to actual persons, events or institutions is purely coincidental.

Story by Phil & Kaja Foglio. Pencils by Phil Foglio. *Beetleburg Clank* inks by Brian Snoddy. Colors by Mark Mc. Nabb (pages 93-192, 195-252, 254-266) and Laurie E. Smith (Pages 253, 267-317). Art on pages 8 and 318 by Kaja Foglio. Selected spot illustrations colored by Kaja Foglio and Cheyenne Wright. Cover colors by Cheyenne Wright. Logos, Lettering, Artist Bullying & Book Design by Kaja.

The story collected in this omnibus is also available in full color as Books 1-3 of the Girl Genius series: *Agatha Heterodyne and the Beetleburg Clank*, *Agatha Heterodyne and the Airship City*, and *Agatha Heterodyne and the Monster Engine*.

ISBN: 978-1-890856-40-3 • Omnibus Edition First Printing: November 2006 • PRINTED IN HONG KONG

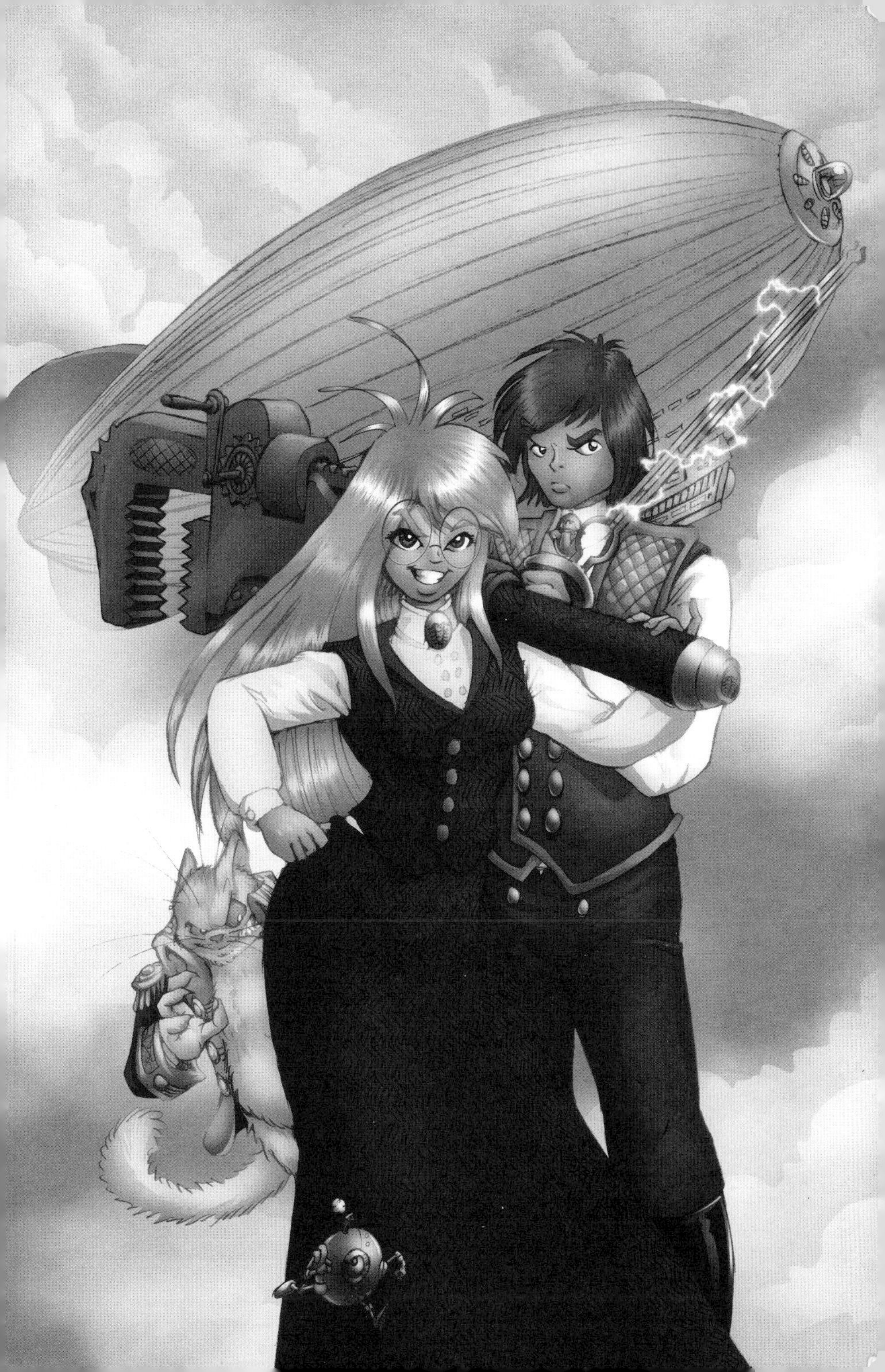

CONTENTS:

This is a story about Science. Or Magic. Or possibly both.

There have always been those with the Spark—people who seem to be able to tinker with the laws of physics as we know them. This sort of person can be the worst of evil mad scientists or a tremendous force for Good.

The last members of the great house Heterodyne stood as the models against which all other heroes of their time were measured. With a collection of like-minded companions, they travelled the globe negotiating peace, stopping monsters and shutting down doomsday devices. Their exploits were the stuff of legends.

And then they disappeared. Our story begins some years later.

SOME CHARACTERS

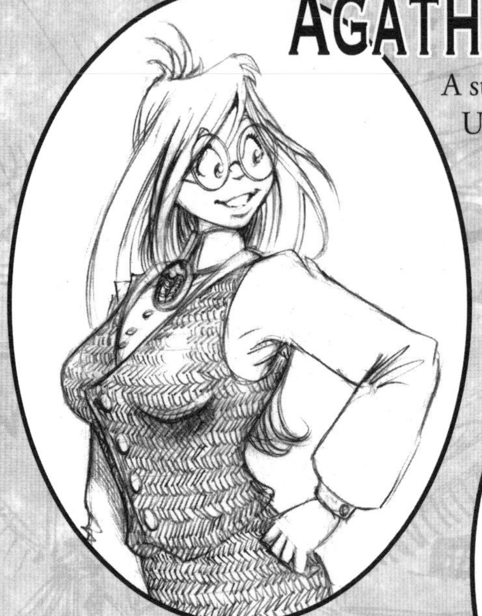

AGATHA CLAY

A student at Transylvania Polygnostic University. Agatha studies hard, but she has trouble concentrating and nothing she builds ever *works.* That's all about to change…

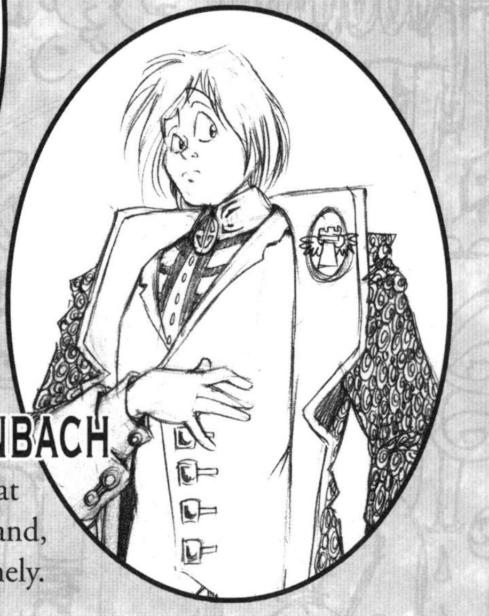

GILGAMESH WULFENBACH

The Baron's son has been away at school for years. He's brilliant, and, now that he's home, kind of lonely.

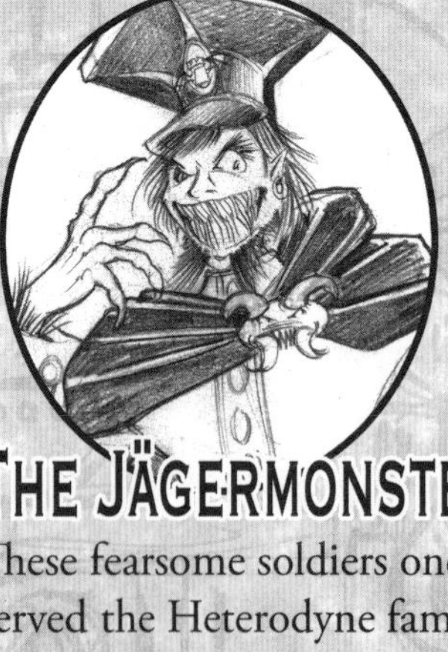

KROSP I

The Emperor of All Cats.

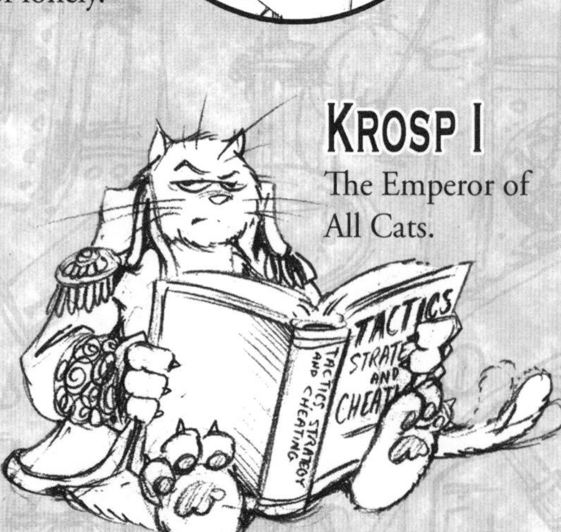
TACTICS, STRATEGY AND CHEATING

THE JÄGERMONSTERS

These fearsome soldiers once served the Heterodyne family. Now, they work for the Baron.

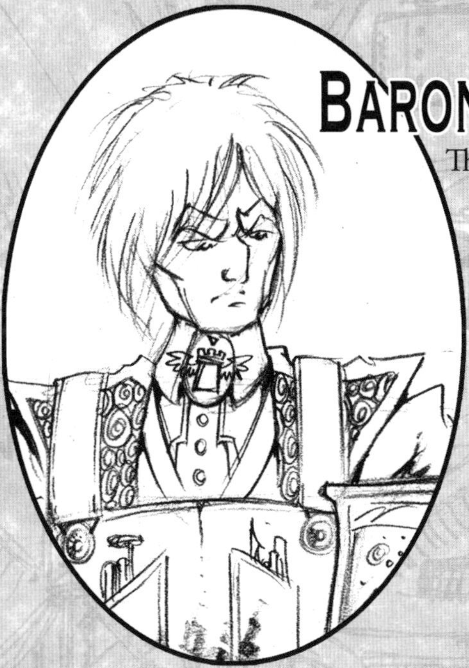

Baron Wulfenbach

The Baron rules the land and keeps the peace–mostly because no one else can. He'd much rather be working in his lab.

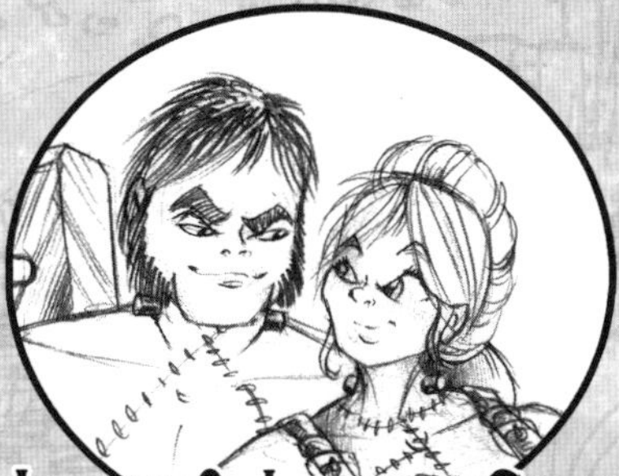

Adam & Lilith Clay

The construct couple who raised Agatha. She thinks of them as her parents.

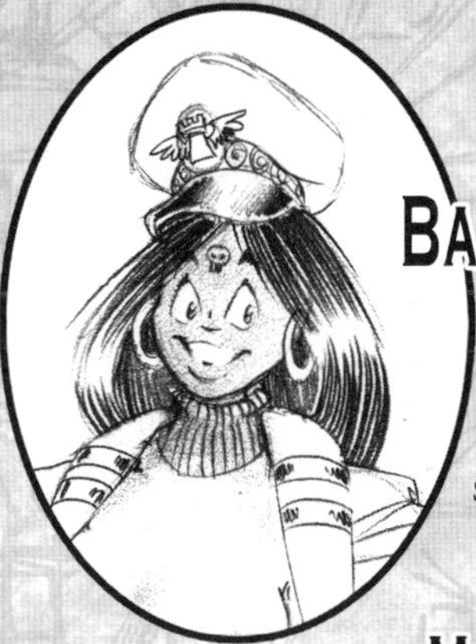

Bangladesh DuPree

Bang was a ruthless pirate queen, but then someone wiped out her fortress, and all her pirates. Now she works for the Baron.

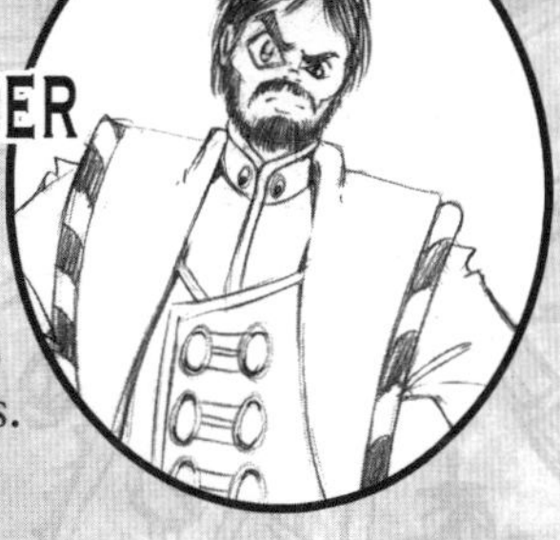

Moloch von Zinzer

A down-on-his-luck soldier and part-time thief. Moloch and his brother Omar have been making their way across the Baron's lands.

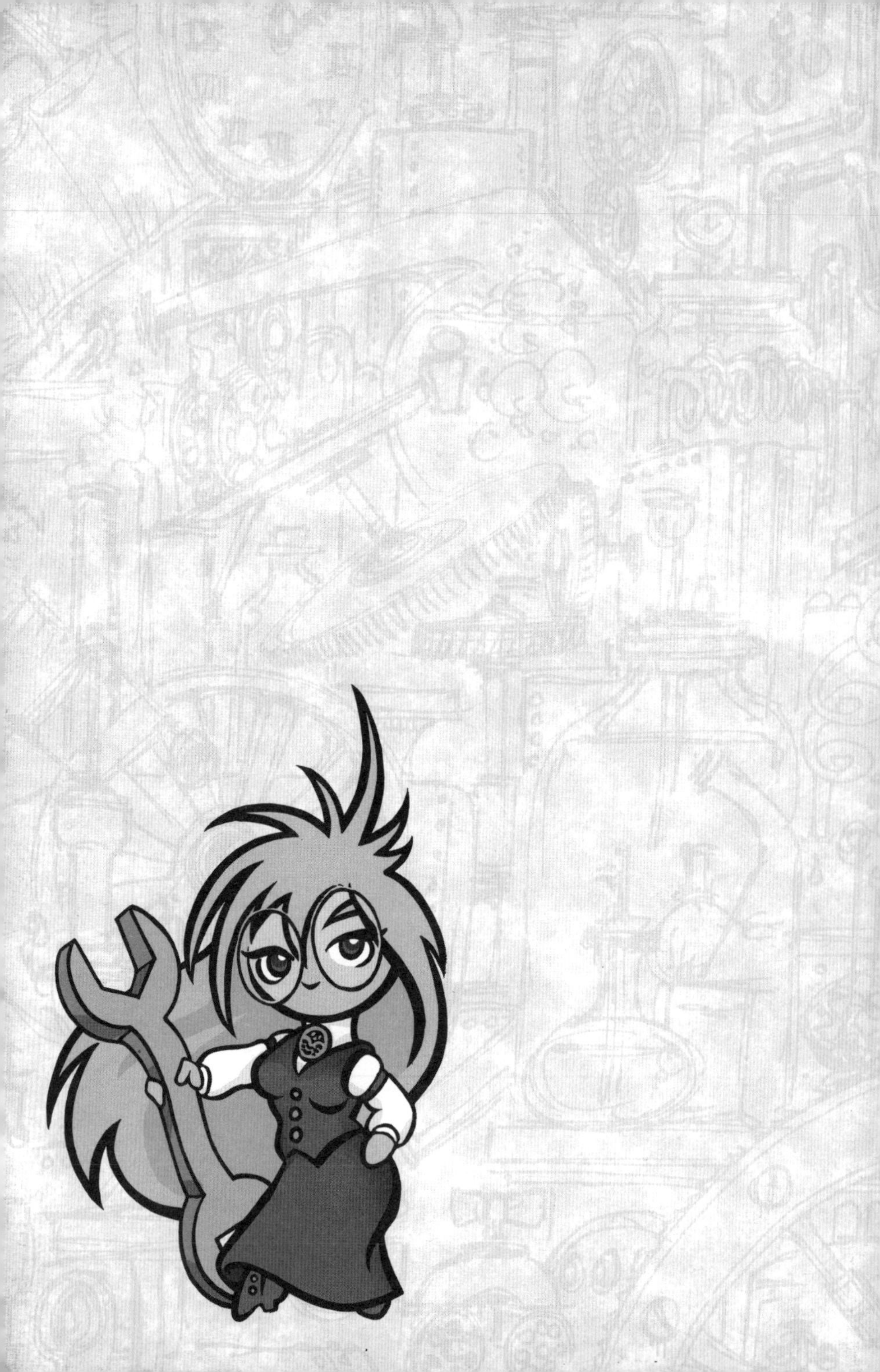

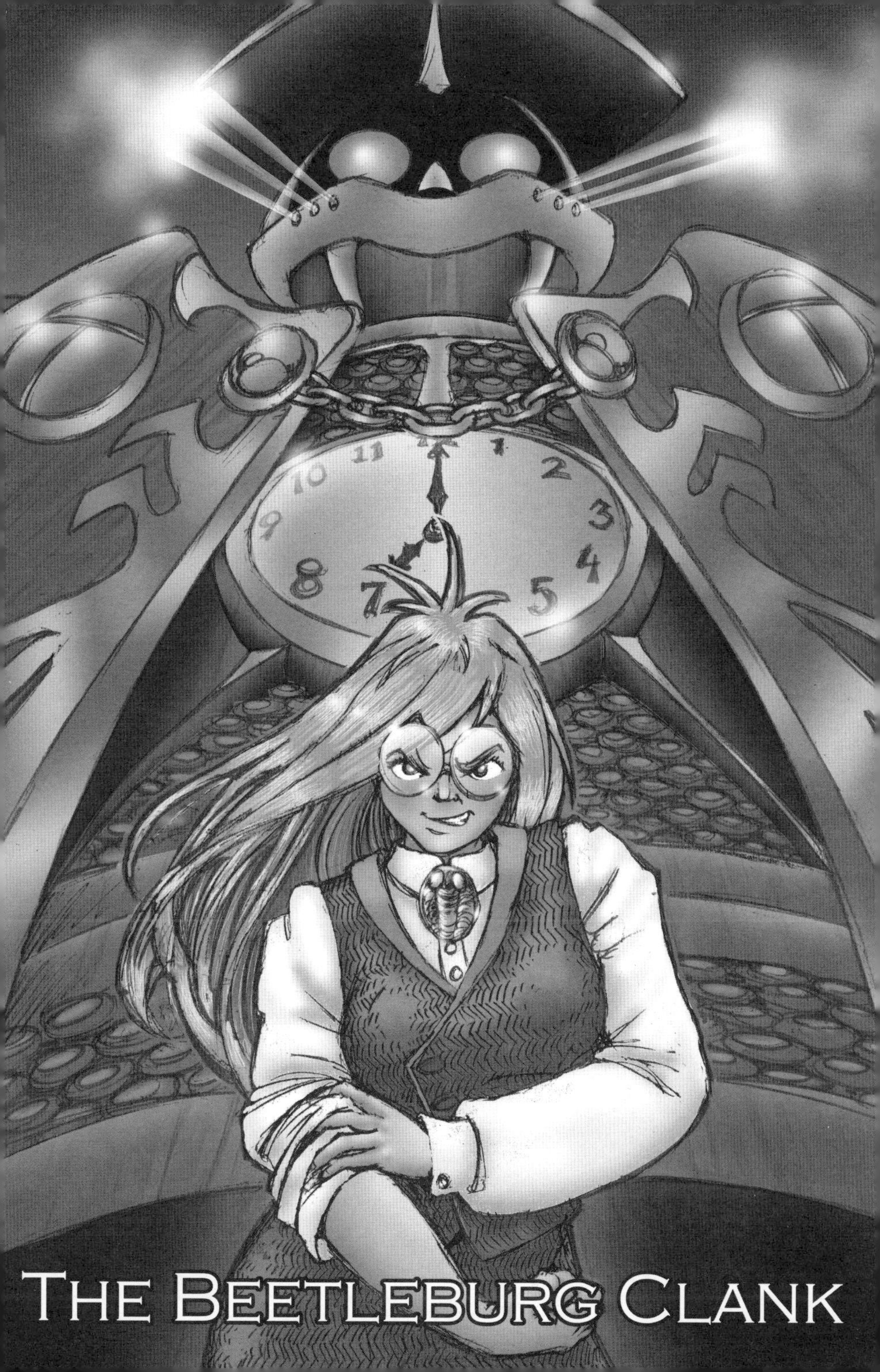
THE BEETLEBURG CLANK

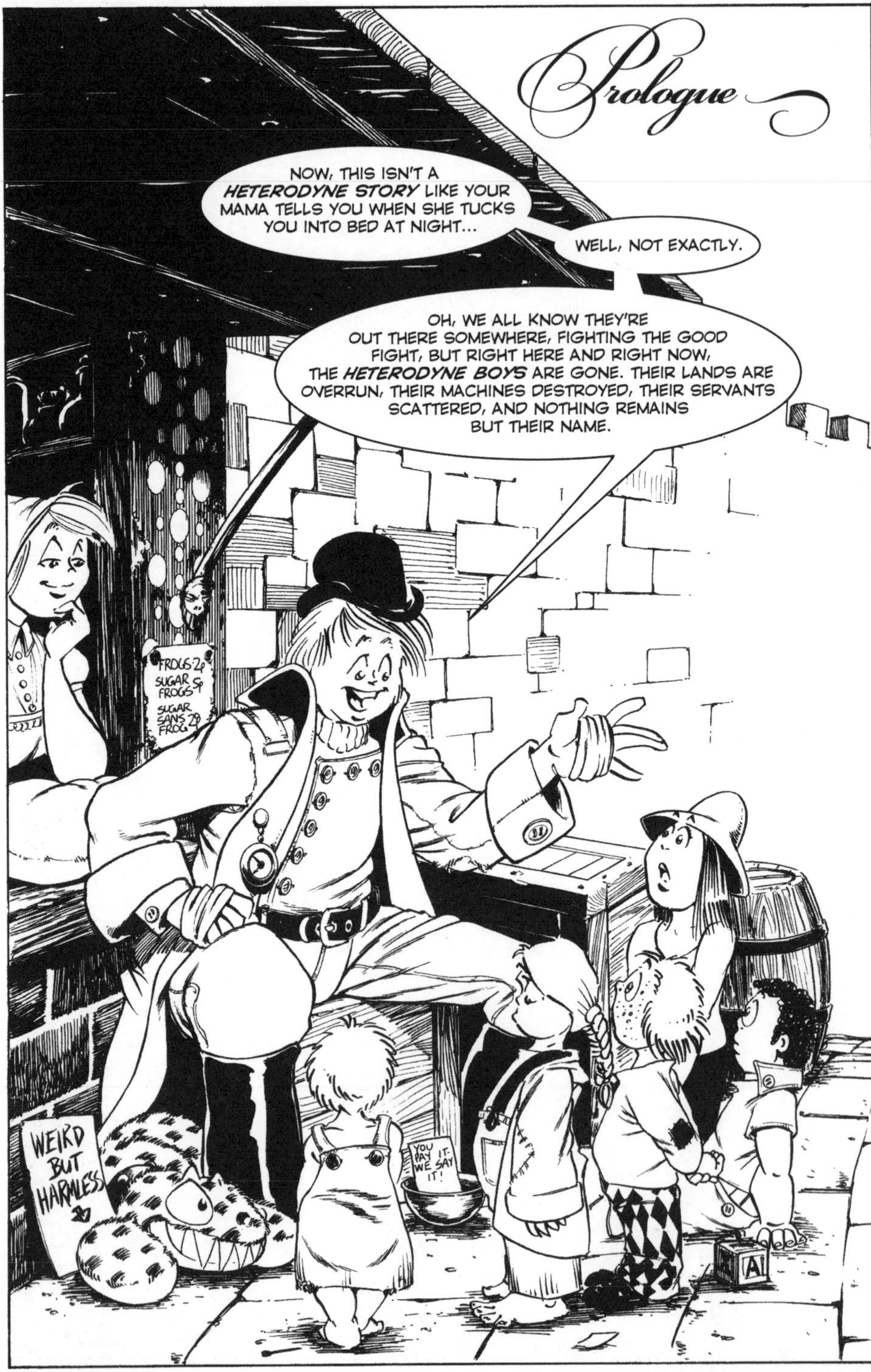
Prologue
NOW, THIS ISN'T A *HETERODYNE STORY* LIKE YOUR MAMA TELLS YOU WHEN SHE TUCKS YOU INTO BED AT NIGHT...
WELL, NOT EXACTLY.
OH, WE ALL KNOW THEY'RE OUT THERE SOMEWHERE, FIGHTING THE GOOD FIGHT, BUT RIGHT HERE AND RIGHT NOW, THE *HETERODYNE BOYS* ARE GONE. THEIR LANDS ARE OVERRUN, THEIR MACHINES DESTROYED, THEIR SERVANTS SCATTERED, AND NOTHING REMAINS BUT THEIR NAME.
FROGS 2p
SUGAR FROGS 5p
SUGAR SANS FROG 2p
WEIRD BUT HARMLESS
YOU PAY IT- WE SAY IT!
A

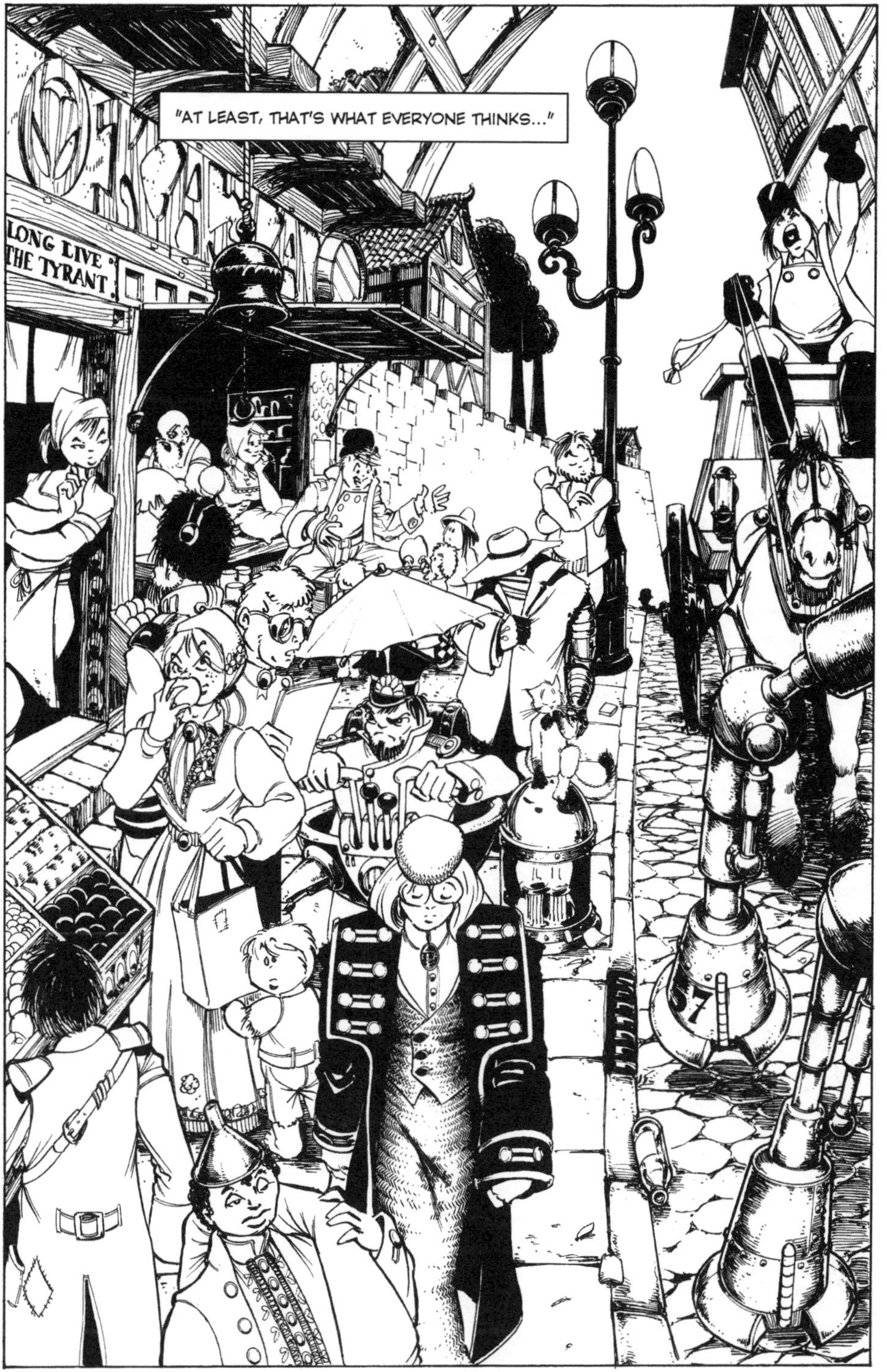
"AT LEAST, THAT'S WHAT EVERYONE THINKS..."
LONG LIVE THE TYRANT.
57

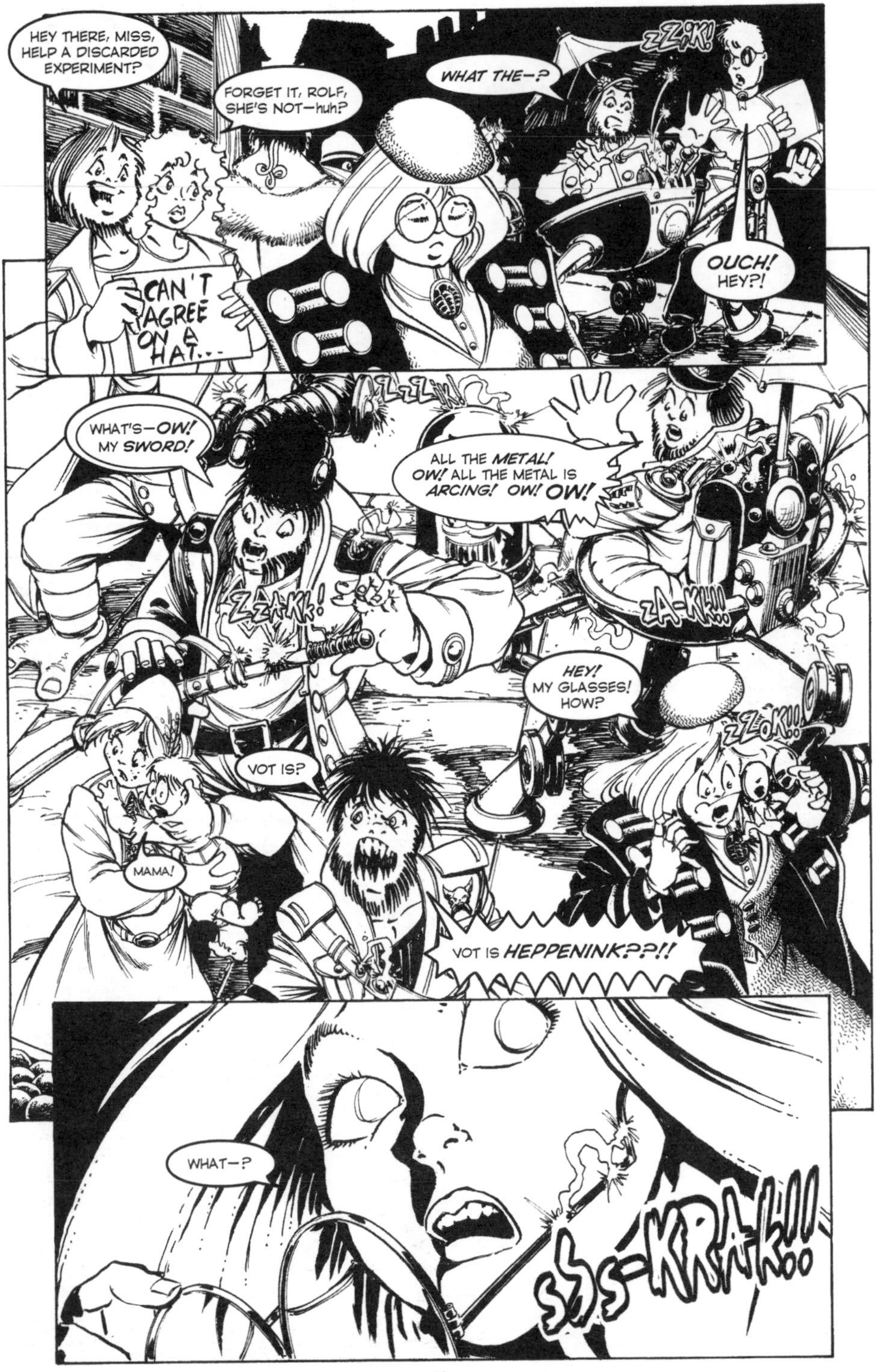
HEY THERE, MISS, HELP A DISCARDED EXPERIMENT?
FORGET IT, ROLF, SHE'S NOT—huh?
CAN'T AGREE ON A HAT...
ZZIK!
WHAT THE—?
OUCH! HEY?!
WHAT'S—OW! MY SWORD!
ALL THE METAL! OW! ALL THE METAL IS ARCING! OW! OW!
ZZAKK!
ZA-KK!!
HEY! MY GLASSES! HOW?
ZZOK!!
VOT IS?
MAMA!
VOT IS HEPPENINK??!!
WHAT—?
SSS-KRAK!!!

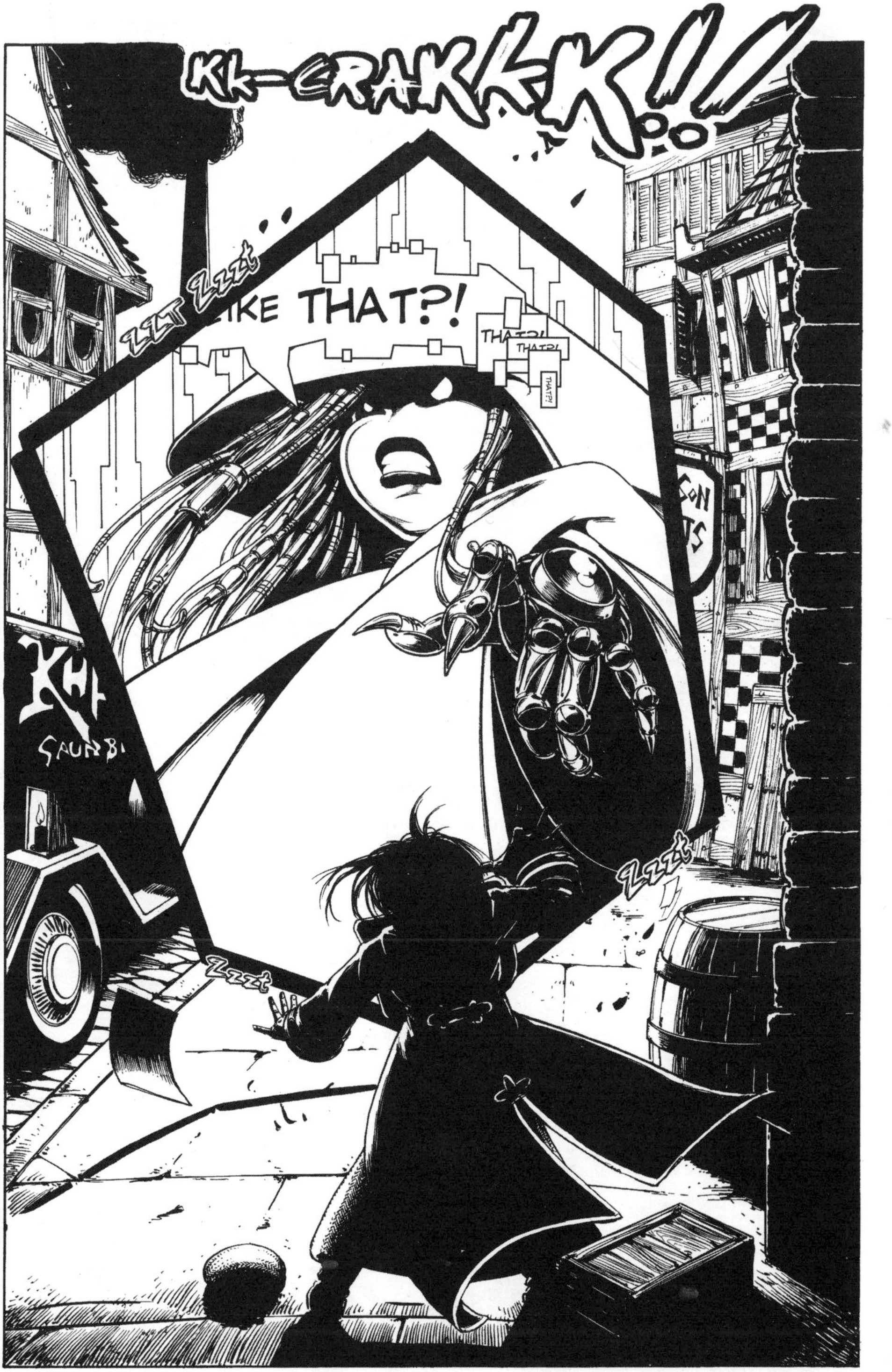
KK-CRAKKK!!
ZZZT ZZZT
LIKE THAT?!
THAT?!
THAT?!
THAT?!
ZZZT
ZZZT

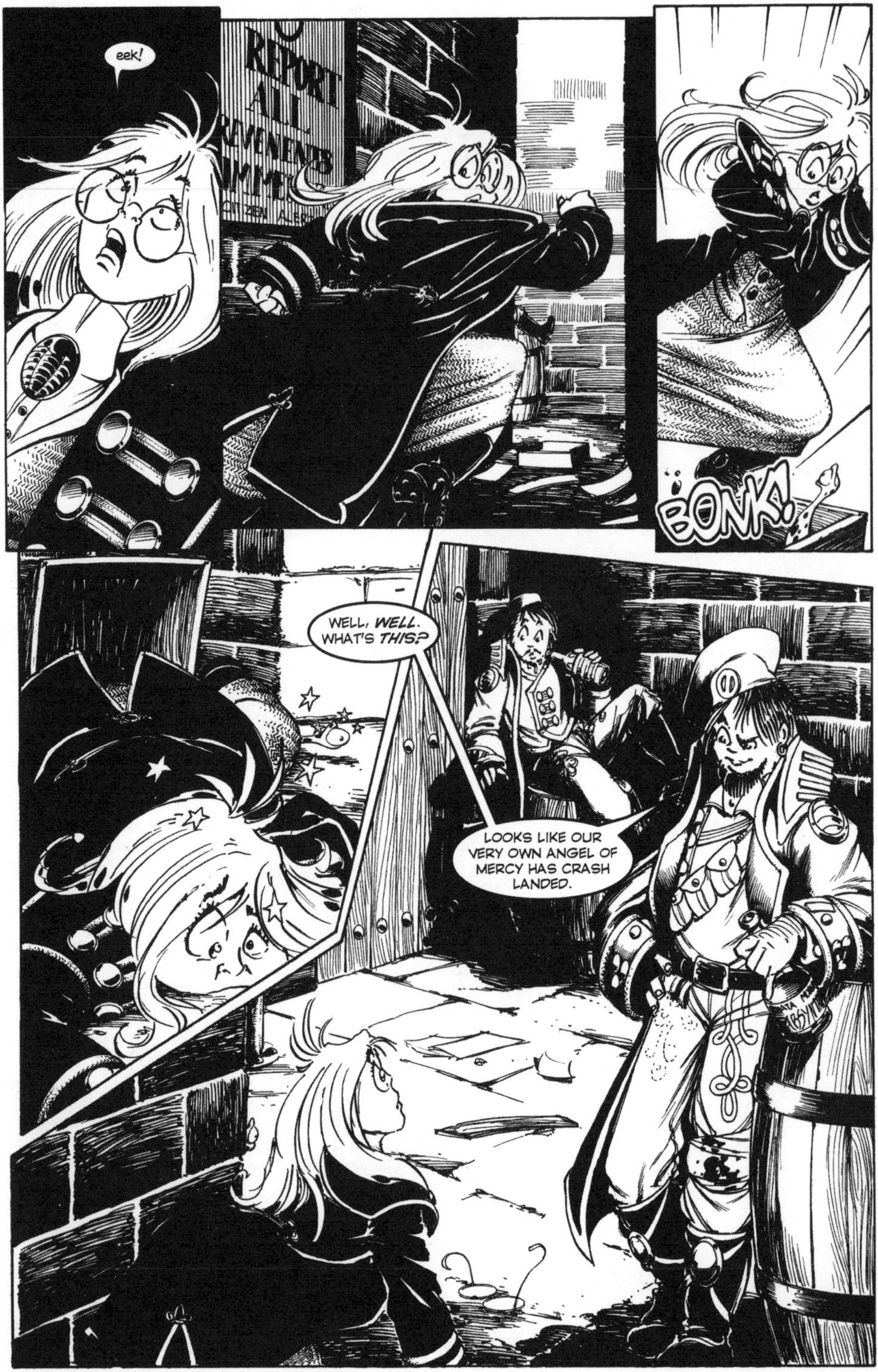
eek!
REPORT
ALL
BONK!
WELL, *WELL*. WHAT'S *THIS?*
LOOKS LIKE OUR VERY OWN ANGEL OF MERCY HAS CRASH LANDED.

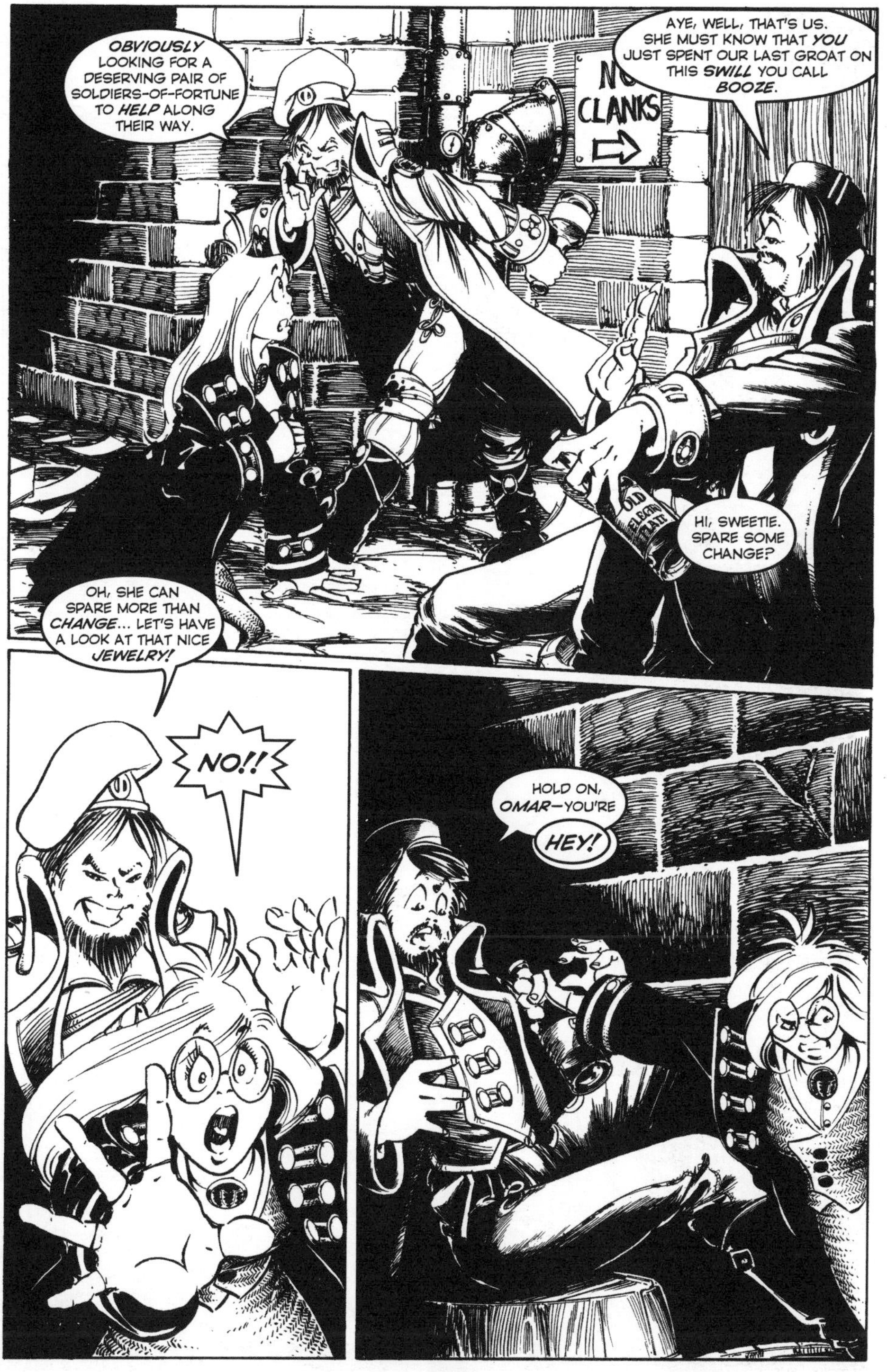
OBVIOUSLY LOOKING FOR A DESERVING PAIR OF SOLDIERS-OF-FORTUNE TO HELP ALONG THEIR WAY.
AYE, WELL, THAT'S US. SHE MUST KNOW THAT YOU JUST SPENT OUR LAST GROAT ON THIS SWILL YOU CALL BOOZE.
NO CLANKS
HI, SWEETIE. SPARE SOME CHANGE?
OH, SHE CAN SPARE MORE THAN CHANGE... LET'S HAVE A LOOK AT THAT NICE JEWELRY!
NO!!
HOLD ON, OMAR—YOU'RE
HEY!

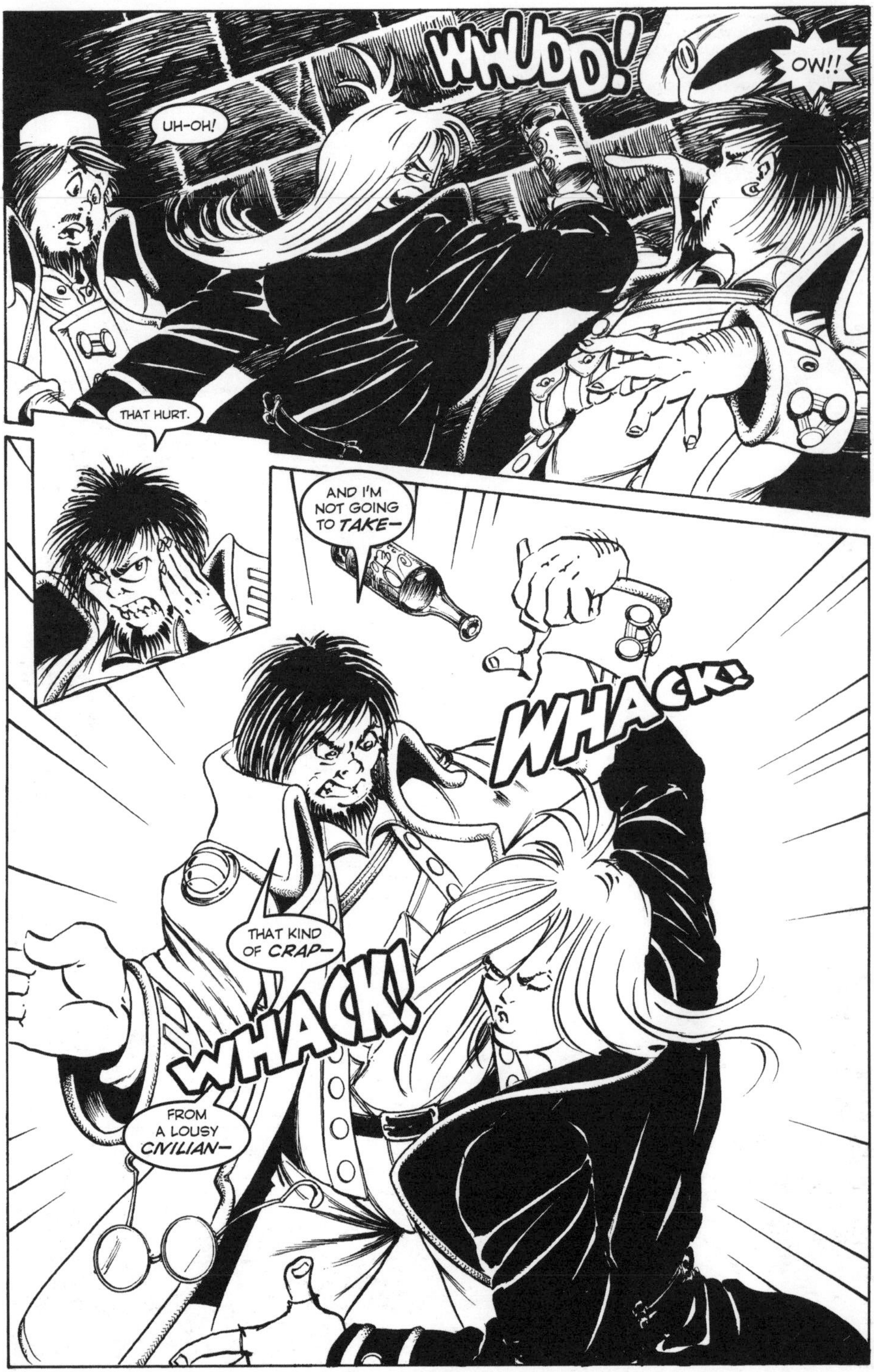
WHUDD!
OW!!
UH-OH!
THAT HURT.
AND I'M NOT GOING TO TAKE—
WHACK!
THAT KIND OF CRAP—
WHACK!
FROM A LOUSY CIVILIAN—

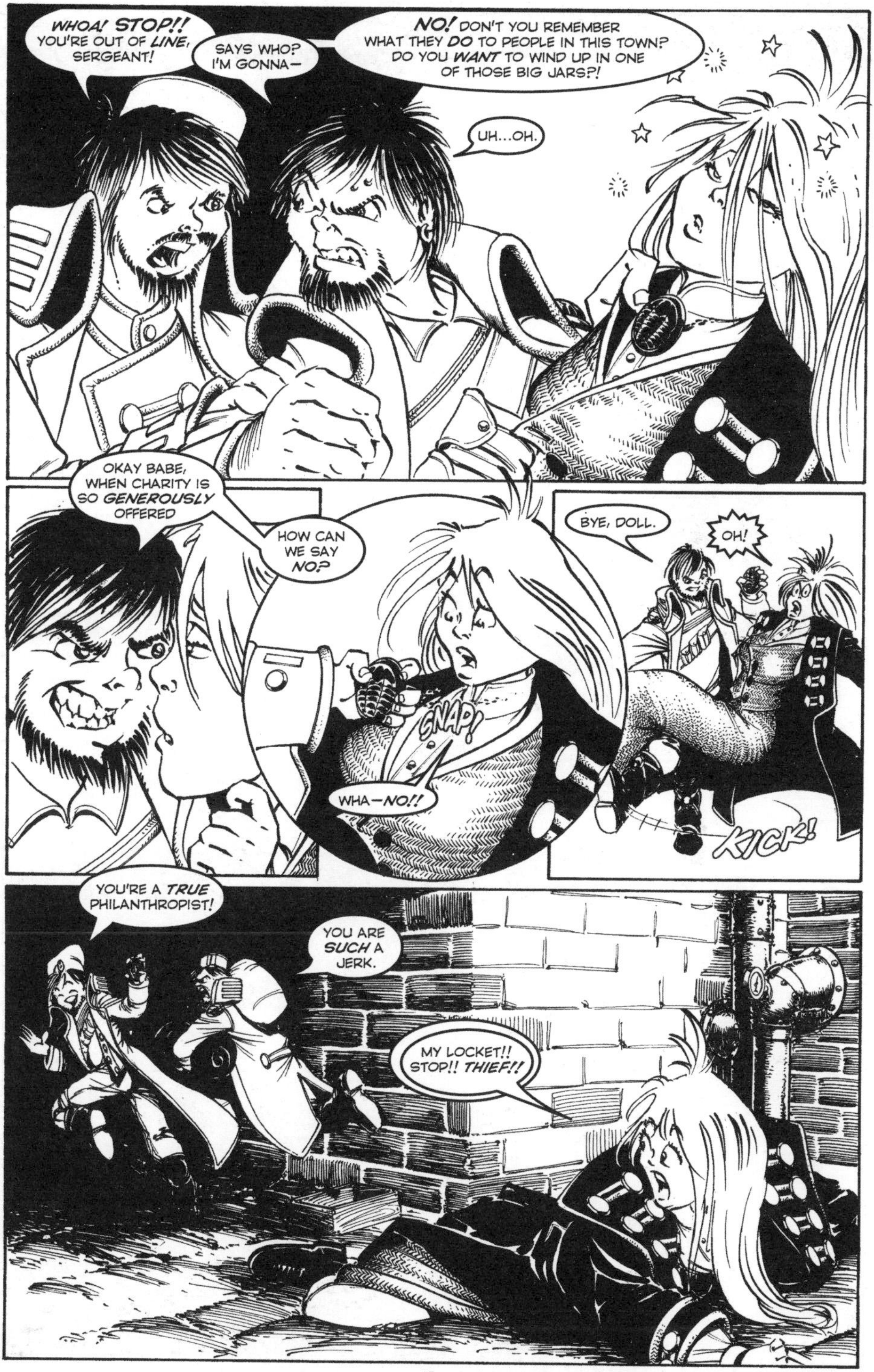
WHOA! STOP!! YOU'RE OUT OF LINE, SERGEANT!
SAYS WHO? I'M GONNA—
NO! DON'T YOU REMEMBER WHAT THEY DO TO PEOPLE IN THIS TOWN? DO YOU WANT TO WIND UP IN ONE OF THOSE BIG JARS?!
UH...OH.
OKAY BABE, WHEN CHARITY IS SO GENEROUSLY OFFERED
HOW CAN WE SAY NO?
SNAP!
WHA—NO!!
BYE, DOLL.
OH!
KICK!
YOU'RE A TRUE PHILANTHROPIST!
YOU ARE SUCH A JERK.
MY LOCKET!! STOP!! THIEF!!

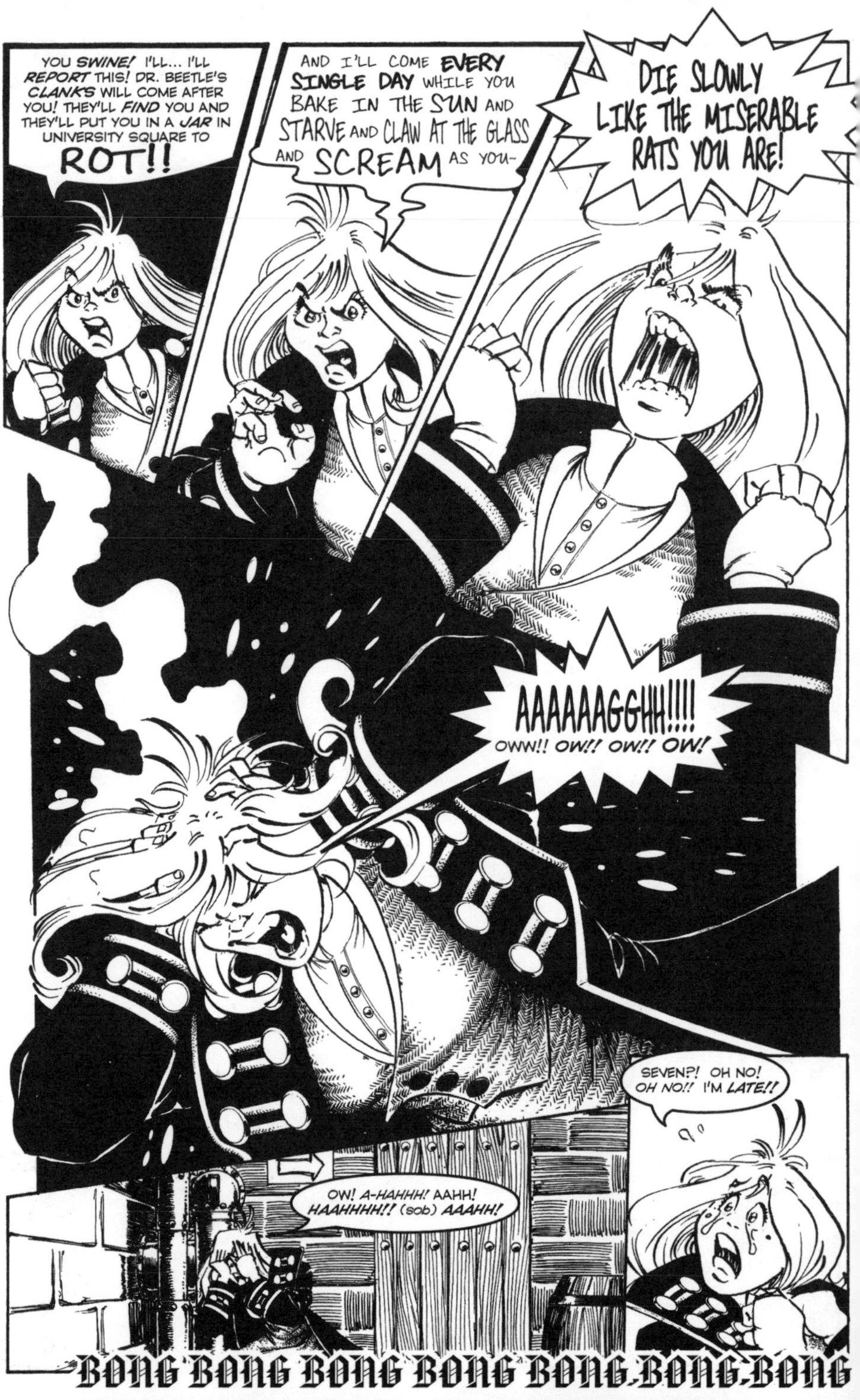
YOU SWINE! I'LL... I'LL REPORT THIS! DR. BEETLE'S CLANKS WILL COME AFTER YOU! THEY'LL FIND YOU AND THEY'LL PUT YOU IN A JAR IN UNIVERSITY SQUARE TO ROT!!
AND I'LL COME EVERY SINGLE DAY WHILE YOU BAKE IN THE SUN AND STARVE AND CLAW AT THE GLASS AND SCREAM AS YOU-
DIE SLOWLY LIKE THE MISERABLE RATS YOU ARE!
AAAAAAGGHH!!!!! OWW!! OW!! OW!! OW!
OW! A-HAHHH! AAHH! HAAHHHH!! (sob) AAAHH!
SEVEN?! OH NO! OH NO!! I'M LATE!!
BONG BONG BONG BONG BONG BONG BONG

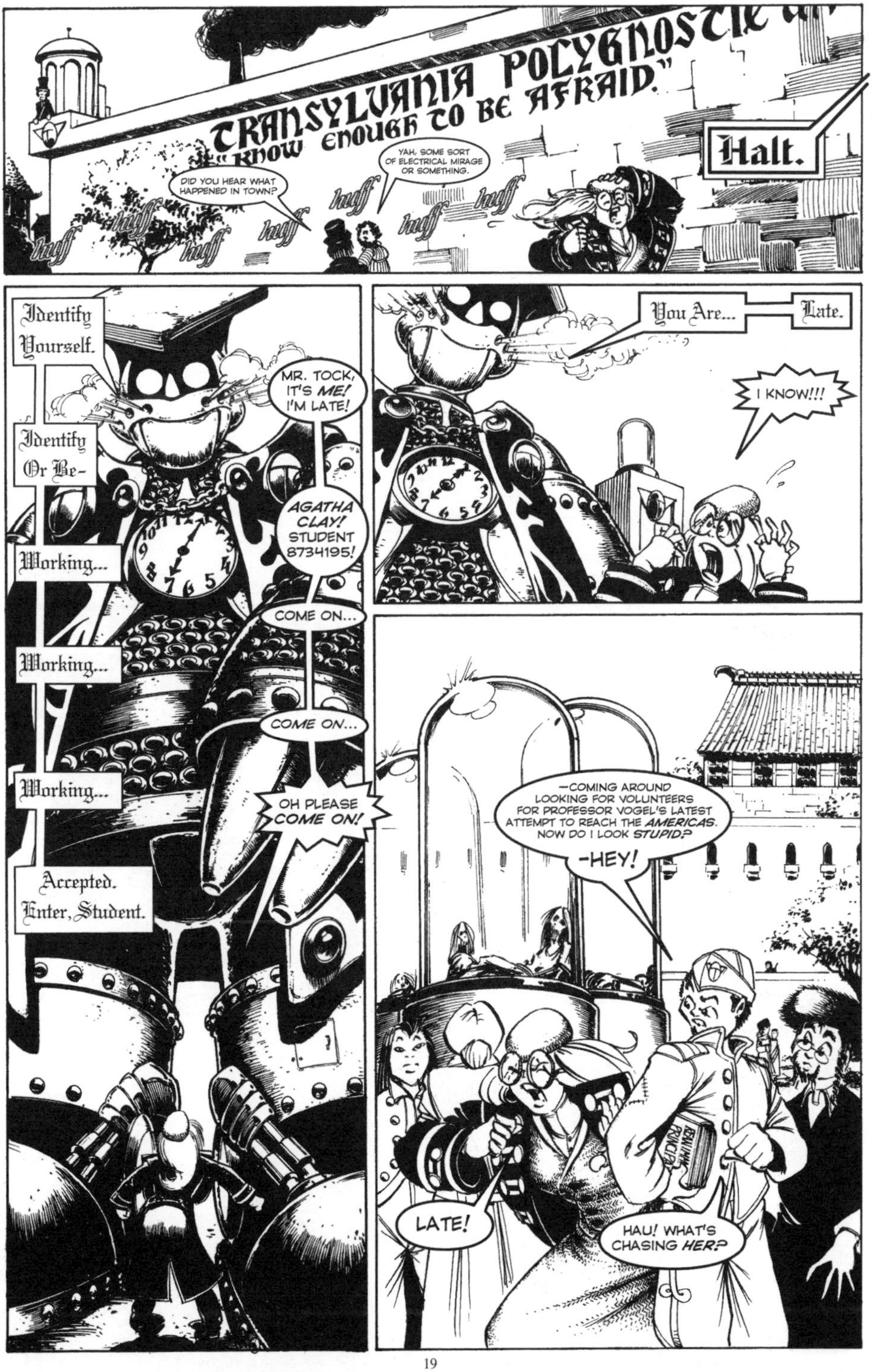

TRANSYLVANIA POLYGNOSTIC
"KNOW ENOUGH TO BE AFRAID."
DID YOU HEAR WHAT HAPPENED IN TOWN?
YAH, SOME SORT OF ELECTRICAL MIRAGE OR SOMETHING.
huff huff huff huff huff huff huff huff
Halt.
Identify Yourself.
MR. TOCK, IT'S ME! I'M LATE!
Identify Or Be-
AGATHA CLAY! STUDENT 8734195!
Working...
COME ON...
Working...
COME ON...
Working...
OH PLEASE COME ON!
Accepted. Enter, Student.
You Are... Late.
I KNOW!!!
—COMING AROUND LOOKING FOR VOLUNTEERS FOR PROFESSOR VOGEL'S LATEST ATTEMPT TO REACH THE AMERICAS. NOW DO I LOOK STUPID?
-HEY!
LATE!
HAU! WHAT'S CHASING HER?

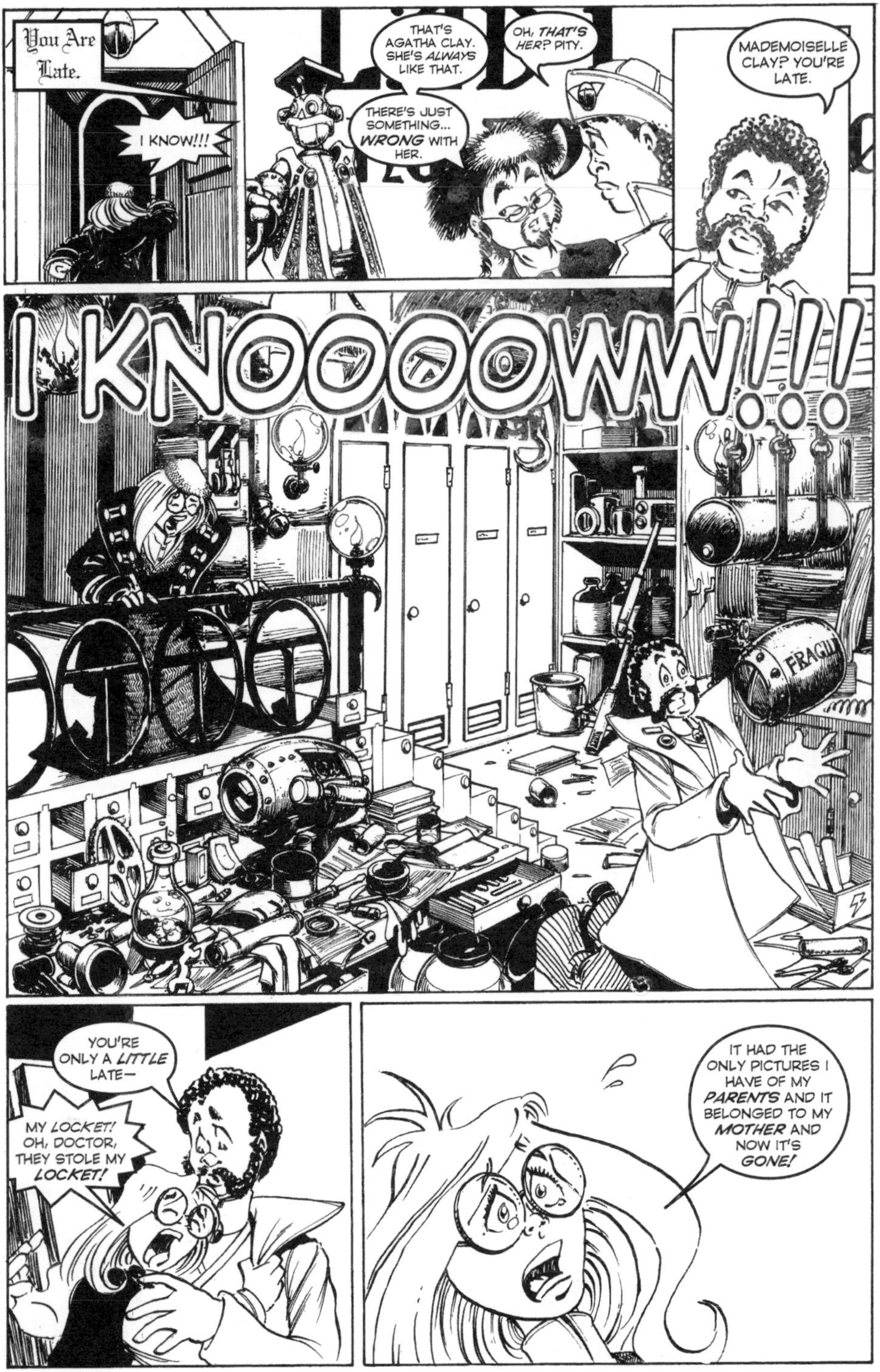
You Are Late.
I KNOW!!!
THAT'S AGATHA CLAY. SHE'S ALWAYS LIKE THAT.
THERE'S JUST SOMETHING... WRONG WITH HER.
OH, THAT'S HER? PITY.
MADEMOISELLE CLAY? YOU'RE LATE.
I KNOOOOWW!!!
YOU'RE ONLY A LITTLE LATE—
MY LOCKET! OH, DOCTOR, THEY STOLE MY LOCKET!
IT HAD THE ONLY PICTURES I HAVE OF MY PARENTS AND IT BELONGED TO MY MOTHER AND NOW IT'S GONE!

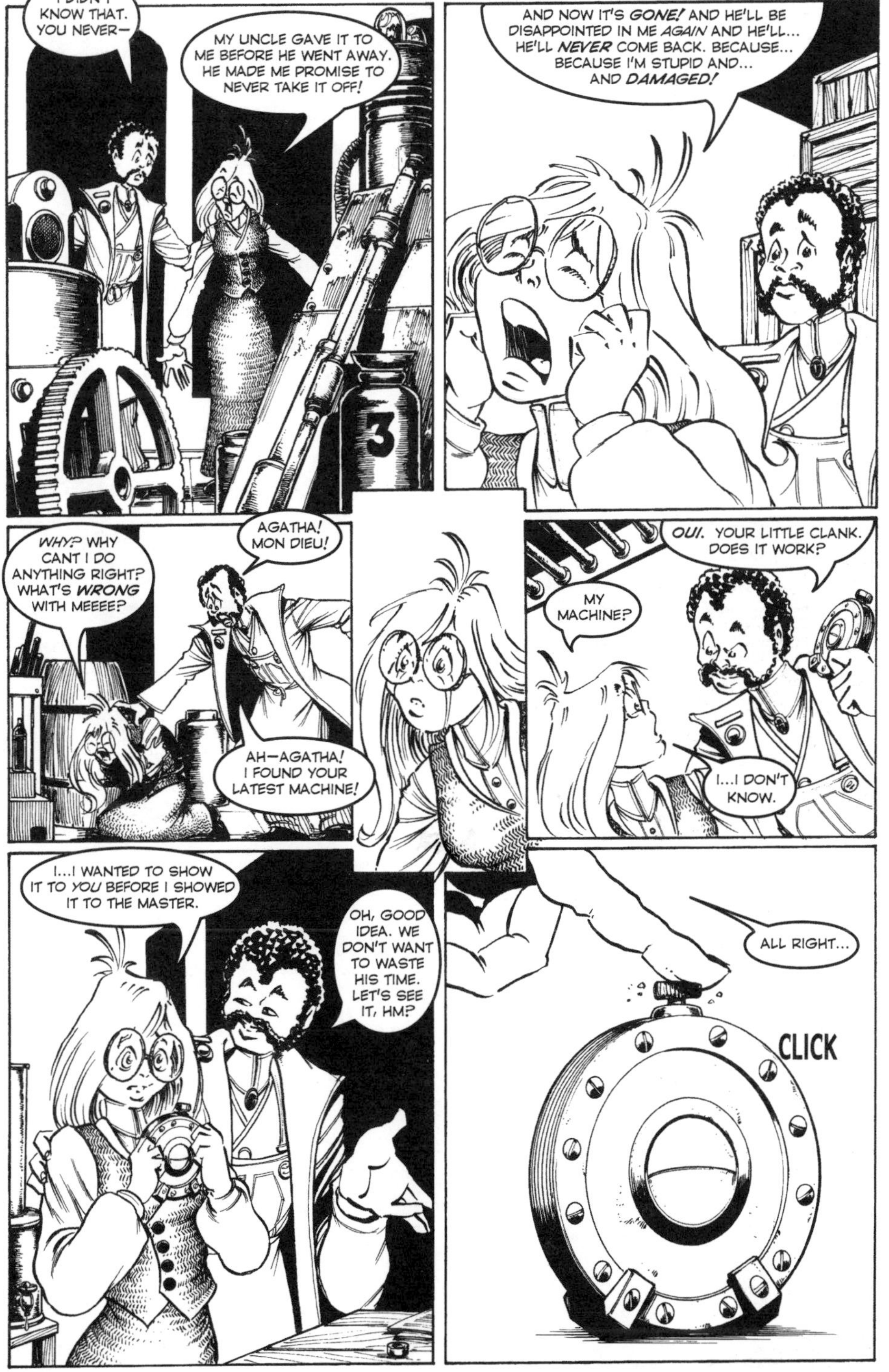
I DIDN'T KNOW THAT. YOU NEVER—
MY UNCLE GAVE IT TO ME BEFORE HE WENT AWAY. HE MADE ME PROMISE TO NEVER TAKE IT OFF!
AND NOW IT'S *GONE!* AND HE'LL BE DISAPPOINTED IN ME *AGAIN* AND HE'LL... HE'LL ***NEVER*** COME BACK. BECAUSE... BECAUSE I'M STUPID AND... AND ***DAMAGED!***
WHY? WHY CANT I DO ANYTHING RIGHT? WHAT'S ***WRONG*** WITH MEEEE?
AGATHA! MON DIEU!
AH—AGATHA! I FOUND YOUR LATEST MACHINE!
MY MACHINE?
OUI. YOUR LITTLE CLANK. DOES IT WORK?
I...I DON'T KNOW.
I...I WANTED TO SHOW IT TO *YOU* BEFORE I SHOWED IT TO THE MASTER.
OH, GOOD IDEA. WE DON'T WANT TO WASTE HIS TIME. LET'S SEE IT, HM?
ALL RIGHT...
CLICK

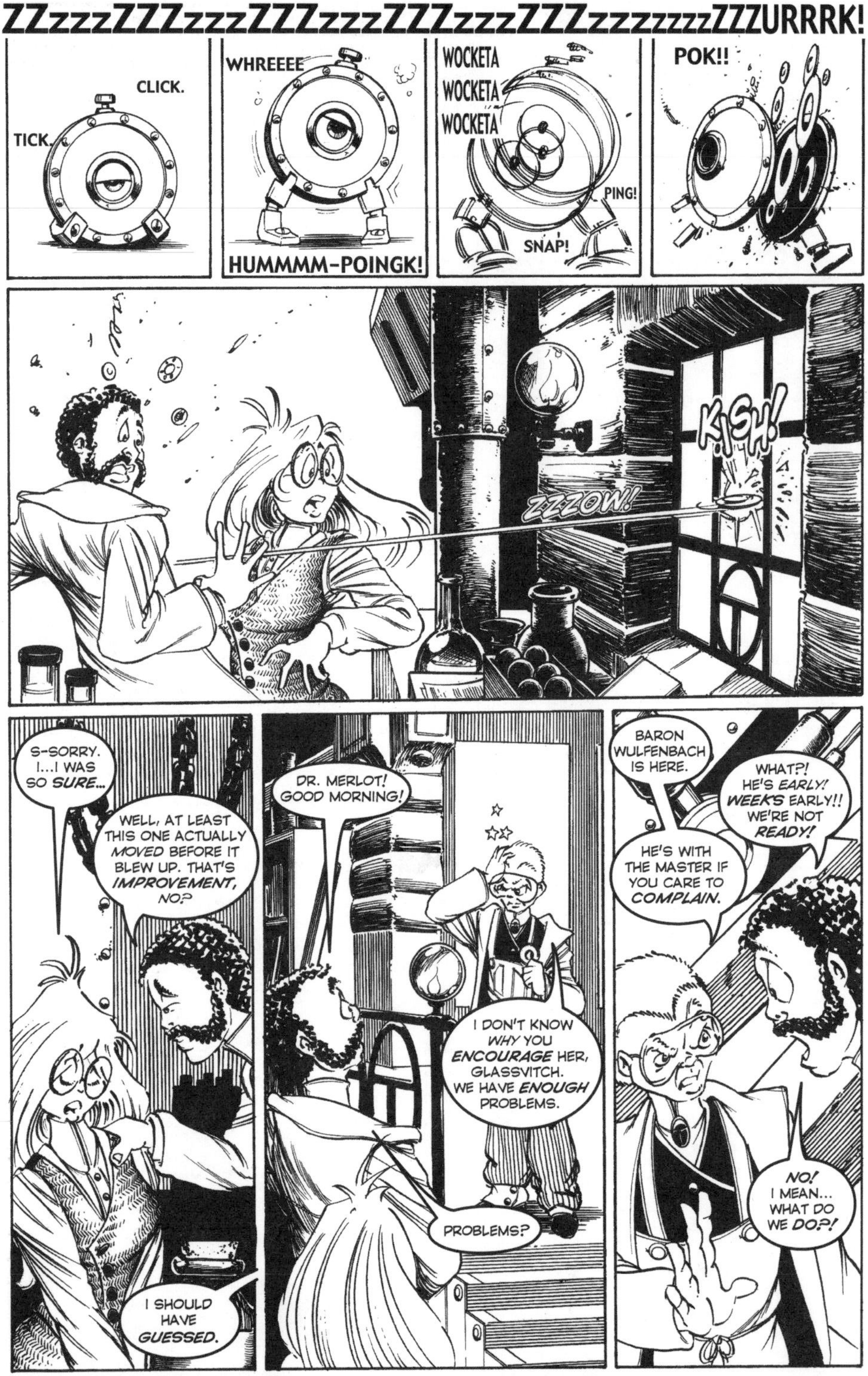
ZZzzzZZZzzzZZZzzzZZZzzzZZZzzzzzzzZZZURRRK!
TICK.
CLICK.
WHREEEE
HUMMMM-POINGK!
WOCKETA
WOCKETA
WOCKETA
PING!
SNAP!
POK!!
KISH!
ZZZOW!
S-SORRY. I...I WAS SO SURE...
WELL, AT LEAST THIS ONE ACTUALLY MOVED BEFORE IT BLEW UP. THAT'S IMPROVEMENT, NO?
I SHOULD HAVE GUESSED.
DR. MERLOT! GOOD MORNING!
I DON'T KNOW WHY YOU ENCOURAGE HER, GLASSVITCH. WE HAVE ENOUGH PROBLEMS.
PROBLEMS?
BARON WULFENBACH IS HERE.
WHAT?! HE'S EARLY! WEEKS EARLY!! WE'RE NOT READY!
HE'S WITH THE MASTER IF YOU CARE TO COMPLAIN.
NO! I MEAN... WHAT DO WE DO?!

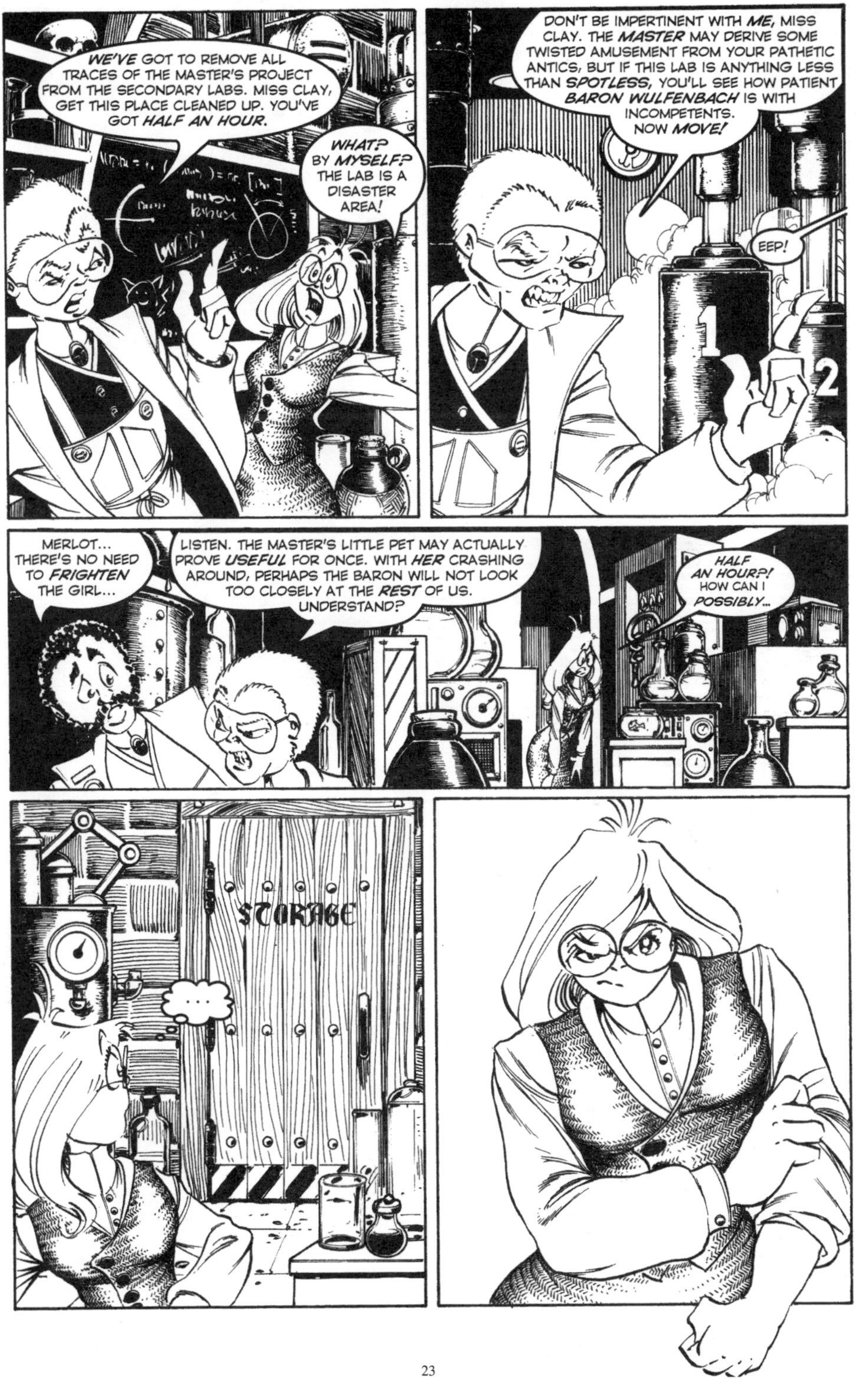
WE'VE GOT TO REMOVE ALL TRACES OF THE MASTER'S PROJECT FROM THE SECONDARY LABS. MISS CLAY, GET THIS PLACE CLEANED UP. YOU'VE GOT HALF AN HOUR.
WHAT? BY MYSELF? THE LAB IS A DISASTER AREA!
DON'T BE IMPERTINENT WITH ME, MISS CLAY. THE MASTER MAY DERIVE SOME TWISTED AMUSEMENT FROM YOUR PATHETIC ANTICS, BUT IF THIS LAB IS ANYTHING LESS THAN SPOTLESS, YOU'LL SEE HOW PATIENT BARON WULFENBACH IS WITH INCOMPETENTS. NOW MOVE!
EEP!
1
2
MERLOT... THERE'S NO NEED TO FRIGHTEN THE GIRL...
LISTEN. THE MASTER'S LITTLE PET MAY ACTUALLY PROVE USEFUL FOR ONCE. WITH HER CRASHING AROUND, PERHAPS THE BARON WILL NOT LOOK TOO CLOSELY AT THE REST OF US. UNDERSTAND?
HALF AN HOUR?! HOW CAN I POSSIBLY...
STORAGE
....

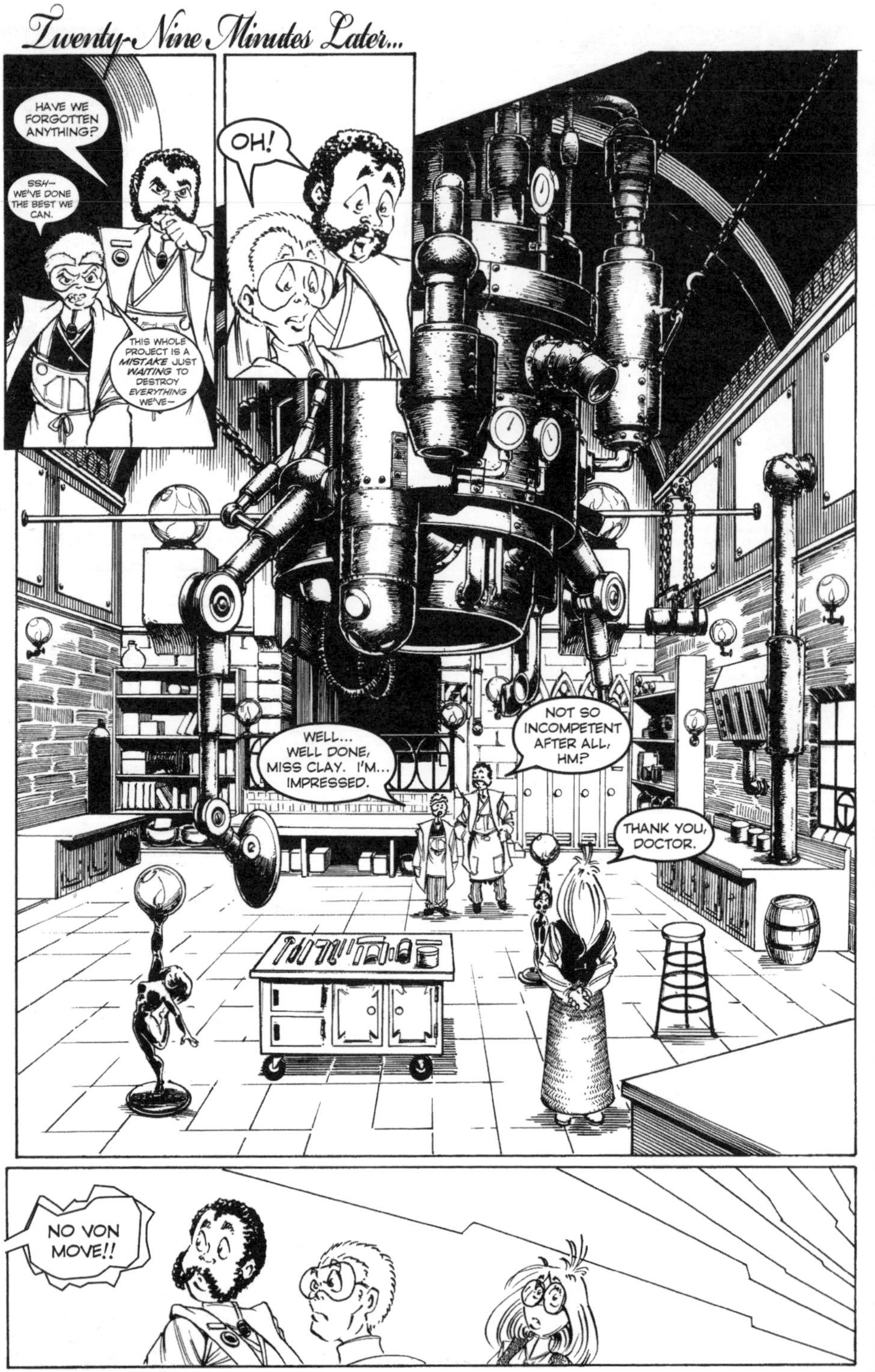
Twenty-Nine Minutes Later...
HAVE WE FORGOTTEN ANYTHING?
SSH— WE'VE DONE THE BEST WE CAN.
THIS WHOLE PROJECT IS A *MISTAKE* JUST *WAITING* TO DESTROY *EVERYTHING* WE'VE—
OH!
WELL... WELL DONE, MISS CLAY. I'M... IMPRESSED.
NOT SO INCOMPETENT AFTER ALL, HM?
THANK YOU, DOCTOR.
NO VON MOVE!!

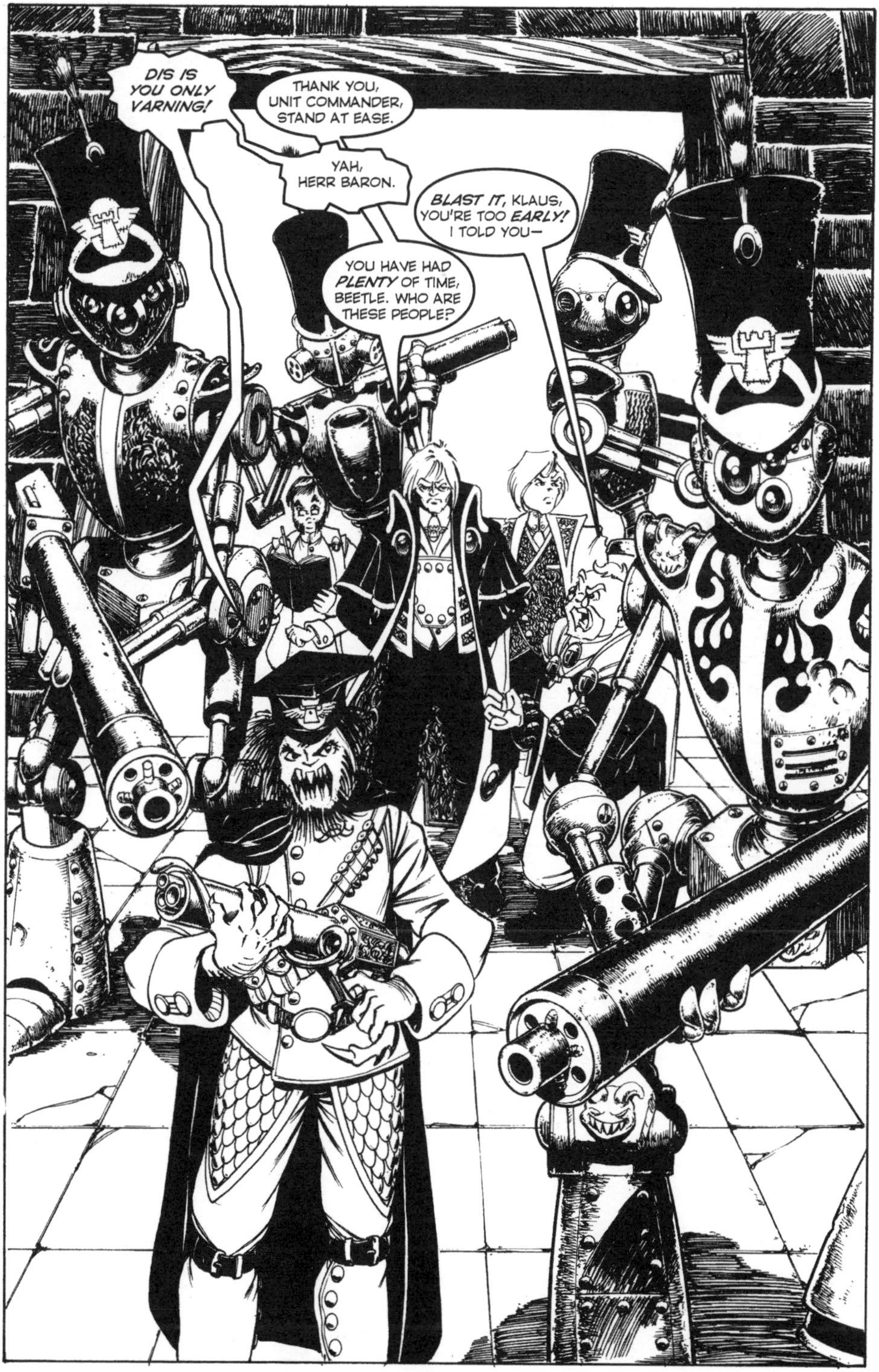
DIS IS YOU ONLY VARNING!
THANK YOU, UNIT COMMANDER, STAND AT EASE.
YAH, HERR BARON.
BLAST IT, KLAUS, YOU'RE TOO EARLY! I TOLD YOU—
YOU HAVE HAD PLENTY OF TIME, BEETLE. WHO ARE THESE PEOPLE?

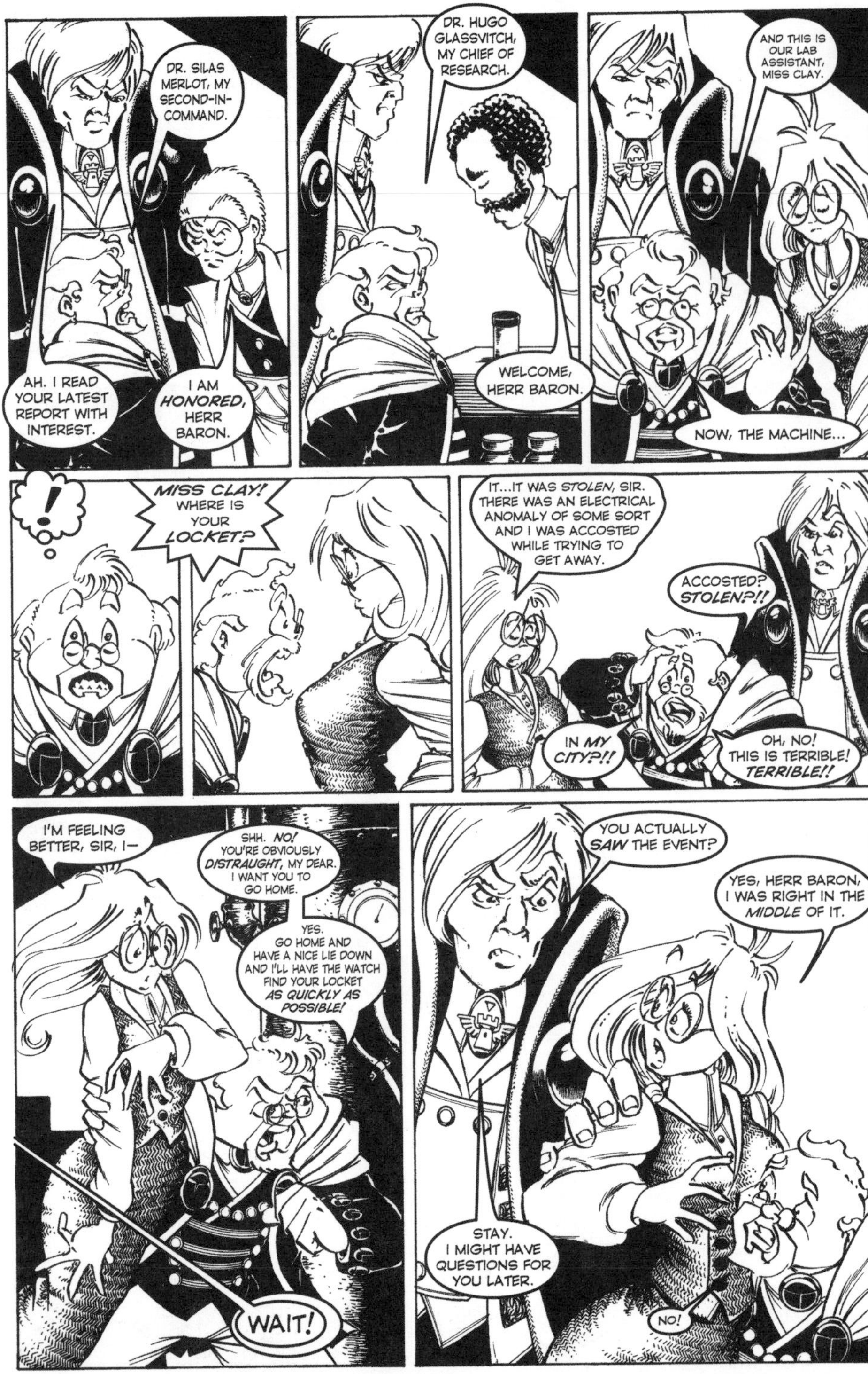
DR. SILAS MERLOT, MY SECOND-IN-COMMAND.
AH. I READ YOUR LATEST REPORT WITH INTEREST.
I AM HONORED, HERR BARON.
DR. HUGO GLASSVITCH, MY CHIEF OF RESEARCH.
WELCOME, HERR BARON.
AND THIS IS OUR LAB ASSISTANT, MISS CLAY.
NOW, THE MACHINE...
!
MISS CLAY! WHERE IS YOUR LOCKET?
IT...IT WAS STOLEN, SIR. THERE WAS AN ELECTRICAL ANOMALY OF SOME SORT AND I WAS ACCOSTED WHILE TRYING TO GET AWAY.
ACCOSTED? STOLEN?!!
IN MY CITY?!!
OH, NO! THIS IS TERRIBLE! TERRIBLE!!
I'M FEELING BETTER, SIR, I—
SHH. NO! YOU'RE OBVIOUSLY DISTRAUGHT, MY DEAR. I WANT YOU TO GO HOME.
YES. GO HOME AND HAVE A NICE LIE DOWN AND I'LL HAVE THE WATCH FIND YOUR LOCKET AS QUICKLY AS POSSIBLE!
WAIT!
YOU ACTUALLY SAW THE EVENT?
YES, HERR BARON, I WAS RIGHT IN THE MIDDLE OF IT.
STAY. I MIGHT HAVE QUESTIONS FOR YOU LATER.
NO!

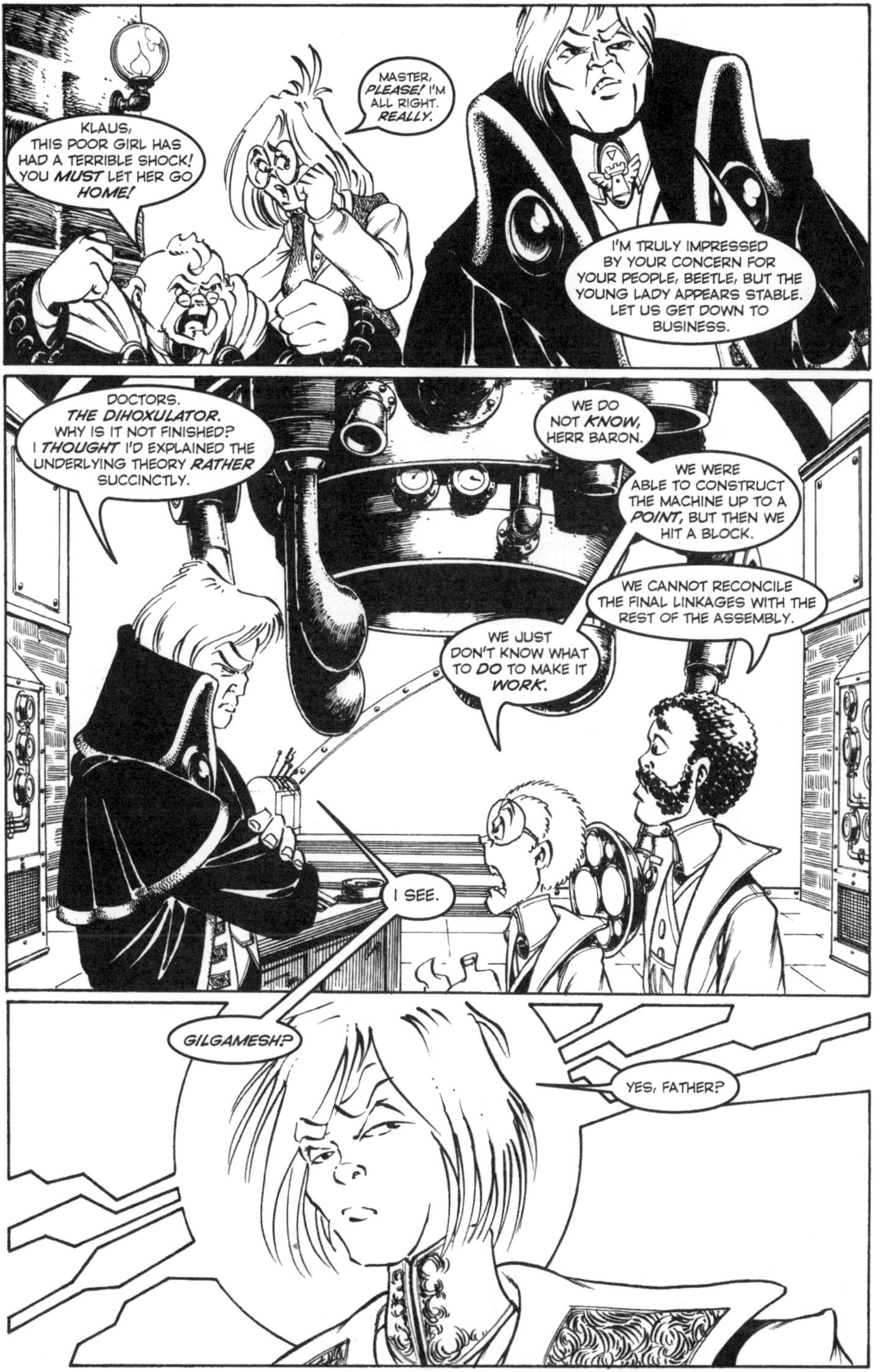
KLAUS, THIS POOR GIRL HAS HAD A TERRIBLE SHOCK! YOU MUST LET HER GO HOME!
MASTER, PLEASE! I'M ALL RIGHT. REALLY.
I'M TRULY IMPRESSED BY YOUR CONCERN FOR YOUR PEOPLE, BEETLE, BUT THE YOUNG LADY APPEARS STABLE. LET US GET DOWN TO BUSINESS.
DOCTORS. THE DIHOXULATOR. WHY IS IT NOT FINISHED? I THOUGHT I'D EXPLAINED THE UNDERLYING THEORY RATHER SUCCINCTLY.
WE DO NOT KNOW, HERR BARON.
WE WERE ABLE TO CONSTRUCT THE MACHINE UP TO A POINT, BUT THEN WE HIT A BLOCK.
WE CANNOT RECONCILE THE FINAL LINKAGES WITH THE REST OF THE ASSEMBLY.
WE JUST DON'T KNOW WHAT TO DO TO MAKE IT WORK.
I SEE.
GILGAMESH?
YES, FATHER?

CAN YOU WORK OUT THE PROBLEMS WITH THIS DEVICE *TONIGHT?*

I CAN TRY, FATHER. IF YOU'D EXPLAIN THE THEORY?

MERLOT, WE'RE *DOOMED!* WE'VE ACCOMPLISHED *NOTHING!* THEY'LL SHIP US TO THE *WAXWORKS!*

...OF *COURSE.* THE BARON *KNOWS* WE DON'T HAVE THE *SPARK.* WE WEREN'T *EXPECTED* TO FINISH THIS. IT'S A *TEST.*

THEN WE'RE *FAILING!*

NOT US, GLASSVITCH, HIS *SON!*

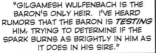

THE BASIC IDEA IS TO PROMOTE SECONDARY OXIDATION...

"GILGAMESH WULFENBACH IS THE BARON'S ONLY HEIR. I'VE HEARD RUMORS THAT THE BARON IS *TESTING* HIM, TRYING TO DETERMINE IF THE SPARK BURNS AS BRIGHTLY IN HIM AS IT DOES IN HIS SIRE."

"AND IF IT DOES NOT?"

DIS IS *BARON WULFENBACH,* SVEETHOT! HE VILL BREAK HIM DOWN FOR *PARTS* AND TRY AGAIN!

MON DIEU!

YES, RATHER *COMFORTING* TO KNOW THERE'S SOMEONE WHOSE LIFE SUCKS MORE THAN YOURS, EH?

MISS CLAY! STOP THAT INFERNAL *HUMMING!*

HAH?! I...I'M SORRY, DOCTOR, BUT I WAS LISTENING TO THE BARON, AND SOMETHING.... SOMETHING ISN'T *RIGHT,* AND—

SILENCE!!

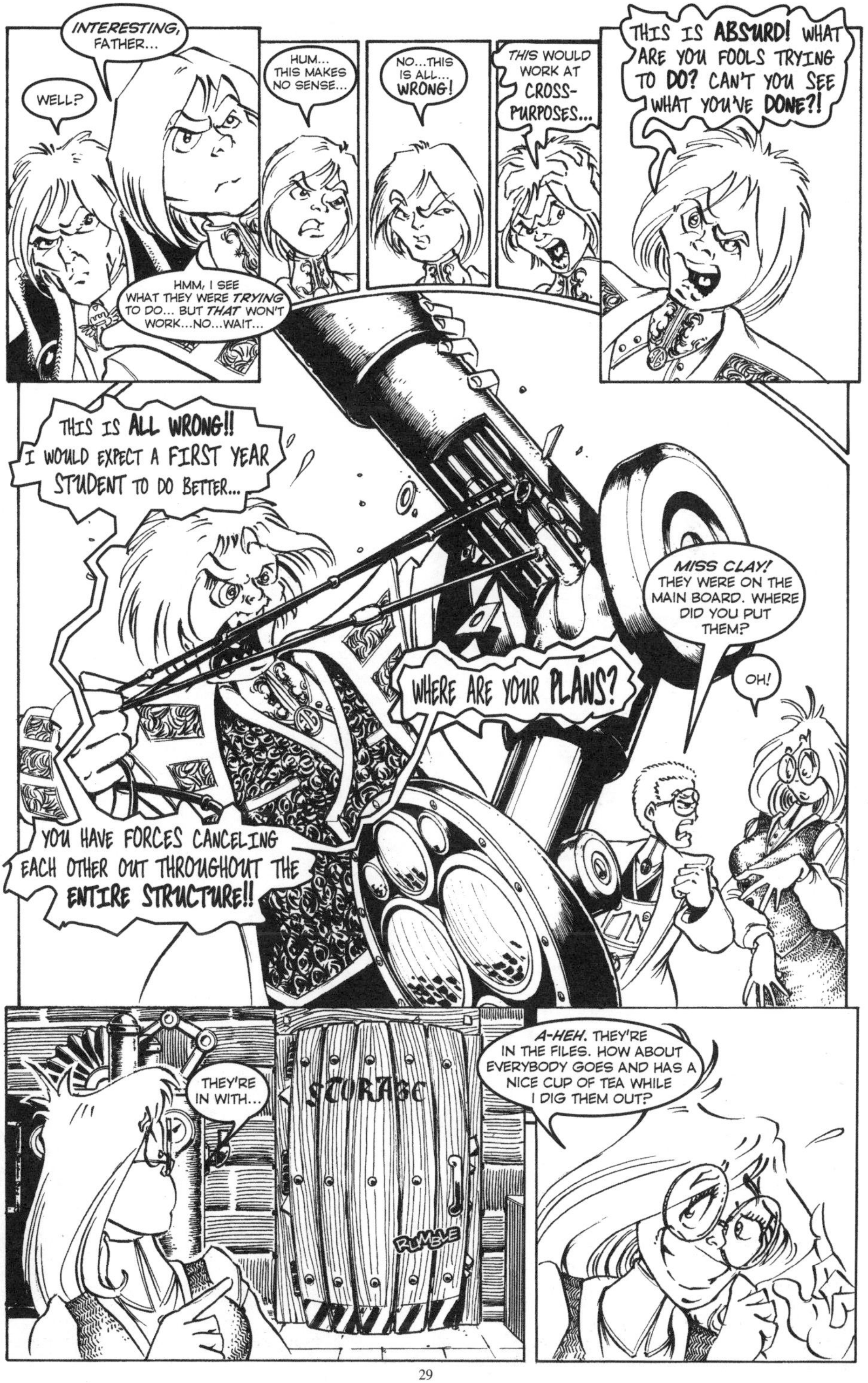
INTERESTING, FATHER...
WELL?
HMM, I SEE WHAT THEY WERE TRYING TO DO... BUT THAT WON'T WORK...NO...WAIT...
HUM... THIS MAKES NO SENSE...
NO...THIS IS ALL... WRONG!
THIS WOULD WORK AT CROSS-PURPOSES...
THIS IS ABSURD! WHAT ARE YOU FOOLS TRYING TO DO? CAN'T YOU SEE WHAT YOU'VE DONE?!
THIS IS ALL WRONG!! I WOULD EXPECT A FIRST YEAR STUDENT TO DO BETTER...
WHERE ARE YOUR PLANS?
YOU HAVE FORCES CANCELING EACH OTHER OUT THROUGHOUT THE ENTIRE STRUCTURE!!
MISS CLAY! THEY WERE ON THE MAIN BOARD. WHERE DID YOU PUT THEM?
OH!
THEY'RE IN WITH...
STORAGE
RUMBLE
A-HEH. THEY'RE IN THE FILES. HOW ABOUT EVERYBODY GOES AND HAS A NICE CUP OF TEA WHILE I DIG THEM OUT?

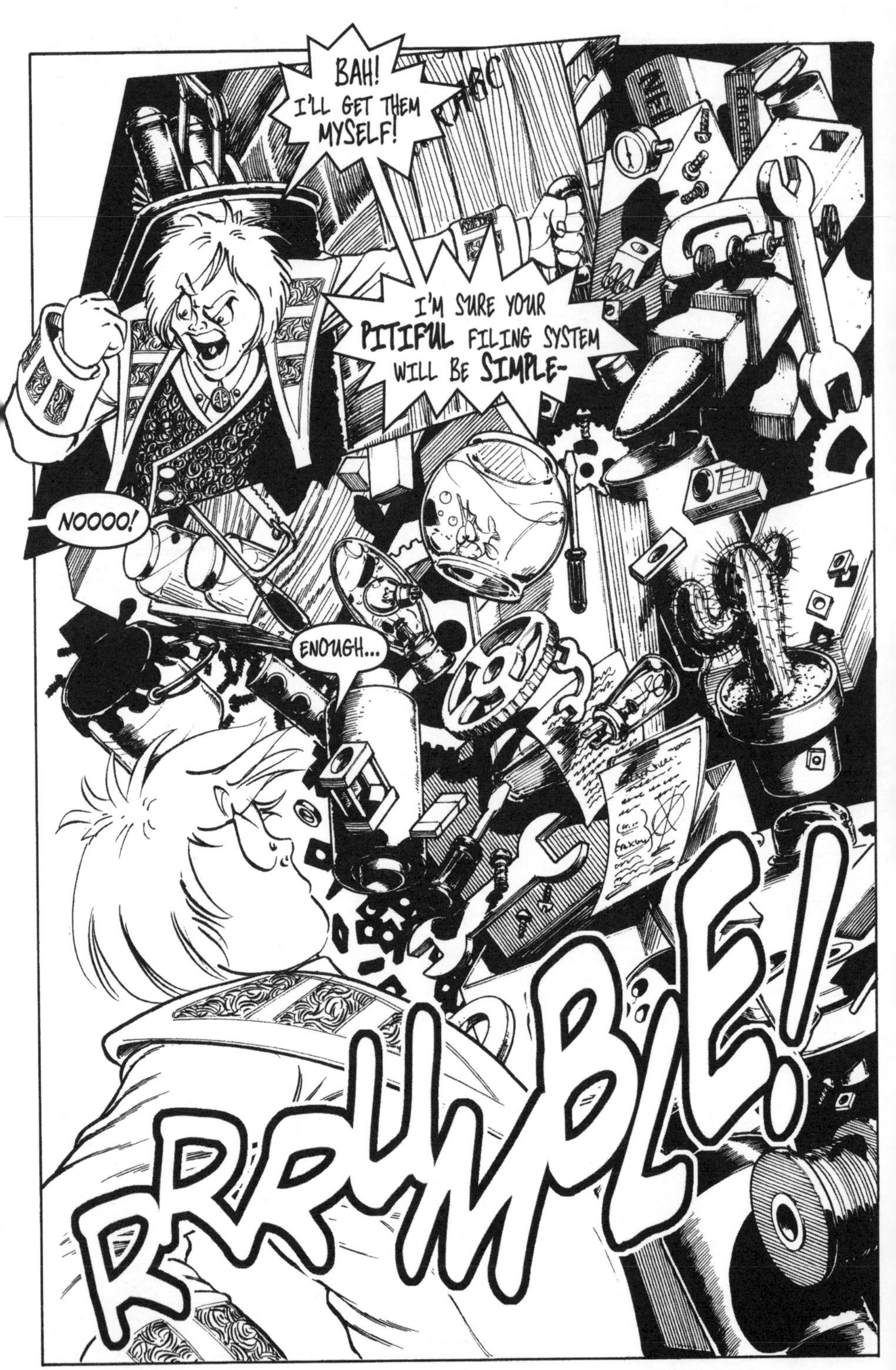
BAH!
I'LL GET THEM MYSELF!
I'M SURE YOUR PITIFUL FILING SYSTEM WILL BE SIMPLE-
NOOOO!
ENOUGH...
BRRUMBLE!

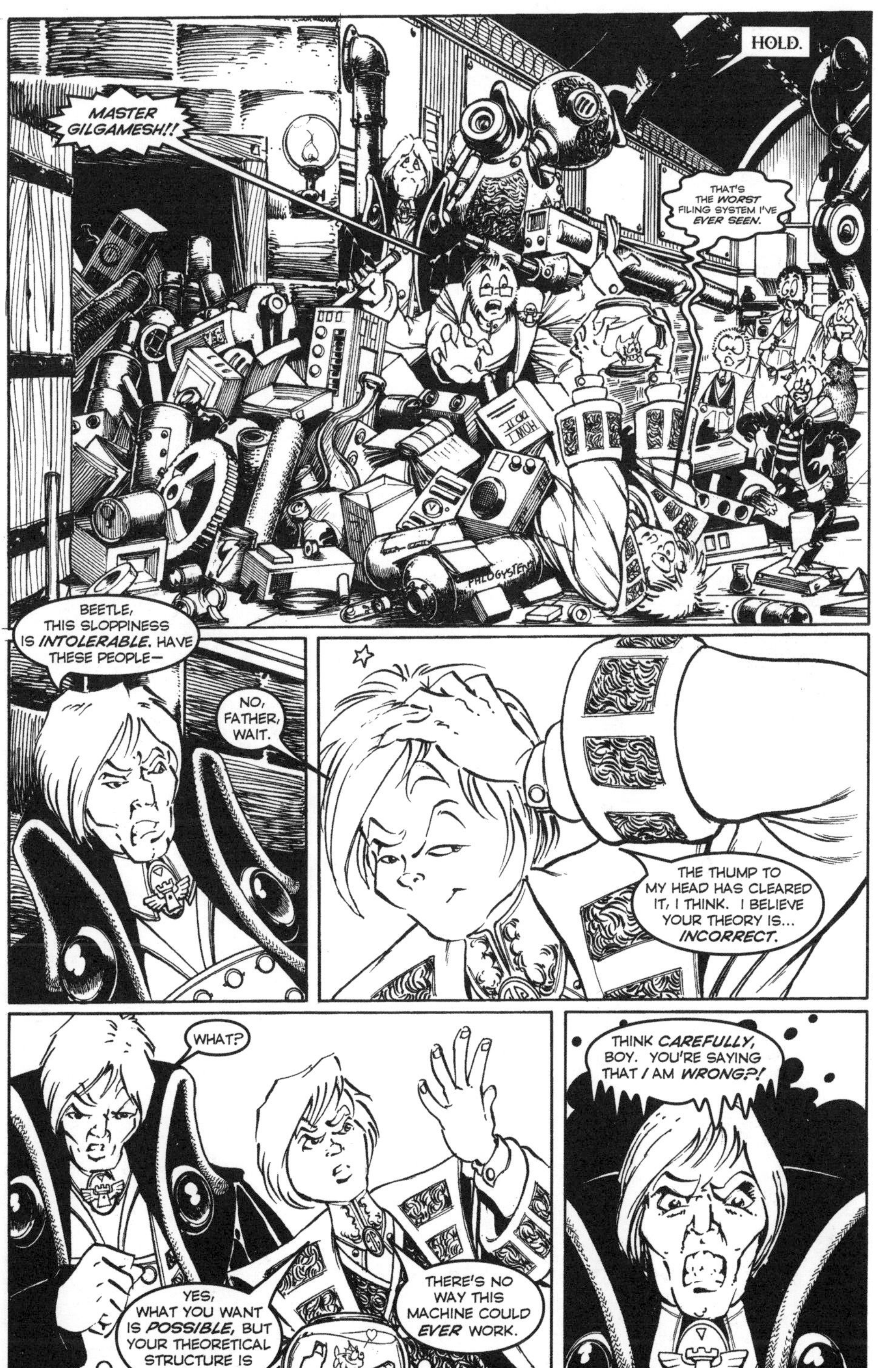
MASTER GILGAMESH!!
HOLD.
THAT'S THE *WORST* FILING SYSTEM I'VE *EVER SEEN.*
BEETLE, THIS SLOPPINESS IS *INTOLERABLE.* HAVE THESE PEOPLE—
NO, FATHER, WAIT.
THE THUMP TO MY HEAD HAS CLEARED IT, I THINK. I BELIEVE YOUR THEORY IS... *INCORRECT.*
WHAT?
YES, WHAT YOU WANT IS *POSSIBLE,* BUT YOUR THEORETICAL STRUCTURE IS FLAWED.
THERE'S NO WAY THIS MACHINE COULD *EVER* WORK.
THINK *CAREFULLY,* BOY. YOU'RE SAYING THAT *I* AM *WRONG?!*

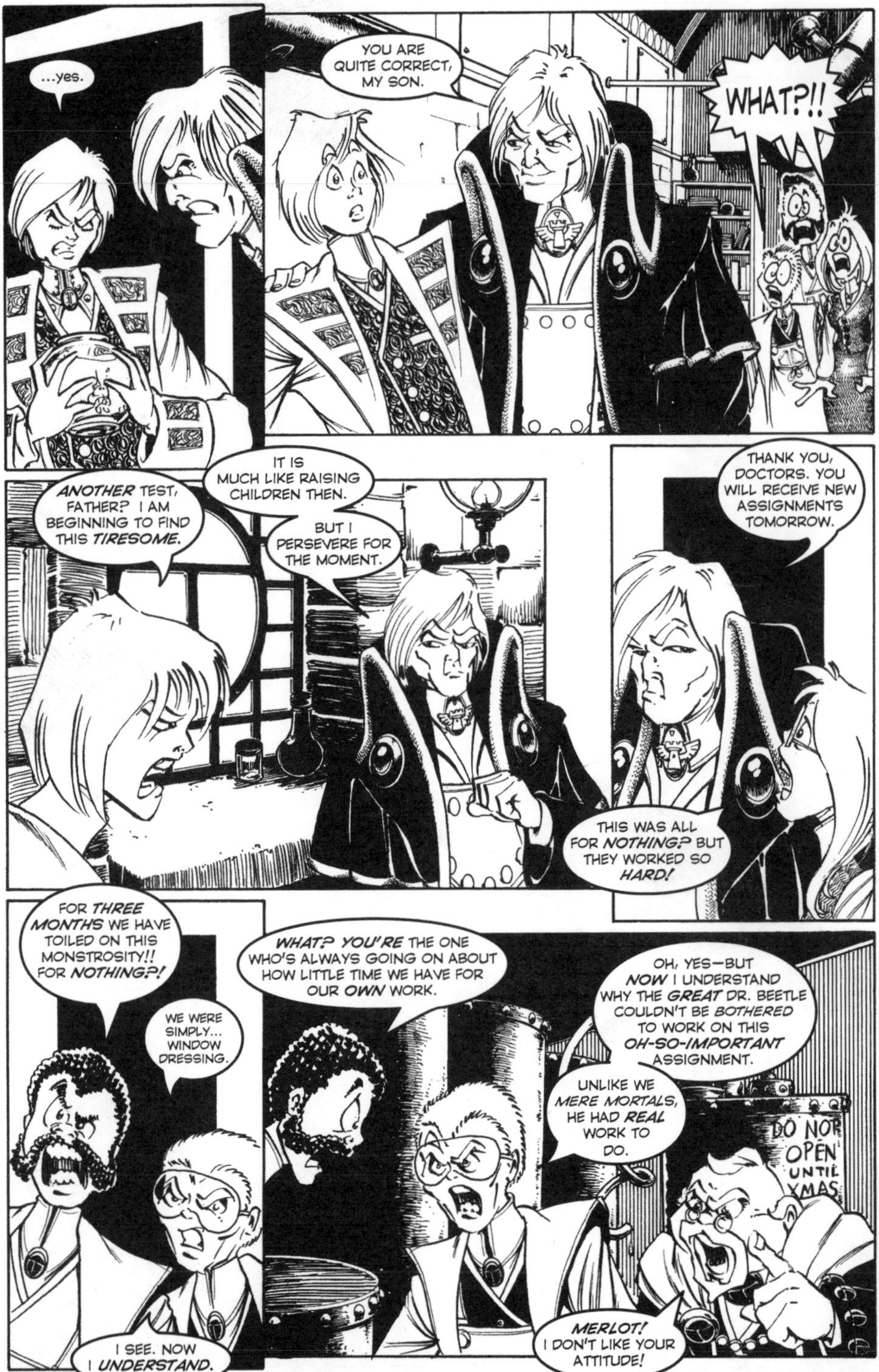
...yes.
YOU ARE QUITE CORRECT, MY SON.
WHAT?!!
ANOTHER TEST, FATHER? I AM BEGINNING TO FIND THIS TIRESOME.
IT IS MUCH LIKE RAISING CHILDREN THEN.
BUT I PERSEVERE FOR THE MOMENT.
THANK YOU, DOCTORS. YOU WILL RECEIVE NEW ASSIGNMENTS TOMORROW.
THIS WAS ALL FOR NOTHING? BUT THEY WORKED SO HARD!
FOR THREE MONTHS WE HAVE TOILED ON THIS MONSTROSITY!! FOR NOTHING?!
WE WERE SIMPLY... WINDOW DRESSING.
I SEE. NOW I UNDERSTAND.
WHAT? YOU'RE THE ONE WHO'S ALWAYS GOING ON ABOUT HOW LITTLE TIME WE HAVE FOR OUR OWN WORK.
OH, YES—BUT NOW I UNDERSTAND WHY THE GREAT DR. BEETLE COULDN'T BE BOTHERED TO WORK ON THIS OH-SO-IMPORTANT ASSIGNMENT.
UNLIKE WE MERE MORTALS, HE HAD REAL WORK TO DO.
DO NOT OPEN UNTIL XMAS
MERLOT! I DON'T LIKE YOUR ATTITUDE!

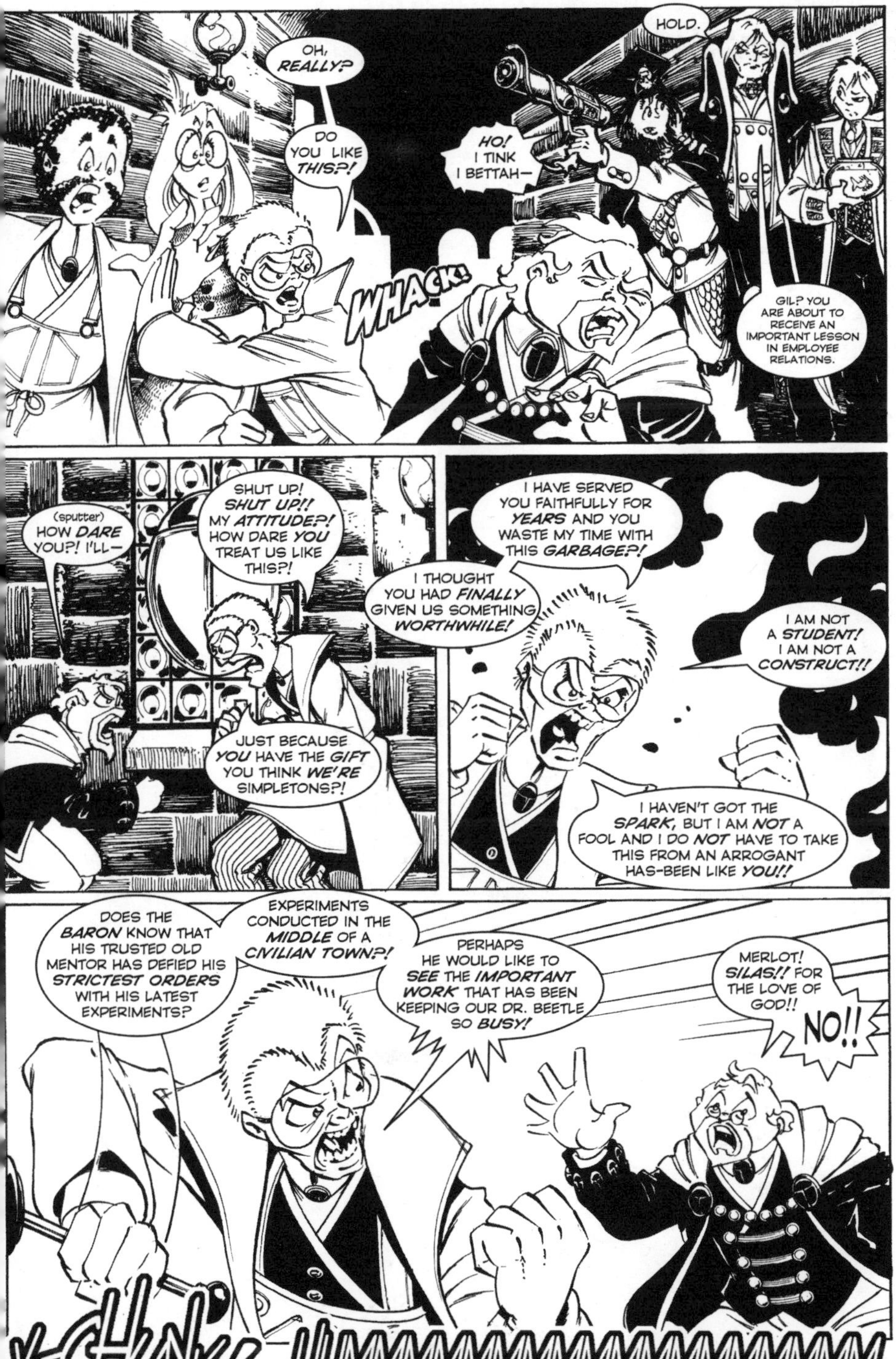
OH, REALLY?
DO YOU LIKE THIS?!
WHACK!
HO! I TINK I BETTAH—
HOLD.
GIL? YOU ARE ABOUT TO RECEIVE AN IMPORTANT LESSON IN EMPLOYEE RELATIONS.
(sputter) HOW DARE YOU?! I'LL—
SHUT UP! SHUT UP!! MY ATTITUDE?! HOW DARE YOU TREAT US LIKE THIS?!
JUST BECAUSE YOU HAVE THE GIFT YOU THINK WE'RE SIMPLETONS?!
I HAVE SERVED YOU FAITHFULLY FOR YEARS AND YOU WASTE MY TIME WITH THIS GARBAGE?!
I THOUGHT YOU HAD FINALLY GIVEN US SOMETHING WORTHWHILE!
I AM NOT A STUDENT! I AM NOT A CONSTRUCT!!
I HAVEN'T GOT THE SPARK, BUT I AM NOT A FOOL AND I DO NOT HAVE TO TAKE THIS FROM AN ARROGANT HAS-BEEN LIKE YOU!!
DOES THE BARON KNOW THAT HIS TRUSTED OLD MENTOR HAS DEFIED HIS STRICTEST ORDERS WITH HIS LATEST EXPERIMENTS?
EXPERIMENTS CONDUCTED IN THE MIDDLE OF A CIVILIAN TOWN?!
PERHAPS HE WOULD LIKE TO SEE THE IMPORTANT WORK THAT HAS BEEN KEEPING OUR DR. BEETLE SO BUSY!
MERLOT! SILAS!! FOR THE LOVE OF GOD!!
NO!!
K-CHUNK!
HUMMMMMMMMMMMMMMMMMMM

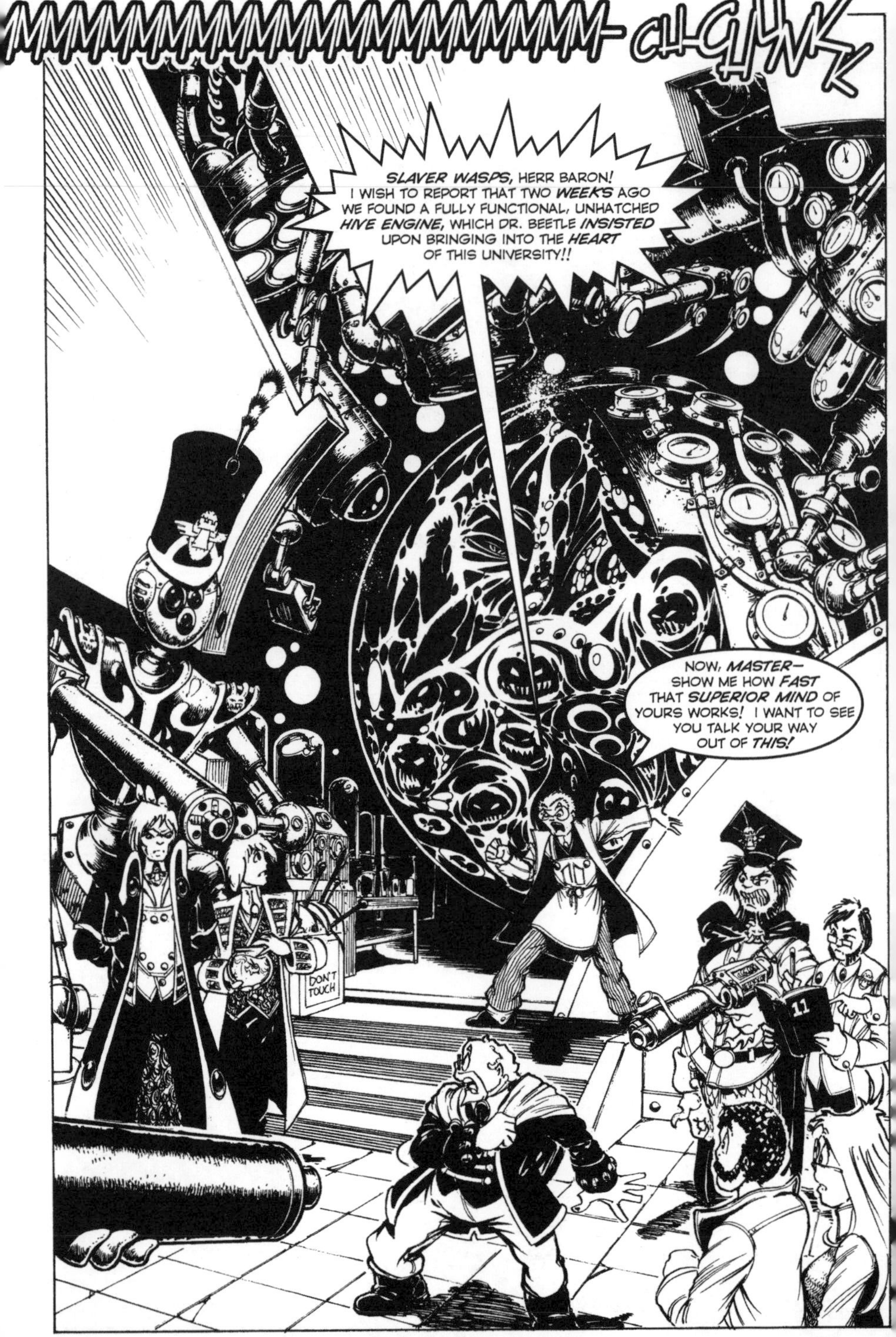

MMMMMMMMMMMMMMMMMMMMM—CH-CHUNK
SLAVER WASPS, HERR BARON! I WISH TO REPORT THAT TWO WEEKS AGO WE FOUND A FULLY FUNCTIONAL, UNHATCHED HIVE ENGINE, WHICH DR. BEETLE INSISTED UPON BRINGING INTO THE HEART OF THIS UNIVERSITY!!
NOW, MASTER— SHOW ME HOW FAST THAT SUPERIOR MIND OF YOURS WORKS! I WANT TO SEE YOU TALK YOUR WAY OUT OF THIS!
DON'T TOUCH
11

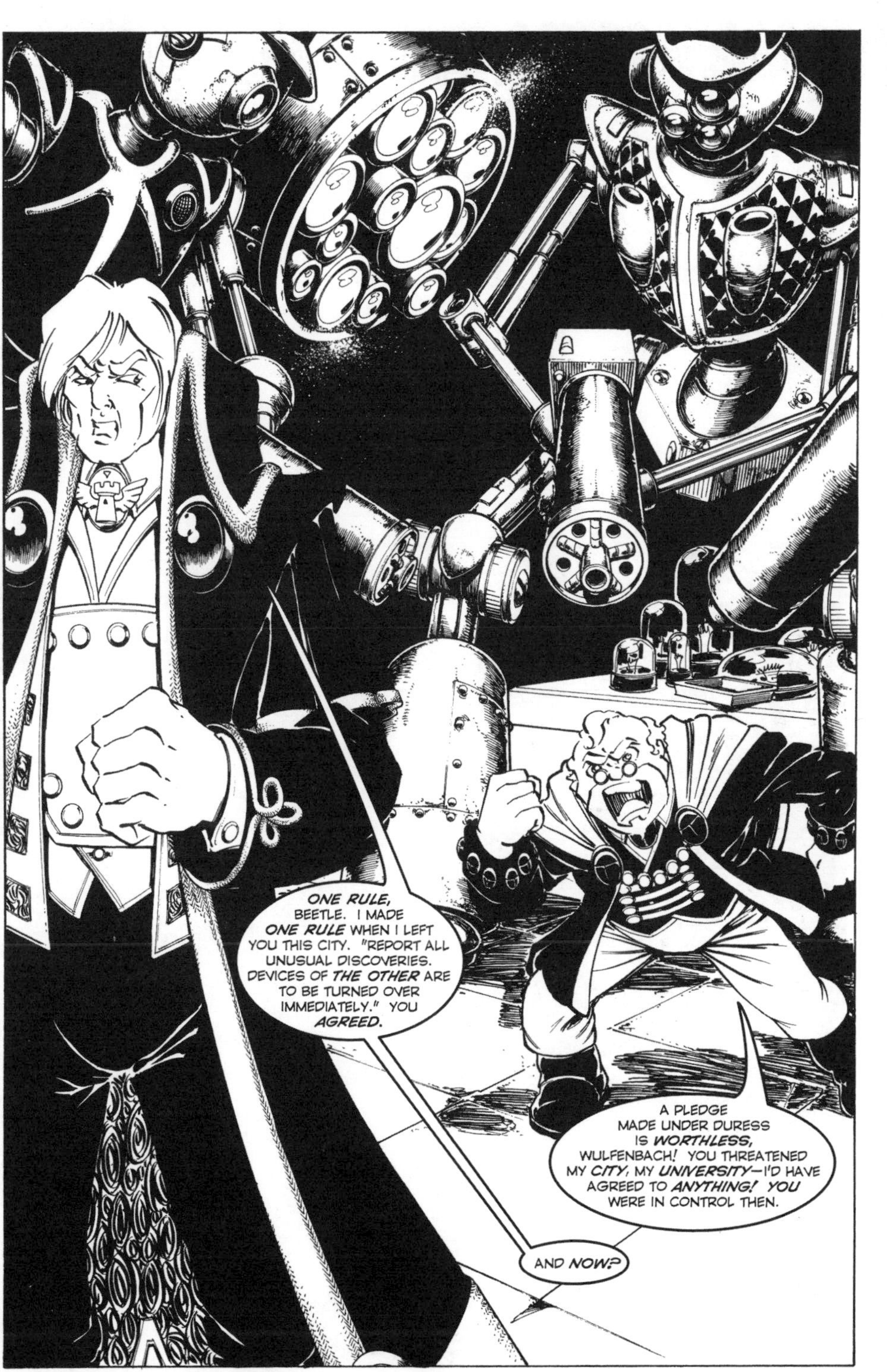
ONE RULE, BEETLE. I MADE ONE RULE WHEN I LEFT YOU THIS CITY. "REPORT ALL UNUSUAL DISCOVERIES. DEVICES OF THE OTHER ARE TO BE TURNED OVER IMMEDIATELY." YOU AGREED.
A PLEDGE MADE UNDER DURESS IS WORTHLESS, WULFENBACH! YOU THREATENED MY CITY, MY UNIVERSITY—I'D HAVE AGREED TO ANYTHING! YOU WERE IN CONTROL THEN.
AND NOW?

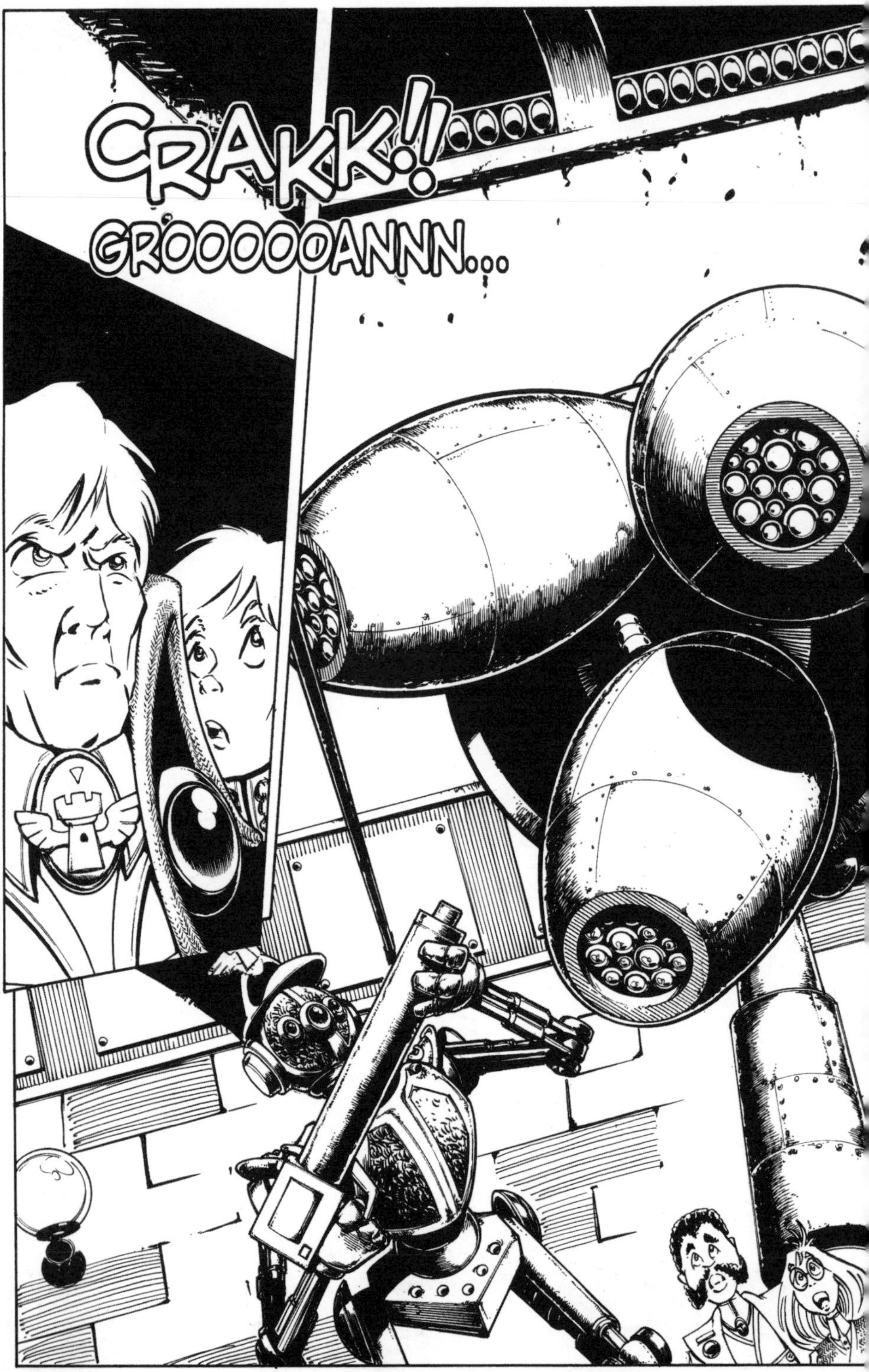
CRAKK!!
GROOOOOOANNN...

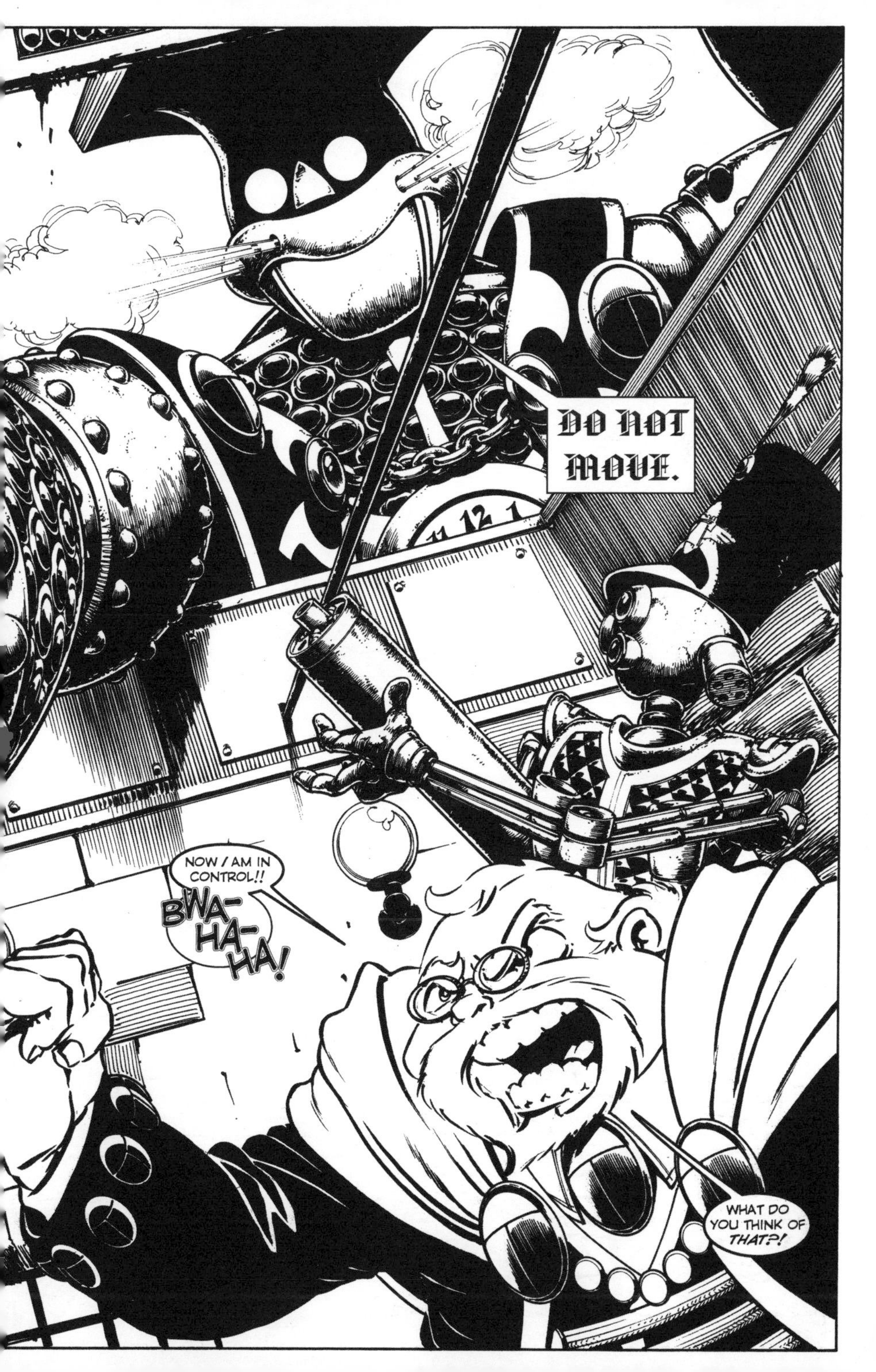
DO NOT MOVE.
NOW I AM IN CONTROL!!
BWA-HA-HA!
WHAT DO YOU THINK OF THAT?!

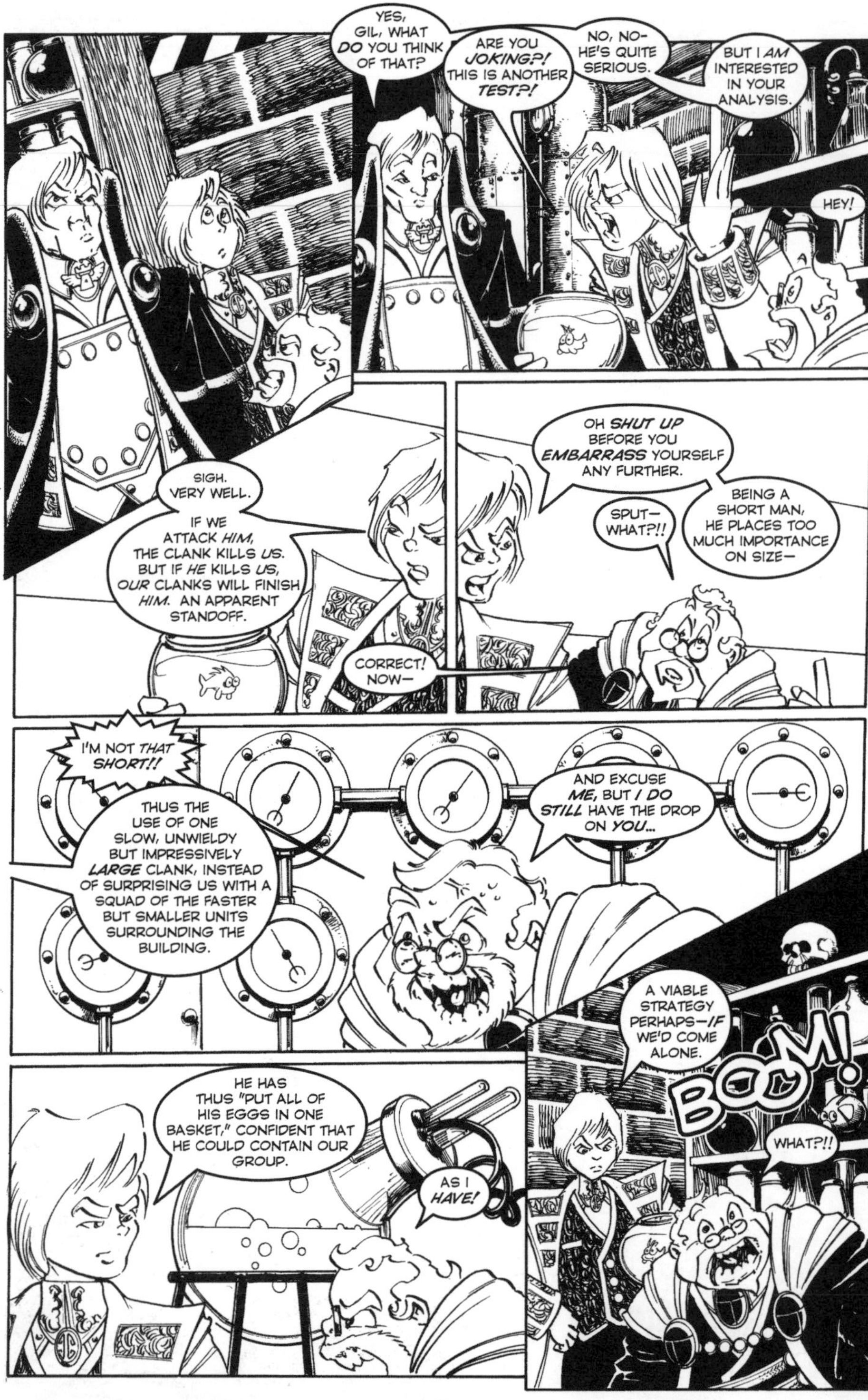
YES, GIL, WHAT DO YOU THINK OF THAT?
ARE YOU JOKING?! THIS IS ANOTHER TEST?!
NO, NO- HE'S QUITE SERIOUS.
BUT I AM INTERESTED IN YOUR ANALYSIS.
HEY!
SIGH. VERY WELL.
IF WE ATTACK HIM, THE CLANK KILLS US. BUT IF HE KILLS US, OUR CLANKS WILL FINISH HIM. AN APPARENT STANDOFF.
CORRECT! NOW—
OH SHUT UP BEFORE YOU EMBARRASS YOURSELF ANY FURTHER.
SPUT— WHAT?!!
BEING A SHORT MAN, HE PLACES TOO MUCH IMPORTANCE ON SIZE—
I'M NOT THAT SHORT!!
THUS THE USE OF ONE SLOW, UNWIELDY BUT IMPRESSIVELY LARGE CLANK, INSTEAD OF SURPRISING US WITH A SQUAD OF THE FASTER BUT SMALLER UNITS SURROUNDING THE BUILDING.
AND EXCUSE ME, BUT I DO STILL HAVE THE DROP ON YOU...
HE HAS THUS "PUT ALL OF HIS EGGS IN ONE BASKET," CONFIDENT THAT HE COULD CONTAIN OUR GROUP.
AS I HAVE!
A VIABLE STRATEGY PERHAPS—IF WE'D COME ALONE.
BOOM!
WHAT?!!

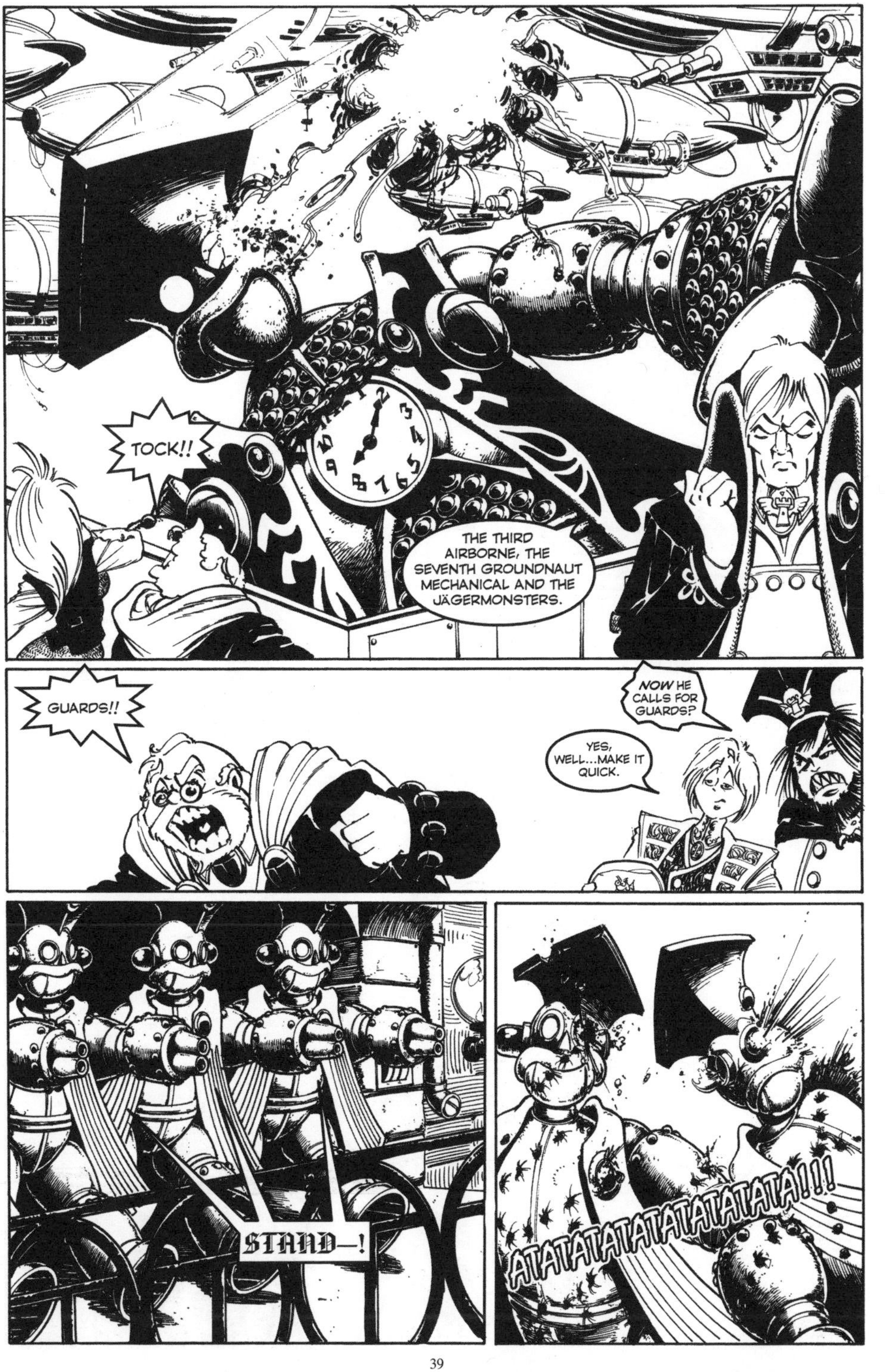
TOCK!!
THE THIRD AIRBORNE, THE SEVENTH GROUNDNAUT MECHANICAL AND THE JÄGERMONSTERS.
GUARDS!!
NOW HE CALLS FOR GUARDS?
YES, WELL...MAKE IT QUICK.
STAND—!
ATATATATATATATATATATA!!!

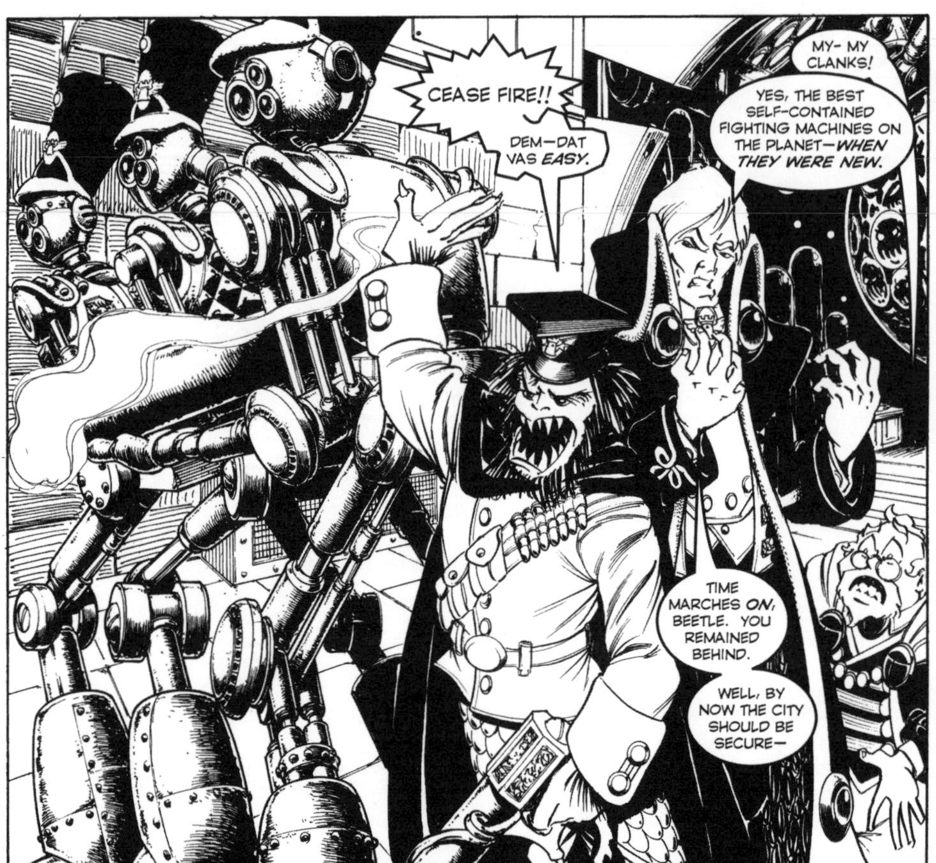
CEASE FIRE!!
DEM—DAT VAS *EASY.*
MY- MY CLANKS!
YES, THE BEST SELF-CONTAINED FIGHTING MACHINES ON THE PLANET—*WHEN THEY WERE NEW.*
TIME MARCHES *ON,* BEETLE. YOU REMAINED BEHIND.
WELL, BY NOW THE CITY SHOULD BE SECURE—

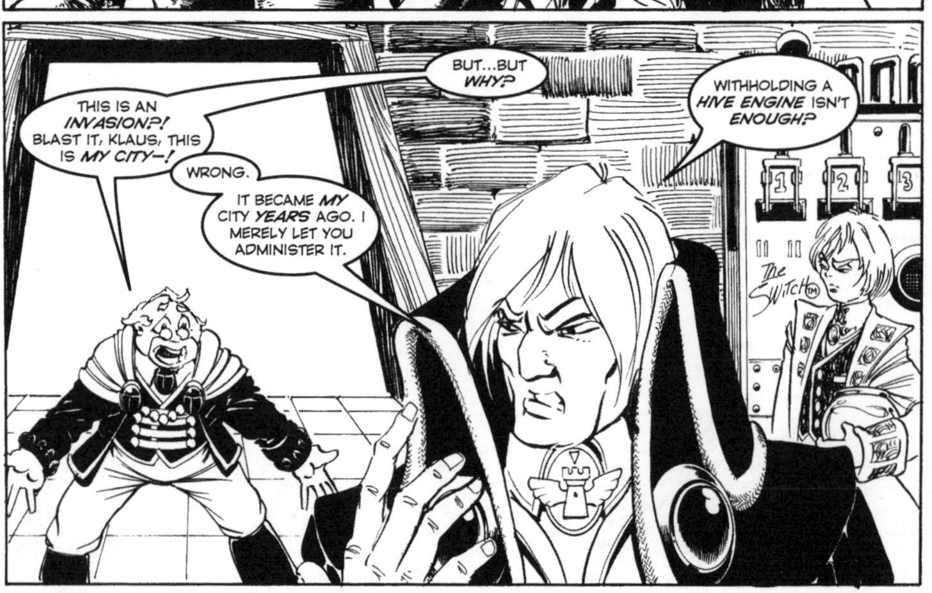
THIS IS AN *INVASION?!* BLAST IT, KLAUS, THIS IS *MY CITY—!*
WRONG.
IT BECAME *MY* CITY *YEARS* AGO. I MERELY LET YOU ADMINISTER IT.
BUT...BUT *WHY?*
WITHHOLDING A *HIVE ENGINE* ISN'T *ENOUGH?*
1
2
3
The SWITCH TM

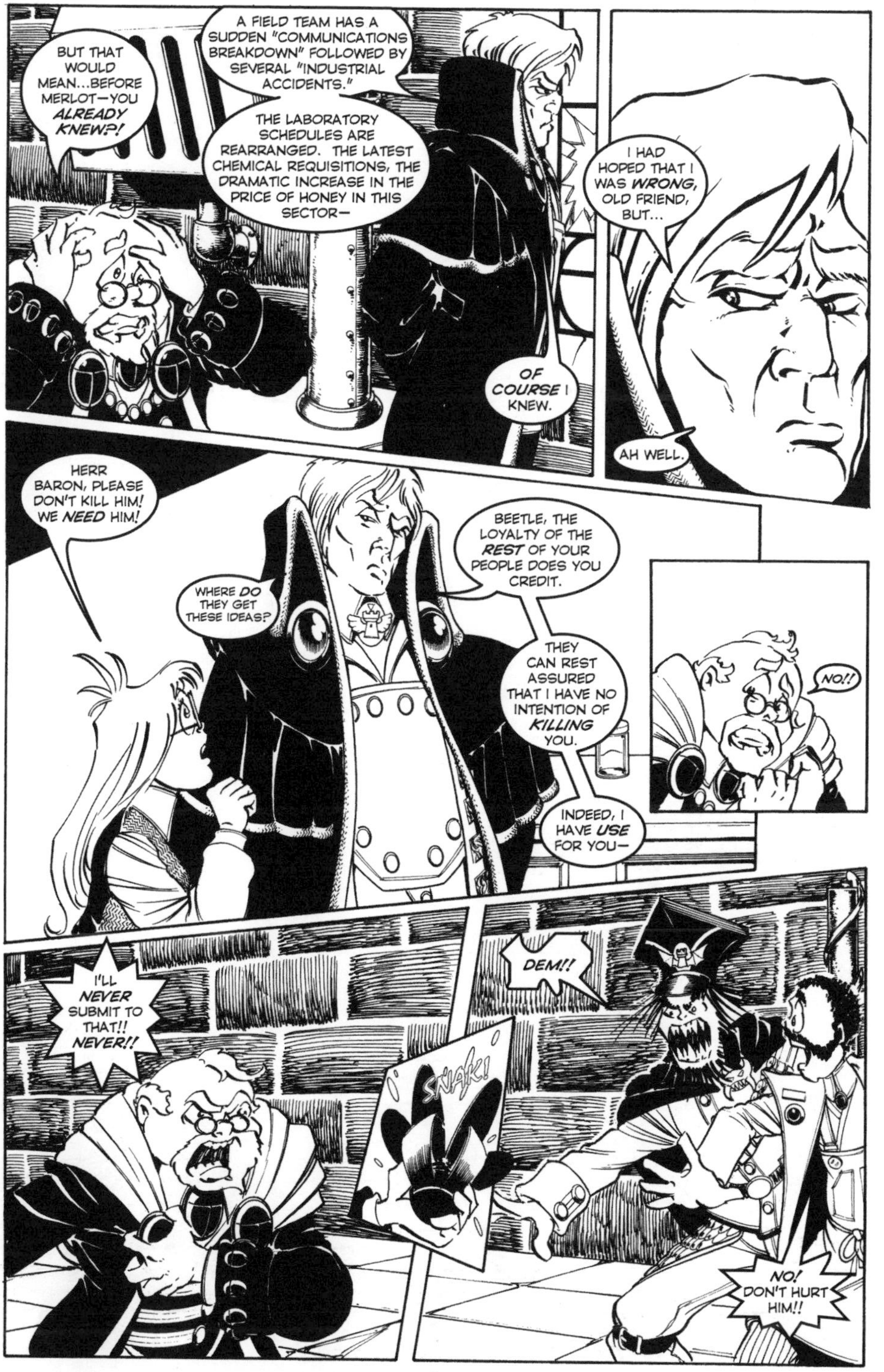
BUT THAT WOULD MEAN...BEFORE MERLOT—YOU ALREADY KNEW?!
A FIELD TEAM HAS A SUDDEN "COMMUNICATIONS BREAKDOWN" FOLLOWED BY SEVERAL "INDUSTRIAL ACCIDENTS."
THE LABORATORY SCHEDULES ARE REARRANGED. THE LATEST CHEMICAL REQUISITIONS, THE DRAMATIC INCREASE IN THE PRICE OF HONEY IN THIS SECTOR—
OF COURSE I KNEW.
I HAD HOPED THAT I WAS WRONG, OLD FRIEND, BUT...
AH WELL.
HERR BARON, PLEASE DON'T KILL HIM! WE NEED HIM!
WHERE DO THEY GET THESE IDEAS?
BEETLE, THE LOYALTY OF THE REST OF YOUR PEOPLE DOES YOU CREDIT.
THEY CAN REST ASSURED THAT I HAVE NO INTENTION OF KILLING YOU.
INDEED, I HAVE USE FOR YOU—
NO!!
I'LL NEVER SUBMIT TO THAT!! NEVER!!
DEM!!
SNAK!
NO! DON'T HURT HIM!!

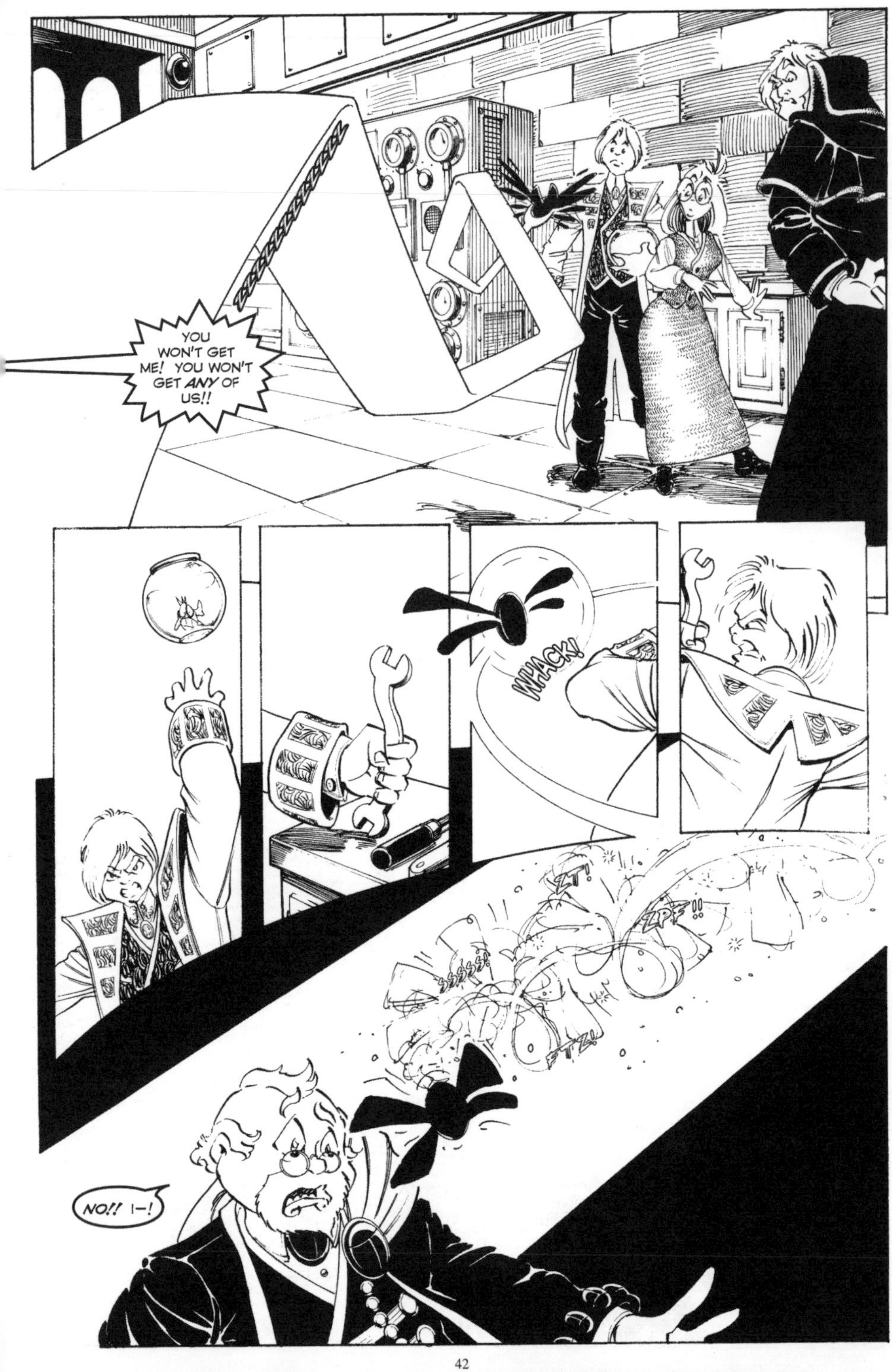
YOU WON'T GET ME! YOU WON'T GET *ANY* OF US!!
WHACK!
ZT!
ZPF!!
SSSSSS!
FTZ!
NO!! I--!

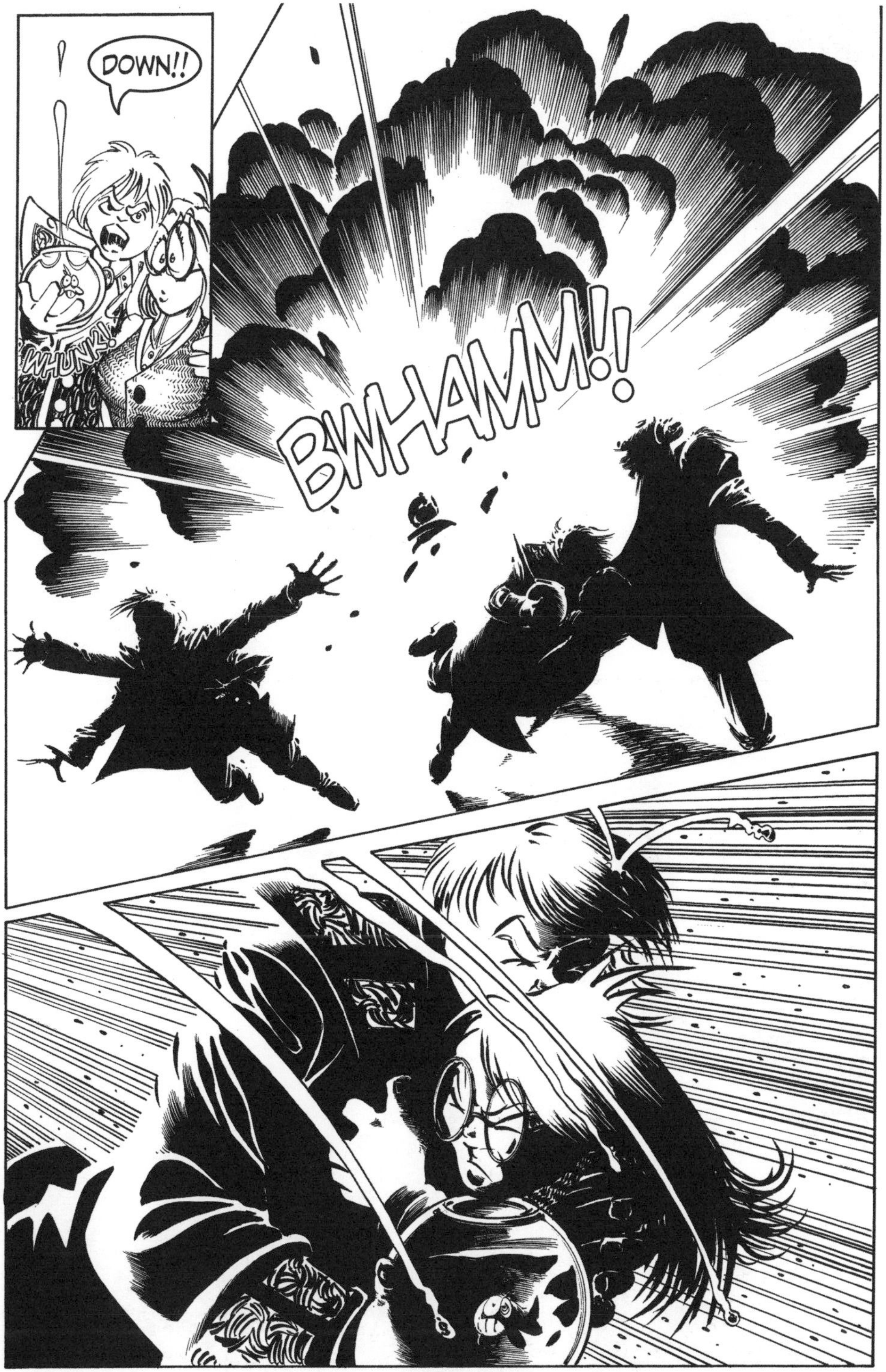
!
DOWN!!
WHUNK!
BWHAMM!!

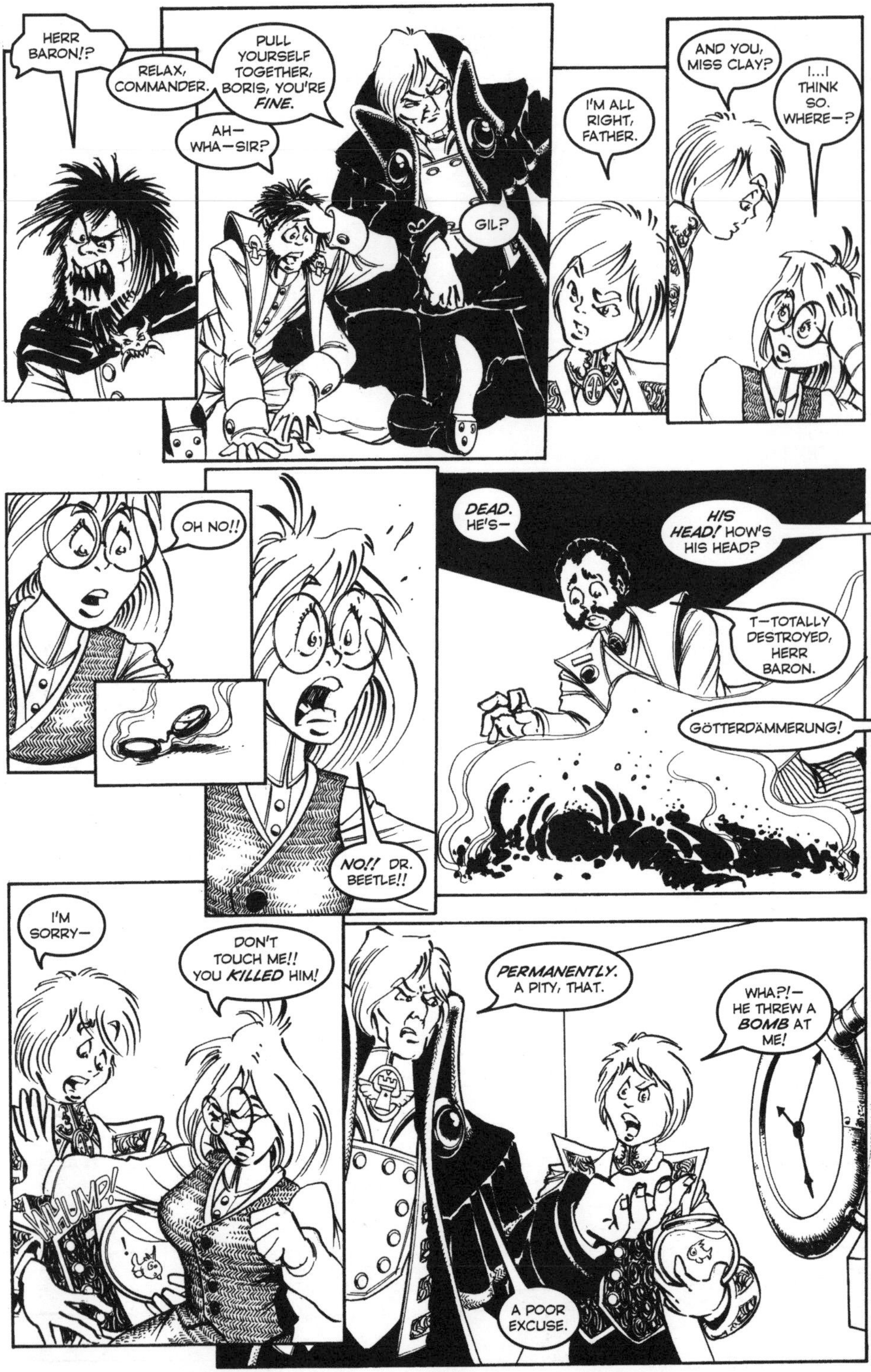

HERR BARON!?
RELAX, COMMANDER.
PULL YOURSELF TOGETHER, BORIS, YOU'RE *FINE*.
AH— WHA—SIR?
GIL?
I'M ALL RIGHT, FATHER.
AND YOU, MISS CLAY?
I...I THINK SO. WHERE—?
OH NO!!
NO!! DR. BEETLE!!
DEAD. HE'S—
HIS HEAD! HOW'S HIS HEAD?
T—TOTALLY DESTROYED, HERR BARON.
GÖTTERDÄMMERUNG!
I'M SORRY—
DON'T TOUCH ME!! YOU *KILLED* HIM!
WHUMP!
!
PERMANENTLY. A PITY, THAT.
WHA?!— HE THREW A *BOMB* AT ME!
A POOR EXCUSE.

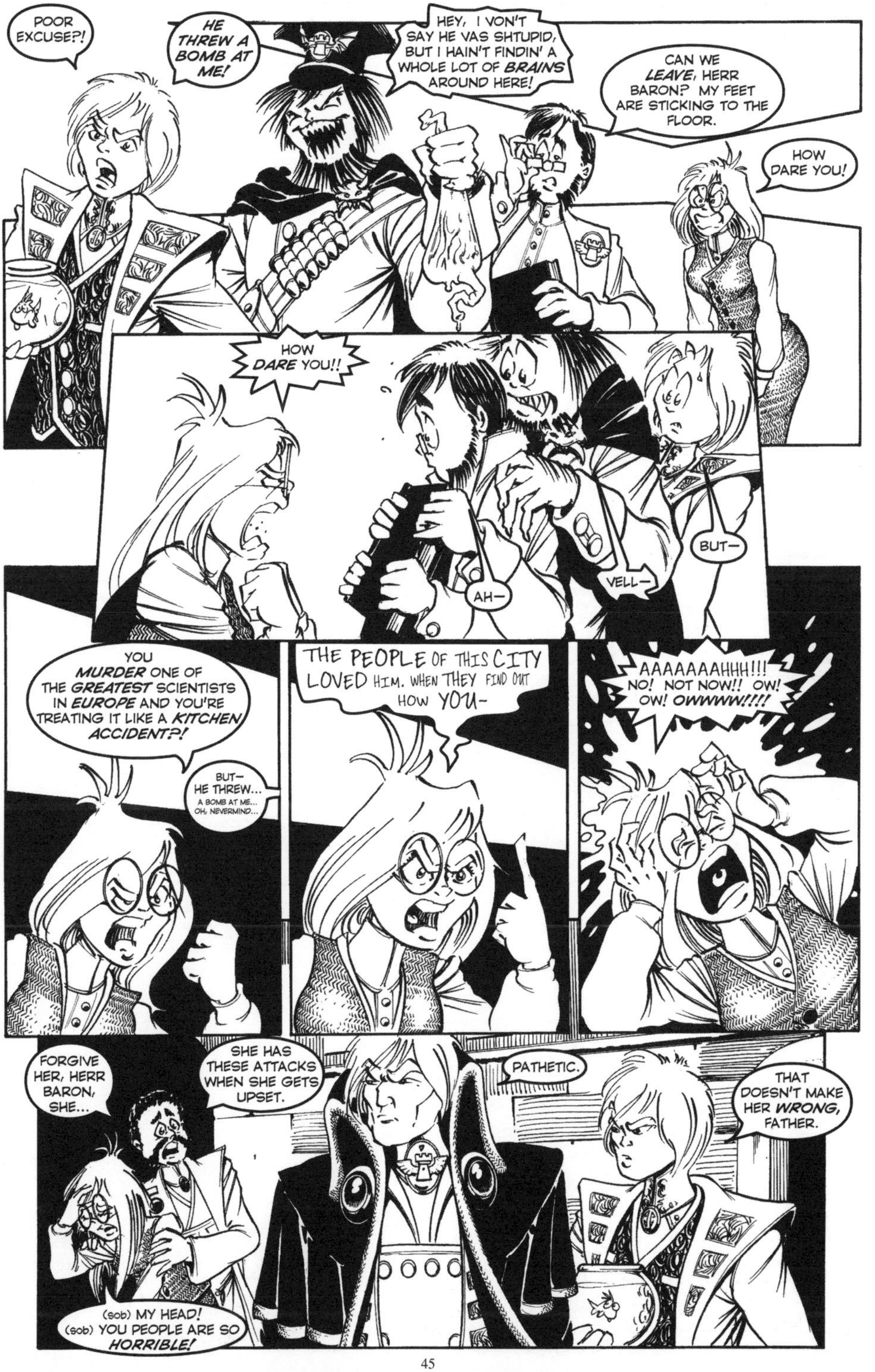
POOR EXCUSE?!
HE THREW A BOMB AT ME!
HEY, I VON'T SAY HE VAS SHTUPID, BUT I HAIN'T FINDIN' A WHOLE LOT OF BRAINS AROUND HERE!
CAN WE LEAVE, HERR BARON? MY FEET ARE STICKING TO THE FLOOR.
HOW DARE YOU!
HOW DARE YOU!!
AH—
VELL—
BUT—
YOU MURDER ONE OF THE GREATEST SCIENTISTS IN EUROPE AND YOU'RE TREATING IT LIKE A KITCHEN ACCIDENT?!
BUT— HE THREW... A BOMB AT ME... OH, NEVERMIND...
THE PEOPLE OF THIS CITY LOVED HIM. WHEN THEY FIND OUT HOW YOU-
AAAAAAAHHH!!! NO! NOT NOW!! OW! OW! OWWWW!!!!
FORGIVE HER, HERR BARON, SHE...
SHE HAS THESE ATTACKS WHEN SHE GETS UPSET.
PATHETIC.
THAT DOESN'T MAKE HER WRONG, FATHER.
(sob) MY HEAD! (sob) YOU PEOPLE ARE SO HORRIBLE!

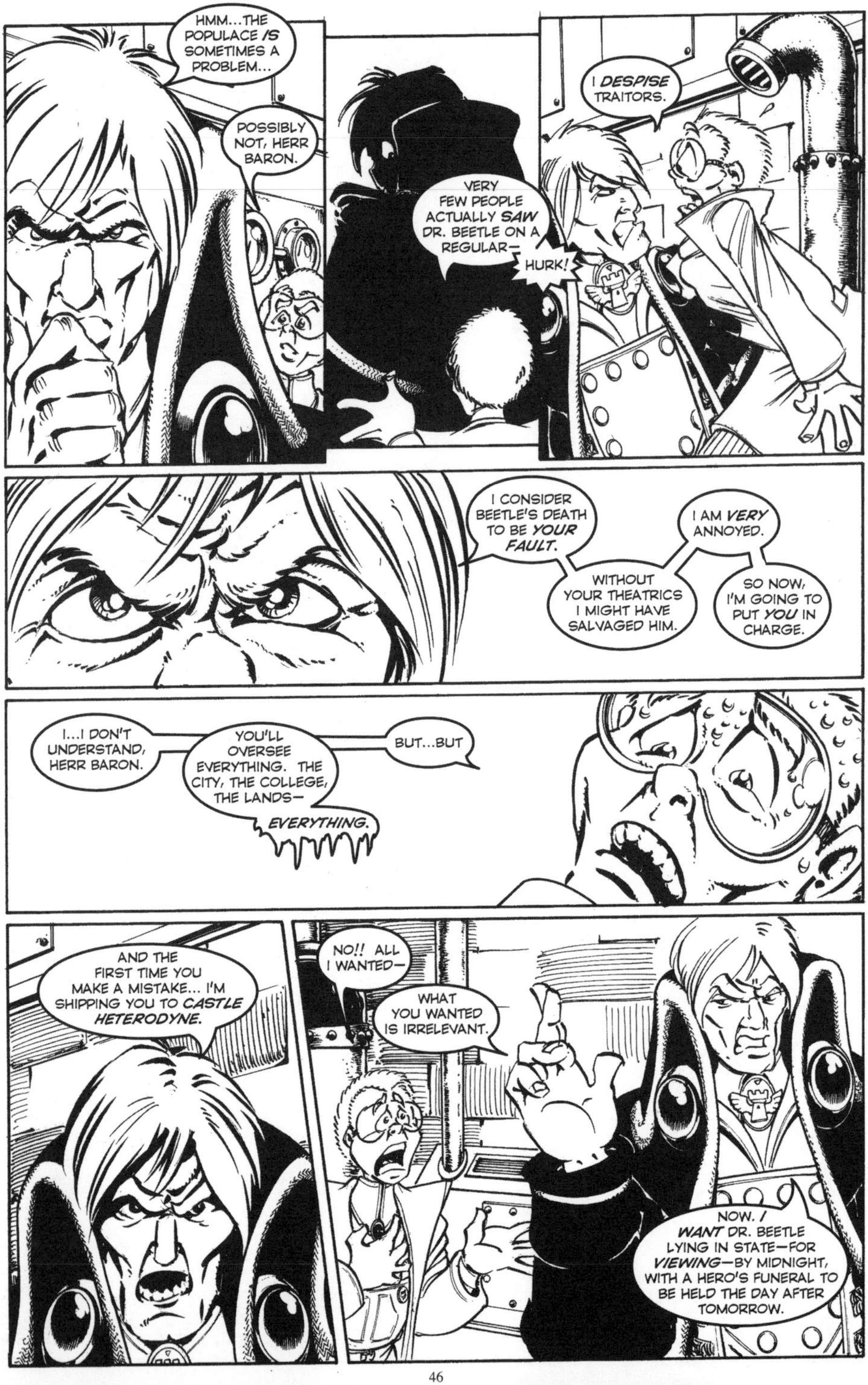
HMM...THE POPULACE *IS* SOMETIMES A PROBLEM...
POSSIBLY NOT, HERR BARON.
VERY FEW PEOPLE ACTUALLY *SAW* DR. BEETLE ON A REGULAR—
HURK!
I *DESPISE* TRAITORS.
I CONSIDER BEETLE'S DEATH TO BE *YOUR FAULT*.
WITHOUT YOUR THEATRICS I MIGHT HAVE SALVAGED HIM.
I AM *VERY* ANNOYED.
SO NOW, I'M GOING TO PUT *YOU* IN CHARGE.
I...I DON'T UNDERSTAND, HERR BARON.
YOU'LL OVERSEE EVERYTHING. THE CITY, THE COLLEGE, THE LANDS—
EVERYTHING.
BUT...BUT
AND THE FIRST TIME YOU MAKE A MISTAKE... I'M SHIPPING YOU TO *CASTLE HETERODYNE*.
NO!! ALL I WANTED—
WHAT YOU WANTED IS IRRELEVANT.
NOW. *I WANT* DR. BEETLE LYING IN STATE—FOR *VIEWING*—BY MIDNIGHT, WITH A HERO'S FUNERAL TO BE HELD THE DAY AFTER TOMORROW.

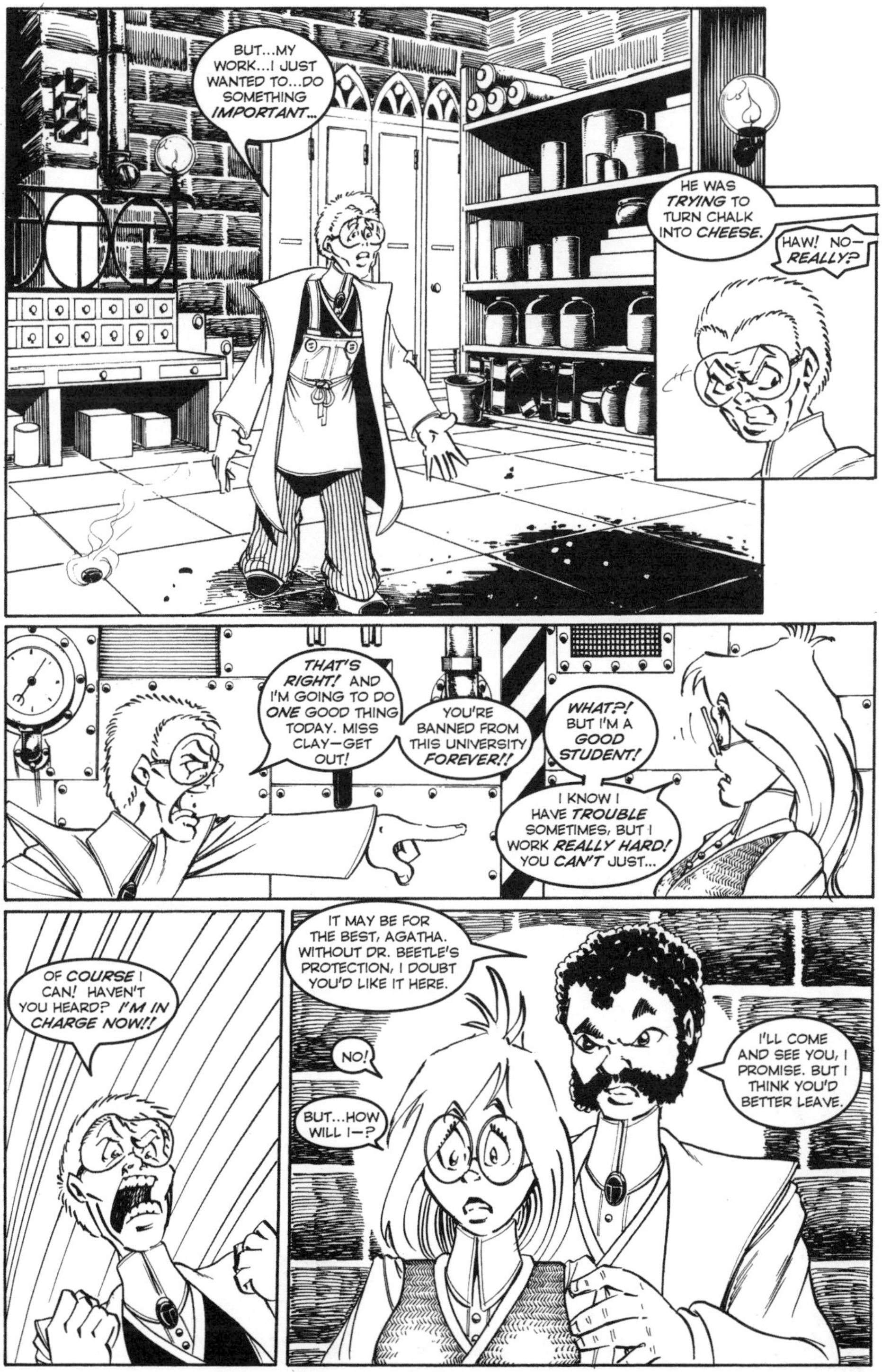
BUT...MY WORK...I JUST WANTED TO...DO SOMETHING IMPORTANT...
HE WAS TRYING TO TURN CHALK INTO CHEESE.
HAW! NO—REALLY?
THAT'S RIGHT! AND I'M GOING TO DO ONE GOOD THING TODAY. MISS CLAY—GET OUT!
YOU'RE BANNED FROM THIS UNIVERSITY FOREVER!!
WHAT?! BUT I'M A GOOD STUDENT!
I KNOW I HAVE TROUBLE SOMETIMES, BUT I WORK REALLY HARD! YOU CAN'T JUST...
OF COURSE I CAN! HAVEN'T YOU HEARD? I'M IN CHARGE NOW!!
IT MAY BE FOR THE BEST, AGATHA. WITHOUT DR. BEETLE'S PROTECTION, I DOUBT YOU'D LIKE IT HERE.
NO!
BUT...HOW WILL I—?
I'LL COME AND SEE YOU, I PROMISE. BUT I THINK YOU'D BETTER LEAVE.

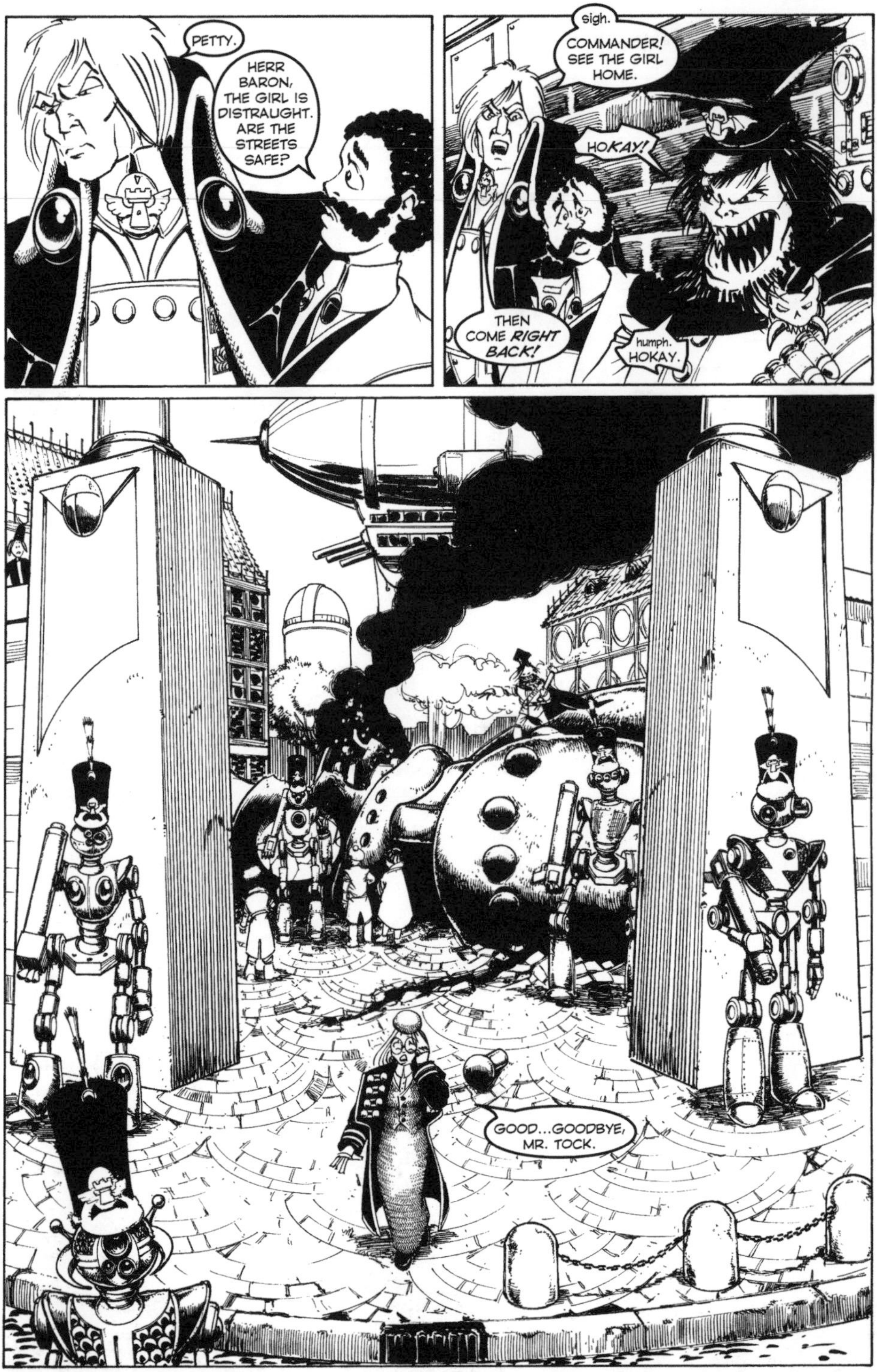
PETTY.
HERR BARON, THE GIRL IS DISTRAUGHT. ARE THE STREETS SAFE?
sigh.
COMMANDER! SEE THE GIRL HOME.
HOKAY!
THEN COME *RIGHT BACK!*
humph. HOKAY.
GOOD...GOODBYE, MR. TOCK.

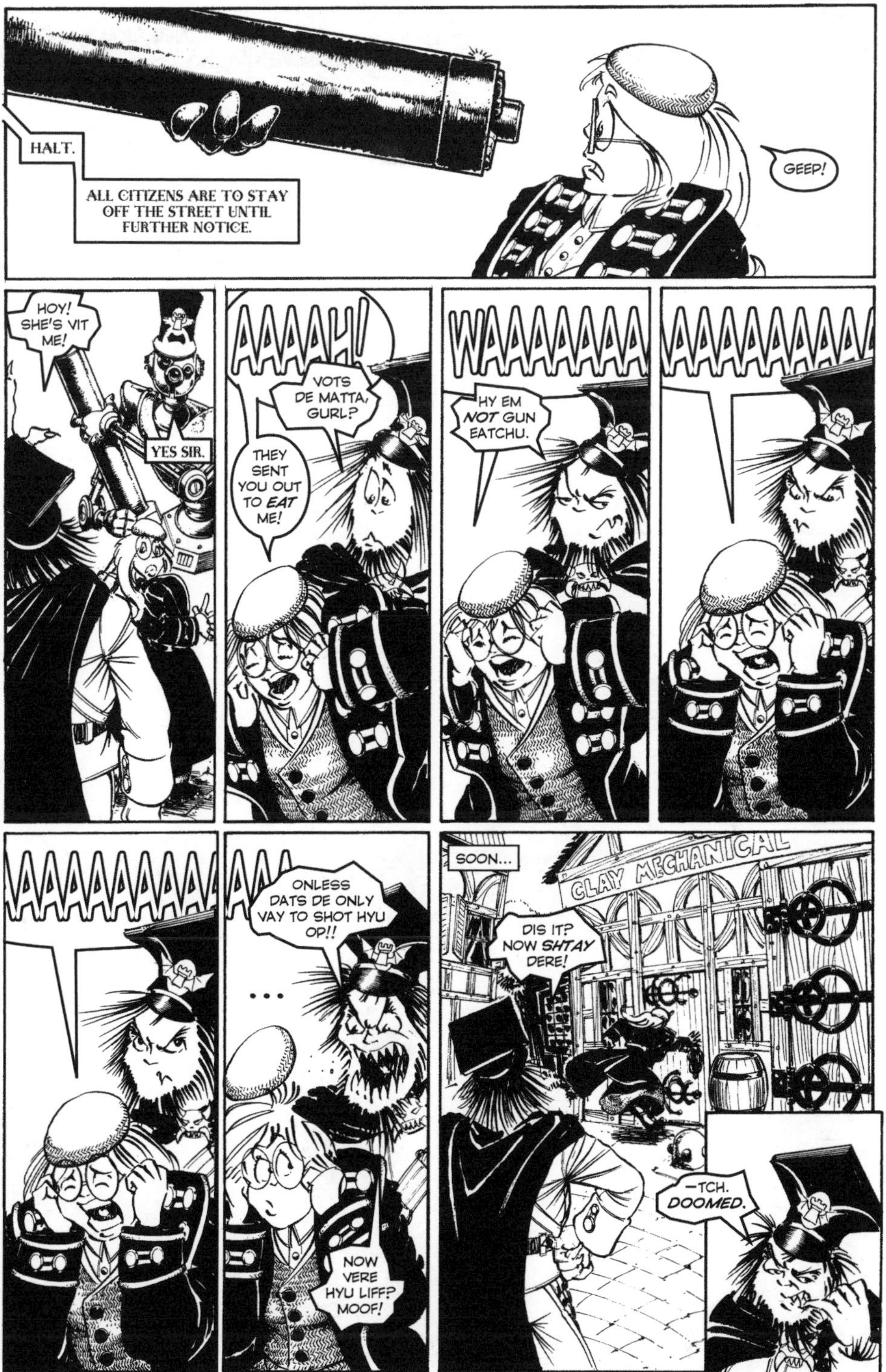
HALT.
ALL CITIZENS ARE TO STAY OFF THE STREET UNTIL FURTHER NOTICE.
GEEP!
HOY! SHE'S VIT ME!
YES SIR.
AAAAH!
VOTS DE MATTA, GURL?
THEY SENT YOU OUT TO EAT ME!
WAAAAAAAA
HY EM NOT GUN EATCHU.
AAAAAAAAAA
AAAAAAAAAA
AAA
ONLESS DATS DE ONLY VAY TO SHOT HYU OP!!
...
NOW VERE HYU LIFF? MOOF!
SOON...
CLAY MECHANICAL
DIS IT? NOW SHTAY DERE!
—TCH. DOOMED.

CLANK!!

SNAP!

WHAMM!!

Huff.

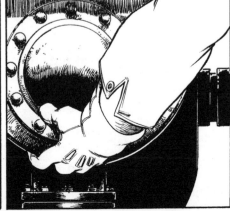

50

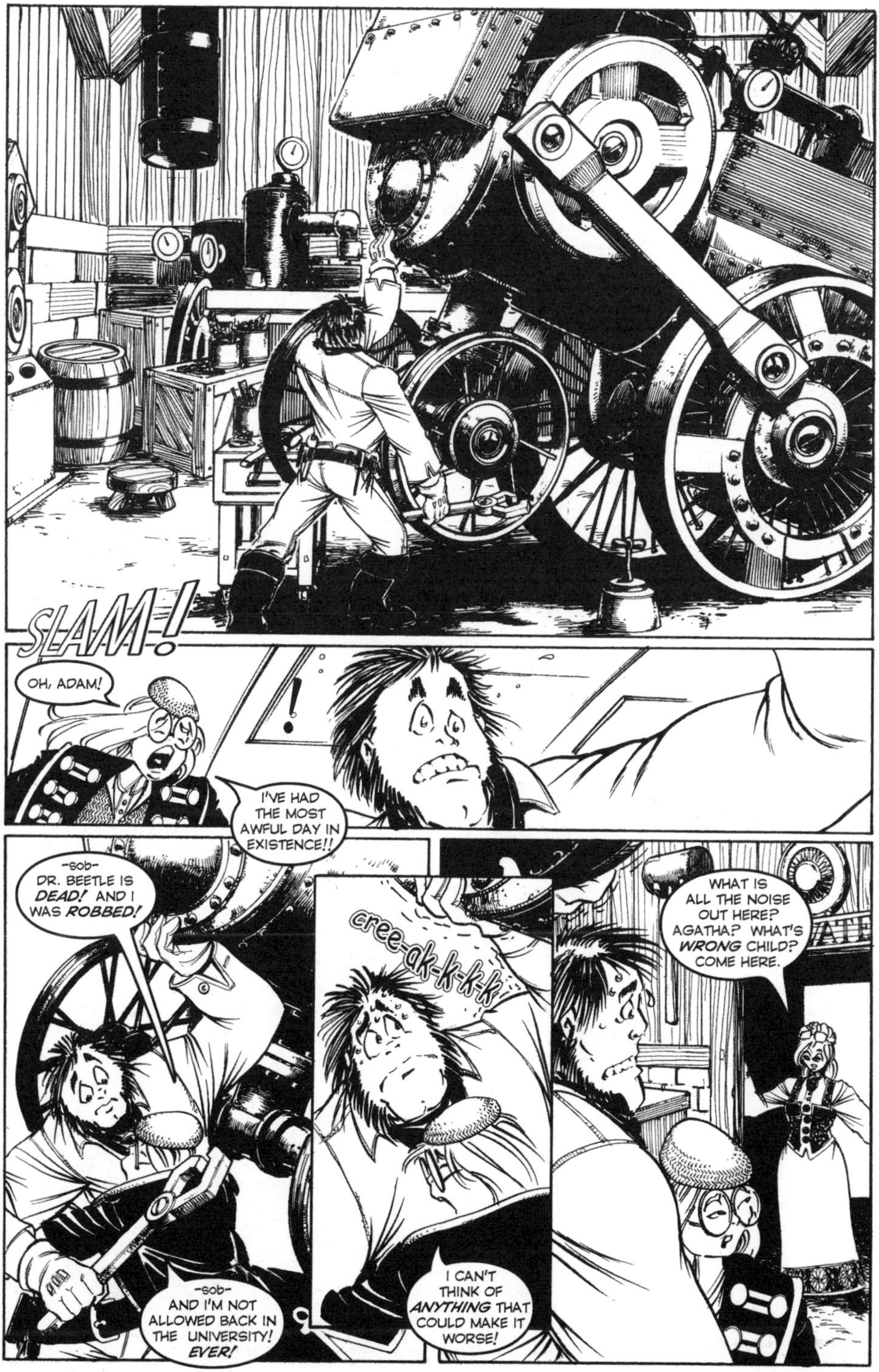

SLAM!
OH, ADAM!
!
I'VE HAD THE MOST AWFUL DAY IN EXISTENCE!!
-sob- DR. BEETLE IS DEAD! AND I WAS ROBBED!
-sob- AND I'M NOT ALLOWED BACK IN THE UNIVERSITY! EVER!
cree-ak-k-k-k
I CAN'T THINK OF ANYTHING THAT COULD MAKE IT WORSE!
WHAT IS ALL THE NOISE OUT HERE? AGATHA? WHAT'S WRONG CHILD? COME HERE.

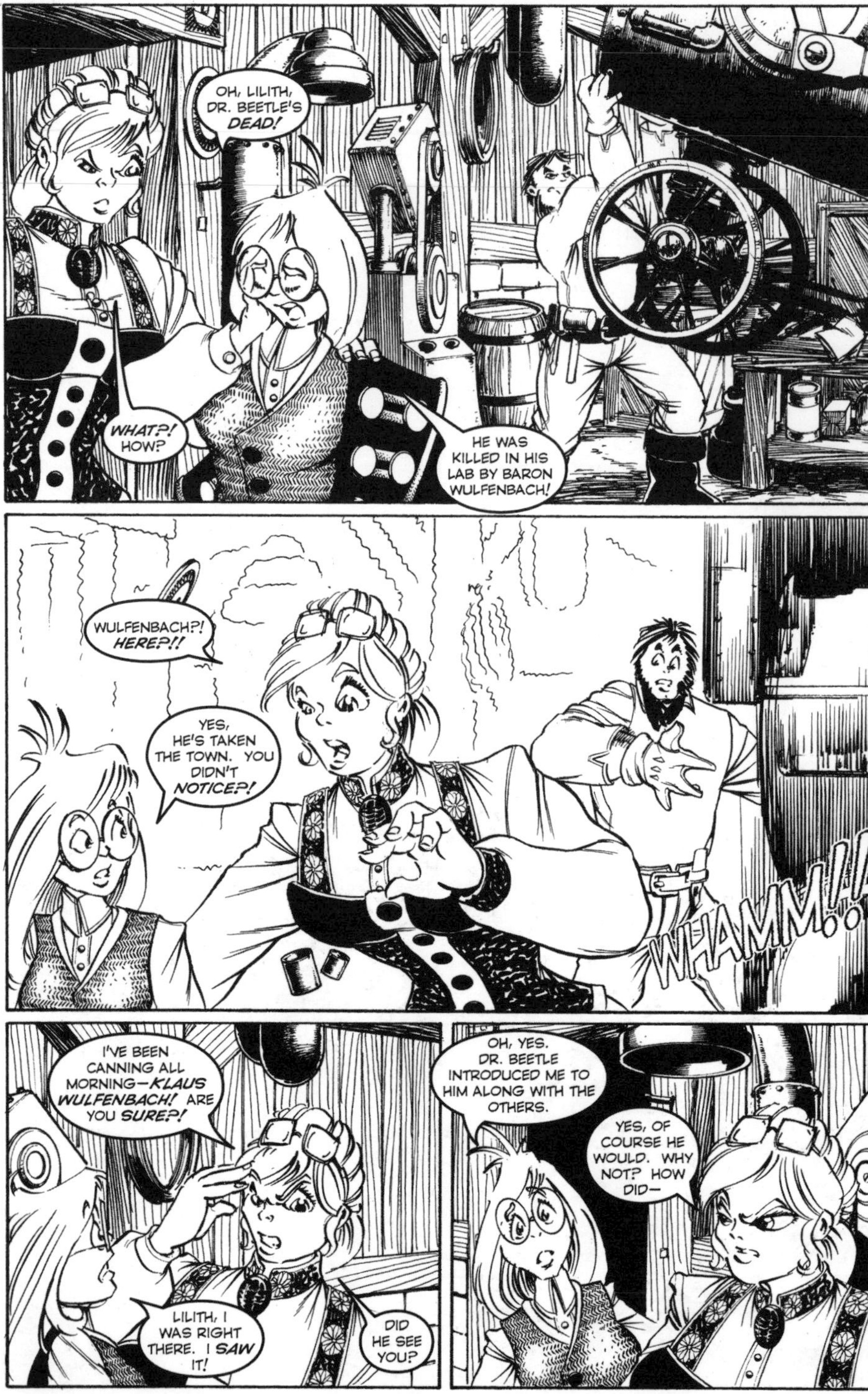
OH, LILITH, DR. BEETLE'S DEAD!
WHAT?! HOW?
HE WAS KILLED IN HIS LAB BY BARON WULFENBACH!
WULFENBACH?! HERE?!!
YES, HE'S TAKEN THE TOWN. YOU DIDN'T NOTICE?!
WHAMM!!
I'VE BEEN CANNING ALL MORNING—KLAUS WULFENBACH! ARE YOU SURE?!
LILITH, I WAS RIGHT THERE. I SAW IT!
DID HE SEE YOU?
OH, YES. DR. BEETLE INTRODUCED ME TO HIM ALONG WITH THE OTHERS.
YES, OF COURSE HE WOULD. WHY NOT? HOW DID—

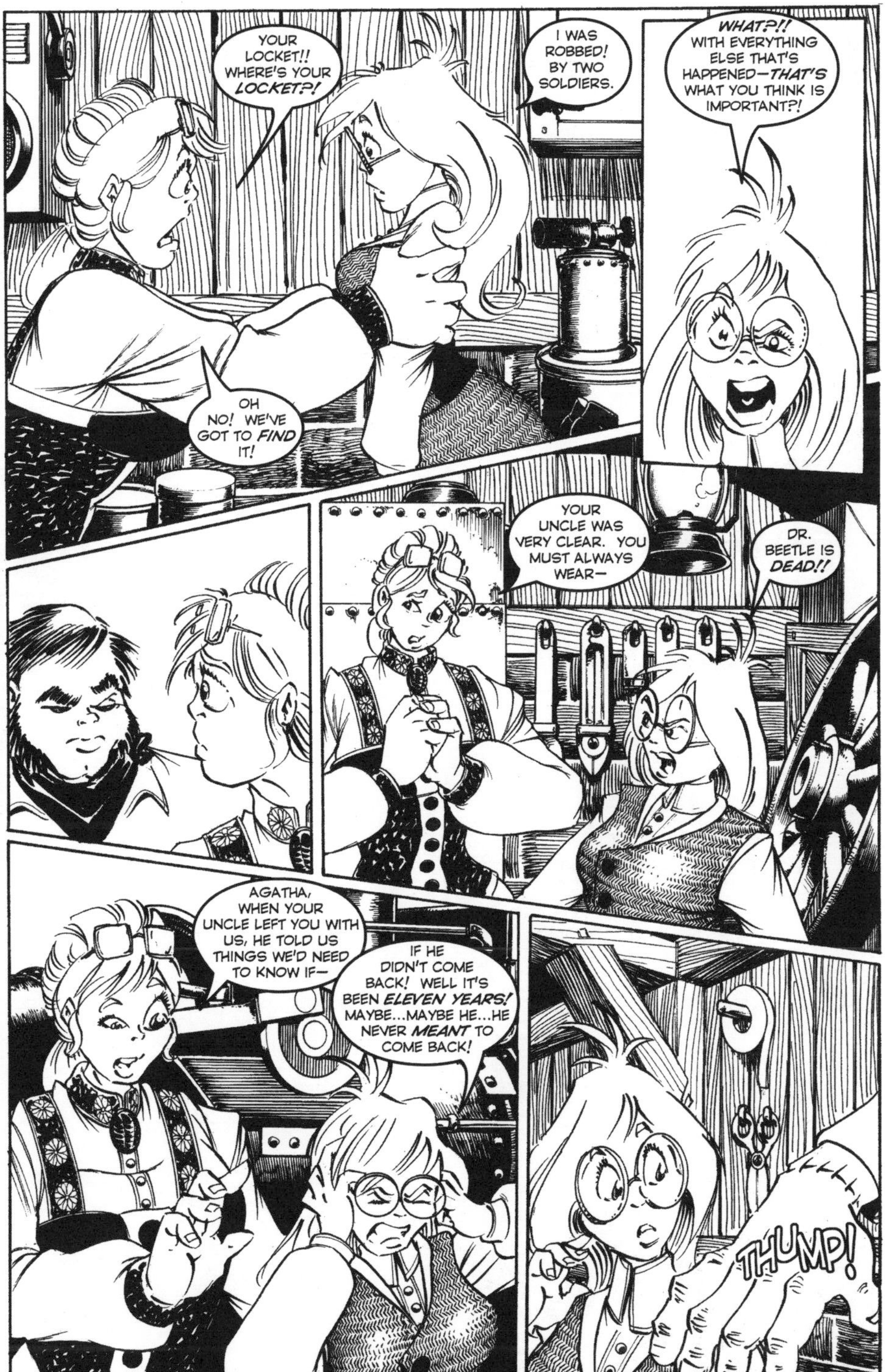
YOUR LOCKET!! WHERE'S YOUR LOCKET?!
OH NO! WE'VE GOT TO FIND IT!
I WAS ROBBED! BY TWO SOLDIERS.
WHAT?!! WITH EVERYTHING ELSE THAT'S HAPPENED—THAT'S WHAT YOU THINK IS IMPORTANT?!
YOUR UNCLE WAS VERY CLEAR. YOU MUST ALWAYS WEAR—
DR. BEETLE IS DEAD!!
AGATHA, WHEN YOUR UNCLE LEFT YOU WITH US, HE TOLD US THINGS WE'D NEED TO KNOW IF—
IF HE DIDN'T COME BACK! WELL IT'S BEEN ELEVEN YEARS! MAYBE...MAYBE HE...HE NEVER MEANT TO COME BACK!
THUMP!

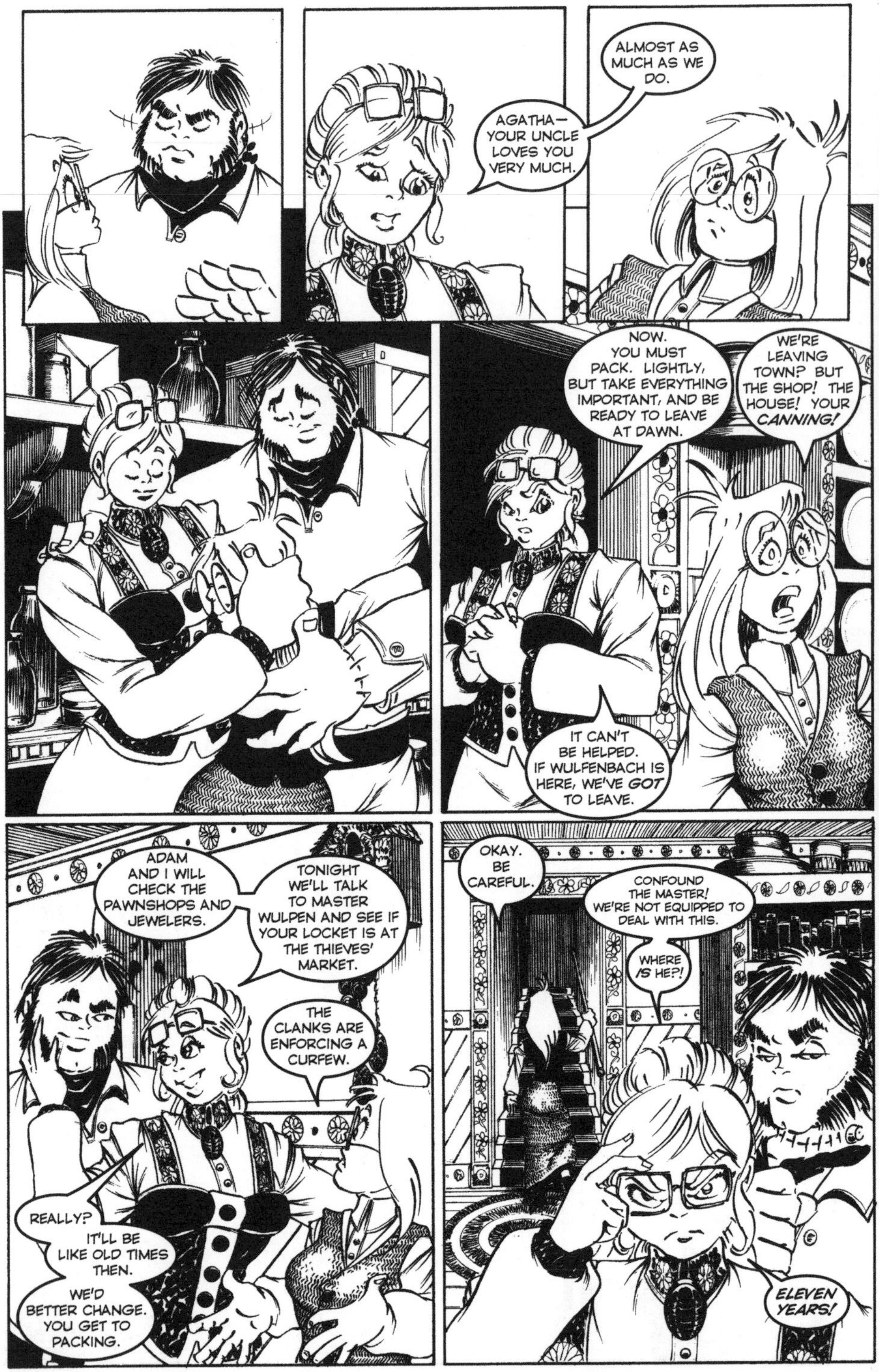
AGATHA— YOUR UNCLE LOVES YOU VERY MUCH.
ALMOST AS MUCH AS WE DO.
NOW. YOU MUST PACK. LIGHTLY, BUT TAKE EVERYTHING IMPORTANT, AND BE READY TO LEAVE AT DAWN.
WE'RE LEAVING TOWN? BUT THE SHOP! THE HOUSE! YOUR CANNING!
IT CAN'T BE HELPED. IF WULFENBACH IS HERE, WE'VE GOT TO LEAVE.
ADAM AND I WILL CHECK THE PAWNSHOPS AND JEWELERS.
TONIGHT WE'LL TALK TO MASTER WULPEN AND SEE IF YOUR LOCKET IS AT THE THIEVES' MARKET.
THE CLANKS ARE ENFORCING A CURFEW.
REALLY?
IT'LL BE LIKE OLD TIMES THEN.
WE'D BETTER CHANGE. YOU GET TO PACKING.
OKAY. BE CAREFUL.
CONFOUND THE MASTER! WE'RE NOT EQUIPPED TO DEAL WITH THIS.
WHERE IS HE?!
ELEVEN YEARS!

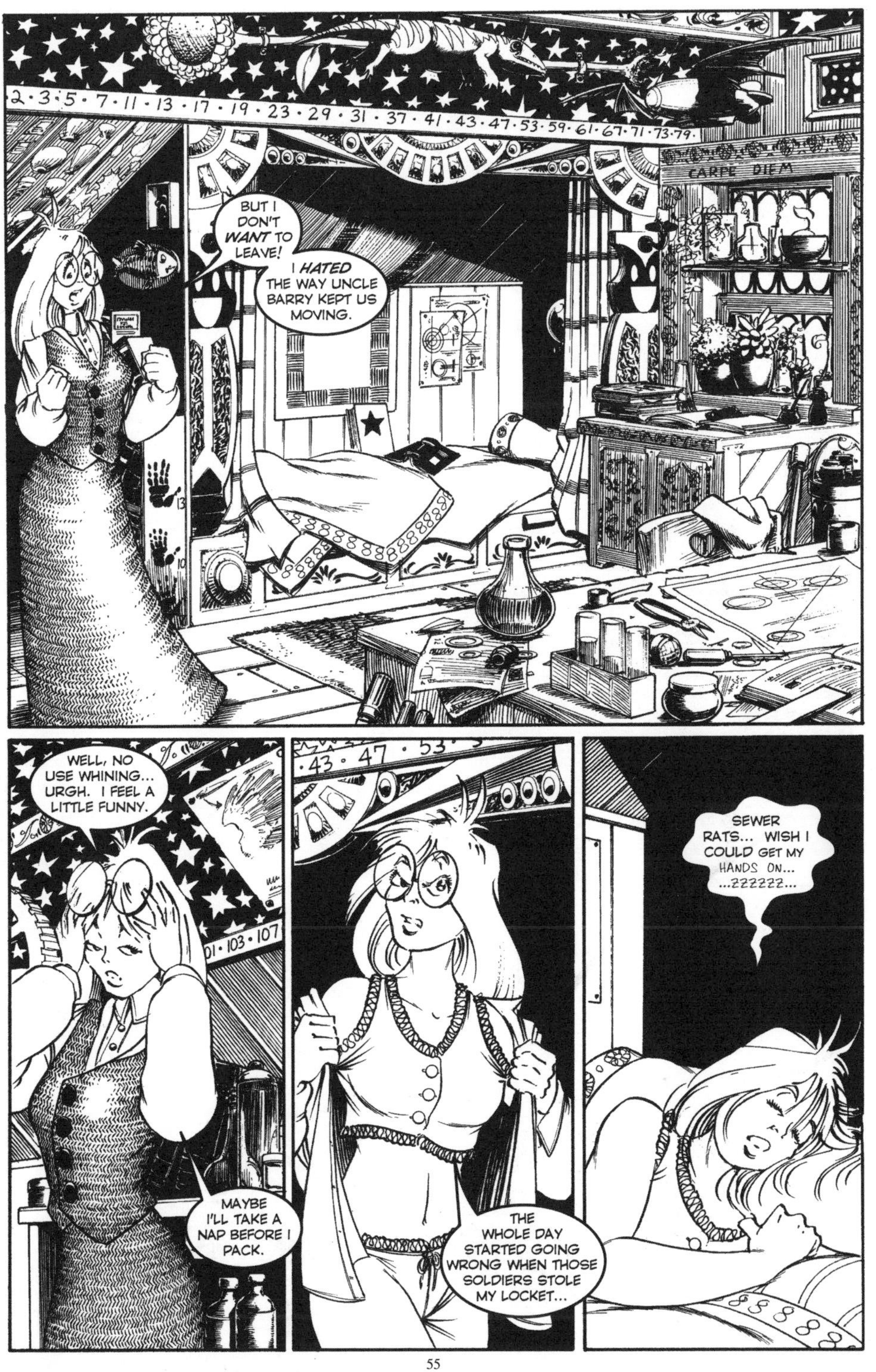
2 · 3 · 5 · 7 · 11 · 13 · 17 · 19 · 23 · 29 · 31 · 37 · 41 · 43 · 47 · 53 · 59 · 61 · 67 · 71 · 73 · 79
CARPE DIEM
BUT I DON'T *WANT* TO LEAVE!
I *HATED* THE WAY UNCLE BARRY KEPT US MOVING.
WELL, NO USE WHINING... URGH. I FEEL A LITTLE FUNNY.
MAYBE I'LL TAKE A NAP BEFORE I PACK.
THE WHOLE DAY STARTED GOING WRONG WHEN THOSE SOLDIERS STOLE MY LOCKET...
SEWER RATS... WISH I COULD GET MY HANDS ON... ...ZZZZZZ...

Early the next morning...

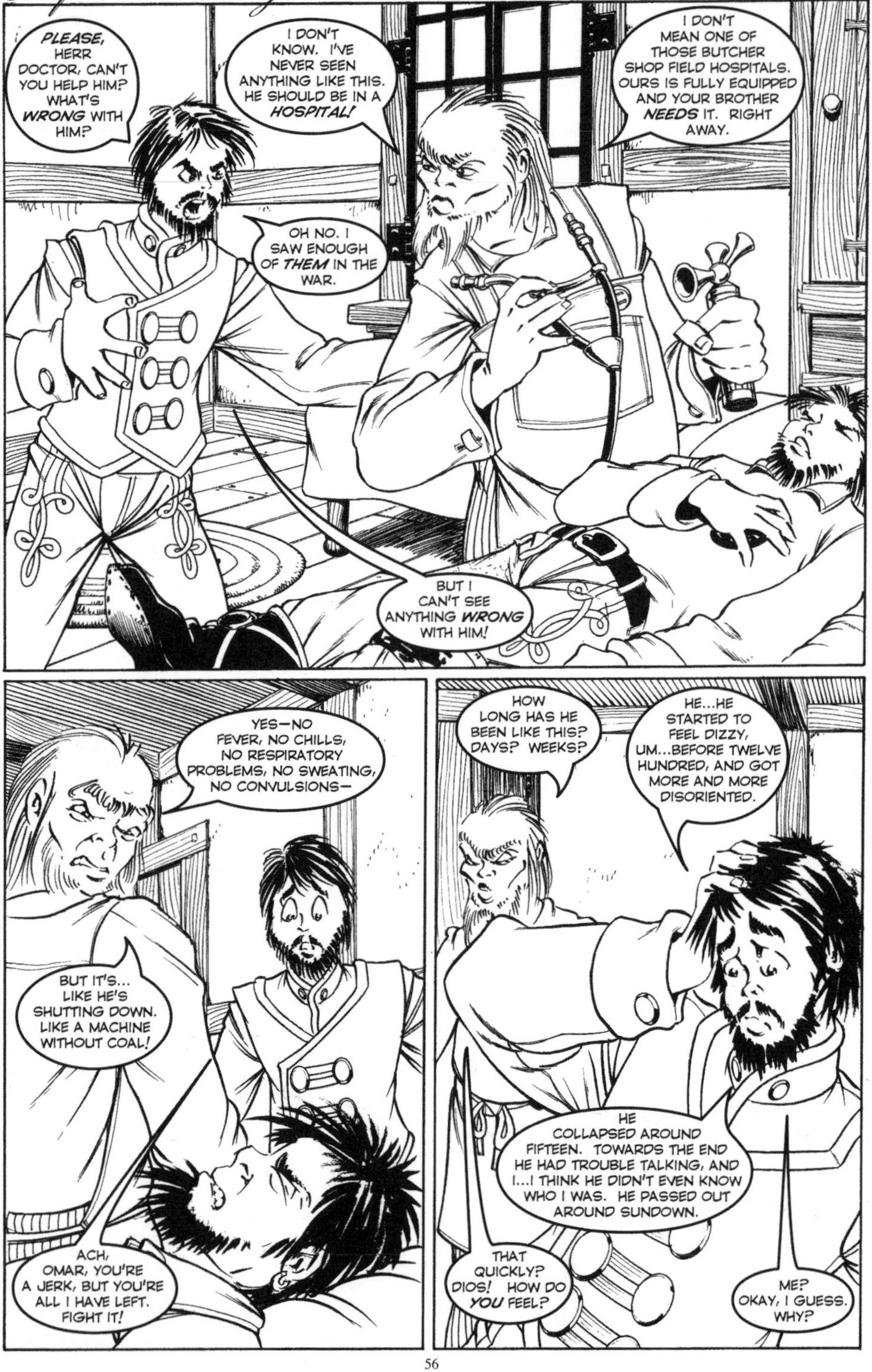
PLEASE, HERR DOCTOR, CAN'T YOU HELP HIM? WHAT'S WRONG WITH HIM?
I DON'T KNOW. I'VE NEVER SEEN ANYTHING LIKE THIS. HE SHOULD BE IN A HOSPITAL!
OH NO. I SAW ENOUGH OF THEM IN THE WAR.
I DON'T MEAN ONE OF THOSE BUTCHER SHOP FIELD HOSPITALS. OURS IS FULLY EQUIPPED AND YOUR BROTHER NEEDS IT. RIGHT AWAY.
BUT I CAN'T SEE ANYTHING WRONG WITH HIM!
YES—NO FEVER, NO CHILLS, NO RESPIRATORY PROBLEMS, NO SWEATING, NO CONVULSIONS—
BUT IT'S... LIKE HE'S SHUTTING DOWN. LIKE A MACHINE WITHOUT COAL!
ACH, OMAR, YOU'RE A JERK, BUT YOU'RE ALL I HAVE LEFT. FIGHT IT!
HOW LONG HAS HE BEEN LIKE THIS? DAYS? WEEKS?
HE...HE STARTED TO FEEL DIZZY, UM...BEFORE TWELVE HUNDRED, AND GOT MORE AND MORE DISORIENTED.
HE COLLAPSED AROUND FIFTEEN. TOWARDS THE END HE HAD TROUBLE TALKING, AND I...I THINK HE DIDN'T EVEN KNOW WHO I WAS. HE PASSED OUT AROUND SUNDOWN.
THAT QUICKLY? DIOS! HOW DO YOU FEEL?
ME? OKAY, I GUESS. WHY?

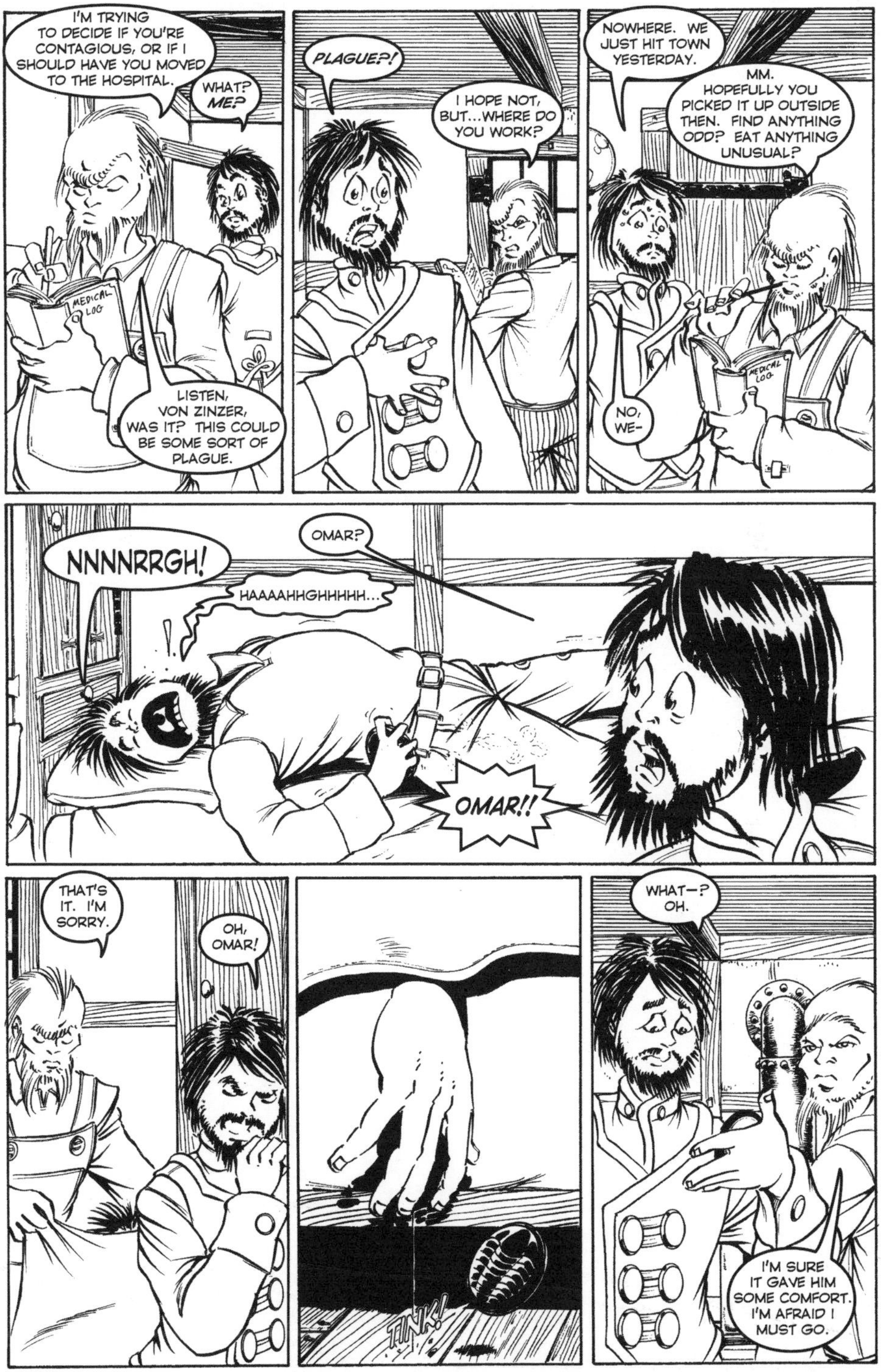
I'M TRYING TO DECIDE IF YOU'RE CONTAGIOUS, OR IF I SHOULD HAVE YOU MOVED TO THE HOSPITAL.
WHAT? ME?
LISTEN, VON ZINZER, WAS IT? THIS COULD BE SOME SORT OF PLAGUE.
MEDICAL LOG
PLAGUE?!
I HOPE NOT, BUT...WHERE DO YOU WORK?
NOWHERE. WE JUST HIT TOWN YESTERDAY.
MM. HOPEFULLY YOU PICKED IT UP OUTSIDE THEN. FIND ANYTHING ODD? EAT ANYTHING UNUSUAL?
NO, WE-
MEDICAL LOG
NNNNRRGH!
OMAR?
HAAAAHHGHHHHH...
!
OMAR!!
THAT'S IT. I'M SORRY.
OH, OMAR!
TINK!
WHAT—? OH.
I'M SURE IT GAVE HIM SOME COMFORT. I'M AFRAID I MUST GO.

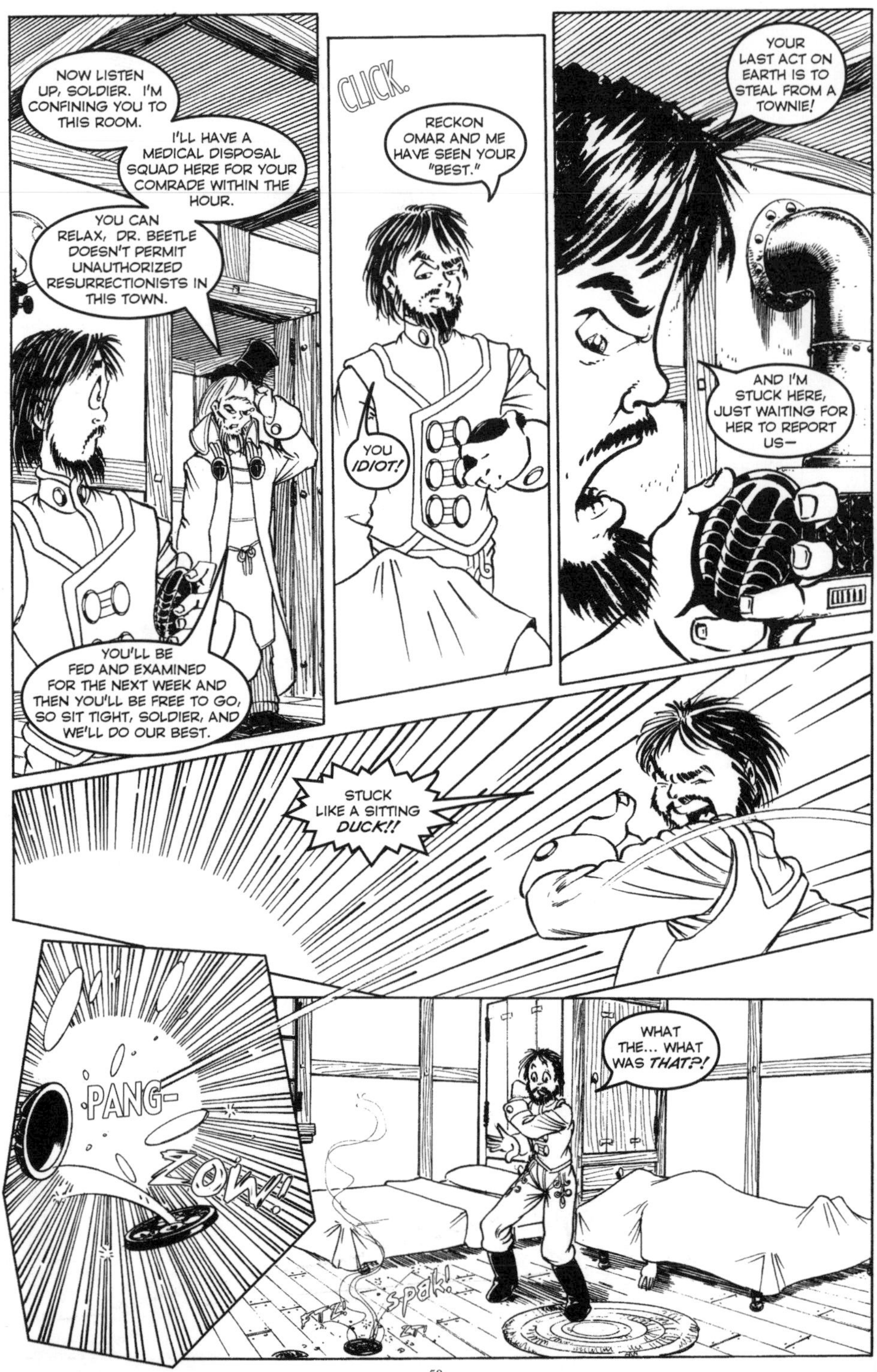
NOW LISTEN UP, SOLDIER. I'M CONFINING YOU TO THIS ROOM.
I'LL HAVE A MEDICAL DISPOSAL SQUAD HERE FOR YOUR COMRADE WITHIN THE HOUR.
YOU CAN RELAX, DR. BEETLE DOESN'T PERMIT UNAUTHORIZED RESURRECTIONISTS IN THIS TOWN.
YOU'LL BE FED AND EXAMINED FOR THE NEXT WEEK AND THEN YOU'LL BE FREE TO GO, SO SIT TIGHT, SOLDIER, AND WE'LL DO OUR BEST.
CLICK.
RECKON OMAR AND ME HAVE SEEN YOUR "BEST."
YOU *IDIOT!*
YOUR LAST ACT ON EARTH IS TO STEAL FROM A TOWNIE!
AND I'M STUCK HERE, JUST WAITING FOR HER TO REPORT US—
STUCK LIKE A SITTING *DUCK!!*
PANG-
ZOW!!
WHAT THE... WHAT WAS *THAT?!*
spak!

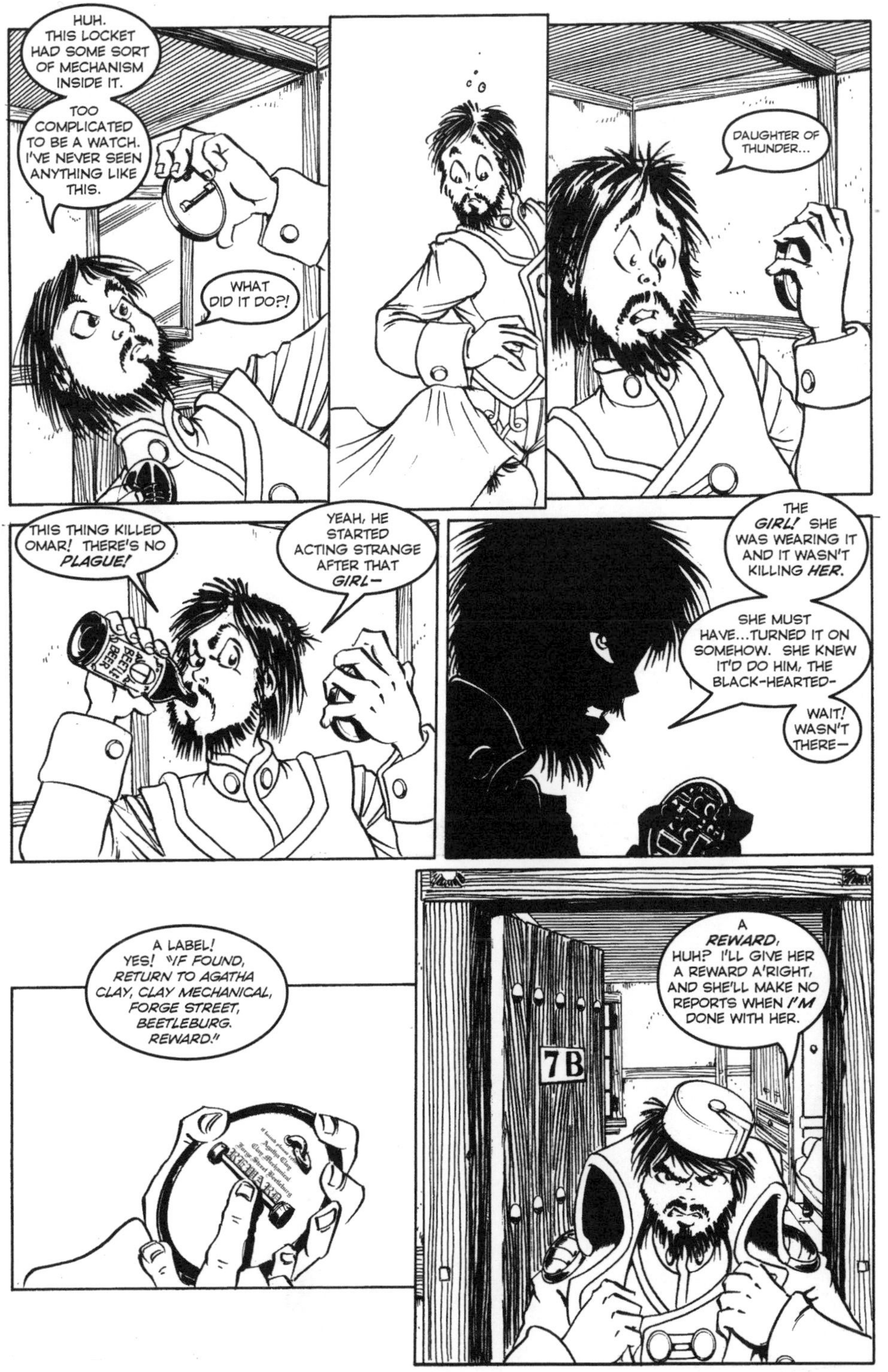
HUH. THIS LOCKET HAD SOME SORT OF MECHANISM INSIDE IT.
TOO COMPLICATED TO BE A WATCH. I'VE NEVER SEEN ANYTHING LIKE THIS.
WHAT DID IT DO?!
DAUGHTER OF THUNDER...
THIS THING KILLED OMAR! THERE'S NO *PLAGUE!*
YEAH, HE STARTED ACTING STRANGE AFTER THAT *GIRL—*
BEETLE BEER
THE *GIRL!* SHE WAS WEARING IT AND IT WASN'T KILLING *HER.*
SHE MUST HAVE...TURNED IT ON SOMEHOW. SHE KNEW IT'D DO HIM, THE BLACK-HEARTED—
WAIT! WASN'T THERE—
A LABEL! YES! *"IF FOUND, RETURN TO AGATHA CLAY, CLAY MECHANICAL, FORGE STREET, BEETLEBURG. REWARD."*
Agatha Clay
Clay Mechanical
Forge Street Beetleburg
REWARD
A *REWARD,* HUH? I'LL GIVE HER A REWARD A'RIGHT, AND SHE'LL MAKE NO REPORTS WHEN *I'M* DONE WITH HER.
7B

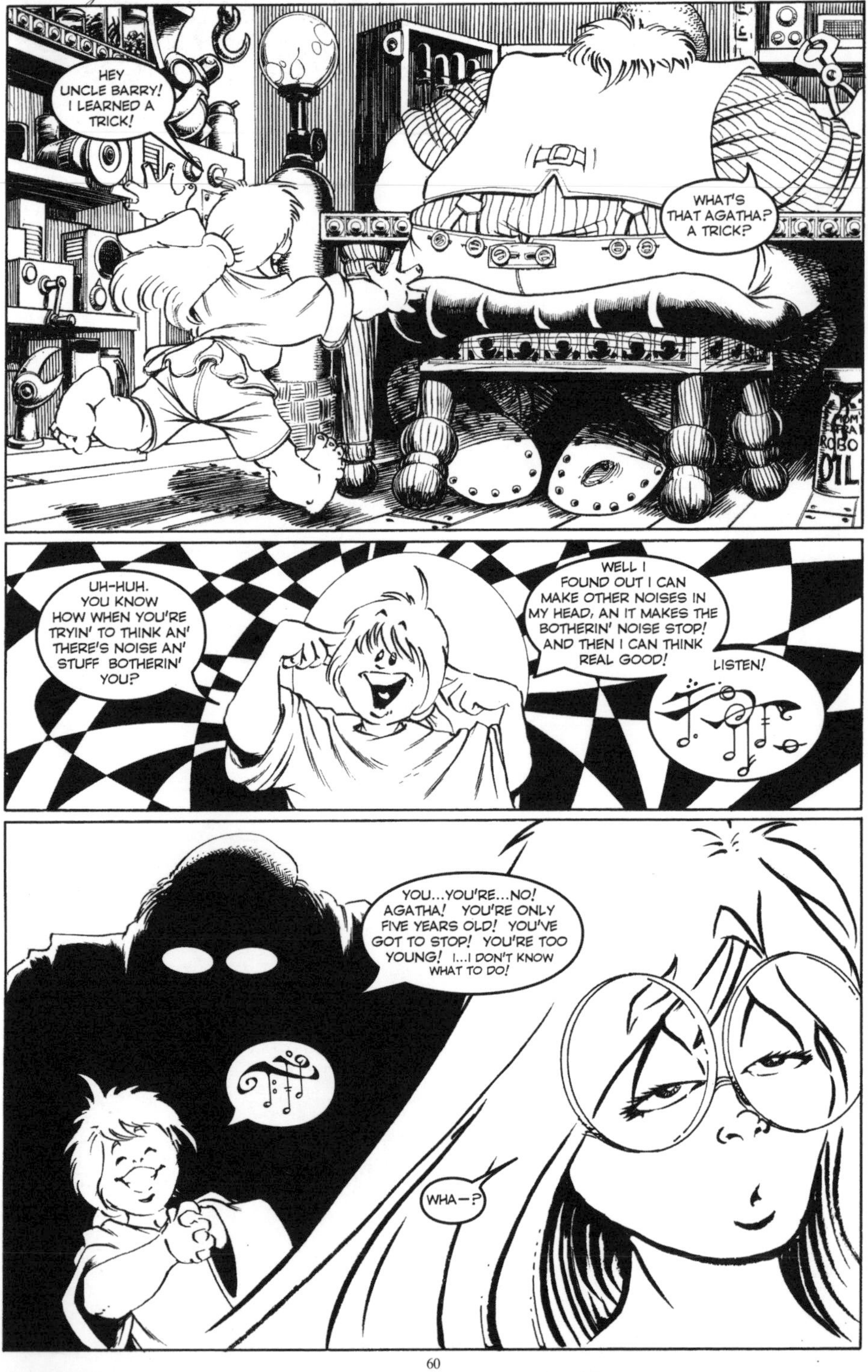
HEY UNCLE BARRY! I LEARNED A TRICK!
WHAT'S THAT AGATHA? A TRICK?
ROBO OIL
UH-HUH. YOU KNOW HOW WHEN YOU'RE TRYIN' TO THINK AN' THERE'S NOISE AN' STUFF BOTHERIN' YOU?
WELL I FOUND OUT I CAN MAKE OTHER NOISES IN MY HEAD, AN IT MAKES THE BOTHERIN' NOISE STOP! AND THEN I CAN THINK REAL GOOD!
LISTEN!
YOU...YOU'RE...NO! AGATHA! YOU'RE ONLY FIVE YEARS OLD! YOU'VE GOT TO STOP! YOU'RE TOO YOUNG! I...I DON'T KNOW WHAT TO DO!
WHA–?

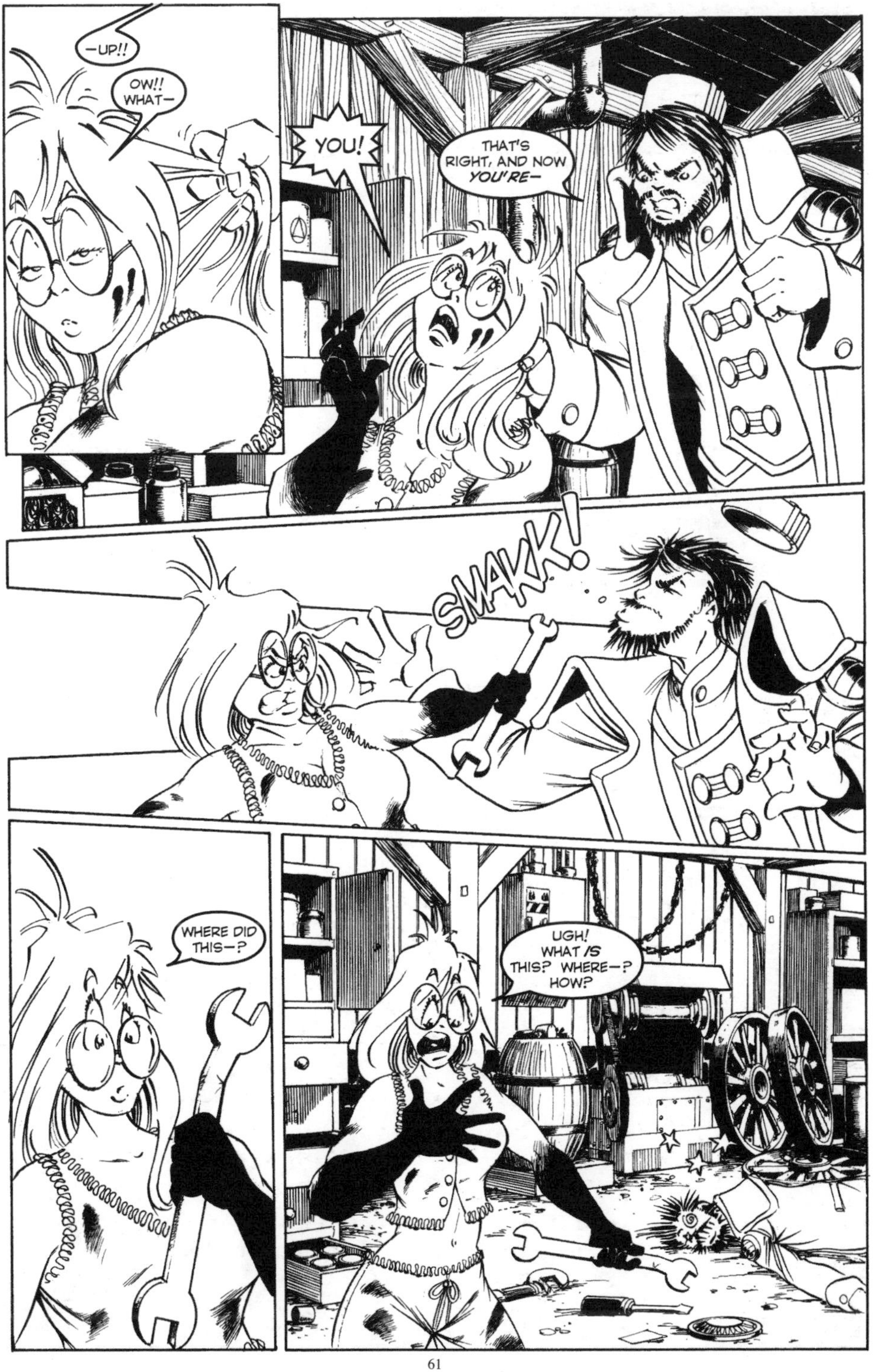

—UP!!
OW!! WHAT—
YOU!
THAT'S RIGHT, AND NOW *YOU'RE*—
SMAKK!
WHERE DID THIS—?
UGH! WHAT *IS* THIS? WHERE—? HOW?

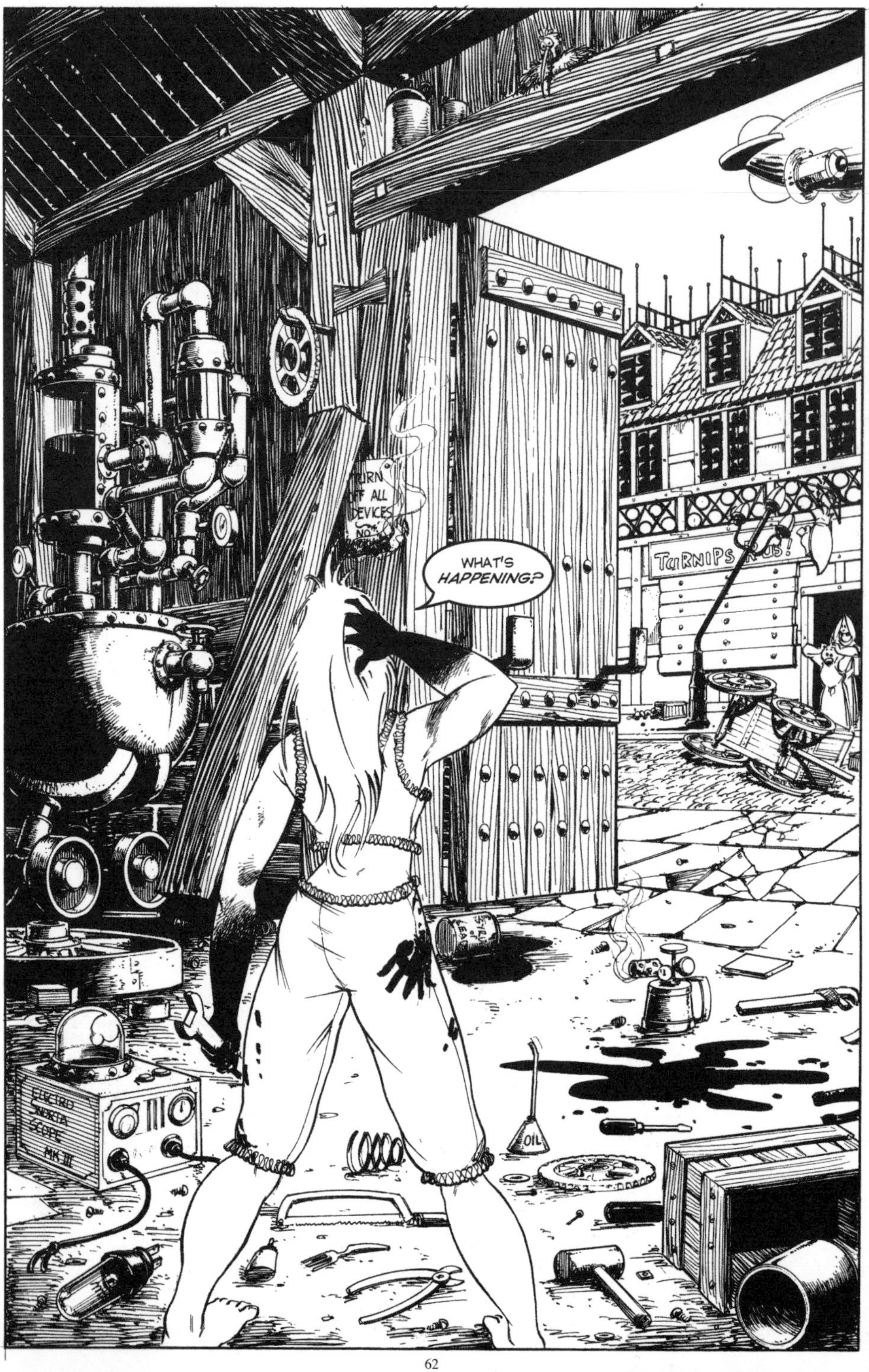
WHAT'S HAPPENING?
TURN
FF ALL
DEVICES
NO
TURNIPS R US!
ELECTRO SNORTA SCOPE MK III
OIL

Meanwhile...

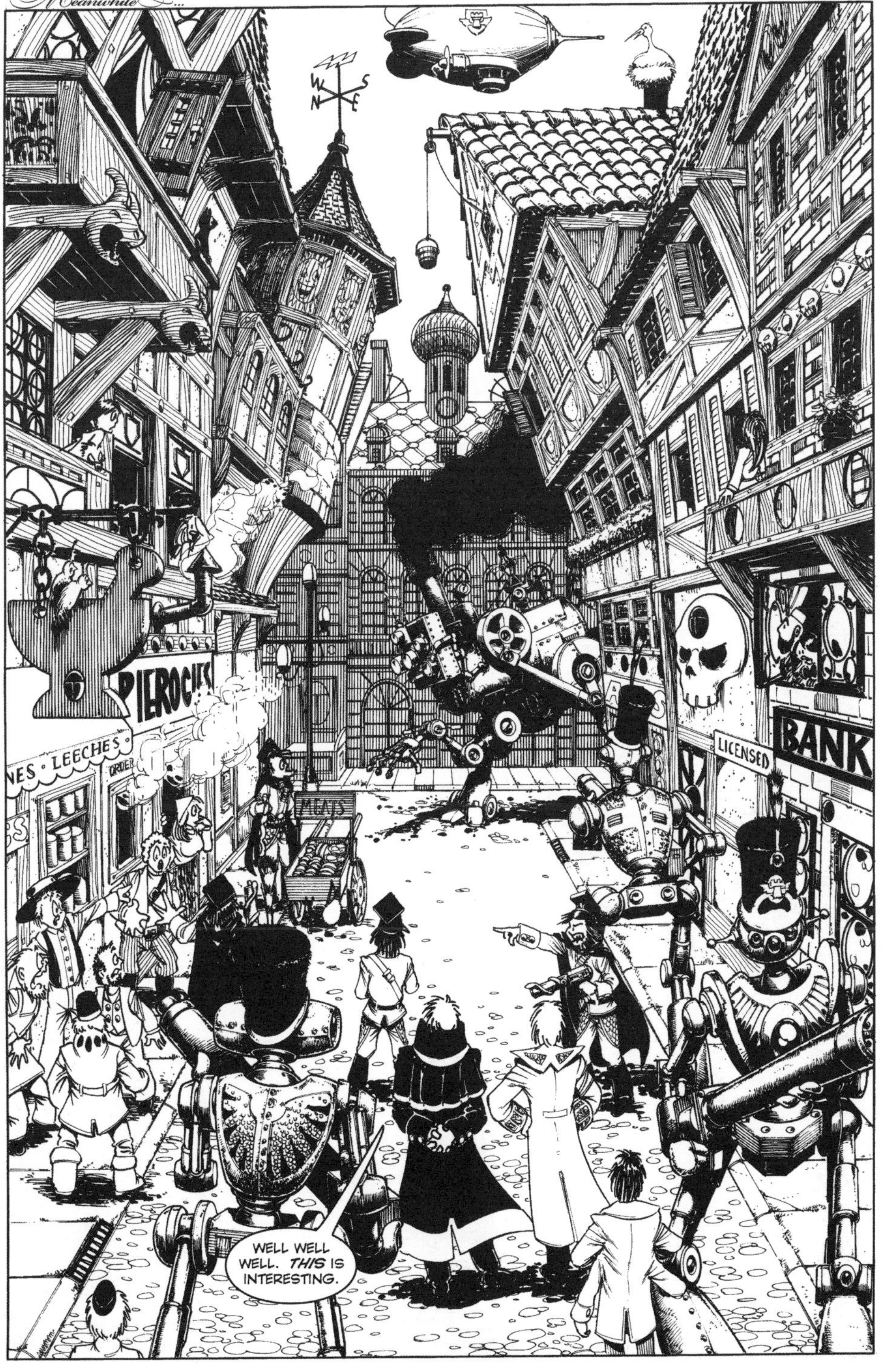
PIEROGIES
NES · LEECHES
ORDER
MEATS
LICENSED
BANK
WELL WELL WELL. *THIS* IS INTERESTING.

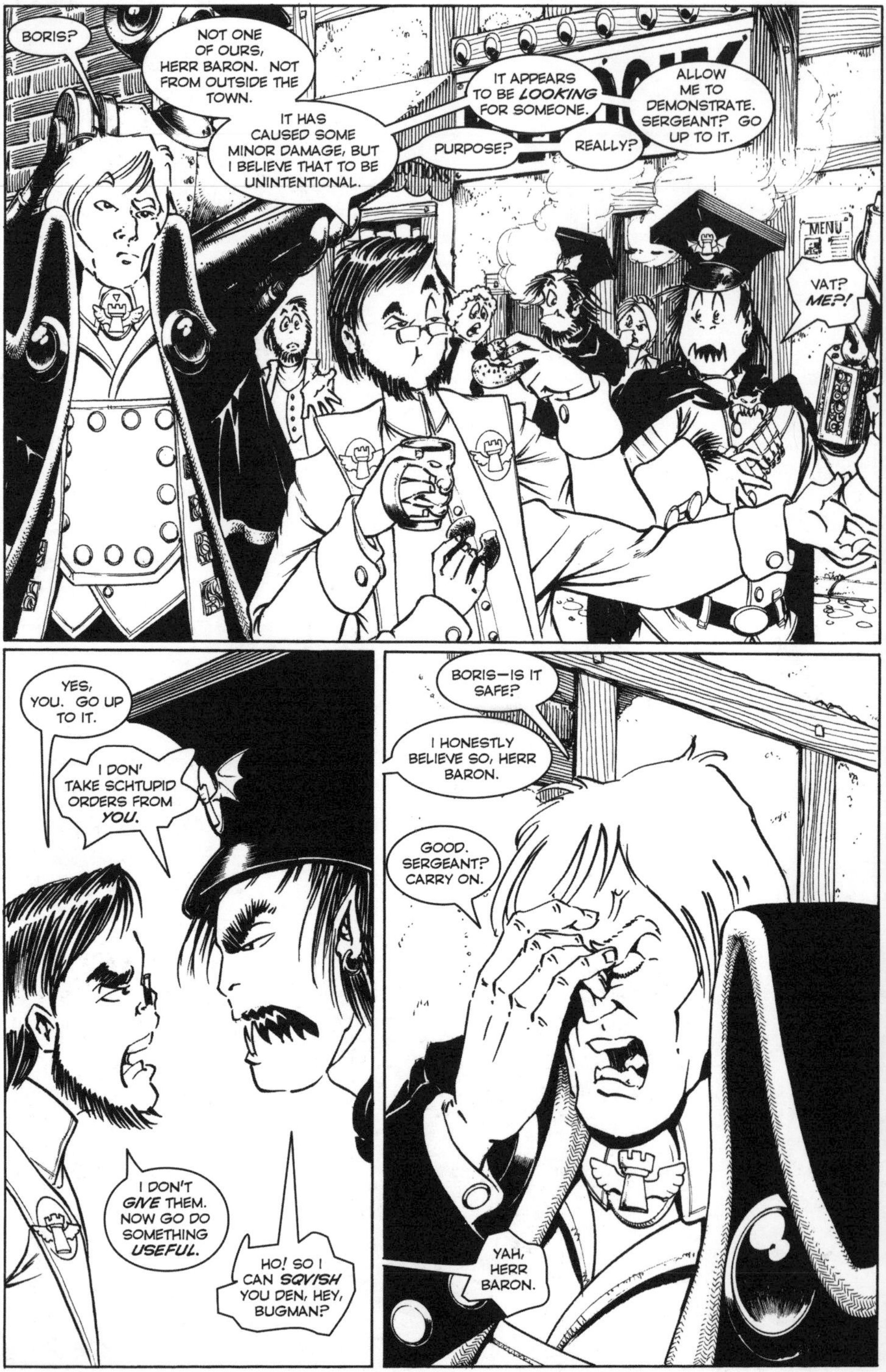
BORIS?
NOT ONE OF OURS, HERR BARON. NOT FROM OUTSIDE THE TOWN.
IT HAS CAUSED SOME MINOR DAMAGE, BUT I BELIEVE THAT TO BE UNINTENTIONAL.
PURPOSE?
IT APPEARS TO BE *LOOKING* FOR SOMEONE.
REALLY?
ALLOW ME TO DEMONSTRATE. SERGEANT? GO UP TO IT.
MENU
VAT? *ME?!*
YES, YOU. GO UP TO IT.
I DON' TAKE SCHTUPID ORDERS FROM *YOU.*
I DON'T *GIVE* THEM. NOW GO DO SOMETHING *USEFUL.*
HO! SO I CAN *SQVISH* YOU DEN, HEY, BUGMAN?
BORIS—IS IT SAFE?
I HONESTLY BELIEVE SO, HERR BARON.
GOOD. SERGEANT? CARRY ON.
YAH, HERR BARON.

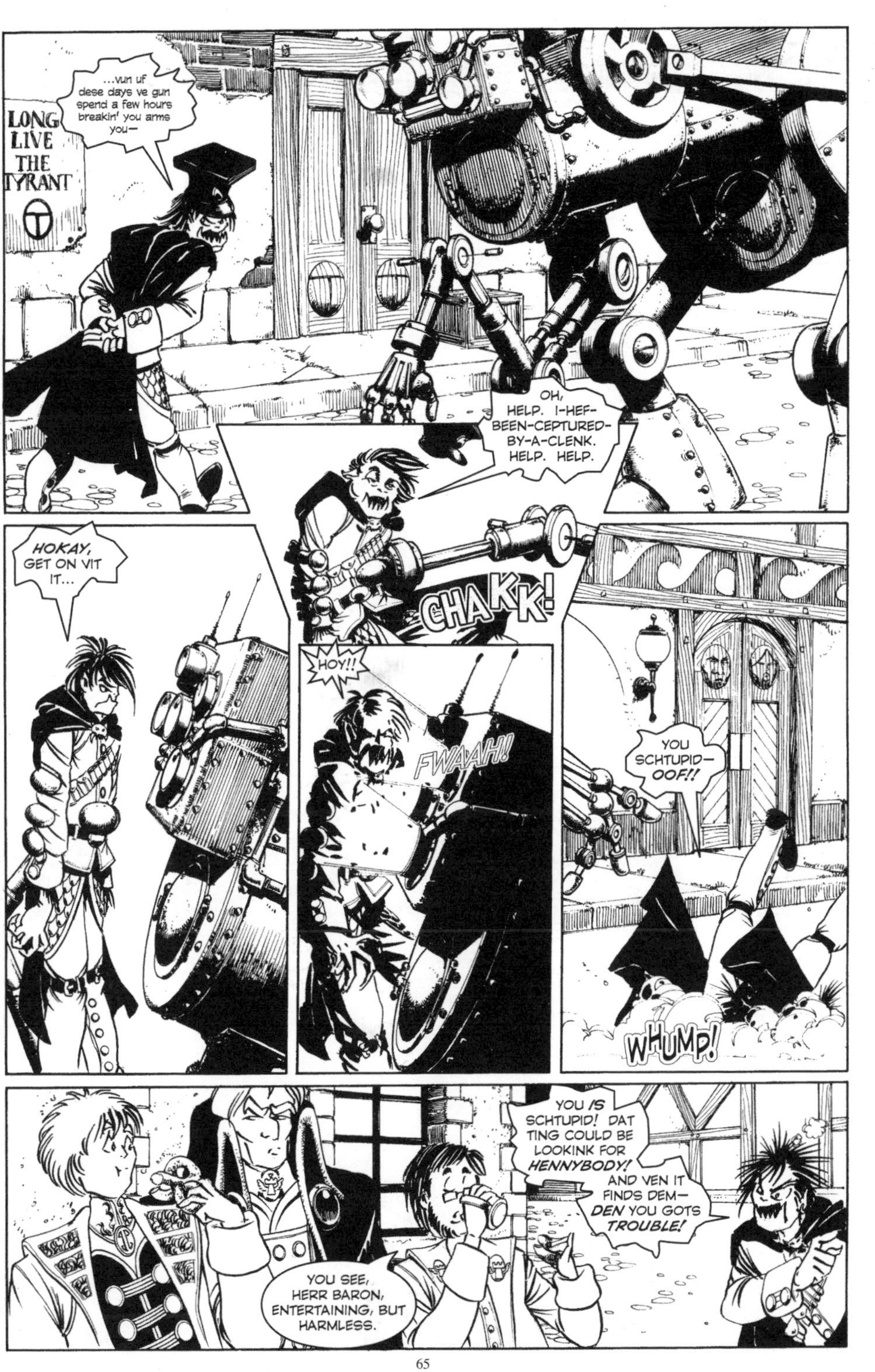

LONG LIVE THE TYRANT
...vun uf dese days ve gun spend a few hours breakin' you arms you—
OH, HELP. I-HEF-BEEN-CEPTURED-BY-A-CLENK. HELP. HELP.
HOKAY, GET ON VIT IT...
CHAKK!
HOY!!
FWAAH!
YOU SCHTUPID—OOF!!
WHUMP!
YOU IS SCHTUPID! DAT TING COULD BE LOOKINK FOR HENNYBODY!
AND VEN IT FINDS DEM—DEN YOU GOTS TROUBLE!
YOU SEE, HERR BARON, ENTERTAINING, BUT HARMLESS.

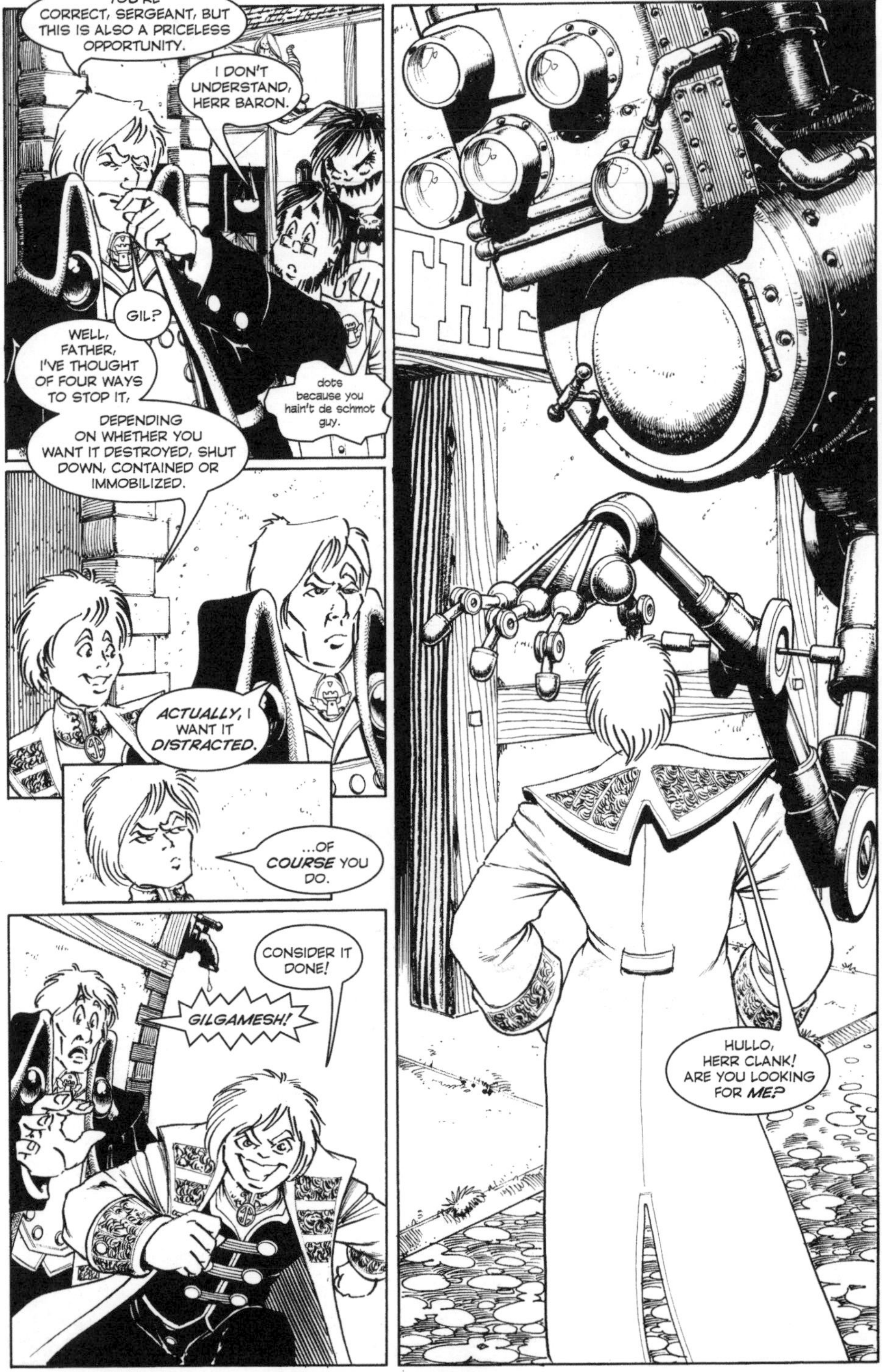

YOU'RE CORRECT, SERGEANT, BUT THIS IS ALSO A PRICELESS OPPORTUNITY.
I DON'T UNDERSTAND, HERR BARON.
GIL?
WELL, FATHER, I'VE THOUGHT OF FOUR WAYS TO STOP IT,
DEPENDING ON WHETHER YOU WANT IT DESTROYED, SHUT DOWN, CONTAINED OR IMMOBILIZED.
dots because you hain't de schmot guy.
ACTUALLY, I WANT IT *DISTRACTED.*
...OF *COURSE* YOU DO.
CONSIDER IT DONE!
GILGAMESH!
THE
HULLO, HERR CLANK! ARE YOU LOOKING FOR *ME?*

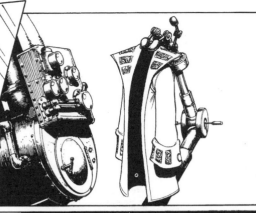

CLINK!

HO! YOU'LL HAVE TO DO BETTER THAN *THAT!*

BEVERAG

THOMB! THOMB! THOM

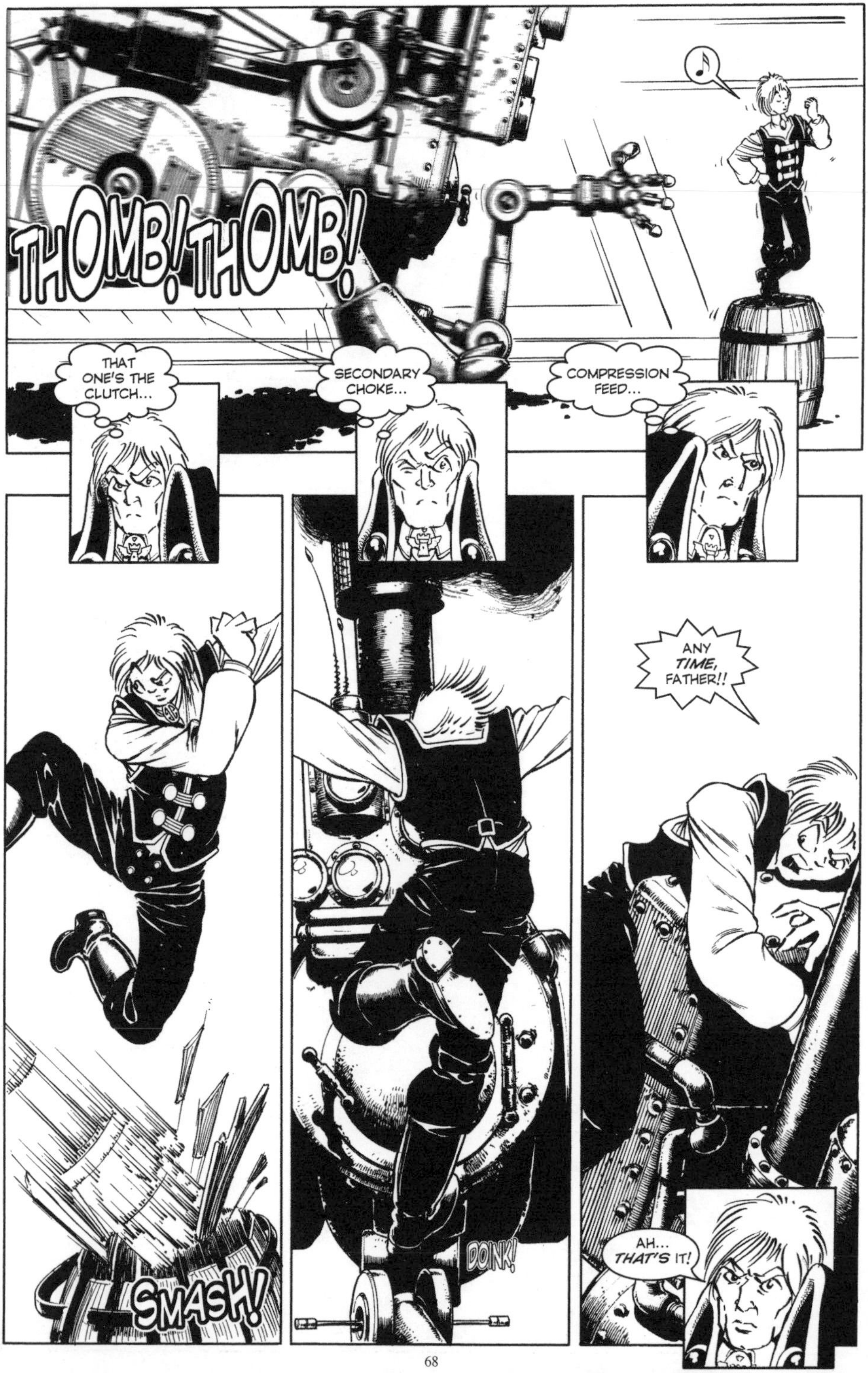

♪
THOMB! THOMB!
THAT ONE'S THE CLUTCH...
SECONDARY CHOKE...
COMPRESSION FEED...
ANY *TIME*, FATHER!!
SMASH!
DOINK!
AH... *THAT'S* IT!

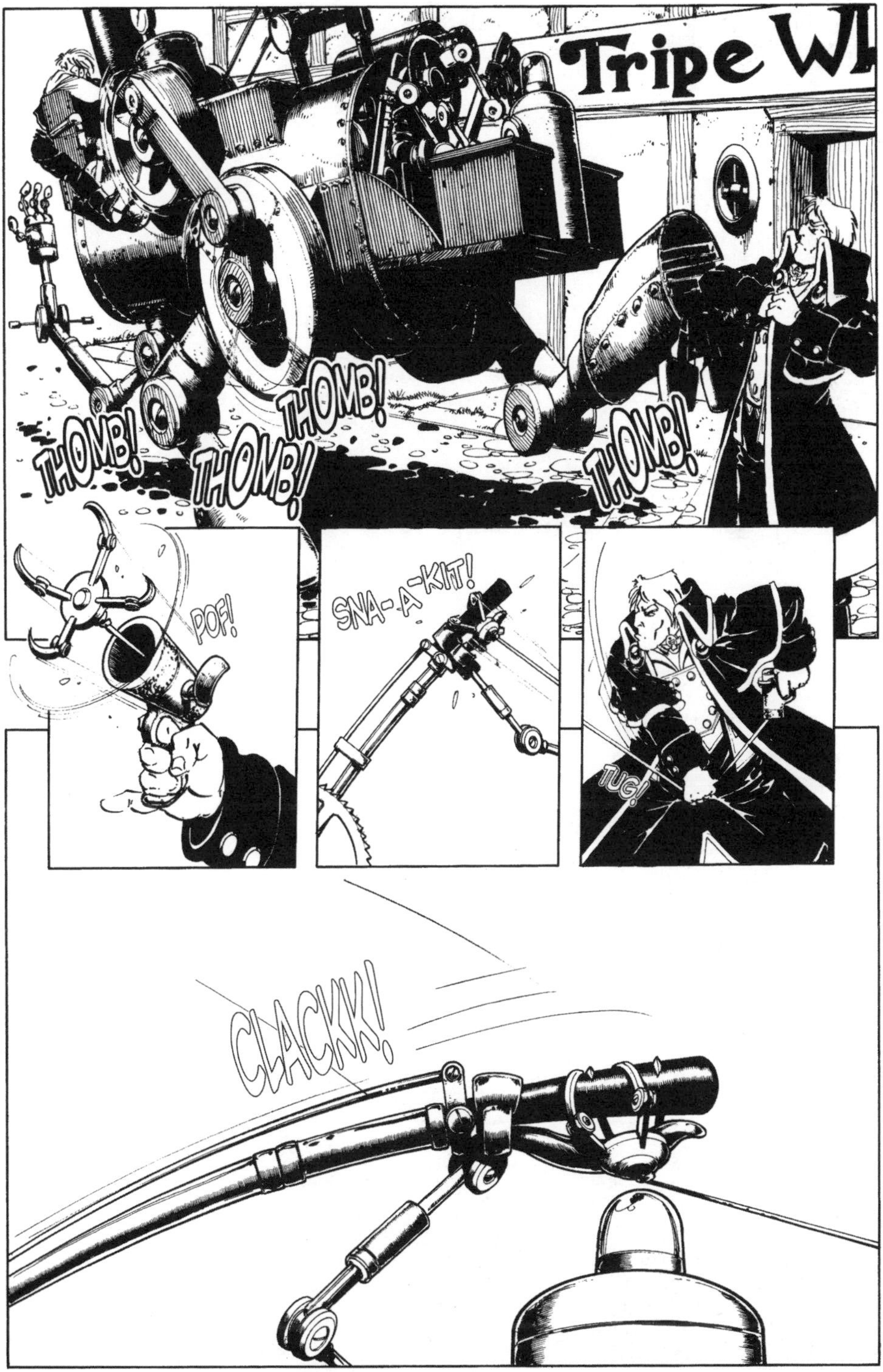
Tripe W
THOMB!
THOMB!
THOMB!
THOMB!
POF!
SNA-A-KIT!
TUG!
CLACKK!

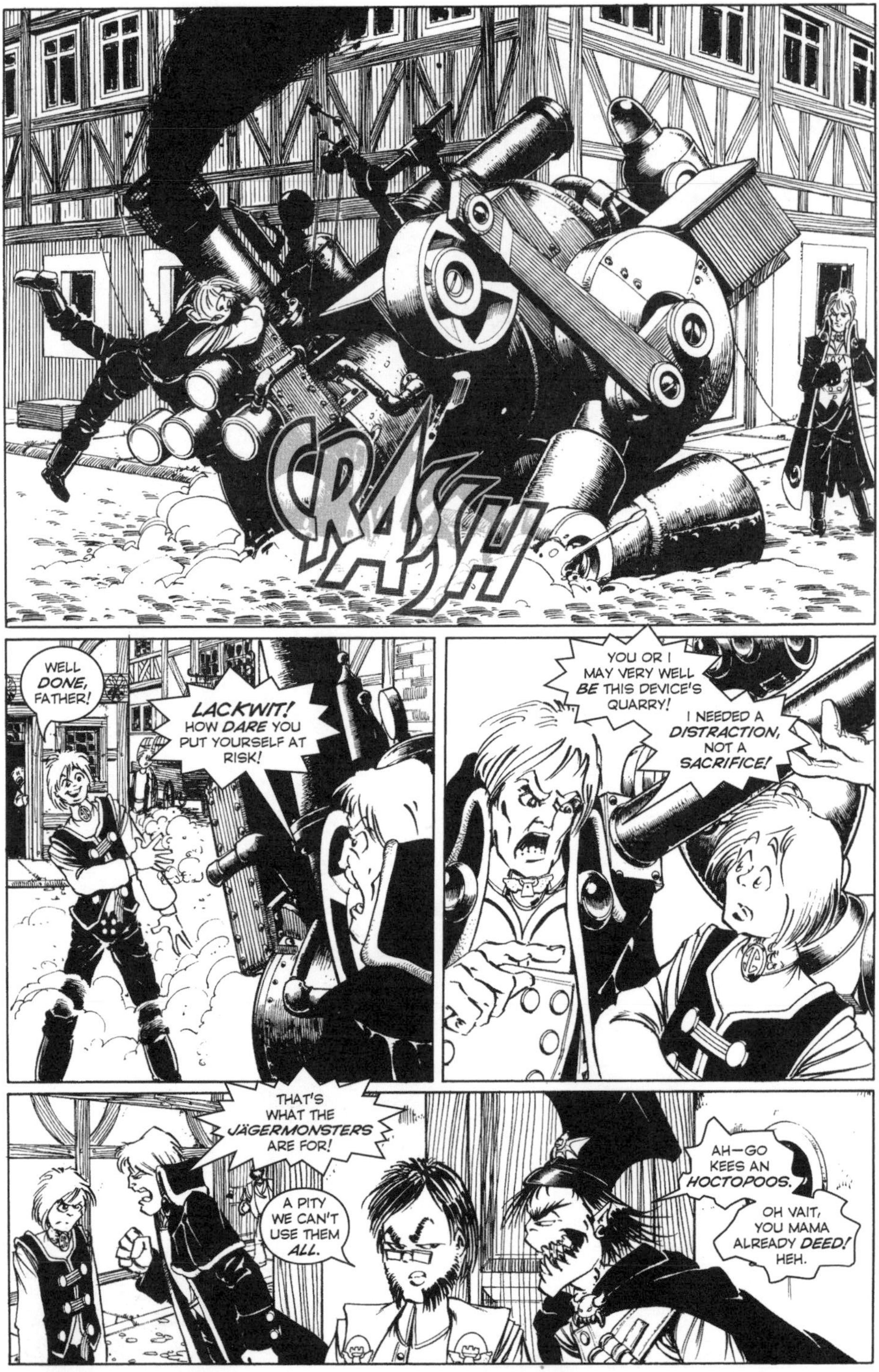
CRASH
WELL DONE, FATHER!
LACKWIT! HOW DARE YOU PUT YOURSELF AT RISK!
YOU OR I MAY VERY WELL BE THIS DEVICE'S QUARRY!
I NEEDED A DISTRACTION, NOT A SACRIFICE!
THAT'S WHAT THE JÄGERMONSTERS ARE FOR!
A PITY WE CAN'T USE THEM ALL.
AH—GO KEES AN HOCTOPOOS.
OH VAIT, YOU MAMA ALREADY DEED! HEH.

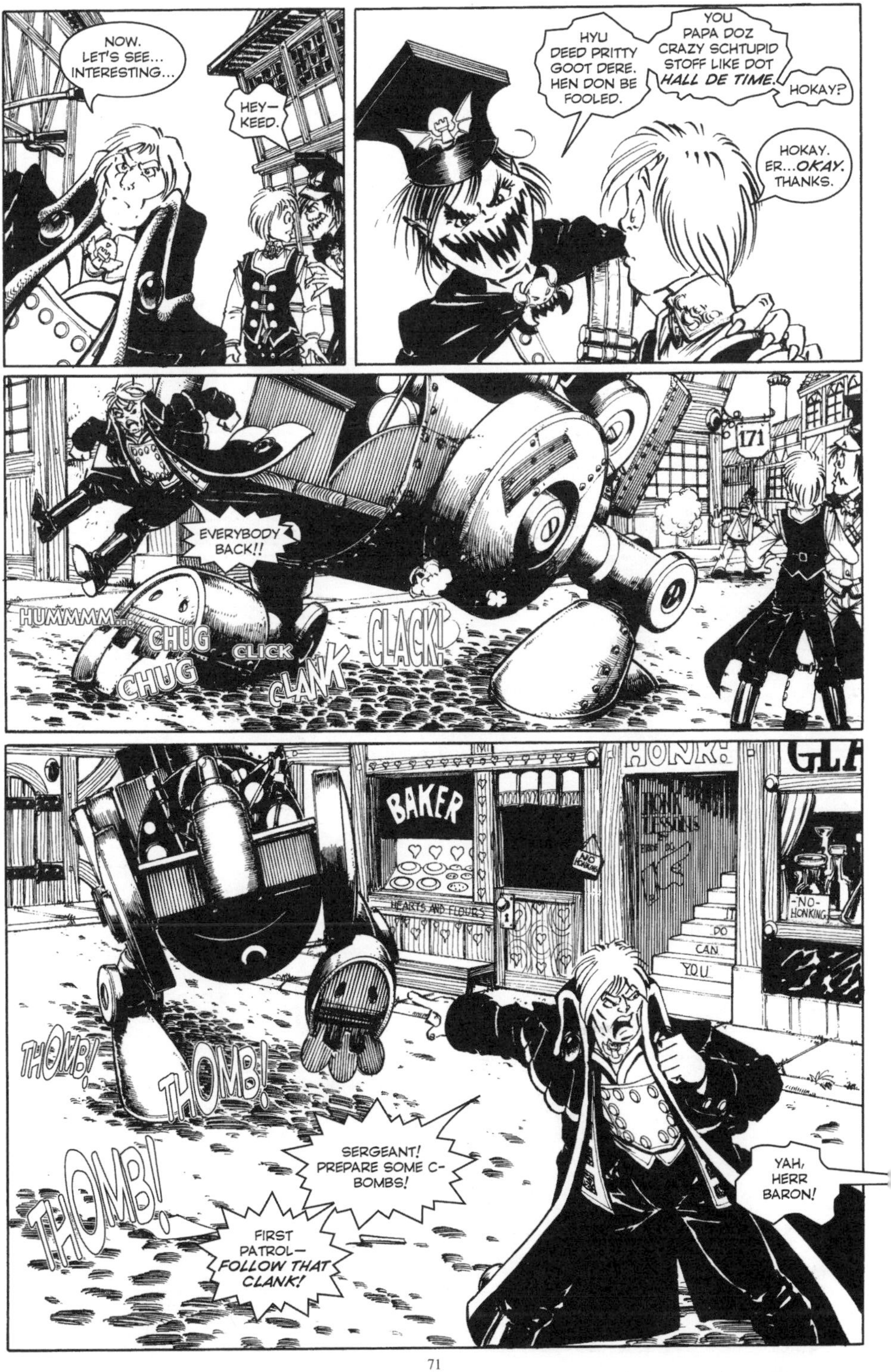
NOW. LET'S SEE... INTERESTING...
HEY— KEED.
HYU DEED PRITTY GOOT DERE. HEN DON BE FOOLED.
YOU PAPA DOZ CRAZY SCHTUPID STOFF LIKE DOT HALL DE TIME.
HOKAY?
HOKAY. ER...OKAY. THANKS.
171
EVERYBODY BACK!!
HUMMMM...
CHUG
CHUG
CLICK
CLANK
CLACK!
BAKER
HEARTS AND FLOURS
HONK!
HONK LESSONS
NO HONKING
-NO- HONKING
DO
CAN
YOU
THOMB!
THOMB!
THOMB!
SERGEANT! PREPARE SOME C-BOMBS!
FIRST PATROL— FOLLOW THAT CLANK!
YAH, HERR BARON!

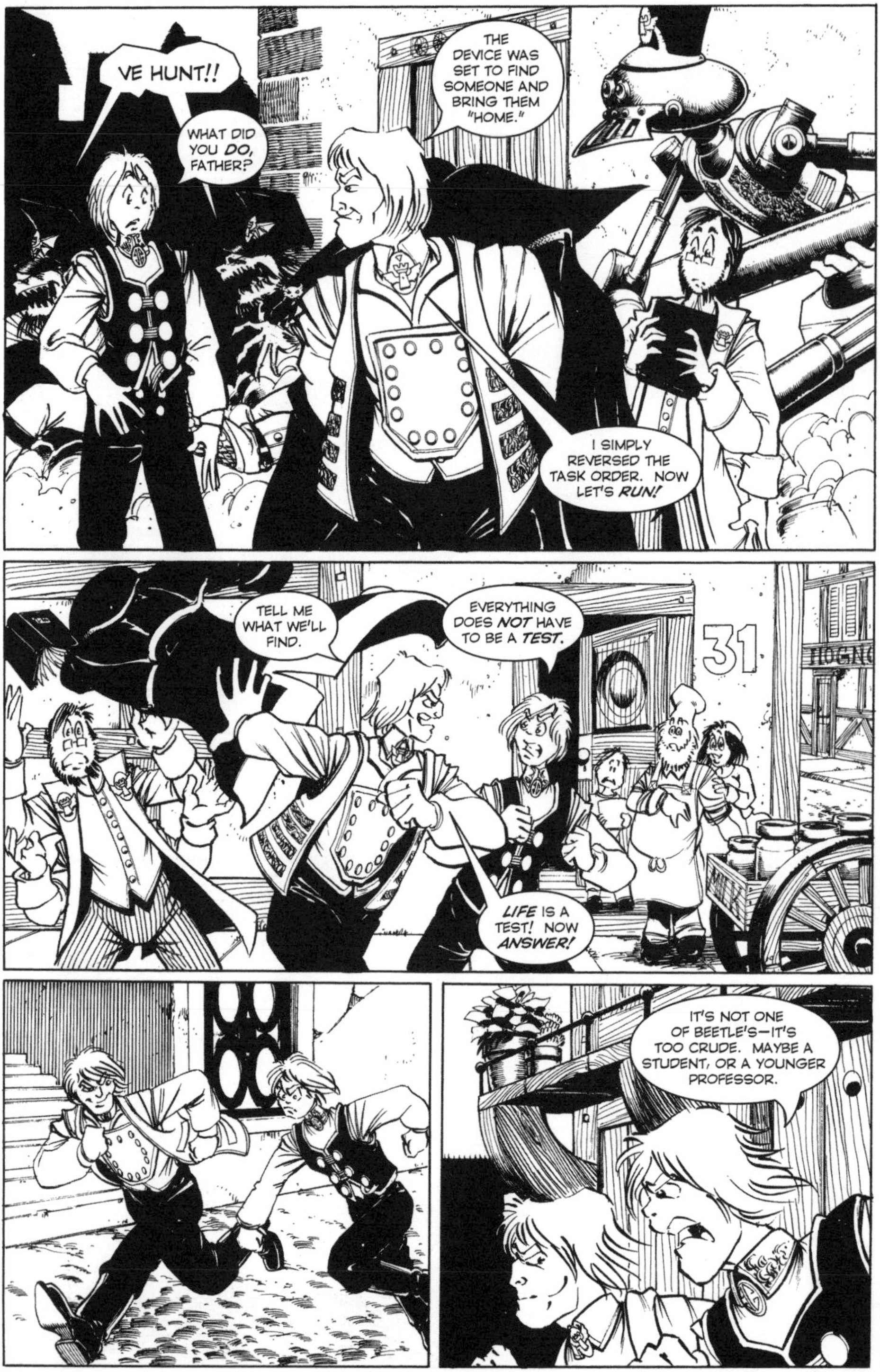
VE HUNT!!
WHAT DID YOU *DO*, FATHER?
THE DEVICE WAS SET TO FIND SOMEONE AND BRING THEM "HOME."
I SIMPLY REVERSED THE TASK ORDER. NOW LET'S *RUN!*
TELL ME WHAT WE'LL FIND.
EVERYTHING DOES ***NOT*** HAVE TO BE A ***TEST.***
31
LIFE IS A TEST! NOW ***ANSWER!***
IT'S NOT ONE OF BEETLE'S—IT'S TOO CRUDE. MAYBE A STUDENT, OR A YOUNGER PROFESSOR.

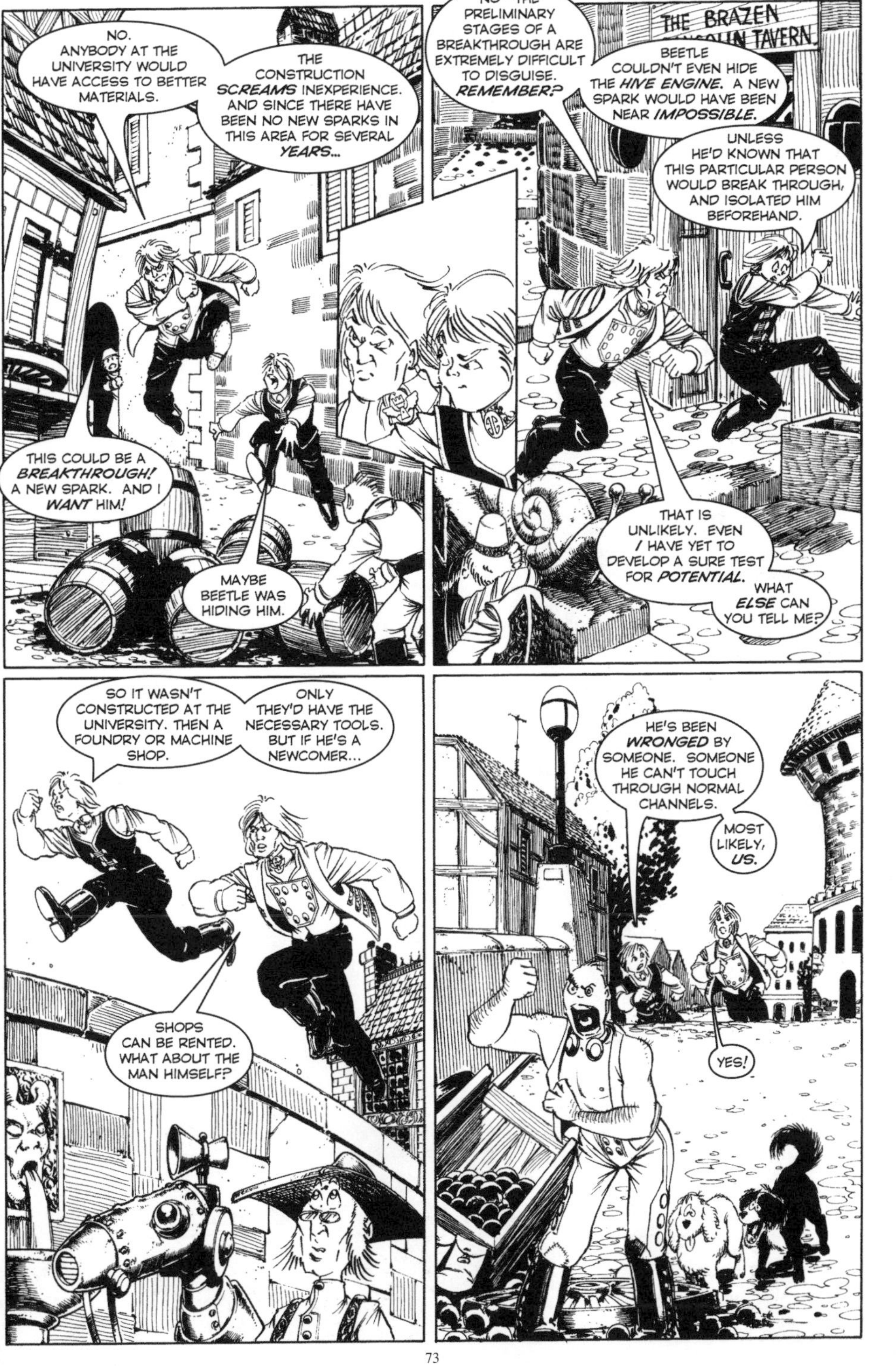
NO. ANYBODY AT THE UNIVERSITY WOULD HAVE ACCESS TO BETTER MATERIALS.
THE CONSTRUCTION SCREAMS INEXPERIENCE. AND SINCE THERE HAVE BEEN NO NEW SPARKS IN THIS AREA FOR SEVERAL YEARS...
THIS COULD BE A BREAKTHROUGH! A NEW SPARK. AND I WANT HIM!
MAYBE BEETLE WAS HIDING HIM.
NO—THE PRELIMINARY STAGES OF A BREAKTHROUGH ARE EXTREMELY DIFFICULT TO DISGUISE. REMEMBER?
THE BRAZEN
TAVERN
BEETLE COULDN'T EVEN HIDE THE HIVE ENGINE. A NEW SPARK WOULD HAVE BEEN NEAR IMPOSSIBLE.
UNLESS HE'D KNOWN THAT THIS PARTICULAR PERSON WOULD BREAK THROUGH, AND ISOLATED HIM BEFOREHAND.
THAT IS UNLIKELY. EVEN I HAVE YET TO DEVELOP A SURE TEST FOR POTENTIAL.
WHAT ELSE CAN YOU TELL ME?
SO IT WASN'T CONSTRUCTED AT THE UNIVERSITY. THEN A FOUNDRY OR MACHINE SHOP.
ONLY THEY'D HAVE THE NECESSARY TOOLS. BUT IF HE'S A NEWCOMER...
SHOPS CAN BE RENTED. WHAT ABOUT THE MAN HIMSELF?
HE'S BEEN WRONGED BY SOMEONE. SOMEONE HE CAN'T TOUCH THROUGH NORMAL CHANNELS.
MOST LIKELY, US.
YES!

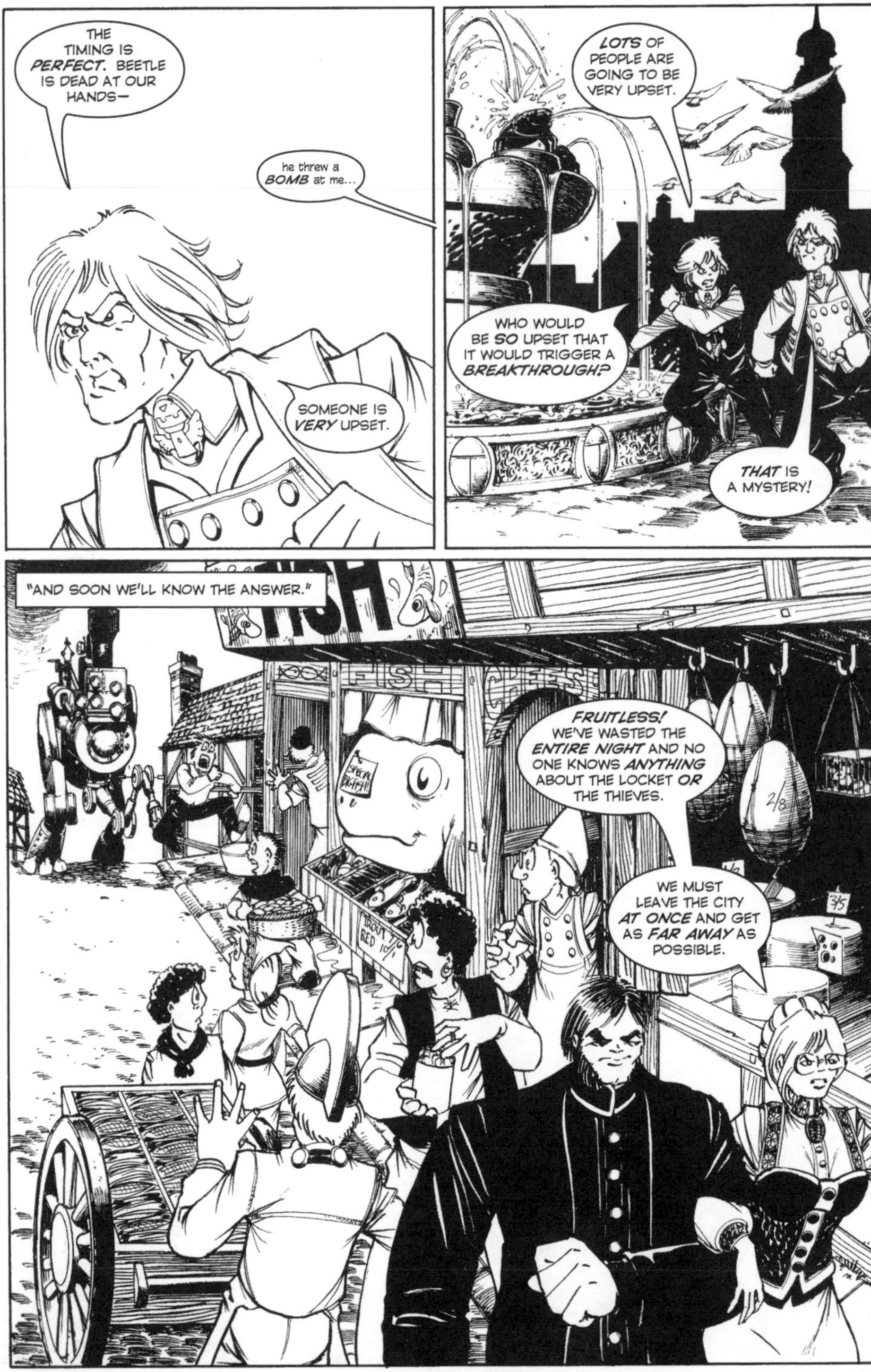
THE TIMING IS PERFECT. BEETLE IS DEAD AT OUR HANDS—
he threw a BOMB at me...
SOMEONE IS VERY UPSET.
LOTS OF PEOPLE ARE GOING TO BE VERY UPSET.
WHO WOULD BE SO UPSET THAT IT WOULD TRIGGER A BREAKTHROUGH?
THAT IS A MYSTERY!
"AND SOON WE'LL KNOW THE ANSWER."
FISH
FRUITLESS! WE'VE WASTED THE ENTIRE NIGHT AND NO ONE KNOWS ANYTHING ABOUT THE LOCKET OR THE THIEVES.
2/8
WE MUST LEAVE THE CITY AT ONCE AND GET AS FAR AWAY AS POSSIBLE.
3/5

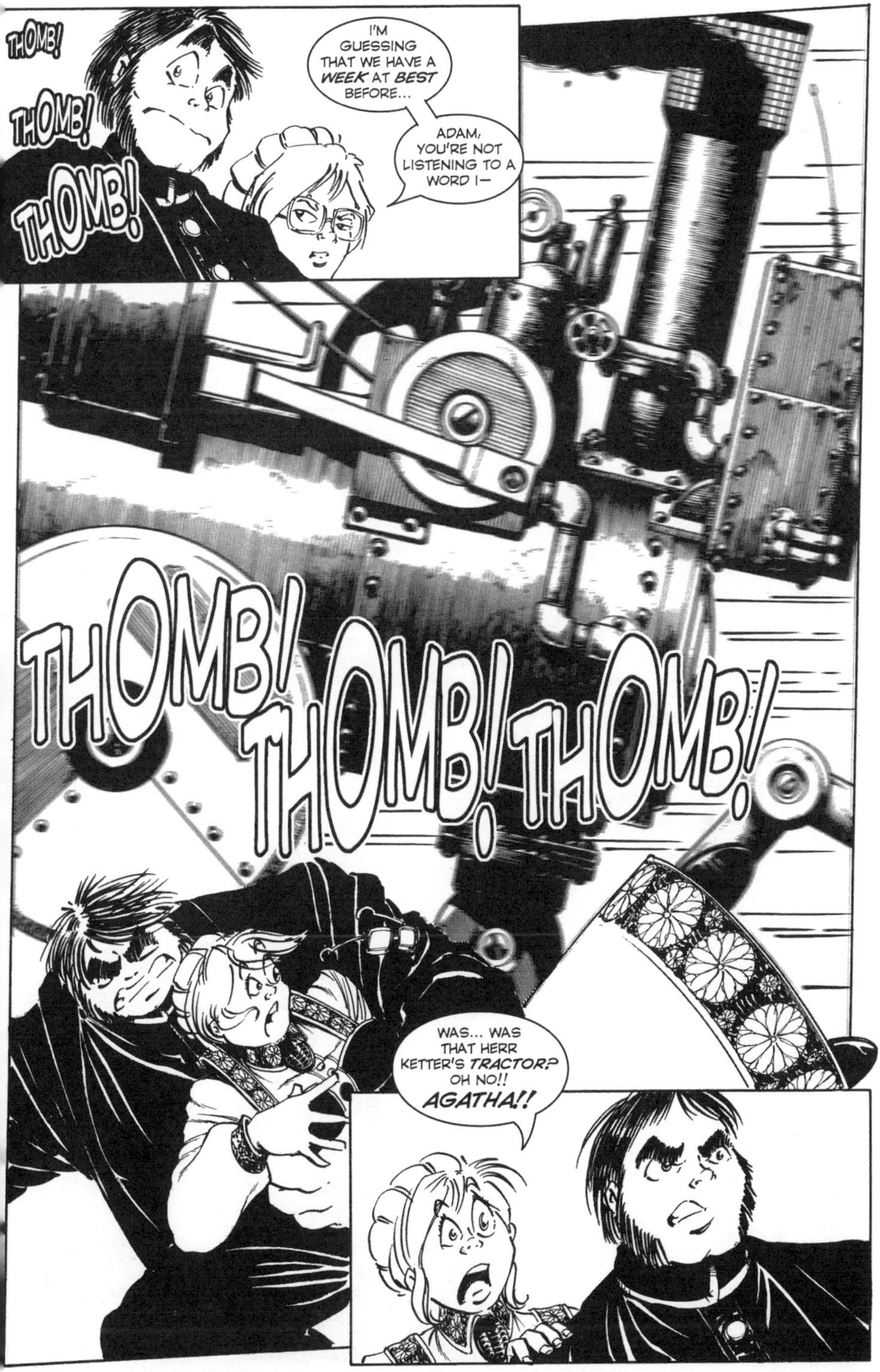
THOMB!
THOMB!
THOMB!
I'M GUESSING THAT WE HAVE A WEEK AT BEST BEFORE...
ADAM, YOU'RE NOT LISTENING TO A WORD I—
THOMB! THOMB! THOMB!
WAS... WAS THAT HERR KETTER'S TRACTOR? OH NO!! AGATHA!!

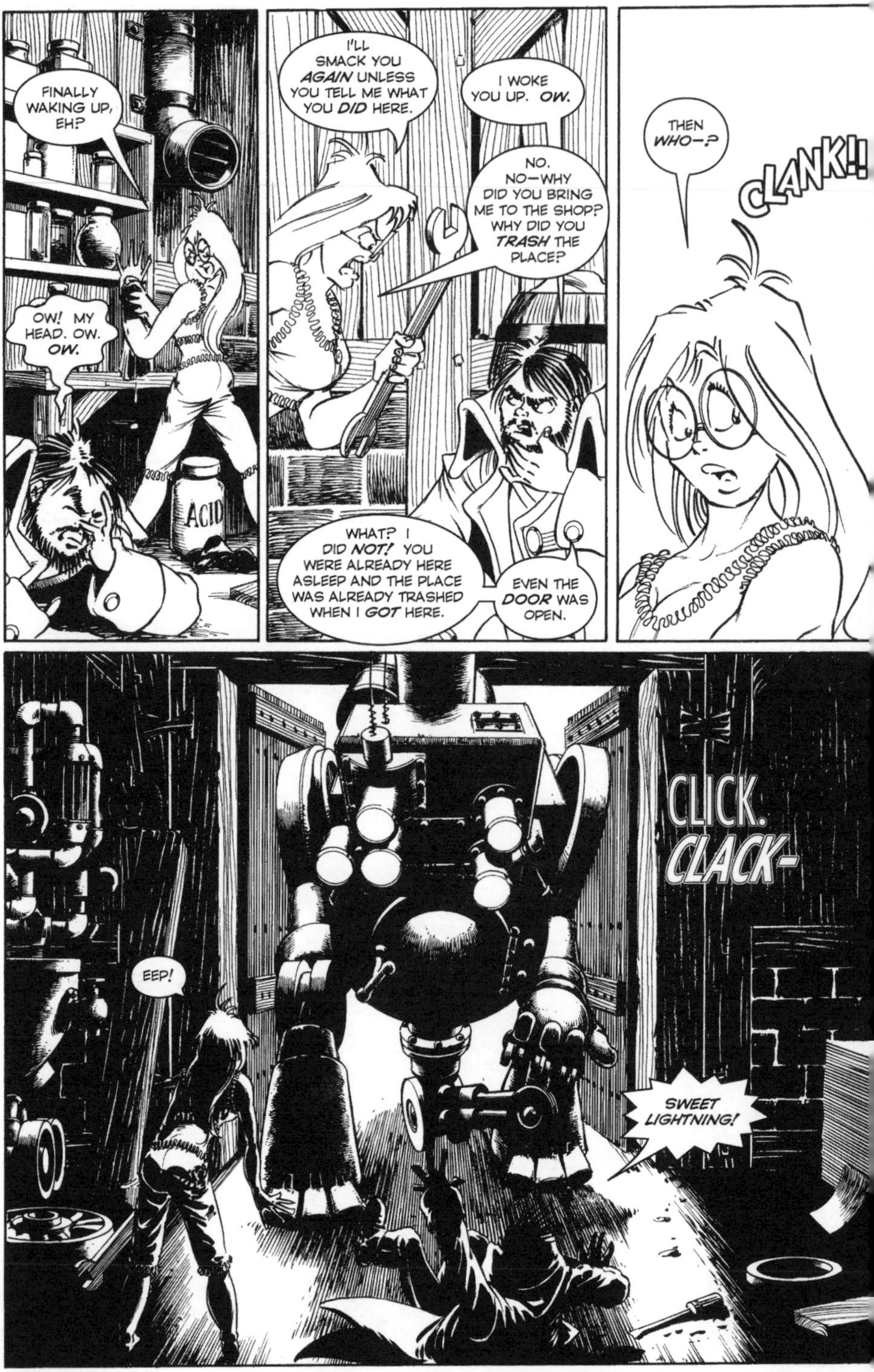
FINALLY WAKING UP, EH?
OW! MY HEAD. OW. OW.
ACID
I'LL SMACK YOU AGAIN UNLESS YOU TELL ME WHAT YOU DID HERE.
I WOKE YOU UP. OW.
NO. NO—WHY DID YOU BRING ME TO THE SHOP? WHY DID YOU TRASH THE PLACE?
WHAT? I DID NOT! YOU WERE ALREADY HERE ASLEEP AND THE PLACE WAS ALREADY TRASHED WHEN I GOT HERE.
EVEN THE DOOR WAS OPEN.
THEN WHO—?
CLANK!!
CLICK.
CLACK-
EEP!
SWEET LIGHTNING!

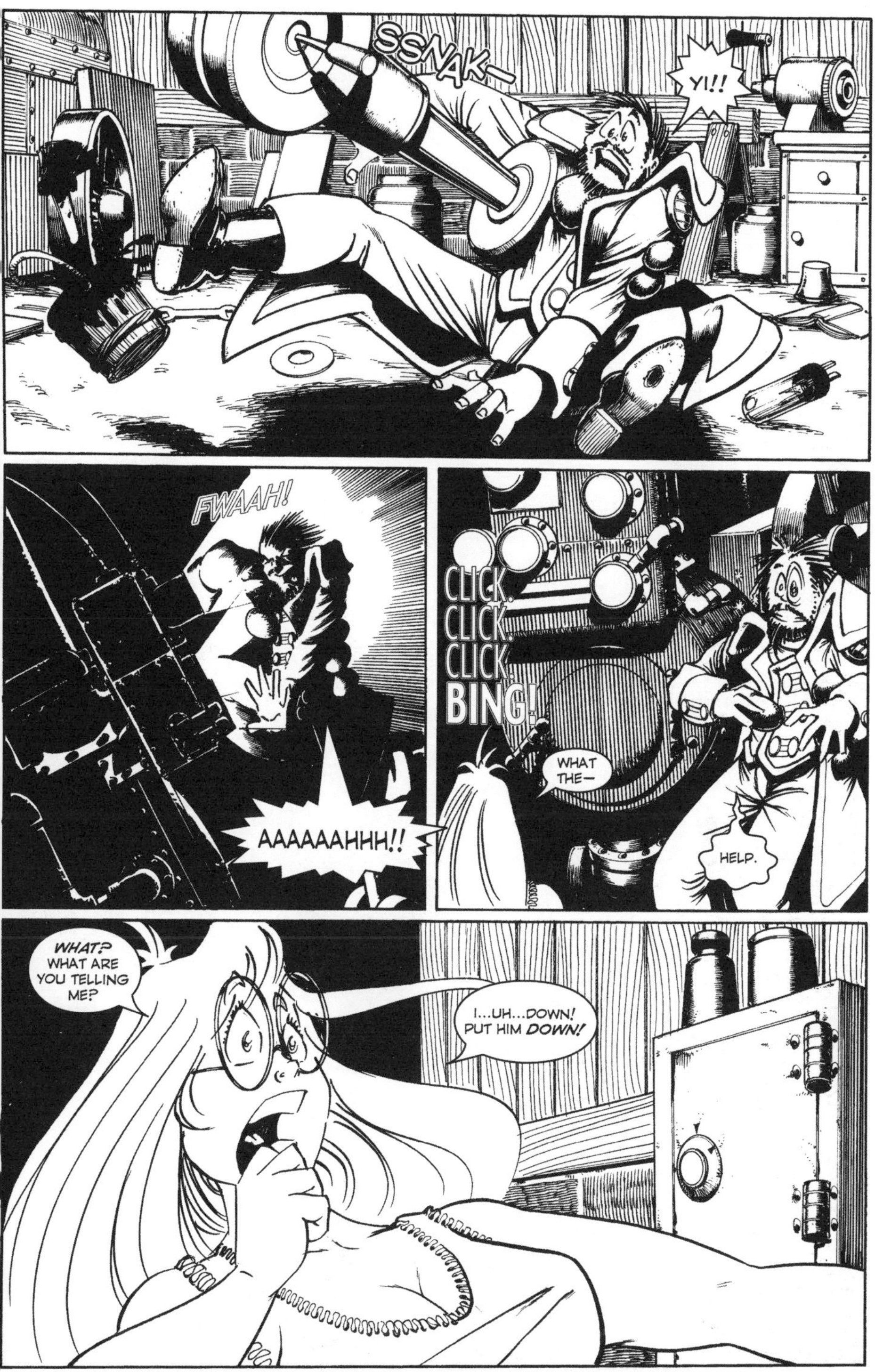
SSNAK—
YI!!
FWAAH!
AAAAAAHHH!!
CLICK.
CLICK.
CLICK.
BING!
WHAT THE—
HELP.
WHAT? WHAT ARE YOU TELLING ME?
I...UH...DOWN! PUT HIM DOWN!

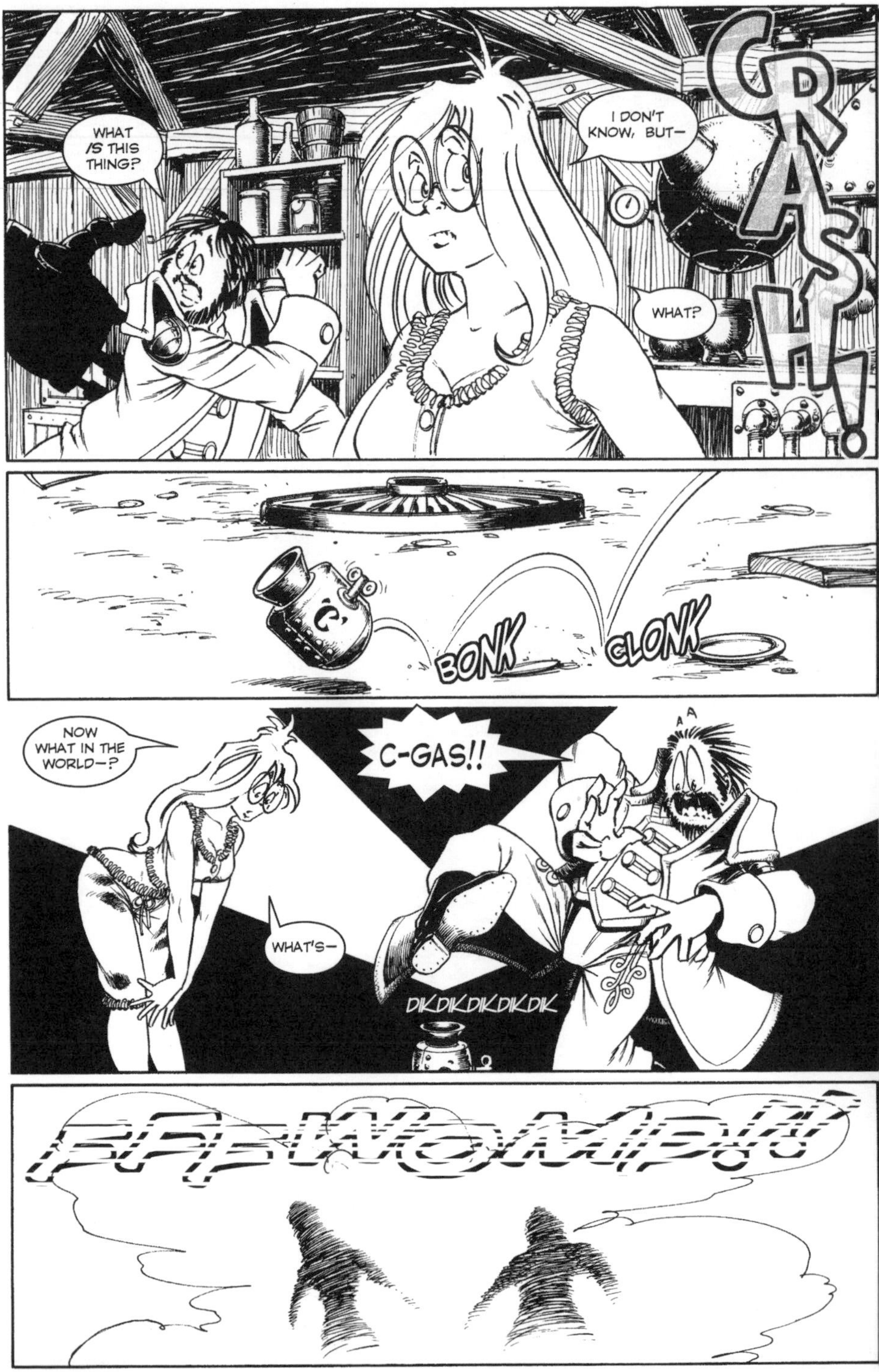
WHAT *IS* THIS THING?
I DON'T KNOW, BUT—
CRASH!
WHAT?
BONK
CLONK
NOW WHAT IN THE WORLD—?
C-GAS!!
WHAT'S—
DIKDIKDIKDIKDIK
FFFWOOMP!!

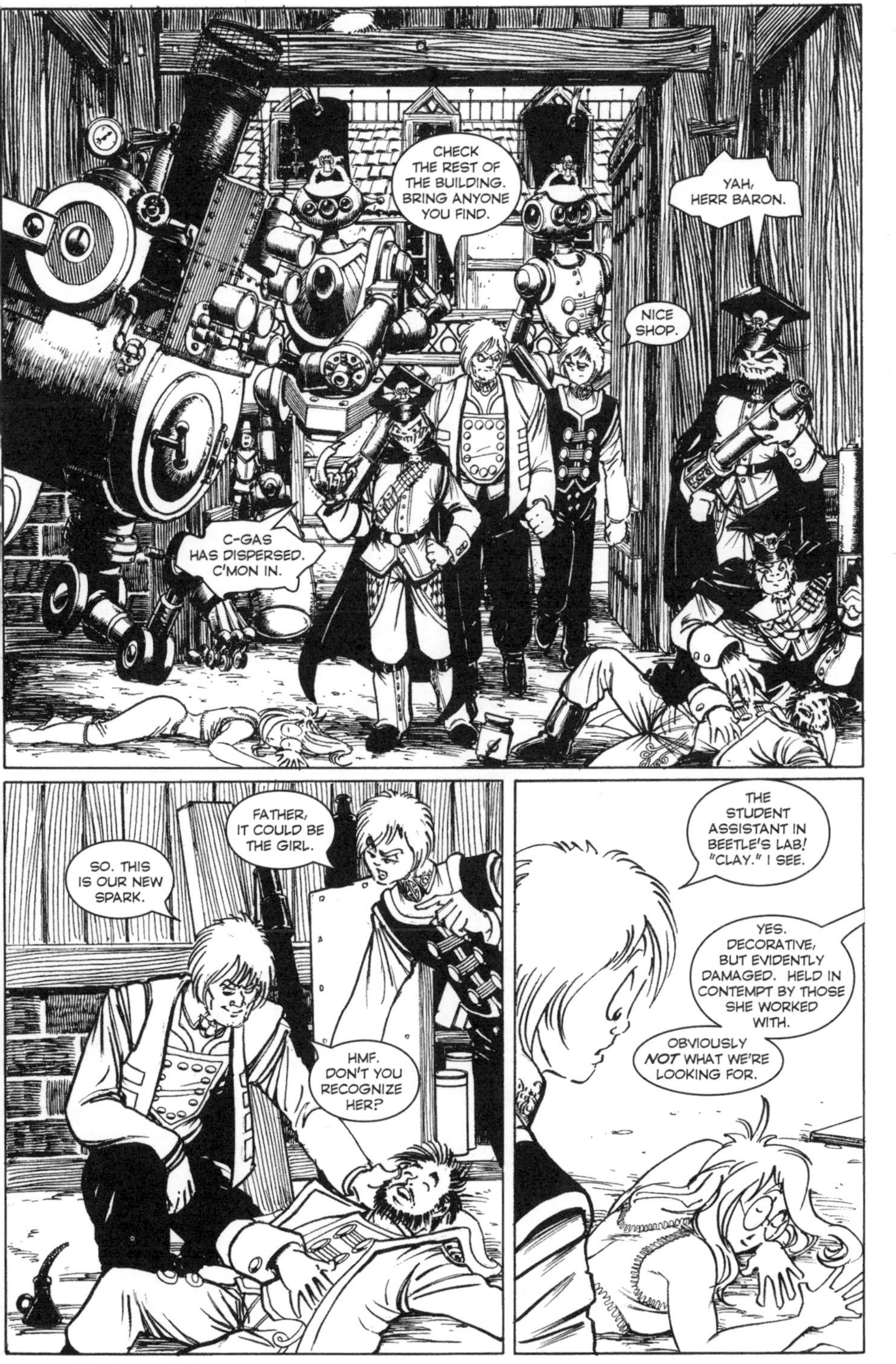
CHECK THE REST OF THE BUILDING. BRING ANYONE YOU FIND.
YAH, HERR BARON.
NICE SHOP.
C-GAS HAS DISPERSED. C'MON IN.
SO. THIS IS OUR NEW SPARK.
FATHER, IT COULD BE THE GIRL.
HMF. DON'T YOU RECOGNIZE HER?
THE STUDENT ASSISTANT IN BEETLE'S LAB! "CLAY." I SEE.
YES. DECORATIVE, BUT EVIDENTLY DAMAGED. HELD IN CONTEMPT BY THOSE SHE WORKED WITH.
OBVIOUSLY *NOT* WHAT WE'RE LOOKING FOR.

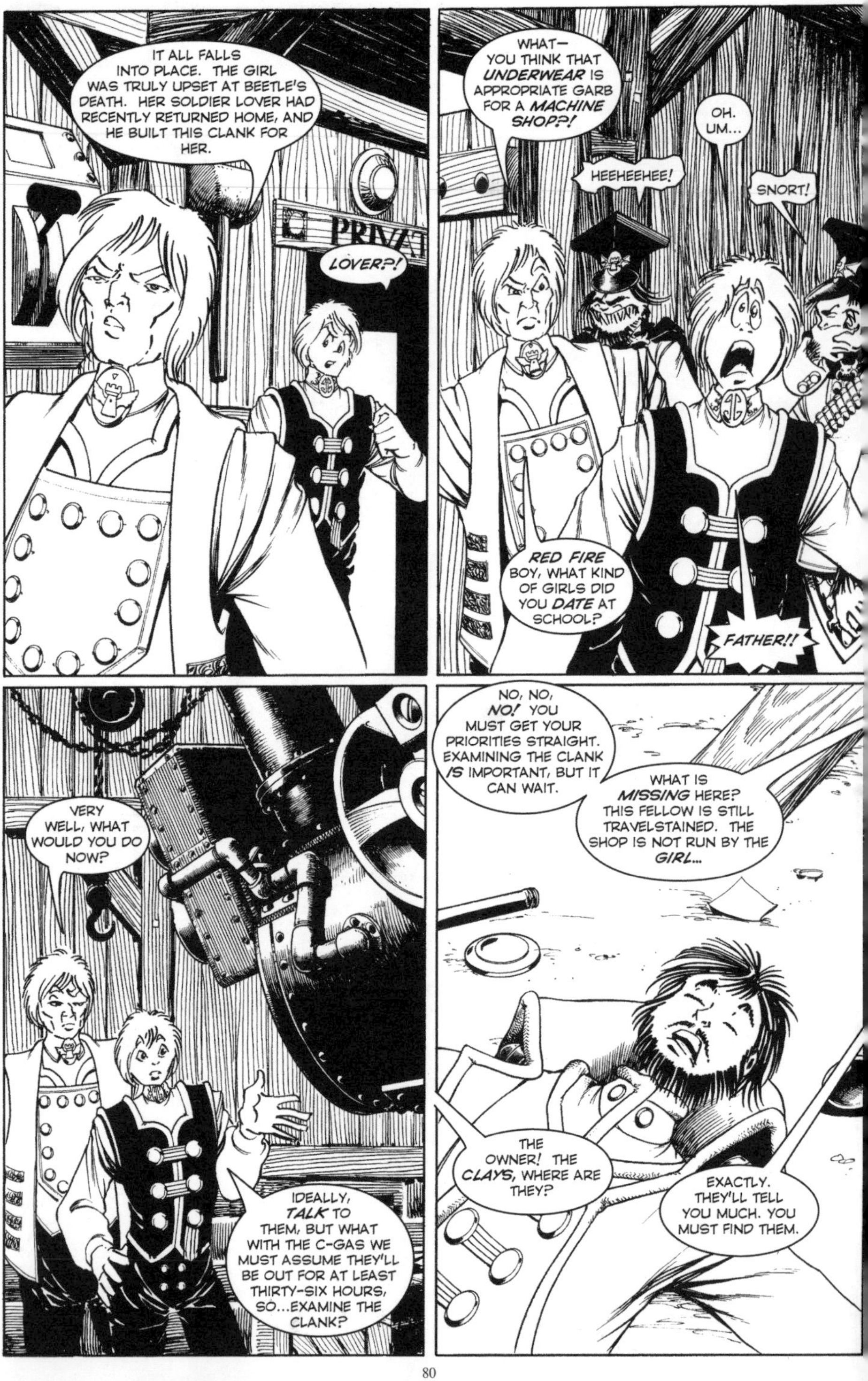
IT ALL FALLS INTO PLACE. THE GIRL WAS TRULY UPSET AT BEETLE'S DEATH. HER SOLDIER LOVER HAD RECENTLY RETURNED HOME, AND HE BUILT THIS CLANK FOR HER.
PRIVAT
LOVER?!
WHAT— YOU THINK THAT UNDERWEAR IS APPROPRIATE GARB FOR A MACHINE SHOP?!
OH. UM...
HEEHEEHEE!
SNORT!
RED FIRE BOY, WHAT KIND OF GIRLS DID YOU DATE AT SCHOOL?
FATHER!!
VERY WELL, WHAT WOULD YOU DO NOW?
IDEALLY, TALK TO THEM, BUT WHAT WITH THE C-GAS WE MUST ASSUME THEY'LL BE OUT FOR AT LEAST THIRTY-SIX HOURS, SO...EXAMINE THE CLANK?
NO, NO, NO! YOU MUST GET YOUR PRIORITIES STRAIGHT. EXAMINING THE CLANK IS IMPORTANT, BUT IT CAN WAIT.
WHAT IS MISSING HERE? THIS FELLOW IS STILL TRAVELSTAINED. THE SHOP IS NOT RUN BY THE GIRL...
THE OWNER! THE CLAYS, WHERE ARE THEY?
EXACTLY. THEY'LL TELL YOU MUCH. YOU MUST FIND THEM.

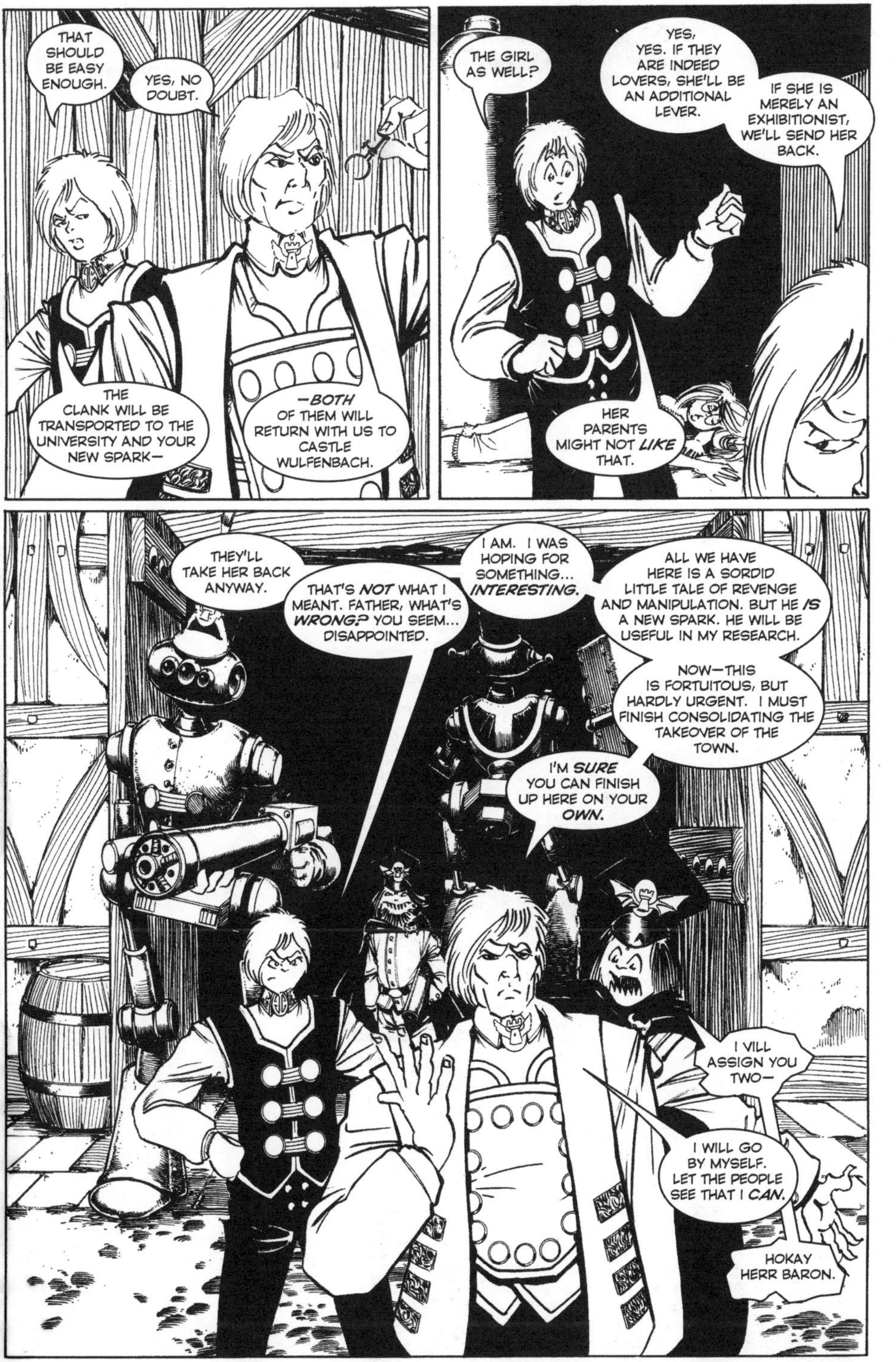

THAT SHOULD BE EASY ENOUGH.
YES, NO DOUBT.
THE CLANK WILL BE TRANSPORTED TO THE UNIVERSITY AND YOUR NEW SPARK—
—BOTH OF THEM WILL RETURN WITH US TO CASTLE WULFENBACH.
THE GIRL AS WELL?
YES, YES. IF THEY ARE INDEED LOVERS, SHE'LL BE AN ADDITIONAL LEVER.
IF SHE IS MERELY AN EXHIBITIONIST, WE'LL SEND HER BACK.
HER PARENTS MIGHT NOT LIKE THAT.
THEY'LL TAKE HER BACK ANYWAY.
THAT'S NOT WHAT I MEANT. FATHER, WHAT'S WRONG? YOU SEEM... DISAPPOINTED.
I AM. I WAS HOPING FOR SOMETHING... INTERESTING.
ALL WE HAVE HERE IS A SORDID LITTLE TALE OF REVENGE AND MANIPULATION. BUT HE IS A NEW SPARK. HE WILL BE USEFUL IN MY RESEARCH.
NOW—THIS IS FORTUITOUS, BUT HARDLY URGENT. I MUST FINISH CONSOLIDATING THE TAKEOVER OF THE TOWN.
I'M SURE YOU CAN FINISH UP HERE ON YOUR OWN.
I VILL ASSIGN YOU TWO—
I WILL GO BY MYSELF. LET THE PEOPLE SEE THAT I CAN.
HOKAY HERR BARON.

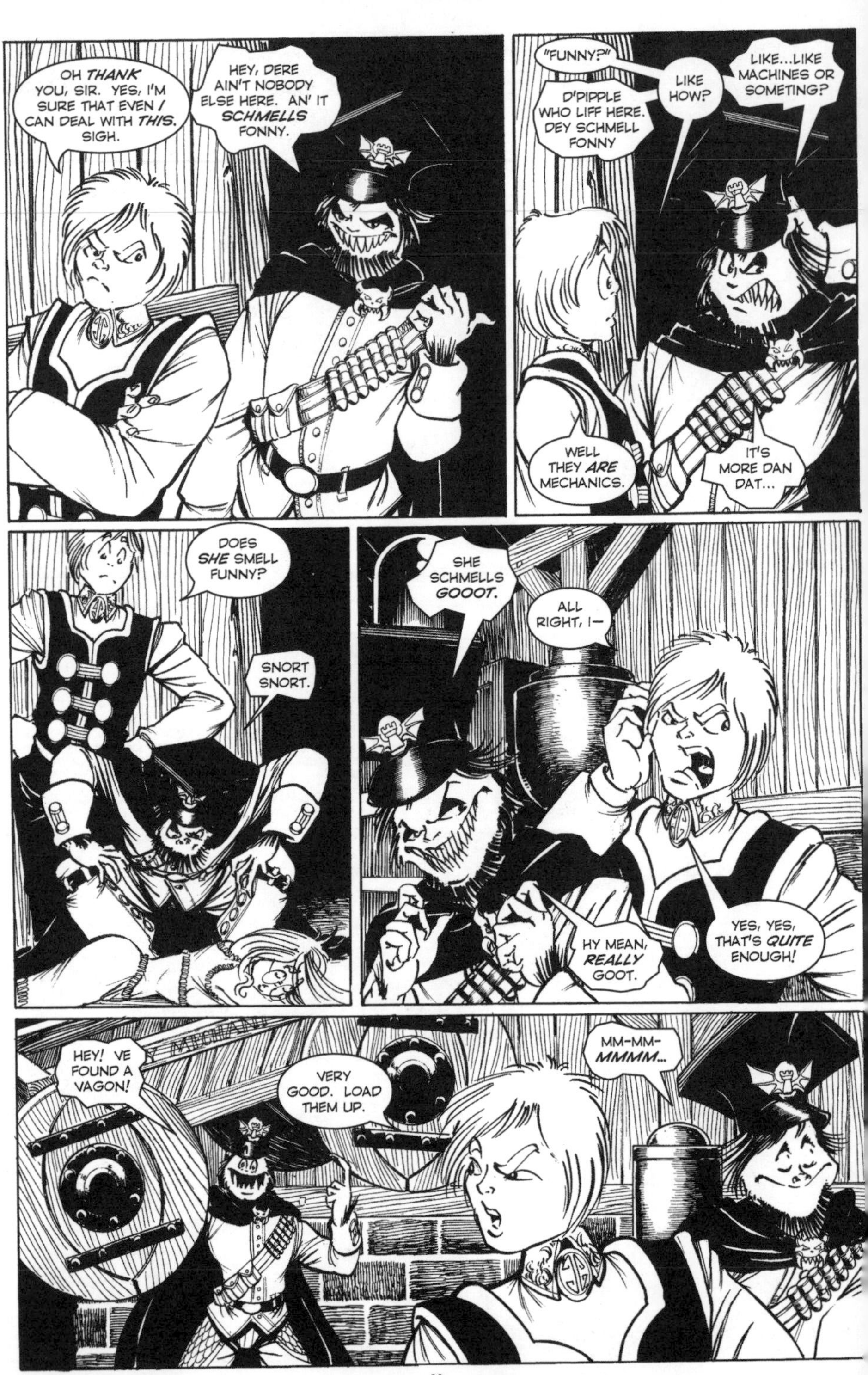
OH THANK YOU, SIR. YES, I'M SURE THAT EVEN I CAN DEAL WITH THIS. SIGH.
HEY, DERE AIN'T NOBODY ELSE HERE. AN' IT SCHMELLS FONNY.
"FUNNY?"
D'PIPPLE WHO LIFF HERE. DEY SCHMELL FONNY
LIKE HOW?
LIKE...LIKE MACHINES OR SOMETING?
WELL THEY ARE MECHANICS.
IT'S MORE DAN DAT...
DOES SHE SMELL FUNNY?
SNORT SNORT.
SHE SCHMELLS GOOOT.
ALL RIGHT, I—
HY MEAN, REALLY GOOT.
YES, YES, THAT'S QUITE ENOUGH!
HEY! VE FOUND A VAGON!
VERY GOOD. LOAD THEM UP.
MM-MM-MMMM...

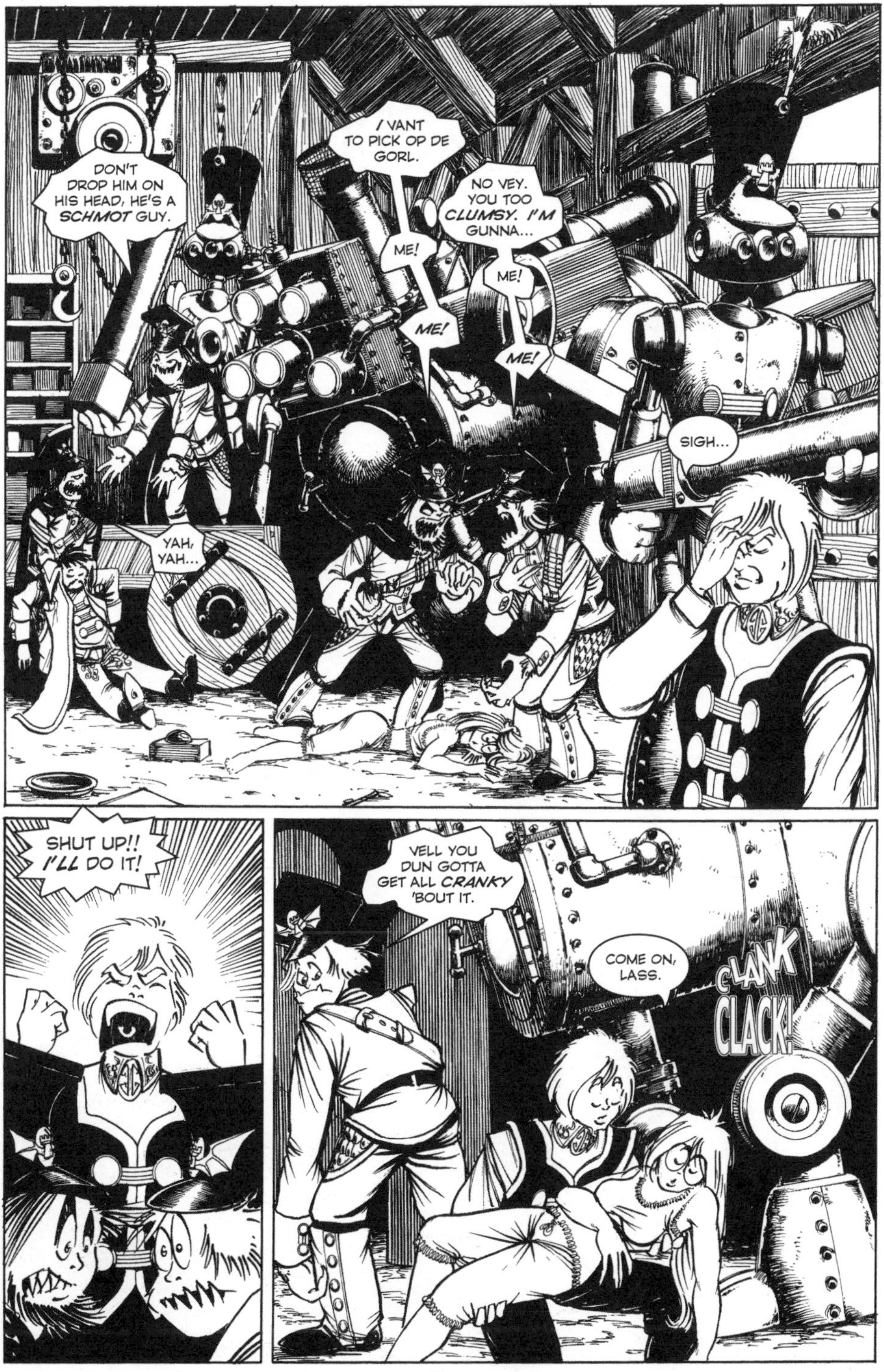
DON'T DROP HIM ON HIS HEAD, HE'S A SCHMOT GUY.
I VANT TO PICK OP DE GORL.
ME!
ME!
NO VEY. YOU TOO CLUMSY. I'M GUNNA...
ME!
ME!
SIGH...
YAH, YAH...
SHUT UP!! I'LL DO IT!
VELL YOU DUN GOTTA GET ALL CRANKY 'BOUT IT.
COME ON, LASS.
CLANK
CLACK!

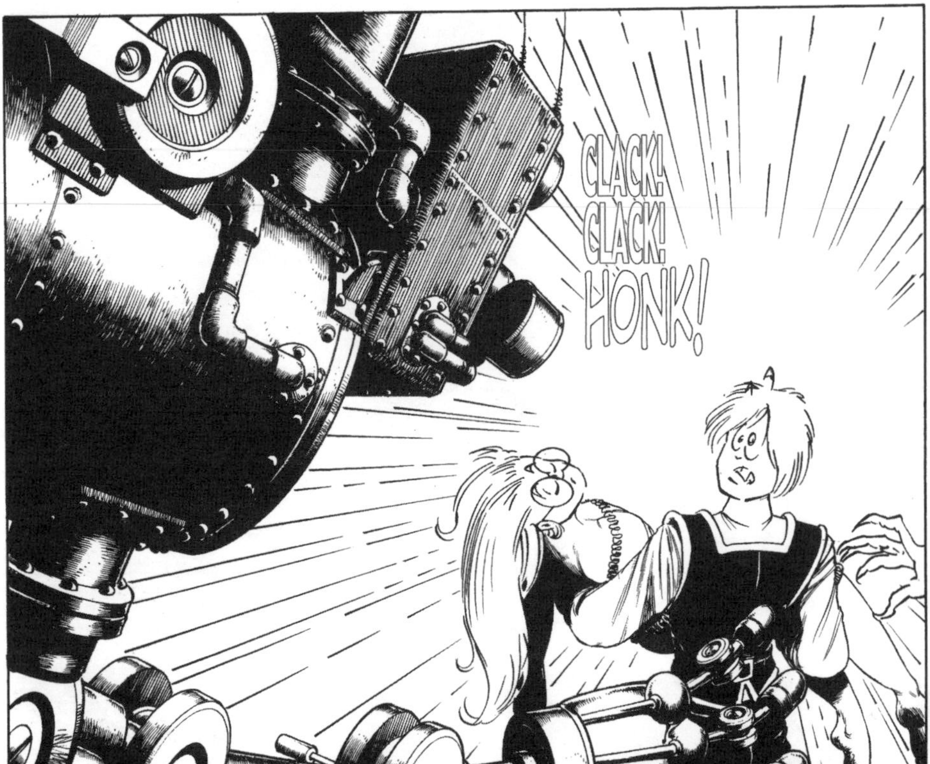
CLACK!
CLACK!
HONK!

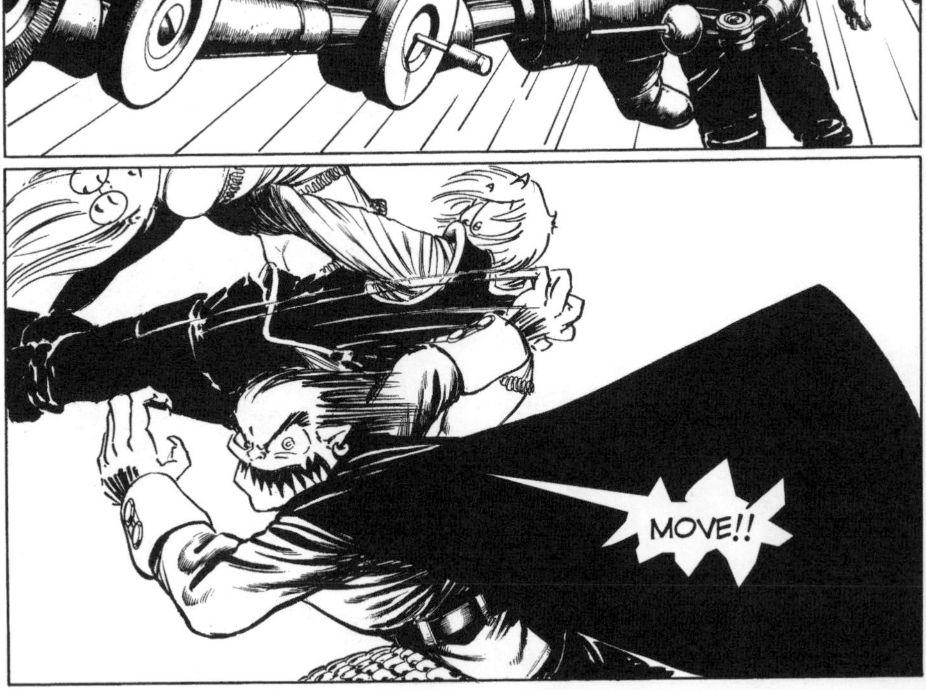
MOVE!!

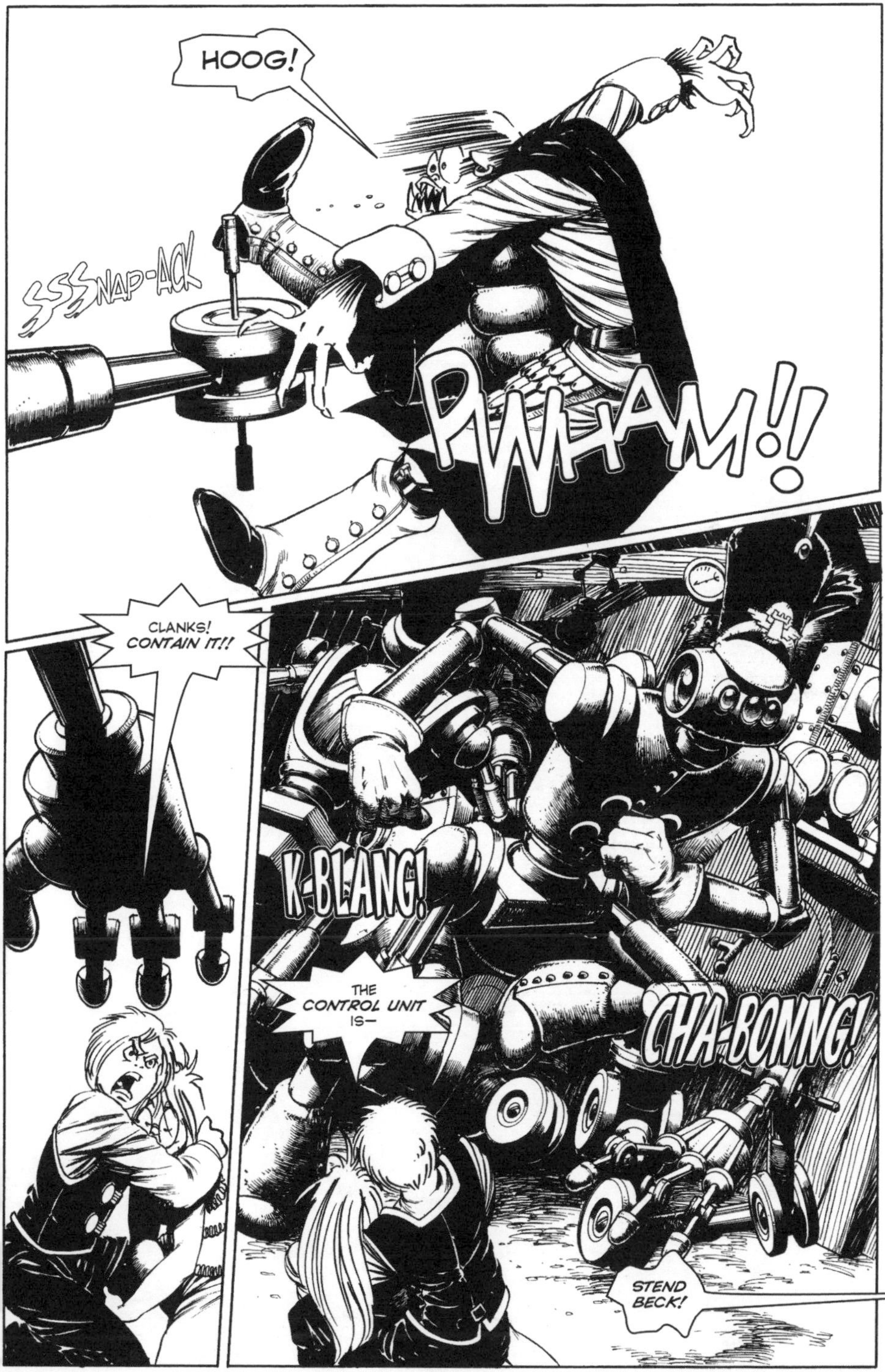
HOOG!
SSSNAP-ACK
PWHAM!!
CLANKS! CONTAIN IT!!
K-BLANG!
THE CONTROL UNIT IS—
CHA-BONNG!
STEND BECK!

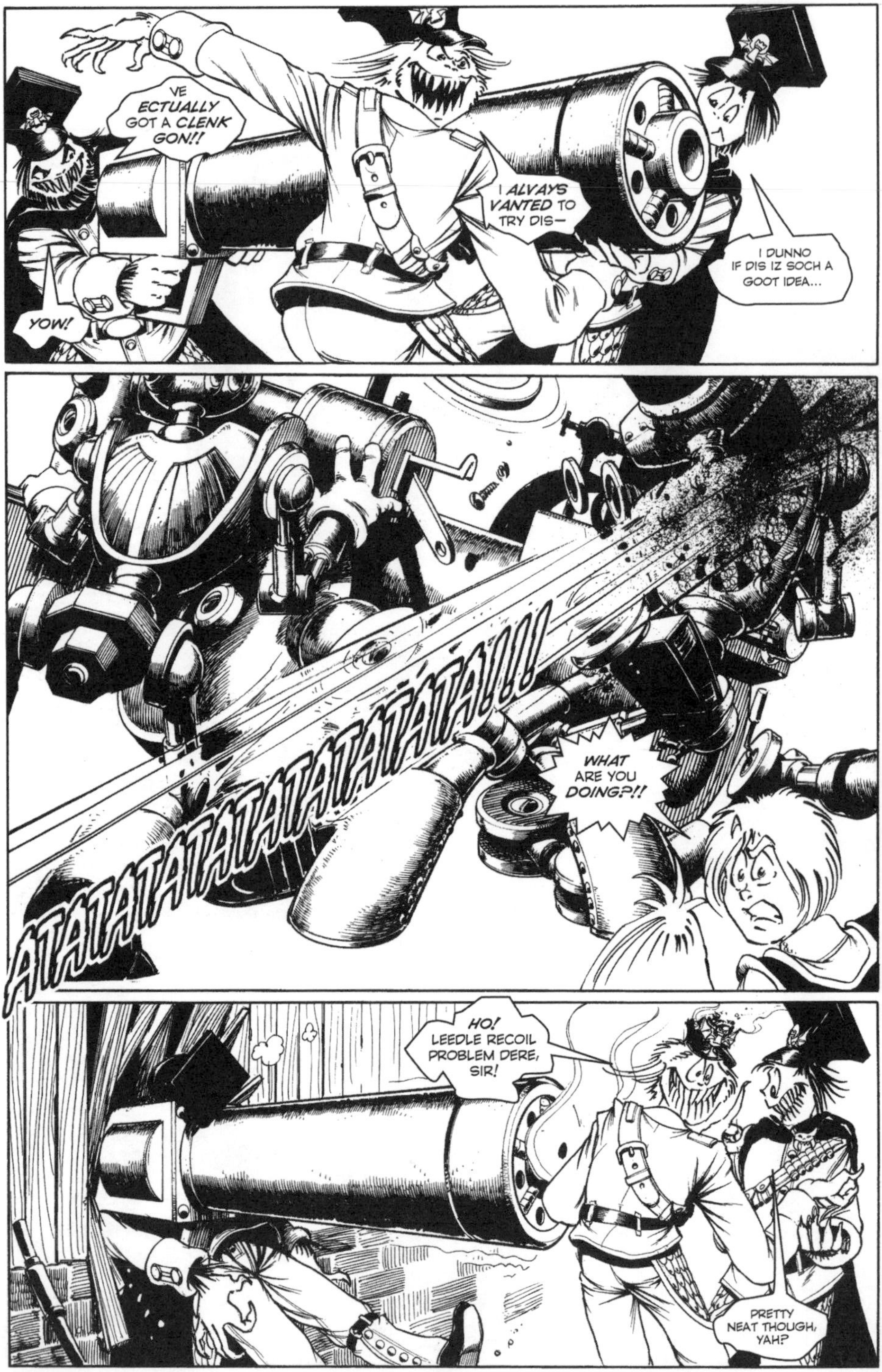
VE ECTUALLY GOT A CLENK GON!!
I ALVAYS VANTED TO TRY DIS—
I DUNNO IF DIS IZ SOCH A GOOT IDEA...
YOW!
ATATATATATATATATATA!!!
WHAT ARE YOU DOING?!!
HO! LEEDLE RECOIL PROBLEM DERE, SIR!
PRETTY NEAT THOUGH, YAH?

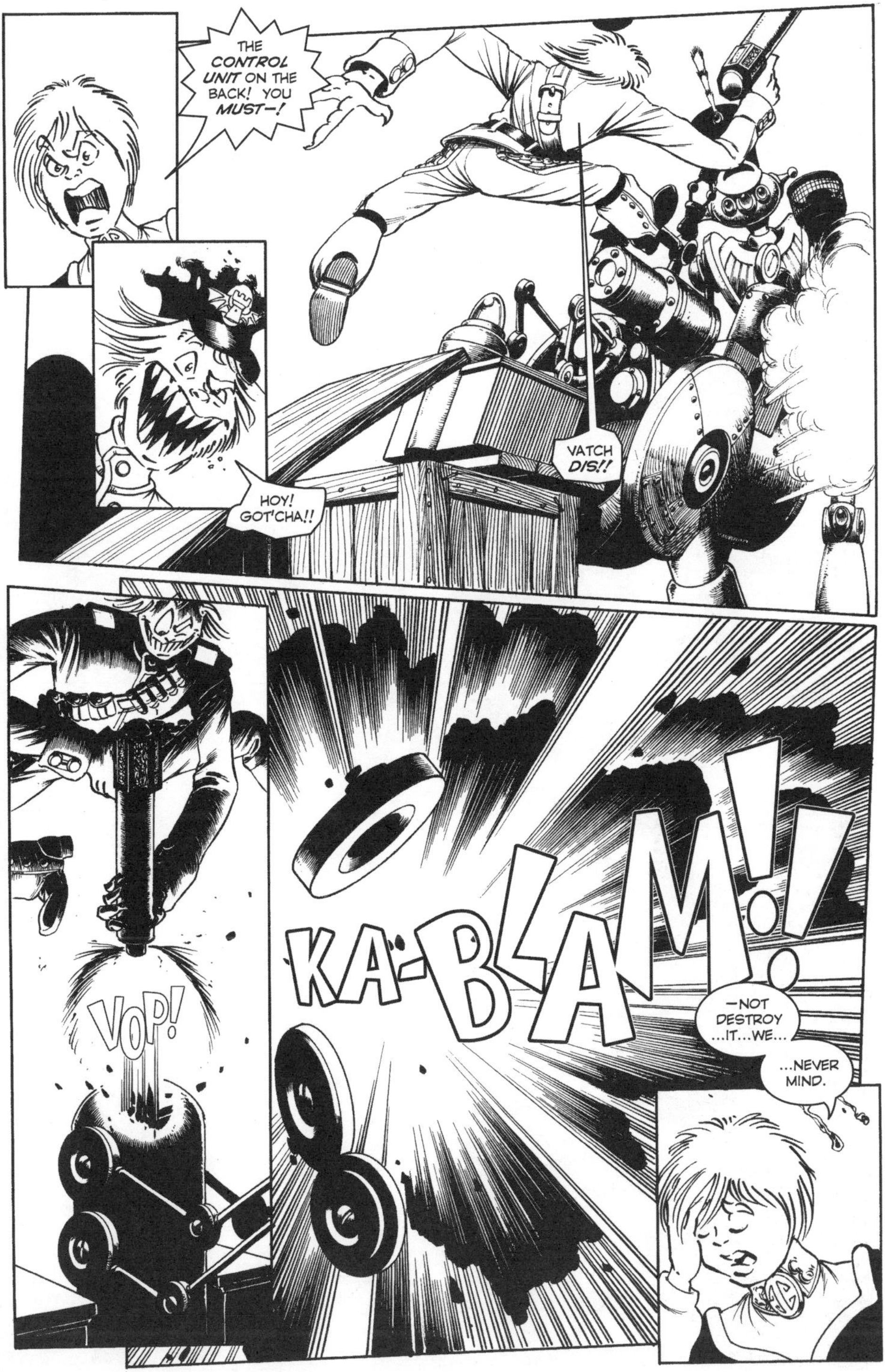
THE CONTROL UNIT ON THE BACK! YOU MUST-!
HOY! GOT'CHA!!
VATCH DIS!!
VOP!
KA-BLAM!!
-NOT DESTROY ...IT...WE...
...NEVER MIND.

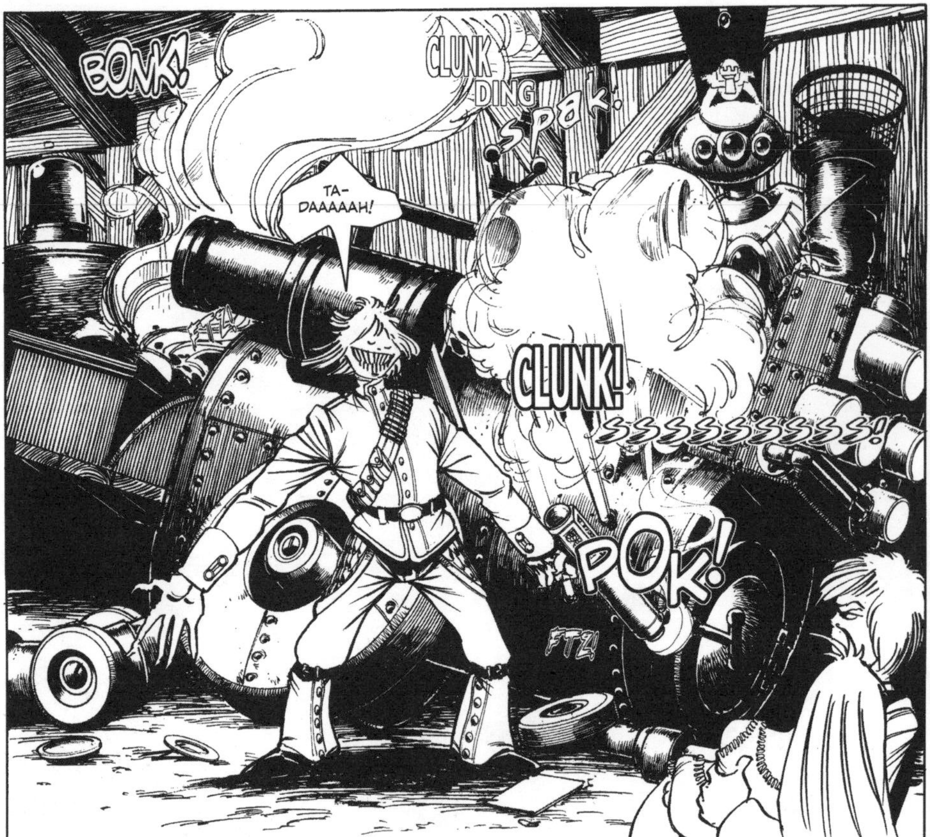
BONK!
CLUNK
DING
spak!
TA-DAAAAAH!
FTZ!
CLUNK!
SSSSSSSSSS!
POK!
FTZ!

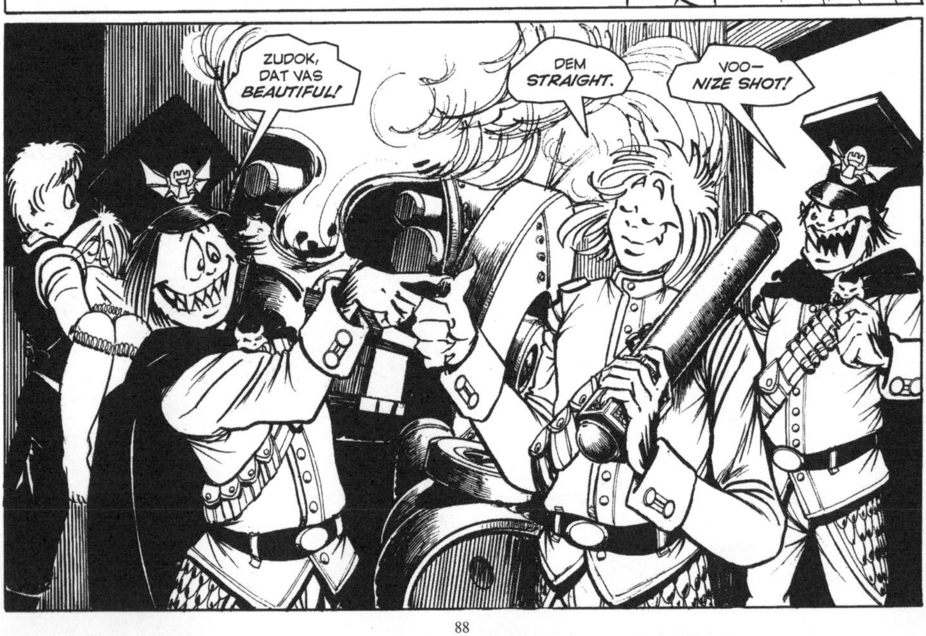
ZUDOK, DAT VAS *BEAUTIFUL!*
DEM *STRAIGHT.*
VOO-NIZE SHOT!

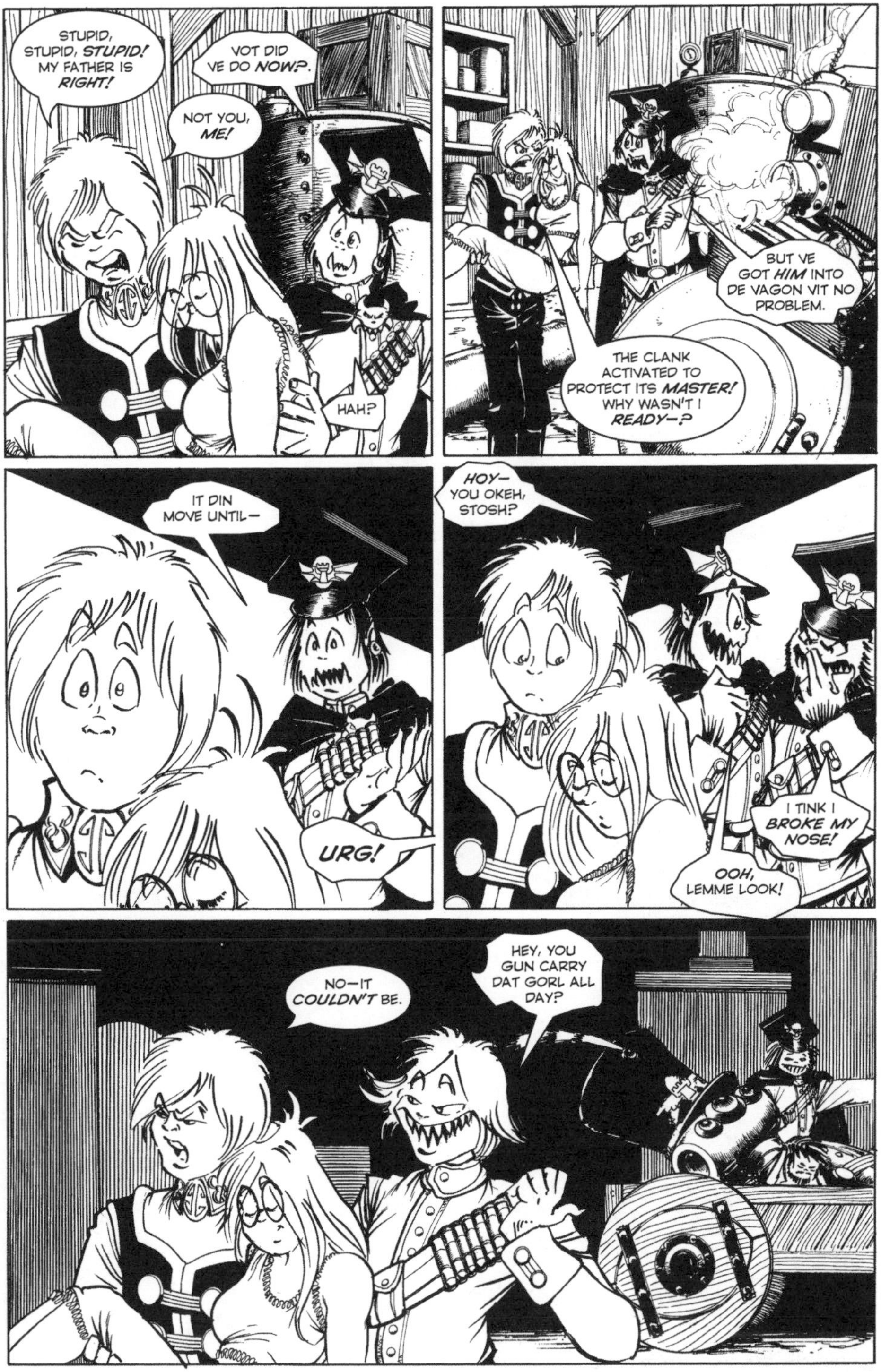
STUPID, STUPID, **STUPID!** MY FATHER IS **RIGHT!**
VOT DID VE DO **NOW?**.
NOT YOU, **ME!**
HAH?
BUT VE GOT **HIM** INTO DE VAGON VIT NO PROBLEM.
THE CLANK ACTIVATED TO PROTECT ITS **MASTER!** WHY WASN'T I **READY—?**
IT DIN MOVE UNTIL—
URG!
HOY— YOU OKEH, STOSH?
I TINK I **BROKE MY NOSE!**
OOH, LEMME LOOK!
NO—IT **COULDN'T** BE.
HEY, YOU GUN CARRY DAT GORL ALL DAY?

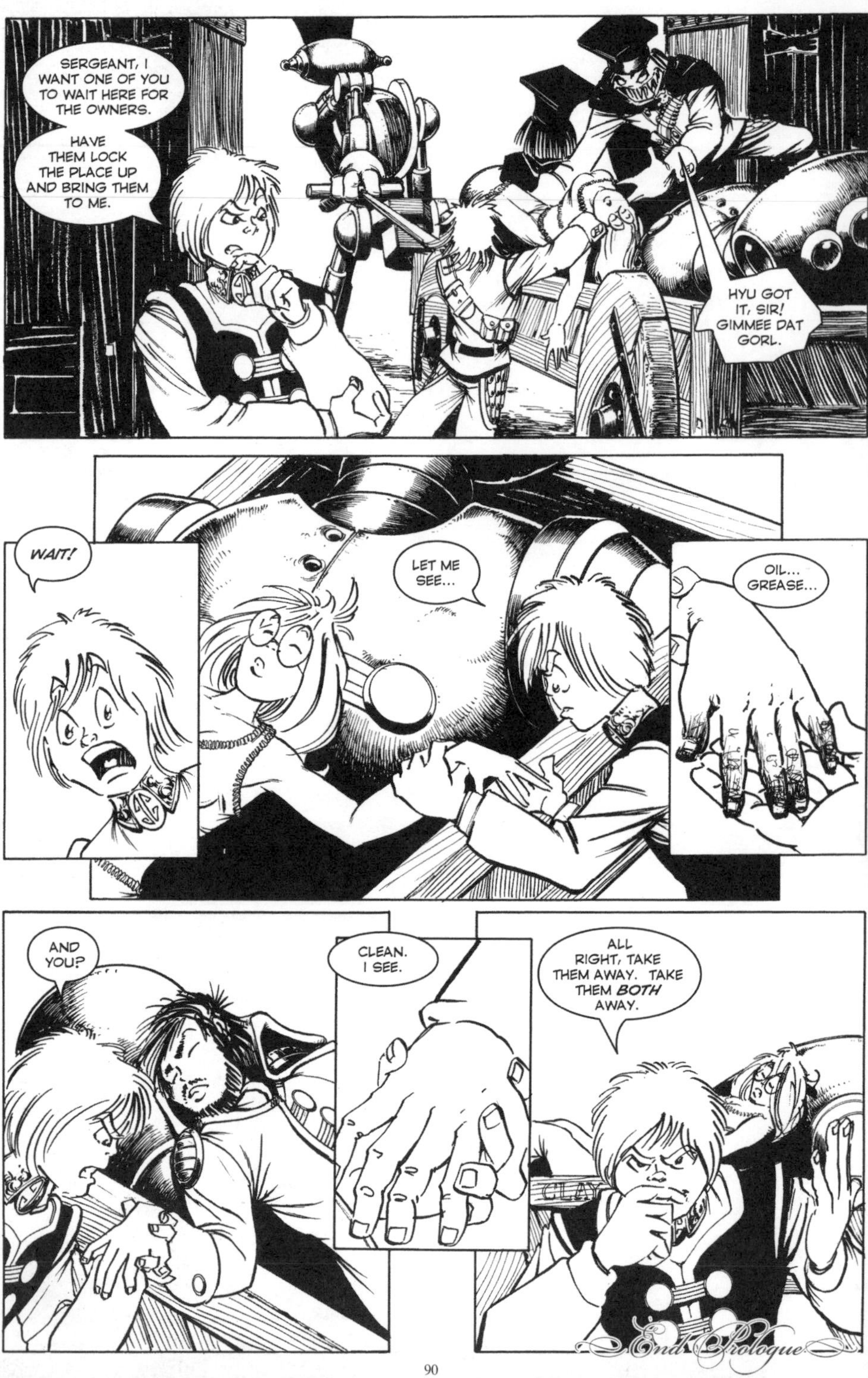
SERGEANT, I WANT ONE OF YOU TO WAIT HERE FOR THE OWNERS.
HAVE THEM LOCK THE PLACE UP AND BRING THEM TO ME.
HYU GOT IT, SIR! GIMMEE DAT GORL.
WAIT!
LET ME SEE...
OIL... GREASE...
AND YOU?
CLEAN. I SEE.
ALL RIGHT, TAKE THEM AWAY. TAKE THEM BOTH AWAY.
CLAY
End Prologue

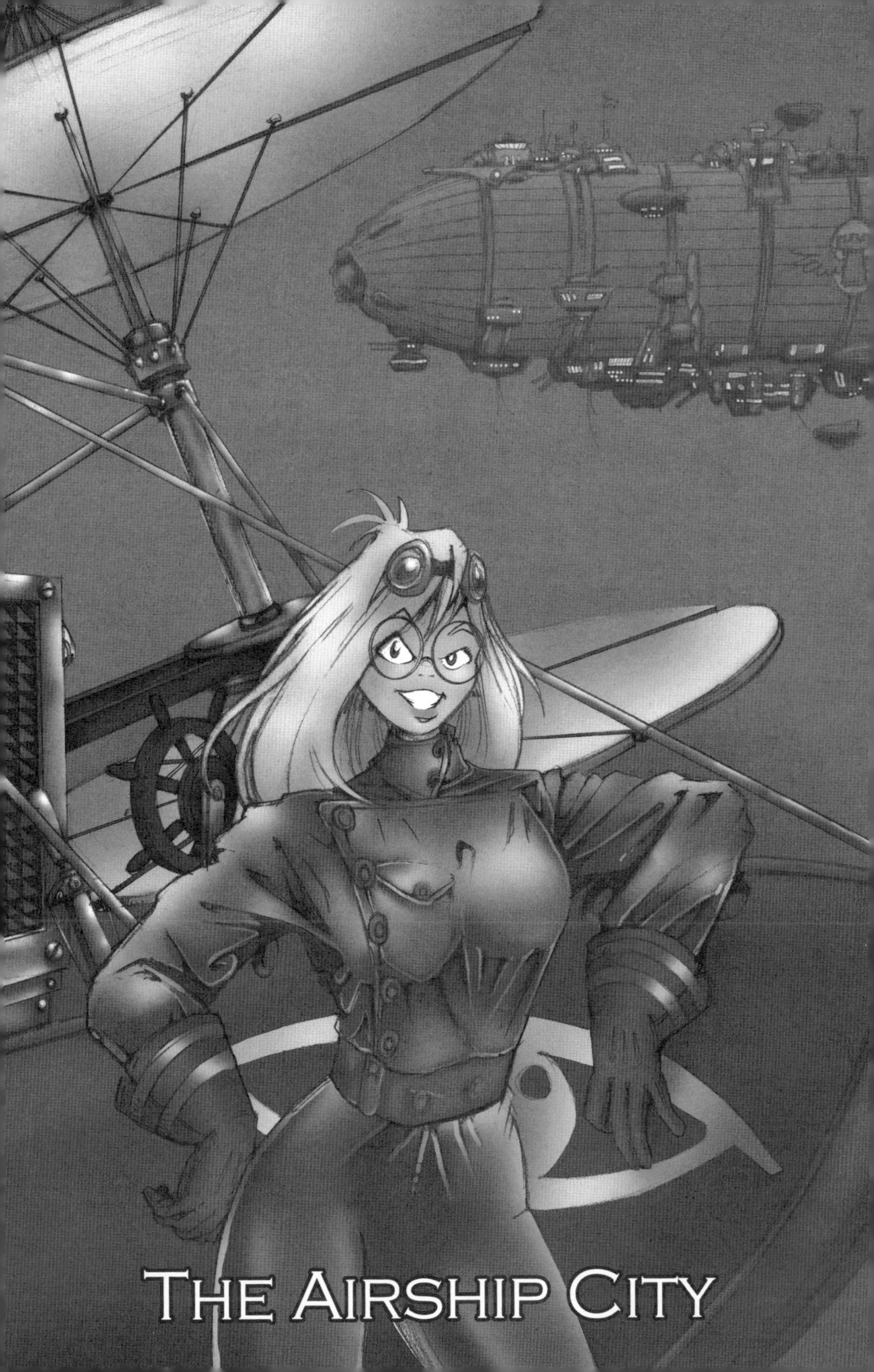

The Airship City

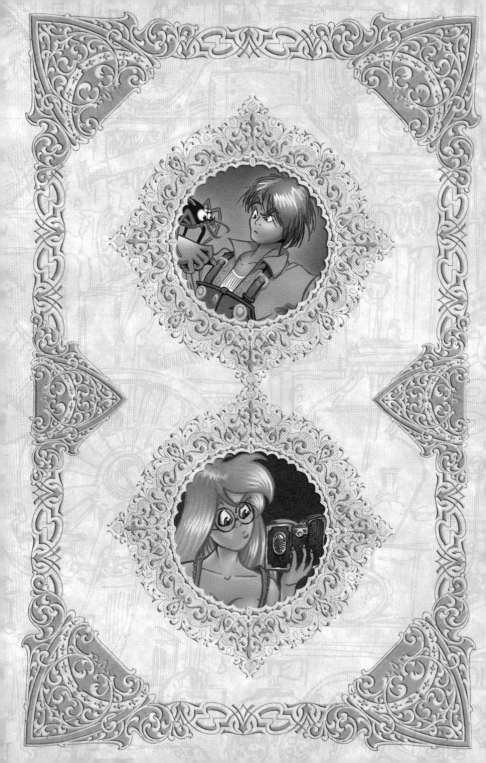

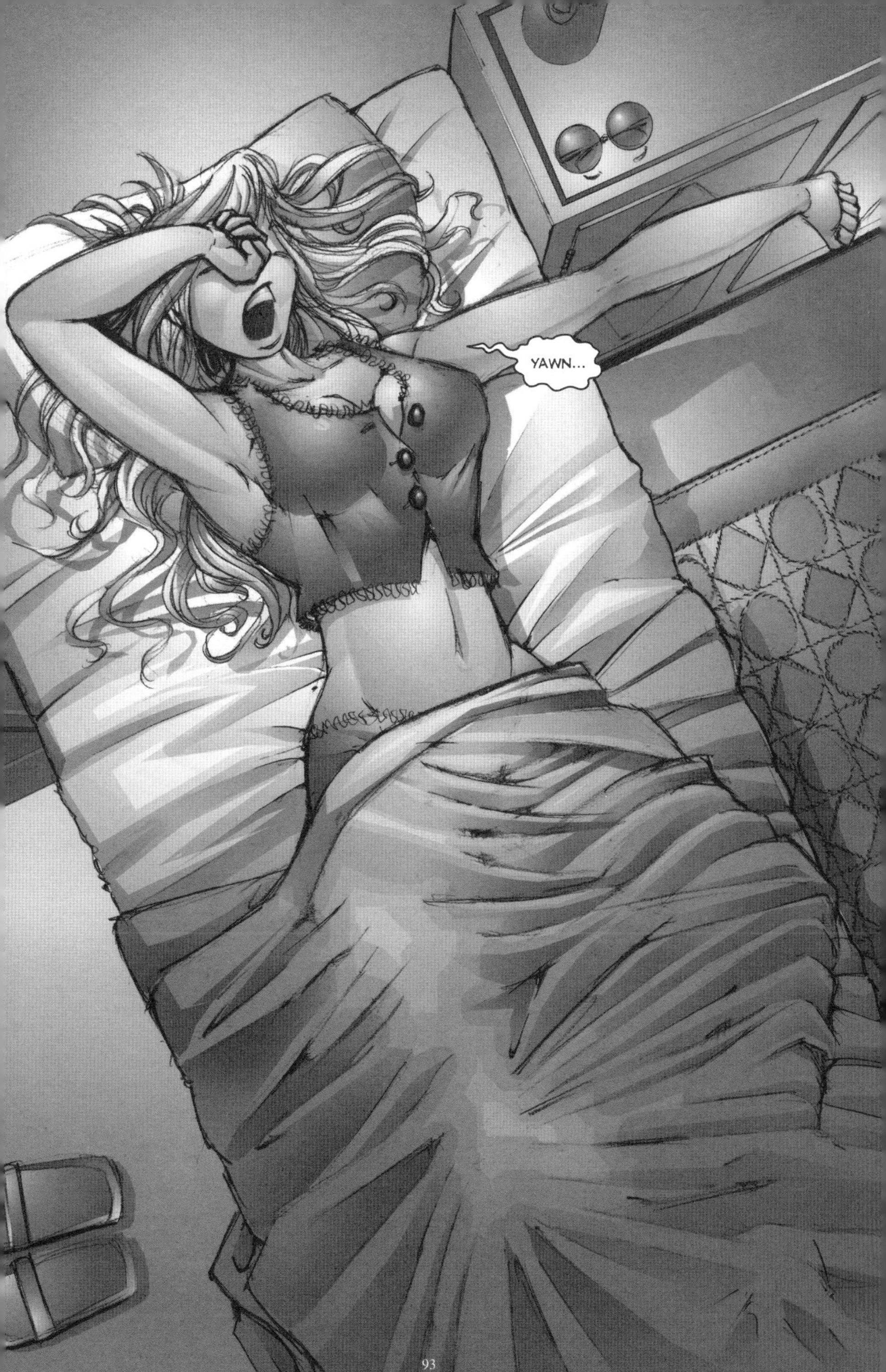
YAWN...

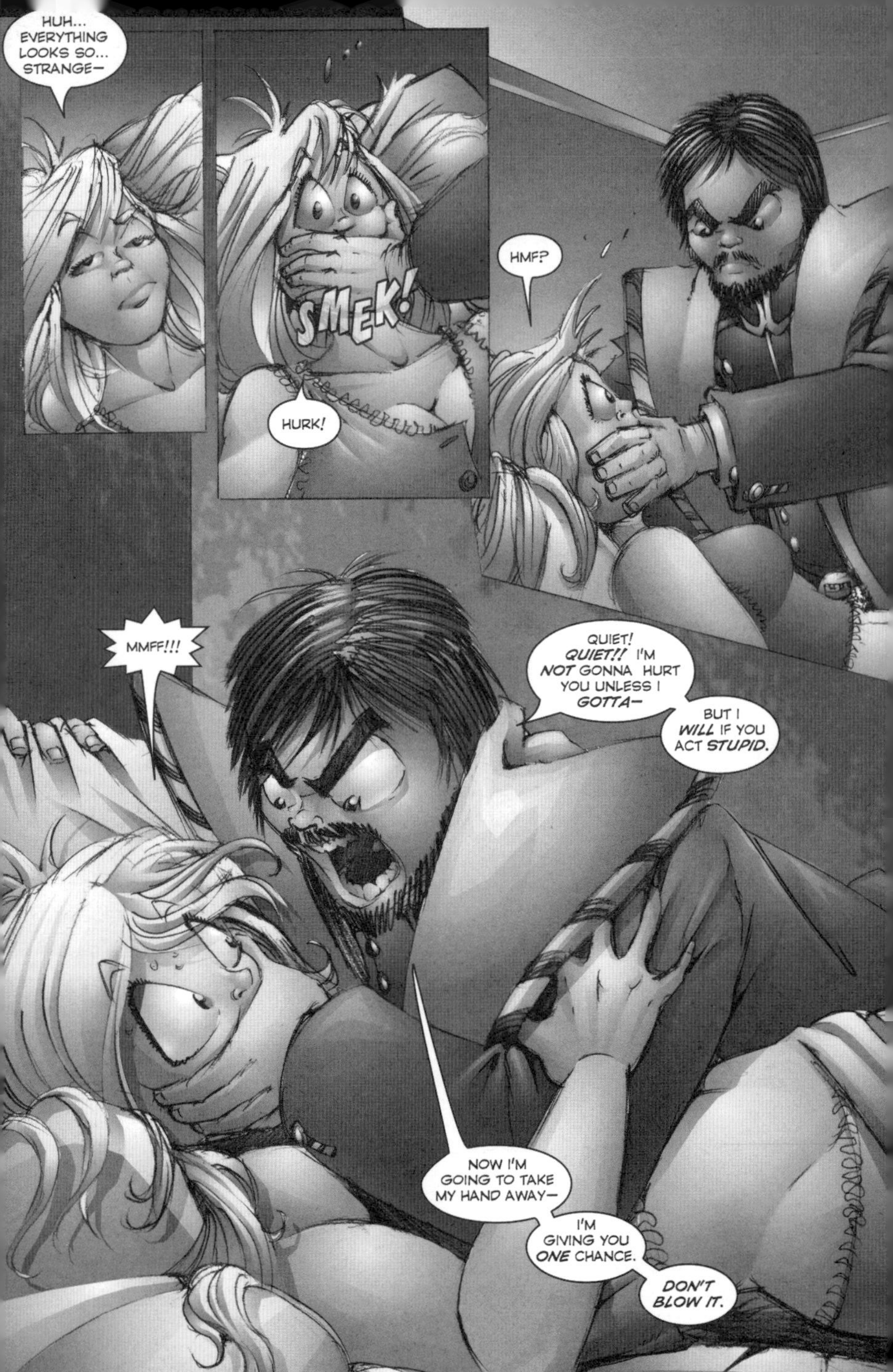
HUH... EVERYTHING LOOKS SO... STRANGE—
SMEK!
HURK!
HMF?
MMFF!!!
QUIET! QUIET!! I'M NOT GONNA HURT YOU UNLESS I GOTTA—
BUT I WILL IF YOU ACT STUPID.
NOW I'M GOING TO TAKE MY HAND AWAY—
I'M GIVING YOU ONE CHANCE.
DON'T BLOW IT.

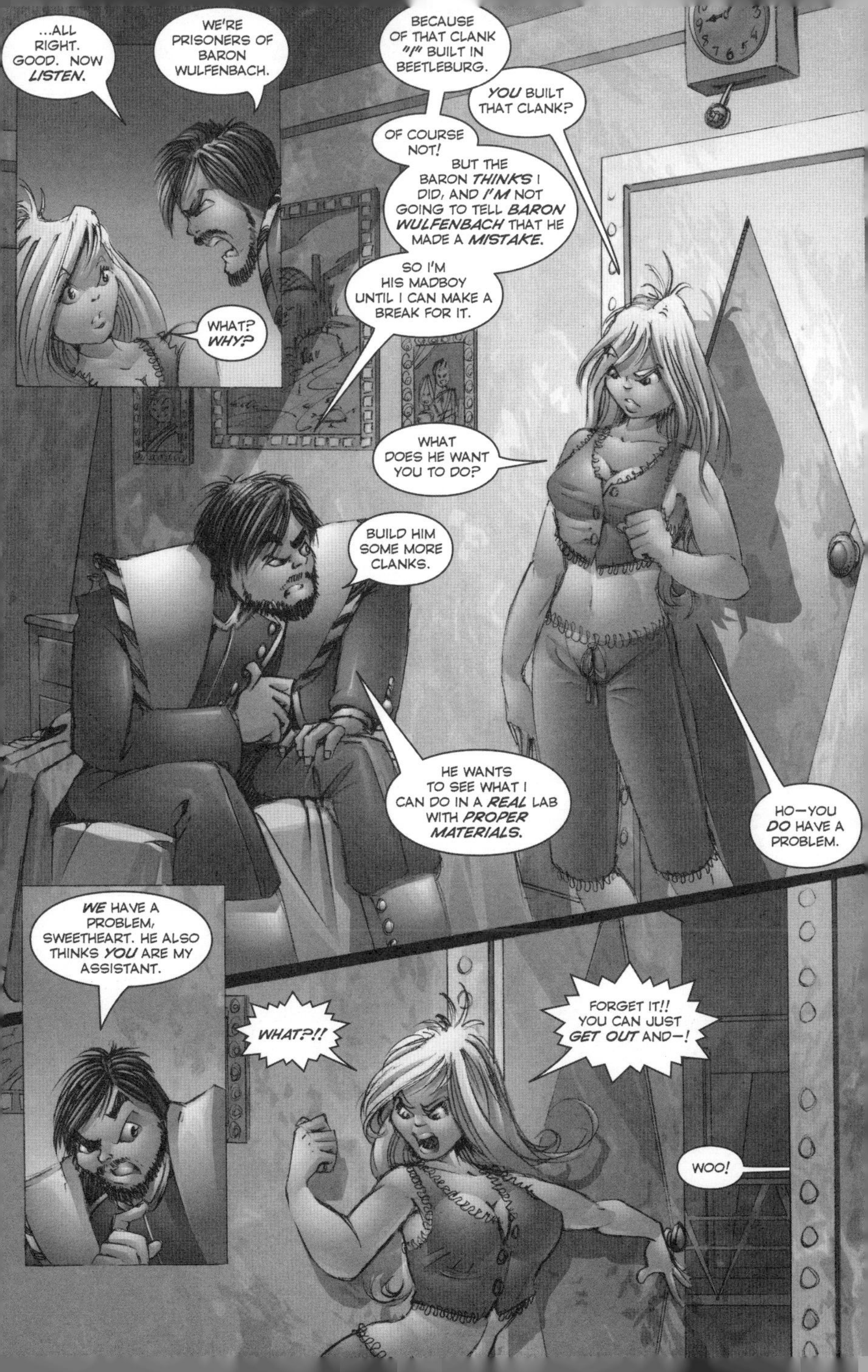
...ALL RIGHT. GOOD. NOW LISTEN.
WE'RE PRISONERS OF BARON WULFENBACH.
WHAT? WHY?
BECAUSE OF THAT CLANK "I" BUILT IN BEETLEBURG.
YOU BUILT THAT CLANK?
OF COURSE NOT!
BUT THE BARON THINKS I DID, AND I'M NOT GOING TO TELL BARON WULFENBACH THAT HE MADE A MISTAKE.
SO I'M HIS MADBOY UNTIL I CAN MAKE A BREAK FOR IT.
WHAT DOES HE WANT YOU TO DO?
BUILD HIM SOME MORE CLANKS.
HE WANTS TO SEE WHAT I CAN DO IN A REAL LAB WITH PROPER MATERIALS.
HO—YOU DO HAVE A PROBLEM.
WE HAVE A PROBLEM, SWEETHEART. HE ALSO THINKS YOU ARE MY ASSISTANT.
WHAT?!!
FORGET IT!! YOU CAN JUST GET OUT AND—!
WOO!

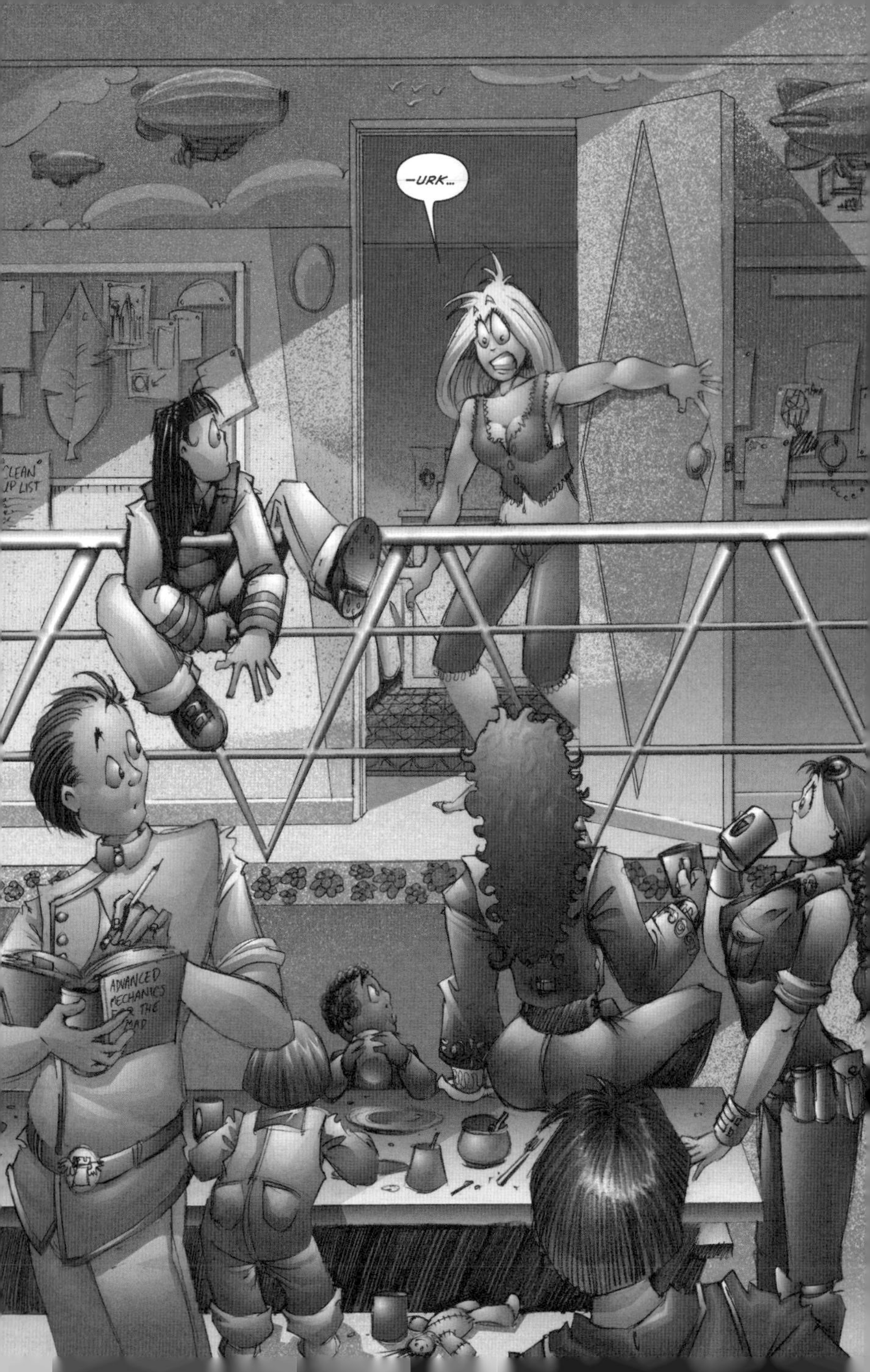
—URK...
CLEAN
UP LIST
ADVANCED
MECHANICS
THE
MAD

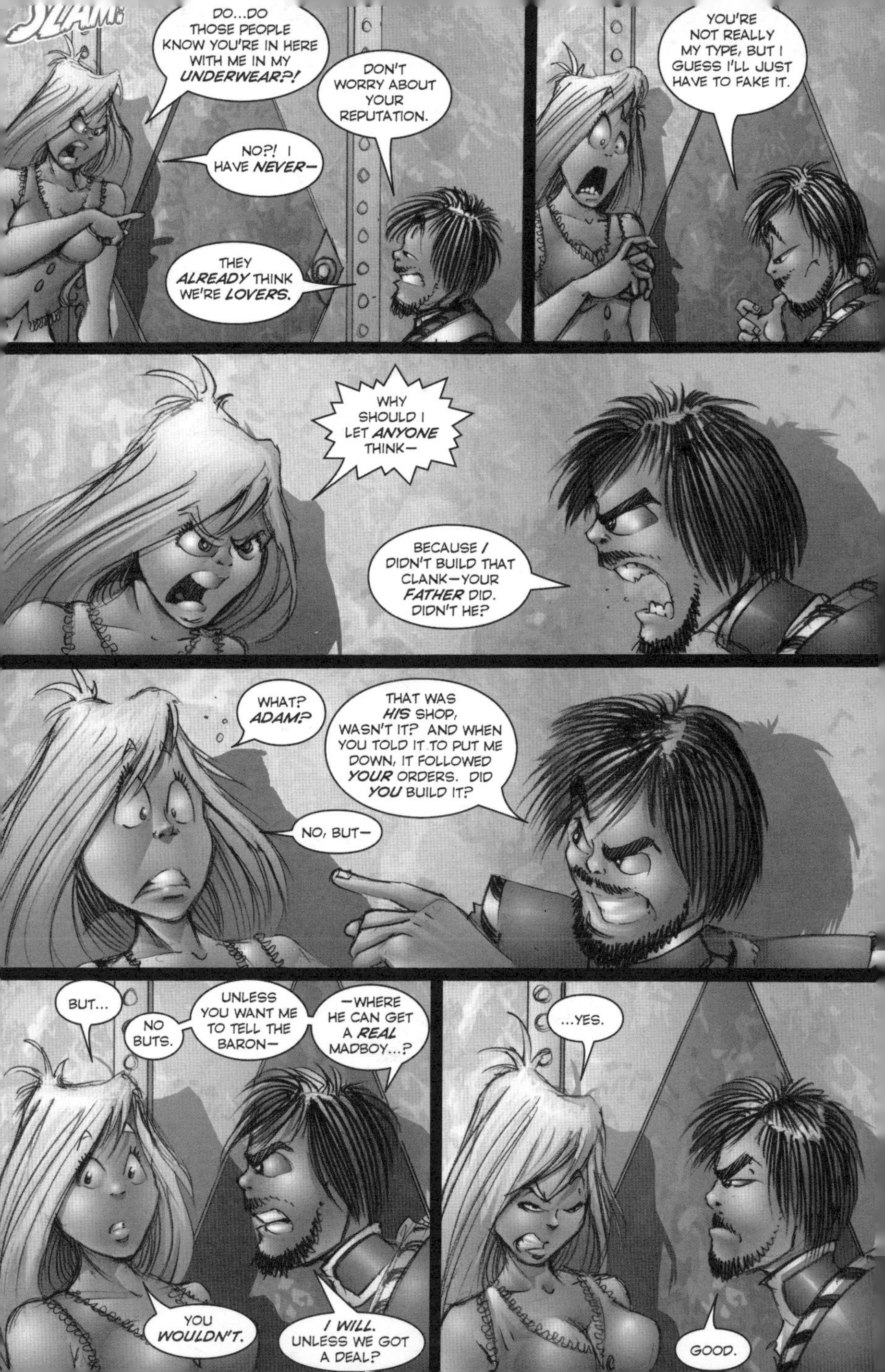
SLAM!
DO...DO THOSE PEOPLE KNOW YOU'RE IN HERE WITH ME IN MY UNDERWEAR?!
DON'T WORRY ABOUT YOUR REPUTATION.
NO?! I HAVE NEVER—
THEY ALREADY THINK WE'RE LOVERS.
YOU'RE NOT REALLY MY TYPE, BUT I GUESS I'LL JUST HAVE TO FAKE IT.
WHY SHOULD I LET ANYONE THINK—
BECAUSE I DIDN'T BUILD THAT CLANK—YOUR FATHER DID. DIDN'T HE?
WHAT? ADAM?
THAT WAS HIS SHOP, WASN'T IT? AND WHEN YOU TOLD IT TO PUT ME DOWN, IT FOLLOWED YOUR ORDERS. DID YOU BUILD IT?
NO, BUT—
BUT...
NO BUTS.
UNLESS YOU WANT ME TO TELL THE BARON—
—WHERE HE CAN GET A REAL MADBOY...?
YOU WOULDN'T.
I WILL. UNLESS WE GOT A DEAL?
...YES.
GOOD.

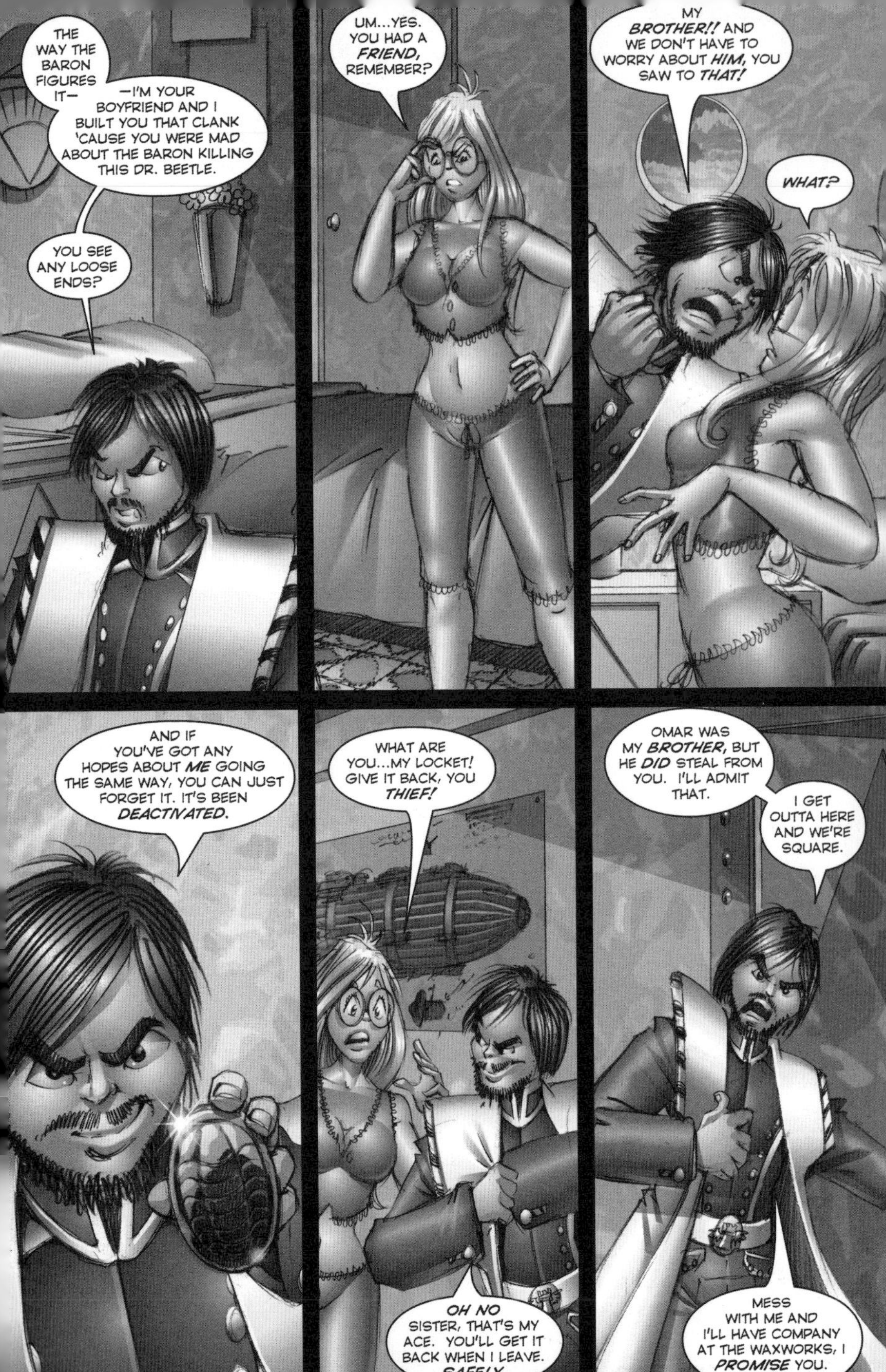
THE WAY THE BARON FIGURES IT—
—I'M YOUR BOYFRIEND AND I BUILT YOU THAT CLANK 'CAUSE YOU WERE MAD ABOUT THE BARON KILLING THIS DR. BEETLE.
YOU SEE ANY LOOSE ENDS?
UM...YES. YOU HAD A *FRIEND,* REMEMBER?
MY *BROTHER!!* AND WE DON'T HAVE TO WORRY ABOUT *HIM,* YOU SAW TO *THAT!*
WHAT?
AND IF YOU'VE GOT ANY HOPES ABOUT *ME* GOING THE SAME WAY, YOU CAN JUST FORGET IT. IT'S BEEN *DEACTIVATED.*
WHAT ARE YOU...MY LOCKET! GIVE IT BACK, YOU *THIEF!*
OH NO SISTER, THAT'S MY ACE. YOU'LL GET IT BACK WHEN I LEAVE. *SAFELY.*
OMAR WAS MY *BROTHER,* BUT HE *DID* STEAL FROM YOU. I'LL ADMIT THAT.
I GET OUTTA HERE AND WE'RE SQUARE.
MESS WITH ME AND I'LL HAVE COMPANY AT THE WAXWORKS, I *PROMISE* YOU.

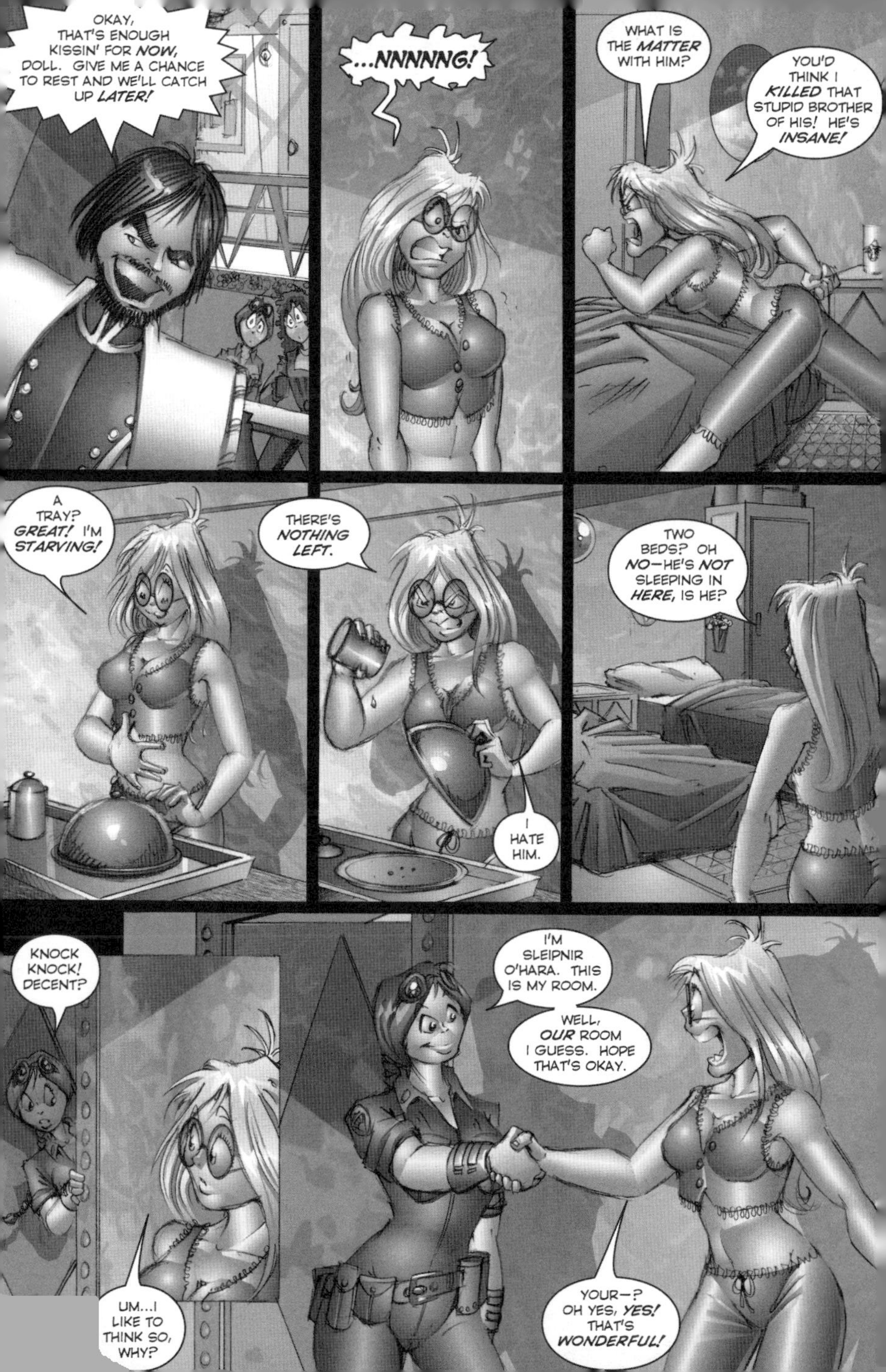
OKAY, THAT'S ENOUGH KISSIN' FOR NOW, DOLL. GIVE ME A CHANCE TO REST AND WE'LL CATCH UP LATER!
...NNNNNG!
WHAT IS THE MATTER WITH HIM?
YOU'D THINK I KILLED THAT STUPID BROTHER OF HIS! HE'S INSANE!
A TRAY? GREAT! I'M STARVING!
THERE'S NOTHING LEFT.
I HATE HIM.
TWO BEDS? OH NO—HE'S NOT SLEEPING IN HERE, IS HE?
KNOCK KNOCK! DECENT?
UM...I LIKE TO THINK SO, WHY?
I'M SLEIPNIR O'HARA. THIS IS MY ROOM.
WELL, OUR ROOM I GUESS. HOPE THAT'S OKAY.
YOUR—? OH YES, YES! THAT'S WONDERFUL!

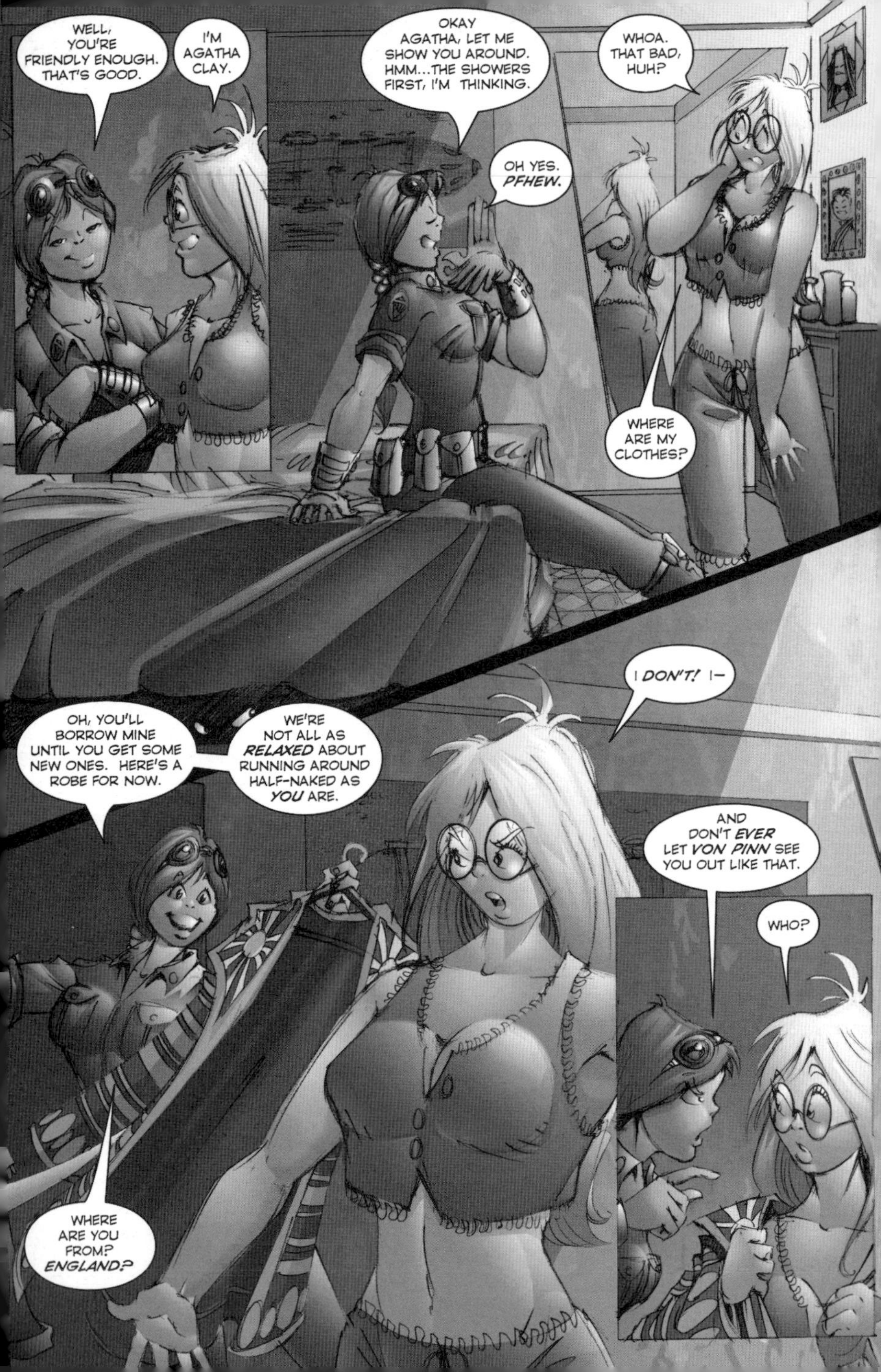

WELL, YOU'RE FRIENDLY ENOUGH. THAT'S GOOD.
I'M AGATHA CLAY.
OKAY AGATHA, LET ME SHOW YOU AROUND. HMM...THE SHOWERS FIRST, I'M THINKING.
OH YES. *PFHEW.*
WHOA. THAT BAD, HUH?
WHERE ARE MY CLOTHES?
OH, YOU'LL BORROW MINE UNTIL YOU GET SOME NEW ONES. HERE'S A ROBE FOR NOW.
WE'RE NOT ALL AS *RELAXED* ABOUT RUNNING AROUND HALF-NAKED AS *YOU* ARE.
I *DON'T!* I—
WHERE ARE YOU FROM? *ENGLAND?*
AND DON'T *EVER* LET *VON PINN* SEE YOU OUT LIKE THAT.
WHO?

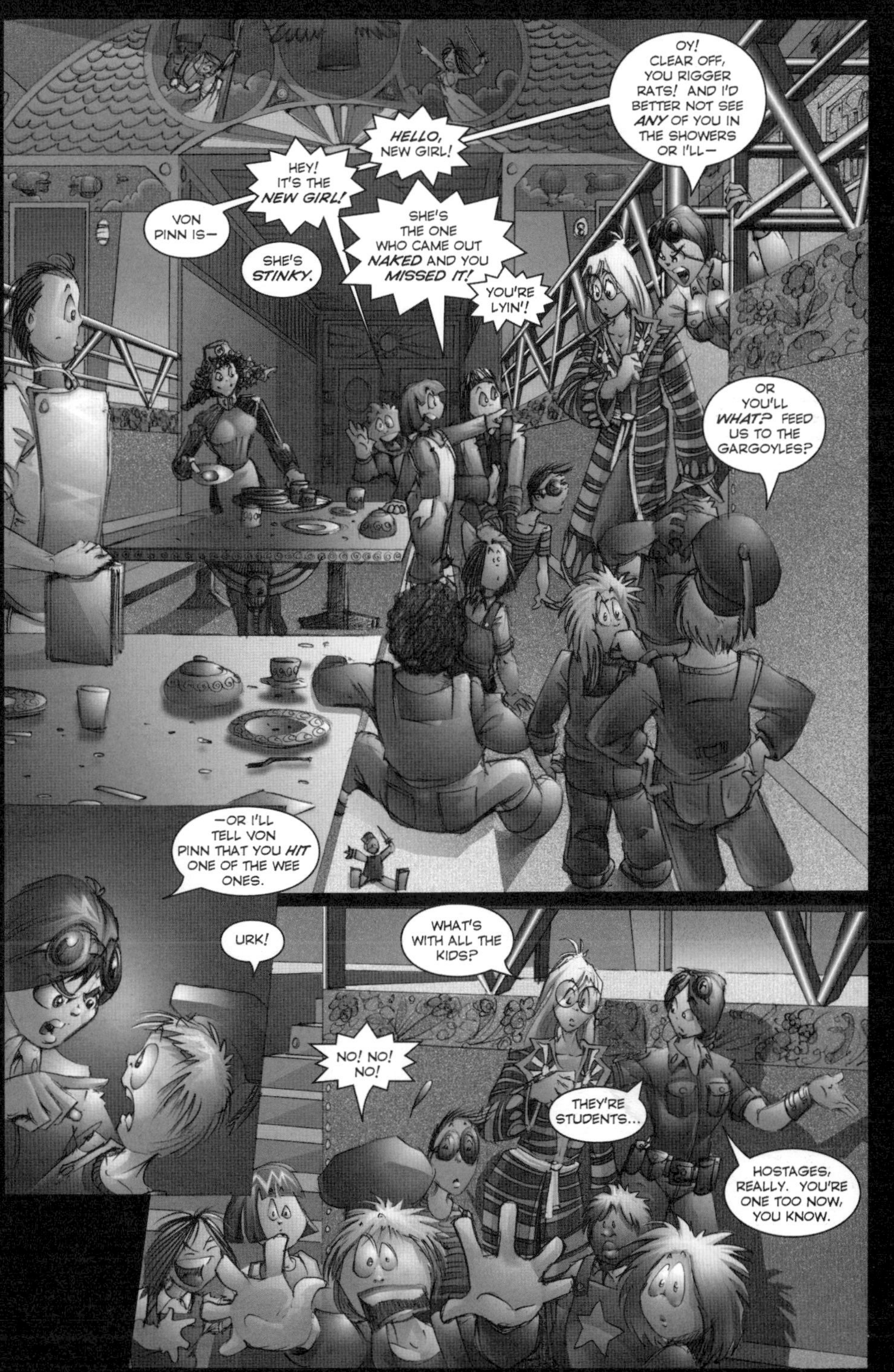
OY! CLEAR OFF, YOU RIGGER RATS! AND I'D BETTER NOT SEE ANY OF YOU IN THE SHOWERS OR I'LL—
HELLO, NEW GIRL!
HEY! IT'S THE NEW GIRL!
VON PINN IS—
SHE'S STINKY.
SHE'S THE ONE WHO CAME OUT NAKED AND YOU MISSED IT!
YOU'RE LYIN'!
OR YOU'LL WHAT? FEED US TO THE GARGOYLES?
—OR I'LL TELL VON PINN THAT YOU HIT ONE OF THE WEE ONES.
URK!
WHAT'S WITH ALL THE KIDS?
NO! NO! NO!
THEY'RE STUDENTS...
HOSTAGES, REALLY. YOU'RE ONE TOO NOW, YOU KNOW.

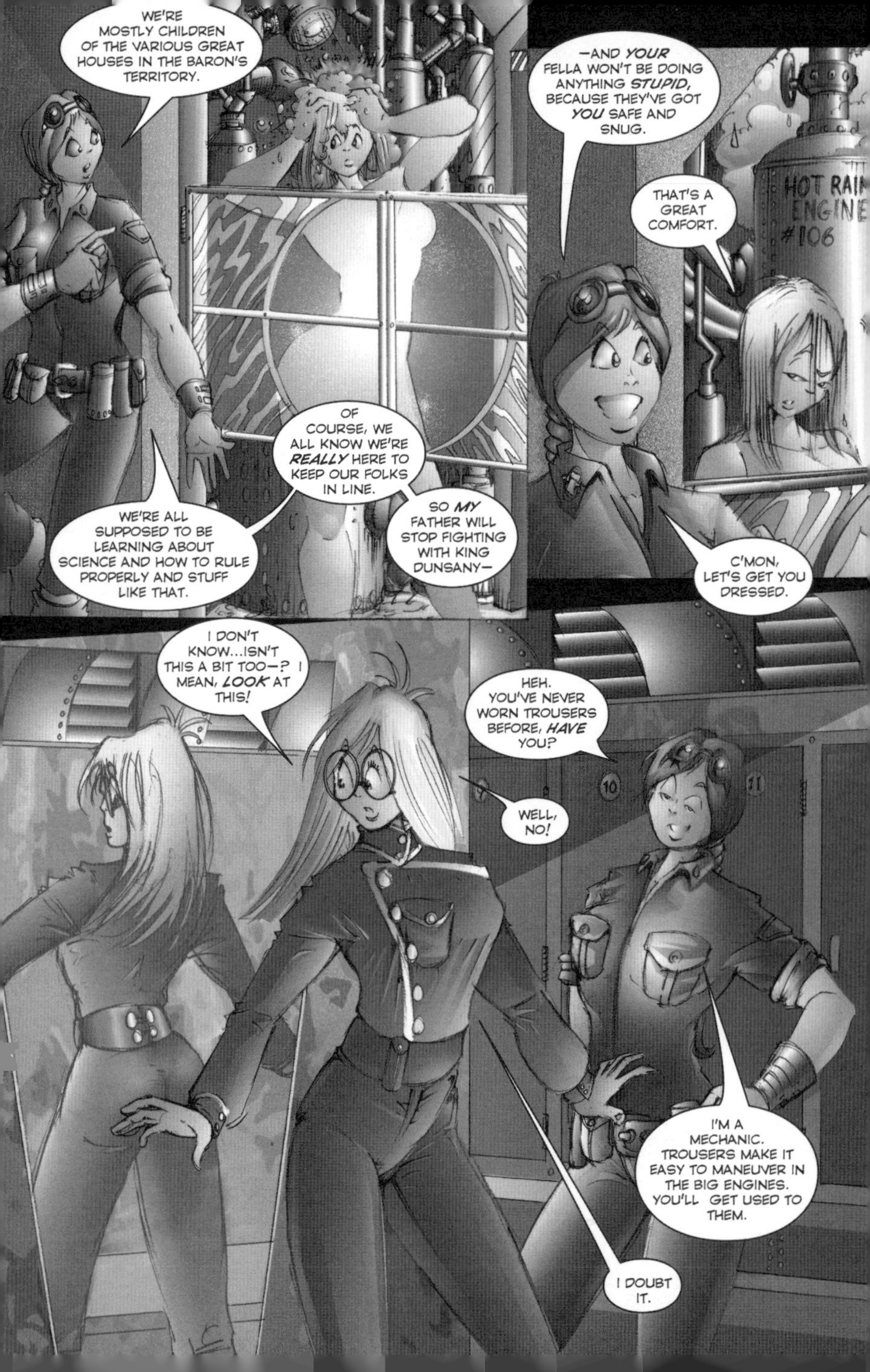
WE'RE MOSTLY CHILDREN OF THE VARIOUS GREAT HOUSES IN THE BARON'S TERRITORY.
WE'RE ALL SUPPOSED TO BE LEARNING ABOUT SCIENCE AND HOW TO RULE PROPERLY AND STUFF LIKE THAT.
OF COURSE, WE ALL KNOW WE'RE REALLY HERE TO KEEP OUR FOLKS IN LINE.
SO MY FATHER WILL STOP FIGHTING WITH KING DUNSANY—
—AND YOUR FELLA WON'T BE DOING ANYTHING STUPID, BECAUSE THEY'VE GOT YOU SAFE AND SNUG.
THAT'S A GREAT COMFORT.
HOT RAIN ENGINE #106
C'MON, LET'S GET YOU DRESSED.
I DON'T KNOW...ISN'T THIS A BIT TOO—? I MEAN, LOOK AT THIS!
HEH. YOU'VE NEVER WORN TROUSERS BEFORE, HAVE YOU?
WELL, NO!
10
11
I'M A MECHANIC. TROUSERS MAKE IT EASY TO MANEUVER IN THE BIG ENGINES. YOU'LL GET USED TO THEM.
I DOUBT IT.

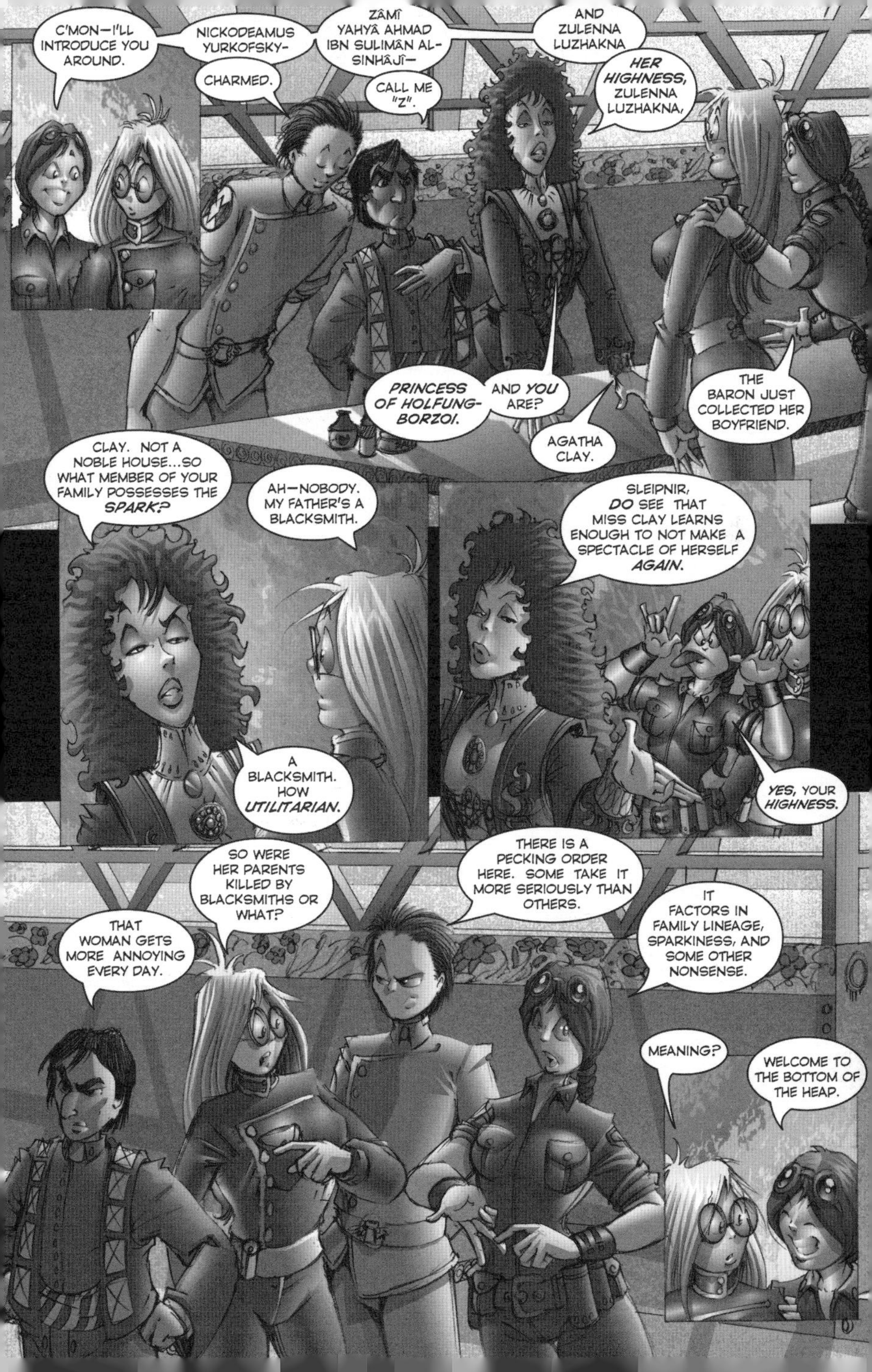
C'MON—I'LL INTRODUCE YOU AROUND.
NICKODEAMUS YURKOFSKY-
CHARMED.
ZÂMÎ YAHYÂ AHMAD IBN SULIMÂN AL-SINHÂJÎ—
CALL ME "Z".
AND ZULENNA LUZHAKNA
HER HIGHNESS, ZULENNA LUZHAKNA,
PRINCESS OF HOLFUNG-BORZOI.
AND YOU ARE?
AGATHA CLAY.
THE BARON JUST COLLECTED HER BOYFRIEND.
CLAY. NOT A NOBLE HOUSE...SO WHAT MEMBER OF YOUR FAMILY POSSESSES THE SPARK?
AH—NOBODY. MY FATHER'S A BLACKSMITH.
A BLACKSMITH. HOW UTILITARIAN.
SLEIPNIR, DO SEE THAT MISS CLAY LEARNS ENOUGH TO NOT MAKE A SPECTACLE OF HERSELF AGAIN.
YES, YOUR HIGHNESS.
THAT WOMAN GETS MORE ANNOYING EVERY DAY.
SO WERE HER PARENTS KILLED BY BLACKSMITHS OR WHAT?
THERE IS A PECKING ORDER HERE. SOME TAKE IT MORE SERIOUSLY THAN OTHERS.
IT FACTORS IN FAMILY LINEAGE, SPARKINESS, AND SOME OTHER NONSENSE.
MEANING?
WELCOME TO THE BOTTOM OF THE HEAP.

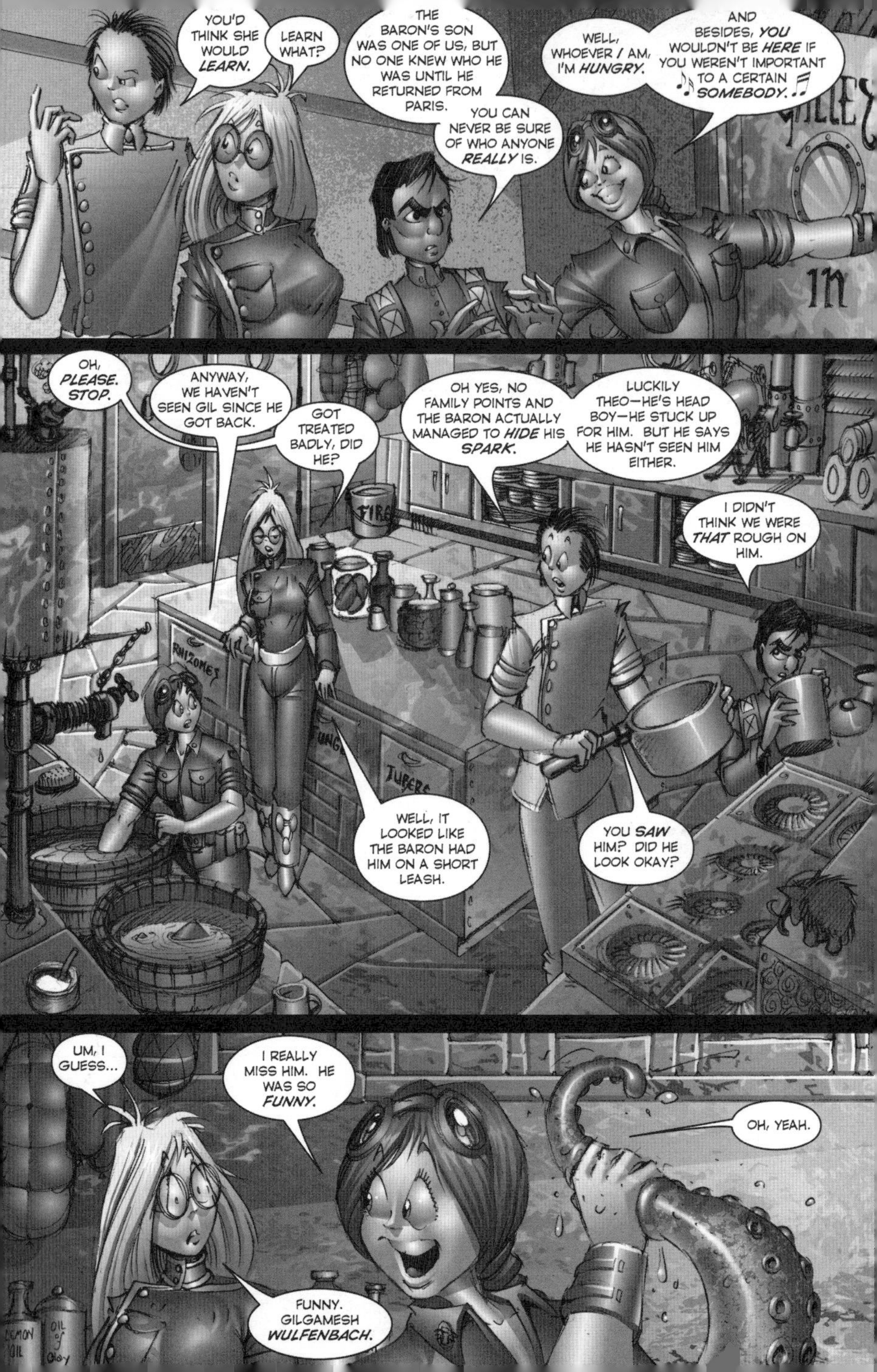
YOU'D THINK SHE WOULD *LEARN*.
LEARN WHAT?
THE BARON'S SON WAS ONE OF US, BUT NO ONE KNEW WHO HE WAS UNTIL HE RETURNED FROM PARIS.
YOU CAN NEVER BE SURE OF WHO ANYONE *REALLY* IS.
WELL, WHOEVER *I* AM, I'M *HUNGRY*.
AND BESIDES, *YOU* WOULDN'T BE *HERE* IF YOU WEREN'T IMPORTANT ♪ TO A CERTAIN *SOMEBODY*. ♫
GALLEY
IN
OH, *PLEASE*. *STOP*.
ANYWAY, WE HAVEN'T SEEN GIL SINCE HE GOT BACK.
GOT TREATED BADLY, DID HE?
OH YES, NO FAMILY POINTS AND THE BARON ACTUALLY MANAGED TO *HIDE* HIS *SPARK*.
LUCKILY THEO—HE'S HEAD BOY—HE STUCK UP FOR HIM. BUT HE SAYS HE HASN'T SEEN HIM EITHER.
I DIDN'T THINK WE WERE *THAT* ROUGH ON HIM.
FIRE
RHIZOMES
TUBERS
WELL, IT LOOKED LIKE THE BARON HAD HIM ON A SHORT LEASH.
YOU *SAW* HIM? DID HE LOOK OKAY?
UM, I GUESS...
I REALLY MISS HIM. HE WAS SO *FUNNY*.
OH, YEAH.
FUNNY. GILGAMESH *WULFENBACH*.
OIL of Glory

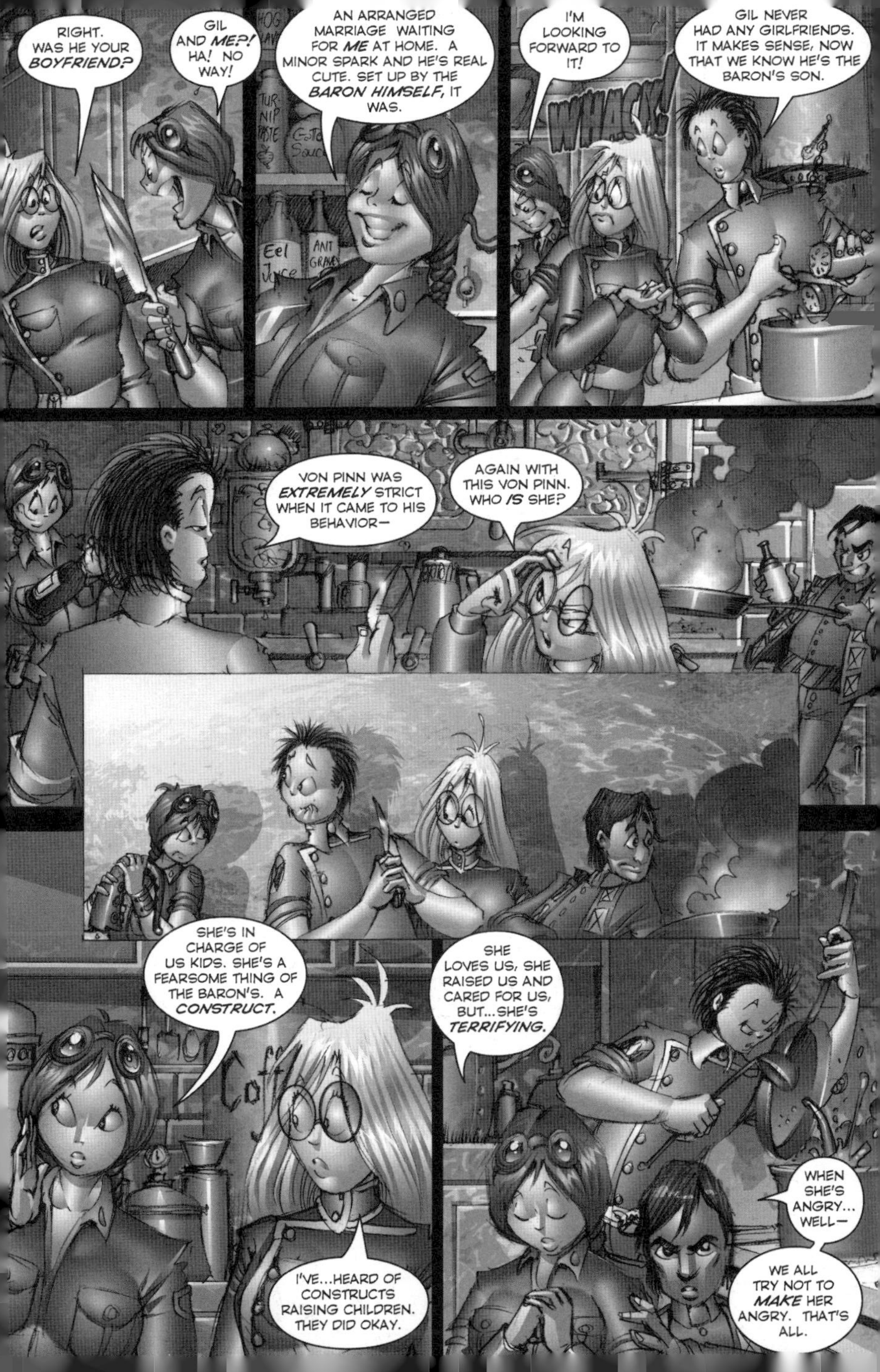
RIGHT. WAS HE YOUR BOYFRIEND?
GIL AND ME?! HA! NO WAY!
AN ARRANGED MARRIAGE WAITING FOR ME AT HOME. A MINOR SPARK AND HE'S REAL CUTE. SET UP BY THE BARON HIMSELF, IT WAS.
I'M LOOKING FORWARD TO IT!
WHACK!
GIL NEVER HAD ANY GIRLFRIENDS. IT MAKES SENSE, NOW THAT WE KNOW HE'S THE BARON'S SON.
VON PINN WAS EXTREMELY STRICT WHEN IT CAME TO HIS BEHAVIOR—
AGAIN WITH THIS VON PINN. WHO IS SHE?
SHE'S IN CHARGE OF US KIDS. SHE'S A FEARSOME THING OF THE BARON'S. A CONSTRUCT.
I'VE...HEARD OF CONSTRUCTS RAISING CHILDREN. THEY DID OKAY.
SHE LOVES US, SHE RAISED US AND CARED FOR US, BUT...SHE'S TERRIFYING.
WHEN SHE'S ANGRY... WELL—
WE ALL TRY NOT TO MAKE HER ANGRY. THAT'S ALL.

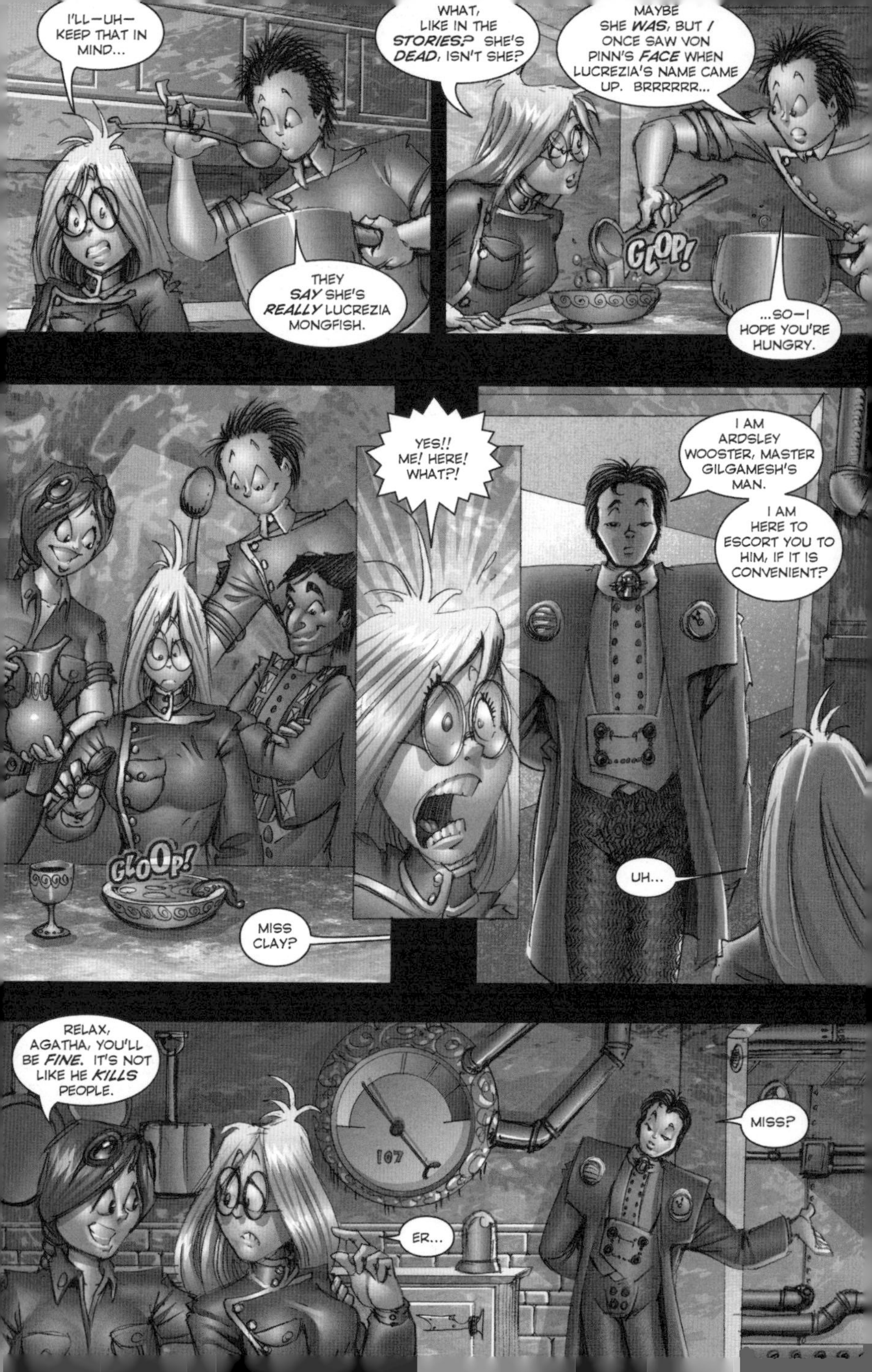
I'LL—UH—KEEP THAT IN MIND...
THEY SAY SHE'S REALLY LUCREZIA MONGFISH.
WHAT, LIKE IN THE STORIES? SHE'S DEAD, ISN'T SHE?
MAYBE SHE WAS, BUT I ONCE SAW VON PINN'S FACE WHEN LUCREZIA'S NAME CAME UP. BRRRRRR...
GLOP!
...SO—I HOPE YOU'RE HUNGRY.
GLOOP!
MISS CLAY?
YES!! ME! HERE! WHAT?!
I AM ARDSLEY WOOSTER, MASTER GILGAMESH'S MAN.
I AM HERE TO ESCORT YOU TO HIM, IF IT IS CONVENIENT?
UH...
RELAX, AGATHA, YOU'LL BE FINE. IT'S NOT LIKE HE KILLS PEOPLE.
ER...
MISS?

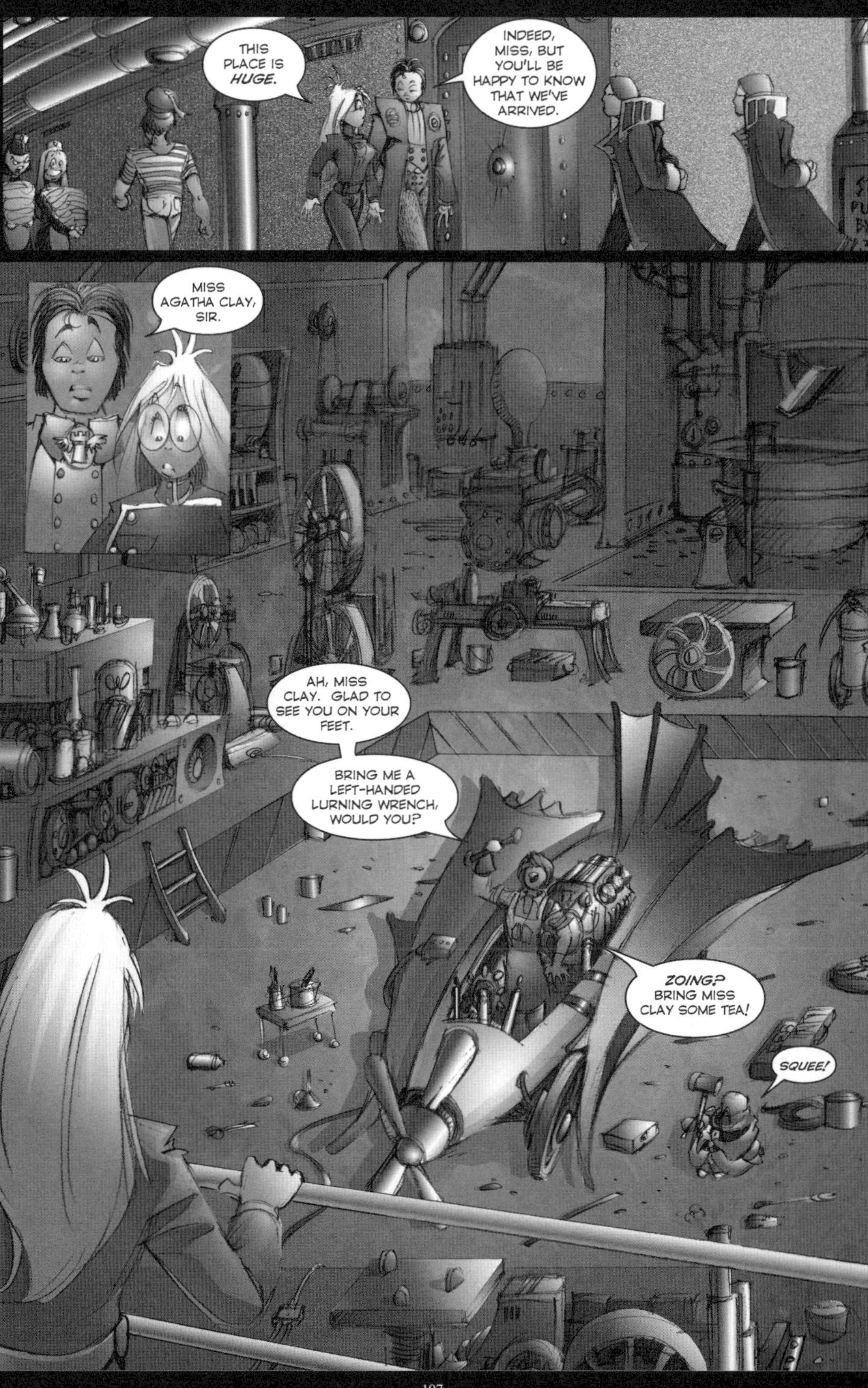
THIS PLACE IS *HUGE*.
INDEED, MISS, BUT YOU'LL BE HAPPY TO KNOW THAT WE'VE ARRIVED.
MISS AGATHA CLAY, SIR.
AH, MISS CLAY. GLAD TO SEE YOU ON YOUR FEET.
BRING ME A LEFT-HANDED LURNING WRENCH, WOULD YOU?
ZOING? BRING MISS CLAY SOME TEA!
SQUEE!

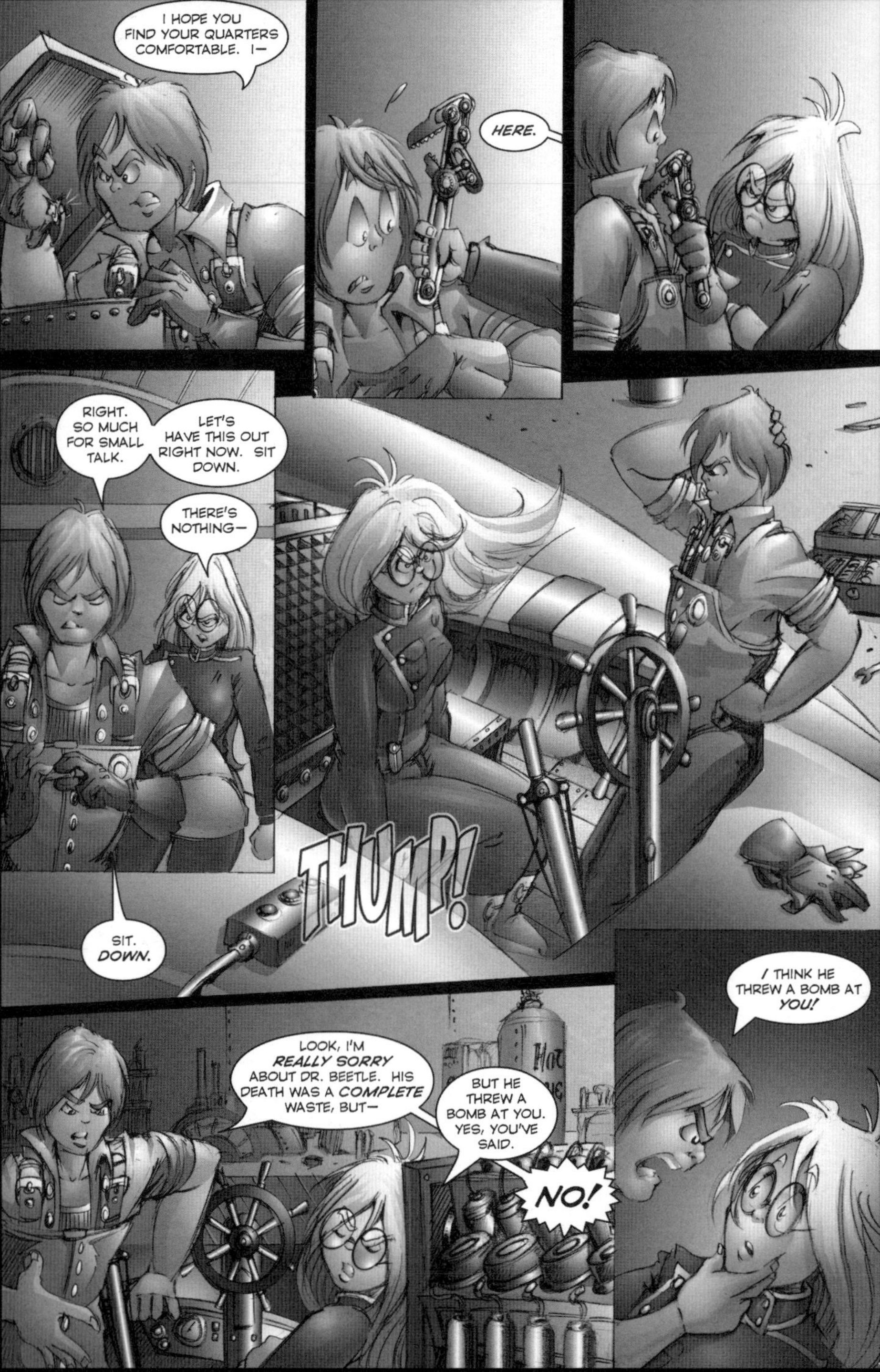
I HOPE YOU FIND YOUR QUARTERS COMFORTABLE. I—
HERE.
RIGHT. SO MUCH FOR SMALL TALK.
LET'S HAVE THIS OUT RIGHT NOW. SIT DOWN.
THERE'S NOTHING—
SIT. *DOWN.*
THUMP!
LOOK, I'M *REALLY SORRY* ABOUT DR. BEETLE. HIS DEATH WAS A *COMPLETE* WASTE, BUT—
BUT HE THREW A BOMB AT YOU. YES, YOU'VE SAID.
NO!
I THINK HE THREW A BOMB AT *YOU!*

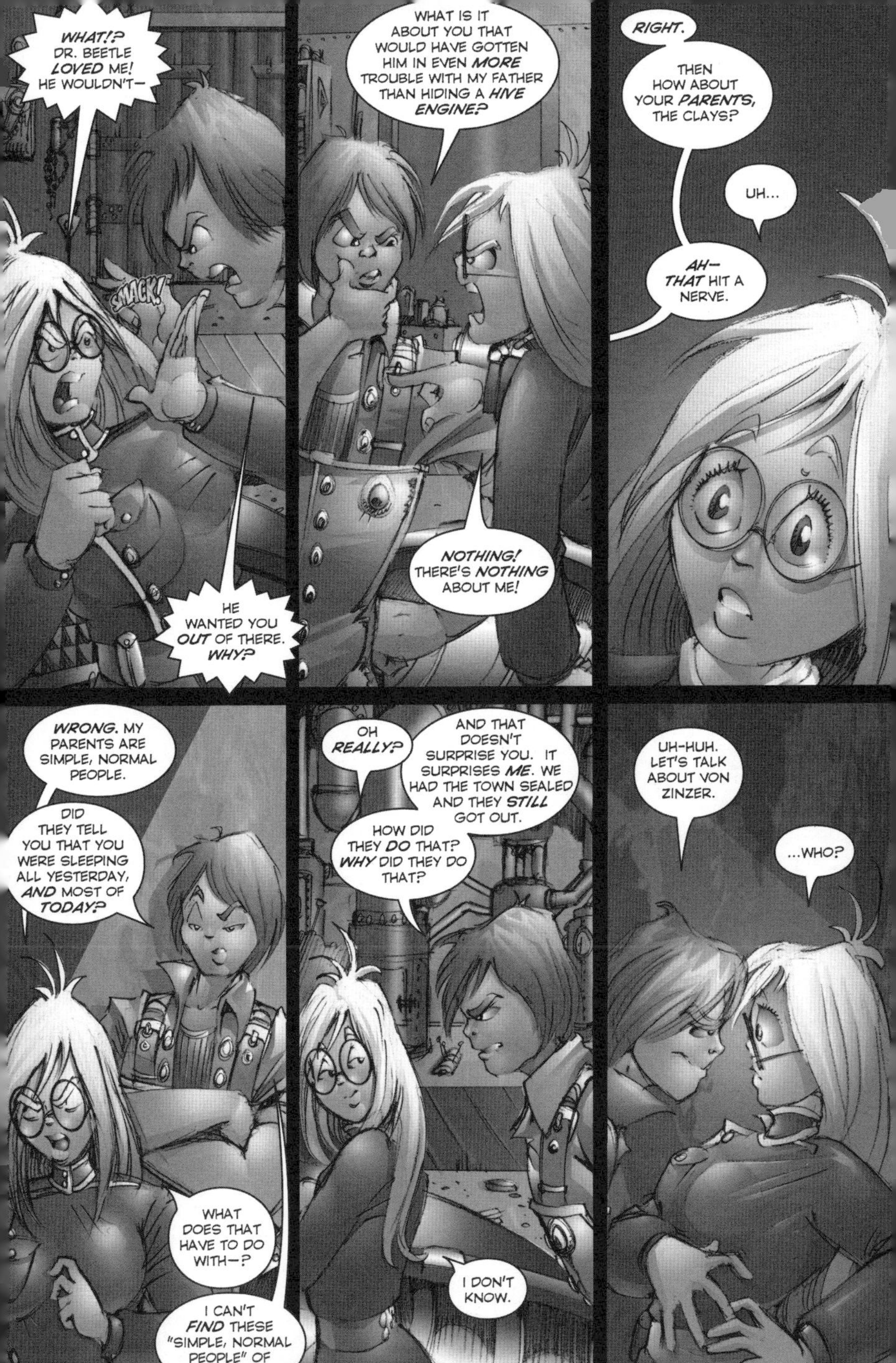
WHAT!? DR. BEETLE LOVED ME! HE WOULDN'T—
SMACK!
HE WANTED YOU OUT OF THERE. WHY?
WHAT IS IT ABOUT YOU THAT WOULD HAVE GOTTEN HIM IN EVEN MORE TROUBLE WITH MY FATHER THAN HIDING A HIVE ENGINE?
NOTHING! THERE'S NOTHING ABOUT ME!
RIGHT.
THEN HOW ABOUT YOUR PARENTS, THE CLAYS?
UH...
AH— THAT HIT A NERVE.
WRONG. MY PARENTS ARE SIMPLE, NORMAL PEOPLE.
DID THEY TELL YOU THAT YOU WERE SLEEPING ALL YESTERDAY, AND MOST OF TODAY?
WHAT DOES THAT HAVE TO DO WITH—?
I CAN'T FIND THESE "SIMPLE, NORMAL PEOPLE" OF YOURS.
OH REALLY?
AND THAT DOESN'T SURPRISE YOU. IT SURPRISES ME. WE HAD THE TOWN SEALED AND THEY STILL GOT OUT.
HOW DID THEY DO THAT? WHY DID THEY DO THAT?
I DON'T KNOW.
UH-HUH. LET'S TALK ABOUT VON ZINZER.
...WHO?

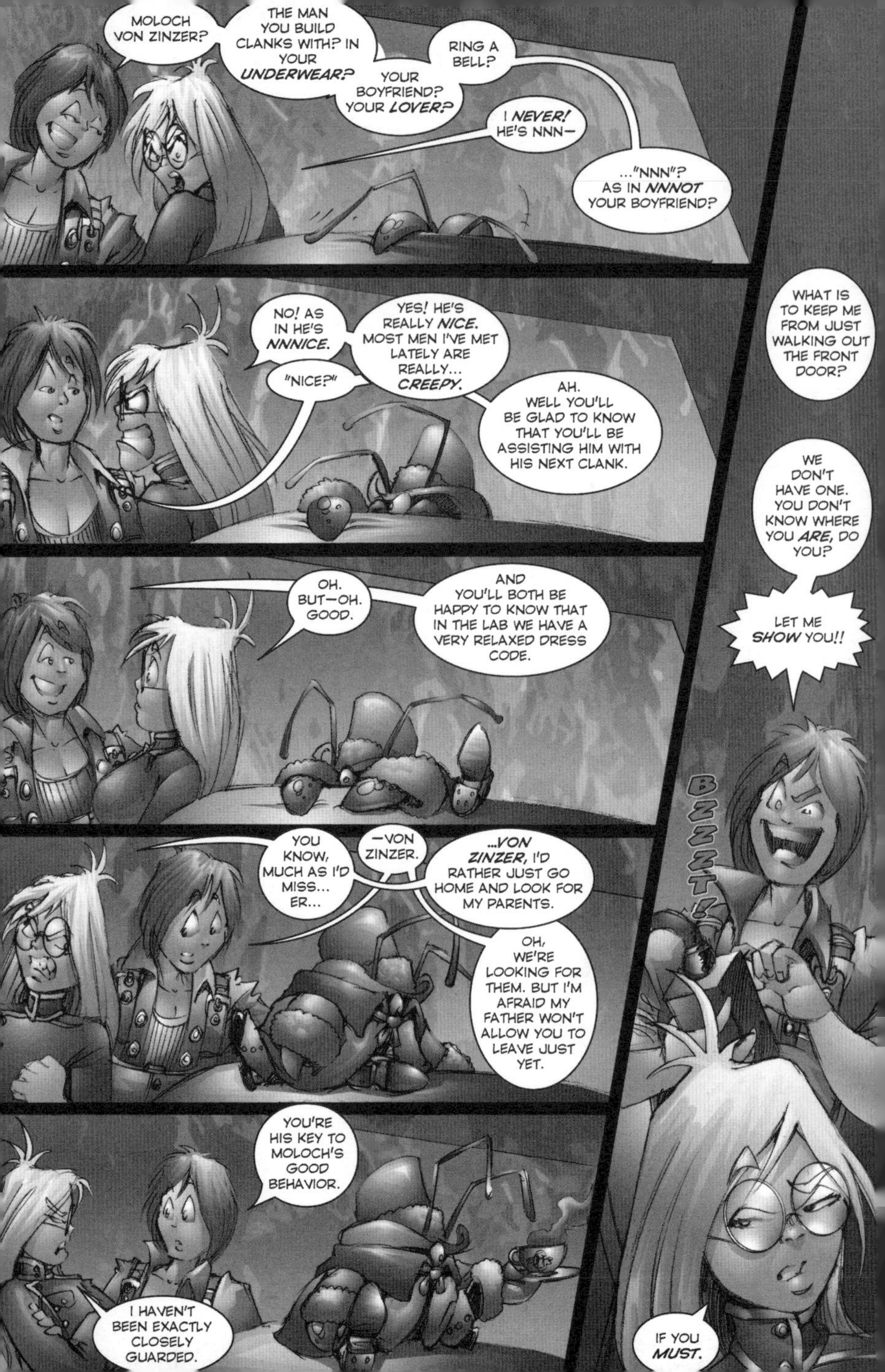
MOLOCH VON ZINZER?
THE MAN YOU BUILD CLANKS WITH? IN YOUR *UNDERWEAR?*
YOUR BOYFRIEND? YOUR *LOVER?*
RING A BELL?
I *NEVER!* HE'S NNN—
..."NNN"? AS IN *NNNOT* YOUR BOYFRIEND?
NO! AS IN HE'S *NNNICE.*
"NICE?"
YES! HE'S REALLY *NICE.* MOST MEN I'VE MET LATELY ARE REALLY... *CREEPY.*
AH. WELL YOU'LL BE GLAD TO KNOW THAT YOU'LL BE ASSISTING HIM WITH HIS NEXT CLANK.
OH. BUT—OH. GOOD.
AND YOU'LL BOTH BE HAPPY TO KNOW THAT IN THE LAB WE HAVE A VERY RELAXED DRESS CODE.
YOU KNOW, MUCH AS I'D MISS... ER...
—VON ZINZER.
...VON ZINZER, I'D RATHER JUST GO HOME AND LOOK FOR MY PARENTS.
OH, WE'RE LOOKING FOR THEM. BUT I'M AFRAID MY FATHER WON'T ALLOW YOU TO LEAVE JUST YET.
YOU'RE HIS KEY TO MOLOCH'S GOOD BEHAVIOR.
I HAVEN'T BEEN EXACTLY CLOSELY GUARDED.
WHAT IS TO KEEP ME FROM JUST WALKING OUT THE FRONT DOOR?
WE DON'T HAVE ONE. YOU DON'T KNOW WHERE YOU *ARE,* DO YOU?
LET ME *SHOW* YOU!!
BZZZZT!
IF YOU *MUST.*

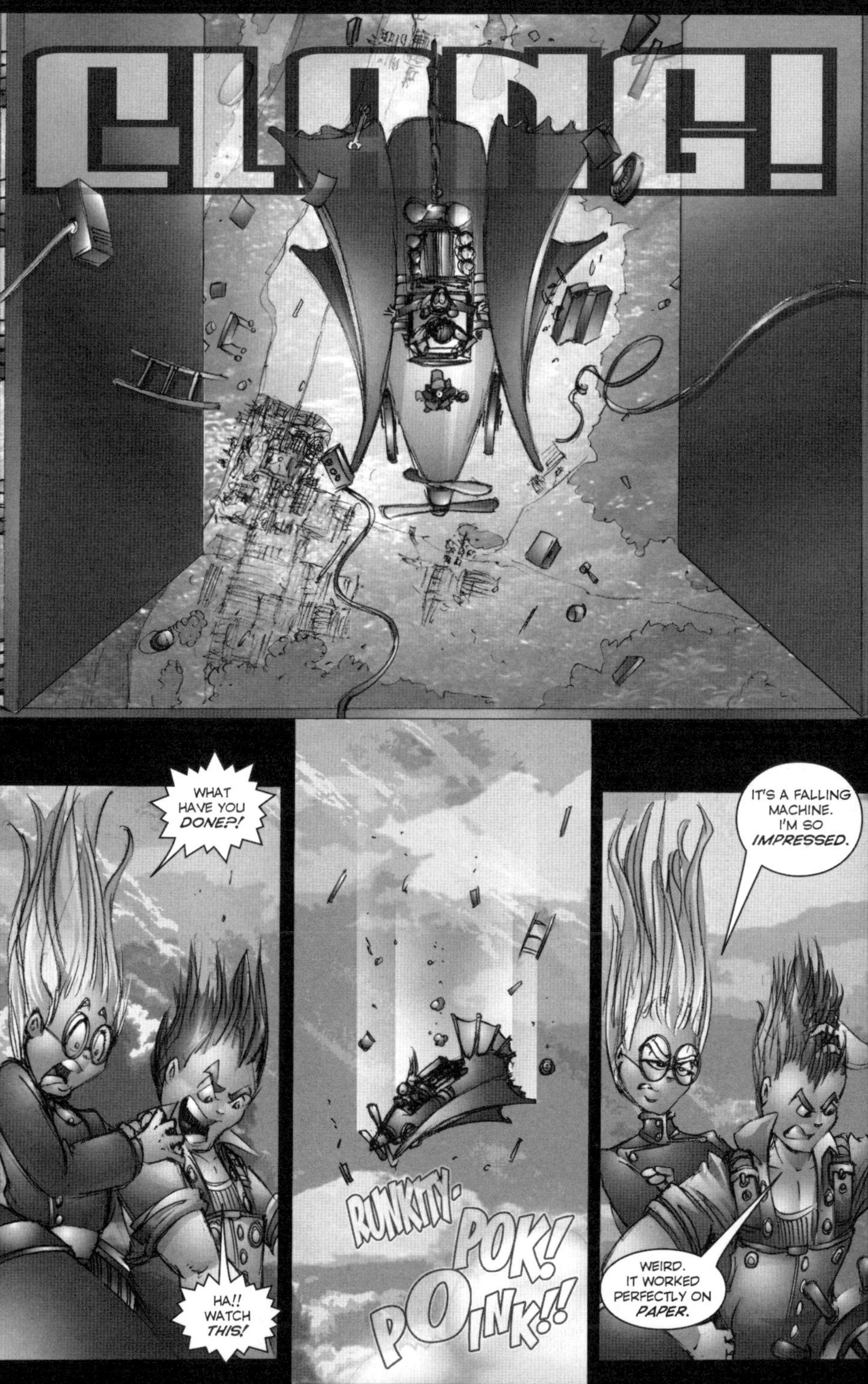
CLONG!
WHAT HAVE YOU DONE?!
HA!! WATCH THIS!
RUNKITY-POK! POINK!!
IT'S A FALLING MACHINE. I'M SO IMPRESSED.
WEIRD. IT WORKED PERFECTLY ON PAPER.

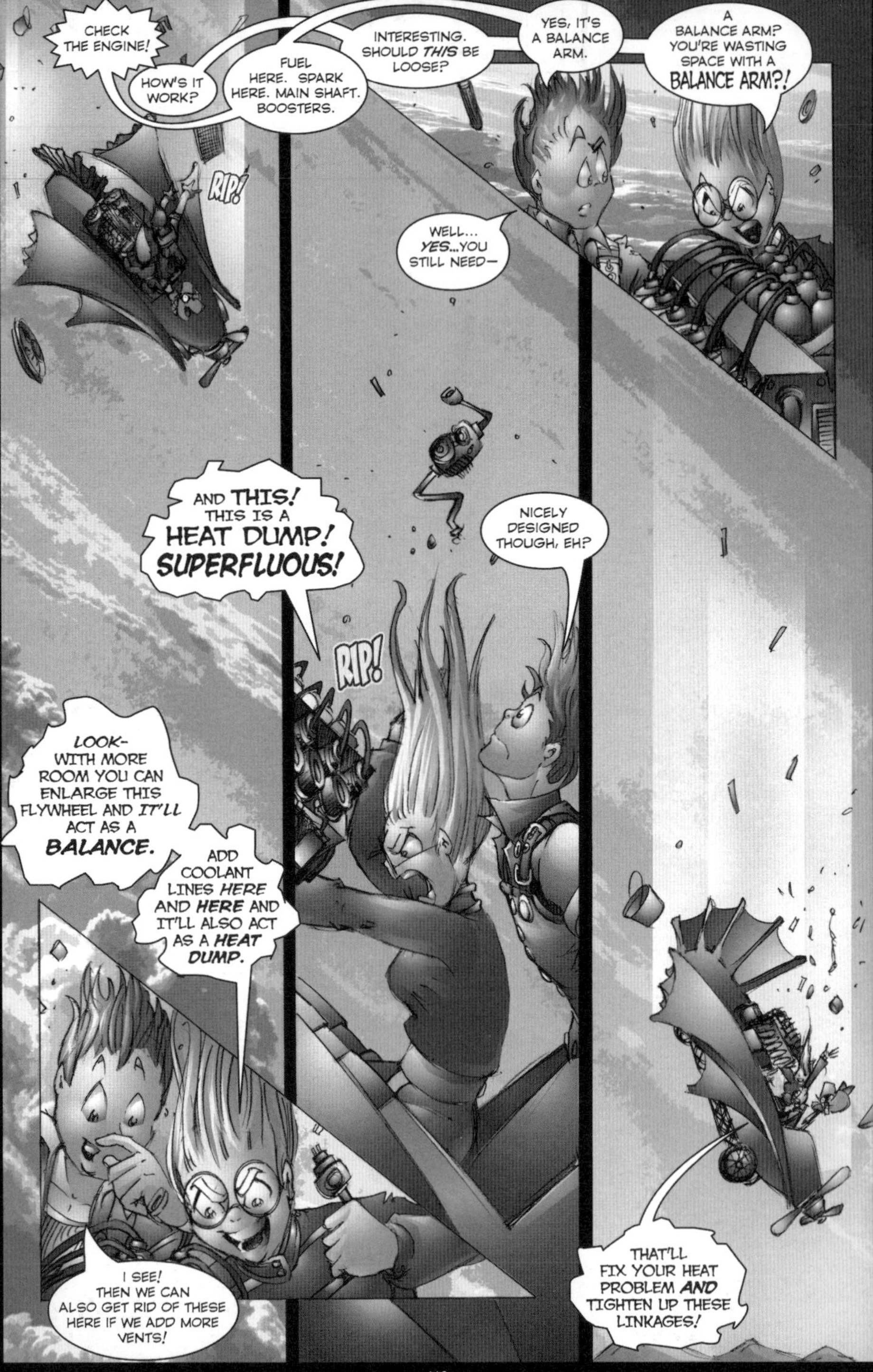
CHECK THE ENGINE!
HOW'S IT WORK?
FUEL HERE. SPARK HERE. MAIN SHAFT. BOOSTERS.
INTERESTING. SHOULD *THIS* BE LOOSE?
YES, IT'S A BALANCE ARM.
A BALANCE ARM? YOU'RE WASTING SPACE WITH A BALANCE ARM?!
RIP!
WELL... *YES*...YOU STILL NEED—
AND **THIS!** THIS IS A HEAT DUMP! ***SUPERFLUOUS!***
NICELY DESIGNED THOUGH, EH?
RIP!
LOOK- WITH MORE ROOM YOU CAN ENLARGE THIS FLYWHEEL AND *IT'LL* ACT AS A ***BALANCE.***
ADD COOLANT LINES *HERE* AND ***HERE*** AND IT'LL ALSO ACT AS A ***HEAT DUMP.***
I SEE! THEN WE CAN ALSO GET RID OF THESE HERE IF WE ADD MORE VENTS!
THAT'LL FIX YOUR HEAT PROBLEM ***AND*** TIGHTEN UP THESE LINKAGES!

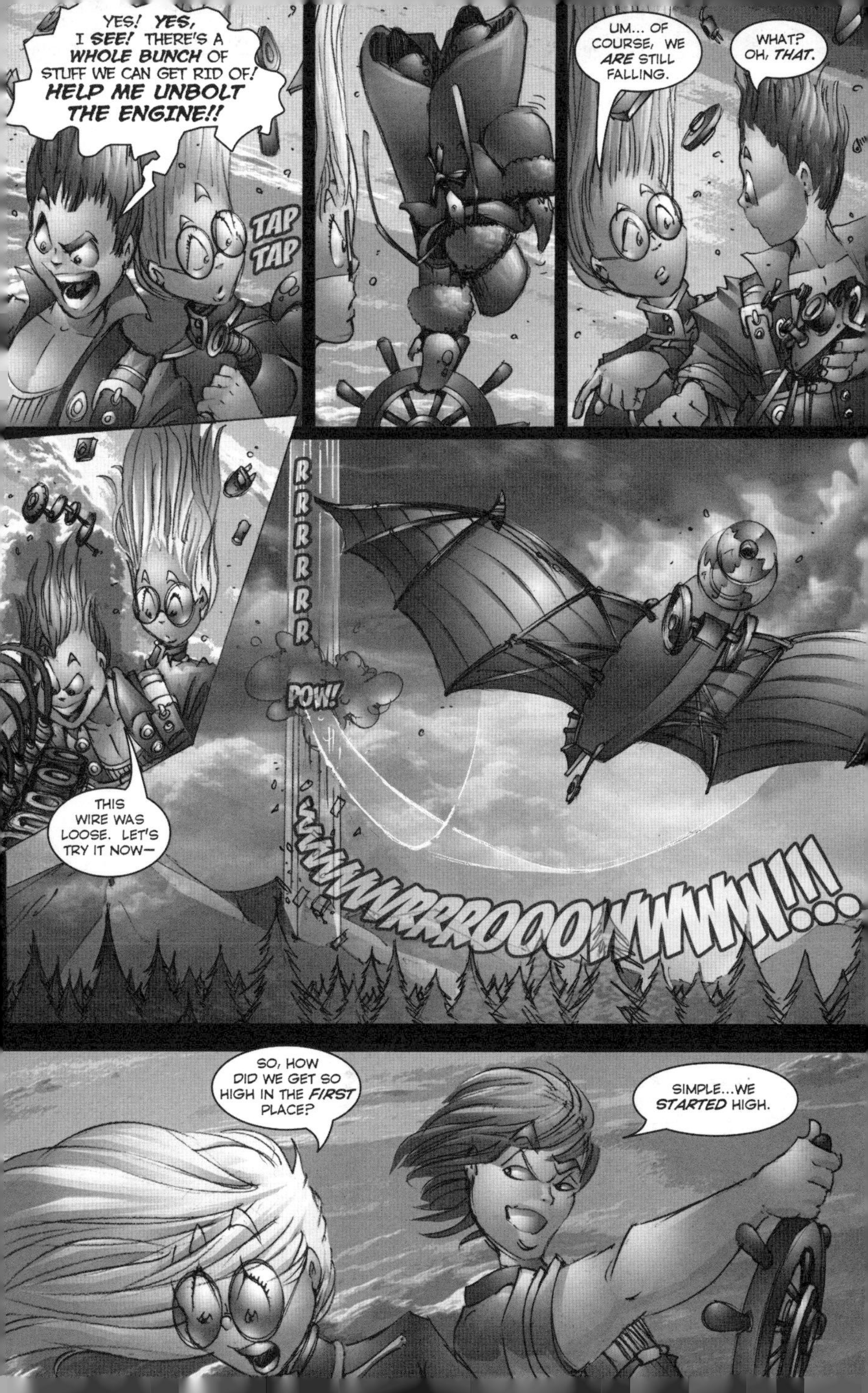
YES! YES, I SEE! THERE'S A WHOLE BUNCH OF STUFF WE CAN GET RID OF! HELP ME UNBOLT THE ENGINE!!
TAP TAP
UM... OF COURSE, WE ARE STILL FALLING.
WHAT? OH, THAT.
THIS WIRE WAS LOOSE. LET'S TRY IT NOW—
RRRRRRR
POW!
WWWWRRRROOOOWWWWN!!!...
SO, HOW DID WE GET SO HIGH IN THE FIRST PLACE?
SIMPLE...WE STARTED HIGH.

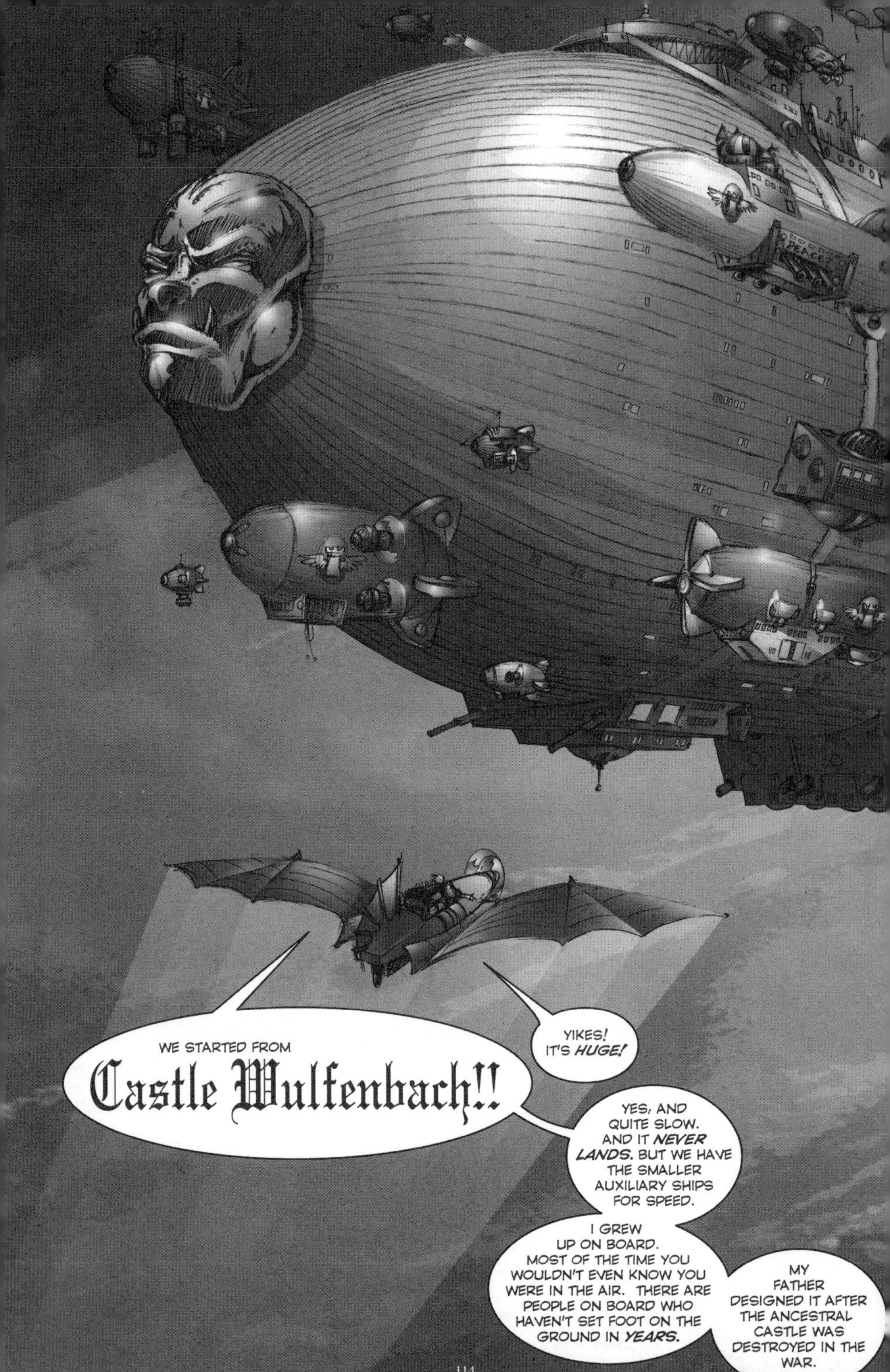
WE STARTED FROM Castle Wulfenbach!!
YIKES! IT'S *HUGE!*
YES, AND QUITE SLOW. AND IT *NEVER LANDS*. BUT WE HAVE THE SMALLER AUXILIARY SHIPS FOR SPEED.
I GREW UP ON BOARD. MOST OF THE TIME YOU WOULDN'T EVEN KNOW YOU WERE IN THE AIR. THERE ARE PEOPLE ON BOARD WHO HAVEN'T SET FOOT ON THE GROUND IN *YEARS*.
MY FATHER DESIGNED IT AFTER THE ANCESTRAL CASTLE WAS DESTROYED IN THE WAR.
PEACE

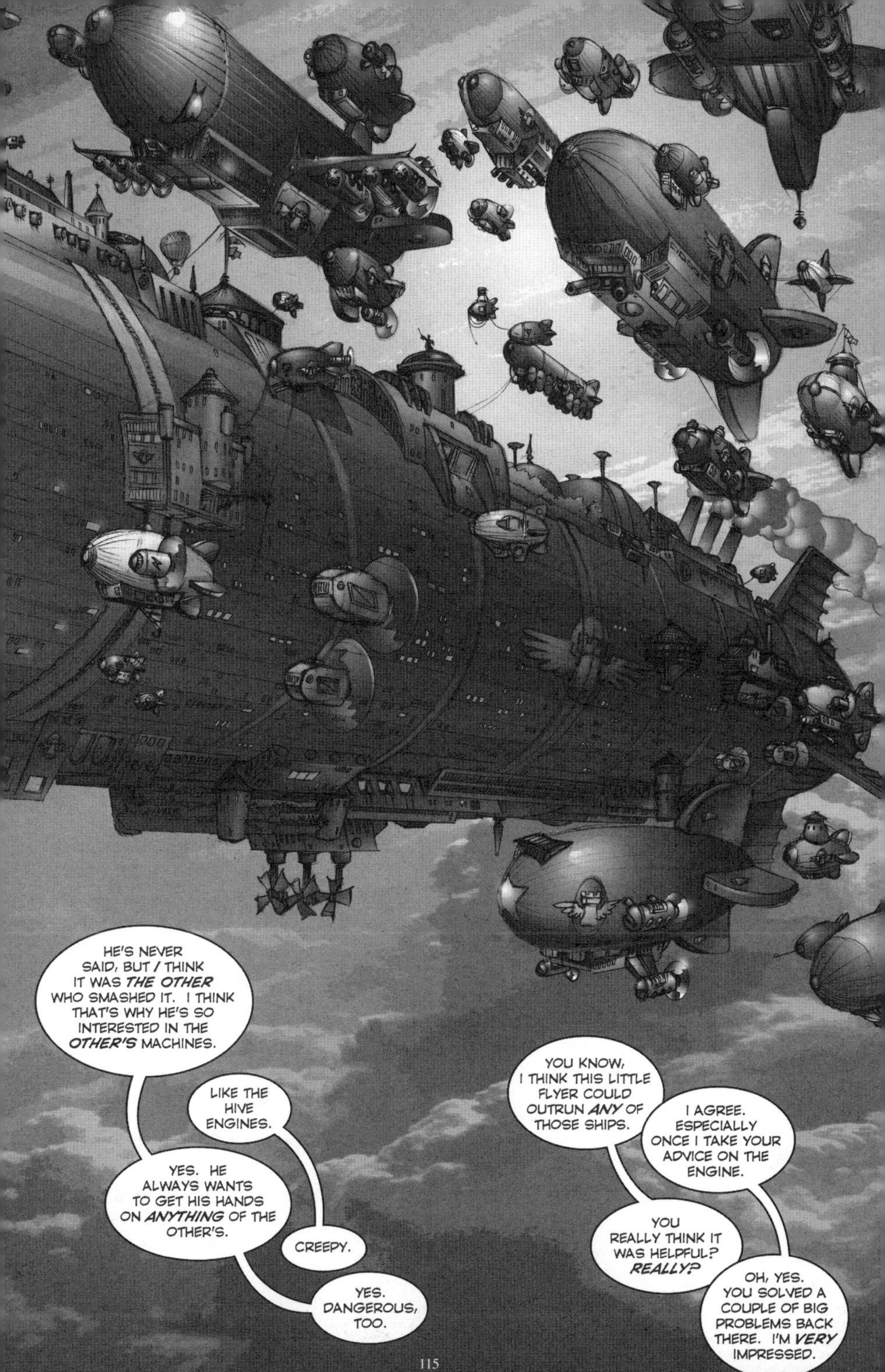
HE'S NEVER SAID, BUT *I* THINK IT WAS ***THE OTHER*** WHO SMASHED IT. I THINK THAT'S WHY HE'S SO INTERESTED IN THE ***OTHER'S*** MACHINES.
LIKE THE HIVE ENGINES.
YES. HE ALWAYS WANTS TO GET HIS HANDS ON ***ANYTHING*** OF THE OTHER'S.
CREEPY.
YES. DANGEROUS, TOO.
YOU KNOW, I THINK THIS LITTLE FLYER COULD OUTRUN ***ANY*** OF THOSE SHIPS.
I AGREE. ESPECIALLY ONCE I TAKE YOUR ADVICE ON THE ENGINE.
YOU REALLY THINK IT WAS HELPFUL? ***REALLY?***
OH, YES. YOU SOLVED A COUPLE OF BIG PROBLEMS BACK THERE. I'M ***VERY*** IMPRESSED.

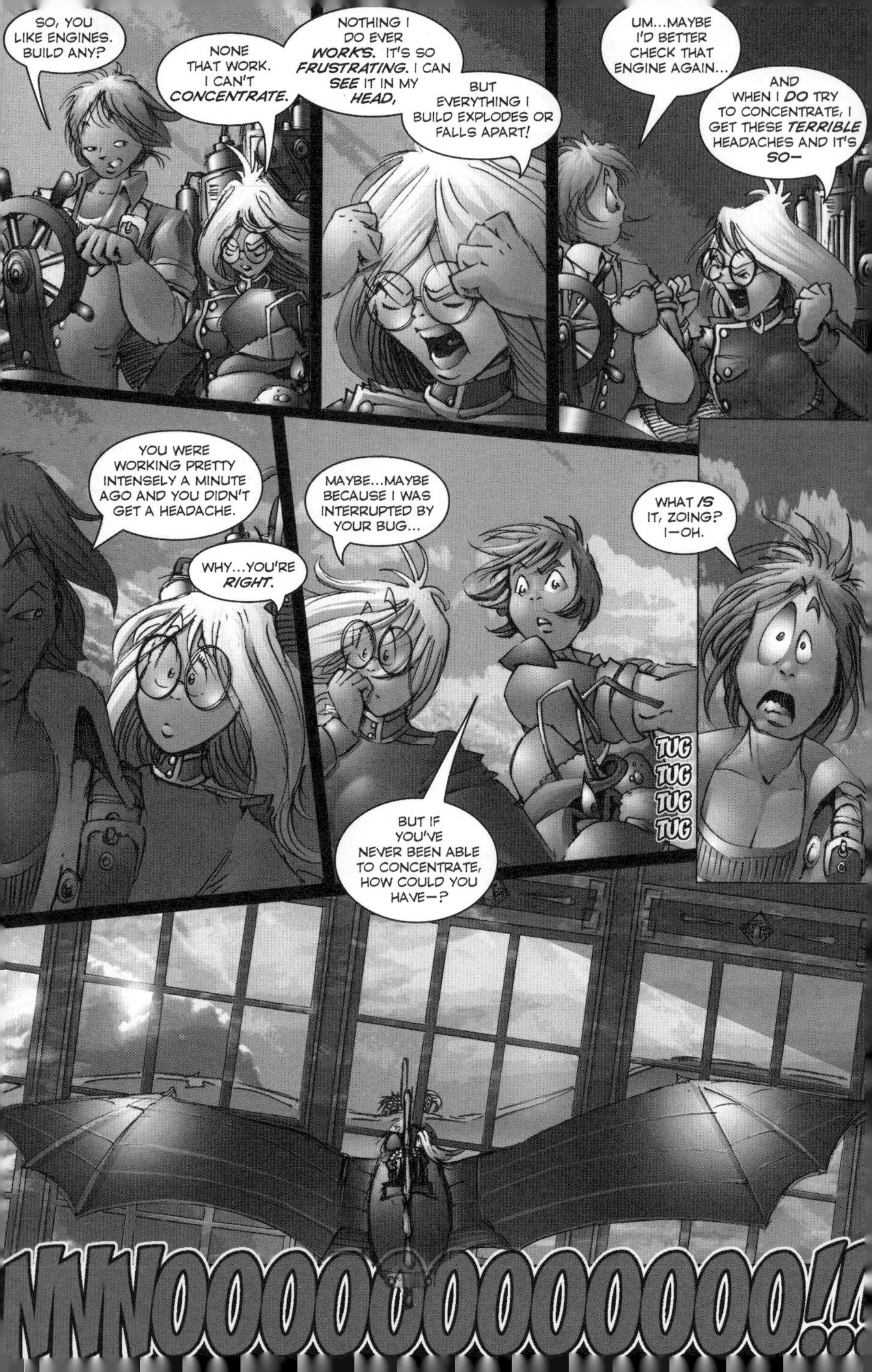

SO, YOU LIKE ENGINES. BUILD ANY?
NONE THAT WORK. I CAN'T *CONCENTRATE.*
NOTHING I DO EVER *WORKS.* IT'S SO *FRUSTRATING.* I CAN *SEE* IT IN MY *HEAD,*
BUT EVERYTHING I BUILD EXPLODES OR FALLS APART!
UM...MAYBE I'D BETTER CHECK THAT ENGINE AGAIN...
AND WHEN I *DO* TRY TO CONCENTRATE, I GET THESE *TERRIBLE* HEADACHES AND IT'S *SO—*
YOU WERE WORKING PRETTY INTENSELY A MINUTE AGO AND YOU DIDN'T GET A HEADACHE.
WHY...YOU'RE *RIGHT.*
MAYBE...MAYBE BECAUSE I WAS INTERRUPTED BY YOUR BUG...
BUT IF YOU'VE NEVER BEEN ABLE TO CONCENTRATE, HOW COULD YOU HAVE—?
WHAT *IS* IT, ZOING? I—OH.
TUG TUG TUG TUG
NNNOOOOOOOOOOOOO!!!

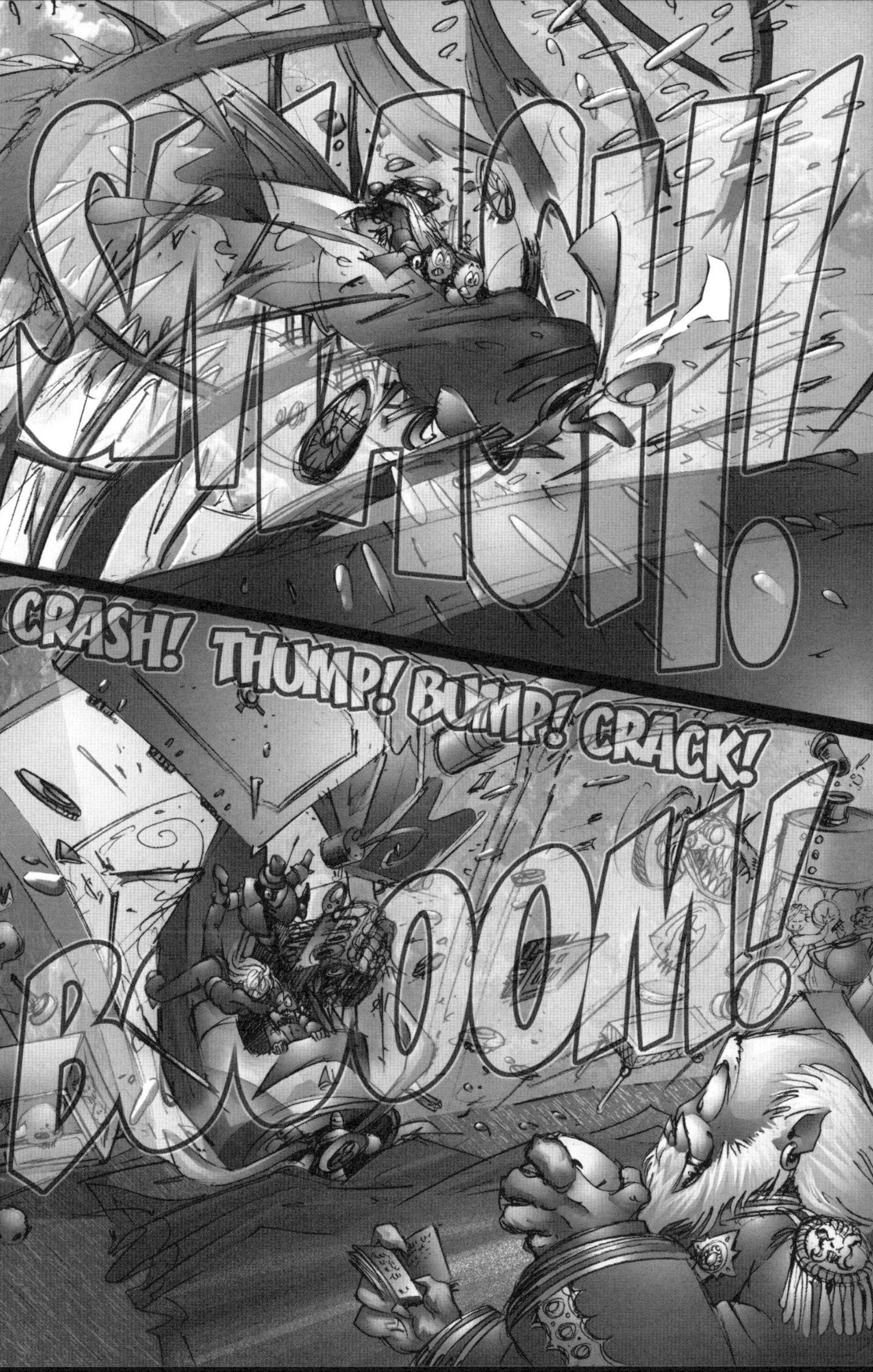
SMASH!
CRASH!
THUMP! BUMP! CRACK!

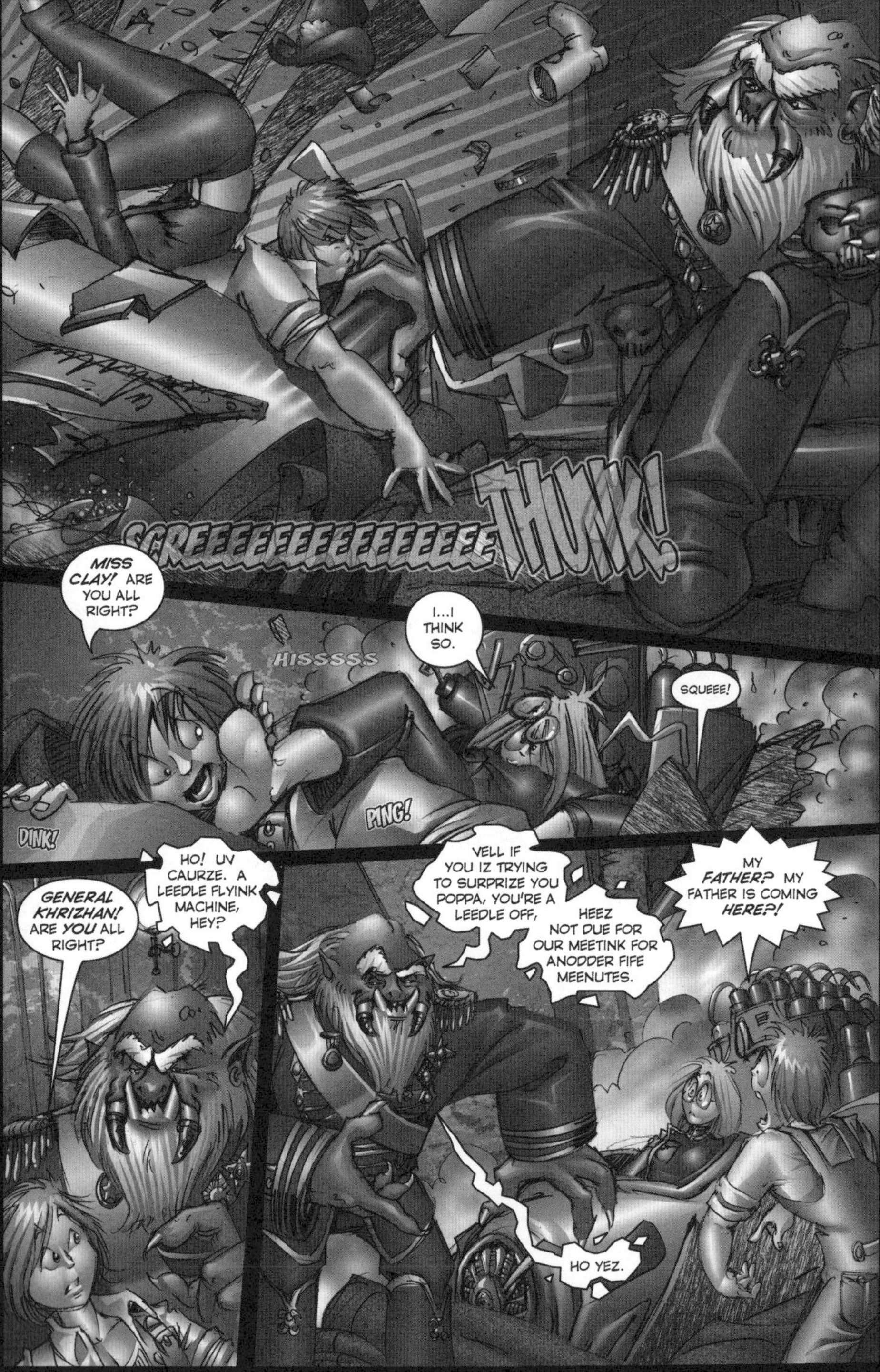
SCREEEEEEEEEEEEEEE
THUNK!
MISS CLAY! ARE YOU ALL RIGHT?
HISSSSS
I...I THINK SO.
SQUEEE!
PING!
DINK!
GENERAL KHRIZHAN! ARE YOU ALL RIGHT?
HO! UV CAURZE. A LEEDLE FLYINK MACHINE, HEY?
VELL IF YOU IZ TRYING TO SURPRIZE YOU POPPA, YOU'RE A LEEDLE OFF,
HEEZ NOT DUE FOR OUR MEETINK FOR ANODDER FIFE MEENUTES.
MY FATHER? MY FATHER IS COMING HERE?!
HO YEZ.

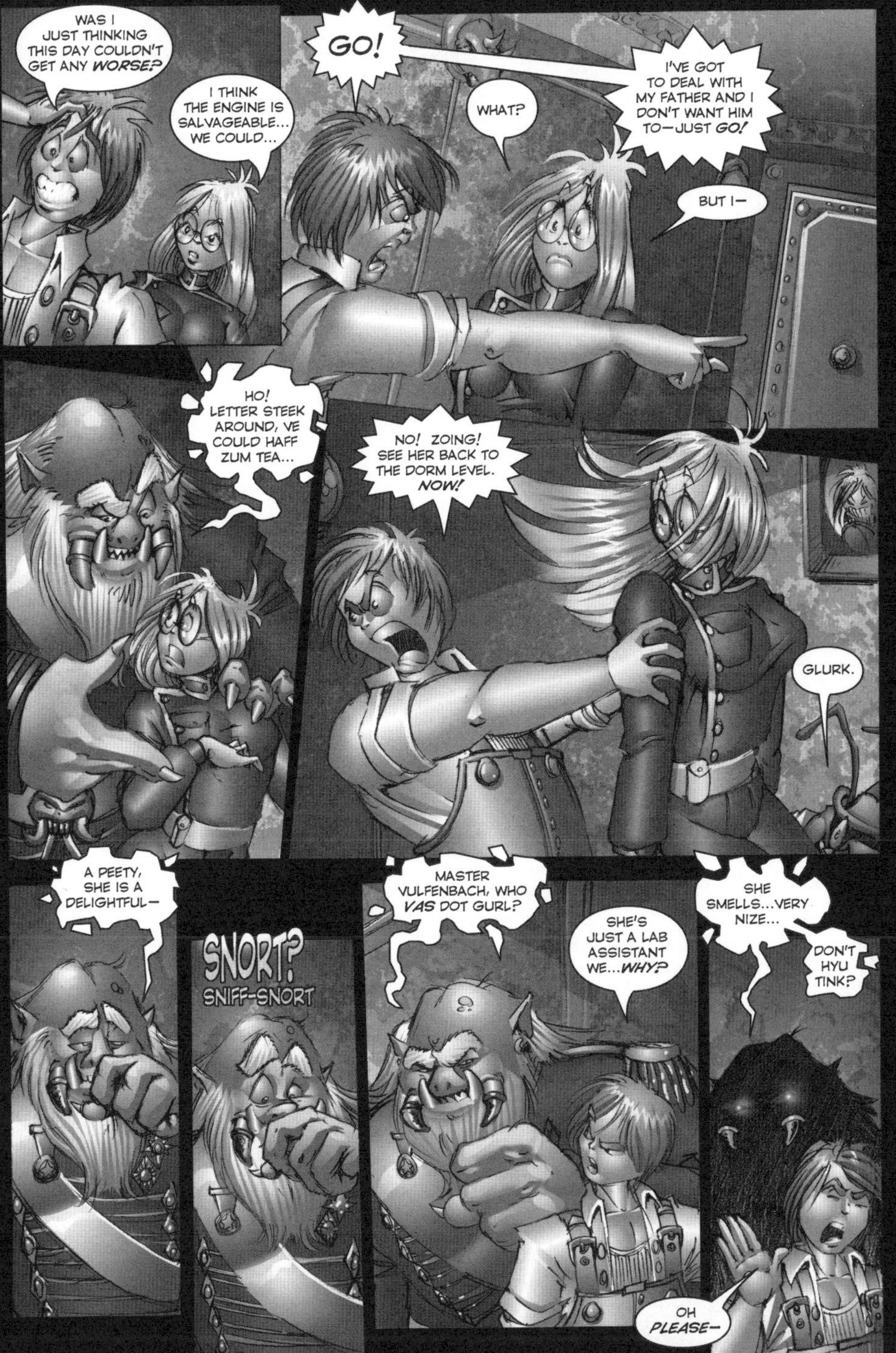
WAS I JUST THINKING THIS DAY COULDN'T GET ANY WORSE?
I THINK THE ENGINE IS SALVAGEABLE... WE COULD...
GO!
WHAT?
I'VE GOT TO DEAL WITH MY FATHER AND I DON'T WANT HIM TO—JUST GO!
BUT I—
HO! LETTER STEEK AROUND, VE COULD HAFF ZUM TEA...
NO! ZOING! SEE HER BACK TO THE DORM LEVEL. NOW!
GLURK.
A PEETY, SHE IS A DELIGHTFUL—
SNORT? SNIFF-SNORT
MASTER VULFENBACH, WHO VAS DOT GURL?
SHE'S JUST A LAB ASSISTANT WE...WHY?
SHE SMELLS...VERY NIZE...
DON'T HYU TINK?
OH PLEASE—

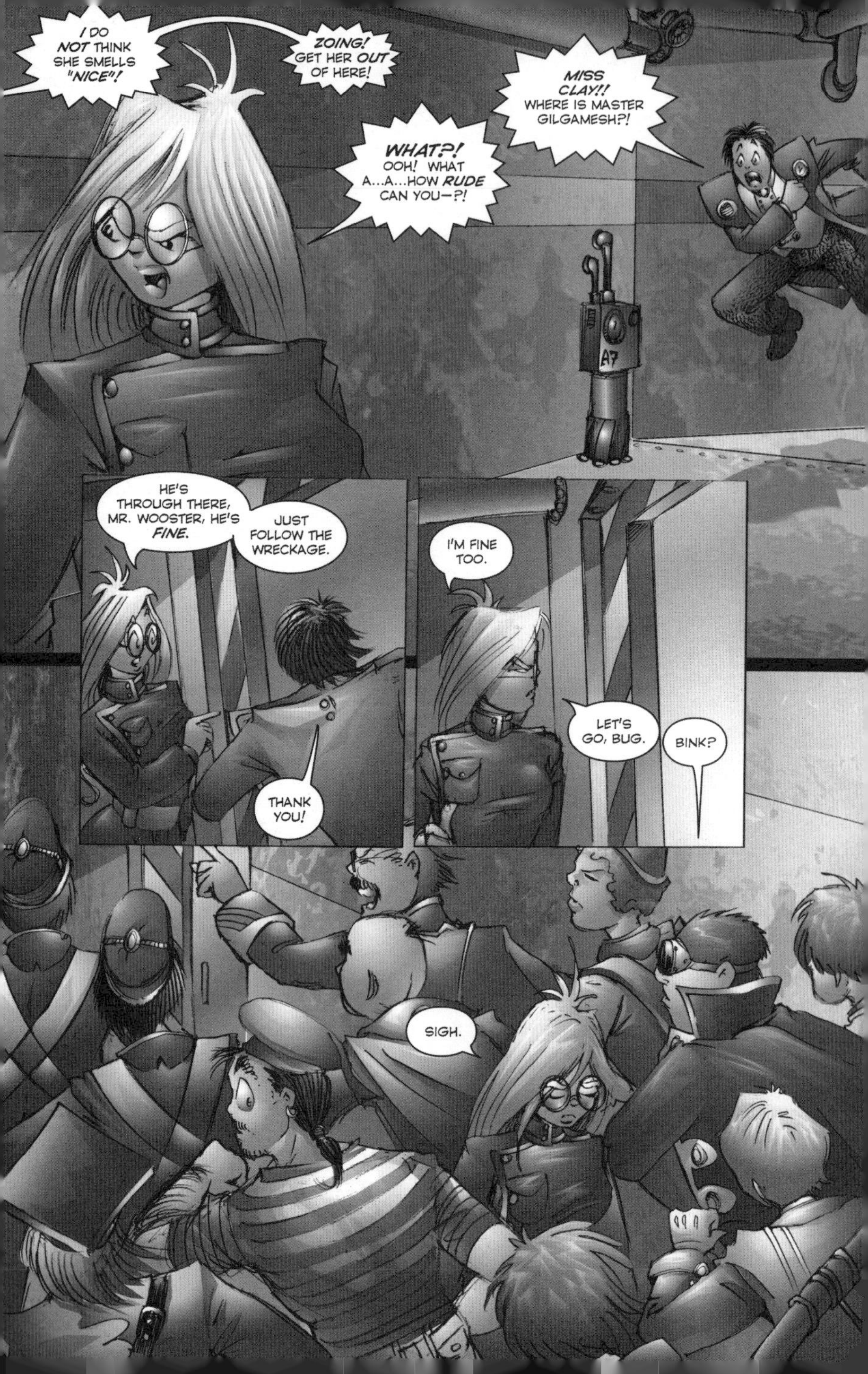
I DO NOT THINK SHE SMELLS "NICE"!
ZOING! GET HER OUT OF HERE!
WHAT?! OOH! WHAT A...A...HOW RUDE CAN YOU—?!
MISS CLAY!! WHERE IS MASTER GILGAMESH?!
A7
HE'S THROUGH THERE, MR. WOOSTER, HE'S FINE.
JUST FOLLOW THE WRECKAGE.
THANK YOU!
I'M FINE TOO.
LET'S GO, BUG.
BINK?
SIGH.

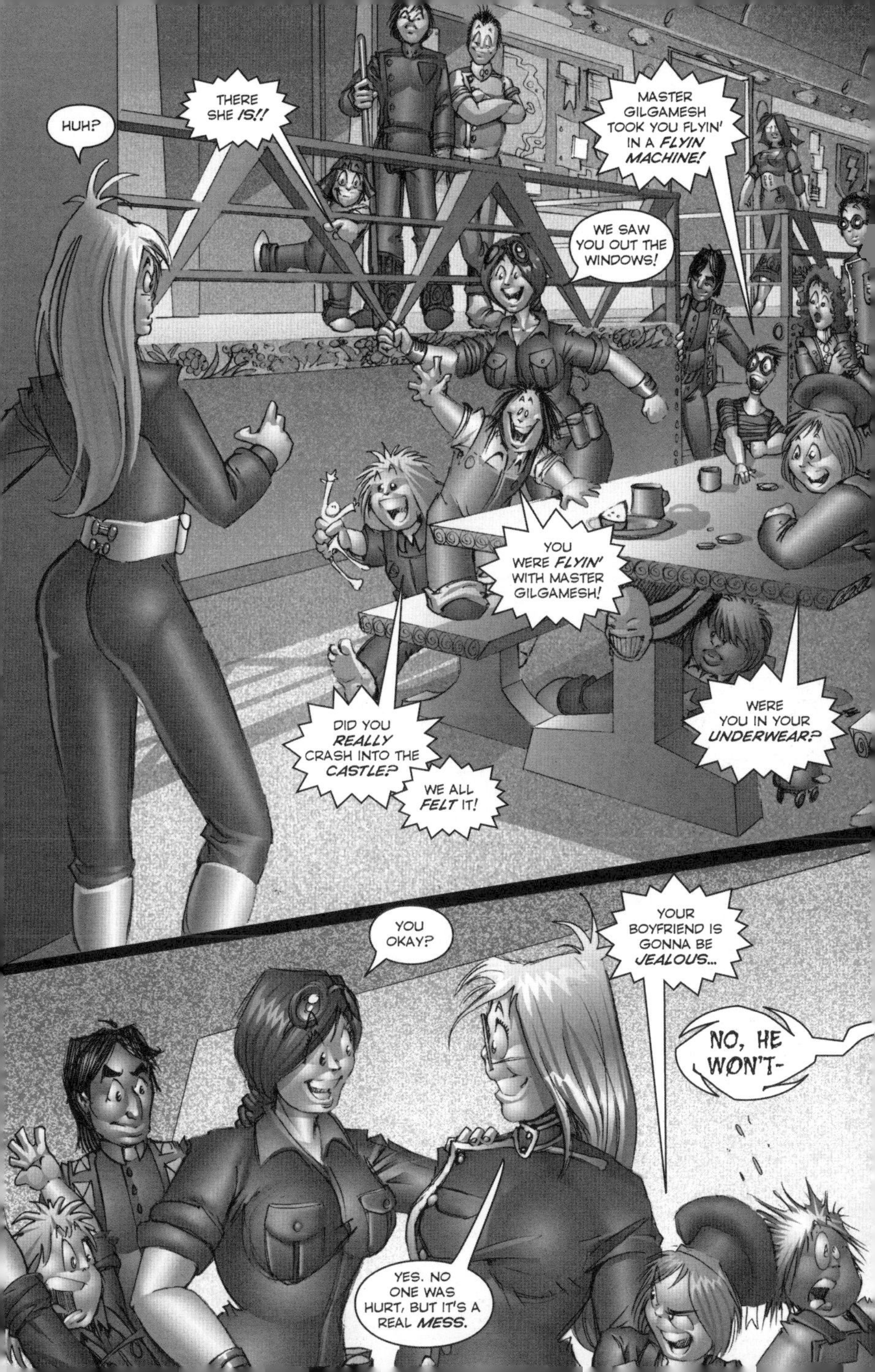
HUH?
THERE SHE IS!!
MASTER GILGAMESH TOOK YOU FLYIN' IN A FLYIN MACHINE!
WE SAW YOU OUT THE WINDOWS!
YOU WERE FLYIN' WITH MASTER GILGAMESH!
DID YOU REALLY CRASH INTO THE CASTLE?
WE ALL FELT IT!
WERE YOU IN YOUR UNDERWEAR?
YOU OKAY?
YES. NO ONE WAS HURT, BUT IT'S A REAL MESS.
YOUR BOYFRIEND IS GONNA BE JEALOUS...
NO, HE WØN'T-

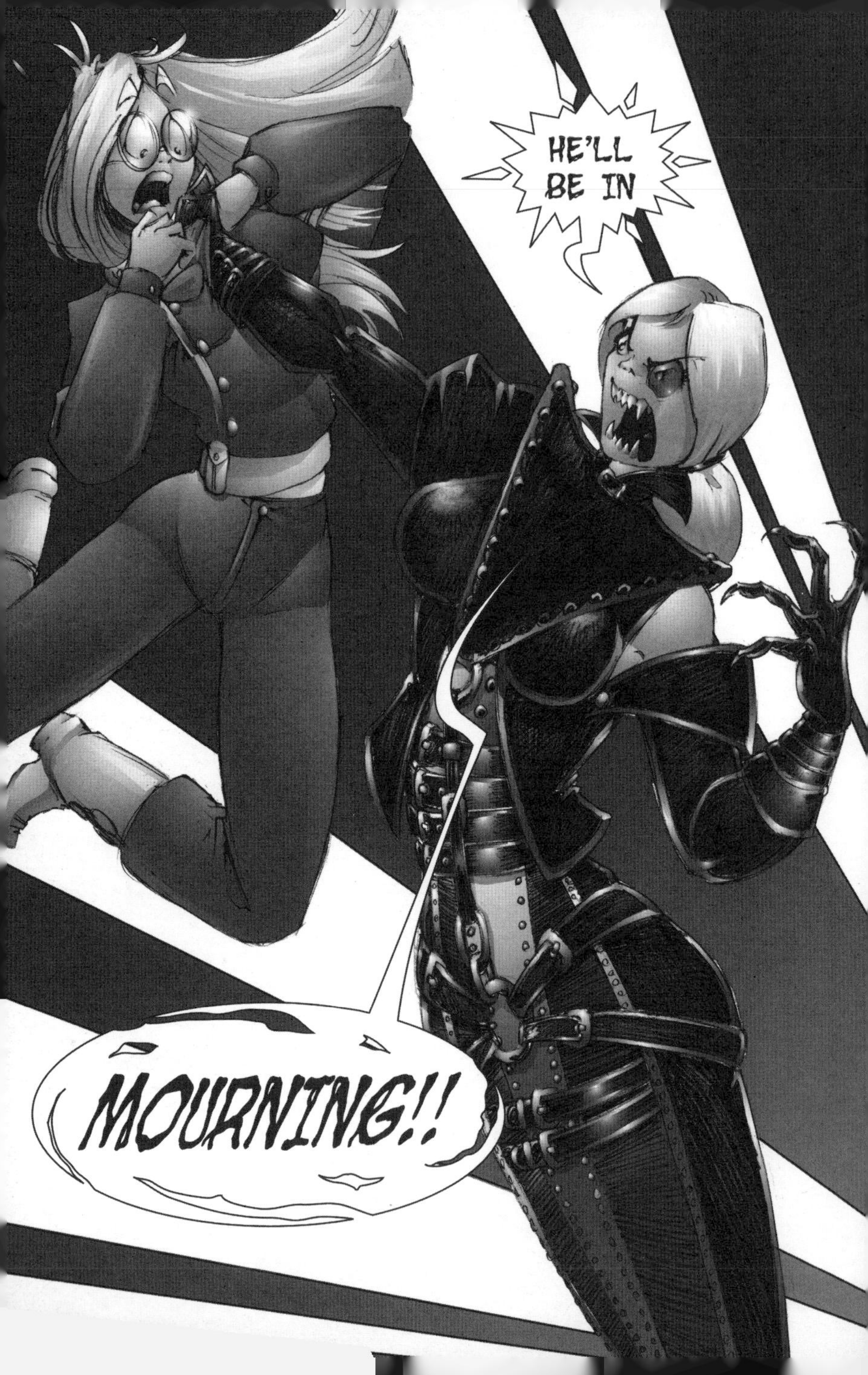
HE'LL BE IN
MOURNING!!

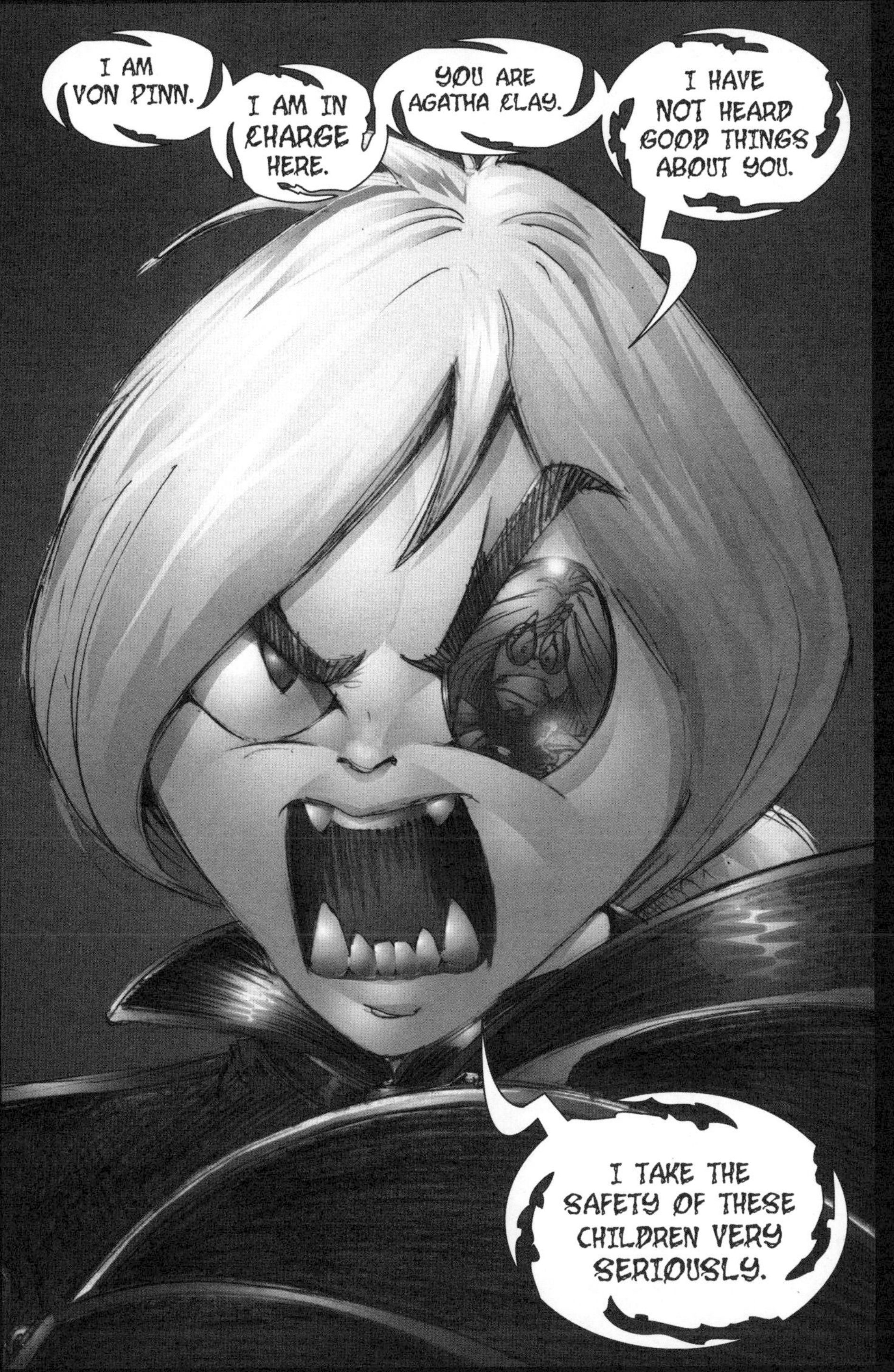
I AM VON PINN.
I AM IN CHARGE HERE.
YOU ARE AGATHA CLAY.
I HAVE NOT HEARD GOOD THINGS ABOUT YOU.
I TAKE THE SAFETY OF THESE CHILDREN VERY SERIOUSLY.

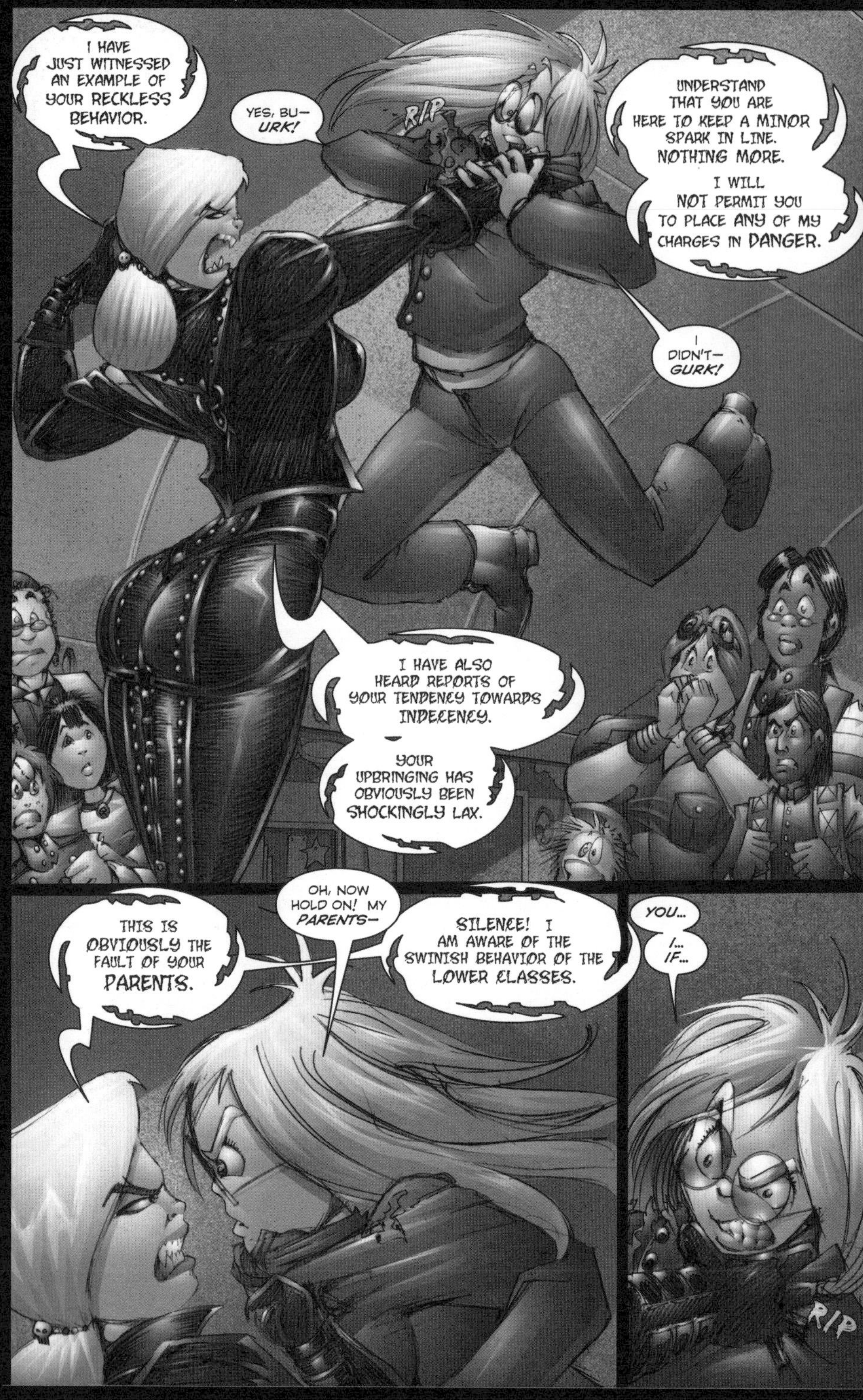

I HAVE JUST WITNESSED AN EXAMPLE OF YOUR RECKLESS BEHAVIOR.
YES, BU— URK!
RIP
UNDERSTAND THAT YOU ARE HERE TO KEEP A MINOR SPARK IN LINE. NOTHING MORE.
I WILL NOT PERMIT YOU TO PLACE ANY OF MY CHARGES IN DANGER.
I DIDN'T— GURK!
I HAVE ALSO HEARD REPORTS OF YOUR TENDENCY TOWARDS INDECENCY.
YOUR UPBRINGING HAS OBVIOUSLY BEEN SHOCKINGLY LAX.
THIS IS OBVIOUSLY THE FAULT OF YOUR PARENTS.
OH, NOW HOLD ON! MY PARENTS—
SILENCE! I AM AWARE OF THE SWINISH BEHAVIOR OF THE LOWER CLASSES.
YOU...
I... IF...
RIP

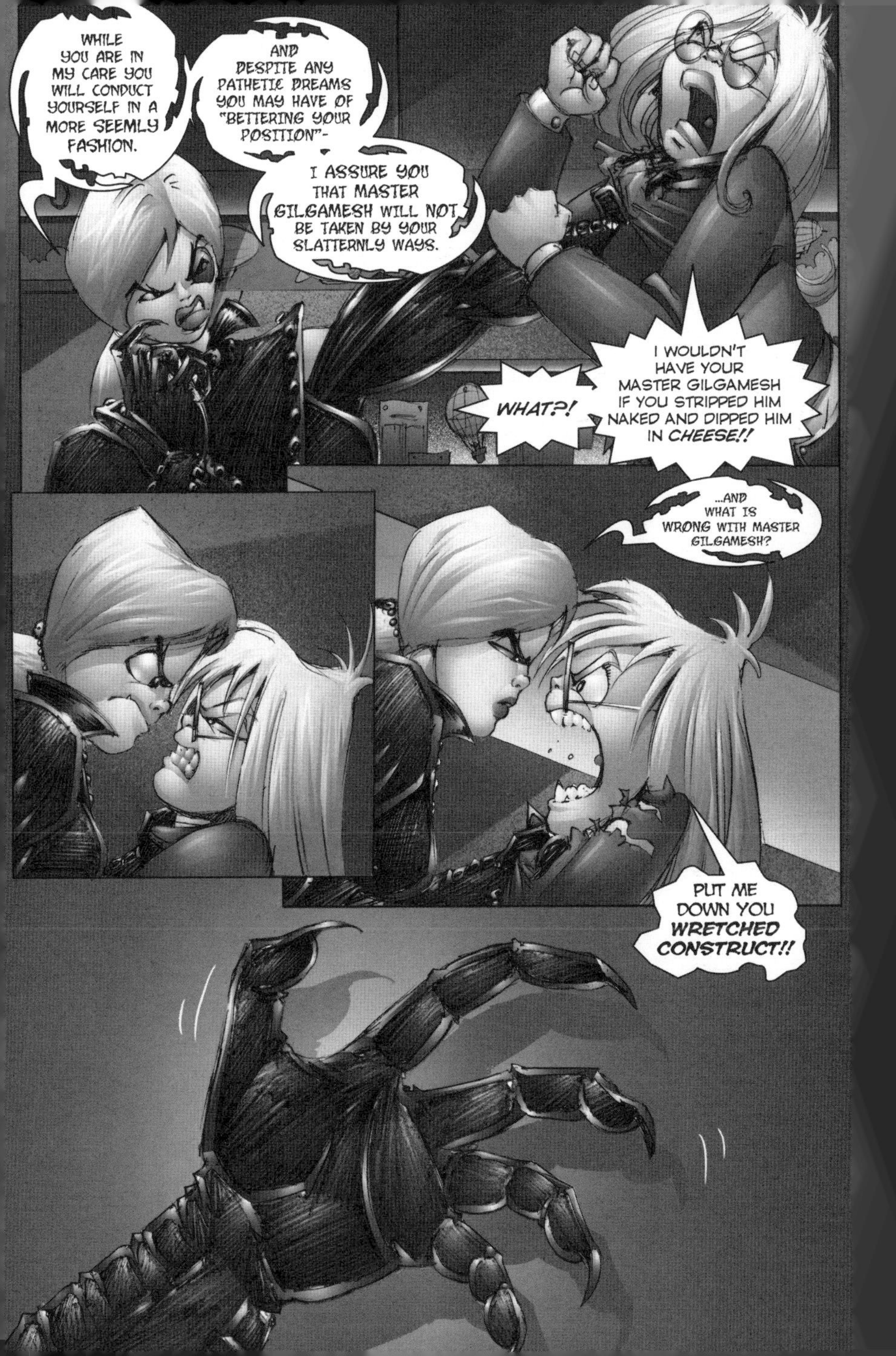
WHILE YOU ARE IN MY CARE YOU WILL CONDUCT YOURSELF IN A MORE SEEMLY FASHION.
AND DESPITE ANY PATHETIC DREAMS YOU MAY HAVE OF "BETTERING YOUR POSITION"-
I ASSURE YOU THAT MASTER GILGAMESH WILL NOT BE TAKEN BY YOUR SLATTERNLY WAYS.
WHAT?!
I WOULDN'T HAVE YOUR MASTER GILGAMESH IF YOU STRIPPED HIM NAKED AND DIPPED HIM IN CHEESE!!
...AND WHAT IS WRONG WITH MASTER GILGAMESH?
PUT ME DOWN YOU WRETCHED CONSTRUCT!!

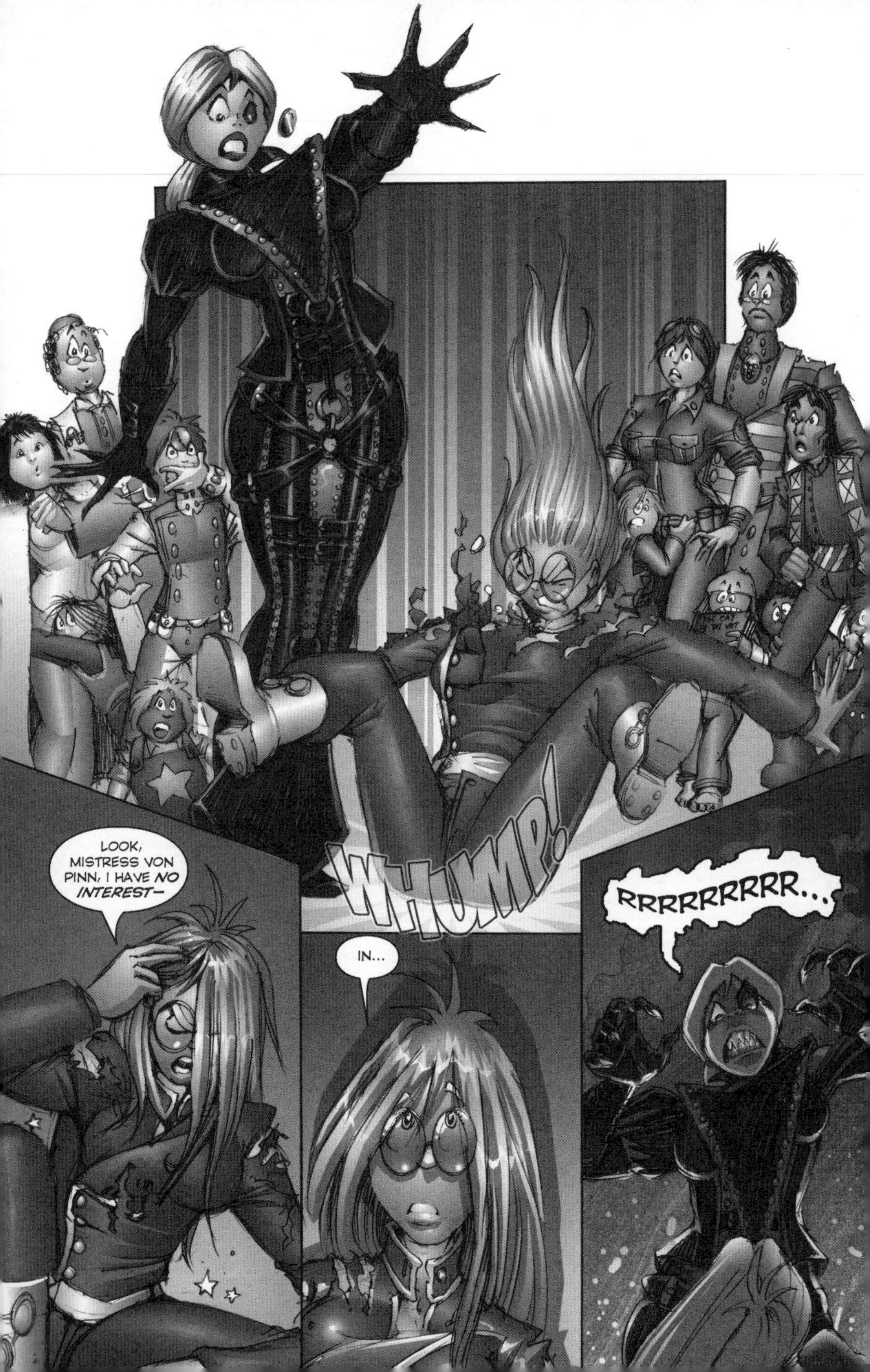
WHUMP!
LOOK, MISTRESS VON PINN, I HAVE *NO INTEREST*—
IN...
RRRRRRRRR...

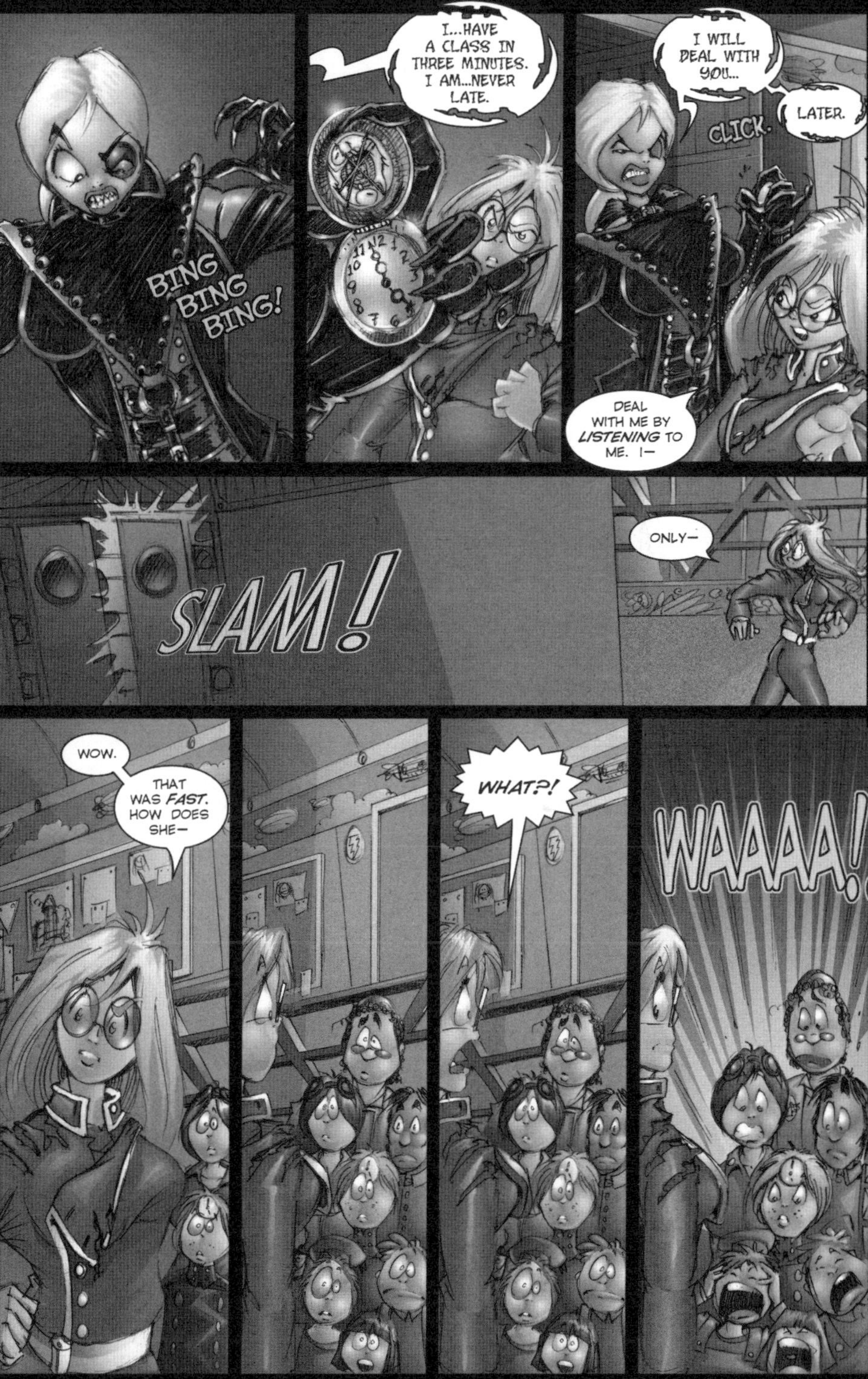
BING BING BING!
I...HAVE A CLASS IN THREE MINUTES. I AM...NEVER LATE.
I WILL DEAL WITH YOU...
CLICK.
LATER.
DEAL WITH ME BY *LISTENING* TO ME. I—
SLAM!
ONLY—
WOW.
THAT WAS *FAST.* HOW DOES SHE—
WHAT?!
WAAAA!

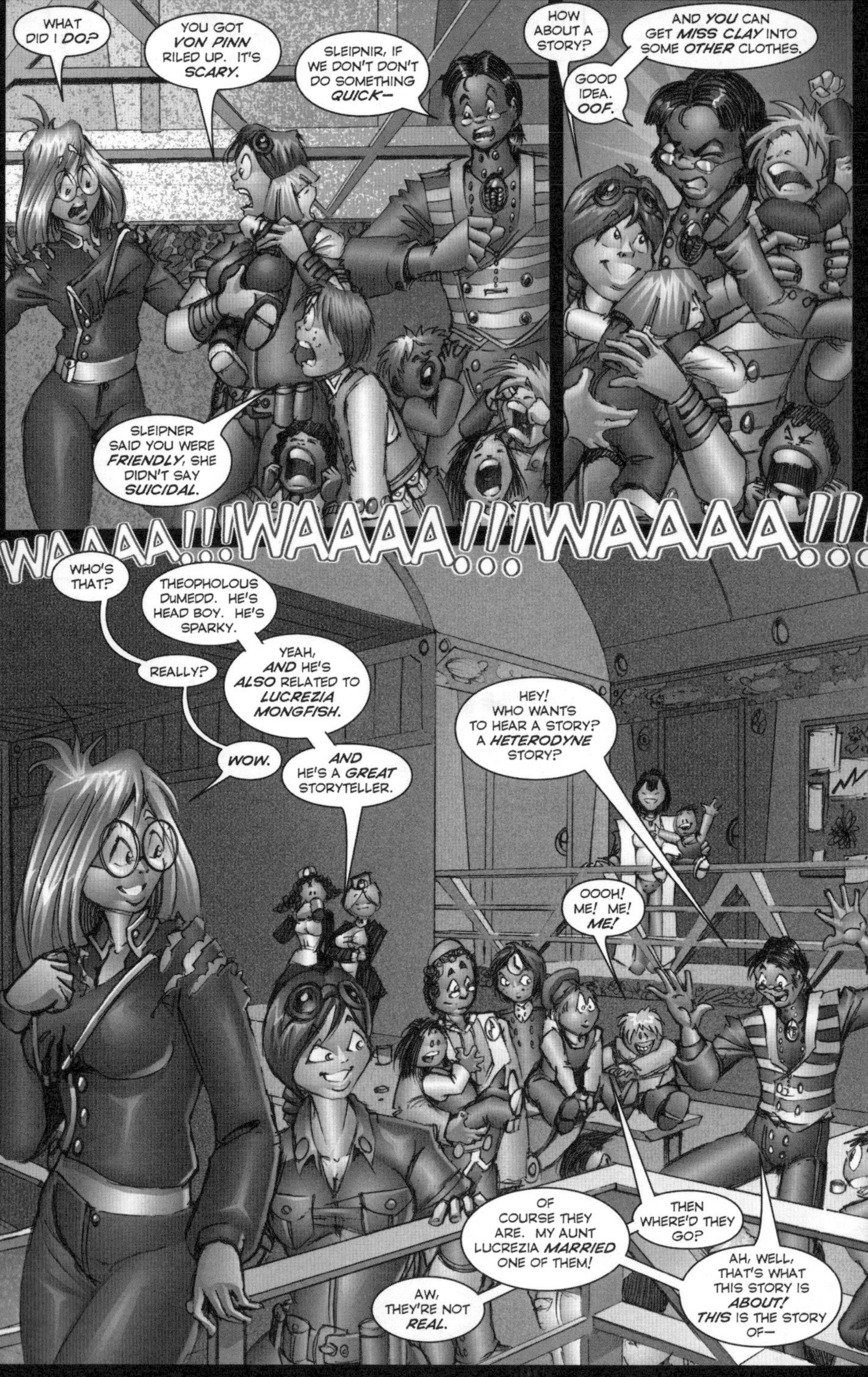
WHAT DID I DO?
YOU GOT VON PINN RILED UP. IT'S SCARY.
SLEIPNIR, IF WE DON'T DON'T DO SOMETHING QUICK—
SLEIPNER SAID YOU WERE FRIENDLY; SHE DIDN'T SAY SUICIDAL.
HOW ABOUT A STORY?
AND YOU CAN GET MISS CLAY INTO SOME OTHER CLOTHES.
GOOD IDEA. OOF.
WAAAA!!!WAAAAA!!!WAAAAA!!!
WHO'S THAT?
THEOPHOLOUS DuMEDD. HE'S HEAD BOY. HE'S SPARKY.
REALLY?
YEAH, AND HE'S ALSO RELATED TO LUCREZIA MONGFISH.
WOW.
AND HE'S A GREAT STORYTELLER.
HEY! WHO WANTS TO HEAR A STORY? A HETERODYNE STORY?
OOOH! ME! ME! ME!
AW, THEY'RE NOT REAL.
OF COURSE THEY ARE. MY AUNT LUCREZIA MARRIED ONE OF THEM!
THEN WHERE'D THEY GO?
AH, WELL, THAT'S WHAT THIS STORY IS ABOUT! THIS IS THE STORY OF—

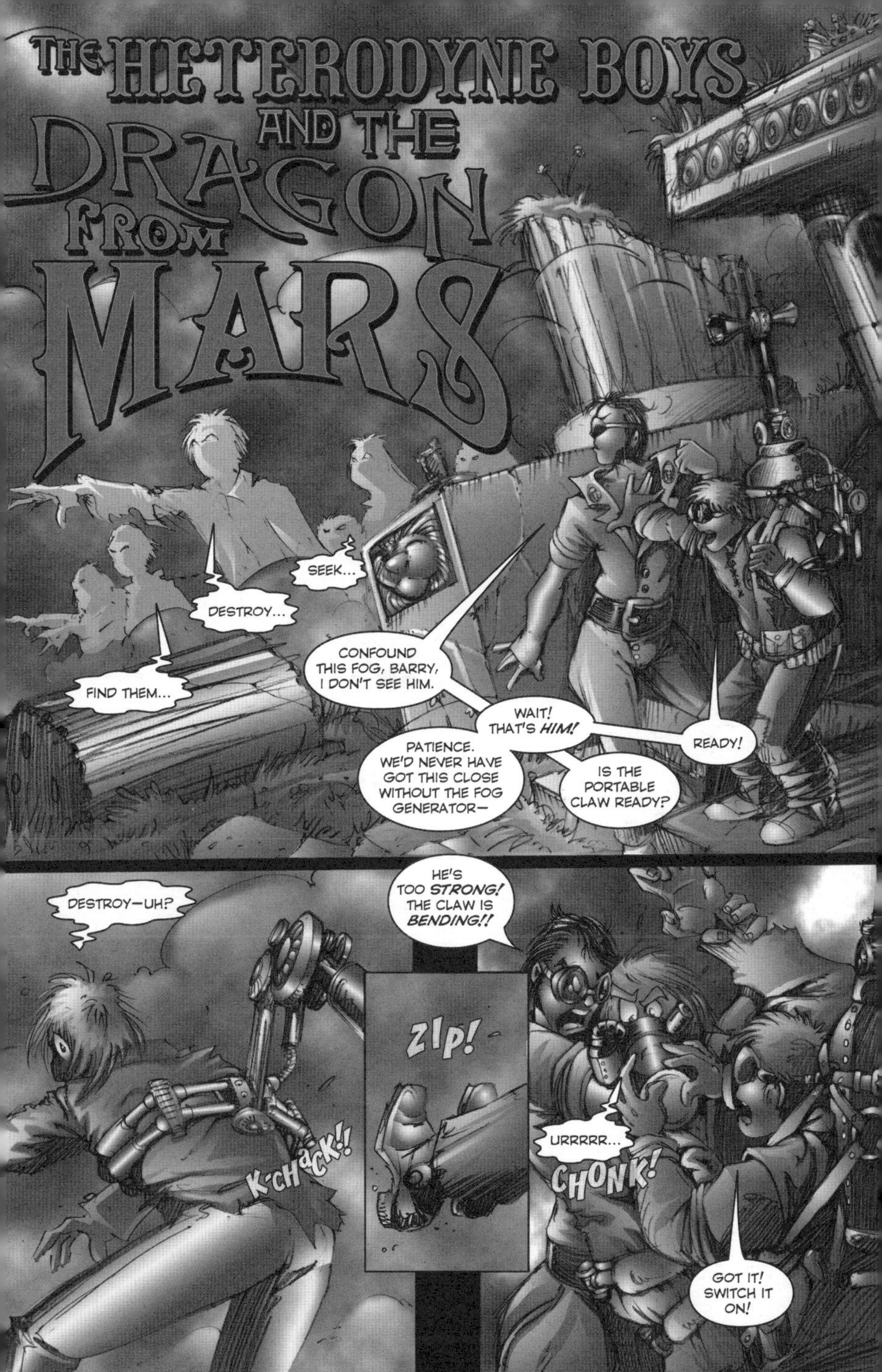
THE HETERODYNE BOYS AND THE DRAGON FROM MARS
SEEK...
DESTROY...
FIND THEM...
CONFOUND THIS FOG, BARRY, I DON'T SEE HIM.
PATIENCE. WE'D NEVER HAVE GOT THIS CLOSE WITHOUT THE FOG GENERATOR—
WAIT! THAT'S *HIM!*
IS THE PORTABLE CLAW READY?
READY!
DESTROY—UH?
K'CHACK!!
ZIP!
HE'S TOO **STRONG!** THE CLAW IS ***BENDING!!***
URRRRR...
CHONK!
GOT IT! SWITCH IT ON!

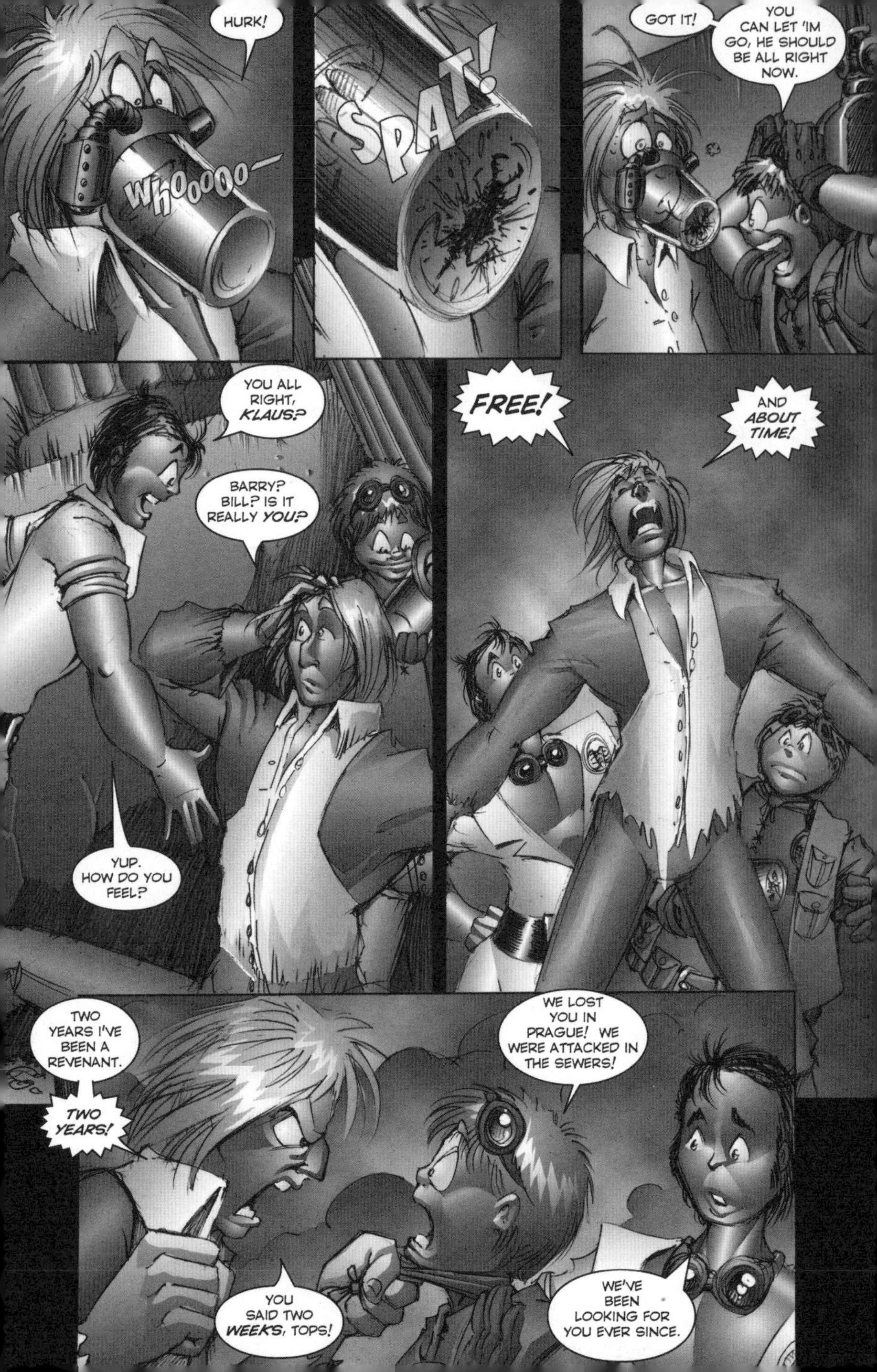
HURK!
WHOOOOO—
SPAT!
GOT IT!
YOU CAN LET 'IM GO, HE SHOULD BE ALL RIGHT NOW.
YOU ALL RIGHT, KLAUS?
BARRY? BILL? IS IT REALLY YOU?
YUP. HOW DO YOU FEEL?
FREE!
AND ABOUT TIME!
TWO YEARS I'VE BEEN A REVENANT.
TWO YEARS!
YOU SAID TWO WEEKS, TOPS!
WE LOST YOU IN PRAGUE! WE WERE ATTACKED IN THE SEWERS!
WE'VE BEEN LOOKING FOR YOU EVER SINCE.

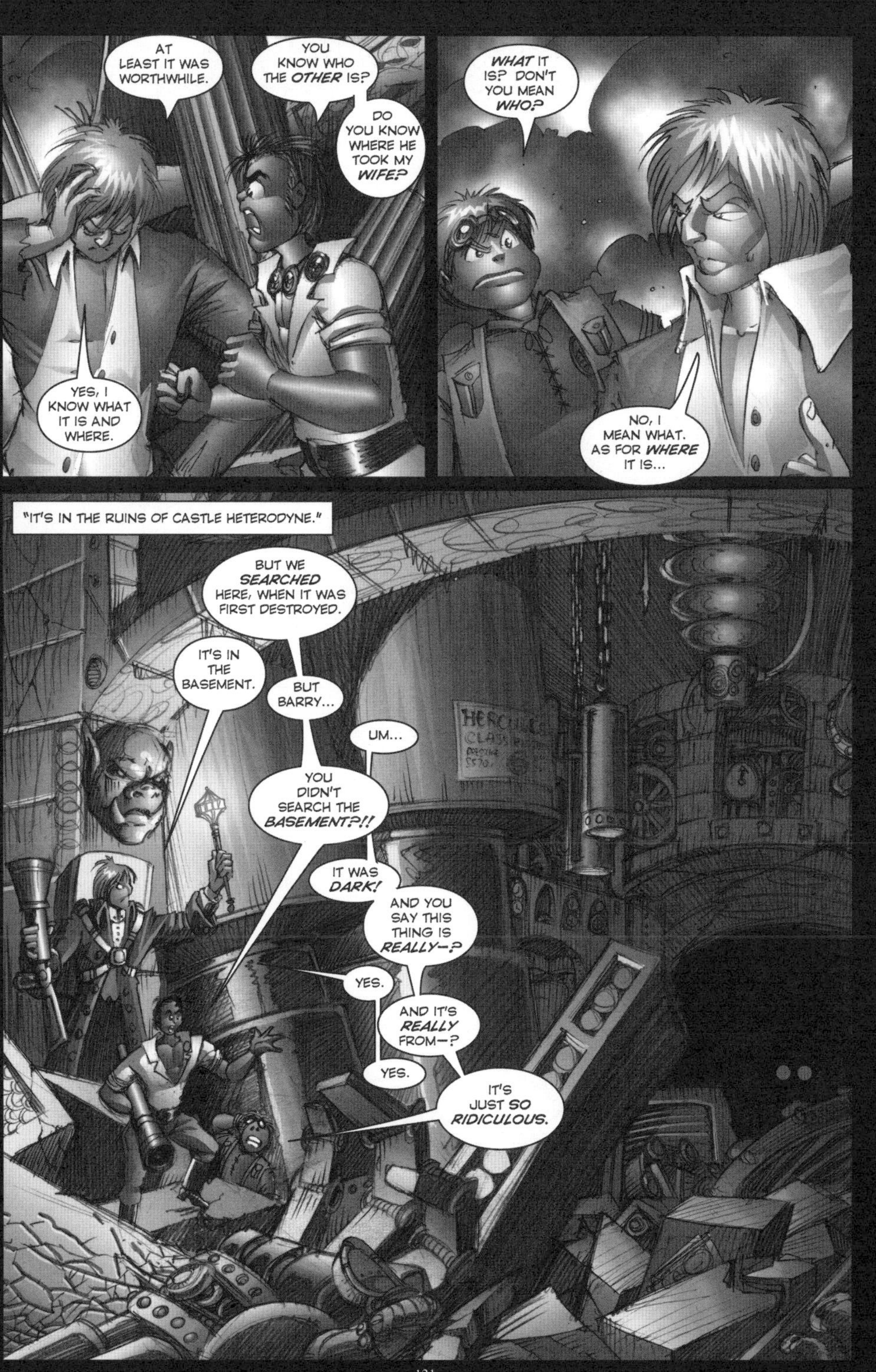
AT LEAST IT WAS WORTHWHILE.
YOU KNOW WHO THE OTHER IS?
DO YOU KNOW WHERE HE TOOK MY WIFE?
YES, I KNOW WHAT IT IS AND WHERE.
WHAT IT IS? DON'T YOU MEAN WHO?
NO, I MEAN WHAT. AS FOR WHERE IT IS...
"IT'S IN THE RUINS OF CASTLE HETERODYNE."
BUT WE SEARCHED HERE, WHEN IT WAS FIRST DESTROYED.
IT'S IN THE BASEMENT.
BUT BARRY...
UM...
YOU DIDN'T SEARCH THE BASEMENT?!!
IT WAS DARK!
AND YOU SAY THIS THING IS REALLY—?
YES.
AND IT'S REALLY FROM—?
YES.
IT'S JUST SO RIDICULOUS.

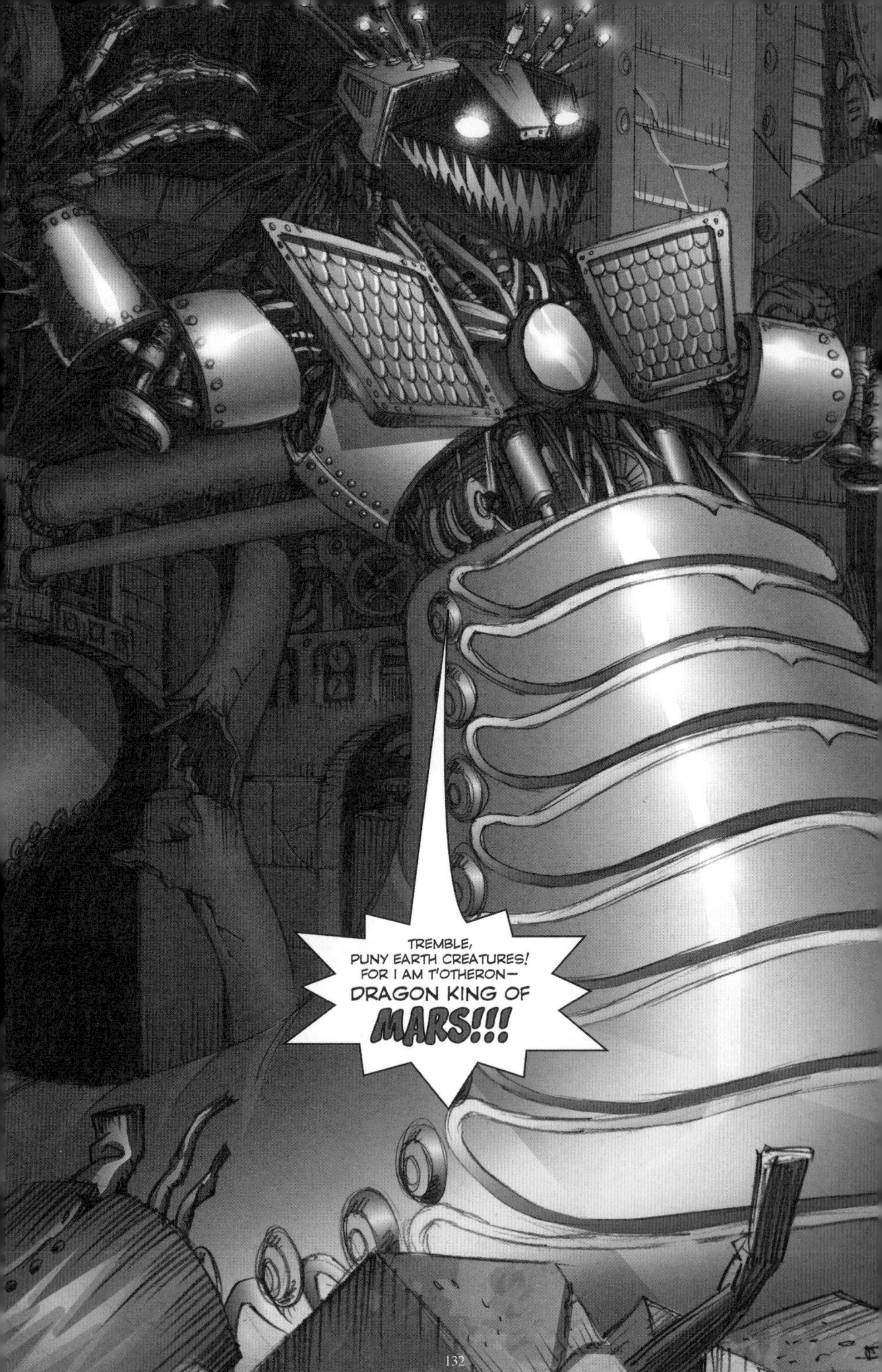
TREMBLE, PUNY EARTH CREATURES! FOR I AM T'OTHERON— DRAGON KING OF MARS!!!

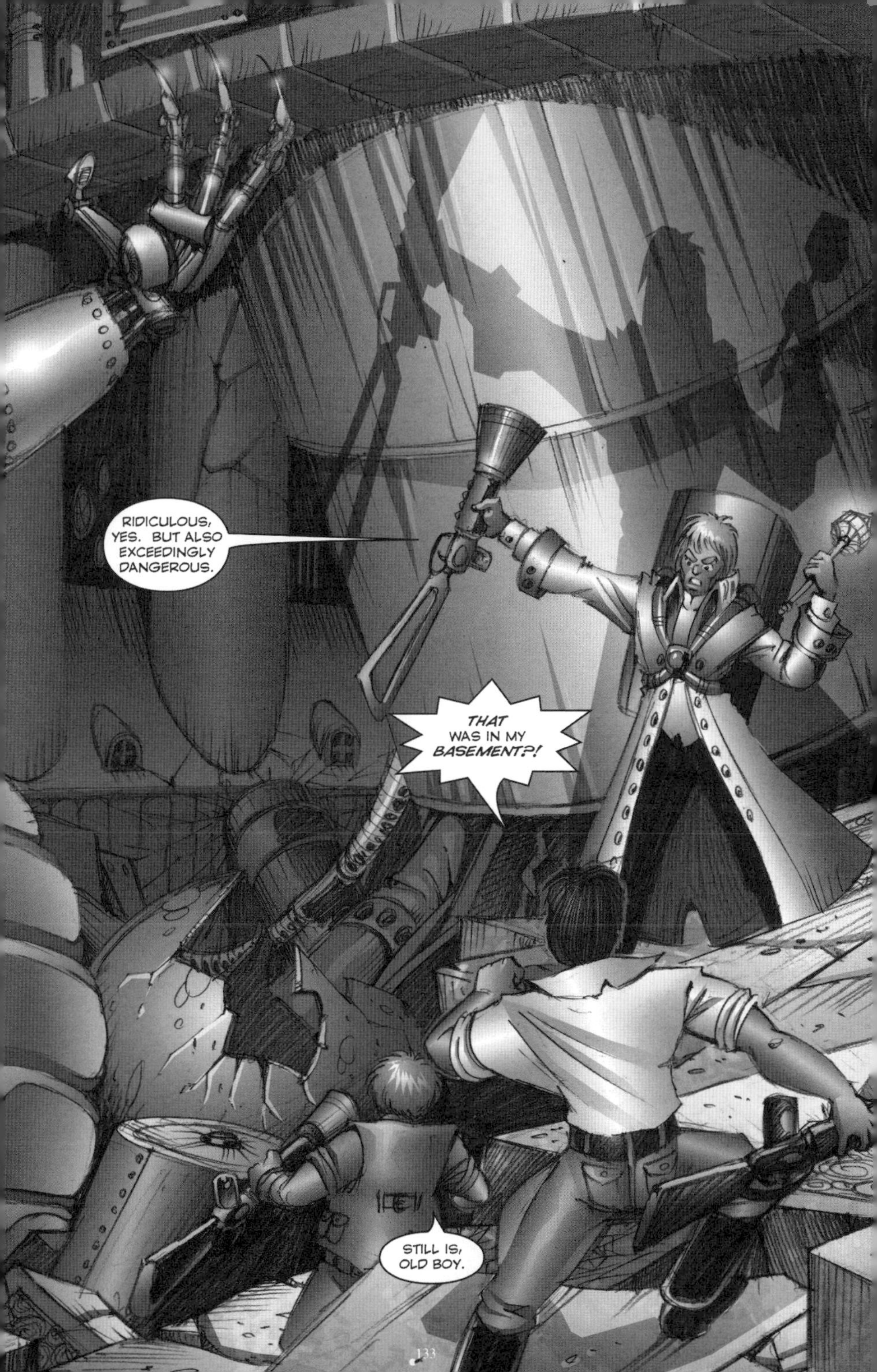
RIDICULOUS, YES. BUT ALSO EXCEEDINGLY DANGEROUS.
THAT WAS IN MY BASEMENT?!
STILL IS, OLD BOY.

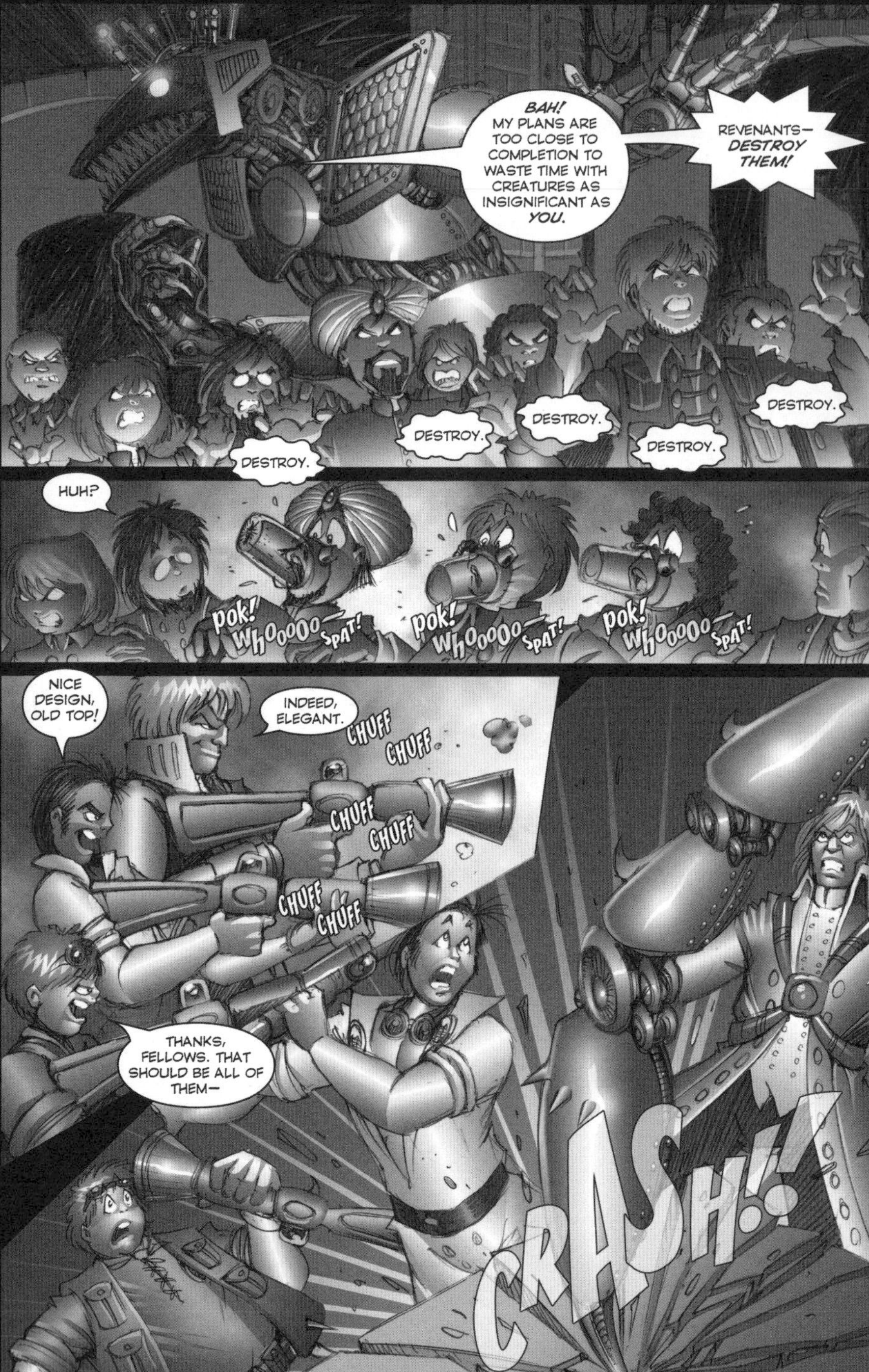
BAH! MY PLANS ARE TOO CLOSE TO COMPLETION TO WASTE TIME WITH CREATURES AS INSIGNIFICANT AS YOU.
REVENANTS— DESTROY THEM!
DESTROY.
DESTROY.
DESTROY.
DESTROY.
DESTROY.
HUH?
pok! Whooooo—SPAT!
pok! Whooooo—SPAT!
pok! Whooooo—SPAT!
NICE DESIGN, OLD TOP!
INDEED, ELEGANT.
CHUFF CHUFF
CHUFF CHUFF
CHUFF CHUFF
THANKS, FELLOWS. THAT SHOULD BE ALL OF THEM—
CRASH!!

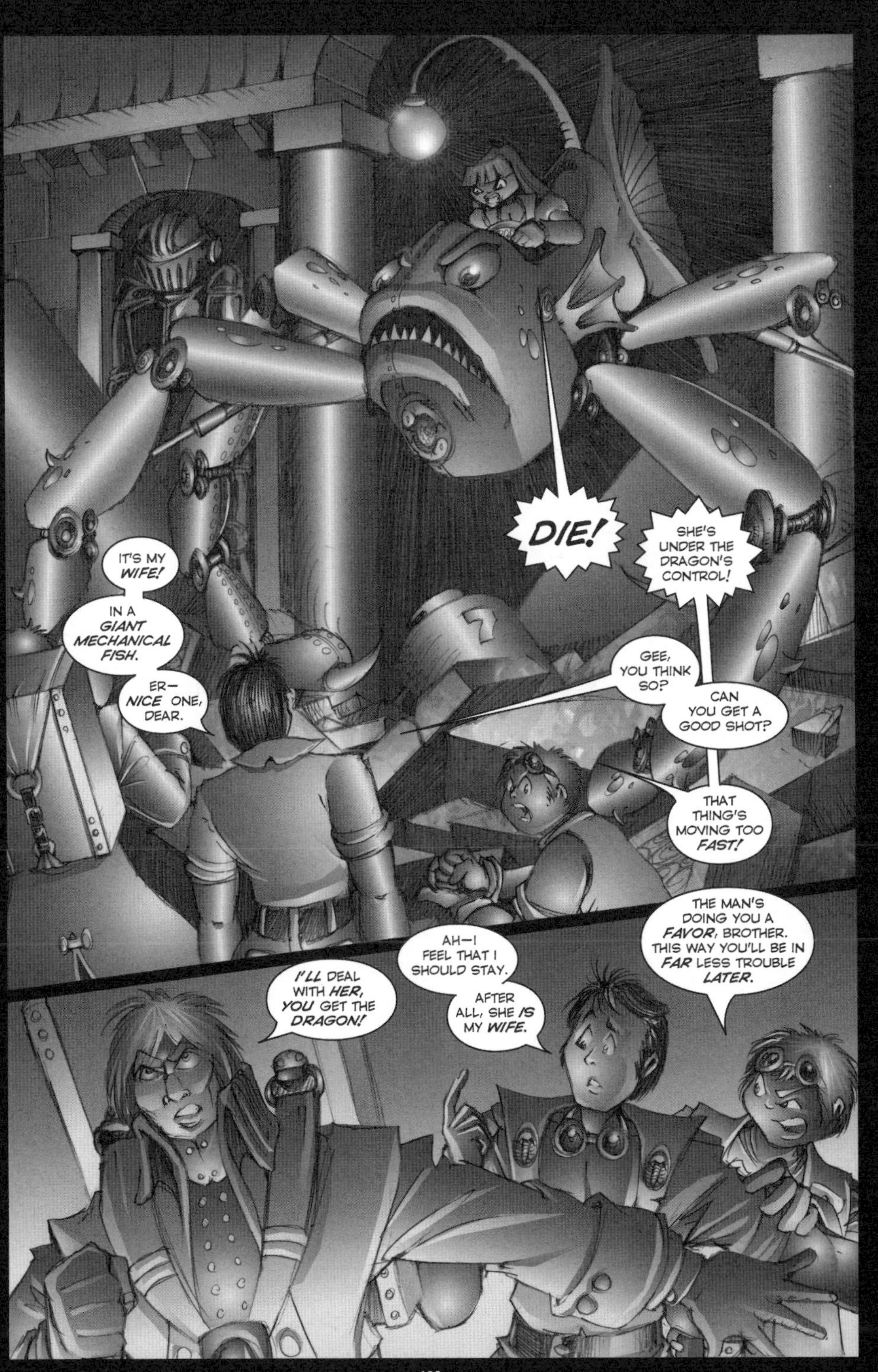
DIE!
SHE'S UNDER THE DRAGON'S CONTROL!
IT'S MY WIFE!
IN A GIANT MECHANICAL FISH.
ER— NICE ONE, DEAR.
GEE, YOU THINK SO?
CAN YOU GET A GOOD SHOT?
THAT THING'S MOVING TOO FAST!
I'LL DEAL WITH HER, YOU GET THE DRAGON!
AH—I FEEL THAT I SHOULD STAY.
AFTER ALL, SHE IS MY WIFE.
THE MAN'S DOING YOU A FAVOR, BROTHER. THIS WAY YOU'LL BE IN FAR LESS TROUBLE LATER.

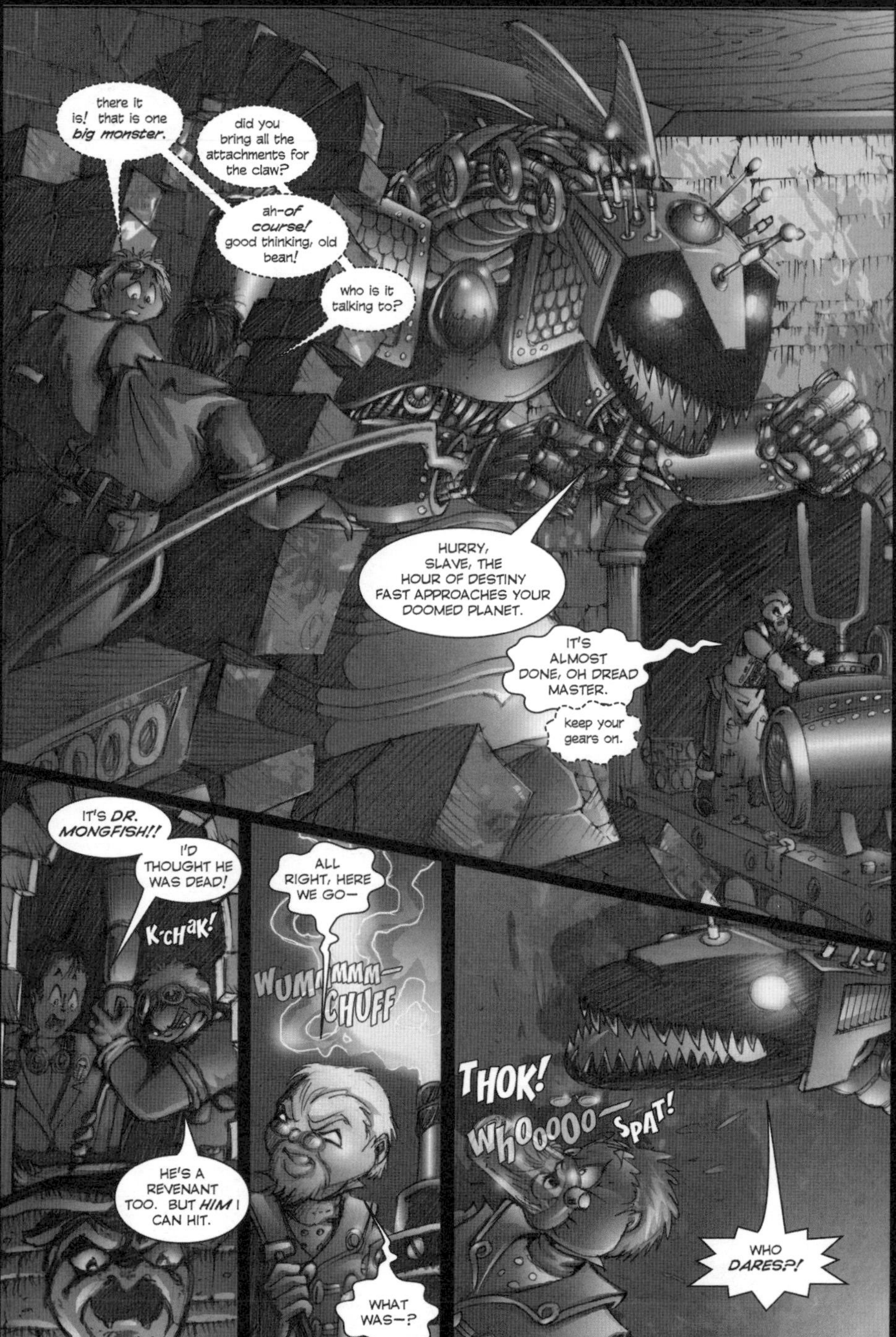
there it is! that is one *big monster*.
did you bring all the attachments for the claw?
ah—*of course!* good thinking, old bean!
who is it talking to?
HURRY, SLAVE, THE HOUR OF DESTINY FAST APPROACHES YOUR DOOMED PLANET.
IT'S ALMOST DONE, OH DREAD MASTER.
keep your gears on.
IT'S *DR. MONGFISH!!*
I'D THOUGHT HE WAS DEAD!
K-CHAK!
HE'S A REVENANT TOO. BUT *HIM* I CAN HIT.
ALL RIGHT, HERE WE GO—
WUMMMMM—CHUFF
WHAT WAS—?
THOK!
WHOOOOO—SPAT!
WHO *DARES?!*

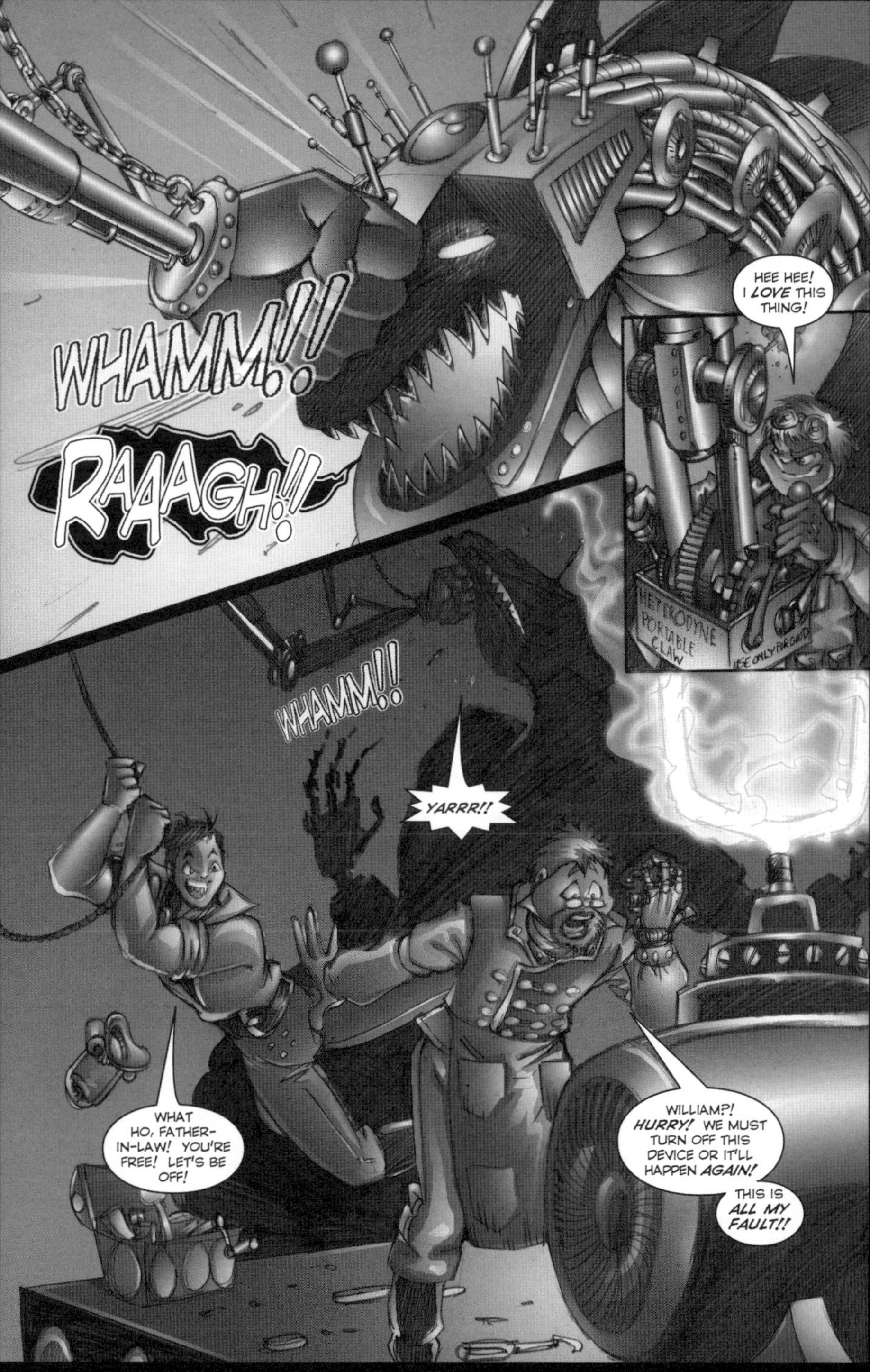
WHAMM!!
RAAAGH!!
HEE HEE! I LOVE THIS THING!
HETERODYNE PORTABLE CLAW
USE ONLY FOR GOOD
WHAMM!!
YARRR!!
WHAT HO, FATHER-IN-LAW! YOU'RE FREE! LET'S BE OFF!
WILLIAM?! HURRY! WE MUST TURN OFF THIS DEVICE OR IT'LL HAPPEN AGAIN!
THIS IS ALL MY FAULT!!

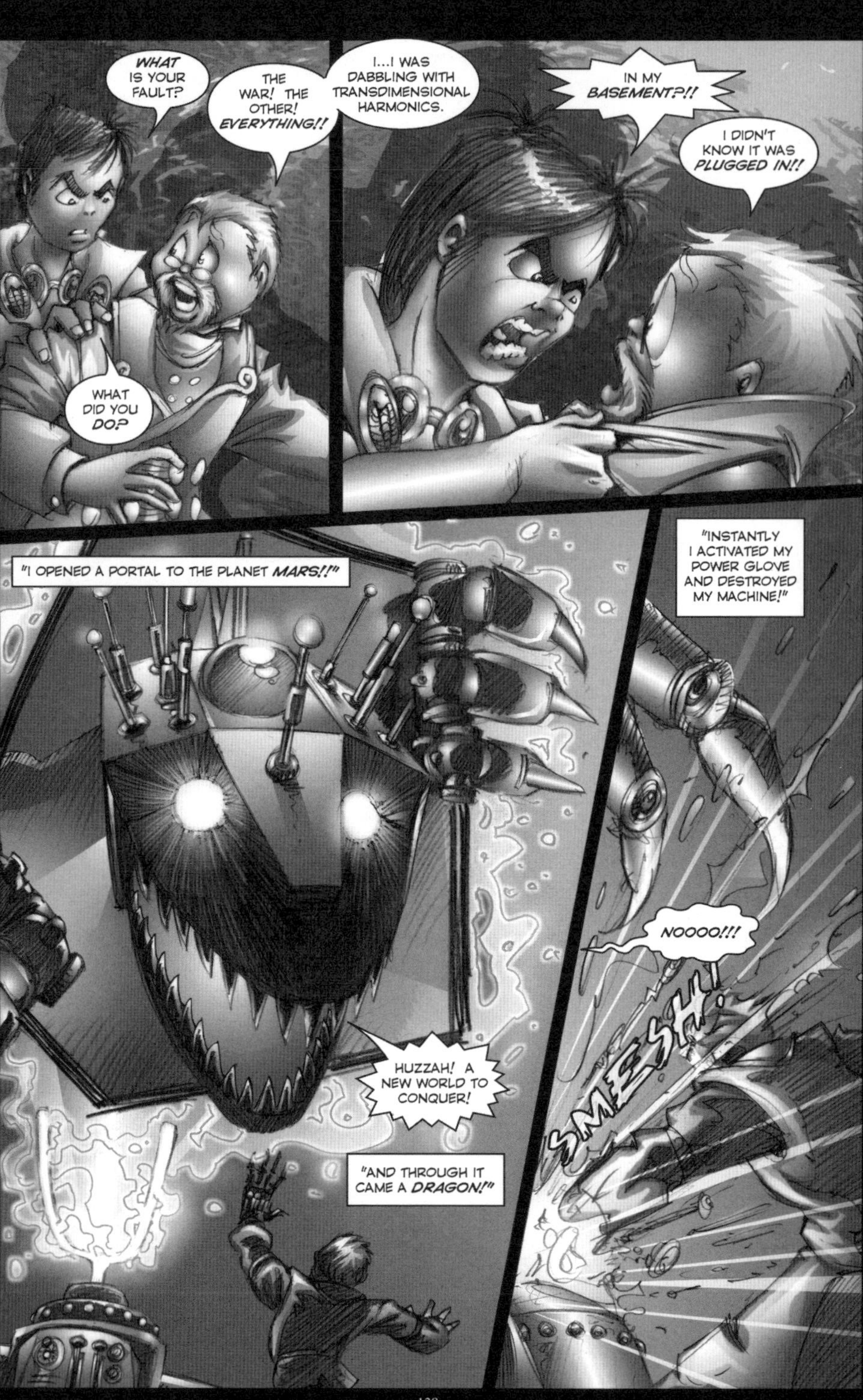
WHAT IS YOUR FAULT?
THE WAR! THE OTHER! EVERYTHING!!
WHAT DID YOU DO?
I...I WAS DABBLING WITH TRANSDIMENSIONAL HARMONICS.
IN MY BASEMENT?!!
I DIDN'T KNOW IT WAS PLUGGED IN!!
"I OPENED A PORTAL TO THE PLANET MARS!!"
HUZZAH! A NEW WORLD TO CONQUER!
"AND THROUGH IT CAME A DRAGON!"
"INSTANTLY I ACTIVATED MY POWER GLOVE AND DESTROYED MY MACHINE!"
NOOOO!!!
SMESH!

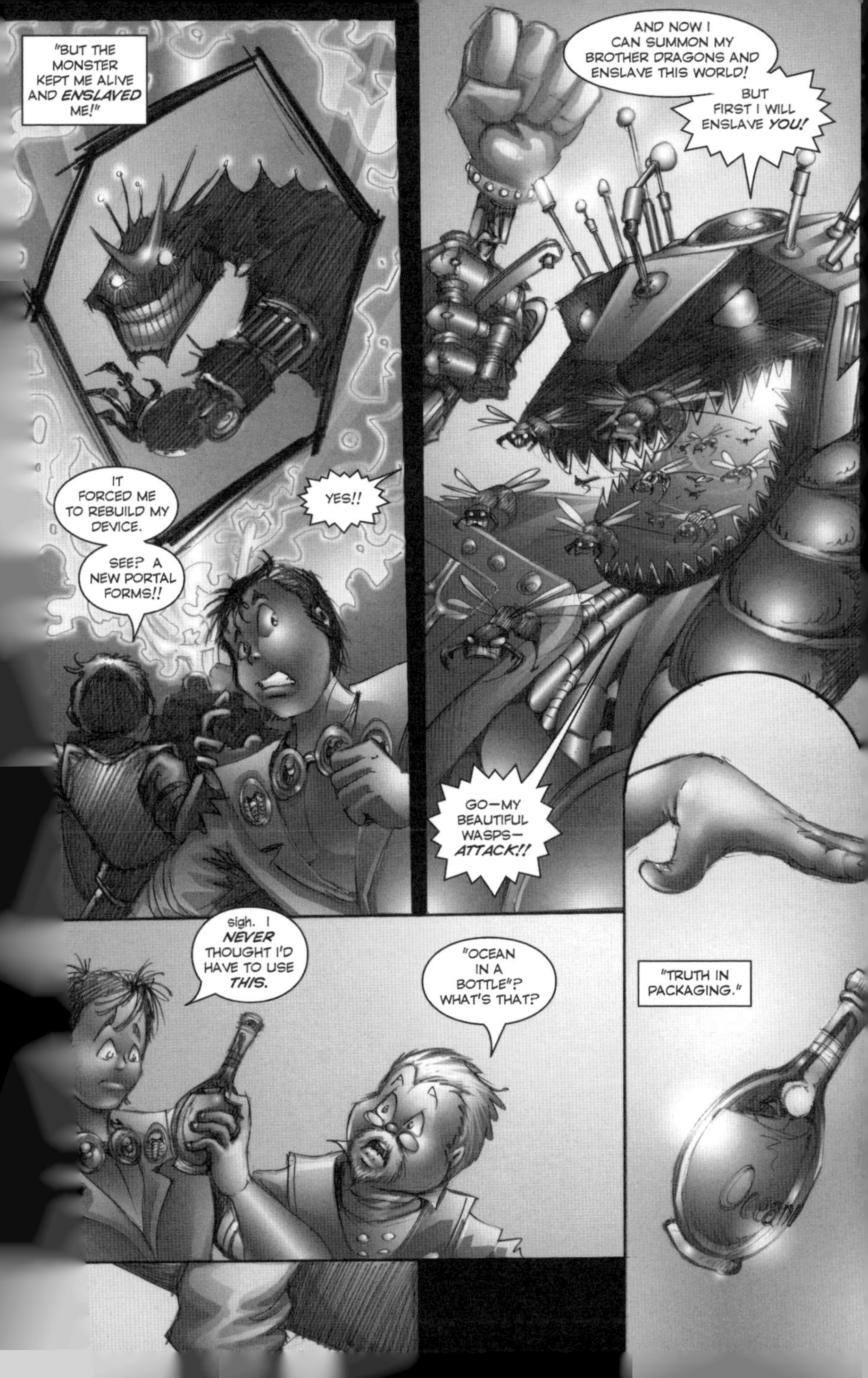
"BUT THE MONSTER KEPT ME ALIVE AND ENSLAVED ME!"
IT FORCED ME TO REBUILD MY DEVICE.
SEE? A NEW PORTAL FORMS!!
YES!!
AND NOW I CAN SUMMON MY BROTHER DRAGONS AND ENSLAVE THIS WORLD!
BUT FIRST I WILL ENSLAVE YOU!
GO—MY BEAUTIFUL WASPS—ATTACK!!
sigh. I NEVER THOUGHT I'D HAVE TO USE THIS.
"OCEAN IN A BOTTLE"? WHAT'S THAT?
"TRUTH IN PACKAGING."
Oceane

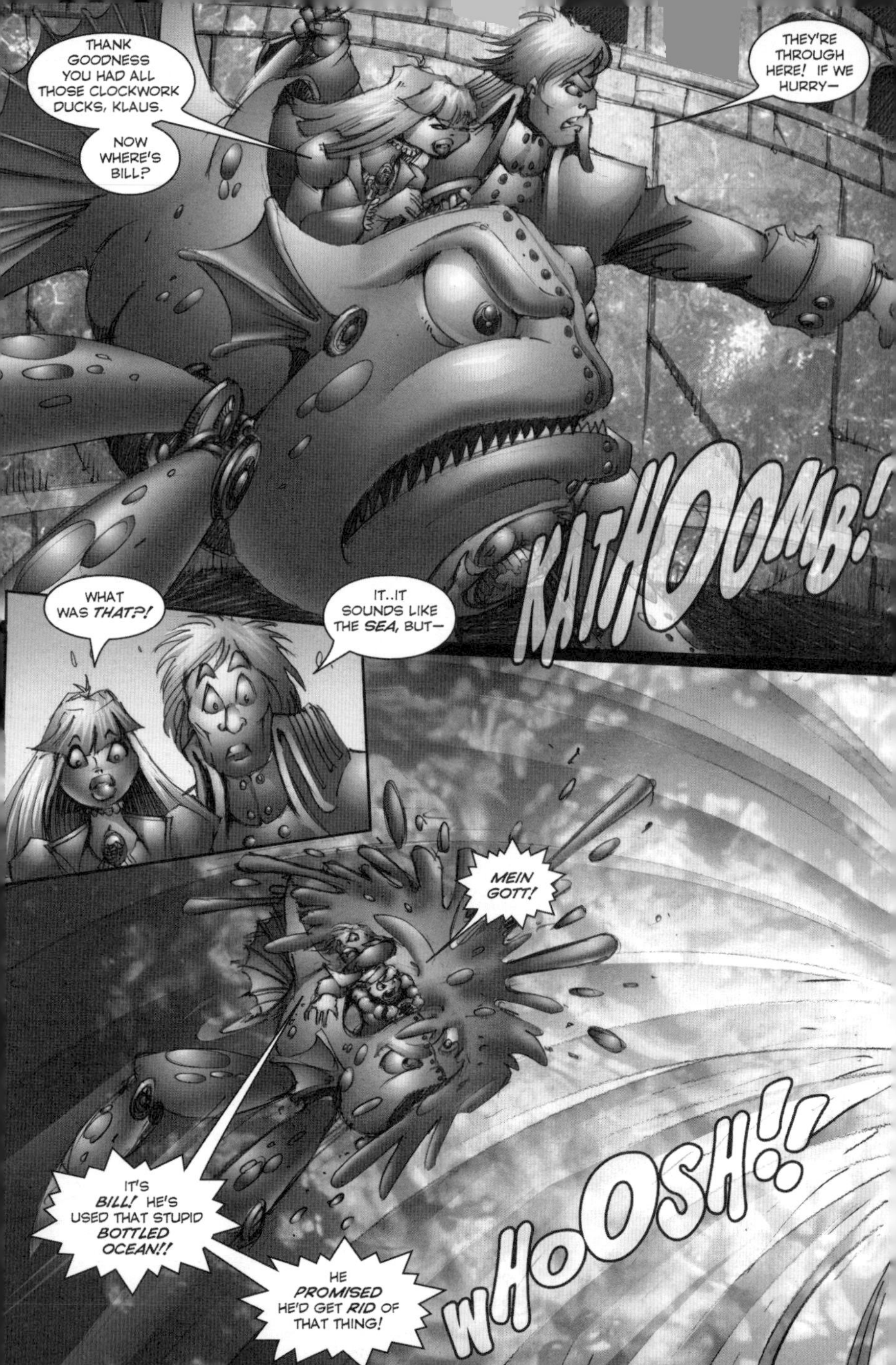
THANK GOODNESS YOU HAD ALL THOSE CLOCKWORK DUCKS, KLAUS.
NOW WHERE'S BILL?
THEY'RE THROUGH HERE! IF WE HURRY—
KATHOOMB!
WHAT WAS THAT?!
IT..IT SOUNDS LIKE THE SEA, BUT—
MEIN GOTT!
IT'S BILL! HE'S USED THAT STUPID BOTTLED OCEAN!!
HE PROMISED HE'D GET RID OF THAT THING!
WHOOSH!!

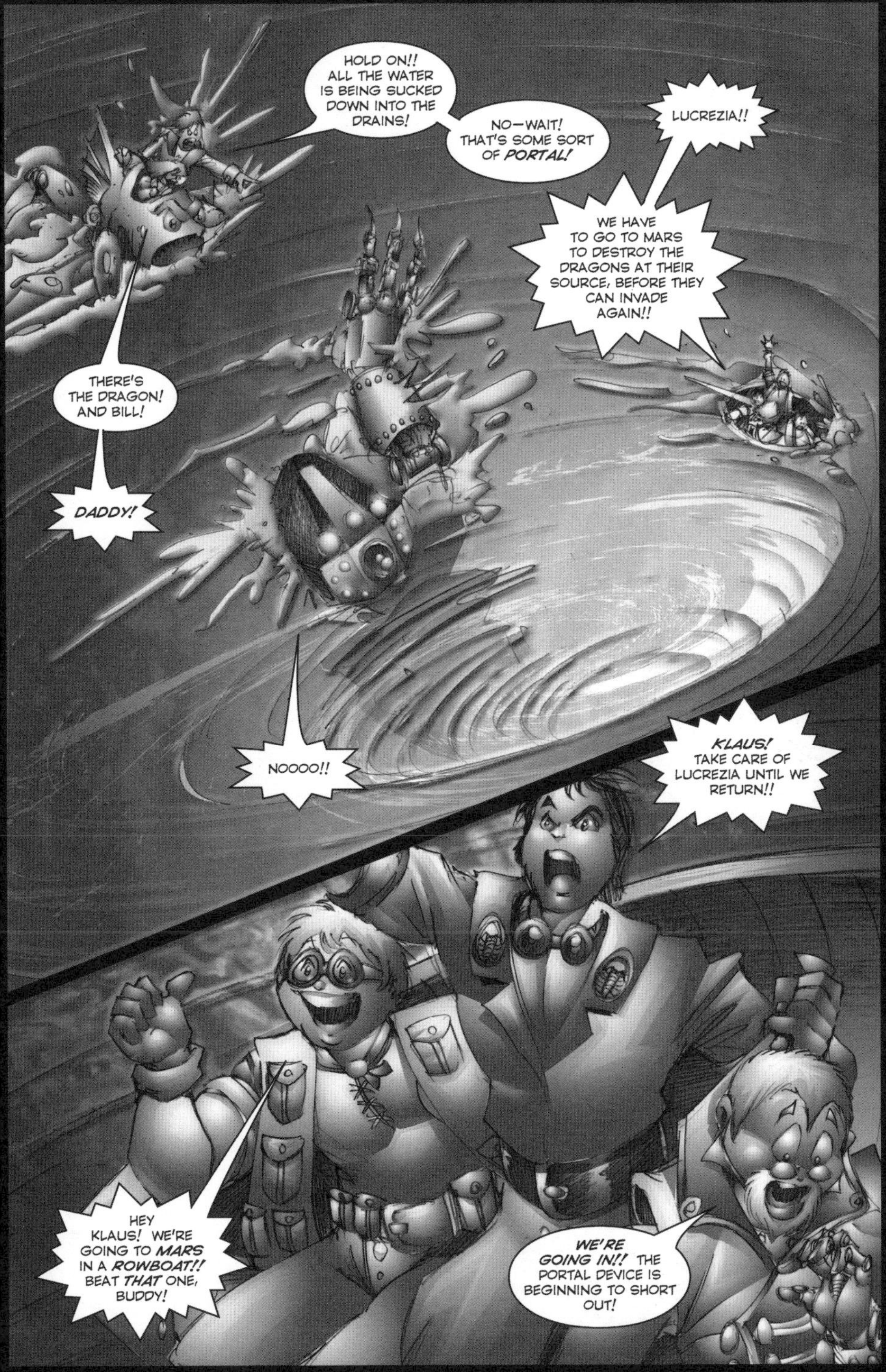
HOLD ON!! ALL THE WATER IS BEING SUCKED DOWN INTO THE DRAINS!
NO—WAIT! THAT'S SOME SORT OF PORTAL!
LUCREZIA!!
WE HAVE TO GO TO MARS TO DESTROY THE DRAGONS AT THEIR SOURCE, BEFORE THEY CAN INVADE AGAIN!!
THERE'S THE DRAGON! AND BILL!
DADDY!
NOOOO!!
KLAUS! TAKE CARE OF LUCREZIA UNTIL WE RETURN!!
HEY KLAUS! WE'RE GOING TO MARS IN A ROWBOAT!! BEAT THAT ONE, BUDDY!
WE'RE GOING IN!! THE PORTAL DEVICE IS BEGINNING TO SHORT OUT!

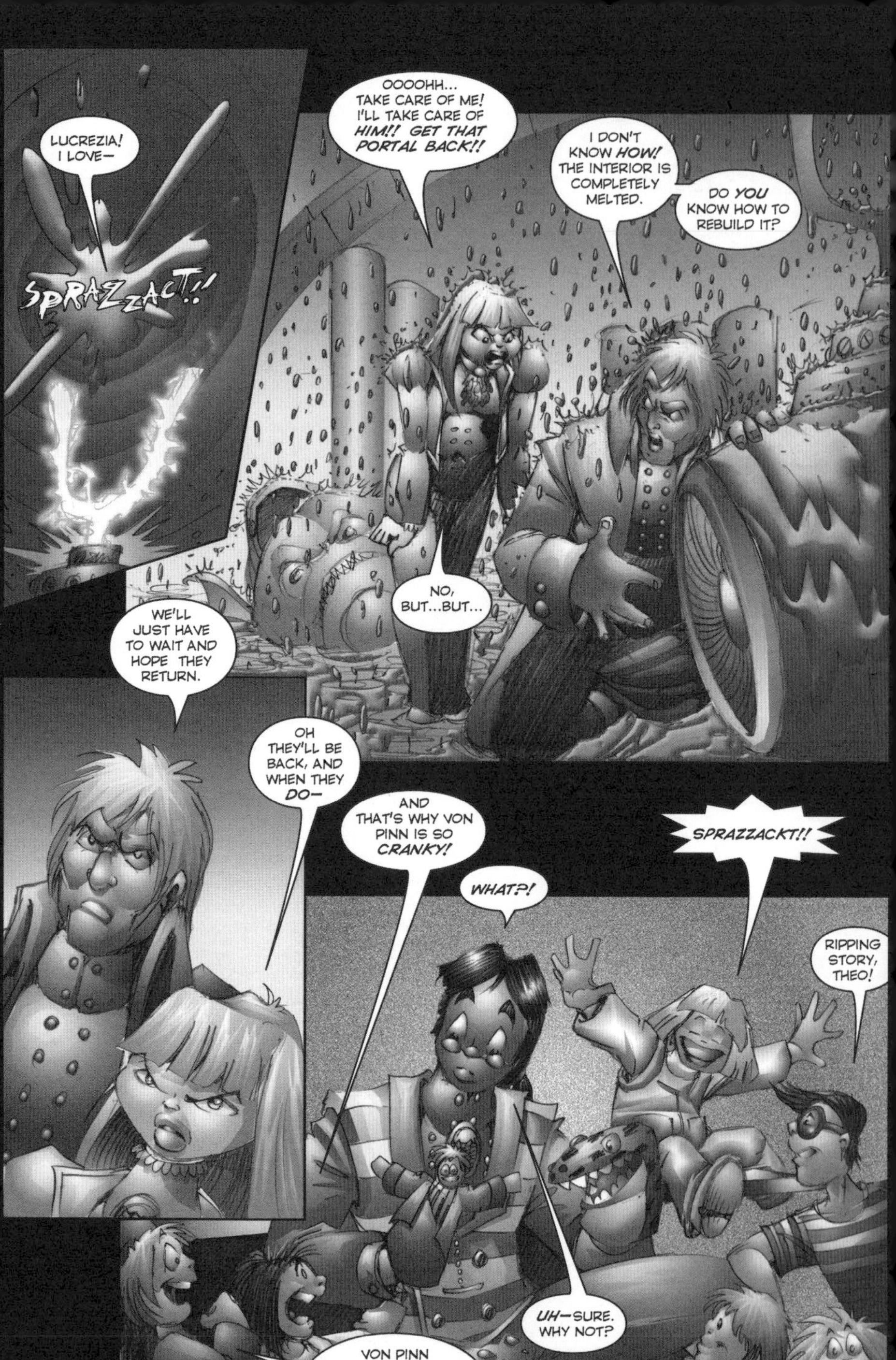
LUCREZIA! I LOVE—
SPRAZZACT!!
OOOOHH... TAKE CARE OF ME! I'LL TAKE CARE OF HIM!! GET THAT PORTAL BACK!!
I DON'T KNOW HOW! THE INTERIOR IS COMPLETELY MELTED.
DO YOU KNOW HOW TO REBUILD IT?
NO, BUT...BUT...
WE'LL JUST HAVE TO WAIT AND HOPE THEY RETURN.
OH THEY'LL BE BACK, AND WHEN THEY DO—
AND THAT'S WHY VON PINN IS SO CRANKY!
SPRAZZACKT!!
WHAT?!
RIPPING STORY, THEO!
UH—SURE. WHY NOT?
VON PINN IS REALLY LUCREZIA! EVERYBODY KNOWS THAT!
I'M HUNGRY!

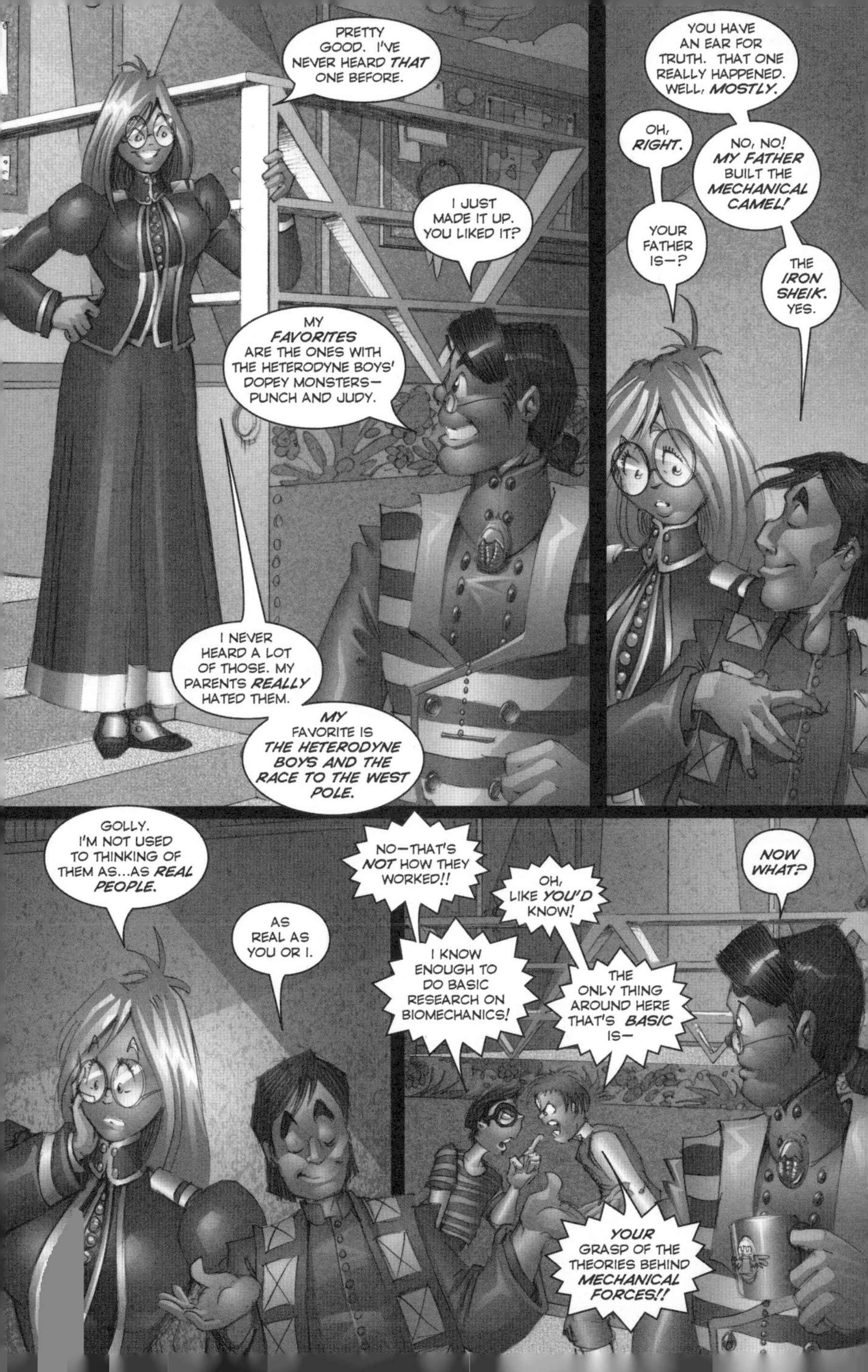

PRETTY GOOD. I'VE NEVER HEARD *THAT* ONE BEFORE.
I JUST MADE IT UP. YOU LIKED IT?
MY *FAVORITES* ARE THE ONES WITH THE HETERODYNE BOYS' DOPEY MONSTERS—PUNCH AND JUDY.
I NEVER HEARD A LOT OF THOSE. MY PARENTS *REALLY* HATED THEM.
MY FAVORITE IS *THE HETERODYNE BOYS AND THE RACE TO THE WEST POLE.*
YOU HAVE AN EAR FOR TRUTH. THAT ONE REALLY HAPPENED. WELL, *MOSTLY.*
OH, *RIGHT.*
NO, NO! *MY FATHER* BUILT THE *MECHANICAL CAMEL!*
YOUR FATHER IS—?
THE *IRON SHEIK.* YES.
GOLLY. I'M NOT USED TO THINKING OF THEM AS...AS *REAL PEOPLE.*
AS REAL AS YOU OR I.
NO—THAT'S *NOT* HOW THEY WORKED!!
OH, LIKE *YOU'D* KNOW!
I KNOW ENOUGH TO DO BASIC RESEARCH ON BIOMECHANICS!
THE ONLY THING AROUND HERE THAT'S *BASIC* IS—
YOUR GRASP OF THE THEORIES BEHIND *MECHANICAL FORCES!!*
NOW WHAT?

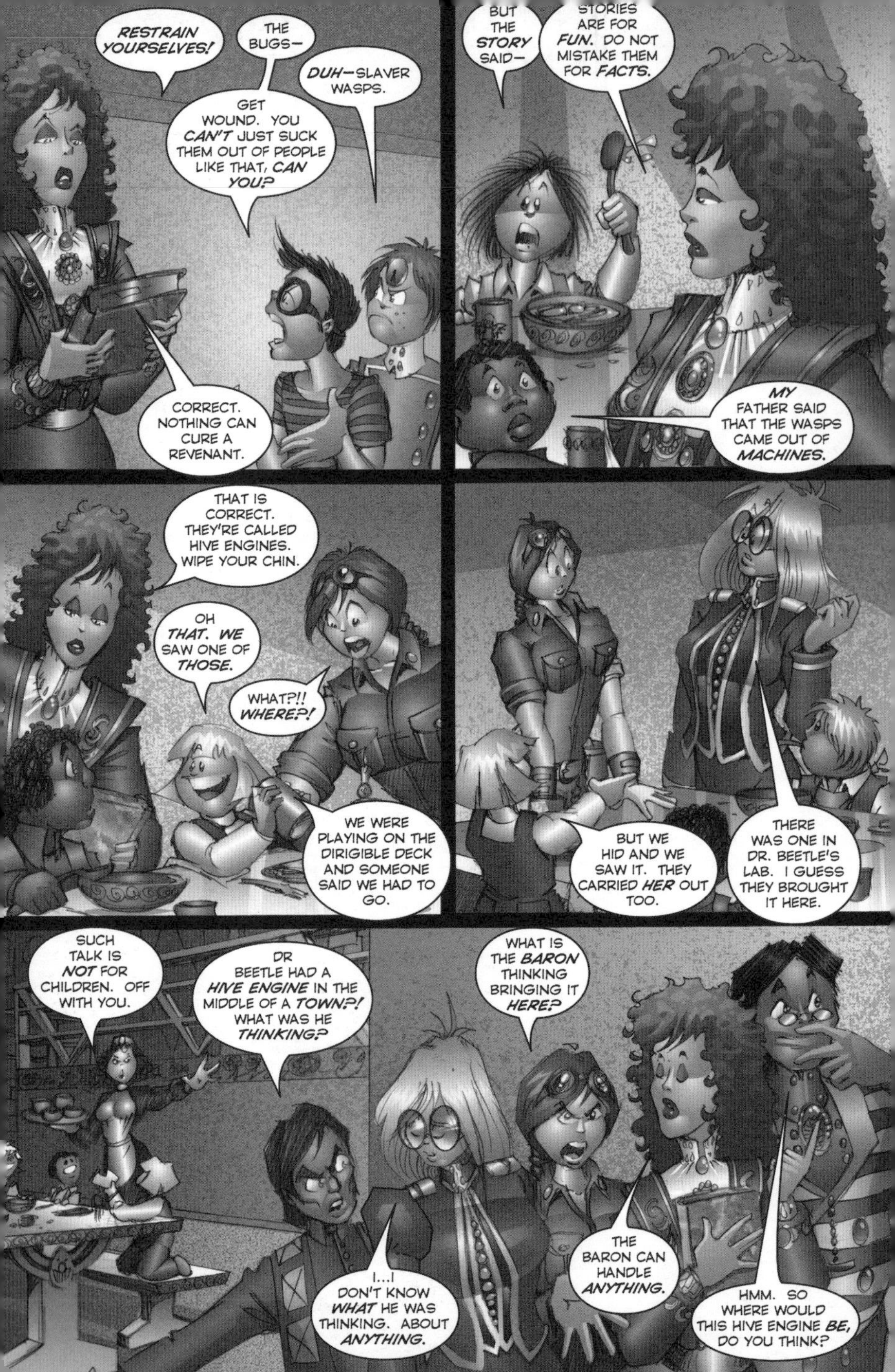

RESTRAIN YOURSELVES!
THE BUGS—
DUH—SLAVER WASPS.
GET WOUND. YOU CAN'T JUST SUCK THEM OUT OF PEOPLE LIKE THAT, CAN YOU?
CORRECT. NOTHING CAN CURE A REVENANT.
BUT THE STORY SAID—
STORIES ARE FOR FUN. DO NOT MISTAKE THEM FOR FACTS.
MY FATHER SAID THAT THE WASPS CAME OUT OF MACHINES.
THAT IS CORRECT. THEY'RE CALLED HIVE ENGINES. WIPE YOUR CHIN.
OH THAT. WE SAW ONE OF THOSE.
WHAT?!! WHERE?!
WE WERE PLAYING ON THE DIRIGIBLE DECK AND SOMEONE SAID WE HAD TO GO.
BUT WE HID AND WE SAW IT. THEY CARRIED HER OUT TOO.
THERE WAS ONE IN DR. BEETLE'S LAB. I GUESS THEY BROUGHT IT HERE.
SUCH TALK IS NOT FOR CHILDREN. OFF WITH YOU.
DR BEETLE HAD A HIVE ENGINE IN THE MIDDLE OF A TOWN?! WHAT WAS HE THINKING?
WHAT IS THE BARON THINKING BRINGING IT HERE?
I...I DON'T KNOW WHAT HE WAS THINKING. ABOUT ANYTHING.
THE BARON CAN HANDLE ANYTHING.
HMM. SO WHERE WOULD THIS HIVE ENGINE BE, DO YOU THINK?

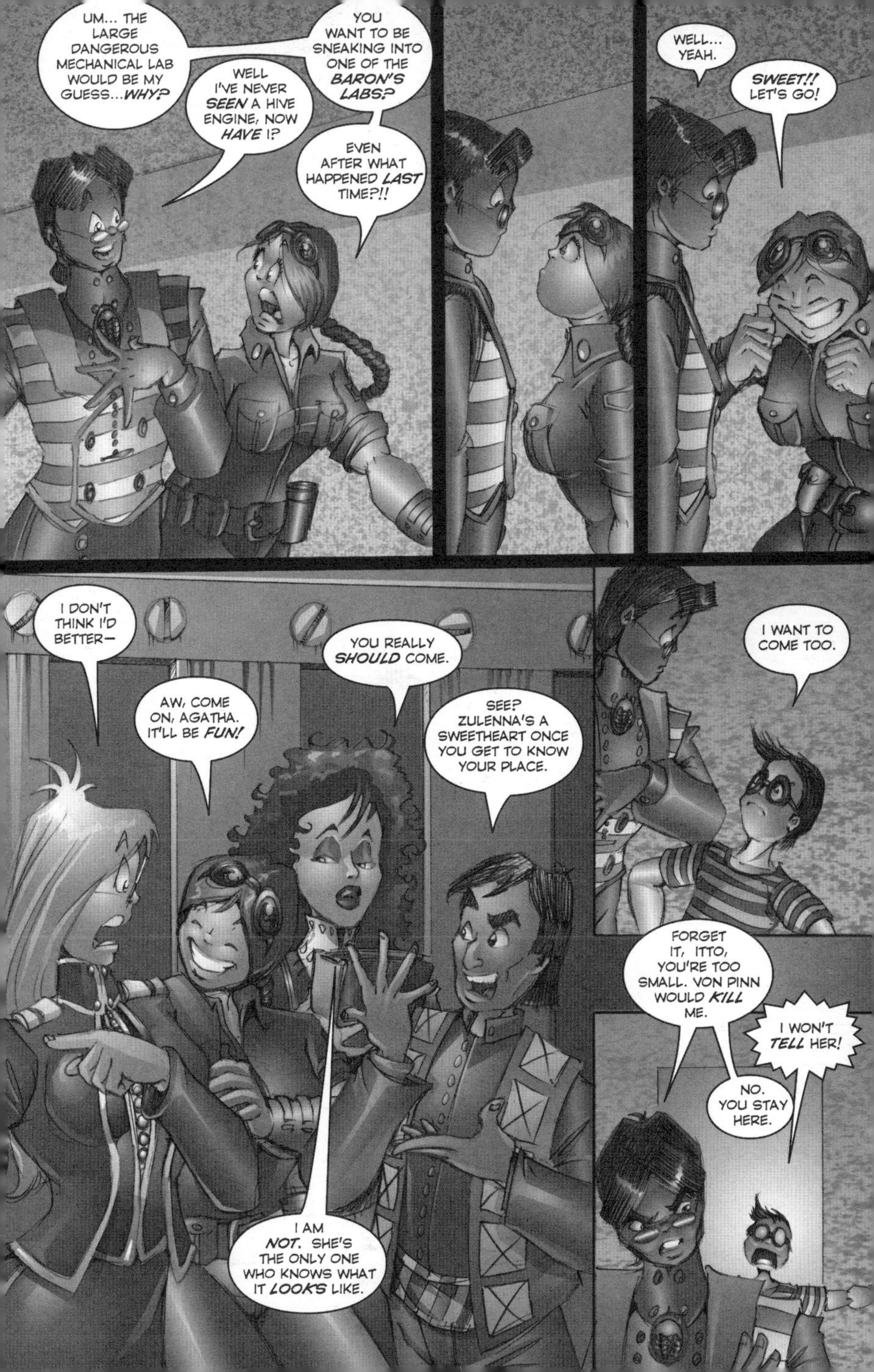
UM... THE LARGE DANGEROUS MECHANICAL LAB WOULD BE MY GUESS...WHY?
YOU WANT TO BE SNEAKING INTO ONE OF THE BARON'S LABS?
WELL I'VE NEVER SEEN A HIVE ENGINE, NOW HAVE I?
EVEN AFTER WHAT HAPPENED LAST TIME?!!
WELL... YEAH.
SWEET!! LET'S GO!
I DON'T THINK I'D BETTER—
YOU REALLY SHOULD COME.
AW, COME ON, AGATHA. IT'LL BE FUN!
SEE? ZULENNA'S A SWEETHEART ONCE YOU GET TO KNOW YOUR PLACE.
I AM NOT. SHE'S THE ONLY ONE WHO KNOWS WHAT IT LOOKS LIKE.
I WANT TO COME TOO.
FORGET IT, ITTO, YOU'RE TOO SMALL. VON PINN WOULD KILL ME.
I WON'T TELL HER!
NO. YOU STAY HERE.

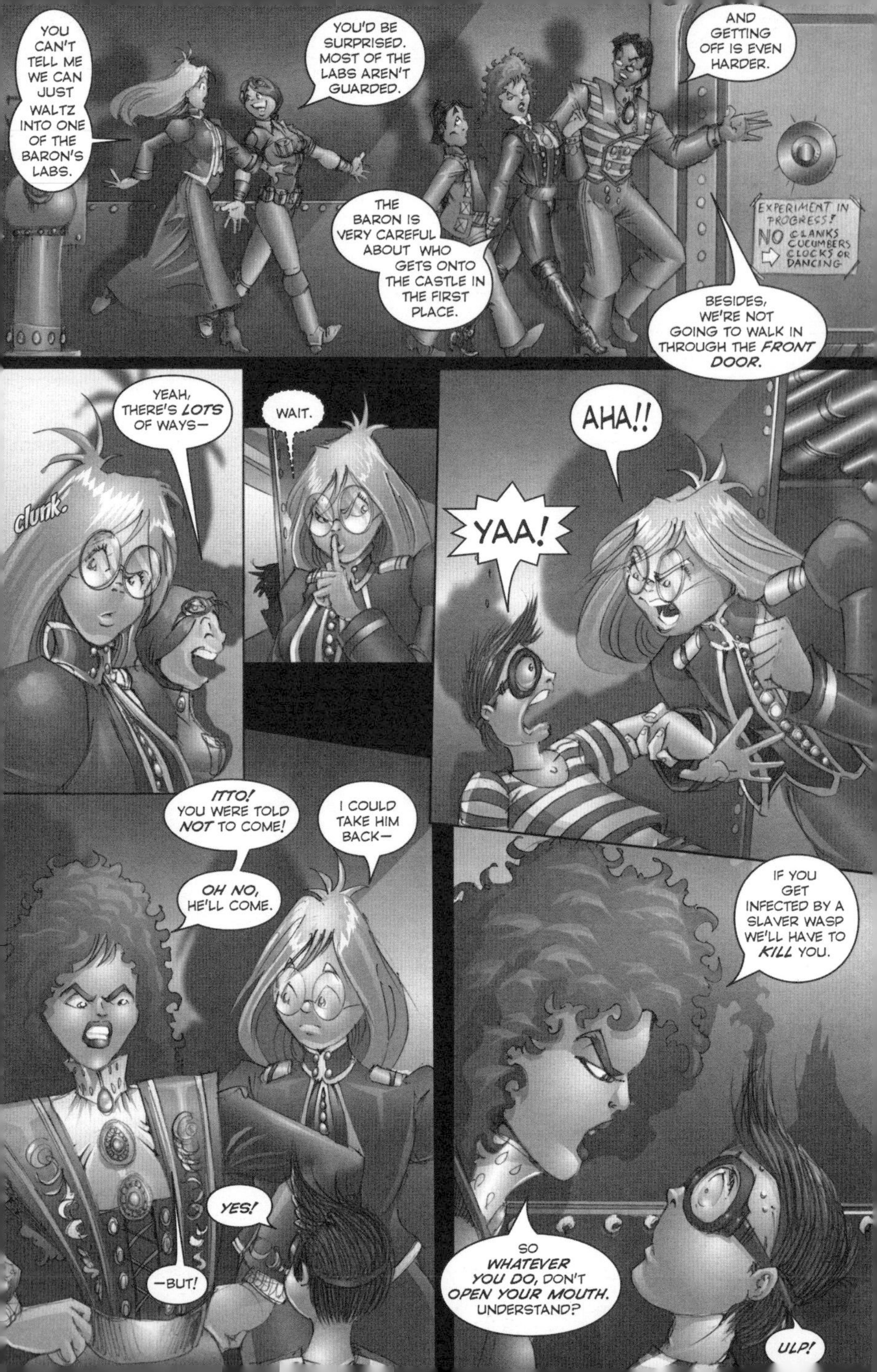
YOU CAN'T TELL ME WE CAN JUST WALTZ INTO ONE OF THE BARON'S LABS.
YOU'D BE SURPRISED. MOST OF THE LABS AREN'T GUARDED.
THE BARON IS VERY CAREFUL ABOUT WHO GETS ONTO THE CASTLE IN THE FIRST PLACE.
AND GETTING OFF IS EVEN HARDER.
EXPERIMENT IN PROGRESS! NO CLANKS CUCUMBERS CLOCKS OR DANCING
BESIDES, WE'RE NOT GOING TO WALK IN THROUGH THE *FRONT DOOR*.
clunk.
YEAH, THERE'S *LOTS* OF WAYS—
WAIT.
AHA!!
YAA!
ITTO! YOU WERE TOLD *NOT* TO COME!
I COULD TAKE HIM BACK—
OH NO, HE'LL COME.
YES!
—BUT!
IF YOU GET INFECTED BY A SLAVER WASP WE'LL HAVE TO *KILL* YOU.
SO *WHATEVER YOU DO,* DON'T *OPEN YOUR MOUTH.* UNDERSTAND?
ULP!

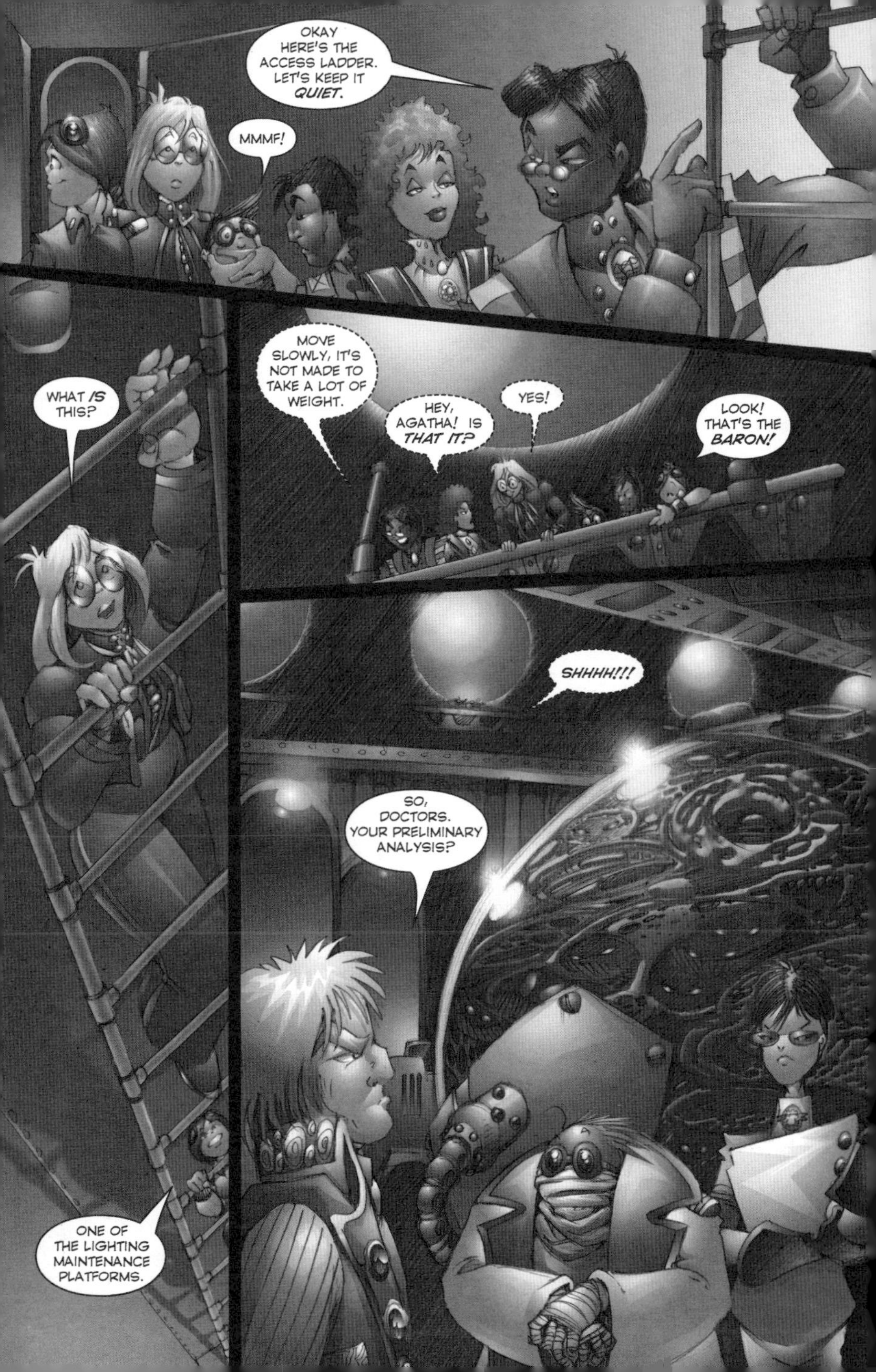
OKAY HERE'S THE ACCESS LADDER. LET'S KEEP IT QUIET.
MMMF!
WHAT IS THIS?
ONE OF THE LIGHTING MAINTENANCE PLATFORMS.
MOVE SLOWLY, IT'S NOT MADE TO TAKE A LOT OF WEIGHT.
HEY, AGATHA! IS THAT IT?
YES!
LOOK! THAT'S THE BARON!
SHHHH!!!
SO, DOCTORS. YOUR PRELIMINARY ANALYSIS?

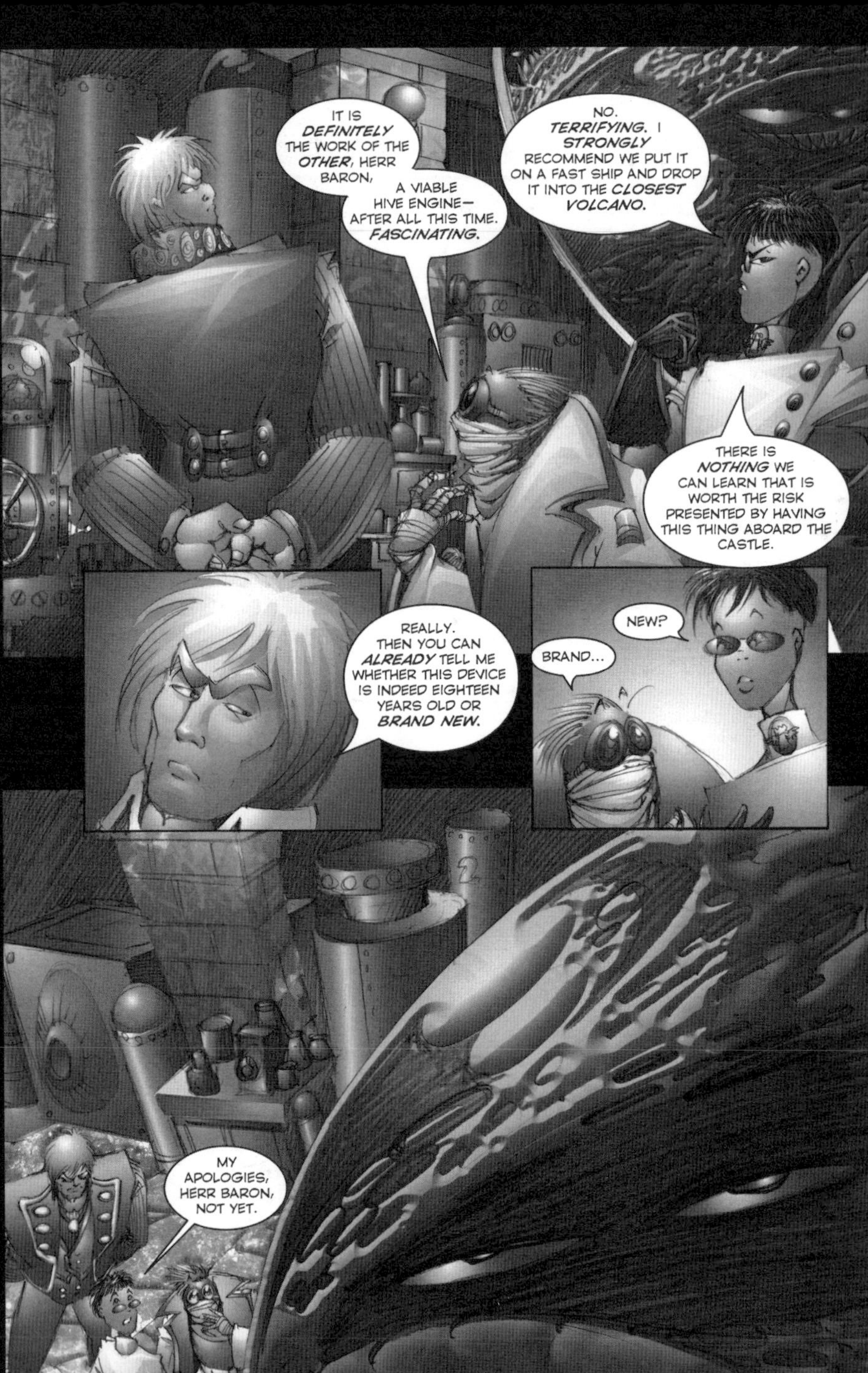

IT IS DEFINITELY THE WORK OF THE OTHER, HERR BARON,
A VIABLE HIVE ENGINE— AFTER ALL THIS TIME. FASCINATING.
NO. TERRIFYING. I STRONGLY RECOMMEND WE PUT IT ON A FAST SHIP AND DROP IT INTO THE CLOSEST VOLCANO.
THERE IS NOTHING WE CAN LEARN THAT IS WORTH THE RISK PRESENTED BY HAVING THIS THING ABOARD THE CASTLE.
REALLY. THEN YOU CAN ALREADY TELL ME WHETHER THIS DEVICE IS INDEED EIGHTEEN YEARS OLD OR BRAND NEW.
BRAND...
NEW?
MY APOLOGIES, HERR BARON, NOT YET.

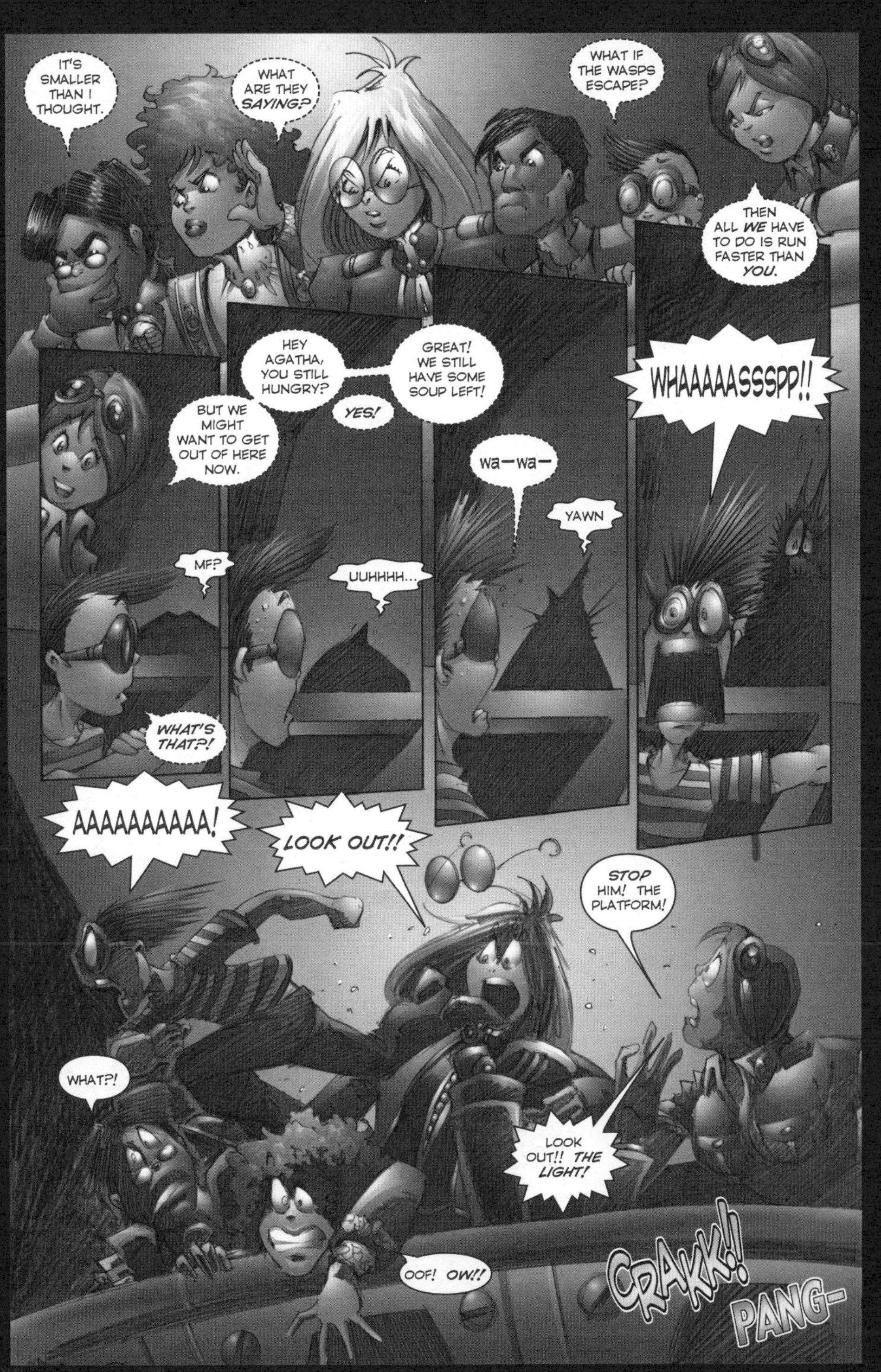

IT'S SMALLER THAN I THOUGHT.
WHAT ARE THEY SAYING?
WHAT IF THE WASPS ESCAPE?
THEN ALL WE HAVE TO DO IS RUN FASTER THAN YOU.
BUT WE MIGHT WANT TO GET OUT OF HERE NOW.
MF?
WHAT'S THAT?!
HEY AGATHA, YOU STILL HUNGRY?
YES!
UUHHHH...
GREAT! WE STILL HAVE SOME SOUP LEFT!
wa-wa-
YAWN
WHAAAAASSSPP!!
AAAAAAAAAA!
LOOK OUT!!
STOP HIM! THE PLATFORM!
WHAT?!
LOOK OUT!! THE LIGHT!
OOF! OW!!
CRAKK!!
PANG-

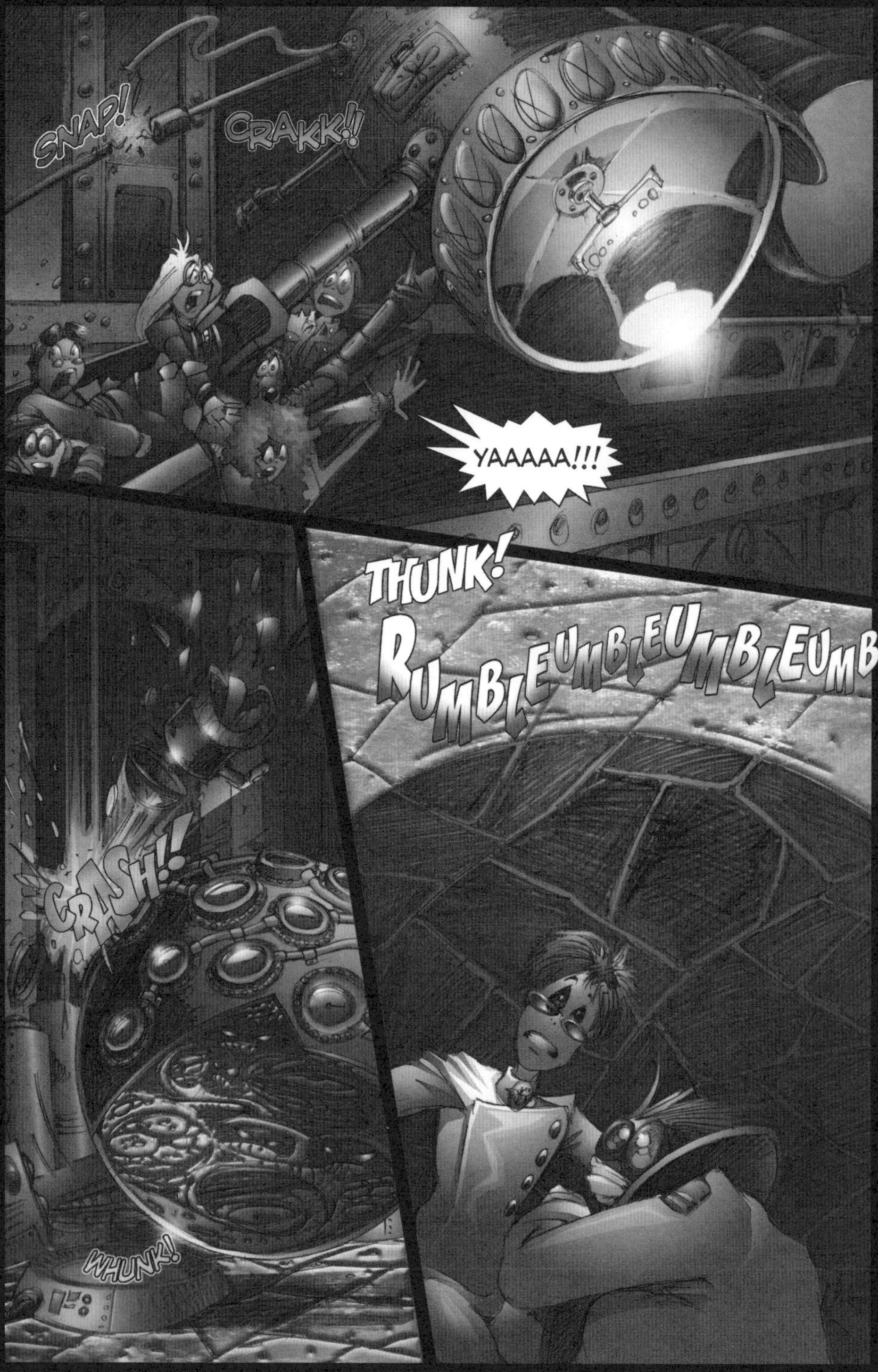
SNAP!
CRAKK!!
YAAAAA!!!
CRASH!!
WHUNK!
THUNK!
RUMBLEUMBLEUMBLEUMB

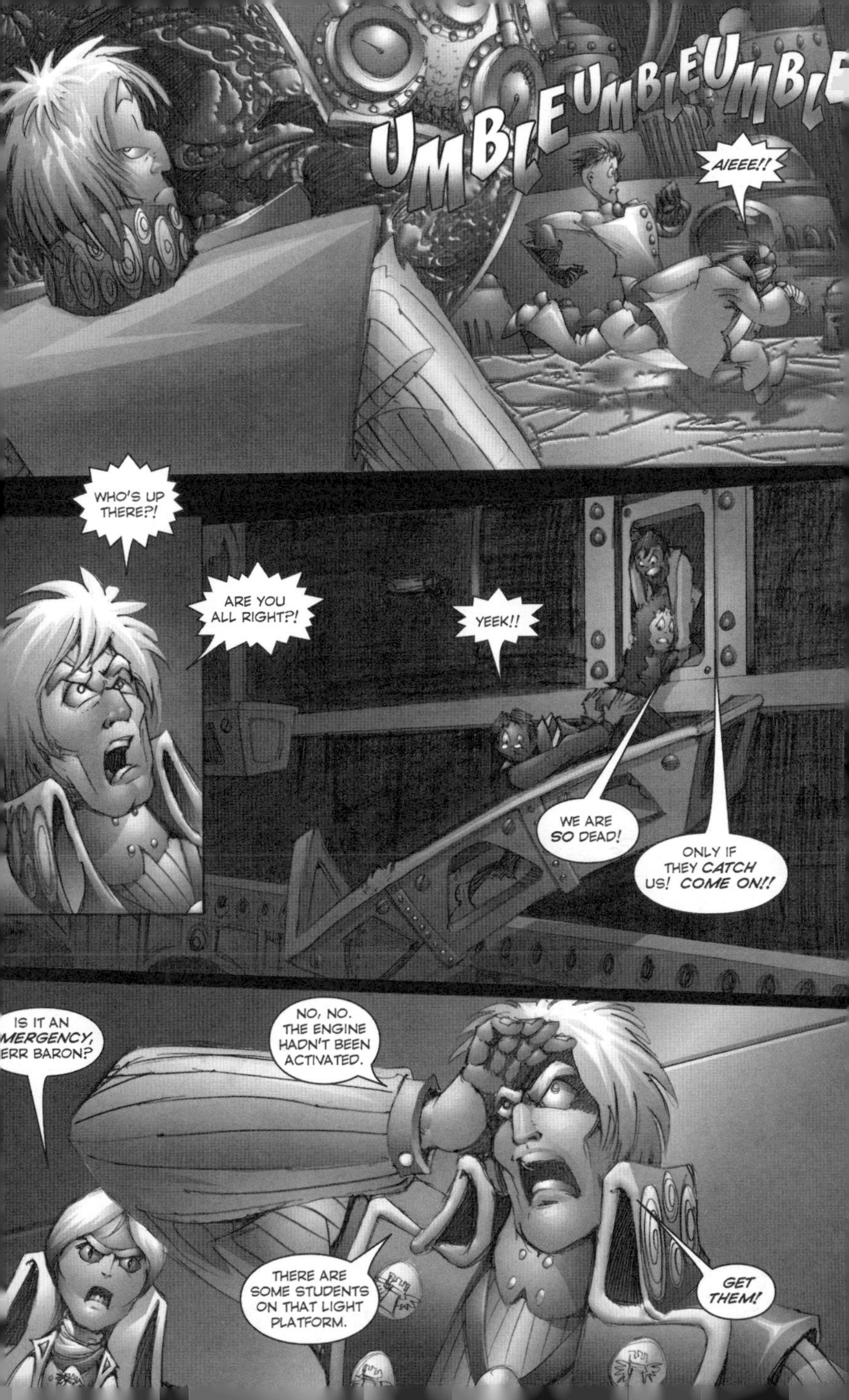
UMBLEUMBLEUMBLE
AIEEE!!
WHO'S UP THERE?!
ARE YOU ALL RIGHT?!
YEEK!!
WE ARE SO DEAD!
ONLY IF THEY CATCH US! COME ON!!
IS IT AN MERGENCY, ERR BARON?
NO, NO. THE ENGINE HADN'T BEEN ACTIVATED.
THERE ARE SOME STUDENTS ON THAT LIGHT PLATFORM.
GET THEM!

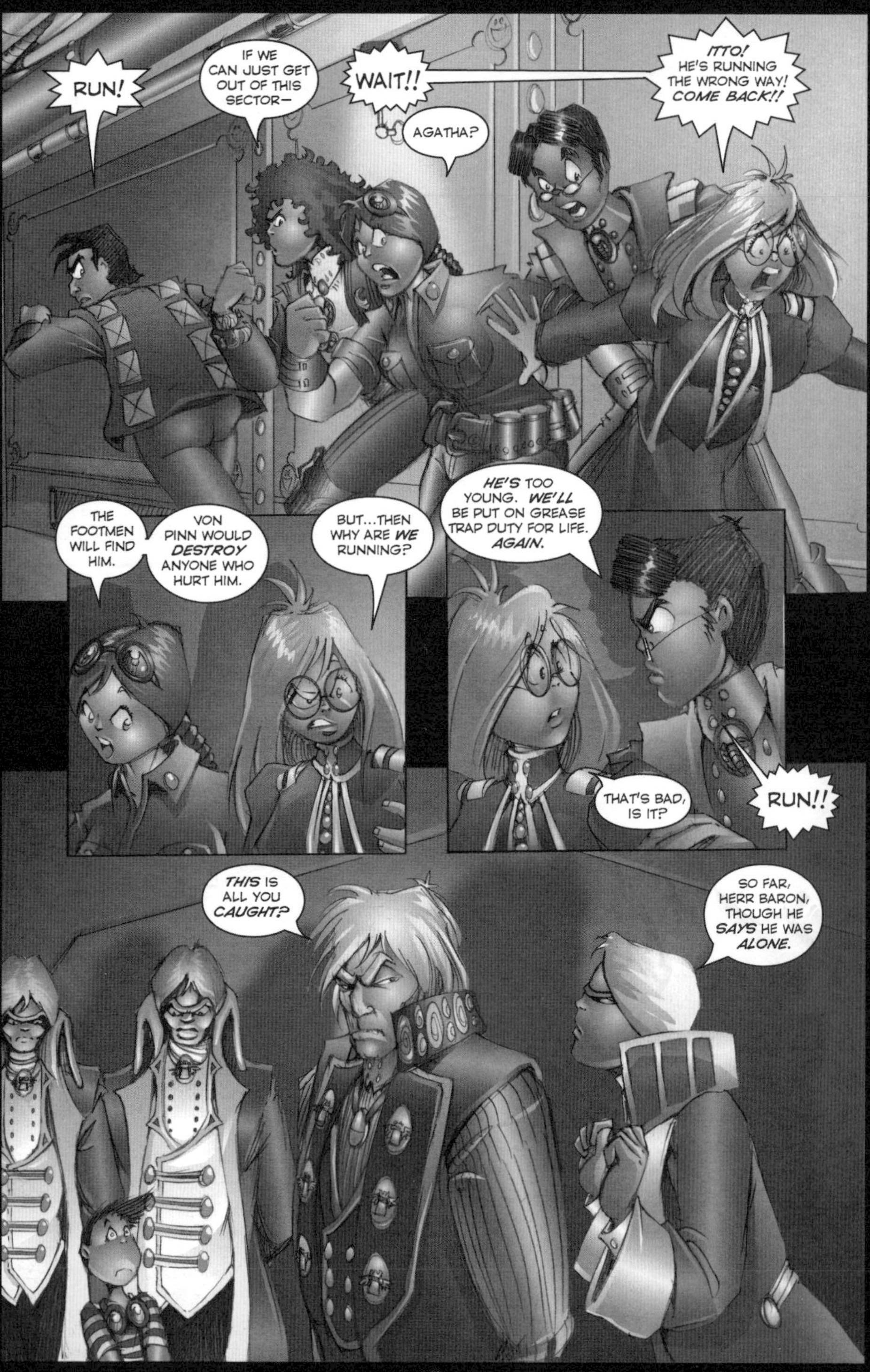
RUN!
IF WE CAN JUST GET OUT OF THIS SECTOR—
WAIT!!
AGATHA?
ITTO! HE'S RUNNING THE WRONG WAY! COME BACK!!
THE FOOTMEN WILL FIND HIM.
VON PINN WOULD DESTROY ANYONE WHO HURT HIM.
BUT...THEN WHY ARE WE RUNNING?
HE'S TOO YOUNG. WE'LL BE PUT ON GREASE TRAP DUTY FOR LIFE. AGAIN.
THAT'S BAD, IS IT?
RUN!!
THIS IS ALL YOU CAUGHT?
SO FAR, HERR BARON, THOUGH HE SAYS HE WAS ALONE.

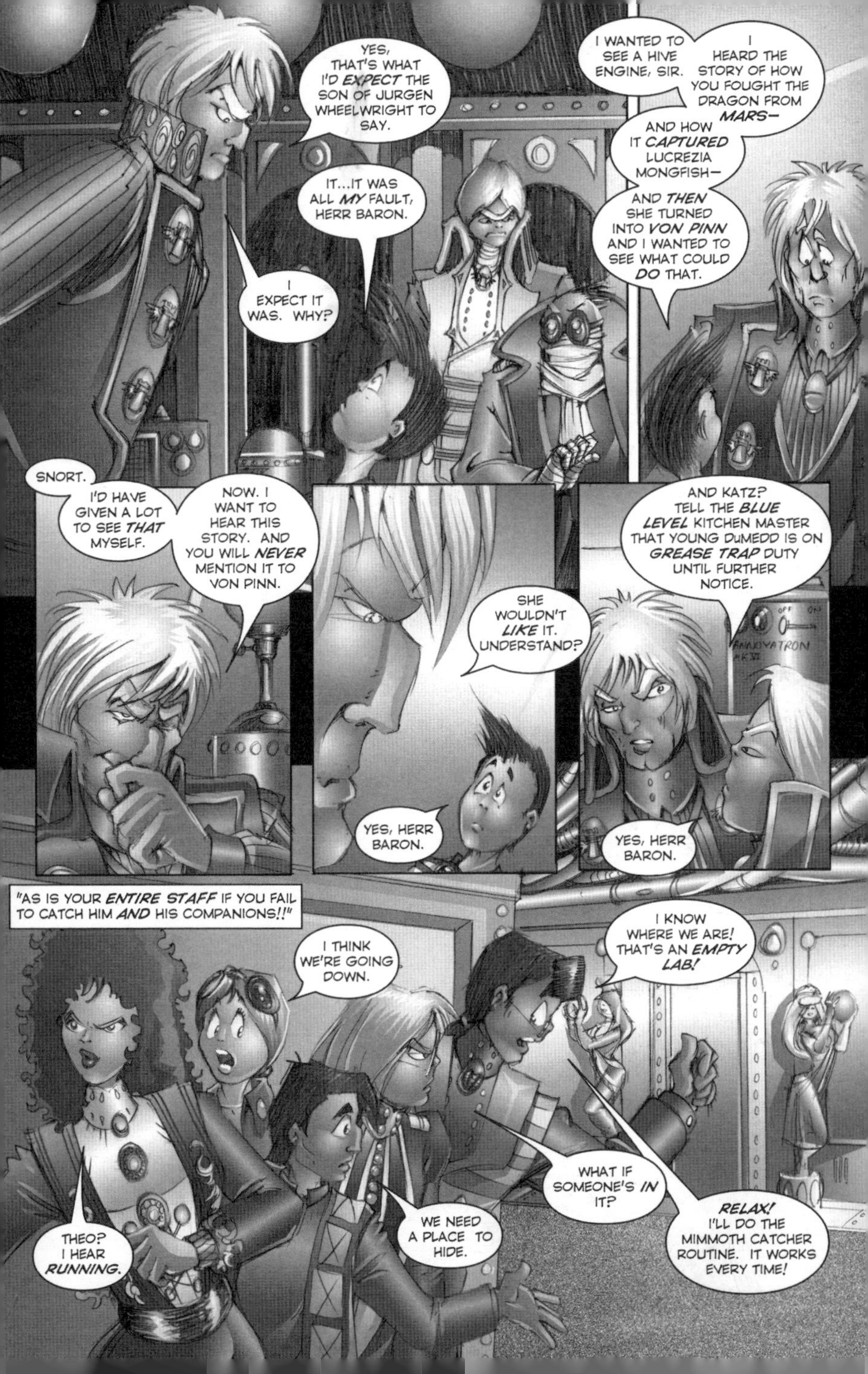
YES, THAT'S WHAT I'D EXPECT THE SON OF JURGEN WHEELWRIGHT TO SAY.
IT...IT WAS ALL MY FAULT, HERR BARON.
I EXPECT IT WAS. WHY?
I WANTED TO SEE A HIVE ENGINE, SIR.
I HEARD THE STORY OF HOW YOU FOUGHT THE DRAGON FROM MARS—
AND HOW IT CAPTURED LUCREZIA MONGFISH—
AND THEN SHE TURNED INTO VON PINN AND I WANTED TO SEE WHAT COULD DO THAT.
SNORT.
I'D HAVE GIVEN A LOT TO SEE THAT MYSELF.
NOW. I WANT TO HEAR THIS STORY. AND YOU WILL NEVER MENTION IT TO VON PINN.
SHE WOULDN'T LIKE IT. UNDERSTAND?
YES, HERR BARON.
AND KATZ? TELL THE BLUE LEVEL KITCHEN MASTER THAT YOUNG DuMEDD IS ON GREASE TRAP DUTY UNTIL FURTHER NOTICE.
OFF ON
YES, HERR BARON.
"AS IS YOUR ENTIRE STAFF IF YOU FAIL TO CATCH HIM AND HIS COMPANIONS!!"
I THINK WE'RE GOING DOWN.
I KNOW WHERE WE ARE! THAT'S AN EMPTY LAB!
THEO? I HEAR RUNNING.
WE NEED A PLACE TO HIDE.
WHAT IF SOMEONE'S IN IT?
RELAX! I'LL DO THE MIMMOTH CATCHER ROUTINE. IT WORKS EVERY TIME!

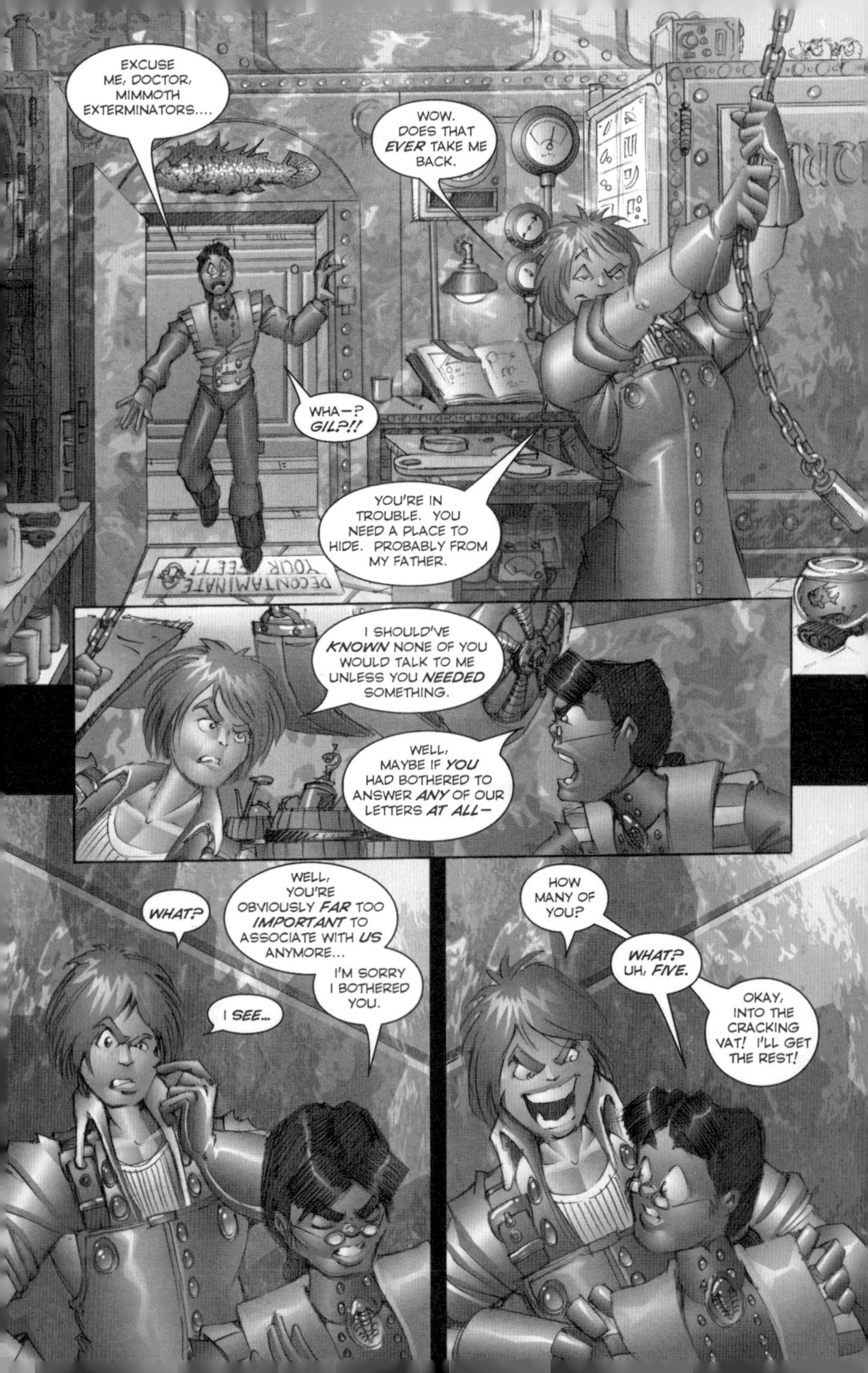
EXCUSE ME, DOCTOR, MIMMOTH EXTERMINATORS....
WOW. DOES THAT EVER TAKE ME BACK.
WHA—? GIL?!!
YOU'RE IN TROUBLE. YOU NEED A PLACE TO HIDE. PROBABLY FROM MY FATHER.
DECONTAMINATE YOUR FEET!
I SHOULD'VE KNOWN NONE OF YOU WOULD TALK TO ME UNLESS YOU NEEDED SOMETHING.
WELL, MAYBE IF YOU HAD BOTHERED TO ANSWER ANY OF OUR LETTERS AT ALL—
WHAT?
WELL, YOU'RE OBVIOUSLY FAR TOO IMPORTANT TO ASSOCIATE WITH US ANYMORE...
I'M SORRY I BOTHERED YOU.
I SEE...
HOW MANY OF YOU?
WHAT? UH, FIVE.
OKAY, INTO THE CRACKING VAT! I'LL GET THE REST!

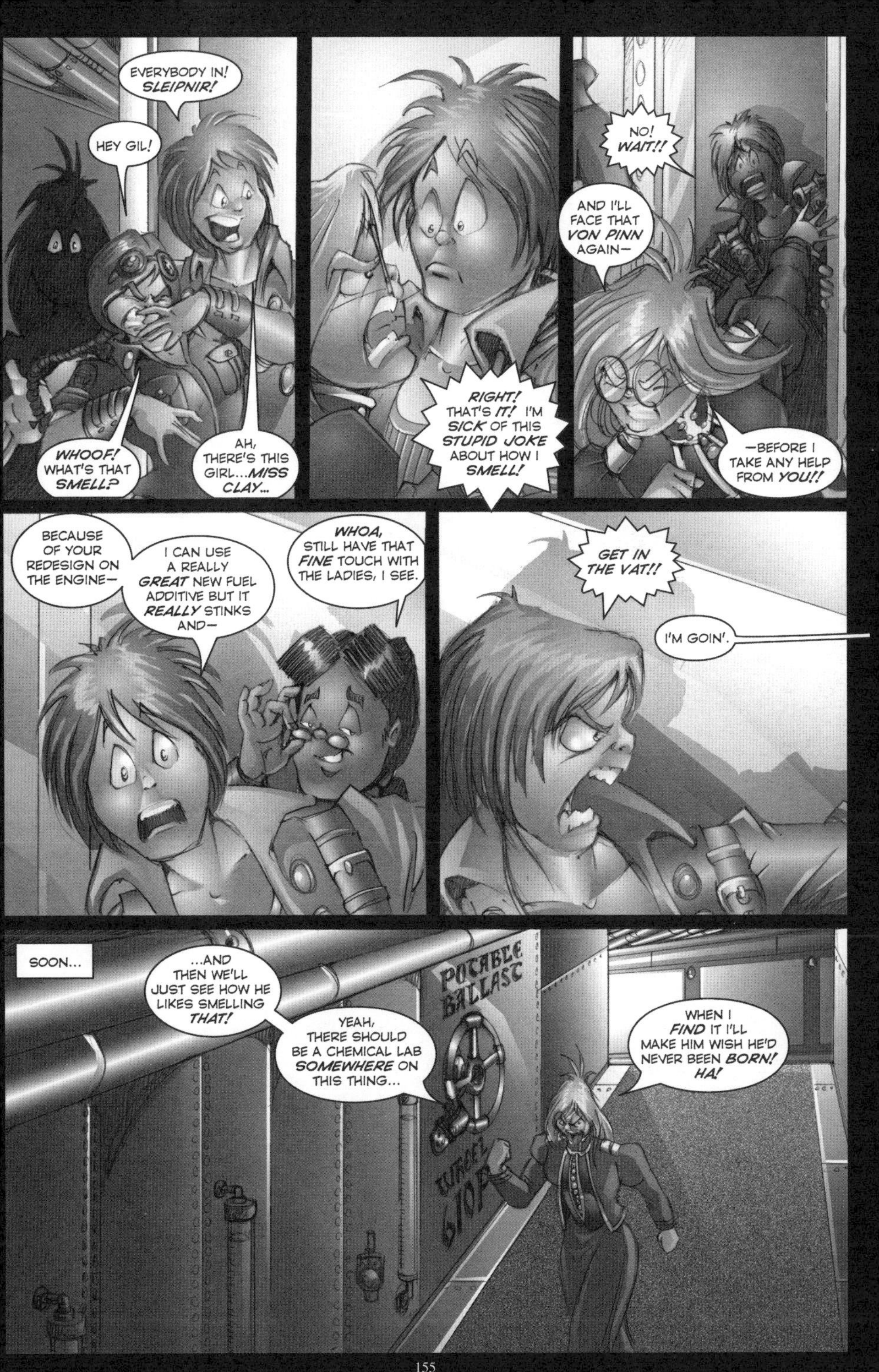
EVERYBODY IN! SLEIPNIR!
HEY GIL!
WHOOF! WHAT'S THAT SMELL?
AH, THERE'S THIS GIRL...MISS CLAY...
RIGHT! THAT'S IT! I'M SICK OF THIS STUPID JOKE ABOUT HOW I SMELL!
NO! WAIT!!
AND I'LL FACE THAT VON PINN AGAIN—
—BEFORE I TAKE ANY HELP FROM YOU!!
BECAUSE OF YOUR REDESIGN ON THE ENGINE—
I CAN USE A REALLY GREAT NEW FUEL ADDITIVE BUT IT REALLY STINKS AND—
WHOA, STILL HAVE THAT FINE TOUCH WITH THE LADIES, I SEE.
GET IN THE VAT!!
I'M GOIN'.
SOON...
...AND THEN WE'LL JUST SEE HOW HE LIKES SMELLING THAT!
POTABLE BALLAST
YEAH, THERE SHOULD BE A CHEMICAL LAB SOMEWHERE ON THIS THING...
WHEN I FIND IT I'LL MAKE HIM WISH HE'D NEVER BEEN BORN! HA!

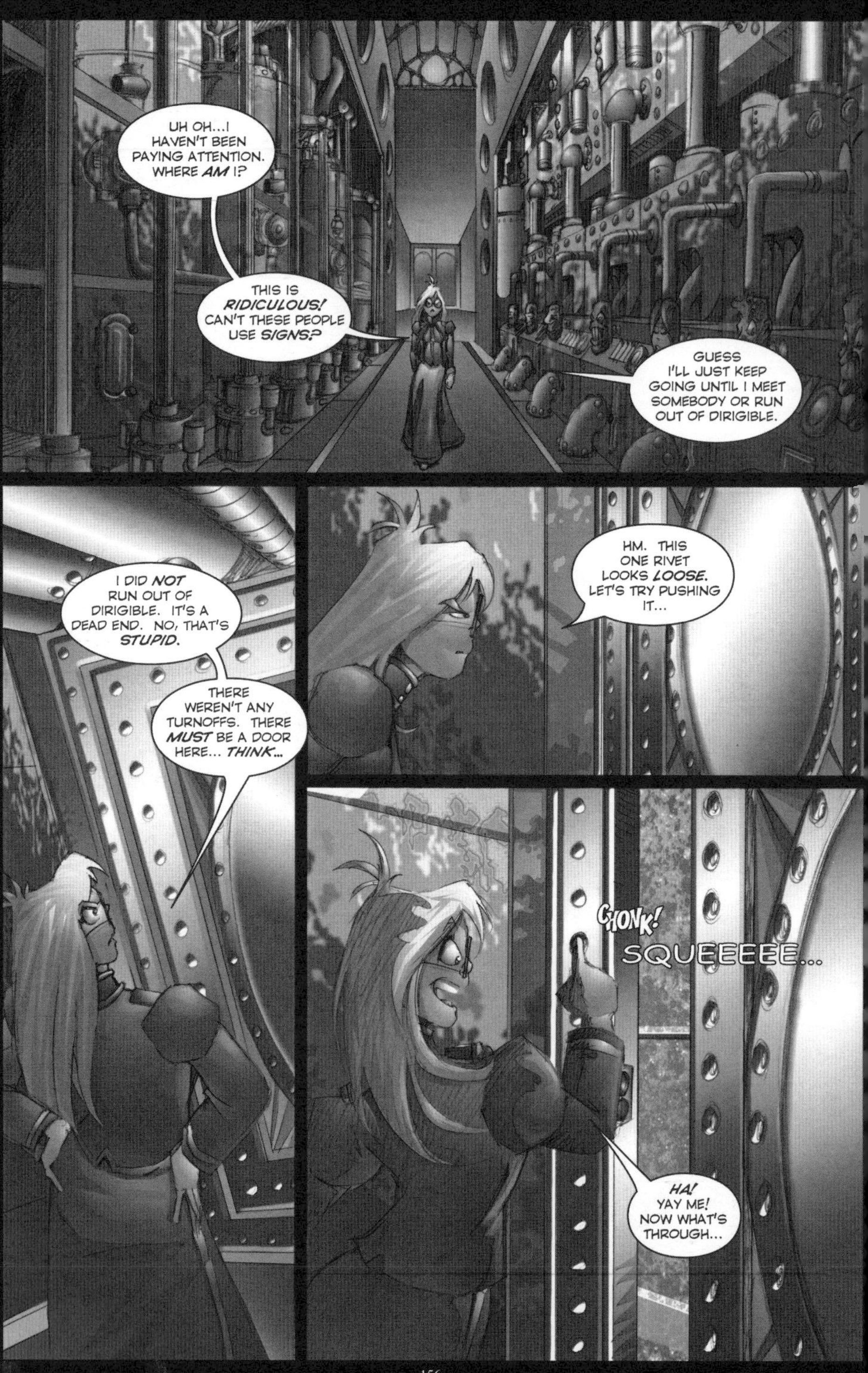
UH OH...I HAVEN'T BEEN PAYING ATTENTION. WHERE *AM* I?
THIS IS *RIDICULOUS!* CAN'T THESE PEOPLE USE *SIGNS?*
GUESS I'LL JUST KEEP GOING UNTIL I MEET SOMEBODY OR RUN OUT OF DIRIGIBLE.
I DID *NOT* RUN OUT OF DIRIGIBLE. IT'S A DEAD END. NO, THAT'S *STUPID.*
THERE WEREN'T ANY TURNOFFS. THERE *MUST* BE A DOOR HERE... *THINK...*
HM. THIS ONE RIVET LOOKS *LOOSE.* LET'S TRY PUSHING IT...
CHONK!
SQUEEEEEE...
HA! YAY ME! NOW WHAT'S THROUGH...

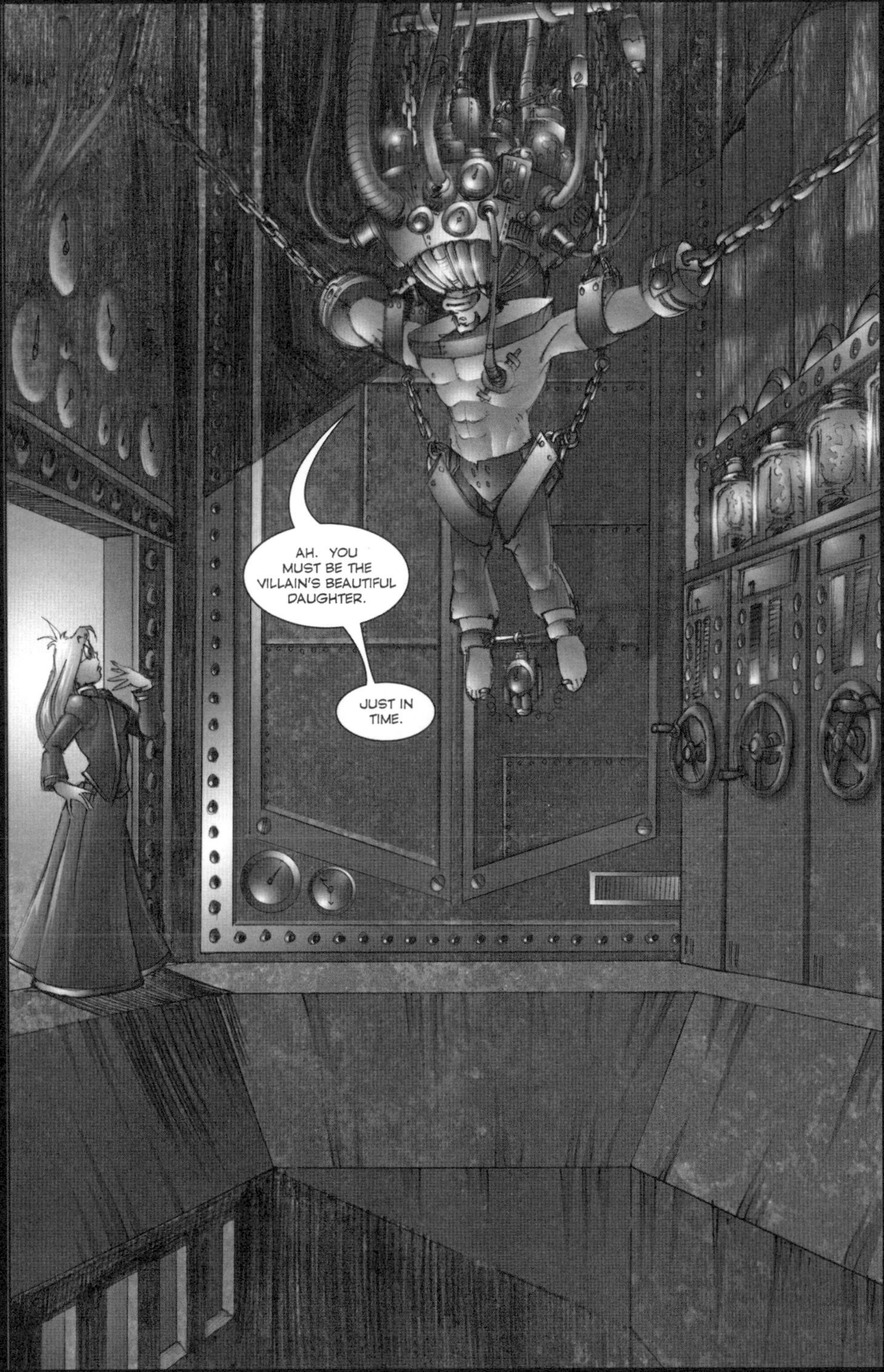
AH. YOU MUST BE THE VILLAIN'S BEAUTIFUL DAUGHTER.
JUST IN TIME.

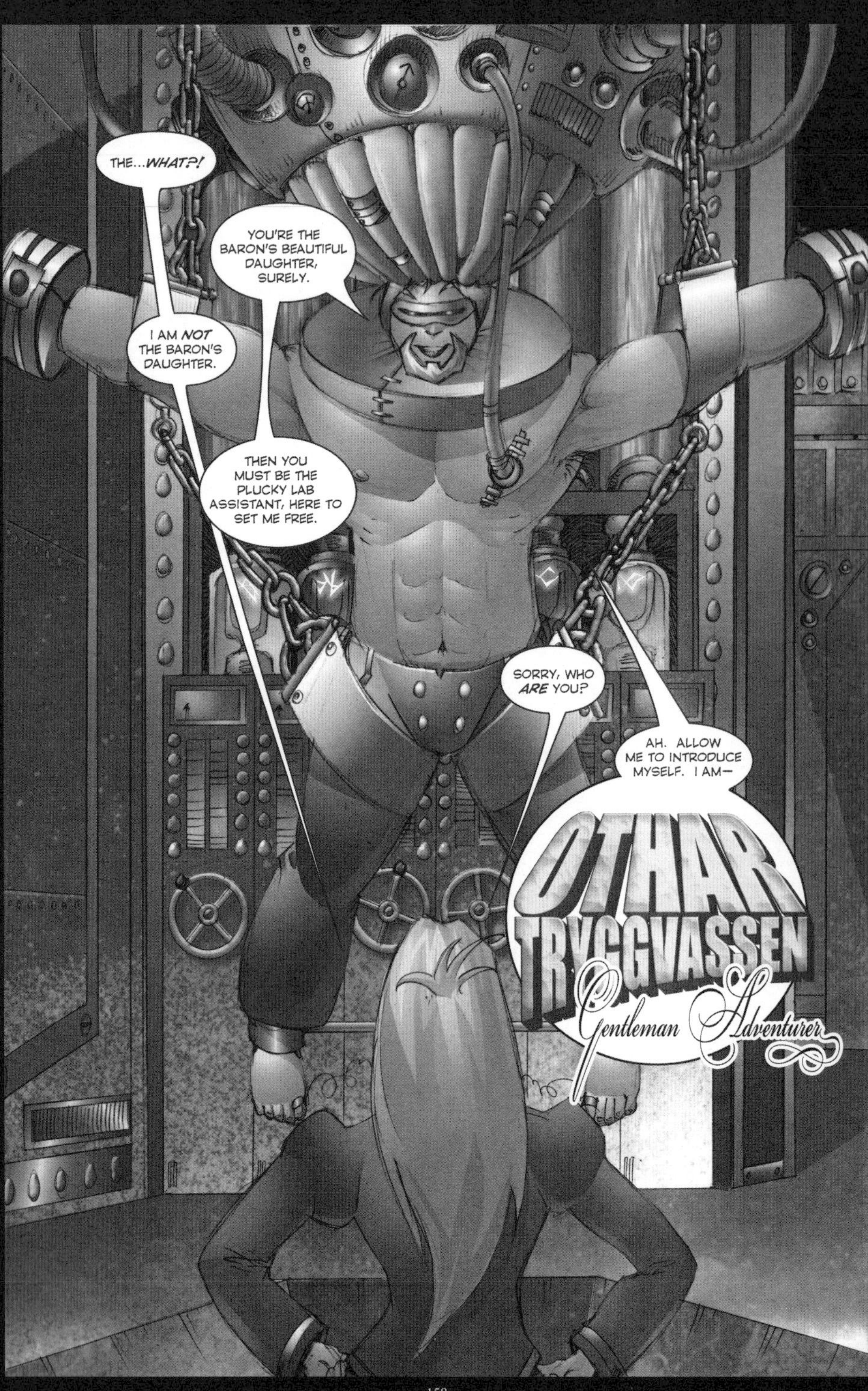
THE...WHAT?!
YOU'RE THE BARON'S BEAUTIFUL DAUGHTER, SURELY.
I AM NOT THE BARON'S DAUGHTER.
THEN YOU MUST BE THE PLUCKY LAB ASSISTANT, HERE TO SET ME FREE.
SORRY, WHO ARE YOU?
AH. ALLOW ME TO INTRODUCE MYSELF. I AM—
OTHAR TRYGGVASSEN
Gentleman Adventurer

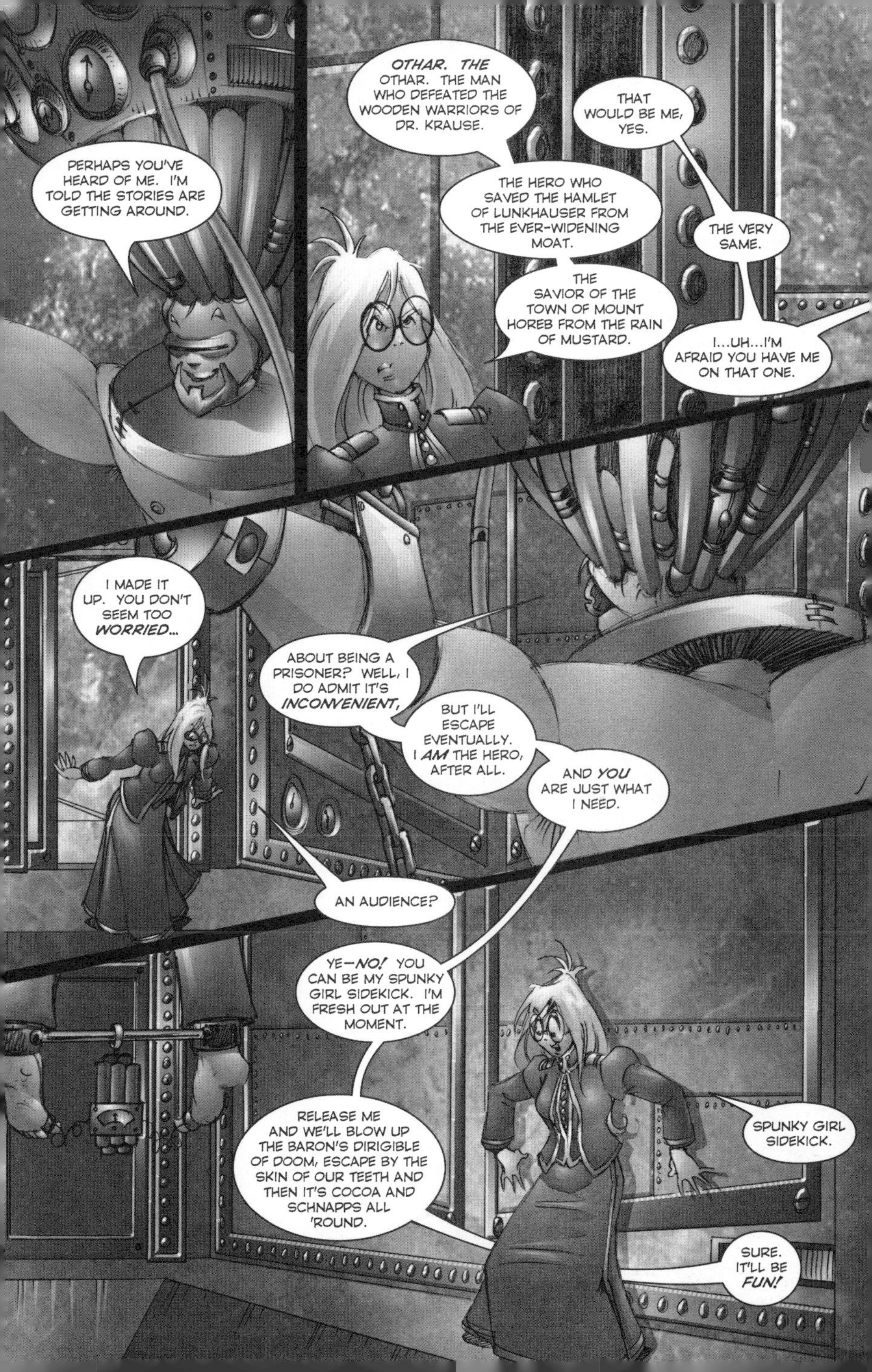
PERHAPS YOU'VE HEARD OF ME. I'M TOLD THE STORIES ARE GETTING AROUND.
OTHAR. THE OTHAR. THE MAN WHO DEFEATED THE WOODEN WARRIORS OF DR. KRAUSE.
THAT WOULD BE ME, YES.
THE HERO WHO SAVED THE HAMLET OF LUNKHAUSER FROM THE EVER-WIDENING MOAT.
THE VERY SAME.
THE SAVIOR OF THE TOWN OF MOUNT HOREB FROM THE RAIN OF MUSTARD.
I...UH...I'M AFRAID YOU HAVE ME ON THAT ONE.
I MADE IT UP. YOU DON'T SEEM TOO *WORRIED...*
ABOUT BEING A PRISONER? WELL, I DO ADMIT IT'S *INCONVENIENT,*
BUT I'LL ESCAPE EVENTUALLY. I *AM* THE HERO, AFTER ALL.
AND *YOU* ARE JUST WHAT I NEED.
AN AUDIENCE?
YE—*NO!* YOU CAN BE MY SPUNKY GIRL SIDEKICK. I'M FRESH OUT AT THE MOMENT.
RELEASE ME AND WE'LL BLOW UP THE BARON'S DIRIGIBLE OF DOOM, ESCAPE BY THE SKIN OF OUR TEETH AND THEN IT'S COCOA AND SCHNAPPS ALL 'ROUND.
SPUNKY GIRL SIDEKICK.
SURE. IT'LL BE *FUN!*

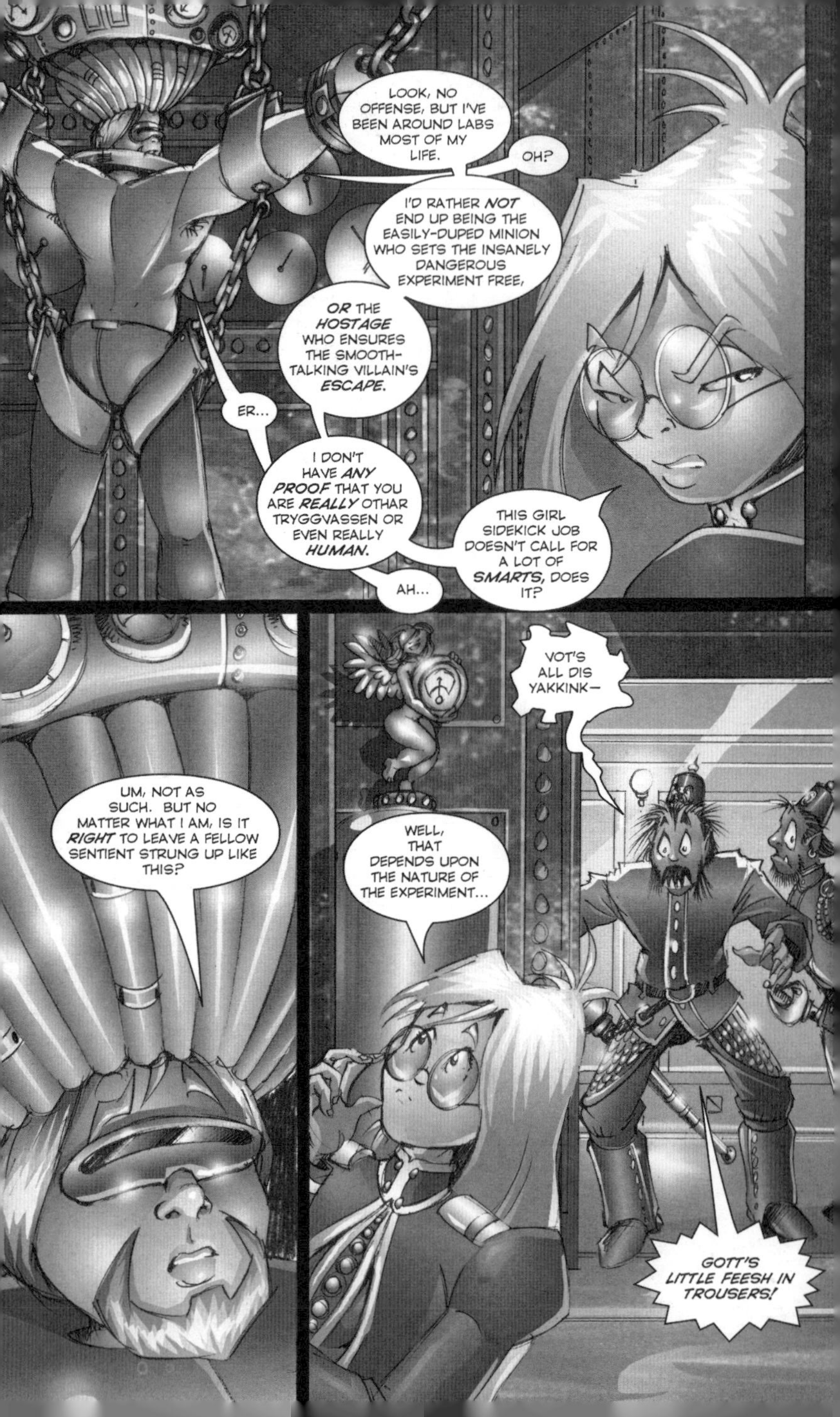
LOOK, NO OFFENSE, BUT I'VE BEEN AROUND LABS MOST OF MY LIFE.
OH?
I'D RATHER *NOT* END UP BEING THE EASILY-DUPED MINION WHO SETS THE INSANELY DANGEROUS EXPERIMENT FREE,
OR THE *HOSTAGE* WHO ENSURES THE SMOOTH-TALKING VILLAIN'S *ESCAPE*.
ER...
I DON'T HAVE *ANY PROOF* THAT YOU ARE *REALLY* OTHAR TRYGGVASSEN OR EVEN REALLY *HUMAN*.
AH...
THIS GIRL SIDEKICK JOB DOESN'T CALL FOR A LOT OF *SMARTS*, DOES IT?
UM, NOT AS SUCH. BUT NO MATTER WHAT I AM, IS IT *RIGHT* TO LEAVE A FELLOW SENTIENT STRUNG UP LIKE THIS?
WELL, THAT DEPENDS UPON THE NATURE OF THE EXPERIMENT...
VOT'S ALL DIS YAKKINK—
GOTT'S LITTLE FEESH IN TROUSERS!

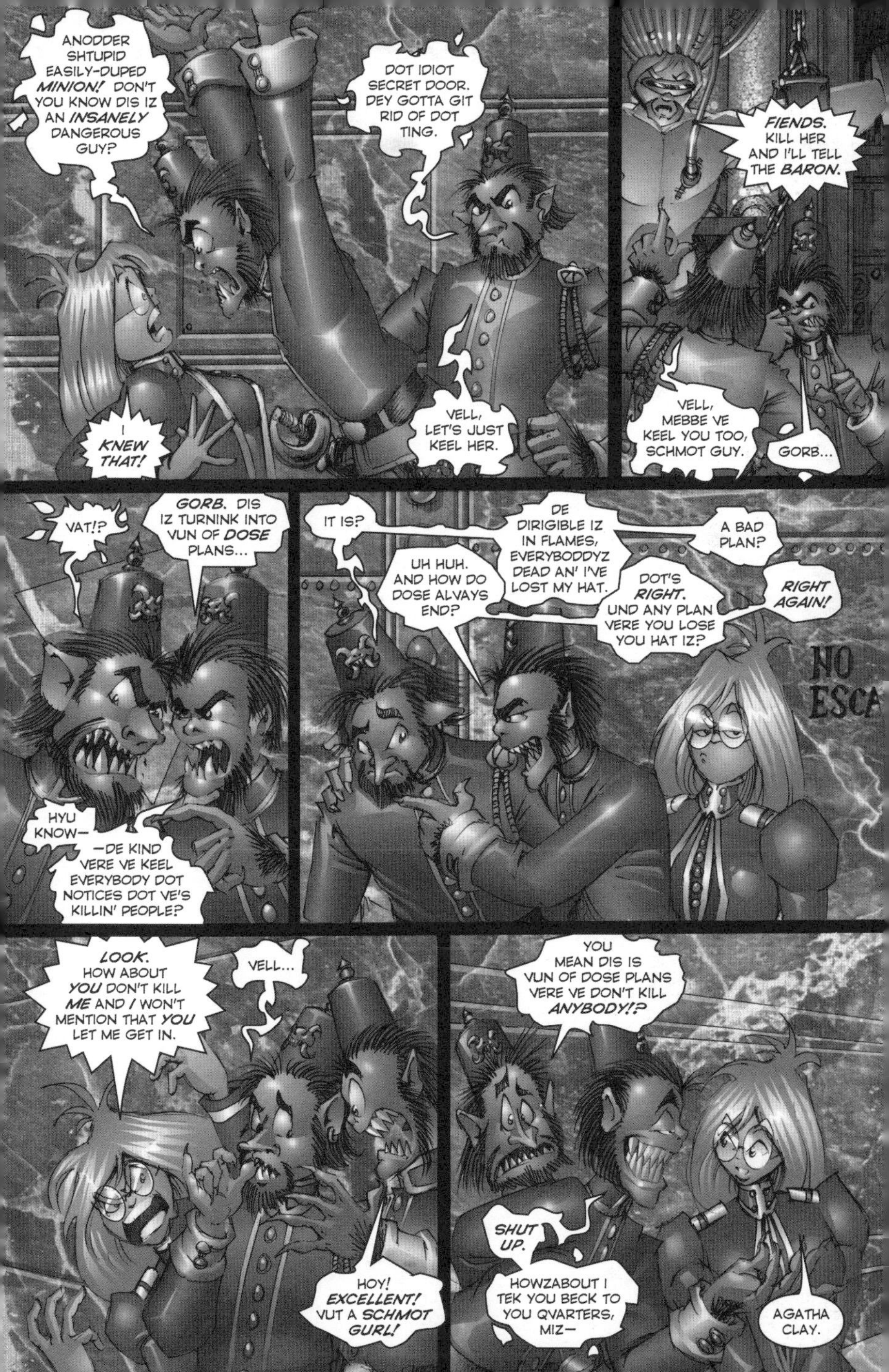
ANODDER SHTUPID EASILY-DUPED MINION! DON'T YOU KNOW DIS IZ AN INSANELY DANGEROUS GUY?
I KNEW THAT!
DOT IDIOT SECRET DOOR. DEY GOTTA GIT RID OF DOT TING.
VELL, LET'S JUST KEEL HER.
FIENDS. KILL HER AND I'LL TELL THE BARON.
VELL, MEBBE VE KEEL YOU TOO, SCHMOT GUY.
GORB...
VAT!?
GORB. DIS IZ TURNINK INTO VUN OF DOSE PLANS...
HYU KNOW—
—DE KIND VERE VE KEEL EVERYBODY DOT NOTICES DOT VE'S KILLIN' PEOPLE?
IT IS?
DE DIRIGIBLE IZ IN FLAMES, EVERYBODDYZ DEAD AN' I'VE LOST MY HAT.
A BAD PLAN?
UH HUH. AND HOW DO DOSE ALVAYS END?
DOT'S RIGHT. UND ANY PLAN VERE YOU LOSE YOU HAT IZ?
RIGHT AGAIN!
NO ESCA
LOOK. HOW ABOUT YOU DON'T KILL ME AND I WON'T MENTION THAT YOU LET ME GET IN.
VELL...
HOY! EXCELLENT! VUT A SCHMOT GURL!
YOU MEAN DIS IS VUN OF DOSE PLANS VERE VE DON'T KILL ANYBODY!?
SHUT UP.
HOWZABOUT I TEK YOU BECK TO YOU QVARTERS, MIZ—
AGATHA CLAY.

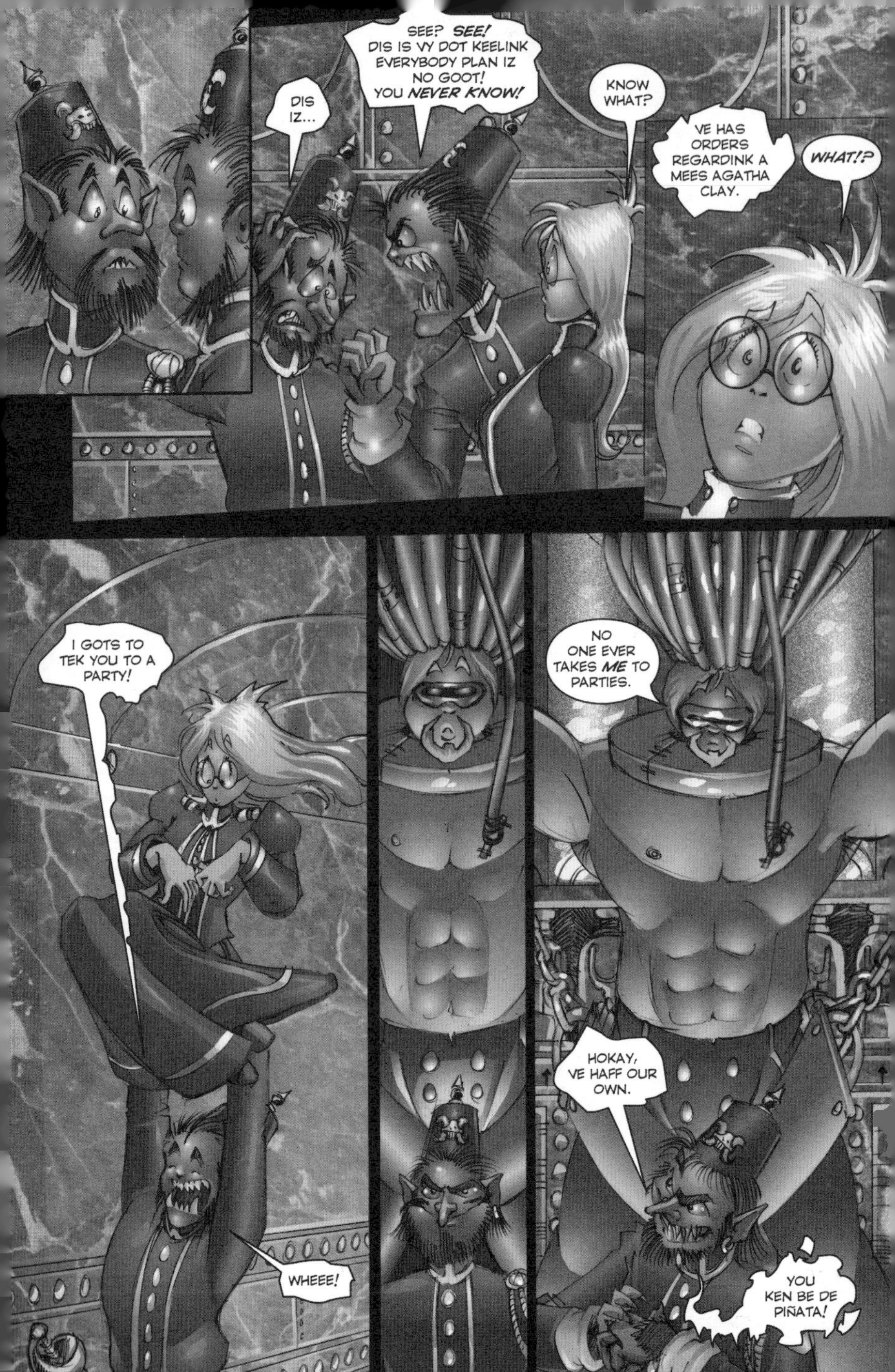

DIS IZ...
SEE? SEE! DIS IS VY DOT KEELINK EVERYBODY PLAN IZ NO GOOT! YOU NEVER KNOW!
KNOW WHAT?
VE HAS ORDERS REGARDINK A MEES AGATHA CLAY.
WHAT!?
I GOTS TO TEK YOU TO A PARTY!
WHEEE!
NO ONE EVER TAKES ME TO PARTIES.
HOKAY, VE HAFF OUR OWN.
YOU KEN BE DE PIÑATA!

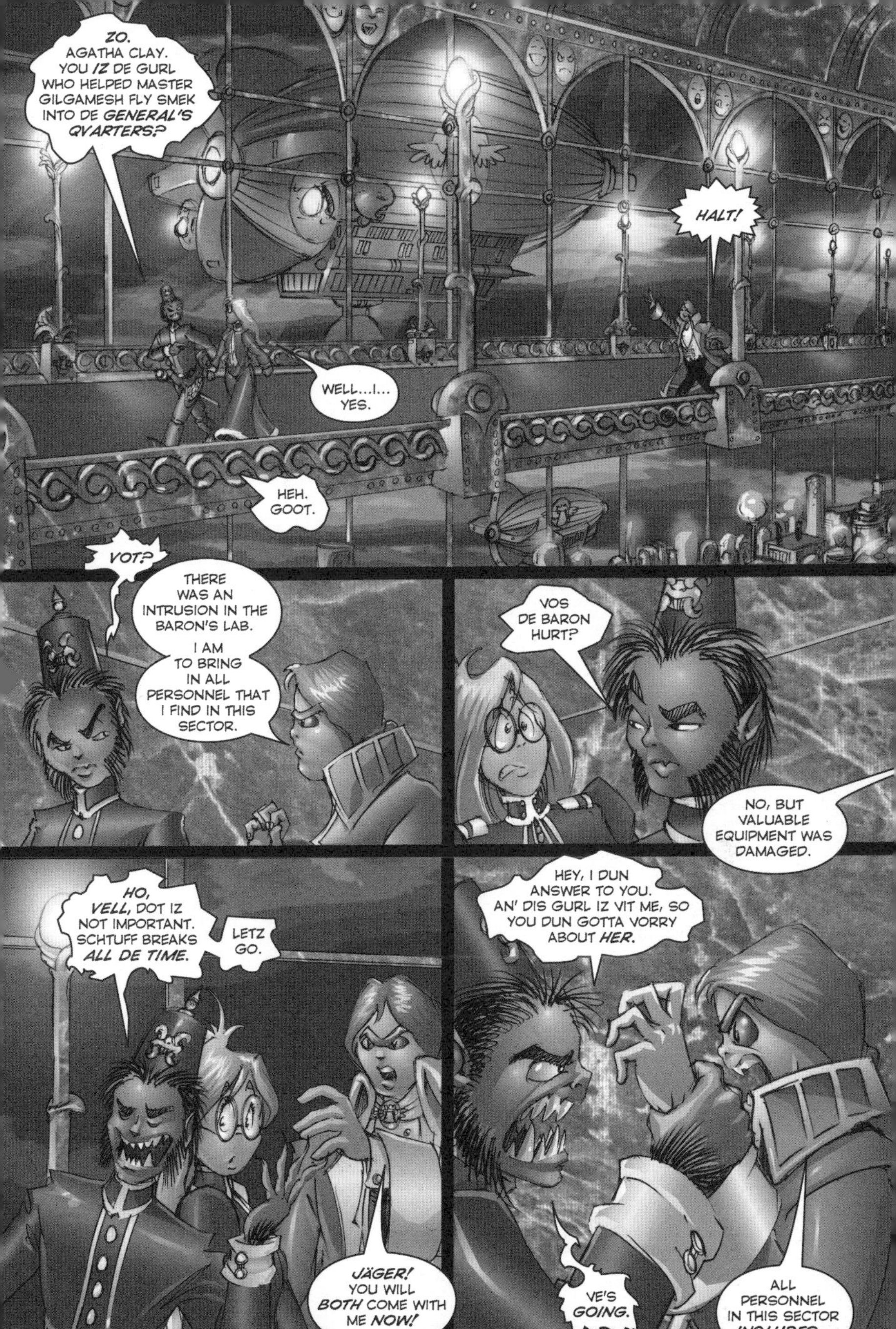
ZO. AGATHA CLAY. YOU IZ DE GURL WHO HELPED MASTER GILGAMESH FLY SMEK INTO DE GENERAL'S QVARTERS?
HALT!
WELL...I... YES.
HEH. GOOT.
VOT?
THERE WAS AN INTRUSION IN THE BARON'S LAB.
I AM TO BRING IN ALL PERSONNEL THAT I FIND IN THIS SECTOR.
VOS DE BARON HURT?
NO, BUT VALUABLE EQUIPMENT WAS DAMAGED.
HO, VELL, DOT IZ NOT IMPORTANT. SCHTUFF BREAKS ALL DE TIME.
LETZ GO.
JÄGER! YOU WILL BOTH COME WITH ME NOW!
HEY, I DUN ANSWER TO YOU. AN' DIS GURL IZ VIT ME, SO YOU DUN GOTTA VORRY ABOUT HER.
VE'S GOING.
ALL PERSONNEL IN THIS SECTOR INCLUDES—

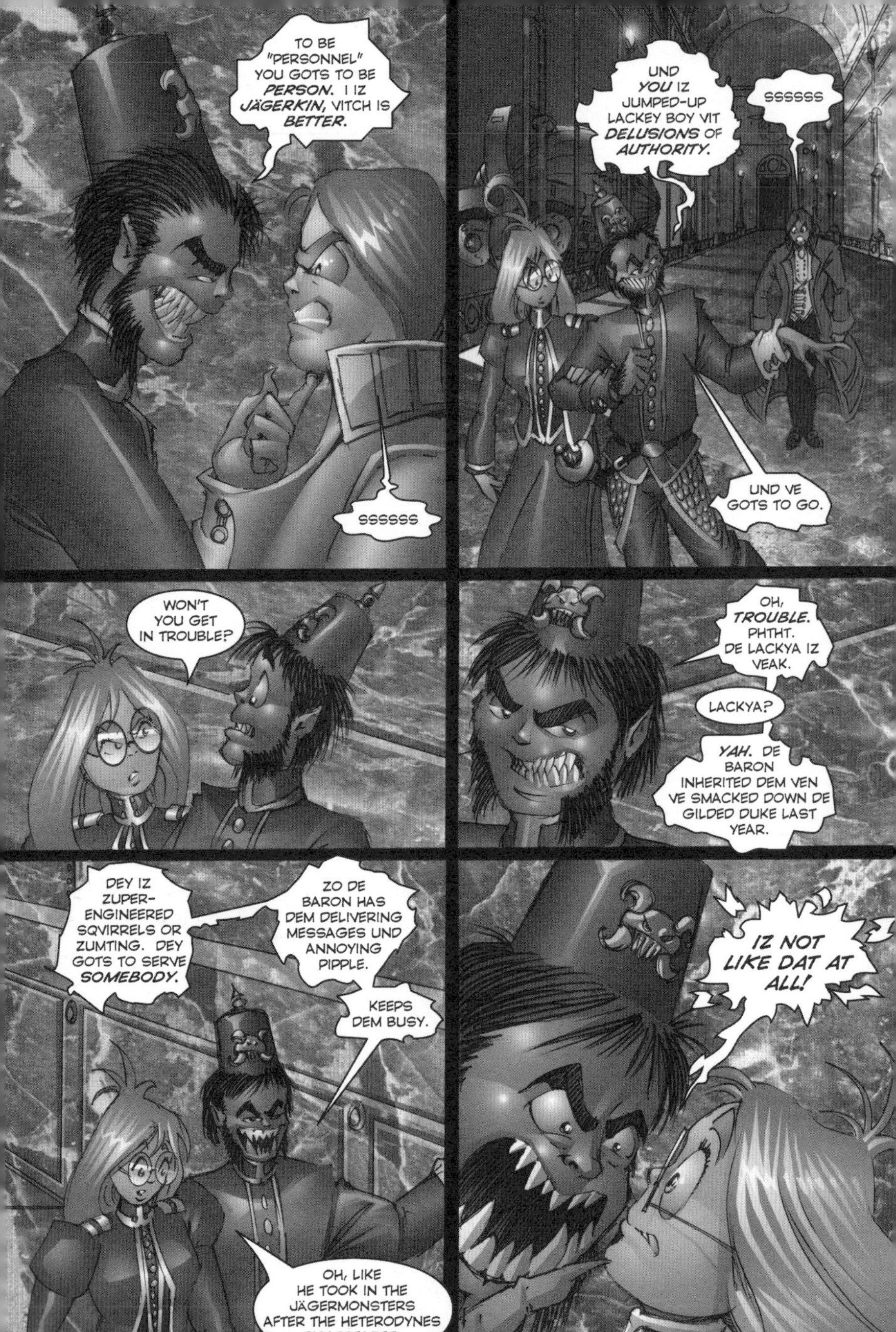
TO BE "PERSONNEL" YOU GOTS TO BE *PERSON.* I IZ *JÄGERKIN,* VITCH IS *BETTER.*
SSSSSS
UND *YOU* IZ JUMPED-UP LACKEY BOY VIT *DELUSIONS* OF *AUTHORITY.*
SSSSSS
UND VE GOTS TO GO.
WON'T YOU GET IN TROUBLE?
OH, *TROUBLE.* PHTHT. DE LACKYA IZ VEAK.
LACKYA?
YAH. DE BARON INHERITED DEM VEN VE SMACKED DOWN DE GILDED DUKE LAST YEAR.
DEY IZ ZUPER-ENGINEERED SQVIRRELS OR ZUMTING. DEY GOTS TO SERVE *SOMEBODY.*
ZO DE BARON HAS DEM DELIVERING MESSAGES UND ANNOYING PIPPLE.
KEEPS DEM BUSY.
OH, LIKE HE TOOK IN THE JÄGERMONSTERS AFTER THE HETERODYNES DISAPPEARED.
IZ NOT LIKE DAT AT ALL!

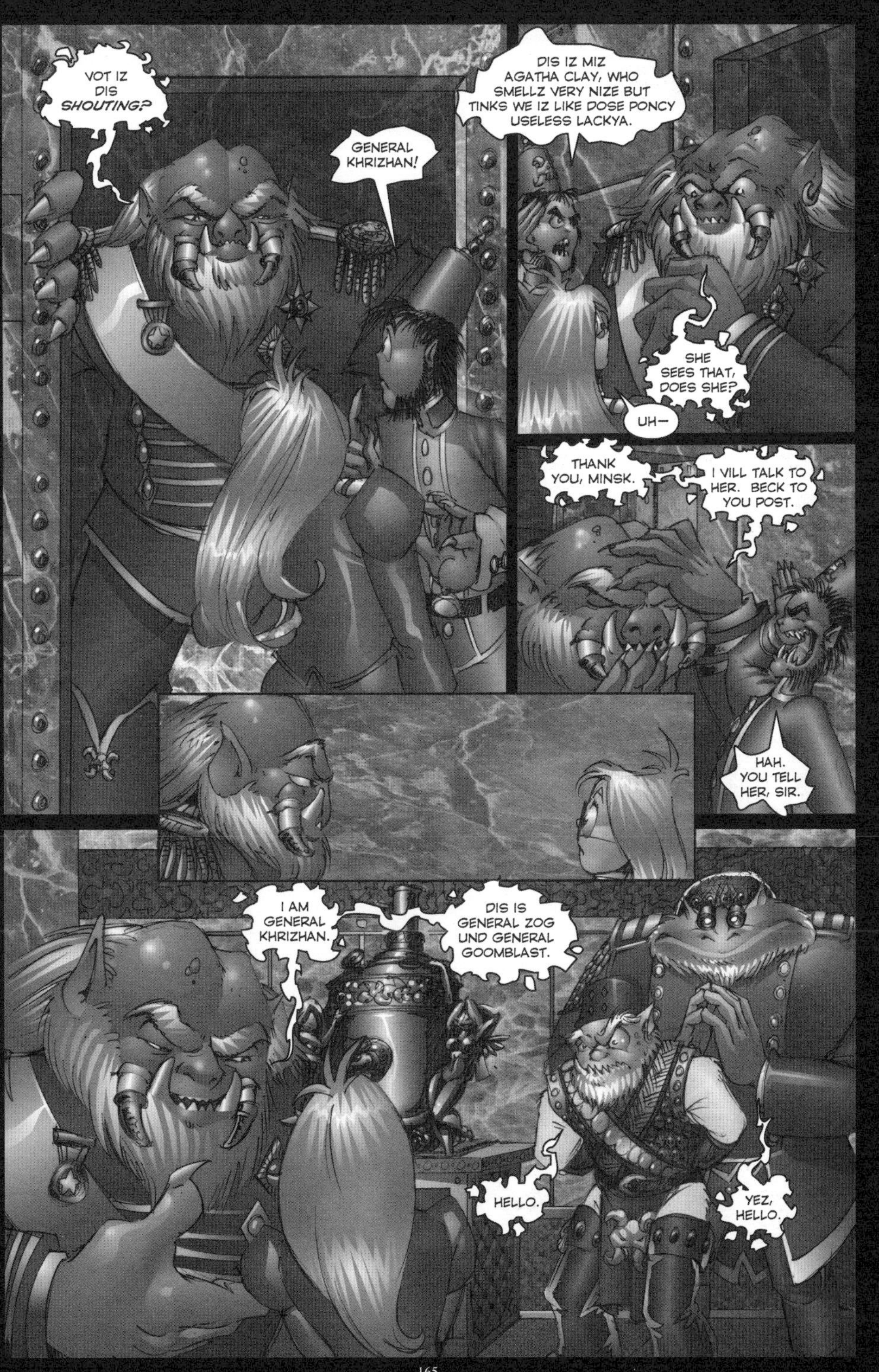
VOT IZ DIS *SHOUTING?*
GENERAL KHRIZHAN!
DIS IZ MIZ AGATHA CLAY, WHO SMELLZ VERY NIZE BUT TINKS WE IZ LIKE DOSE PONCY USELESS LACKYA.
SHE SEES THAT, DOES SHE?
UH—
THANK YOU, MINSK.
I VILL TALK TO HER. BECK TO YOU POST.
HAH. YOU TELL HER, SIR.
I AM GENERAL KHRIZHAN.
DIS IS GENERAL ZOG UND GENERAL GOOMBLAST.
HELLO.
YEZ, HELLO.

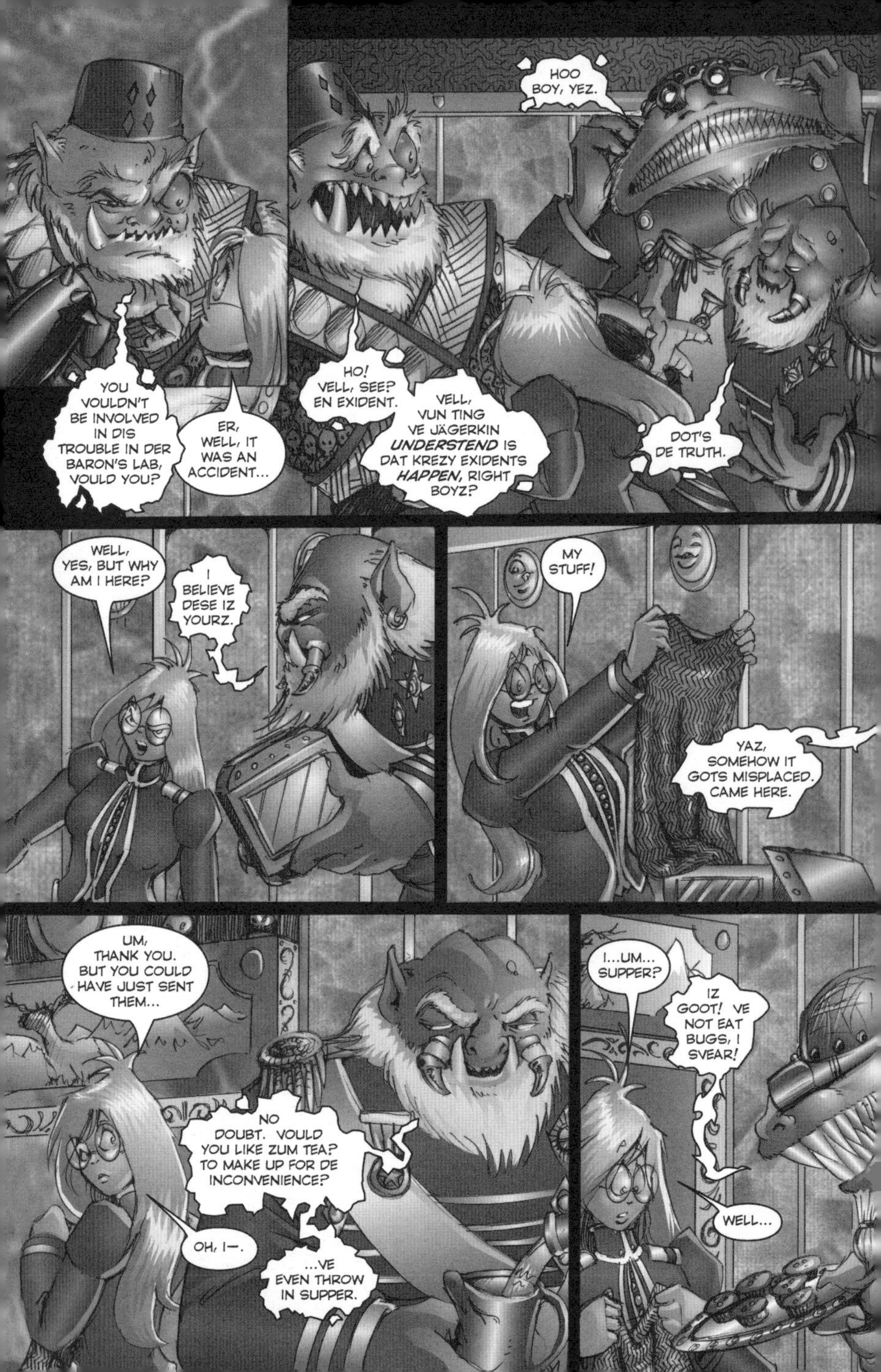

YOU VOULDN'T BE INVOLVED IN DIS TROUBLE IN DER BARON'S LAB, VOULD YOU?
ER, WELL, IT WAS AN ACCIDENT...
HO! VELL, SEE? EN EXIDENT.
VELL, VUN TING VE JÄGERKIN UNDERSTEND IS DAT KREZY EXIDENTS HAPPEN, RIGHT BOYZ?
HOO BOY, YEZ.
DOT'S DE TRUTH.
WELL, YES, BUT WHY AM I HERE?
I BELIEVE DESE IZ YOURZ.
MY STUFF!
YAZ, SOMEHOW IT GOTS MISPLACED. CAME HERE.
UM, THANK YOU. BUT YOU COULD HAVE JUST SENT THEM...
NO DOUBT. VOULD YOU LIKE ZUM TEA? TO MAKE UP FOR DE INCONVENIENCE?
OH, I—.
...VE EVEN THROW IN SUPPER.
I...UM... SUPPER?
IZ GOOT! VE NOT EAT BUGS, I SVEAR!
WELL...

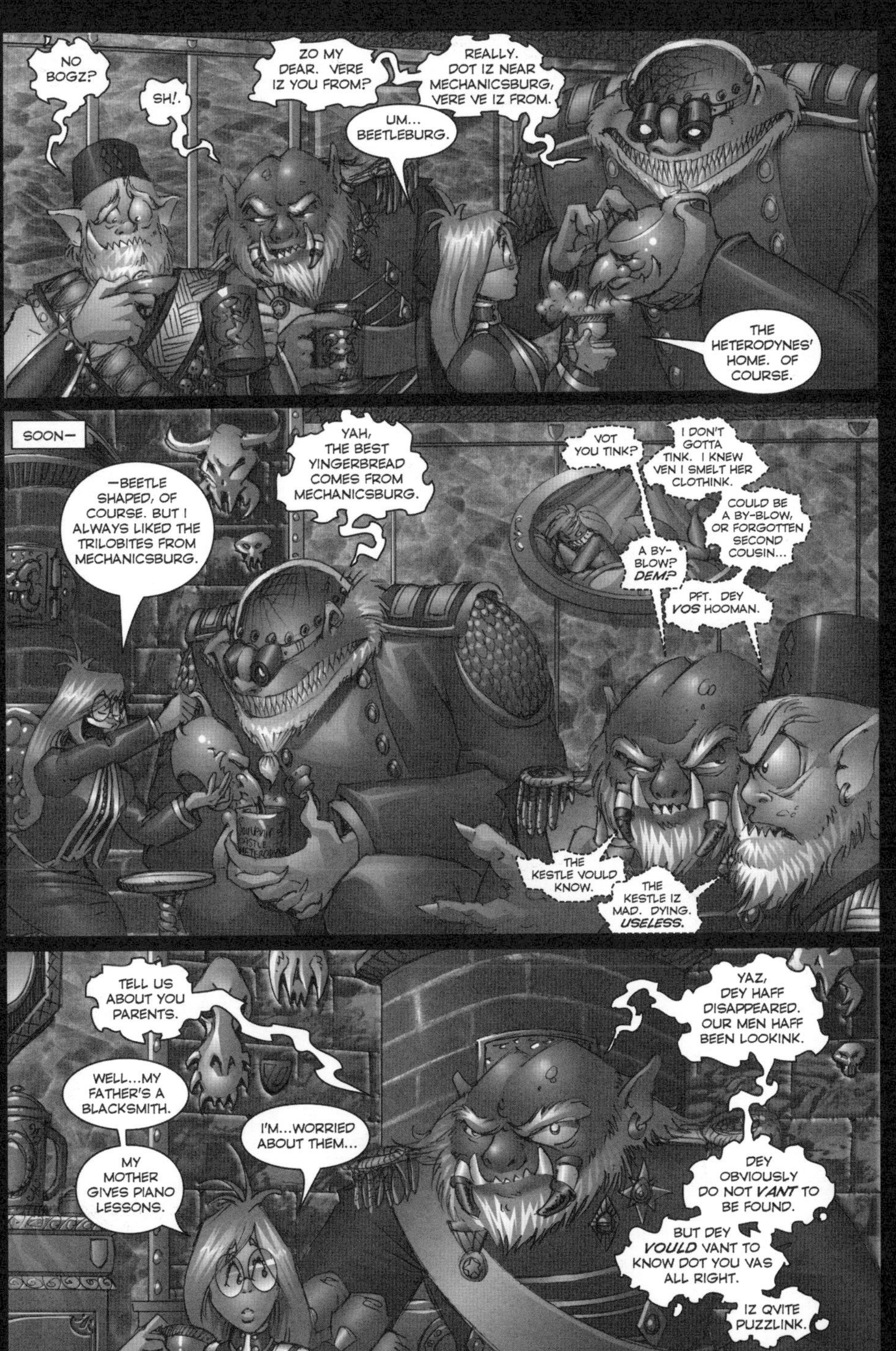
NO BOGZ?
SH!.
ZO MY DEAR. VERE IZ YOU FROM?
UM... BEETLEBURG.
REALLY. DOT IZ NEAR MECHANICSBURG, VERE VE IZ FROM.
THE HETERODYNES' HOME. OF COURSE.
SOON—
—BEETLE SHAPED, OF COURSE. BUT I ALWAYS LIKED THE TRILOBITES FROM MECHANICSBURG.
YAH, THE BEST YINGERBREAD COMES FROM MECHANICSBURG.
VOT YOU TINK?
I DON'T GOTTA TINK. I KNEW VEN I SMELT HER CLOTHINK.
COULD BE A BY-BLOW, OR FORGOTTEN SECOND COUSIN...
A BY-BLOW? DEM?
PFT. DEY VOS HOOMAN.
THE KESTLE VOULD KNOW.
THE KESTLE IZ MAD. DYING. USELESS.
TELL US ABOUT YOU PARENTS.
WELL...MY FATHER'S A BLACKSMITH.
MY MOTHER GIVES PIANO LESSONS.
I'M...WORRIED ABOUT THEM...
YAZ, DEY HAFF DISAPPEARED. OUR MEN HAFF BEEN LOOKINK.
DEY OBVIOUSLY DO NOT VANT TO BE FOUND.
BUT DEY VOULD VANT TO KNOW DOT YOU VAS ALL RIGHT.
IZ QVITE PUZZLINK.

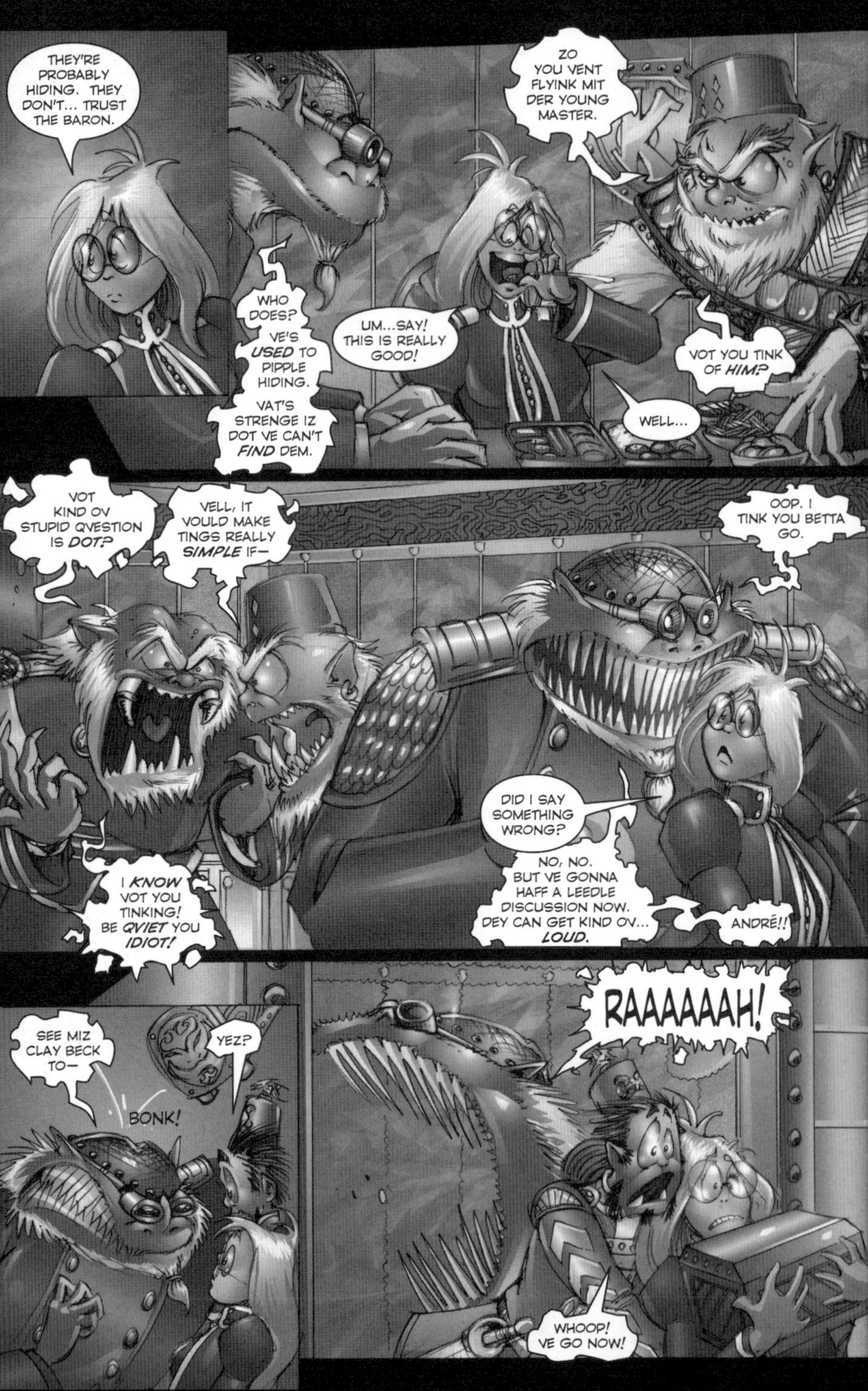
THEY'RE PROBABLY HIDING. THEY DON'T... TRUST THE BARON.
WHO DOES? VE'S *USED* TO PIPPLE HIDING.
VAT'S STRENGE IZ DOT VE CAN'T *FIND* DEM.
ZO YOU VENT FLYINK MIT DER YOUNG MASTER.
UM...SAY! THIS IS REALLY GOOD!
VOT YOU TINK OF *HIM?*
WELL...
VOT KIND OV STUPID QVESTION IS *DOT?*
VELL, IT VOULD MAKE TINGS REALLY *SIMPLE* IF—
OOP. I TINK YOU BETTA GO.
DID I SAY SOMETHING WRONG?
I *KNOW* VOT YOU TINKING! BE *QVIET* YOU *IDIOT!*
NO, NO. BUT VE GONNA HAFF A LEEDLE DISCUSSION NOW. DEY CAN GET KIND OV... *LOUD*.
ANDRÉ!!
SEE MIZ CLAY BECK TO—
YEZ?
BONK!
RAAAAAAH!
WHOOP! VE GO NOW!

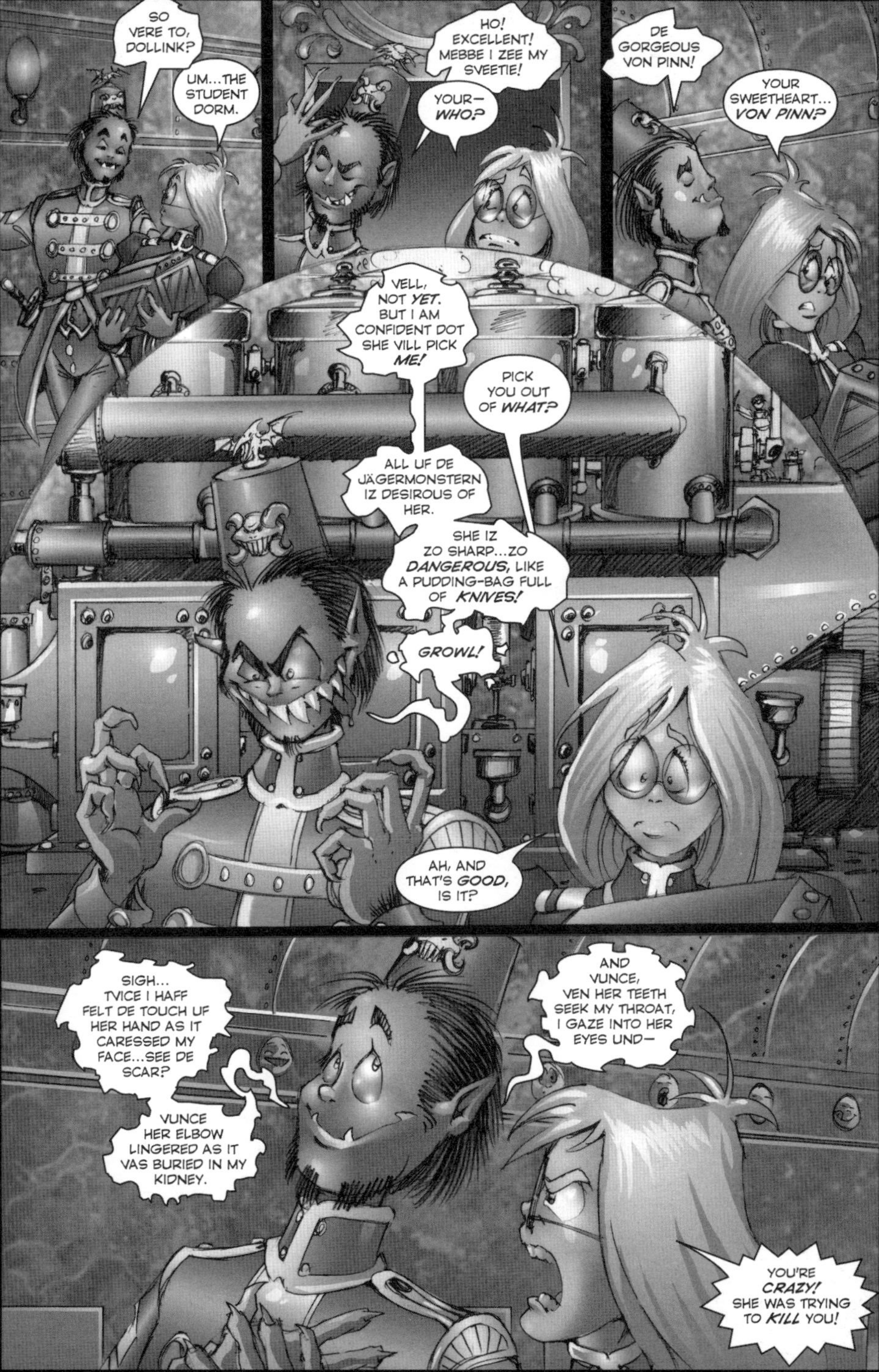
SO VERE TO, DOLLINK?
UM...THE STUDENT DORM.
HO! EXCELLENT! MEBBE I ZEE MY SVEETIE!
YOUR— WHO?
DE GORGEOUS VON PINN!
YOUR SWEETHEART... VON PINN?
VELL, NOT YET. BUT I AM CONFIDENT DOT SHE VILL PICK ME!
PICK YOU OUT OF WHAT?
ALL UF DE JÄGERMONSTERN IZ DESIROUS OF HER.
SHE IZ ZO SHARP...ZO DANGEROUS, LIKE A PUDDING-BAG FULL OF KNIVES!
GROWL!
AH, AND THAT'S GOOD, IS IT?
SIGH... TVICE I HAFF FELT DE TOUCH UF HER HAND AS IT CARESSED MY FACE...SEE DE SCAR?
VUNCE HER ELBOW LINGERED AS IT VAS BURIED IN MY KIDNEY.
AND VUNCE, VEN HER TEETH SEEK MY THROAT, I GAZE INTO HER EYES UND—
YOU'RE CRAZY! SHE WAS TRYING TO KILL YOU!

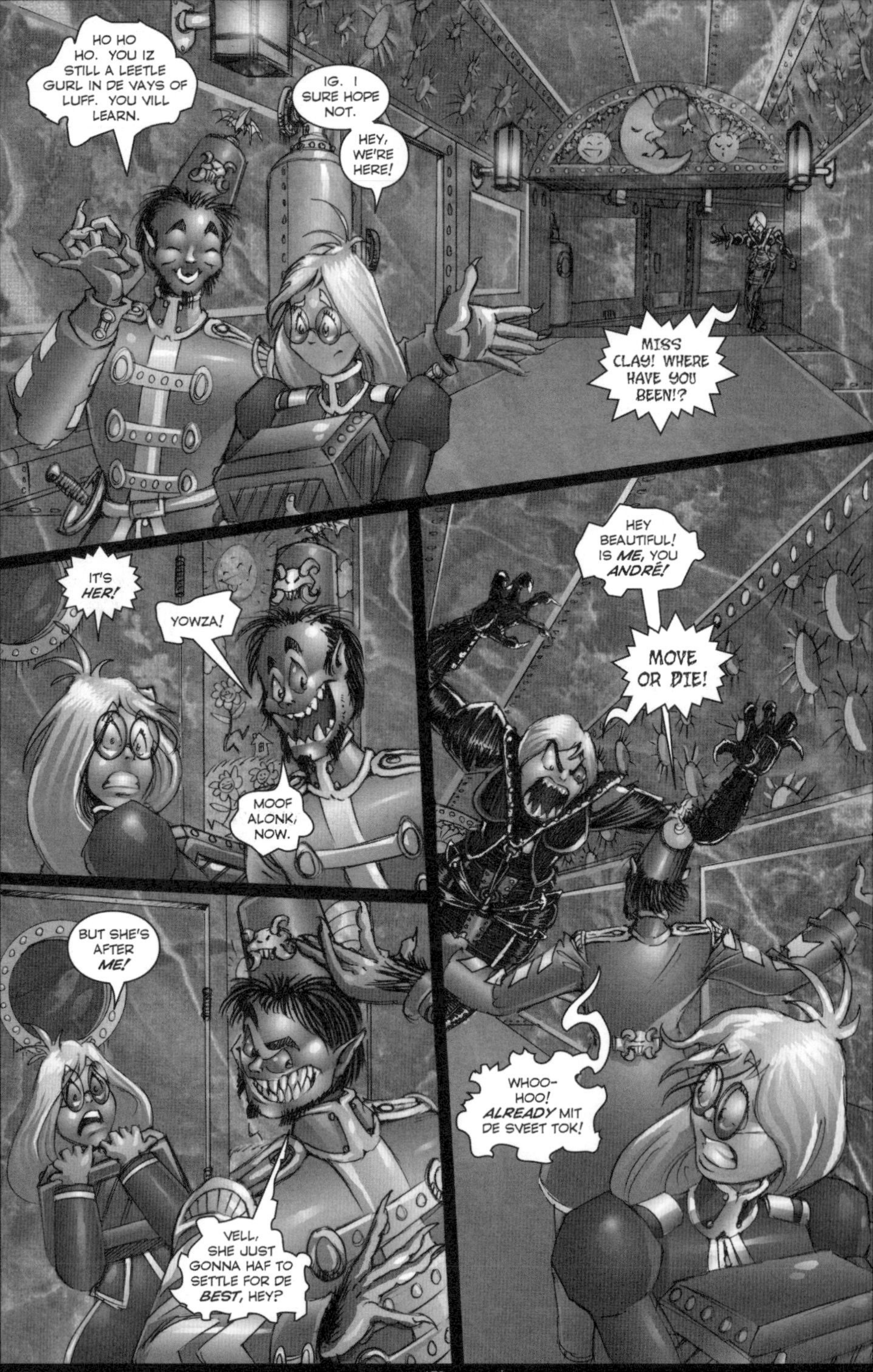
HO HO HO. YOU IZ STILL A LEETLE GURL IN DE VAYS OF LUFF. YOU VILL LEARN.
IG. I SURE HOPE NOT.
HEY, WE'RE HERE!
MISS CLAY! WHERE HAVE YOU BEEN!?
IT'S HER!
YOWZA!
MOOF ALONK, NOW.
HEY BEAUTIFUL! IS ME, YOU ANDRÉ!
MOVE OR DIE!
BUT SHE'S AFTER ME!
VELL, SHE JUST GONNA HAF TO SETTLE FOR DE BEST, HEY?
WHOO-HOO! ALREADY MIT DE SVEET TOK!

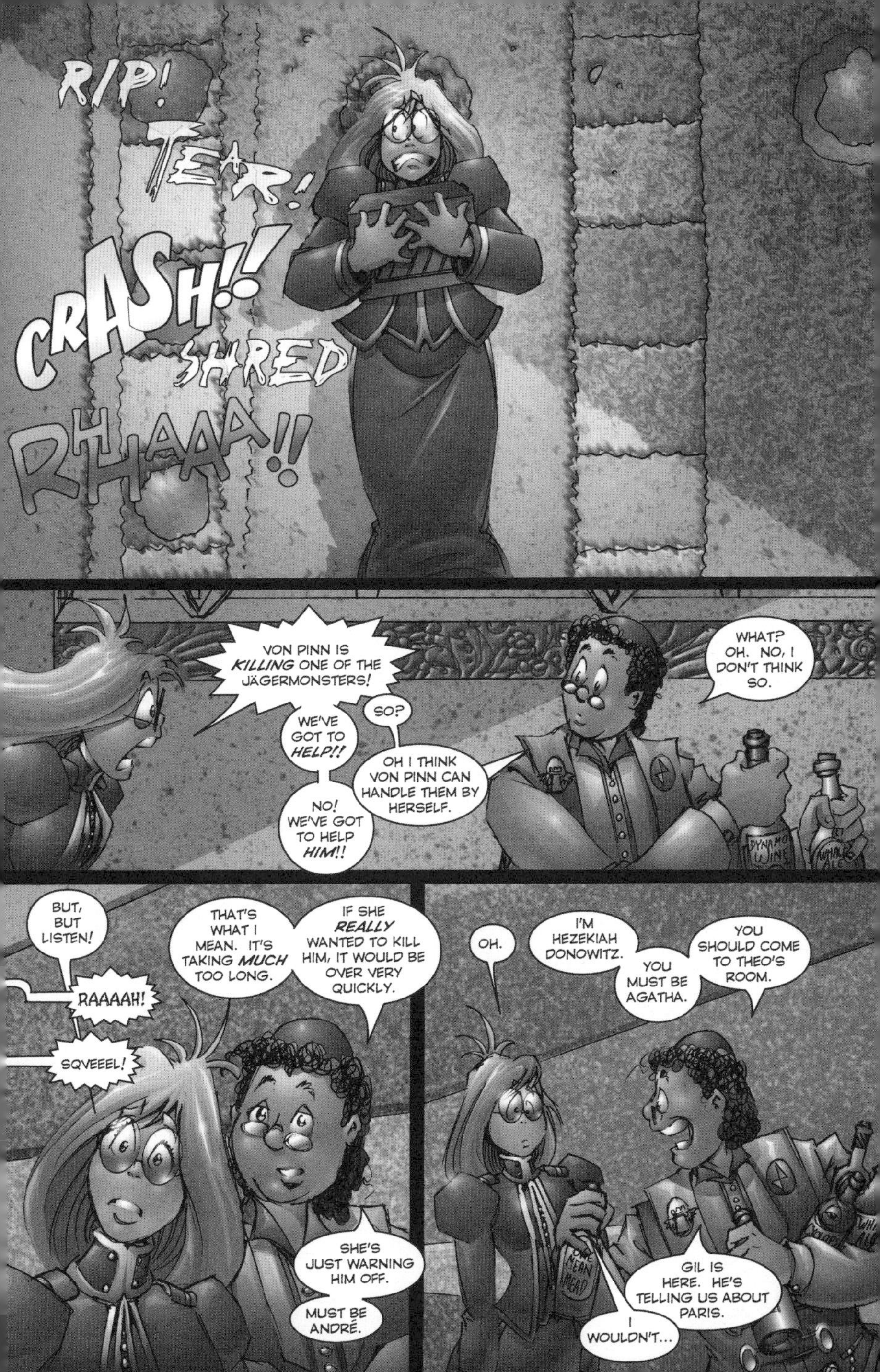
RIP!
TEAR!
CRASH!!
SHRED
RHAAA!!
VON PINN IS KILLING ONE OF THE JÄGERMONSTERS!
WHAT? OH. NO, I DON'T THINK SO.
WE'VE GOT TO HELP!!
SO?
OH I THINK VON PINN CAN HANDLE THEM BY HERSELF.
NO! WE'VE GOT TO HELP HIM!!
DYNAMO WINE
BUT, BUT LISTEN!
RAAAAH!
SQVEEEL!
THAT'S WHAT I MEAN. IT'S TAKING MUCH TOO LONG.
IF SHE REALLY WANTED TO KILL HIM, IT WOULD BE OVER VERY QUICKLY.
SHE'S JUST WARNING HIM OFF.
MUST BE ANDRÉ.
OH.
I'M HEZEKIAH DONOWITZ.
YOU MUST BE AGATHA.
YOU SHOULD COME TO THEO'S ROOM.
GIL IS HERE. HE'S TELLING US ABOUT PARIS.
I WOULDN'T...
ONE MEAN MEAD

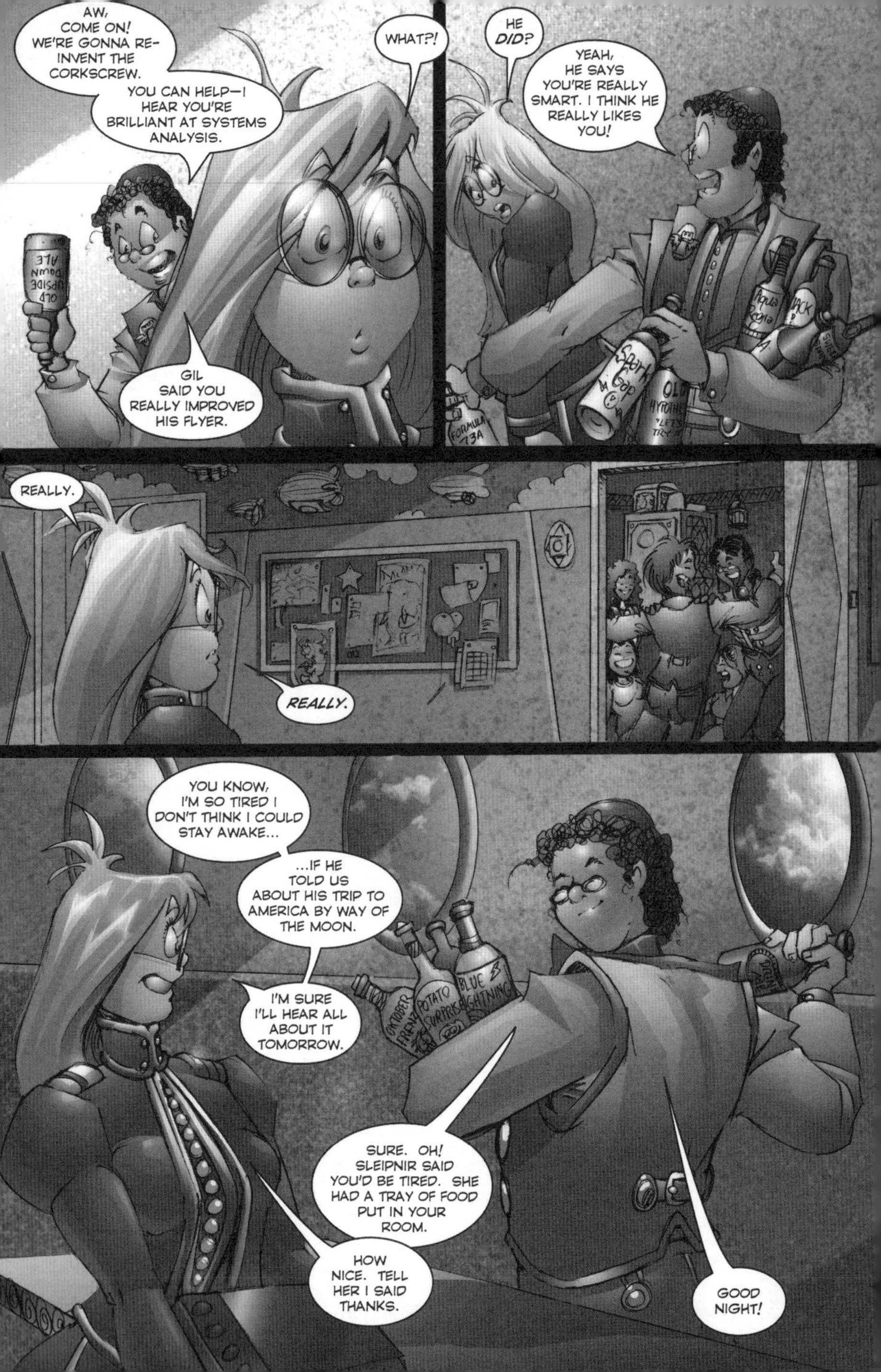

AW, COME ON! WE'RE GONNA RE-INVENT THE CORKSCREW.
YOU CAN HELP—I HEAR YOU'RE BRILLIANT AT SYSTEMS ANALYSIS.
WHAT?!
GIL SAID YOU REALLY IMPROVED HIS FLYER.
HE *DID*?
YEAH, HE SAYS YOU'RE REALLY SMART. I THINK HE REALLY LIKES YOU!
REALLY.
REALLY.
YOU KNOW, I'M SO TIRED I DON'T THINK I COULD STAY AWAKE...
...IF HE TOLD US ABOUT HIS TRIP TO AMERICA BY WAY OF THE MOON.
I'M SURE I'LL HEAR ALL ABOUT IT TOMORROW.
SURE. OH! SLEIPNIR SAID YOU'D BE TIRED. SHE HAD A TRAY OF FOOD PUT IN YOUR ROOM.
HOW NICE. TELL HER I SAID THANKS.
GOOD NIGHT!

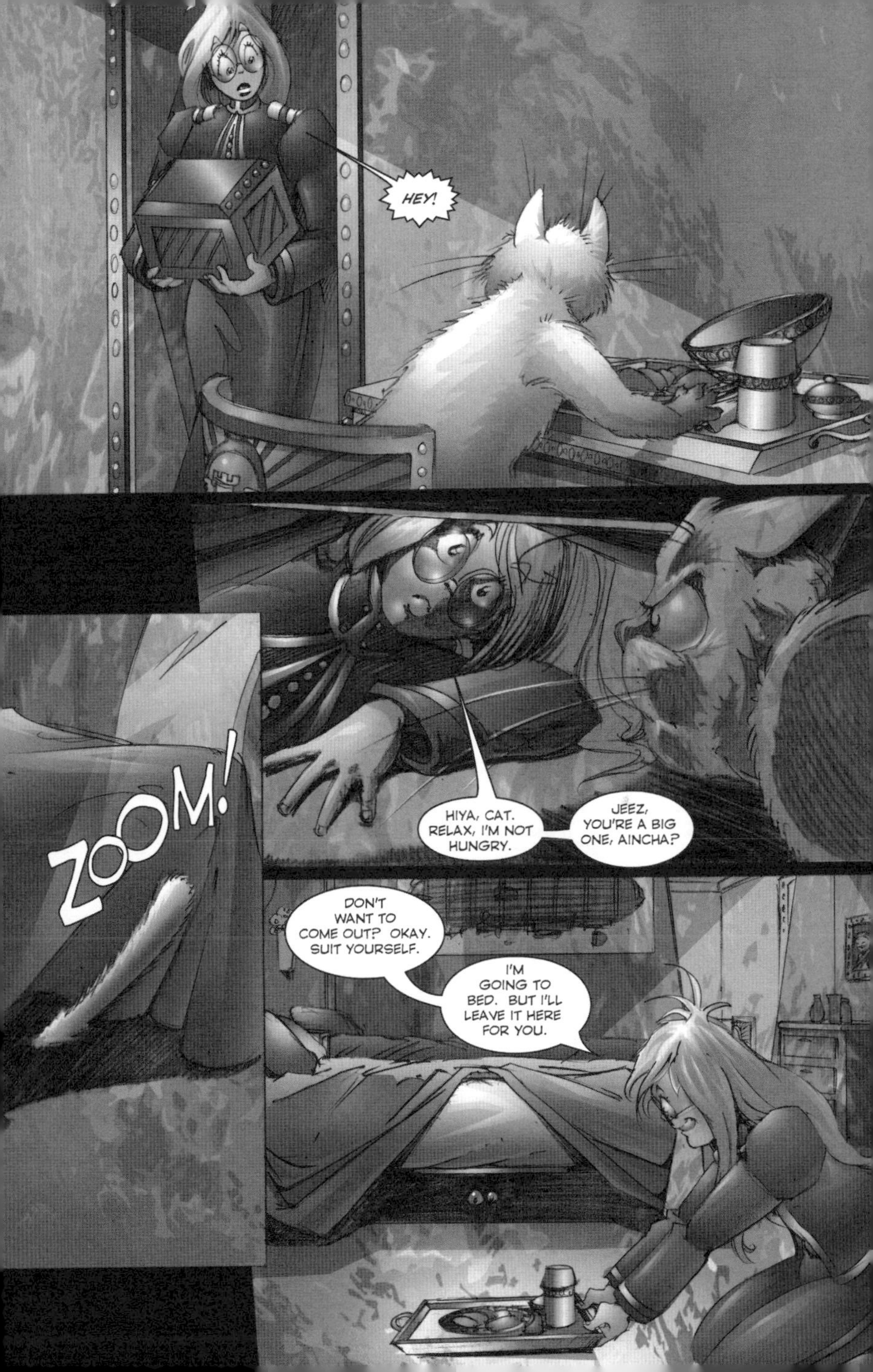
HEY!
HIYA, CAT. RELAX, I'M NOT HUNGRY.
JEEZ, YOU'RE A BIG ONE, AINCHA?
ZOOM!
DON'T WANT TO COME OUT? OKAY. SUIT YOURSELF.
I'M GOING TO BED. BUT I'LL LEAVE IT HERE FOR YOU.

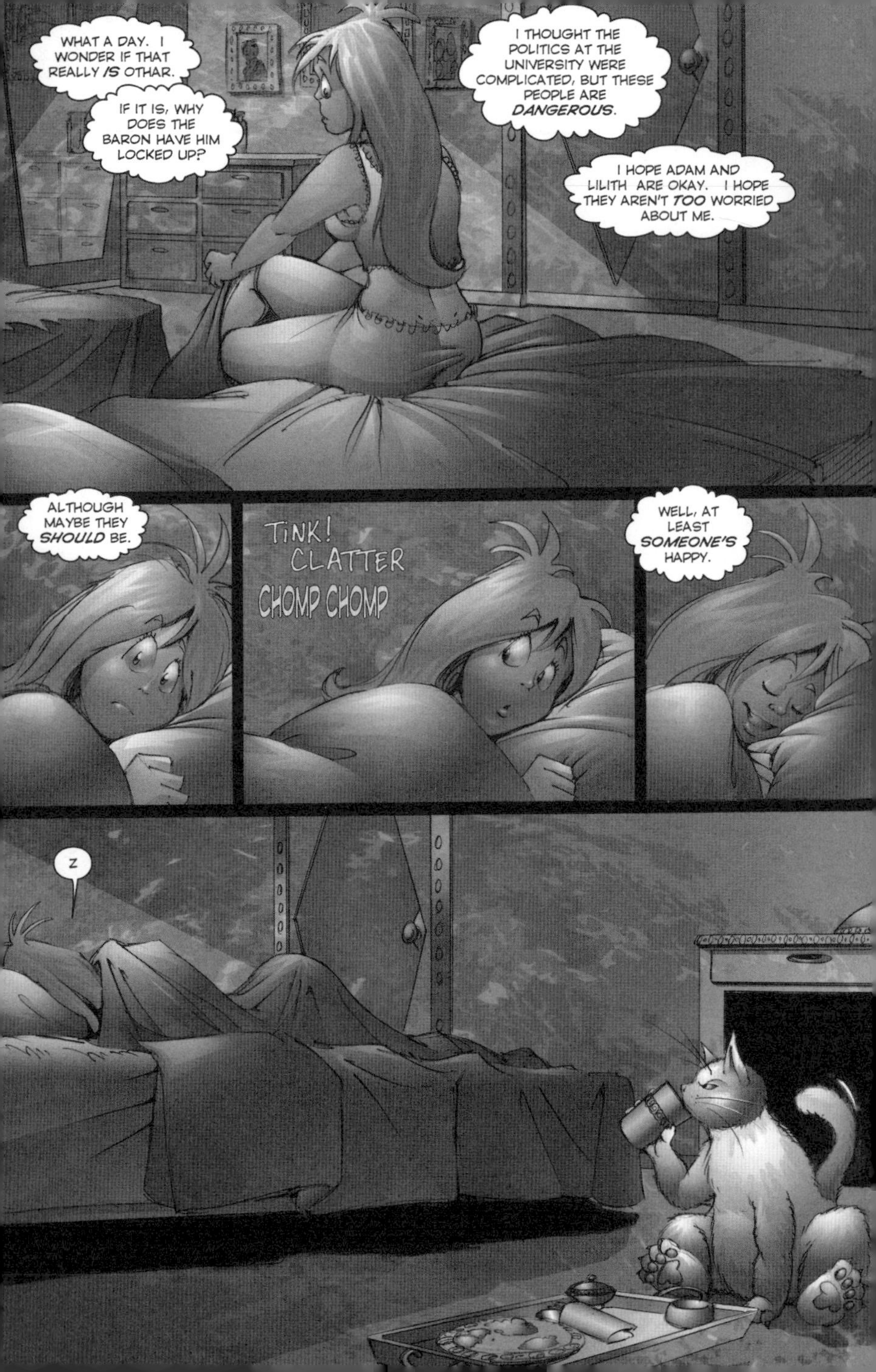
WHAT A DAY. I WONDER IF THAT REALLY *IS* OTHAR.
IF IT IS, WHY DOES THE BARON HAVE HIM LOCKED UP?
I THOUGHT THE POLITICS AT THE UNIVERSITY WERE COMPLICATED, BUT THESE PEOPLE ARE *DANGEROUS*.
I HOPE ADAM AND LILITH ARE OKAY. I HOPE THEY AREN'T *TOO* WORRIED ABOUT ME.
ALTHOUGH MAYBE THEY *SHOULD* BE.
TINK! CLATTER
CHOMP CHOMP
WELL, AT LEAST *SOMEONE'S* HAPPY.
Z

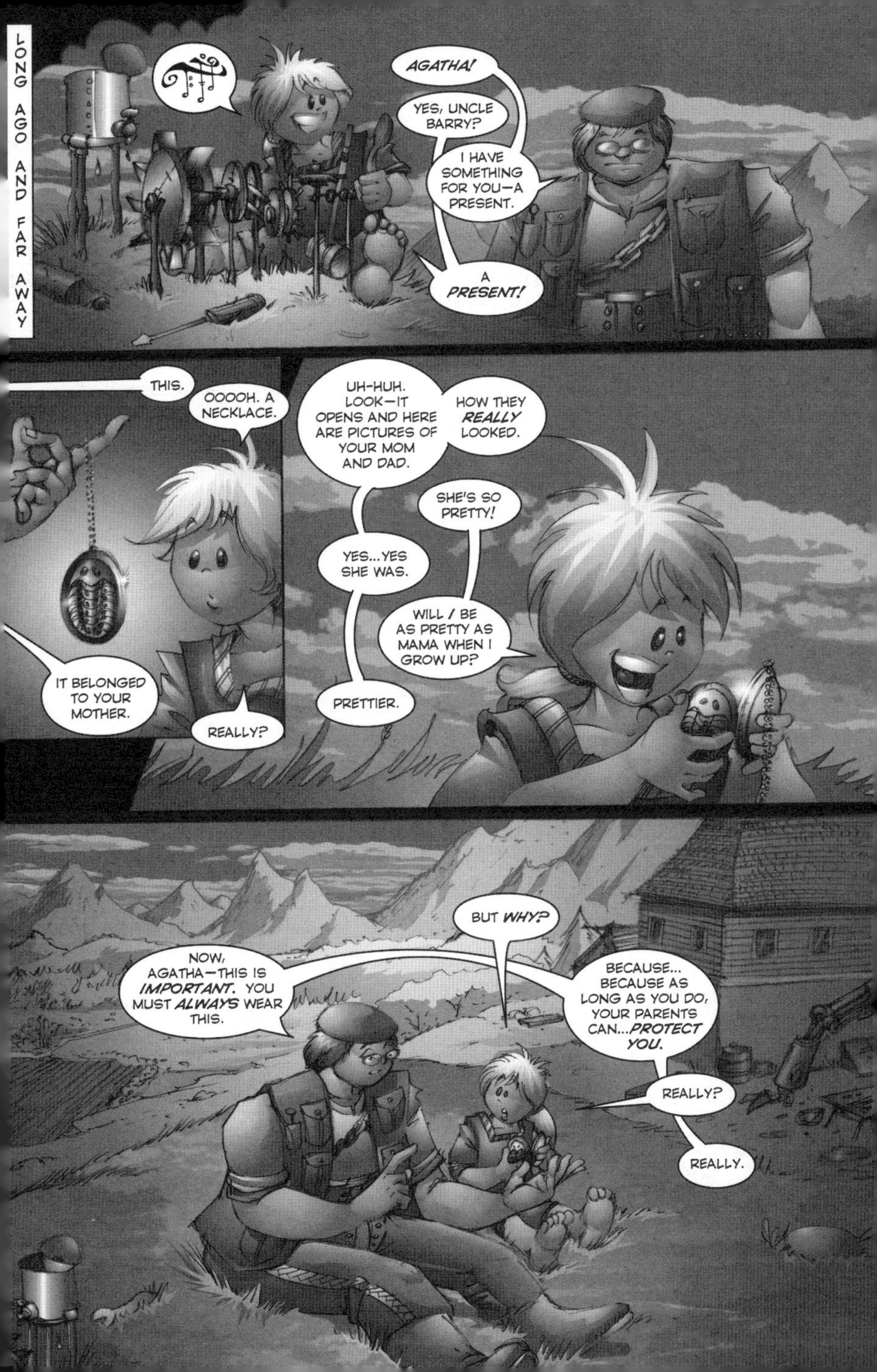
LONG AGO AND FAR AWAY
AGATHA!
YES, UNCLE BARRY?
I HAVE SOMETHING FOR YOU—A PRESENT.
A PRESENT!
THIS.
OOOOH. A NECKLACE.
IT BELONGED TO YOUR MOTHER.
REALLY?
UH-HUH. LOOK—IT OPENS AND HERE ARE PICTURES OF YOUR MOM AND DAD.
HOW THEY REALLY LOOKED.
SHE'S SO PRETTY!
YES...YES SHE WAS.
WILL I BE AS PRETTY AS MAMA WHEN I GROW UP?
PRETTIER.
NOW, AGATHA—THIS IS IMPORTANT. YOU MUST ALWAYS WEAR THIS.
BUT WHY?
BECAUSE... BECAUSE AS LONG AS YOU DO, YOUR PARENTS CAN...PROTECT YOU.
REALLY?
REALLY.

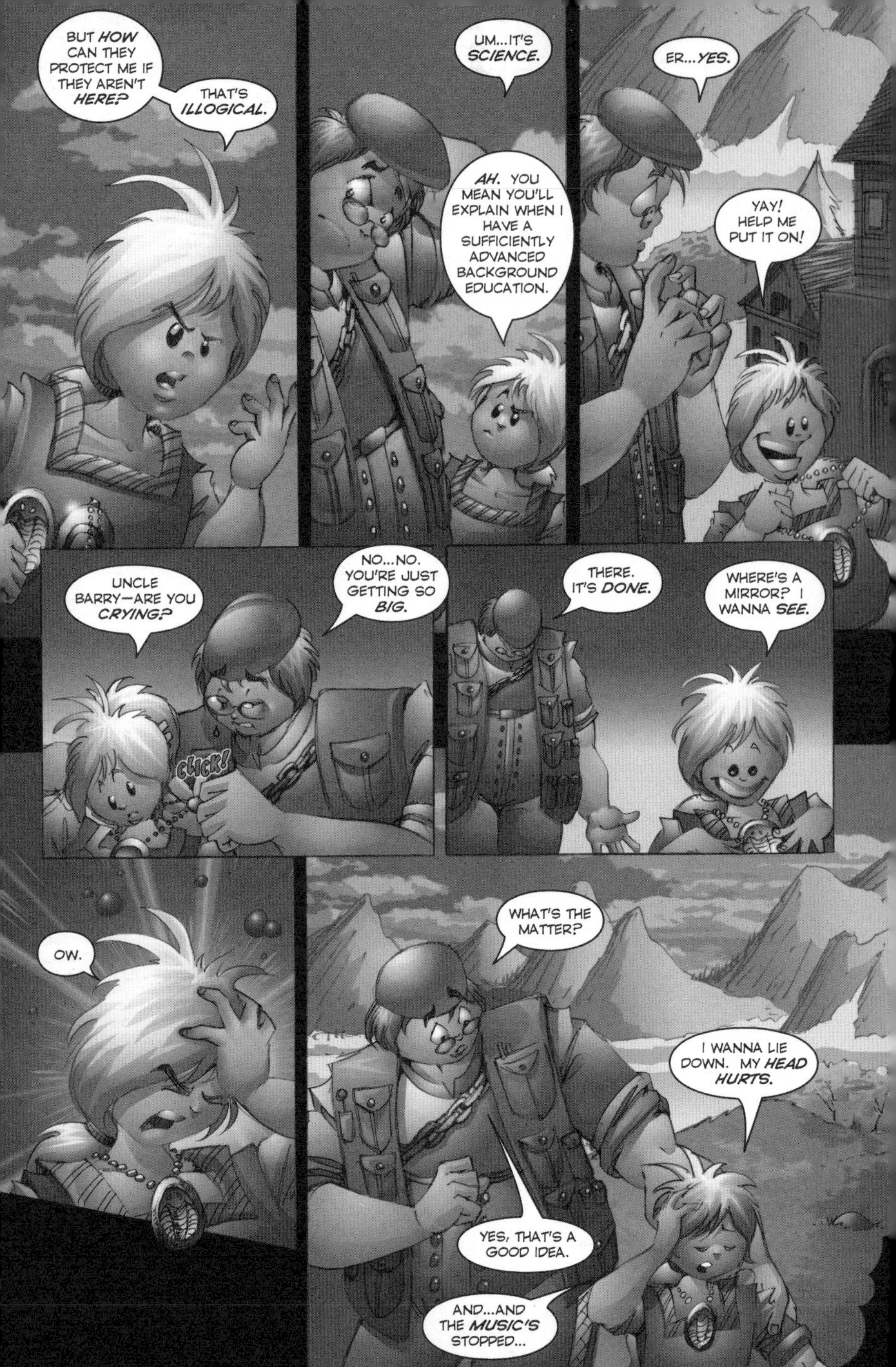
BUT *HOW* CAN THEY PROTECT ME IF THEY AREN'T *HERE?*
THAT'S *ILLOGICAL.*
UM...IT'S *SCIENCE.*
AH. YOU MEAN YOU'LL EXPLAIN WHEN I HAVE A SUFFICIENTLY ADVANCED BACKGROUND EDUCATION.
ER...*YES.*
YAY! HELP ME PUT IT ON!
UNCLE BARRY—ARE YOU *CRYING?*
NO...NO. YOU'RE JUST GETTING SO *BIG.*
CLICK!
THERE. IT'S *DONE.*
WHERE'S A MIRROR? I WANNA *SEE.*
OW.
WHAT'S THE MATTER?
I WANNA LIE DOWN. MY *HEAD HURTS.*
YES, THAT'S A GOOD IDEA.
AND...AND THE *MUSIC'S* STOPPED...

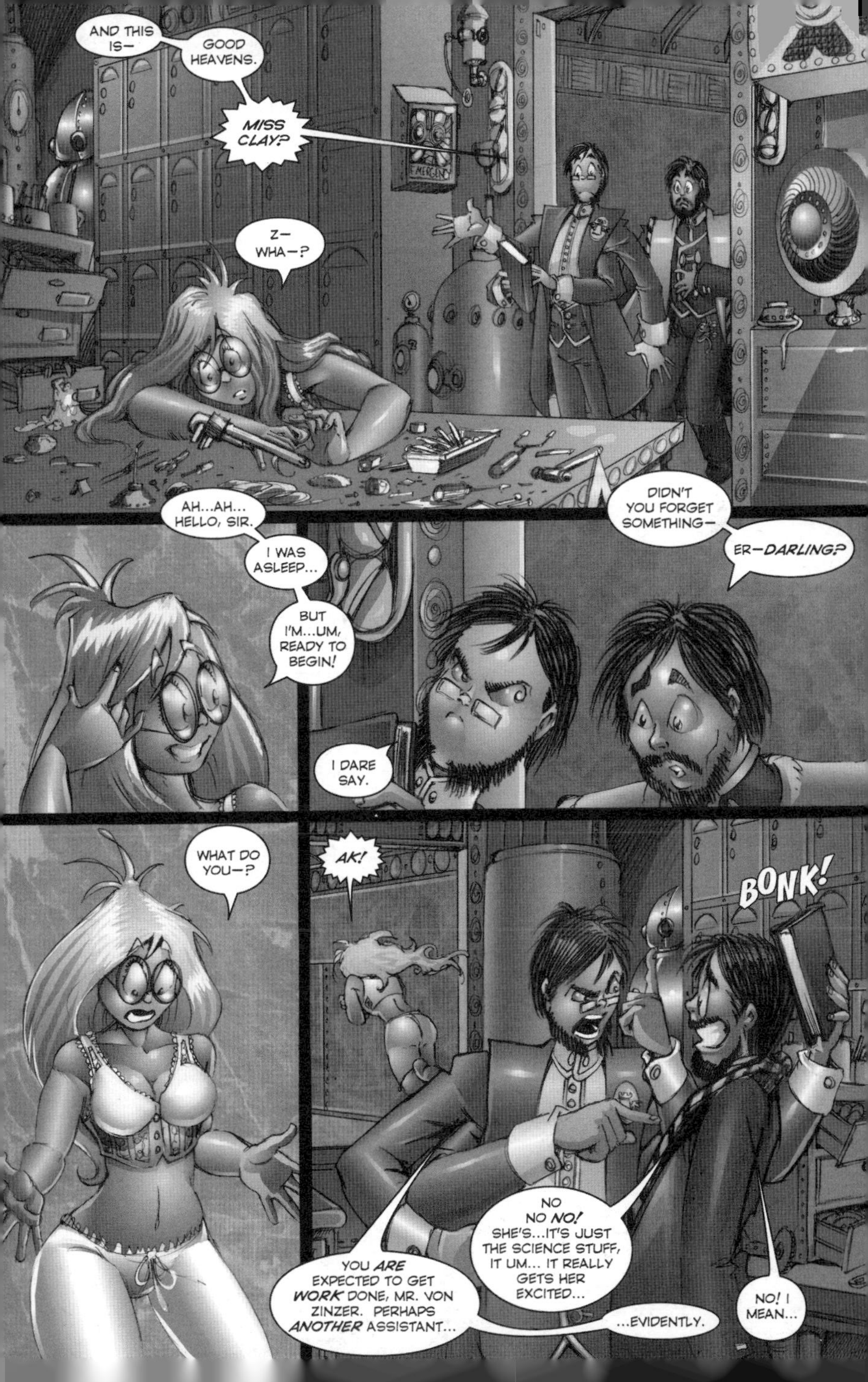
AND THIS IS—
GOOD HEAVENS.
MISS CLAY?
Z—WHA—?
AH...AH... HELLO, SIR.
I WAS ASLEEP...
BUT I'M...UM, READY TO BEGIN!
DIDN'T YOU FORGET SOMETHING—
ER—DARLING?
I DARE SAY.
WHAT DO YOU—?
AK!
BONK!
NO NO NO! SHE'S...IT'S JUST THE SCIENCE STUFF, IT UM... IT REALLY GETS HER EXCITED...
YOU ARE EXPECTED TO GET WORK DONE, MR. VON ZINZER. PERHAPS ANOTHER ASSISTANT...
...EVIDENTLY.
NO! I MEAN...

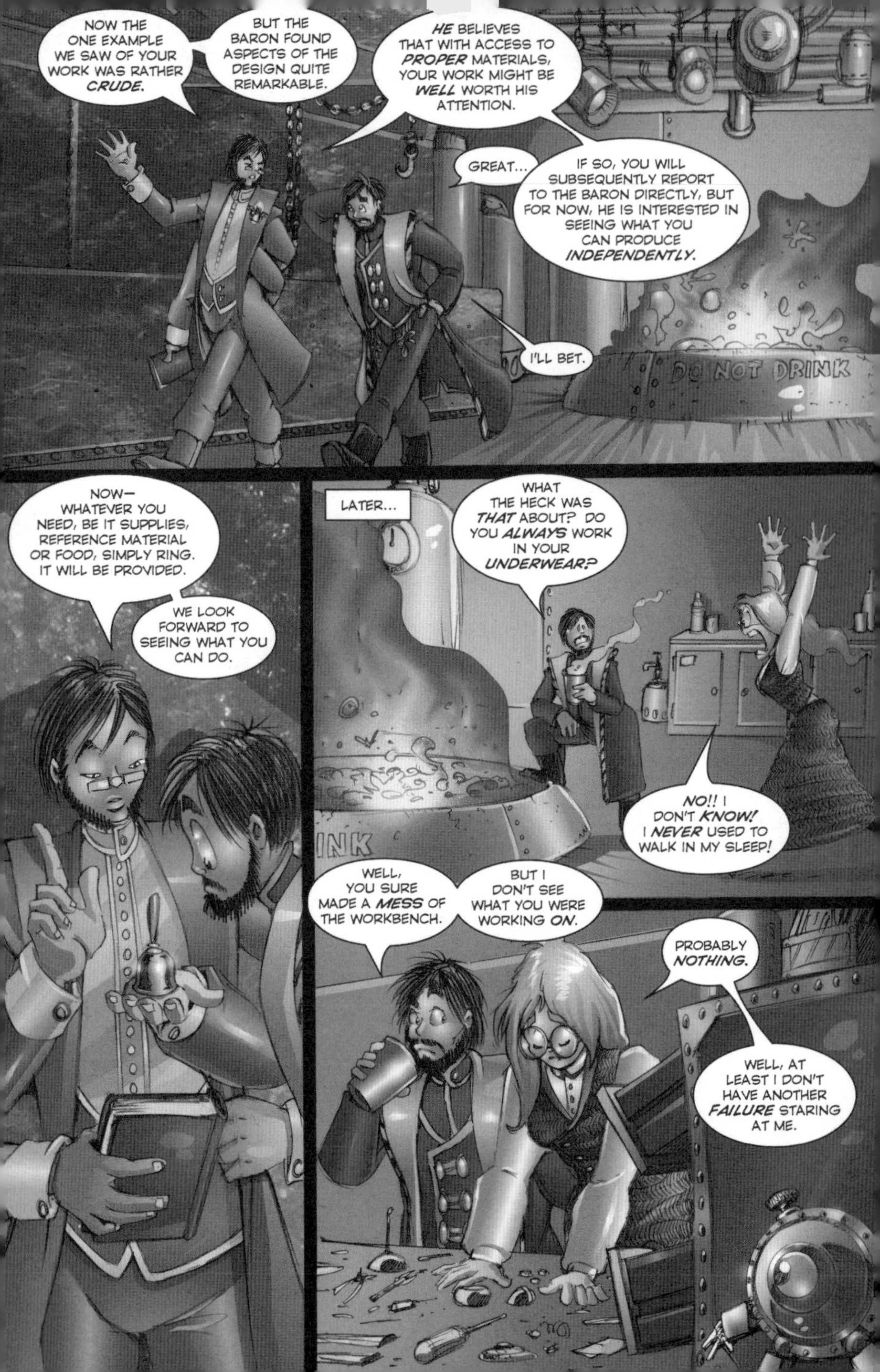
NOW THE ONE EXAMPLE WE SAW OF YOUR WORK WAS RATHER *CRUDE.*
BUT THE BARON FOUND ASPECTS OF THE DESIGN QUITE REMARKABLE.
HE BELIEVES THAT WITH ACCESS TO *PROPER* MATERIALS, YOUR WORK MIGHT BE *WELL* WORTH HIS ATTENTION.
GREAT...
IF SO, YOU WILL SUBSEQUENTLY REPORT TO THE BARON DIRECTLY, BUT FOR NOW, HE IS INTERESTED IN SEEING WHAT YOU CAN PRODUCE *INDEPENDENTLY.*
I'LL BET.
DO NOT DRINK
NOW— WHATEVER YOU NEED, BE IT SUPPLIES, REFERENCE MATERIAL OR FOOD, SIMPLY RING. IT WILL BE PROVIDED.
WE LOOK FORWARD TO SEEING WHAT YOU CAN DO.
LATER...
WHAT THE HECK WAS *THAT* ABOUT? DO YOU *ALWAYS* WORK IN YOUR *UNDERWEAR?*
NO!! I DON'T *KNOW!* I *NEVER* USED TO WALK IN MY SLEEP!
INK
WELL, YOU SURE MADE A *MESS* OF THE WORKBENCH.
BUT I DON'T SEE WHAT YOU WERE WORKING *ON.*
PROBABLY *NOTHING.*
WELL, AT LEAST I DON'T HAVE ANOTHER *FAILURE* STARING AT ME.

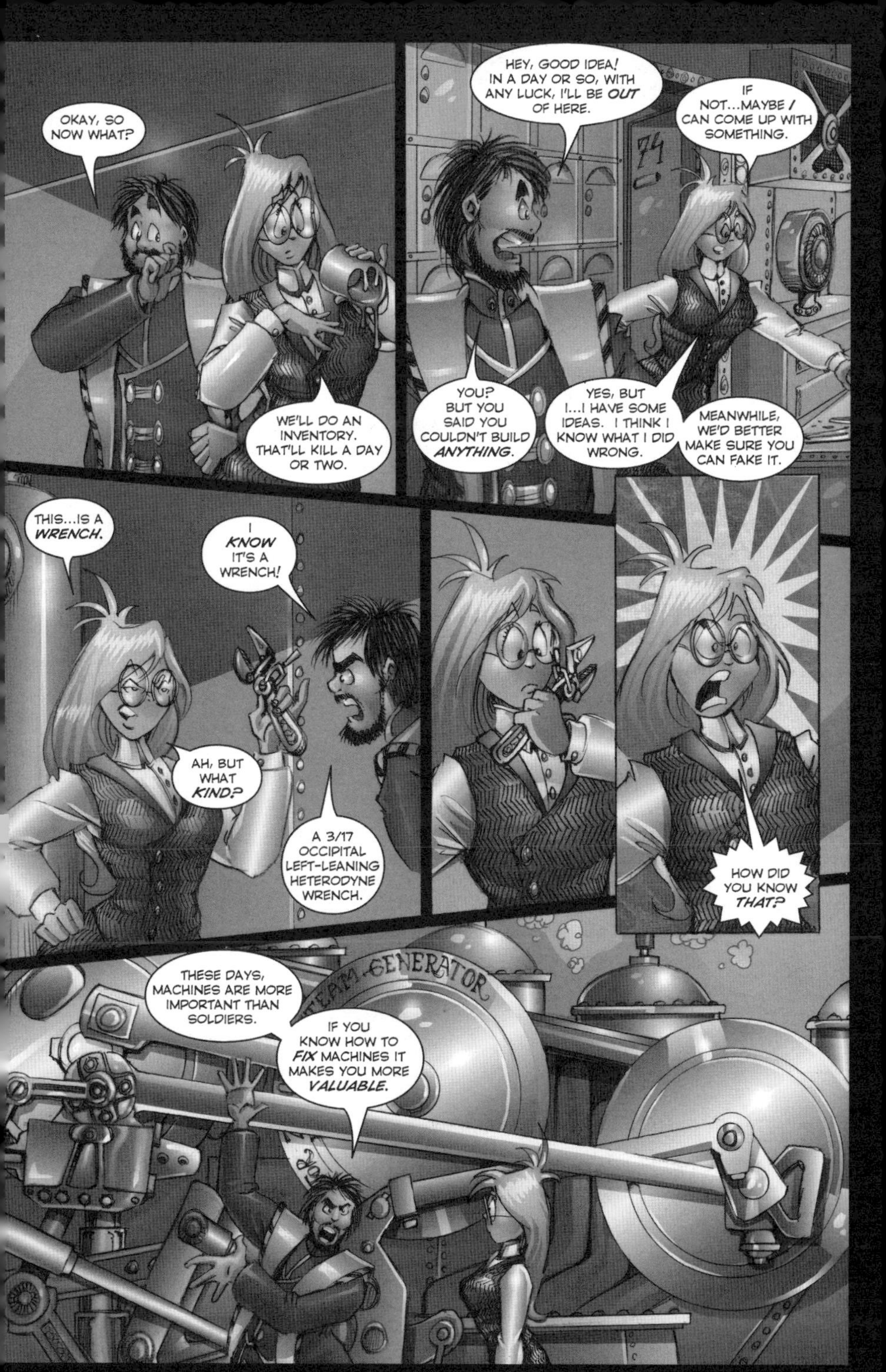
OKAY, SO NOW WHAT?
WE'LL DO AN INVENTORY. THAT'LL KILL A DAY OR TWO.
HEY, GOOD IDEA! IN A DAY OR SO, WITH ANY LUCK, I'LL BE *OUT* OF HERE.
IF NOT...MAYBE *I* CAN COME UP WITH SOMETHING.
YOU? BUT YOU SAID YOU COULDN'T BUILD *ANYTHING*.
YES, BUT I...I HAVE SOME IDEAS. I THINK I KNOW WHAT I DID WRONG.
MEANWHILE, WE'D BETTER MAKE SURE YOU CAN FAKE IT.
74
THIS...IS A *WRENCH*.
I *KNOW* IT'S A WRENCH!
AH, BUT WHAT *KIND?*
A 3/17 OCCIPITAL LEFT-LEANING HETERODYNE WRENCH.
HOW DID YOU KNOW *THAT?*
STEAM GENERATOR
THESE DAYS, MACHINES ARE MORE IMPORTANT THAN SOLDIERS.
IF YOU KNOW HOW TO *FIX* MACHINES IT MAKES YOU MORE *VALUABLE*.

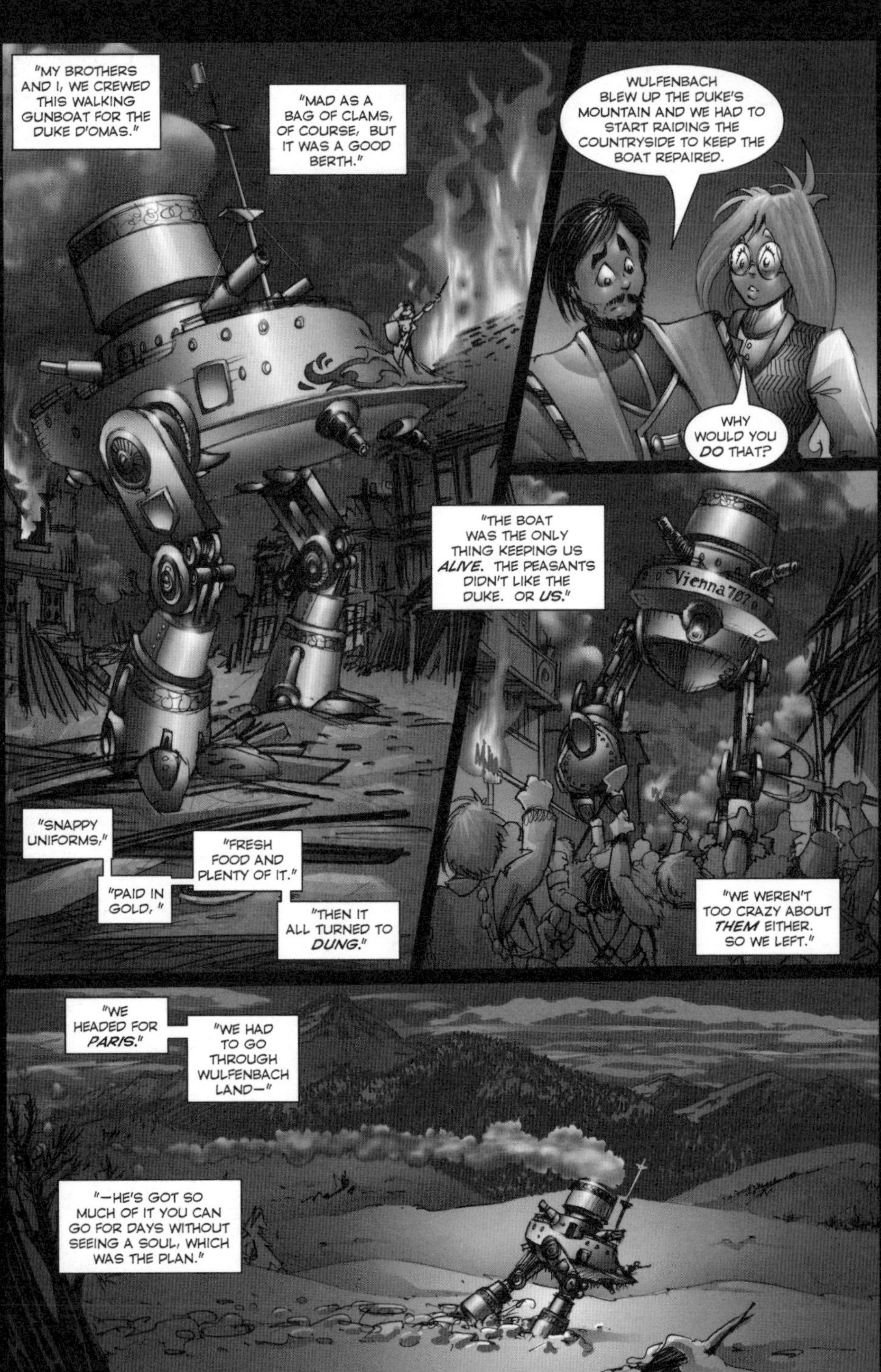
"MY BROTHERS AND I, WE CREWED THIS WALKING GUNBOAT FOR THE DUKE D'OMAS."
"MAD AS A BAG OF CLAMS, OF COURSE, BUT IT WAS A GOOD BERTH."
"SNAPPY UNIFORMS,"
"PAID IN GOLD,"
"FRESH FOOD AND PLENTY OF IT."
"THEN IT ALL TURNED TO DUNG."
WULFENBACH BLEW UP THE DUKE'S MOUNTAIN AND WE HAD TO START RAIDING THE COUNTRYSIDE TO KEEP THE BOAT REPAIRED.
WHY WOULD YOU DO THAT?
"THE BOAT WAS THE ONLY THING KEEPING US ALIVE. THE PEASANTS DIDN'T LIKE THE DUKE. OR US."
Vienna 707
"WE WEREN'T TOO CRAZY ABOUT THEM EITHER. SO WE LEFT."
"WE HEADED FOR PARIS."
"WE HAD TO GO THROUGH WULFENBACH LAND—"
"—HE'S GOT SO MUCH OF IT YOU CAN GO FOR DAYS WITHOUT SEEING A SOUL, WHICH WAS THE PLAN."

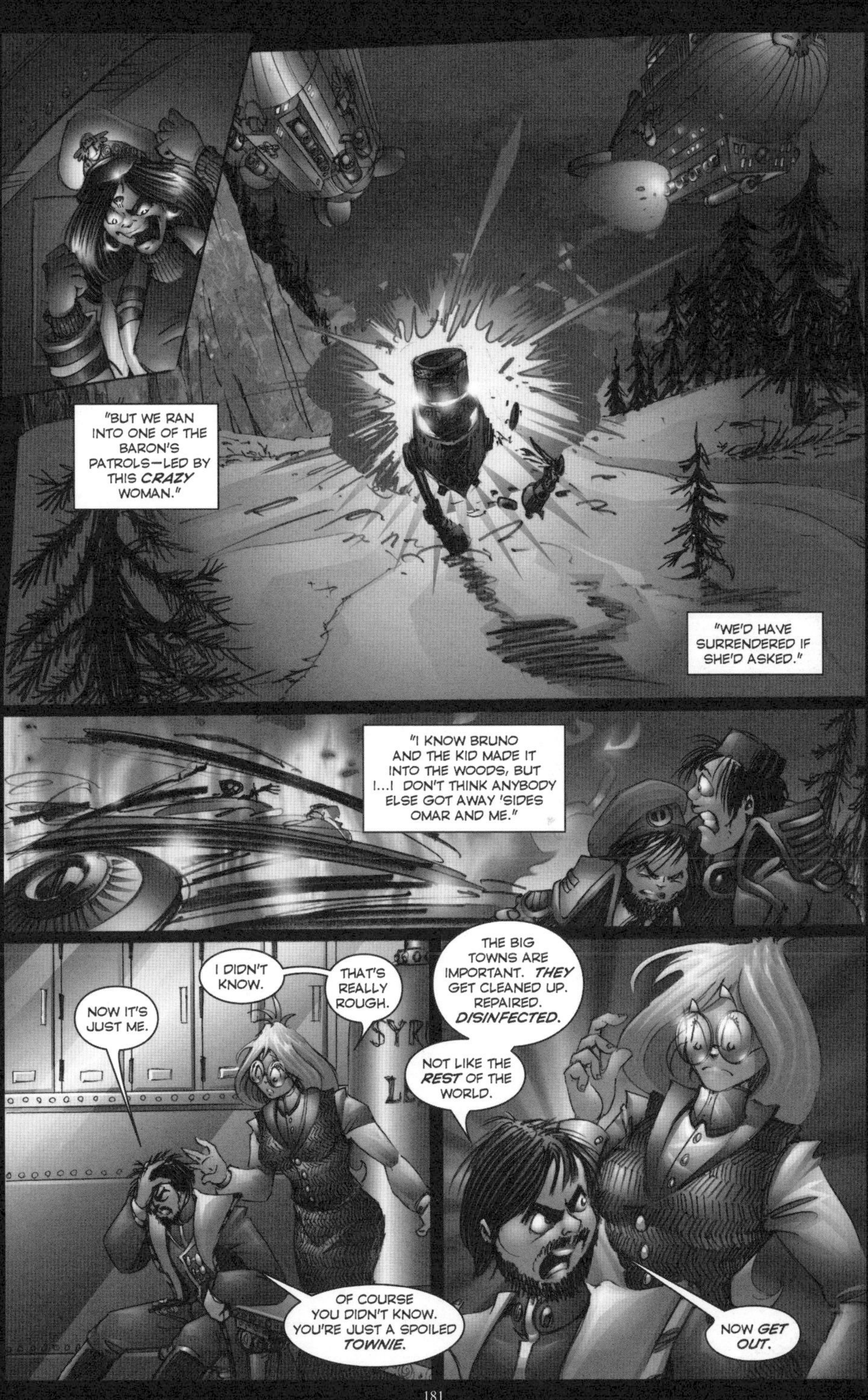
"BUT WE RAN INTO ONE OF THE BARON'S PATROLS—LED BY THIS *CRAZY* WOMAN."
"WE'D HAVE SURRENDERED IF SHE'D ASKED."
"I KNOW BRUNO AND THE KID MADE IT INTO THE WOODS, BUT I...I DON'T THINK ANYBODY ELSE GOT AWAY 'SIDES OMAR AND ME."
NOW IT'S JUST ME.
I DIDN'T KNOW.
THAT'S REALLY ROUGH.
OF COURSE YOU DIDN'T KNOW. YOU'RE JUST A SPOILED *TOWNIE*.
THE BIG TOWNS ARE IMPORTANT. *THEY* GET CLEANED UP. REPAIRED. *DISINFECTED*.
NOT LIKE THE *REST* OF THE WORLD.
NOW *GET OUT*.

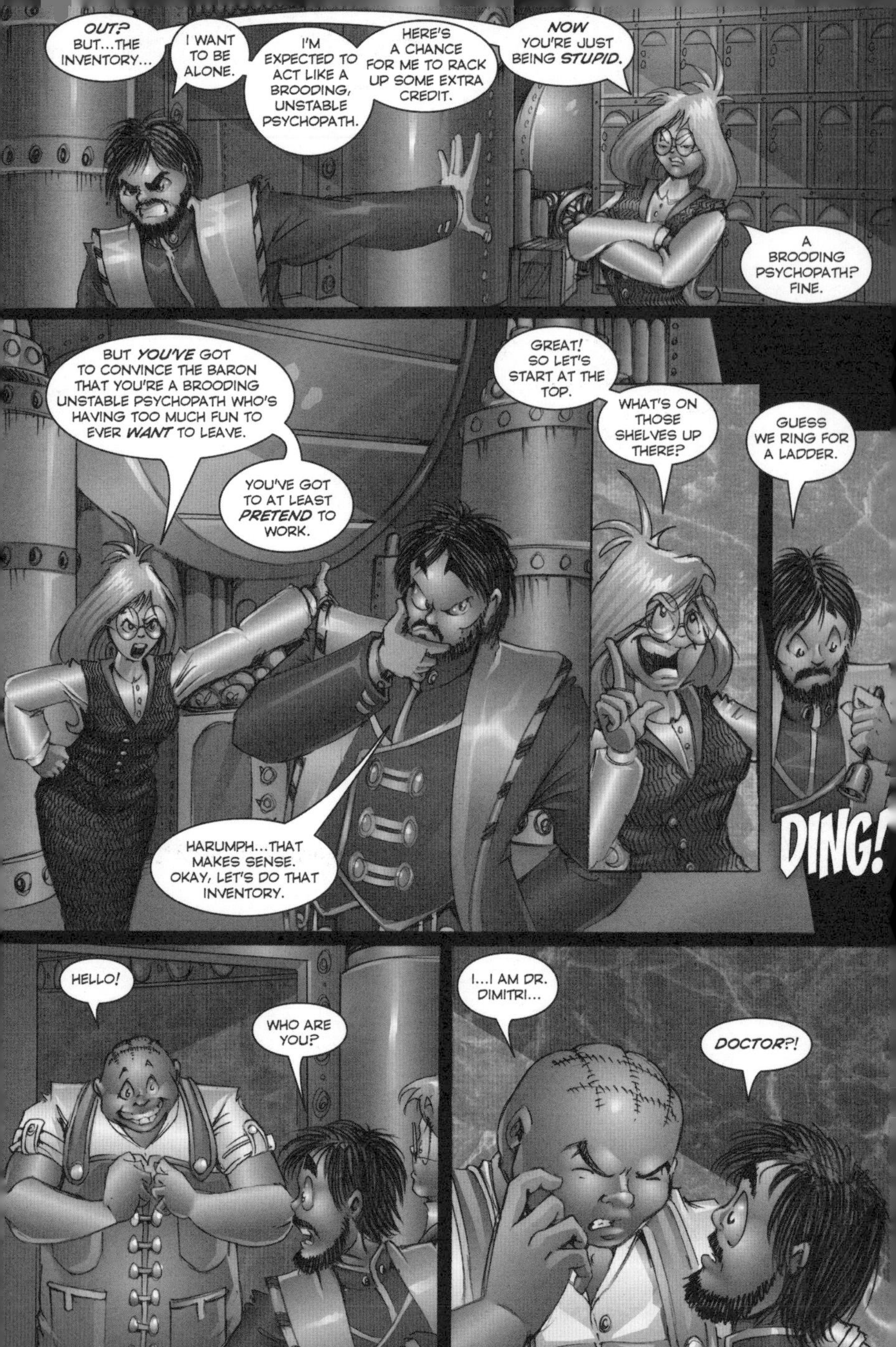
OUT? BUT...THE INVENTORY...
I WANT TO BE ALONE.
I'M EXPECTED TO ACT LIKE A BROODING, UNSTABLE PSYCHOPATH.
HERE'S A CHANCE FOR ME TO RACK UP SOME EXTRA CREDIT.
NOW YOU'RE JUST BEING STUPID.
A BROODING PSYCHOPATH? FINE.
BUT YOU'VE GOT TO CONVINCE THE BARON THAT YOU'RE A BROODING UNSTABLE PSYCHOPATH WHO'S HAVING TOO MUCH FUN TO EVER WANT TO LEAVE.
YOU'VE GOT TO AT LEAST PRETEND TO WORK.
HARUMPH...THAT MAKES SENSE. OKAY, LET'S DO THAT INVENTORY.
GREAT! SO LET'S START AT THE TOP.
WHAT'S ON THOSE SHELVES UP THERE?
GUESS WE RING FOR A LADDER.
DING!
HELLO!
WHO ARE YOU?
I...I AM DR. DIMITRI...
DOCTOR?!

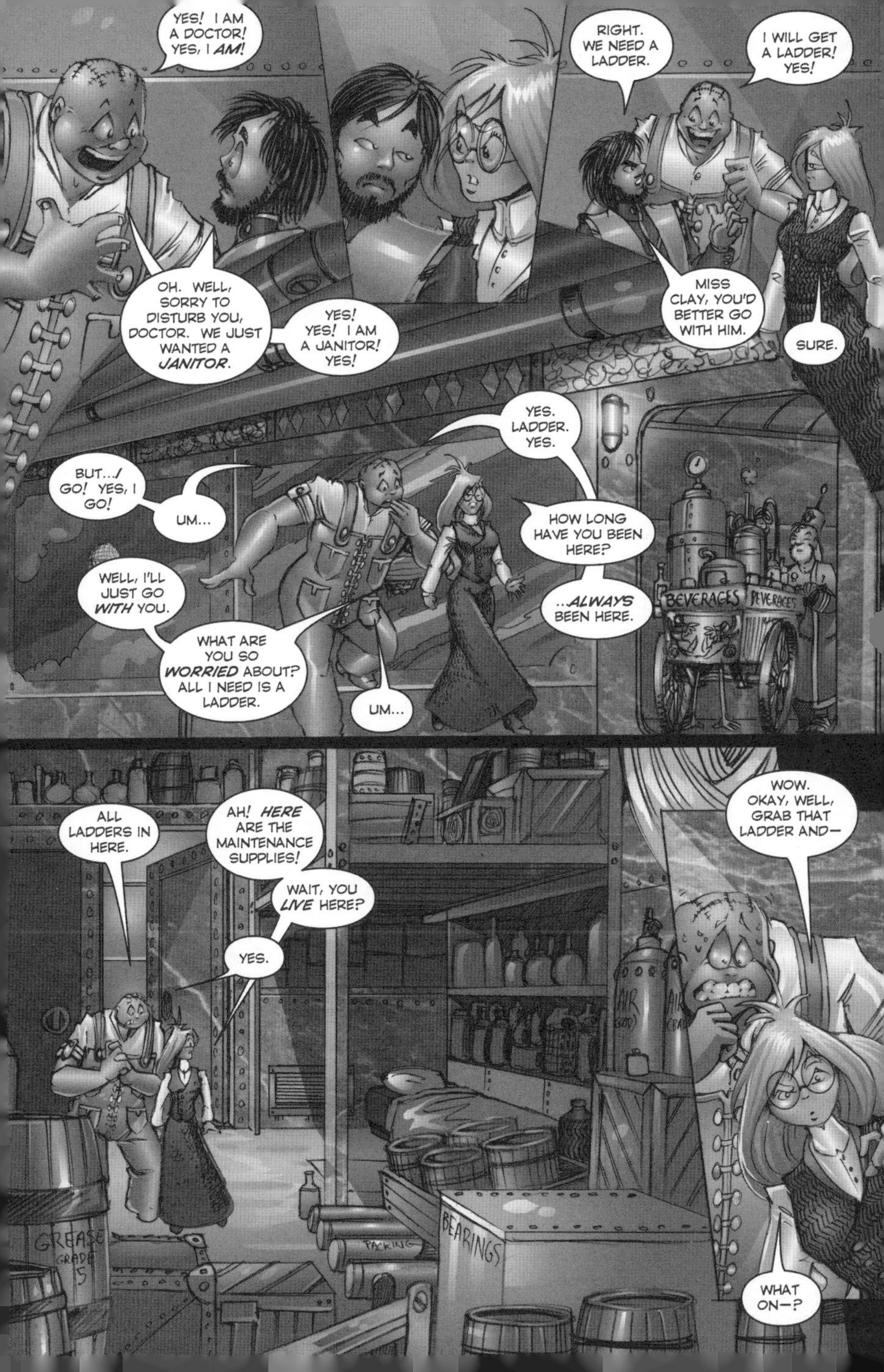
YES! I AM A DOCTOR! YES, I AM!
OH. WELL, SORRY TO DISTURB YOU, DOCTOR. WE JUST WANTED A JANITOR.
YES! YES! I AM A JANITOR! YES!
RIGHT. WE NEED A LADDER.
I WILL GET A LADDER! YES!
MISS CLAY, YOU'D BETTER GO WITH HIM.
SURE.
BUT.../ GO! YES, I GO!
UM...
YES. LADDER. YES.
HOW LONG HAVE YOU BEEN HERE?
WELL, I'LL JUST GO WITH YOU.
...ALWAYS BEEN HERE.
WHAT ARE YOU SO WORRIED ABOUT? ALL I NEED IS A LADDER.
UM...
BEVERAGES
BEVERAGES
ALL LADDERS IN HERE.
AH! HERE ARE THE MAINTENANCE SUPPLIES!
WAIT, YOU LIVE HERE?
YES.
WOW. OKAY, WELL, GRAB THAT LADDER AND—
GREASE GRADE 5
PACKING
BEARINGS
WHAT ON—?

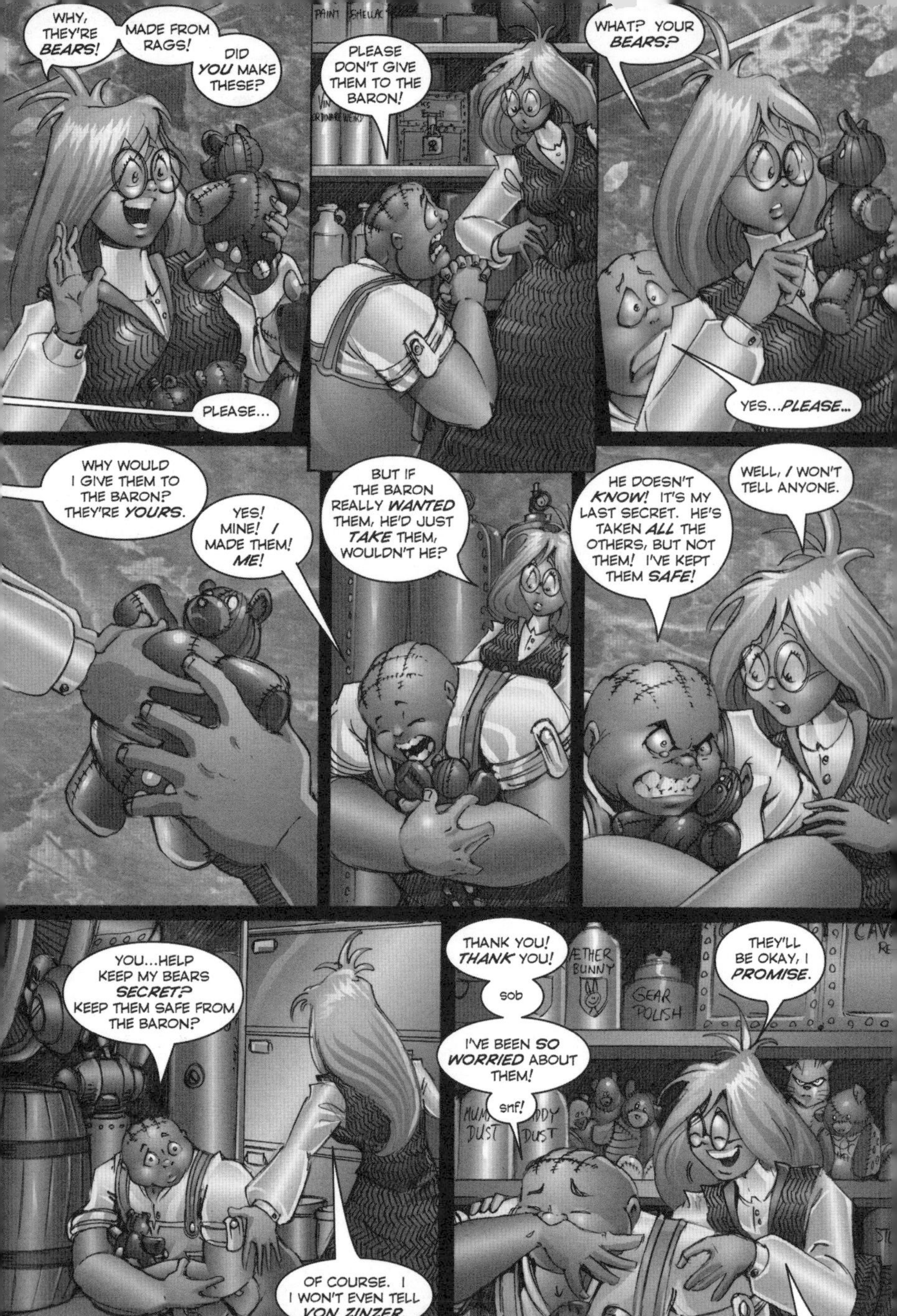
WHY, THEY'RE BEARS!
MADE FROM RAGS!
DID YOU MAKE THESE?
PLEASE...
PAINT
SHELLAC
PLEASE DON'T GIVE THEM TO THE BARON!
WHAT? YOUR BEARS?
YES...PLEASE...
WHY WOULD I GIVE THEM TO THE BARON? THEY'RE YOURS.
YES! MINE! I MADE THEM! ME!
BUT IF THE BARON REALLY WANTED THEM, HE'D JUST TAKE THEM, WOULDN'T HE?
HE DOESN'T KNOW! IT'S MY LAST SECRET. HE'S TAKEN ALL THE OTHERS, BUT NOT THEM! I'VE KEPT THEM SAFE!
WELL, I WON'T TELL ANYONE.
YOU...HELP KEEP MY BEARS SECRET? KEEP THEM SAFE FROM THE BARON?
OF COURSE. I I WON'T EVEN TELL VON ZINZER.
THANK YOU! THANK YOU!
sob
ÆTHER BUNNY
GEAR POLISH
I'VE BEEN SO WORRIED ABOUT THEM!
snf!
DUST
DUST
THEY'LL BE OKAY, I PROMISE.
NOW, LET'S GET THAT LADDER.

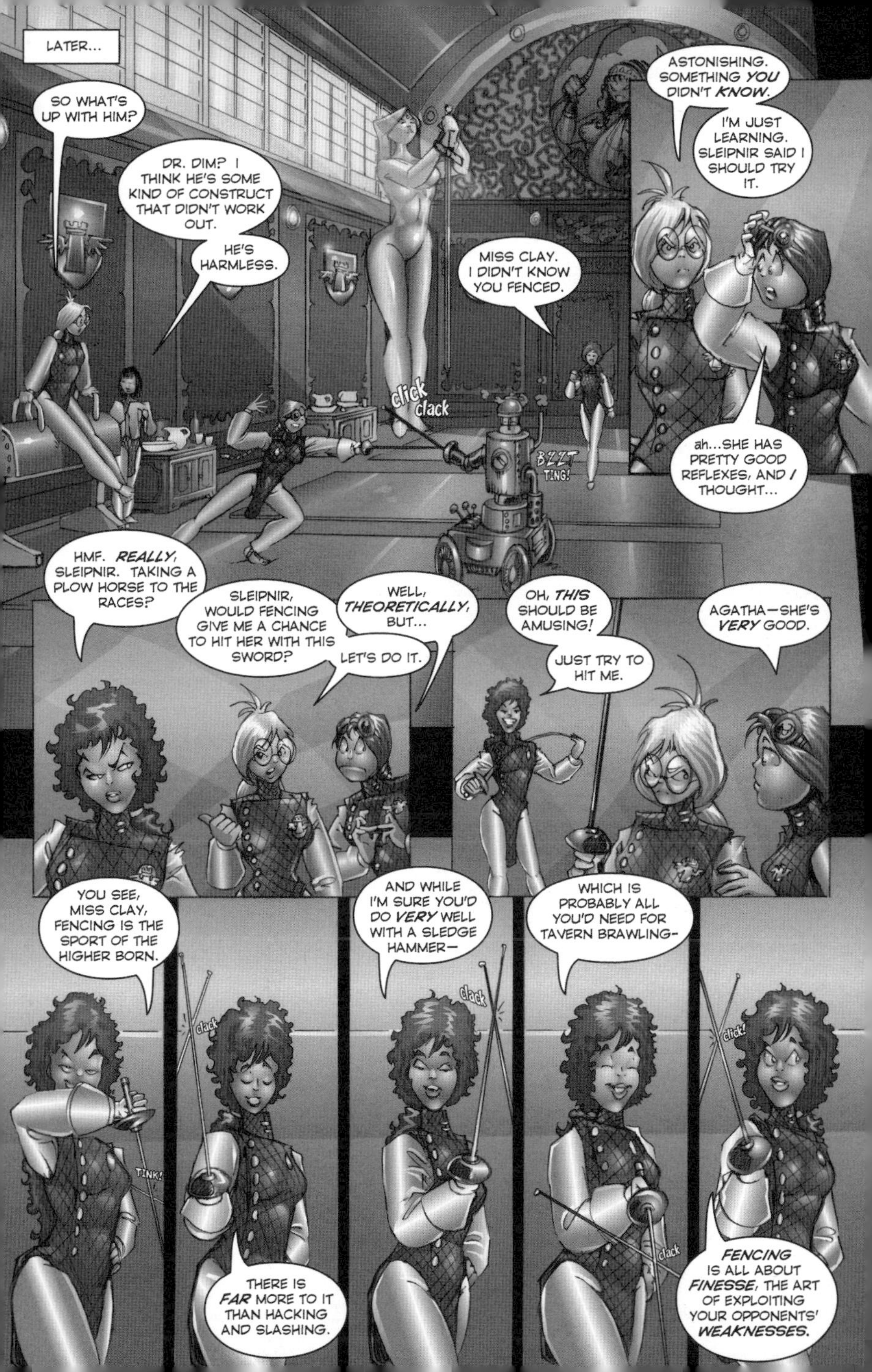
LATER...
SO WHAT'S UP WITH HIM?
DR. DIM? I THINK HE'S SOME KIND OF CONSTRUCT THAT DIDN'T WORK OUT.
HE'S HARMLESS.
click
clack
MISS CLAY. I DIDN'T KNOW YOU FENCED.
BZZT
TING!
ASTONISHING. SOMETHING YOU DIDN'T KNOW.
I'M JUST LEARNING. SLEIPNIR SAID I SHOULD TRY IT.
ah...SHE HAS PRETTY GOOD REFLEXES, AND I THOUGHT...
HMF. REALLY, SLEIPNIR. TAKING A PLOW HORSE TO THE RACES?
SLEIPNIR, WOULD FENCING GIVE ME A CHANCE TO HIT HER WITH THIS SWORD?
WELL, THEORETICALLY, BUT...
LET'S DO IT.
OH, THIS SHOULD BE AMUSING!
JUST TRY TO HIT ME.
AGATHA—SHE'S VERY GOOD.
YOU SEE, MISS CLAY, FENCING IS THE SPORT OF THE HIGHER BORN.
TINK!
clack
THERE IS FAR MORE TO IT THAN HACKING AND SLASHING.
AND WHILE I'M SURE YOU'D DO VERY WELL WITH A SLEDGE HAMMER—
clack
WHICH IS PROBABLY ALL YOU'D NEED FOR TAVERN BRAWLING-
clack
click!
FENCING IS ALL ABOUT FINESSE, THE ART OF EXPLOITING YOUR OPPONENTS' WEAKNESSES.

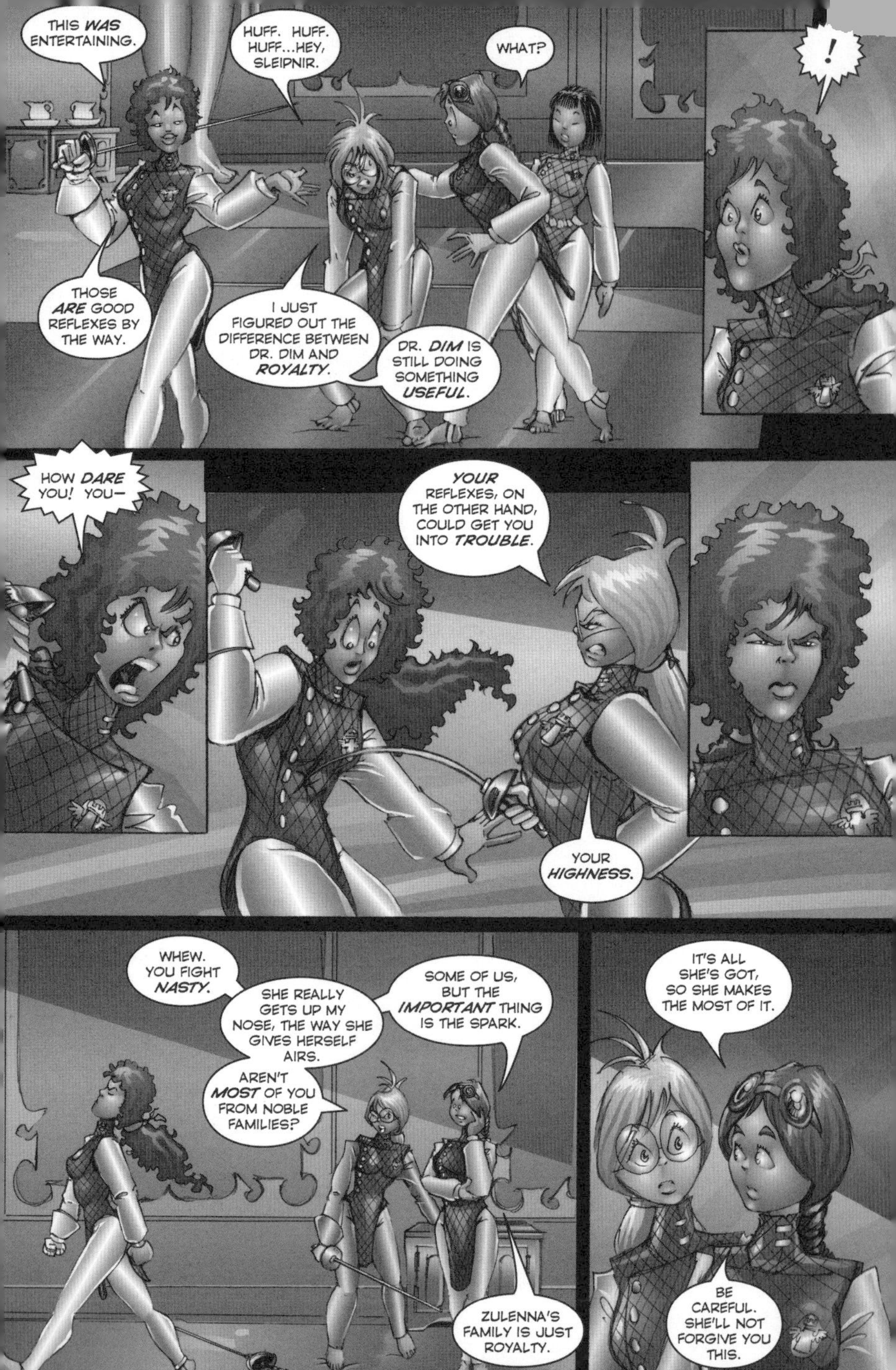
THIS WAS ENTERTAINING.
HUFF. HUFF. HUFF...HEY, SLEIPNIR.
WHAT?
THOSE ARE GOOD REFLEXES BY THE WAY.
I JUST FIGURED OUT THE DIFFERENCE BETWEEN DR. DIM AND ROYALTY.
DR. DIM IS STILL DOING SOMETHING USEFUL.
!
HOW DARE YOU! YOU—
YOUR REFLEXES, ON THE OTHER HAND, COULD GET YOU INTO TROUBLE.
YOUR HIGHNESS.
WHEW. YOU FIGHT NASTY.
SHE REALLY GETS UP MY NOSE, THE WAY SHE GIVES HERSELF AIRS.
AREN'T MOST OF YOU FROM NOBLE FAMILIES?
SOME OF US, BUT THE IMPORTANT THING IS THE SPARK.
ZULENNA'S FAMILY IS JUST ROYALTY.
IT'S ALL SHE'S GOT, SO SHE MAKES THE MOST OF IT.
BE CAREFUL. SHE'LL NOT FORGIVE YOU THIS.

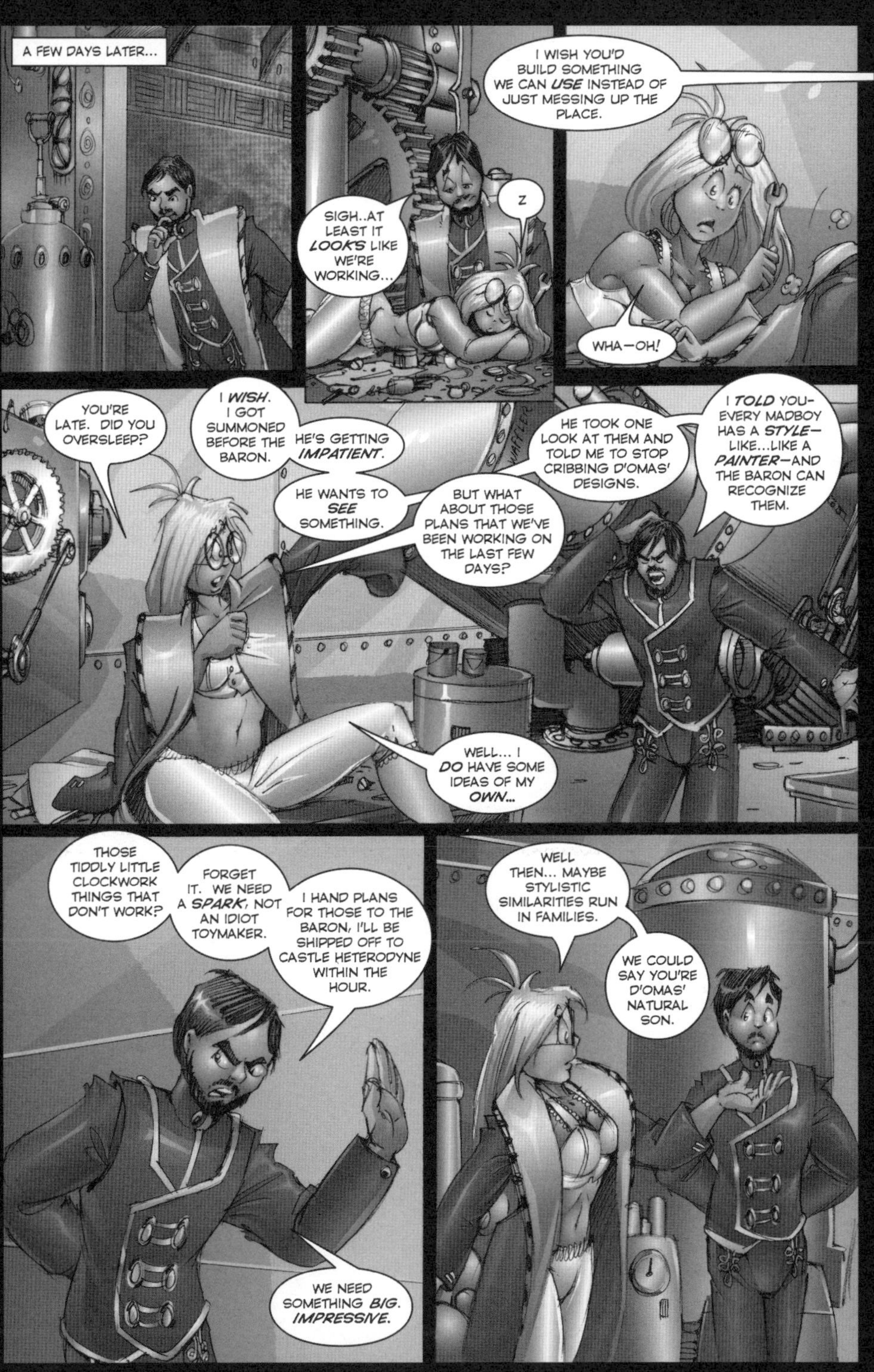
A FEW DAYS LATER...
I WISH YOU'D BUILD SOMETHING WE CAN USE INSTEAD OF JUST MESSING UP THE PLACE.
SIGH..AT LEAST IT LOOKS LIKE WE'RE WORKING...
Z
WHA—OH!
YOU'RE LATE. DID YOU OVERSLEEP?
I WISH. I GOT SUMMONED BEFORE THE BARON.
HE'S GETTING IMPATIENT.
HE WANTS TO SEE SOMETHING.
BUT WHAT ABOUT THOSE PLANS THAT WE'VE BEEN WORKING ON THE LAST FEW DAYS?
HE TOOK ONE LOOK AT THEM AND TOLD ME TO STOP CRIBBING D'OMAS' DESIGNS.
I TOLD YOU—EVERY MADBOY HAS A STYLE—LIKE...LIKE A PAINTER—AND THE BARON CAN RECOGNIZE THEM.
WELL... I DO HAVE SOME IDEAS OF MY OWN...
THOSE TIDDLY LITTLE CLOCKWORK THINGS THAT DON'T WORK?
FORGET IT. WE NEED A SPARK, NOT AN IDIOT TOYMAKER.
I HAND PLANS FOR THOSE TO THE BARON, I'LL BE SHIPPED OFF TO CASTLE HETERODYNE WITHIN THE HOUR.
WE NEED SOMETHING BIG. IMPRESSIVE.
WELL THEN... MAYBE STYLISTIC SIMILARITIES RUN IN FAMILIES.
WE COULD SAY YOU'RE D'OMAS' NATURAL SON.

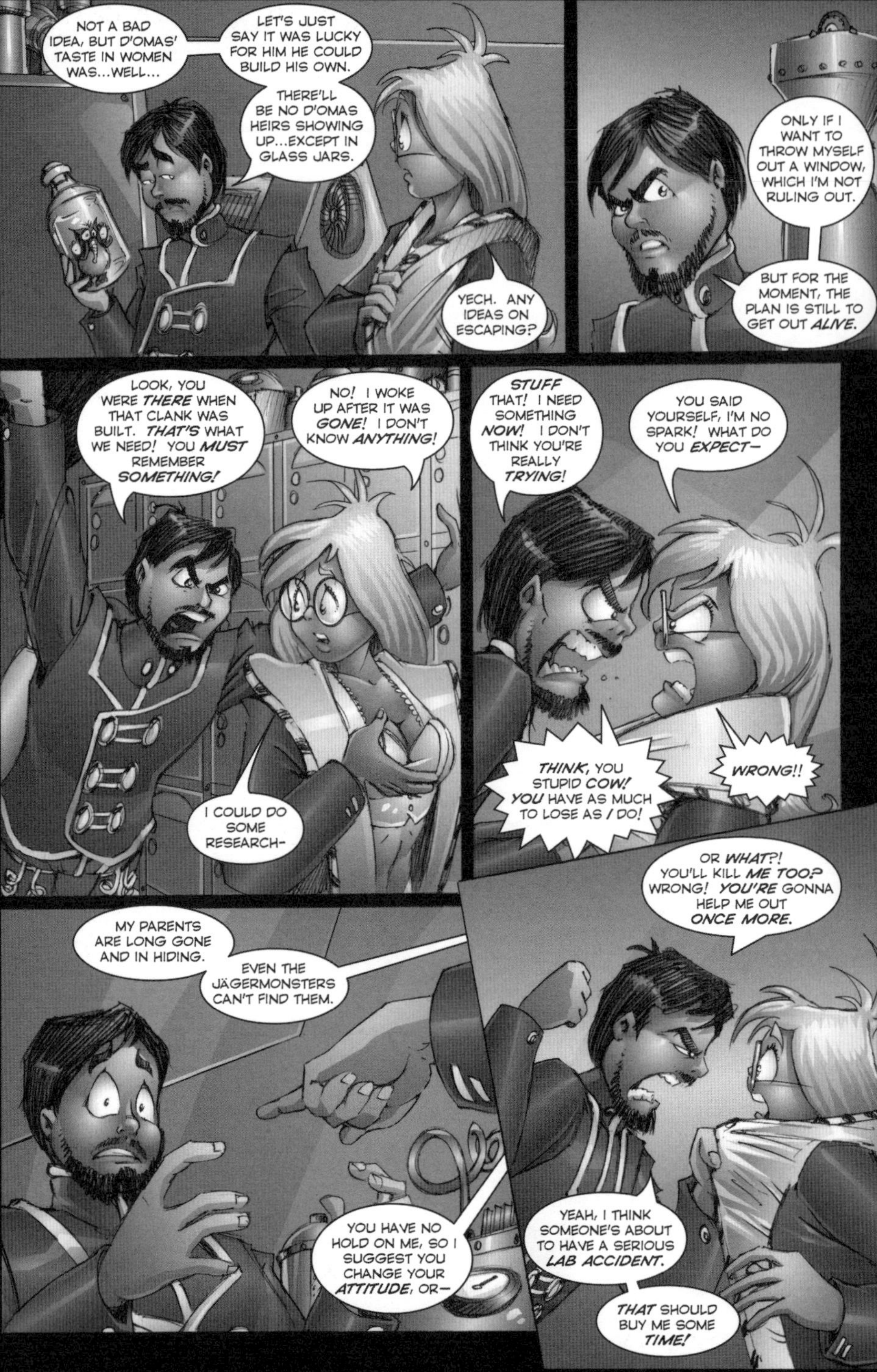
NOT A BAD IDEA, BUT D'OMAS' TASTE IN WOMEN WAS...WELL...
LET'S JUST SAY IT WAS LUCKY FOR HIM HE COULD BUILD HIS OWN.
THERE'LL BE NO D'OMAS HEIRS SHOWING UP...EXCEPT IN GLASS JARS.
YECH. ANY IDEAS ON ESCAPING?
ONLY IF I WANT TO THROW MYSELF OUT A WINDOW, WHICH I'M NOT RULING OUT.
BUT FOR THE MOMENT, THE PLAN IS STILL TO GET OUT ALIVE.
LOOK, YOU WERE THERE WHEN THAT CLANK WAS BUILT. THAT'S WHAT WE NEED! YOU MUST REMEMBER SOMETHING!
NO! I WOKE UP AFTER IT WAS GONE! I DON'T KNOW ANYTHING!
I COULD DO SOME RESEARCH-
STUFF THAT! I NEED SOMETHING NOW! I DON'T THINK YOU'RE REALLY TRYING!
YOU SAID YOURSELF, I'M NO SPARK! WHAT DO YOU EXPECT—
THINK, YOU STUPID COW! YOU HAVE AS MUCH TO LOSE AS I DO!
WRONG!!
MY PARENTS ARE LONG GONE AND IN HIDING.
EVEN THE JÄGERMONSTERS CAN'T FIND THEM.
YOU HAVE NO HOLD ON ME, SO I SUGGEST YOU CHANGE YOUR ATTITUDE, OR—
OR WHAT?! YOU'LL KILL ME TOO? WRONG! YOU'RE GONNA HELP ME OUT ONCE MORE.
YEAH, I THINK SOMEONE'S ABOUT TO HAVE A SERIOUS LAB ACCIDENT.
THAT SHOULD BUY ME SOME TIME!

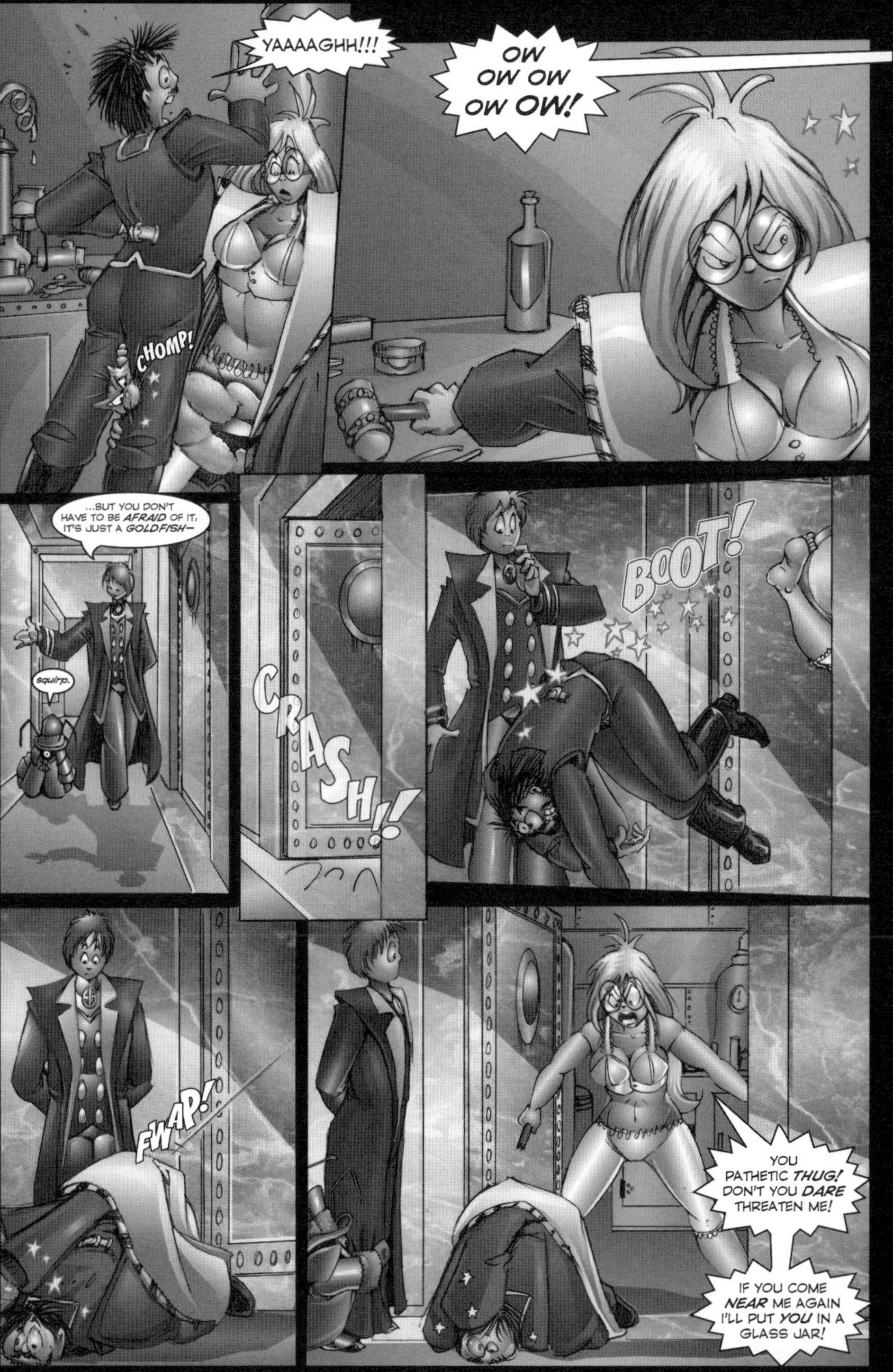
YAAAAGHH!!!
CHOMP!
OW OW OW OW OW!
...BUT YOU DON'T HAVE TO BE AFRAID OF IT, IT'S JUST A GOLDFISH—
squirp.
CRASH!!
BOOT!
FWAP!
YOU PATHETIC THUG! DON'T YOU DARE THREATEN ME!
IF YOU COME NEAR ME AGAIN I'LL PUT YOU IN A GLASS JAR!

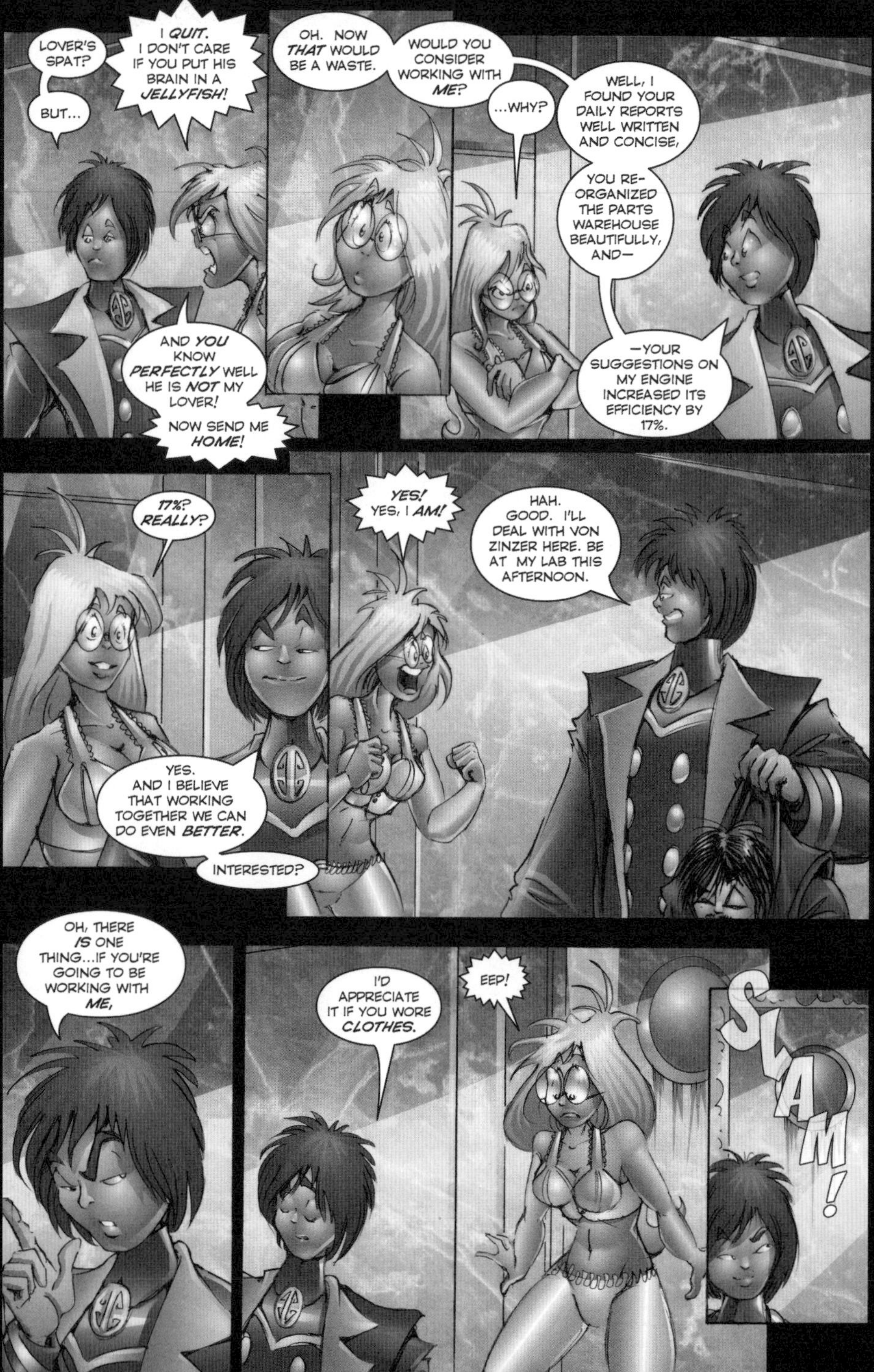
LOVER'S SPAT?
BUT...
I QUIT. I DON'T CARE IF YOU PUT HIS BRAIN IN A JELLYFISH!
AND YOU KNOW PERFECTLY WELL HE IS NOT MY LOVER!
NOW SEND ME HOME!
OH. NOW THAT WOULD BE A WASTE.
WOULD YOU CONSIDER WORKING WITH ME?
...WHY?
WELL, I FOUND YOUR DAILY REPORTS WELL WRITTEN AND CONCISE,
YOU RE-ORGANIZED THE PARTS WAREHOUSE BEAUTIFULLY, AND—
—YOUR SUGGESTIONS ON MY ENGINE INCREASED ITS EFFICIENCY BY 17%.
17%? REALLY?
YES. AND I BELIEVE THAT WORKING TOGETHER WE CAN DO EVEN BETTER.
INTERESTED?
YES! YES, I AM!
HAH. GOOD. I'LL DEAL WITH VON ZINZER HERE. BE AT MY LAB THIS AFTERNOON.
OH, THERE IS ONE THING...IF YOU'RE GOING TO BE WORKING WITH ME,
I'D APPRECIATE IT IF YOU WORE CLOTHES.
EEP!
SLAM!

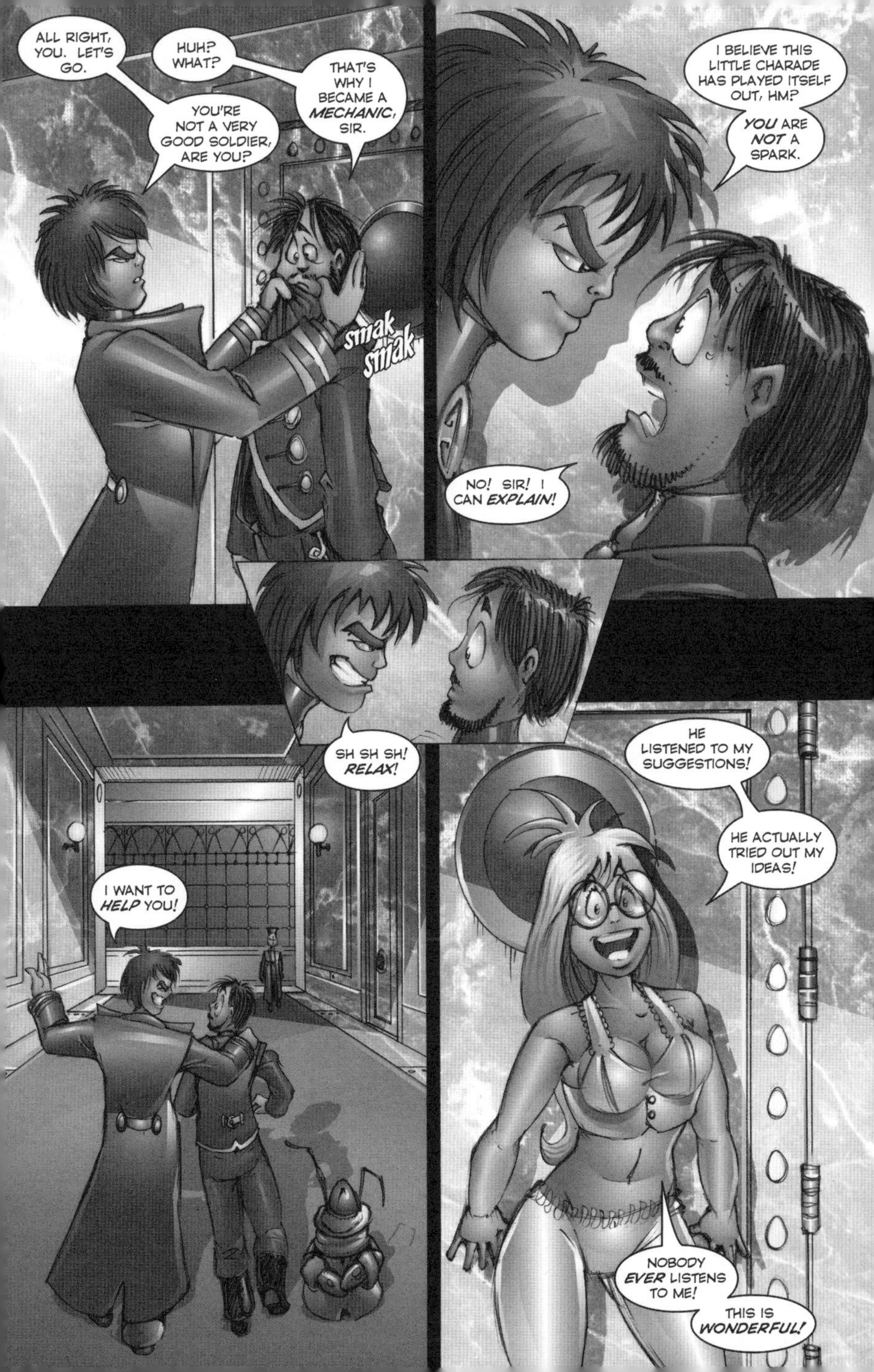
ALL RIGHT, YOU. LET'S GO.
HUH? WHAT?
YOU'RE NOT A VERY GOOD SOLDIER, ARE YOU?
THAT'S WHY I BECAME A *MECHANIC*, SIR.
SMAK SMAK
I BELIEVE THIS LITTLE CHARADE HAS PLAYED ITSELF OUT, HM?
YOU ARE *NOT* A SPARK.
NO! SIR! I CAN *EXPLAIN*!
SH SH SH! *RELAX*!
I WANT TO *HELP* YOU!
HE LISTENED TO MY SUGGESTIONS!
HE ACTUALLY TRIED OUT MY IDEAS!
NOBODY *EVER* LISTENS TO ME!
THIS IS *WONDERFUL*!

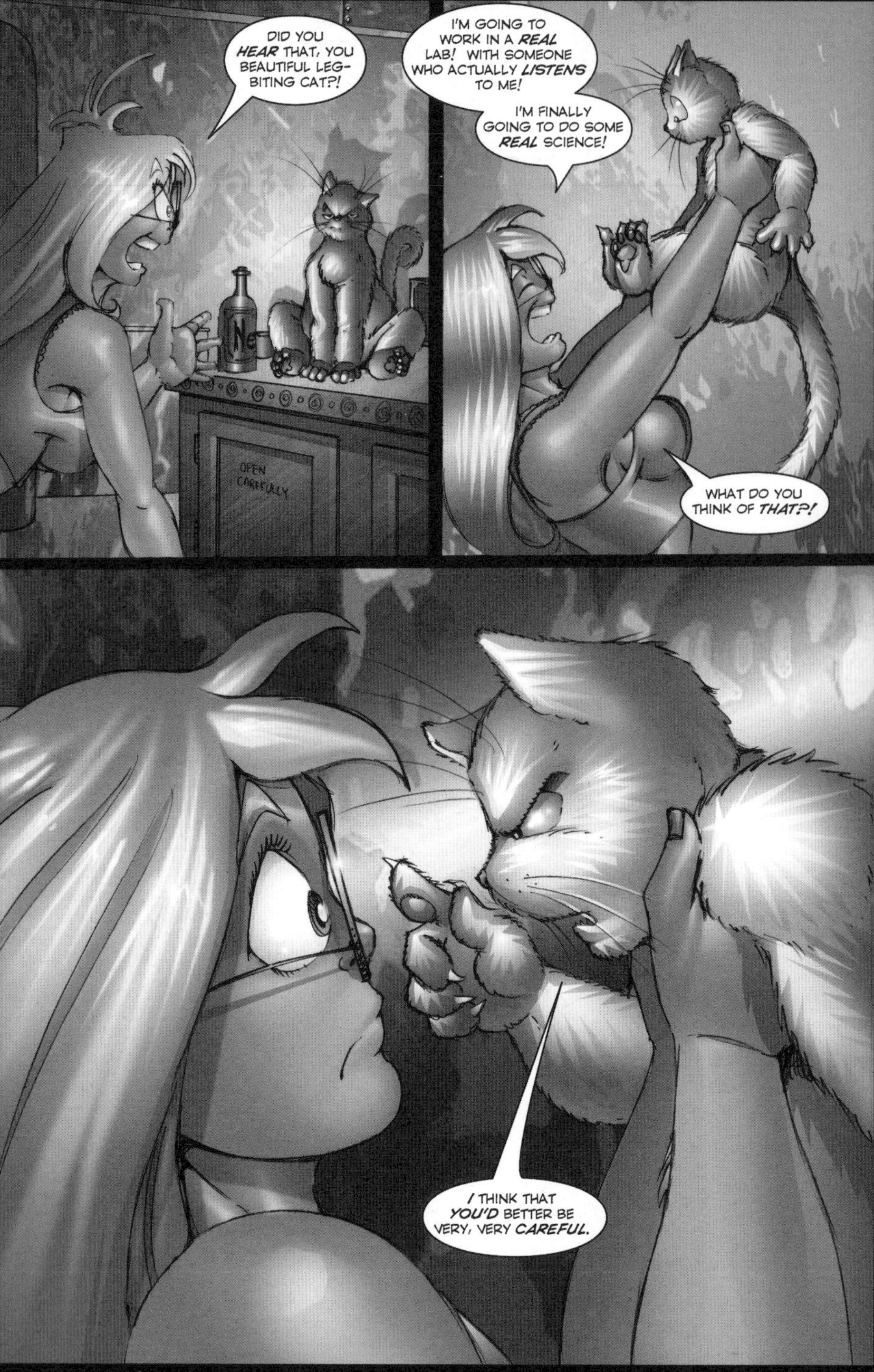
DID YOU HEAR THAT, YOU BEAUTIFUL LEG-BITING CAT?!
OPEN CAREFULLY
I'M GOING TO WORK IN A REAL LAB! WITH SOMEONE WHO ACTUALLY LISTENS TO ME!
I'M FINALLY GOING TO DO SOME REAL SCIENCE!
WHAT DO YOU THINK OF THAT?!
I THINK THAT YOU'D BETTER BE VERY, VERY CAREFUL.

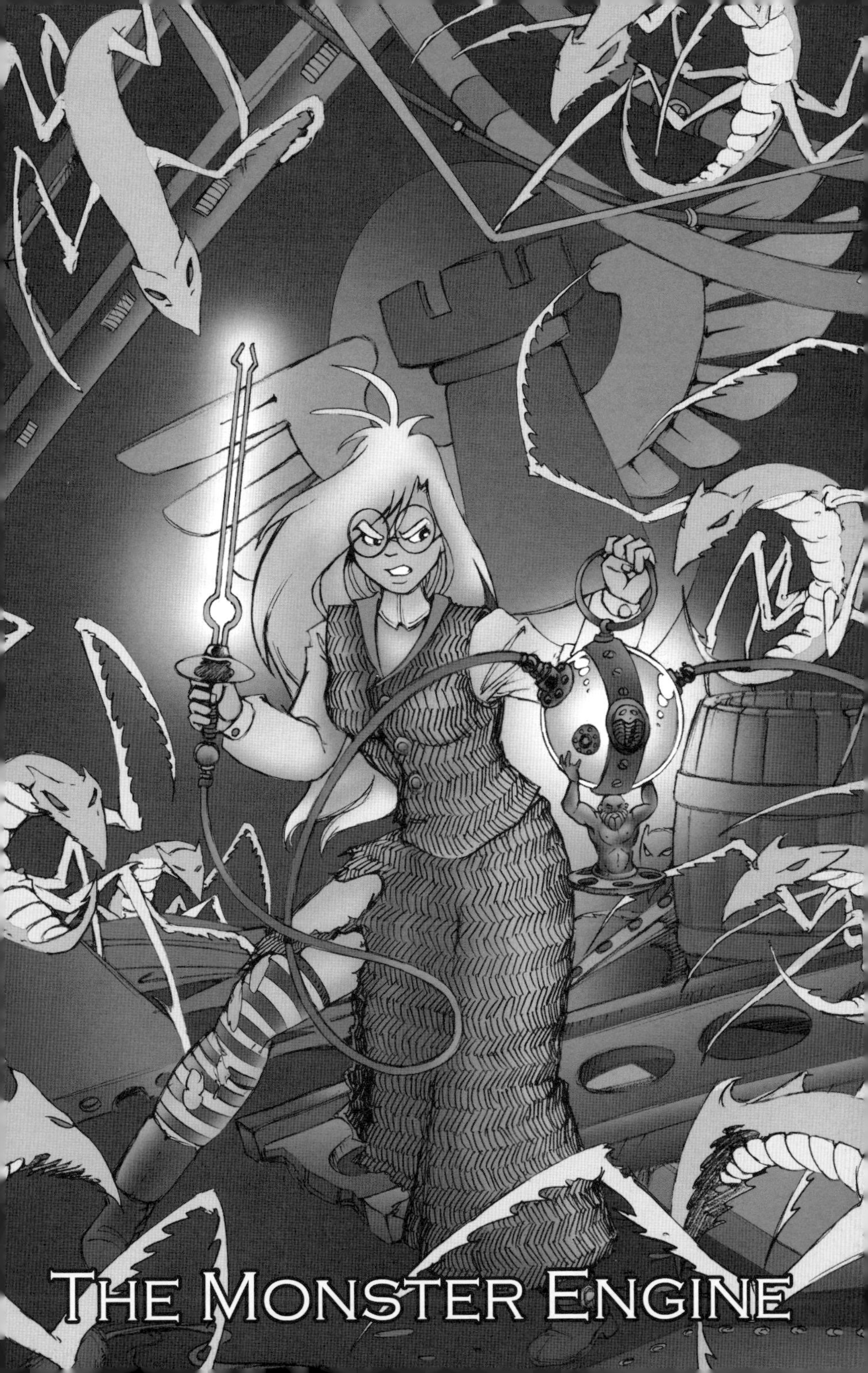
THE MONSTER ENGINE

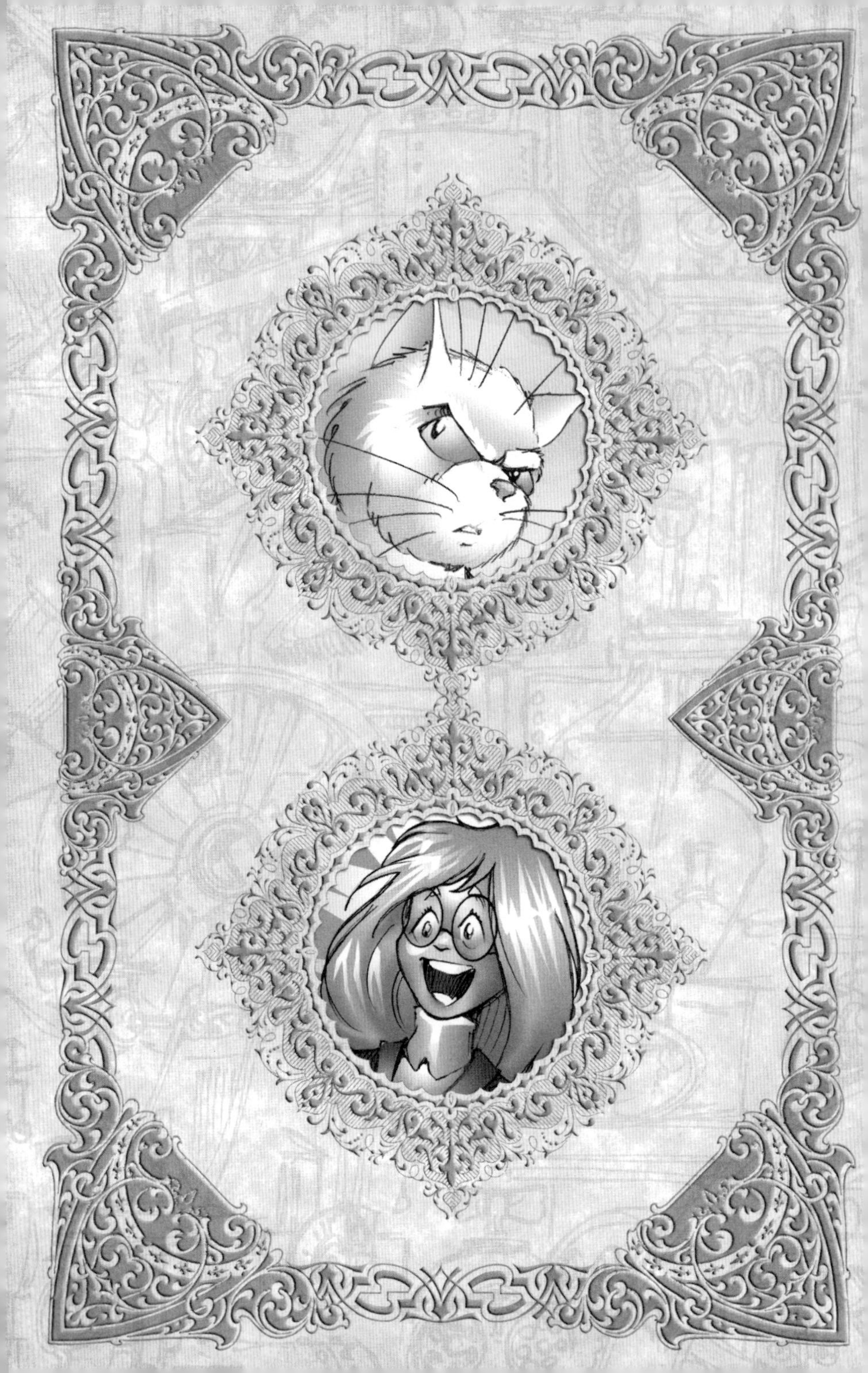

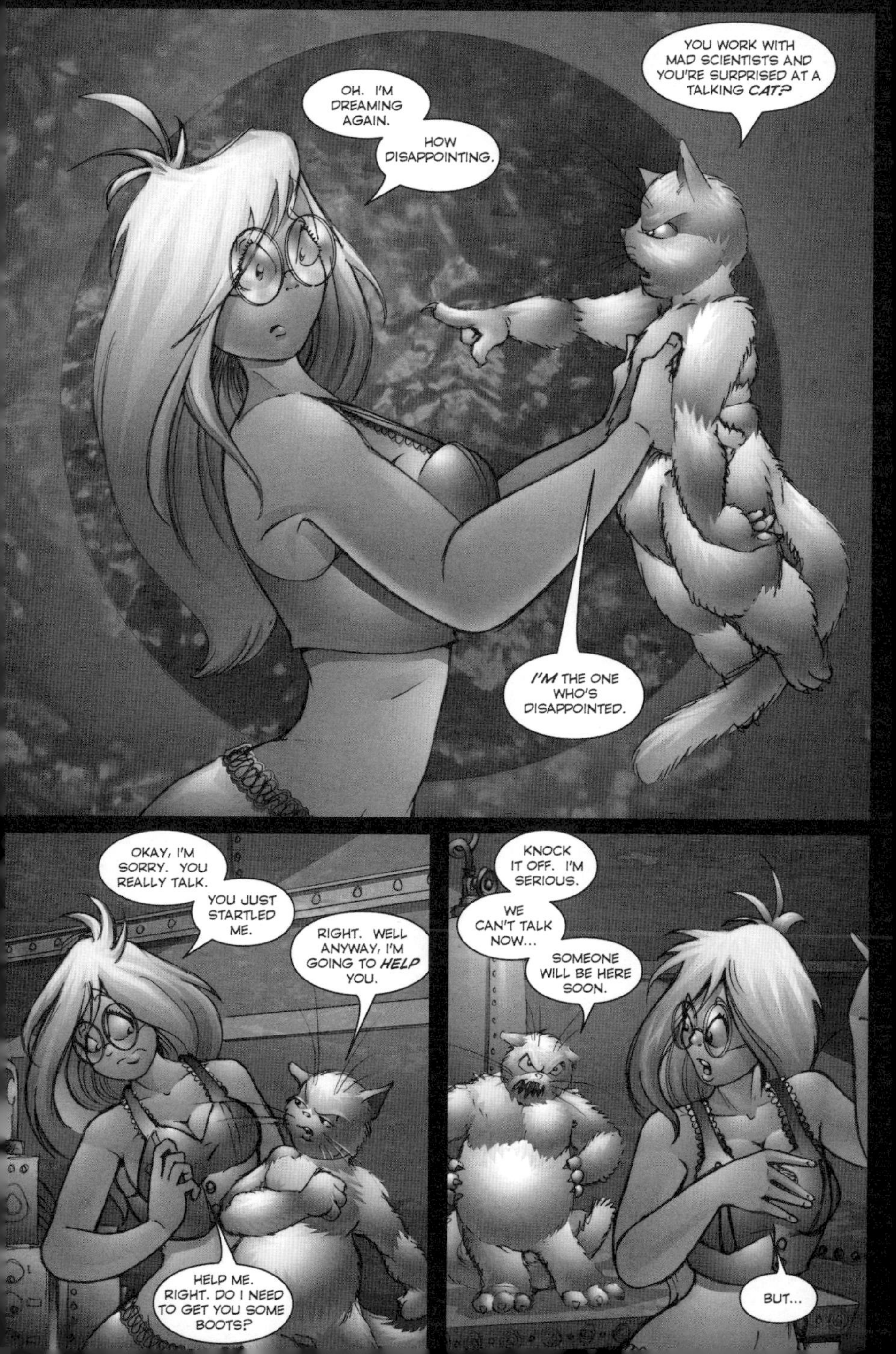
OH. I'M DREAMING AGAIN.
HOW DISAPPOINTING.
YOU WORK WITH MAD SCIENTISTS AND YOU'RE SURPRISED AT A TALKING *CAT?*
I'M THE ONE WHO'S DISAPPOINTED.
OKAY, I'M SORRY. YOU REALLY TALK.
YOU JUST STARTLED ME.
RIGHT. WELL ANYWAY, I'M GOING TO *HELP* YOU.
HELP ME. RIGHT. DO I NEED TO GET YOU SOME BOOTS?
KNOCK IT OFF. I'M SERIOUS.
WE CAN'T TALK NOW...
SOMEONE WILL BE HERE SOON.
BUT...

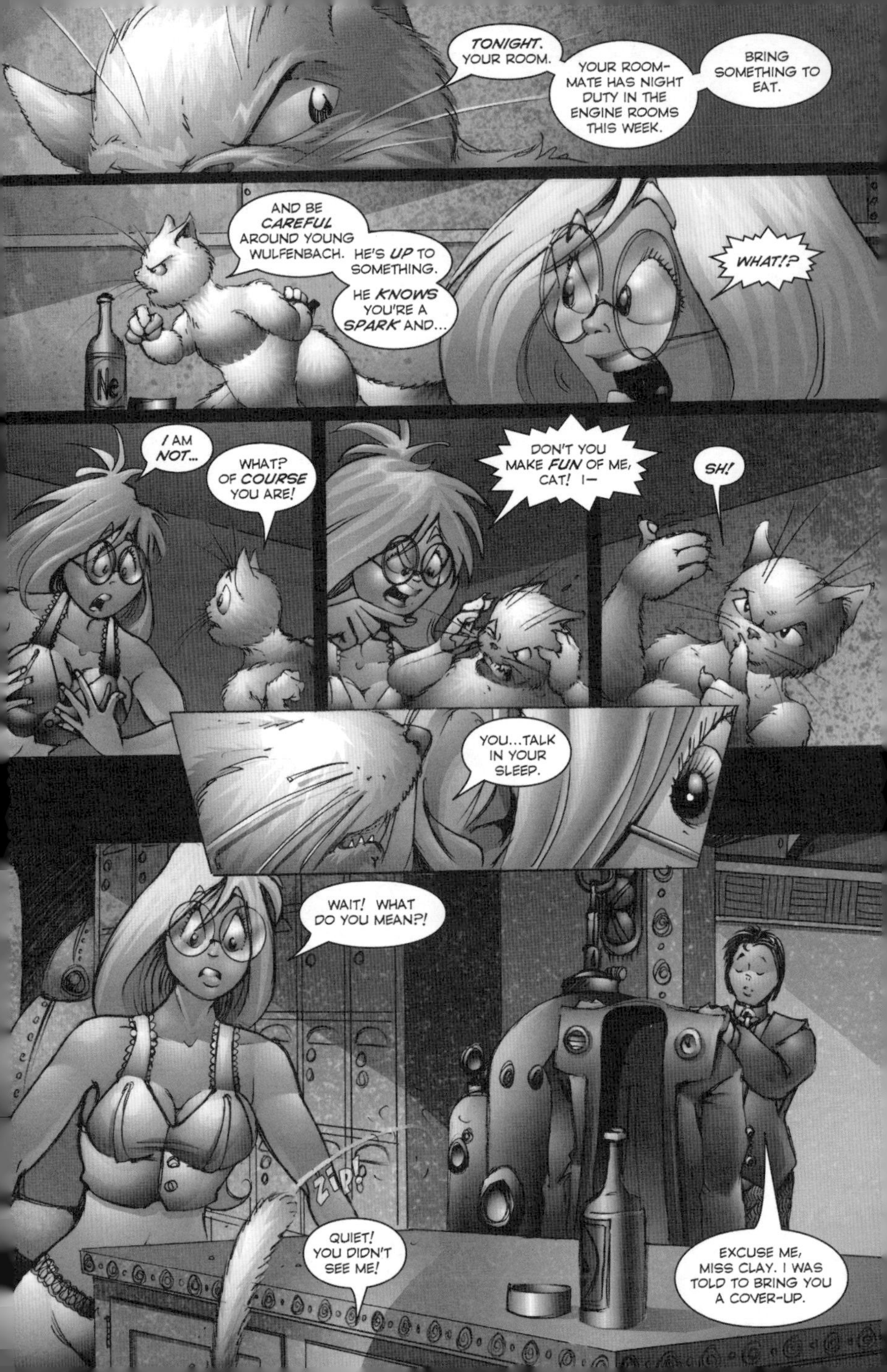
TONIGHT. YOUR ROOM.
YOUR ROOM-MATE HAS NIGHT DUTY IN THE ENGINE ROOMS THIS WEEK.
BRING SOMETHING TO EAT.
AND BE CAREFUL AROUND YOUNG WULFENBACH. HE'S UP TO SOMETHING.
HE KNOWS YOU'RE A SPARK AND...
WHAT!?
I AM NOT...
WHAT? OF COURSE YOU ARE!
DON'T YOU MAKE FUN OF ME, CAT! I—
SH!
YOU...TALK IN YOUR SLEEP.
WAIT! WHAT DO YOU MEAN?!
ZIP!
QUIET! YOU DIDN'T SEE ME!
EXCUSE ME, MISS CLAY. I WAS TOLD TO BRING YOU A COVER-UP.
Ne

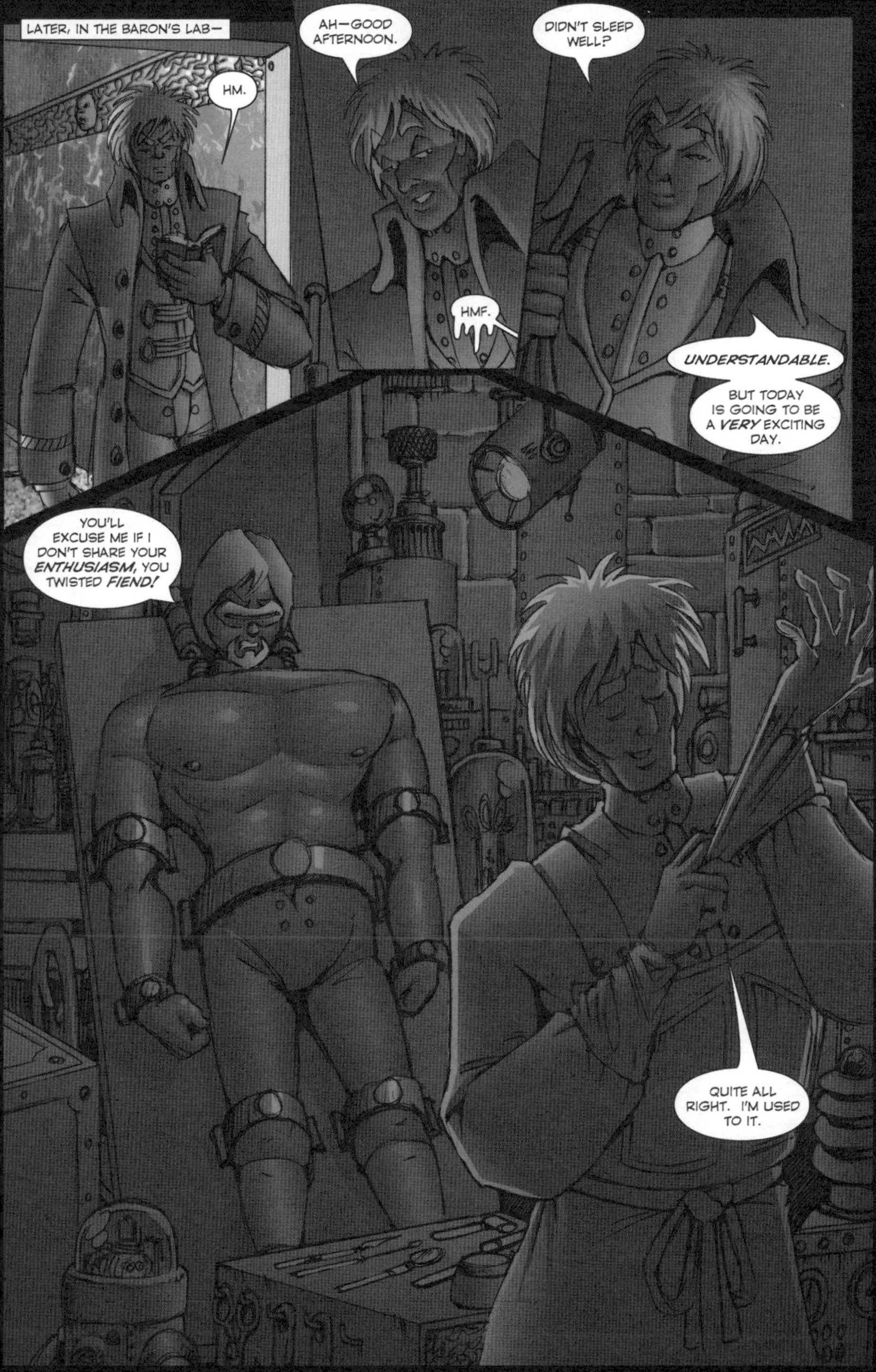
LATER, IN THE BARON'S LAB—
HM.
AH—GOOD AFTERNOON.
DIDN'T SLEEP WELL?
HMF.
UNDERSTANDABLE.
BUT TODAY IS GOING TO BE A *VERY* EXCITING DAY.
YOU'LL EXCUSE ME IF I DON'T SHARE YOUR *ENTHUSIASM,* YOU TWISTED *FIEND!*
QUITE ALL RIGHT. I'M USED TO IT.

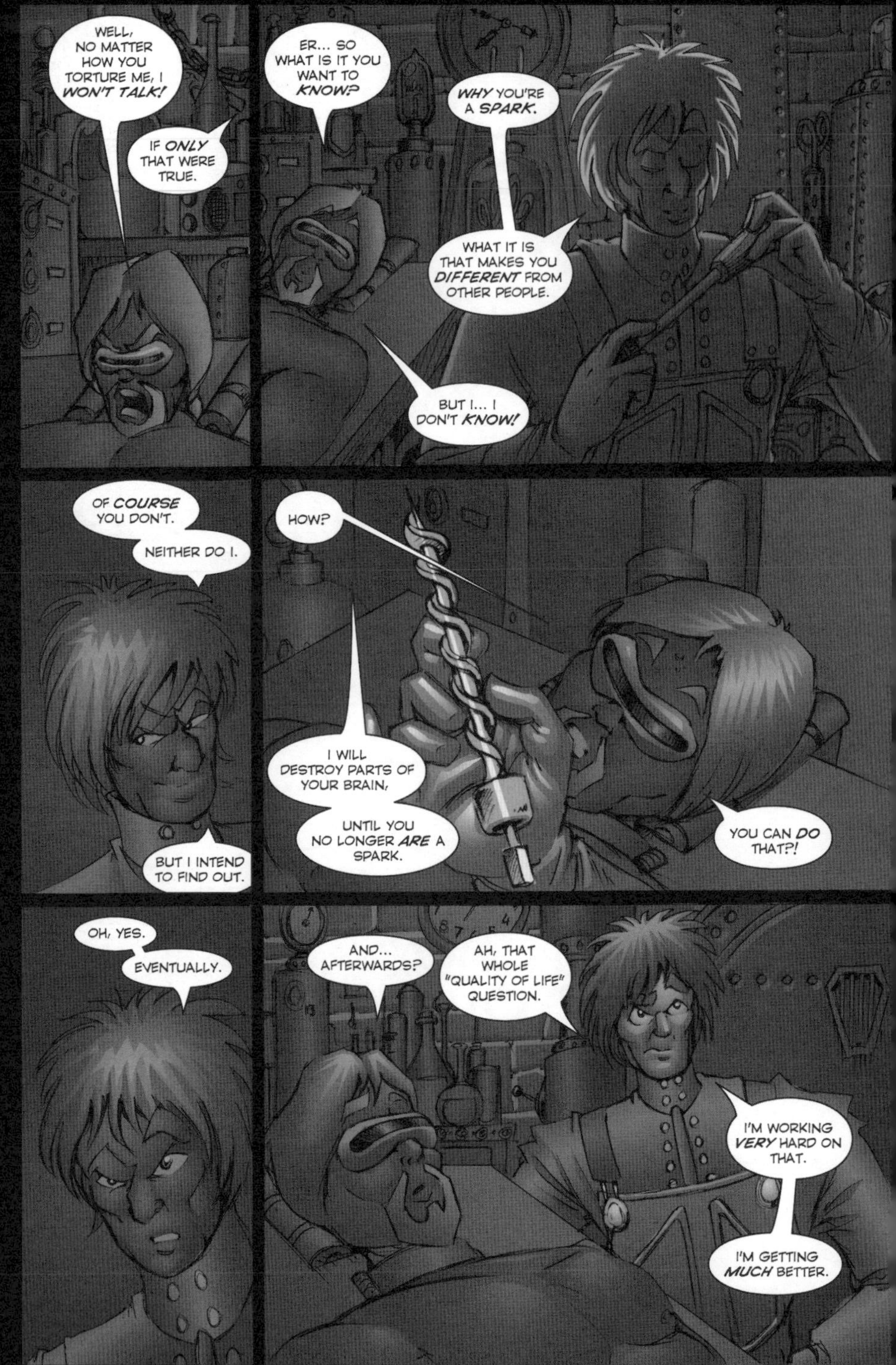
WELL, NO MATTER HOW YOU TORTURE ME, I WON'T TALK!
IF ONLY THAT WERE TRUE.
ER... SO WHAT IS IT YOU WANT TO KNOW?
WHY YOU'RE A SPARK.
WHAT IT IS THAT MAKES YOU DIFFERENT FROM OTHER PEOPLE.
BUT I... I DON'T KNOW!
OF COURSE YOU DON'T.
NEITHER DO I.
BUT I INTEND TO FIND OUT.
HOW?
I WILL DESTROY PARTS OF YOUR BRAIN,
UNTIL YOU NO LONGER ARE A SPARK.
YOU CAN DO THAT?!
OH, YES.
EVENTUALLY.
AND... AFTERWARDS?
AH, THAT WHOLE "QUALITY OF LIFE" QUESTION.
I'M WORKING VERY HARD ON THAT.
I'M GETTING MUCH BETTER.

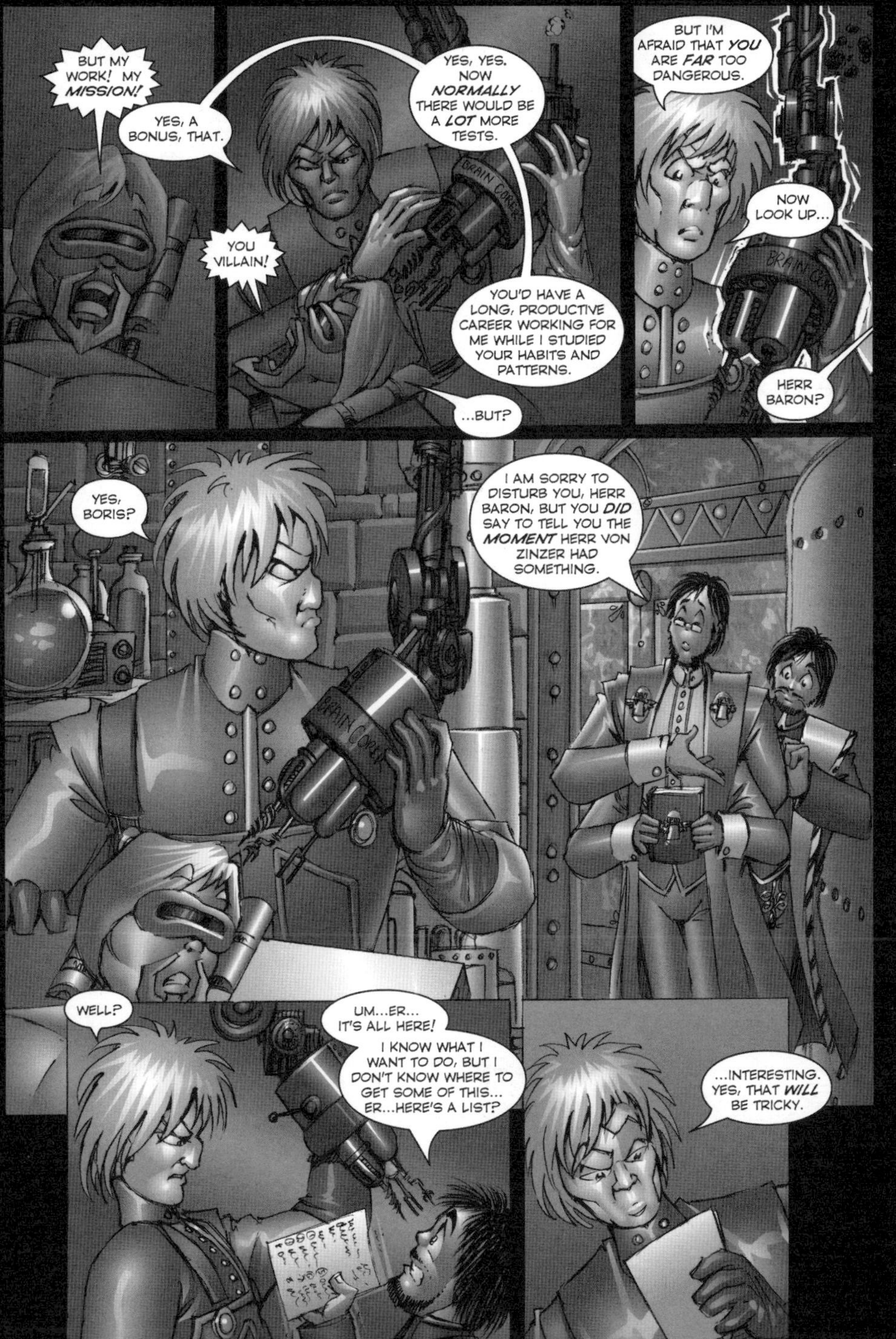
BUT MY WORK! MY MISSION!
YES, A BONUS, THAT.
YES, YES. NOW NORMALLY THERE WOULD BE A LOT MORE TESTS.
YOU VILLAIN!
YOU'D HAVE A LONG, PRODUCTIVE CAREER WORKING FOR ME WHILE I STUDIED YOUR HABITS AND PATTERNS.
...BUT?
BUT I'M AFRAID THAT YOU ARE FAR TOO DANGEROUS.
NOW LOOK UP...
HERR BARON?
YES, BORIS?
I AM SORRY TO DISTURB YOU, HERR BARON, BUT YOU DID SAY TO TELL YOU THE MOMENT HERR VON ZINZER HAD SOMETHING.
WELL?
UM...ER... IT'S ALL HERE!
I KNOW WHAT I WANT TO DO, BUT I DON'T KNOW WHERE TO GET SOME OF THIS... ER...HERE'S A LIST?
...INTERESTING. YES, THAT WILL BE TRICKY.

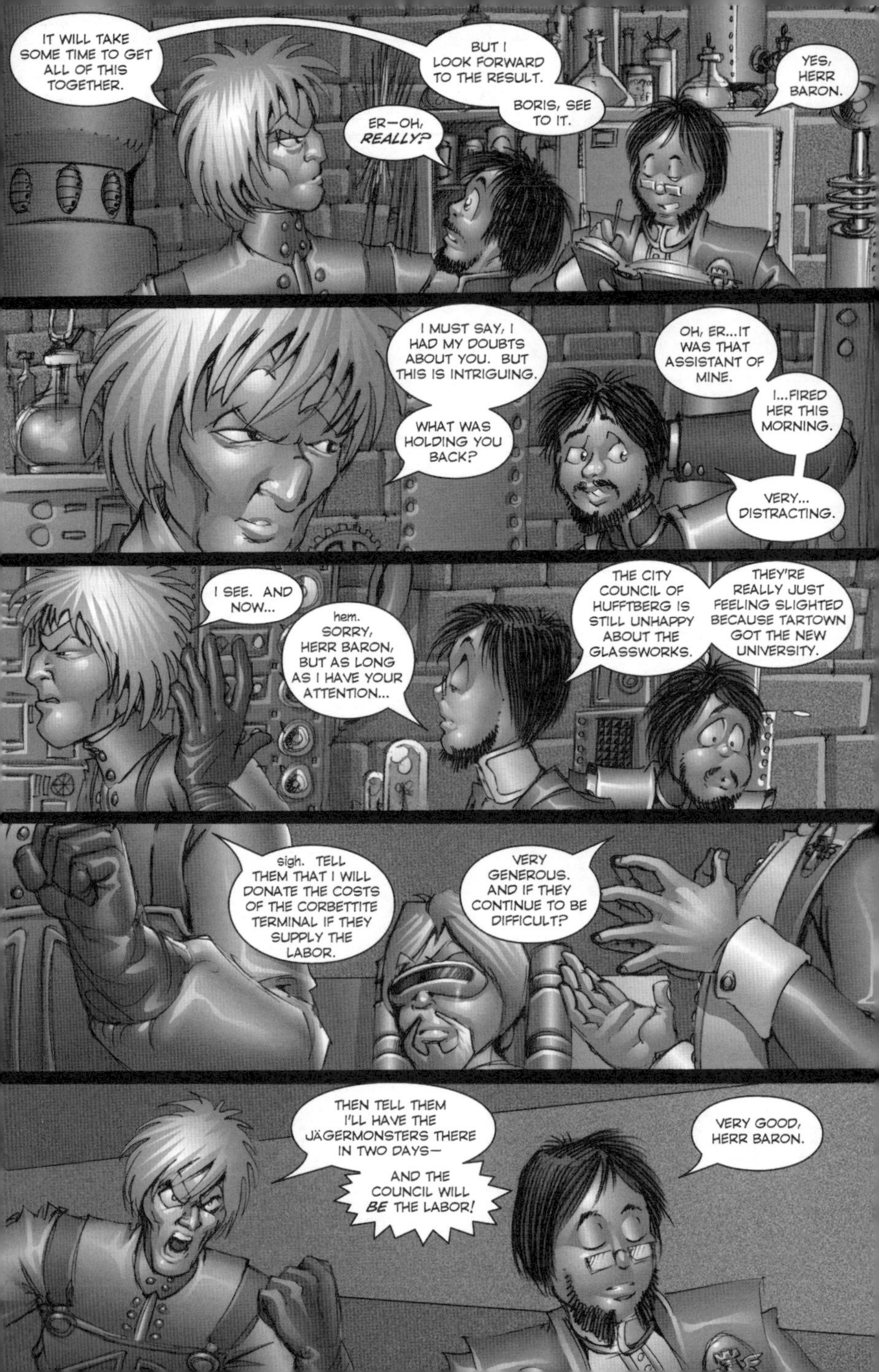
IT WILL TAKE SOME TIME TO GET ALL OF THIS TOGETHER.
BUT I LOOK FORWARD TO THE RESULT.
BORIS, SEE TO IT.
ER—OH, *REALLY?*
YES, HERR BARON.
I MUST SAY, I HAD MY DOUBTS ABOUT YOU. BUT THIS IS INTRIGUING.
WHAT WAS HOLDING YOU BACK?
OH, ER...IT WAS THAT ASSISTANT OF MINE.
I...FIRED HER THIS MORNING.
VERY... DISTRACTING.
I SEE. AND NOW...
hem. SORRY, HERR BARON, BUT AS LONG AS I HAVE YOUR ATTENTION...
THE CITY COUNCIL OF HUFFTBERG IS STILL UNHAPPY ABOUT THE GLASSWORKS.
THEY'RE REALLY JUST FEELING SLIGHTED BECAUSE TARTOWN GOT THE NEW UNIVERSITY.
sigh. TELL THEM THAT I WILL DONATE THE COSTS OF THE CORBETTITE TERMINAL IF THEY SUPPLY THE LABOR.
VERY GENEROUS. AND IF THEY CONTINUE TO BE DIFFICULT?
THEN TELL THEM I'LL HAVE THE JÄGERMONSTERS THERE IN TWO DAYS—
AND THE COUNCIL WILL *BE* THE LABOR!
VERY GOOD, HERR BARON.

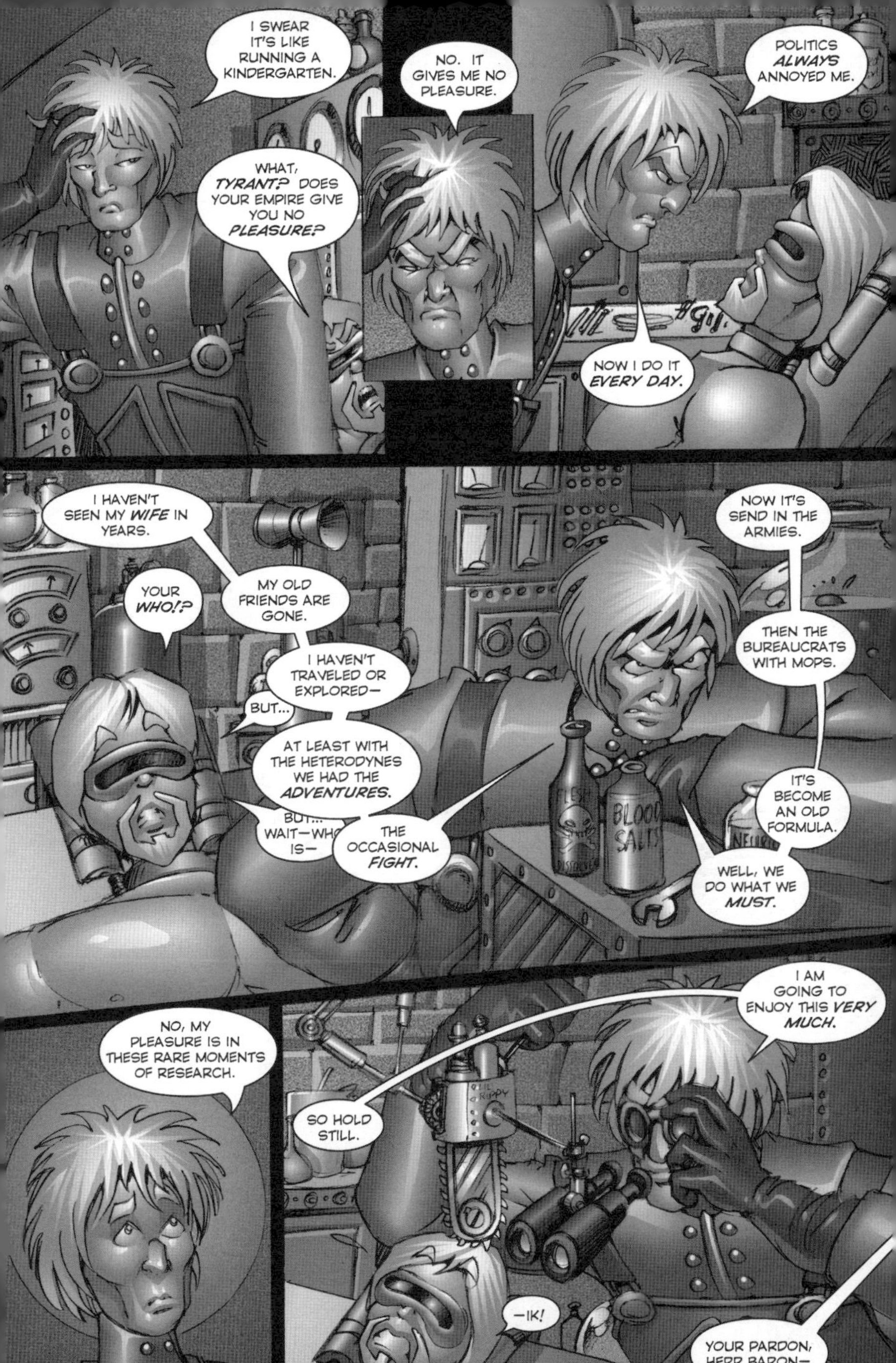
I SWEAR IT'S LIKE RUNNING A KINDERGARTEN.
WHAT, *TYRANT?* DOES YOUR EMPIRE GIVE YOU NO *PLEASURE?*
NO. IT GIVES ME NO PLEASURE.
POLITICS *ALWAYS* ANNOYED ME.
NOW I DO IT *EVERY DAY.*
I HAVEN'T SEEN MY *WIFE* IN YEARS.
YOUR *WHO!?*
MY OLD FRIENDS ARE GONE.
I HAVEN'T TRAVELED OR EXPLORED—
BUT...
AT LEAST WITH THE HETERODYNES WE HAD THE *ADVENTURES.*
BUT... WAIT—WHO IS—
THE OCCASIONAL *FIGHT.*
NOW IT'S SEND IN THE ARMIES.
THEN THE BUREAUCRATS WITH MOPS.
IT'S BECOME AN OLD FORMULA.
WELL, WE DO WHAT WE *MUST.*
BLOOD SALTS
NO, MY PLEASURE IS IN THESE RARE MOMENTS OF RESEARCH.
I AM GOING TO ENJOY THIS *VERY MUCH.*
SO HOLD STILL.
—IK!
YOUR PARDON, HERR BARON—

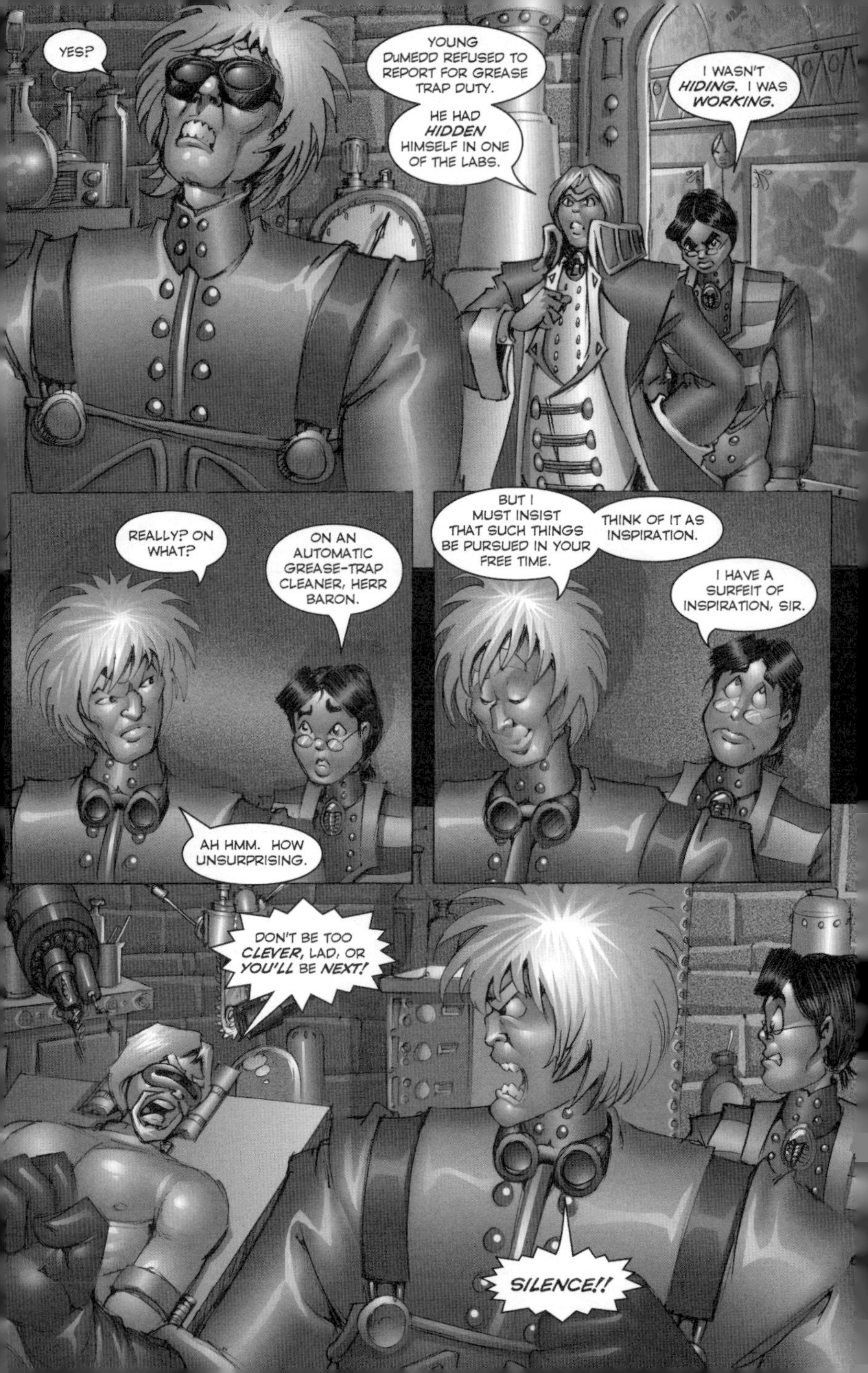
YES?
YOUNG DuMEDD REFUSED TO REPORT FOR GREASE TRAP DUTY.
HE HAD *HIDDEN* HIMSELF IN ONE OF THE LABS.
I WASN'T *HIDING*. I WAS *WORKING*.
REALLY? ON WHAT?
ON AN AUTOMATIC GREASE-TRAP CLEANER, HERR BARON.
AH HMM. HOW UNSURPRISING.
BUT I MUST INSIST THAT SUCH THINGS BE PURSUED IN YOUR FREE TIME.
THINK OF IT AS INSPIRATION.
I HAVE A SURFEIT OF INSPIRATION, SIR.
DON'T BE TOO *CLEVER*, LAD, OR *YOU'LL* BE *NEXT!*
SILENCE!!

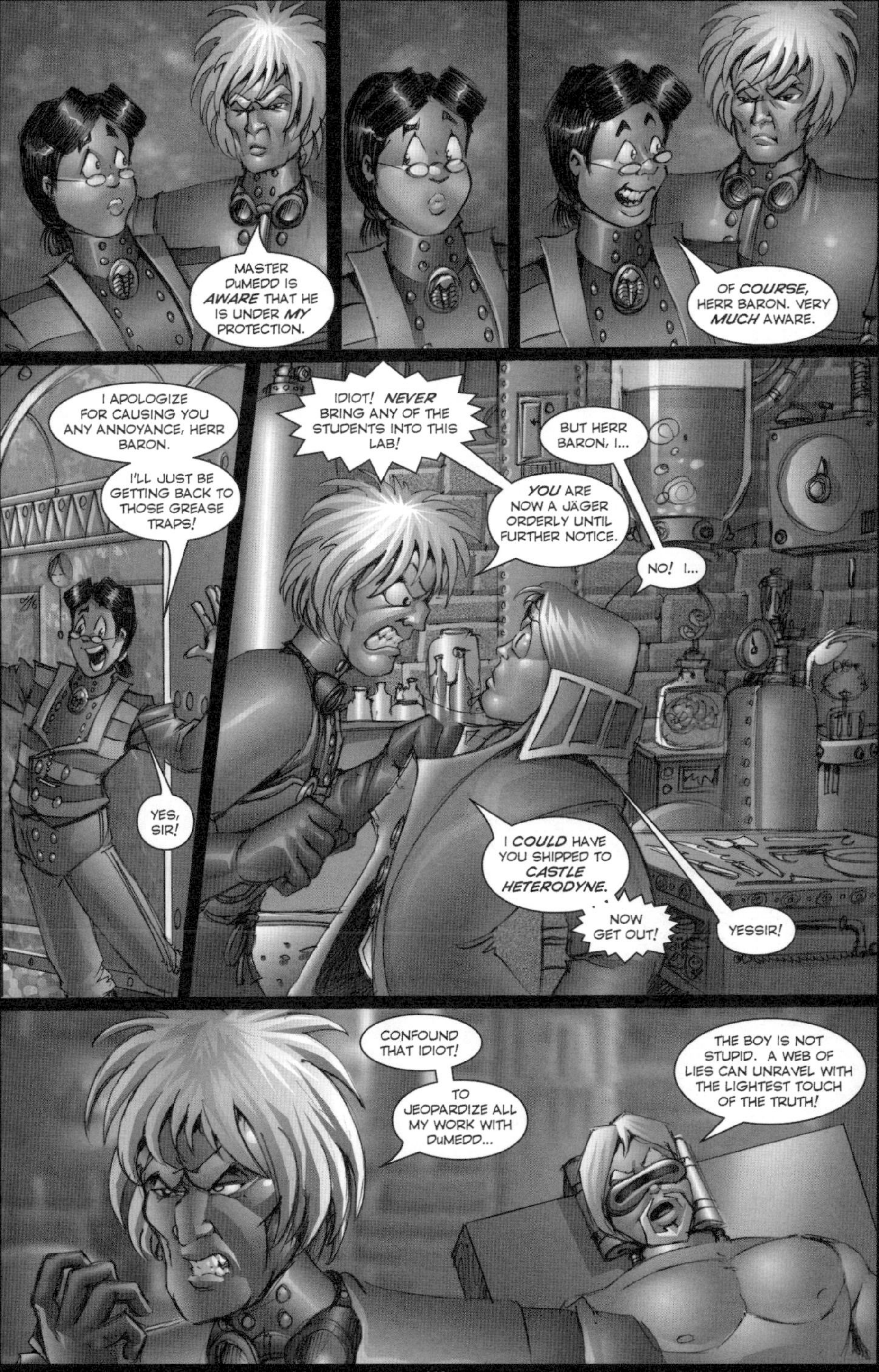
MASTER DuMEDD IS AWARE THAT HE IS UNDER MY PROTECTION.
OF COURSE, HERR BARON. VERY MUCH AWARE.
I APOLOGIZE FOR CAUSING YOU ANY ANNOYANCE, HERR BARON.
I'LL JUST BE GETTING BACK TO THOSE GREASE TRAPS!
YES, SIR!
IDIOT! NEVER BRING ANY OF THE STUDENTS INTO THIS LAB!
BUT HERR BARON, I...
YOU ARE NOW A JÄGER ORDERLY UNTIL FURTHER NOTICE.
NO! I...
I COULD HAVE YOU SHIPPED TO CASTLE HETERODYNE.
NOW GET OUT!
YESSIR!
CONFOUND THAT IDIOT!
TO JEOPARDIZE ALL MY WORK WITH DuMEDD...
THE BOY IS NOT STUPID. A WEB OF LIES CAN UNRAVEL WITH THE LIGHTEST TOUCH OF THE TRUTH!

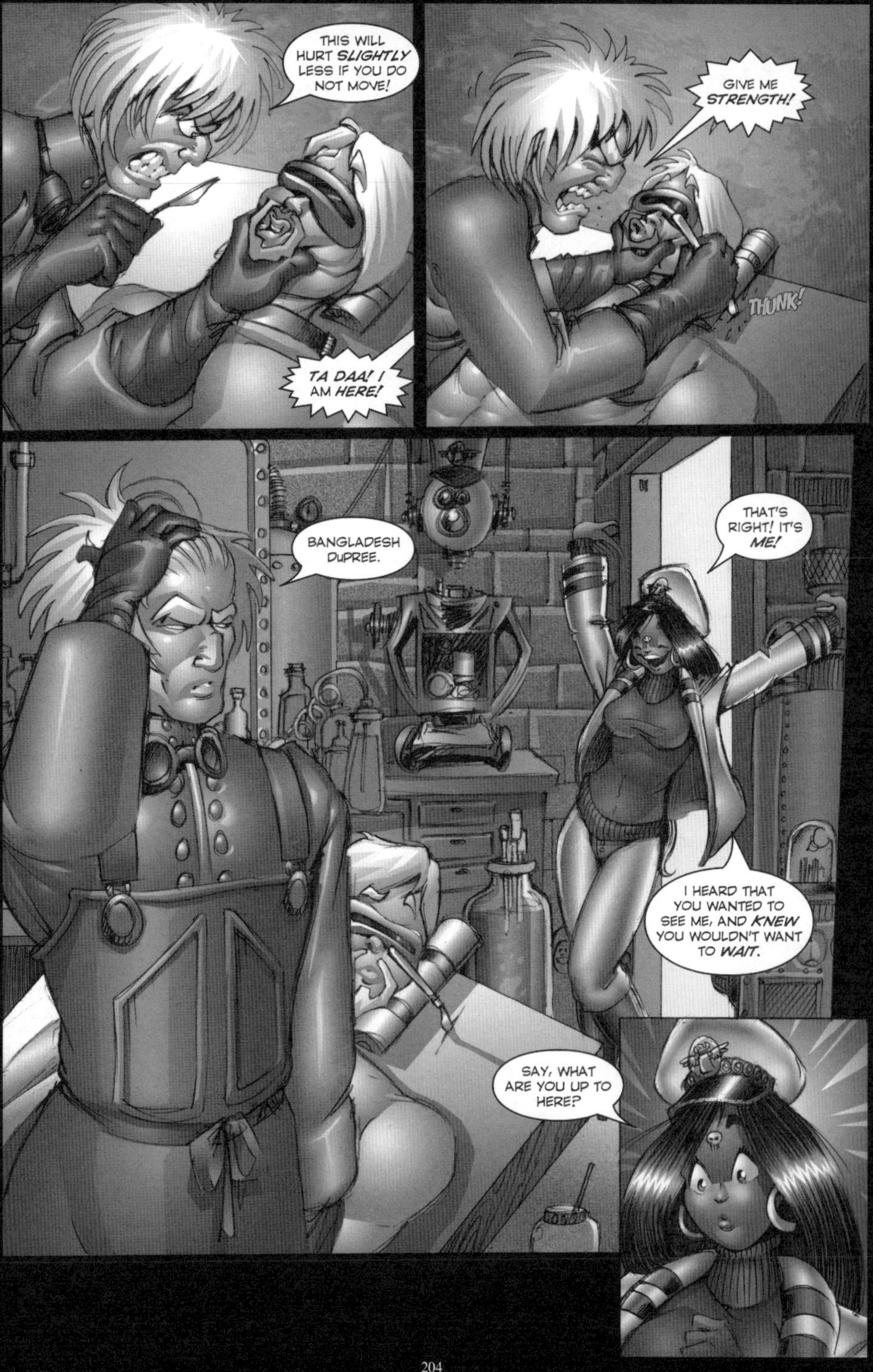
THIS WILL HURT SLIGHTLY LESS IF YOU DO NOT MOVE!
TA DAA! I AM HERE!
GIVE ME STRENGTH!
THUNK!
BANGLADESH DuPREE.
THAT'S RIGHT! IT'S ME!
I HEARD THAT YOU WANTED TO SEE ME, AND KNEW YOU WOULDN'T WANT TO WAIT.
SAY, WHAT ARE YOU UP TO HERE?

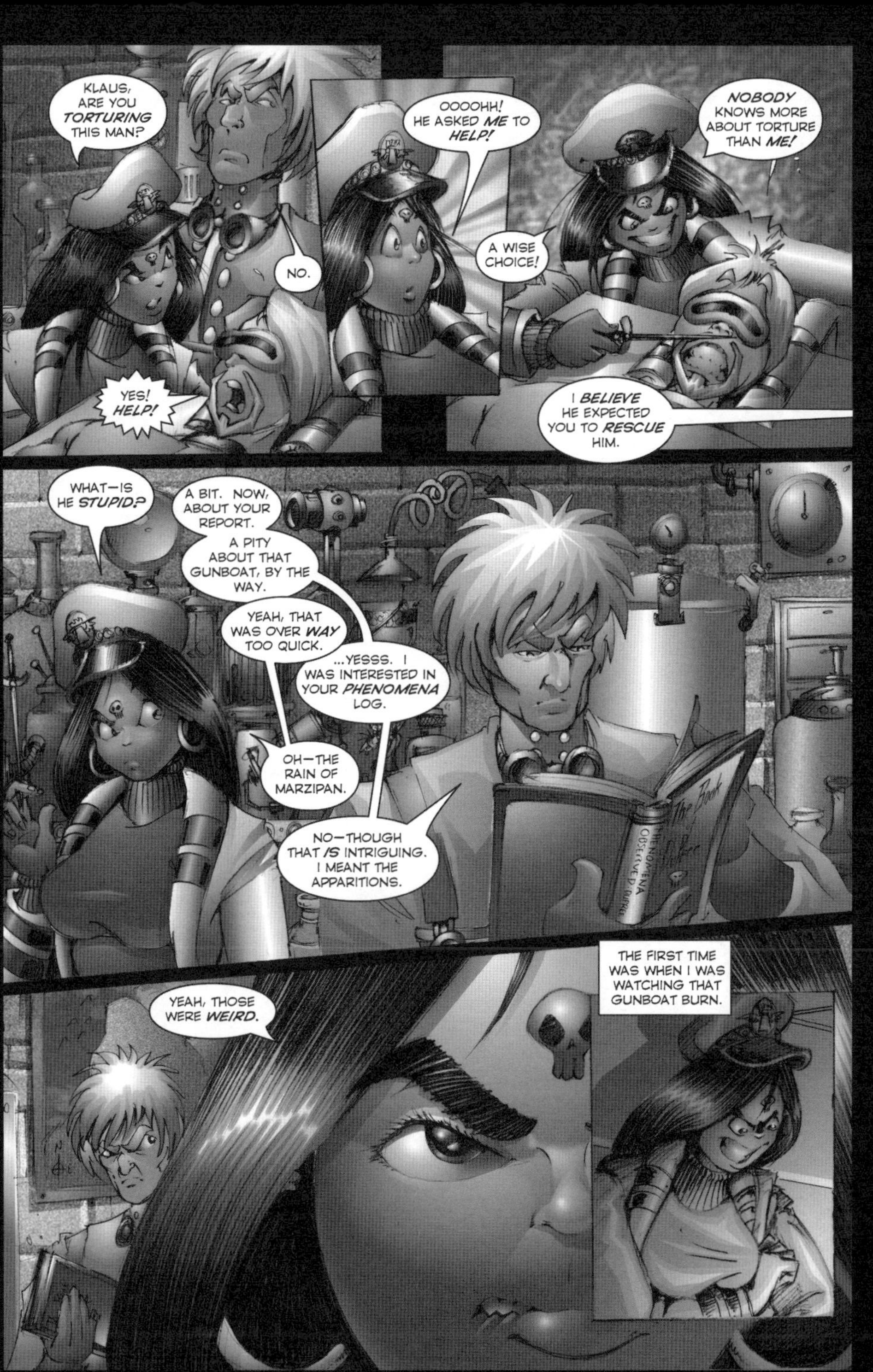
KLAUS, ARE YOU TORTURING THIS MAN?
NO.
YES! HELP!
OOOOHH! HE ASKED ME TO HELP!
A WISE CHOICE!
NOBODY KNOWS MORE ABOUT TORTURE THAN ME!
I BELIEVE HE EXPECTED YOU TO RESCUE HIM.
WHAT—IS HE STUPID?
A BIT. NOW, ABOUT YOUR REPORT.
A PITY ABOUT THAT GUNBOAT, BY THE WAY.
YEAH, THAT WAS OVER WAY TOO QUICK.
...YESSS. I WAS INTERESTED IN YOUR PHENOMENA LOG.
OH—THE RAIN OF MARZIPAN.
NO—THOUGH THAT IS INTRIGUING. I MEANT THE APPARITIONS.
YEAH, THOSE WERE WEIRD.
THE FIRST TIME WAS WHEN I WAS WATCHING THAT GUNBOAT BURN.

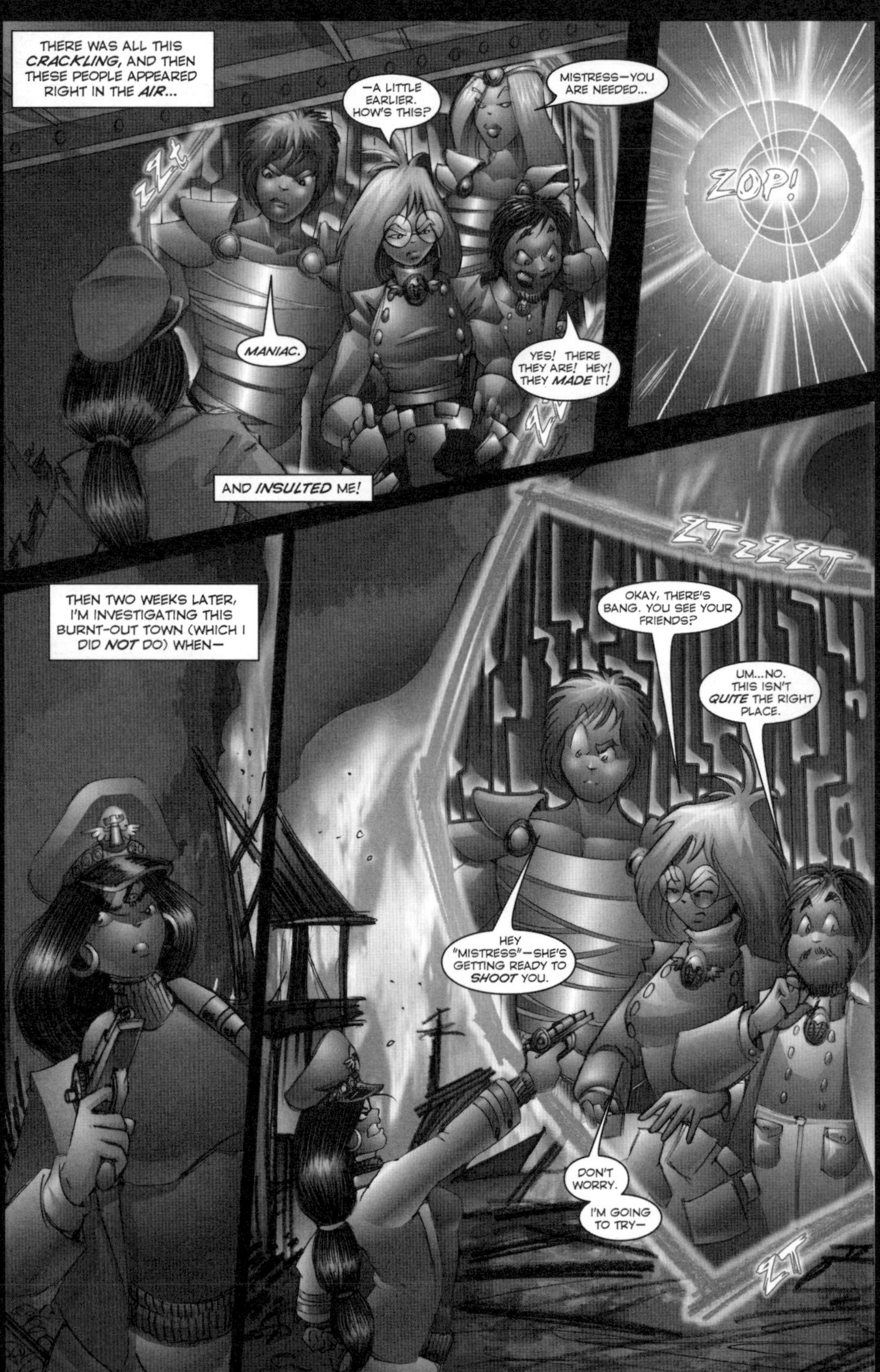

THERE WAS ALL THIS CRACKLING, AND THEN THESE PEOPLE APPEARED RIGHT IN THE AIR...
—A LITTLE EARLIER. HOW'S THIS?
MISTRESS—YOU ARE NEEDED...
ZZt
MANIAC.
YES! THERE THEY ARE! HEY! THEY MADE IT!
ZOP!
AND INSULTED ME!
ZT zZZT
THEN TWO WEEKS LATER, I'M INVESTIGATING THIS BURNT-OUT TOWN (WHICH I DID NOT DO) WHEN—
OKAY, THERE'S BANG. YOU SEE YOUR FRIENDS?
UM...NO. THIS ISN'T QUITE THE RIGHT PLACE.
HEY "MISTRESS"—SHE'S GETTING READY TO SHOOT YOU.
DON'T WORRY.
I'M GOING TO TRY—
ZT

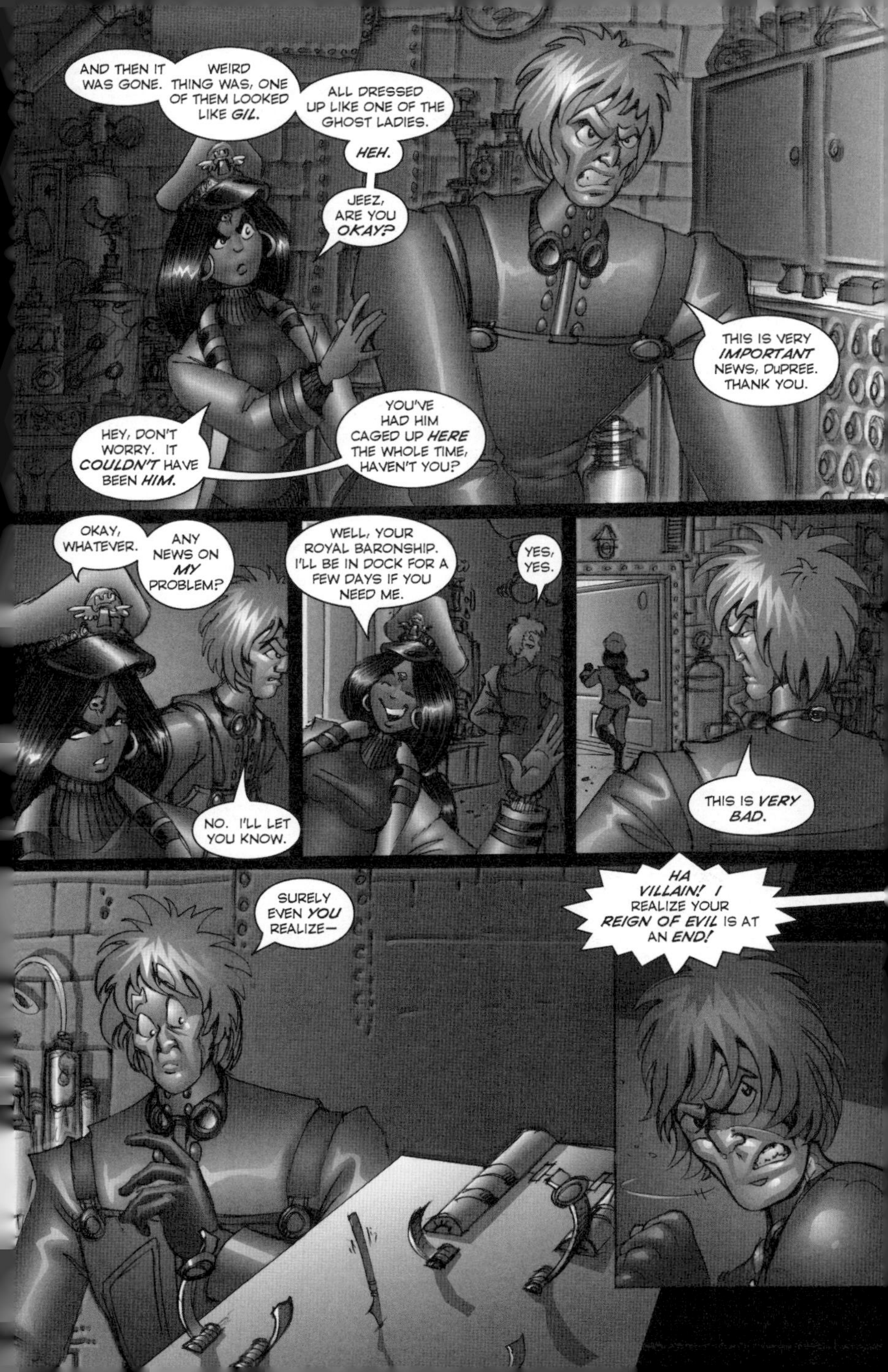
AND THEN IT WAS GONE.
WEIRD THING WAS, ONE OF THEM LOOKED LIKE GIL.
ALL DRESSED UP LIKE ONE OF THE GHOST LADIES.
HEH.
JEEZ, ARE YOU OKAY?
THIS IS VERY IMPORTANT NEWS, DuPREE. THANK YOU.
HEY, DON'T WORRY. IT COULDN'T HAVE BEEN HIM.
YOU'VE HAD HIM CAGED UP HERE THE WHOLE TIME, HAVEN'T YOU?
OKAY, WHATEVER.
ANY NEWS ON MY PROBLEM?
NO. I'LL LET YOU KNOW.
WELL, YOUR ROYAL BARONSHIP. I'LL BE IN DOCK FOR A FEW DAYS IF YOU NEED ME.
YES, YES.
THIS IS VERY BAD.
SURELY EVEN YOU REALIZE—
HA VILLAIN! I REALIZE YOUR REIGN OF EVIL IS AT AN END!

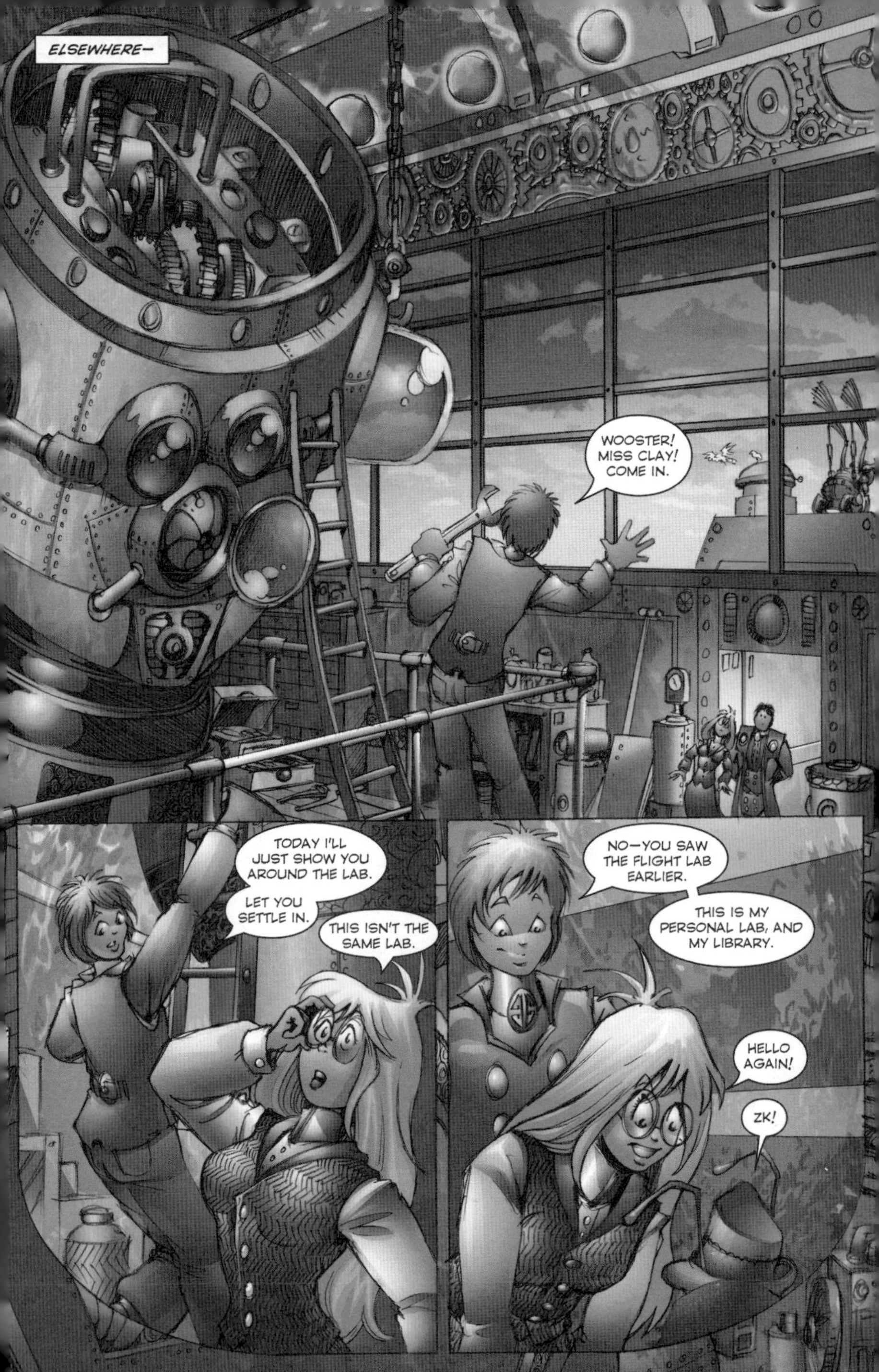
ELSEWHERE—
WOOSTER! MISS CLAY! COME IN.
TODAY I'LL JUST SHOW YOU AROUND THE LAB.
LET YOU SETTLE IN.
THIS ISN'T THE SAME LAB.
NO—YOU SAW THE FLIGHT LAB EARLIER.
THIS IS MY PERSONAL LAB, AND MY LIBRARY.
HELLO AGAIN!
ZK!

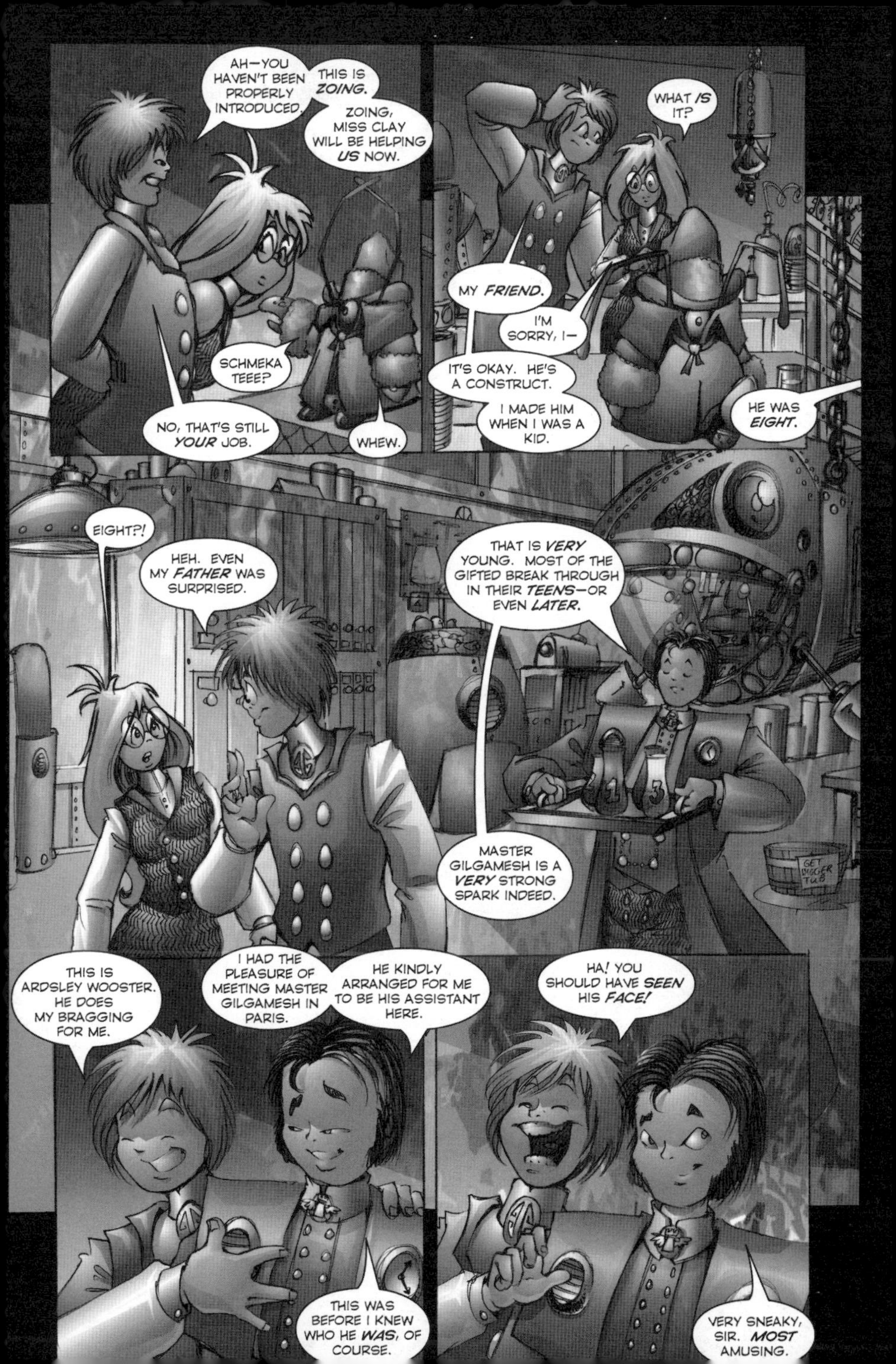
AH—YOU HAVEN'T BEEN PROPERLY INTRODUCED.
THIS IS ZOING.
ZOING, MISS CLAY WILL BE HELPING US NOW.
SCHMEKA TEEE?
NO, THAT'S STILL YOUR JOB.
WHEW.
WHAT IS IT?
MY FRIEND.
I'M SORRY, I—
IT'S OKAY. HE'S A CONSTRUCT.
I MADE HIM WHEN I WAS A KID.
HE WAS EIGHT.
EIGHT?!
HEH. EVEN MY FATHER WAS SURPRISED.
THAT IS VERY YOUNG. MOST OF THE GIFTED BREAK THROUGH IN THEIR TEENS—OR EVEN LATER.
MASTER GILGAMESH IS A VERY STRONG SPARK INDEED.
GET BIGGER TUB
THIS IS ARDSLEY WOOSTER. HE DOES MY BRAGGING FOR ME.
I HAD THE PLEASURE OF MEETING MASTER GILGAMESH IN PARIS.
HE KINDLY ARRANGED FOR ME TO BE HIS ASSISTANT HERE.
THIS WAS BEFORE I KNEW WHO HE WAS, OF COURSE.
HA! YOU SHOULD HAVE SEEN HIS FACE!
VERY SNEAKY, SIR. MOST AMUSING.

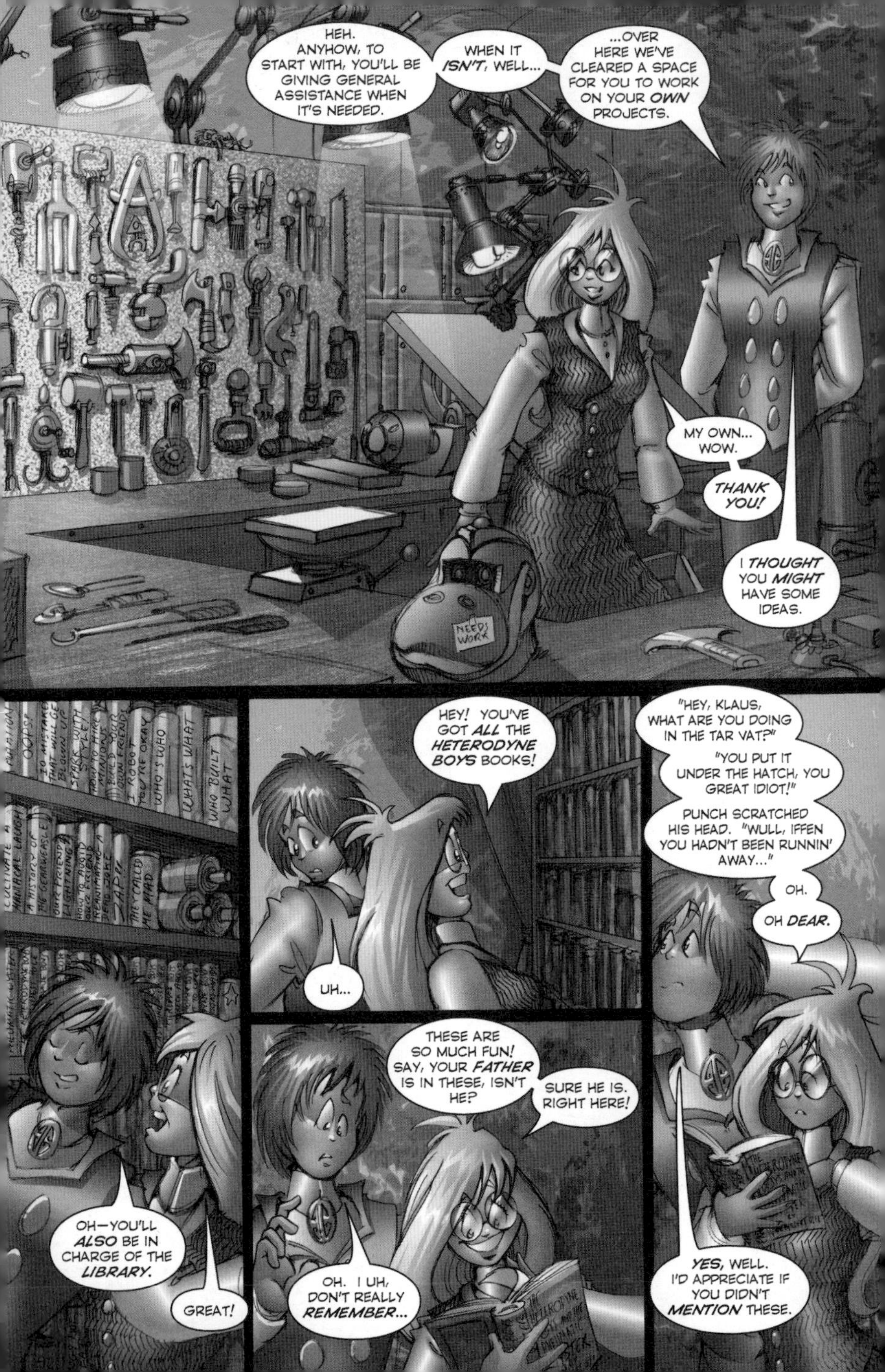
HEH. ANYHOW, TO START WITH, YOU'LL BE GIVING GENERAL ASSISTANCE WHEN IT'S NEEDED.
WHEN IT *ISN'T*, WELL...
...OVER HERE WE'VE CLEARED A SPACE FOR YOU TO WORK ON YOUR *OWN* PROJECTS.
MY OWN... WOW.
THANK YOU!
I *THOUGHT* YOU *MIGHT* HAVE SOME IDEAS.
NEEDS WORK
OH—YOU'LL *ALSO* BE IN CHARGE OF THE *LIBRARY*.
GREAT!
HEY! YOU'VE GOT *ALL* THE *HETERODYNE BOYS* BOOKS!
UH...
THESE ARE SO MUCH FUN! SAY, YOUR *FATHER* IS IN THESE, ISN'T HE?
SURE HE IS. RIGHT HERE!
OH. I UH, DON'T REALLY *REMEMBER*...
"HEY, KLAUS, WHAT ARE YOU DOING IN THE TAR VAT?"
"YOU PUT IT UNDER THE HATCH, YOU GREAT IDIOT!"
PUNCH SCRATCHED HIS HEAD. "WULL, IFFEN YOU HADN'T BEEN RUNNIN' AWAY..."
OH.
OH *DEAR*.
YES, WELL. I'D APPRECIATE IF YOU DIDN'T *MENTION* THESE.

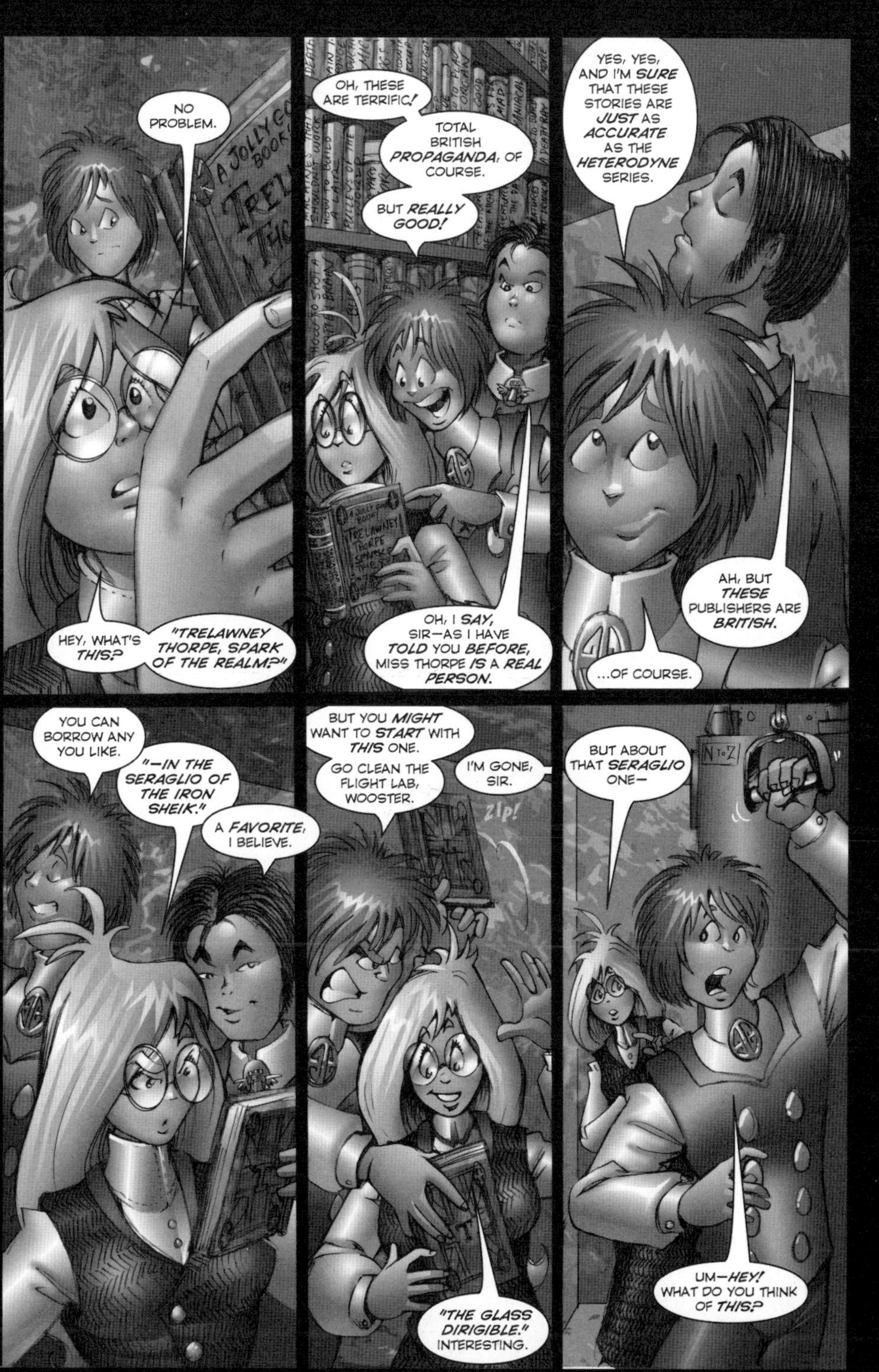
NO PROBLEM.
HEY, WHAT'S THIS?
"TRELAWNEY THORPE, SPARK OF THE REALM?"
OH, THESE ARE TERRIFIC!
TOTAL BRITISH PROPAGANDA, OF COURSE.
BUT REALLY GOOD!
OH, I SAY, SIR—AS I HAVE TOLD YOU BEFORE, MISS THORPE IS A REAL PERSON.
YES, YES, AND I'M SURE THAT THESE STORIES ARE JUST AS ACCURATE AS THE HETERODYNE SERIES.
AH, BUT THESE PUBLISHERS ARE BRITISH.
...OF COURSE.
YOU CAN BORROW ANY YOU LIKE.
"—IN THE SERAGLIO OF THE IRON SHEIK."
A FAVORITE, I BELIEVE.
BUT YOU MIGHT WANT TO START WITH THIS ONE.
GO CLEAN THE FLIGHT LAB, WOOSTER.
I'M GONE, SIR.
ZIP!
"THE GLASS DIRIGIBLE." INTERESTING.
BUT ABOUT THAT SERAGLIO ONE—
N to Z
UM—HEY! WHAT DO YOU THINK OF THIS?

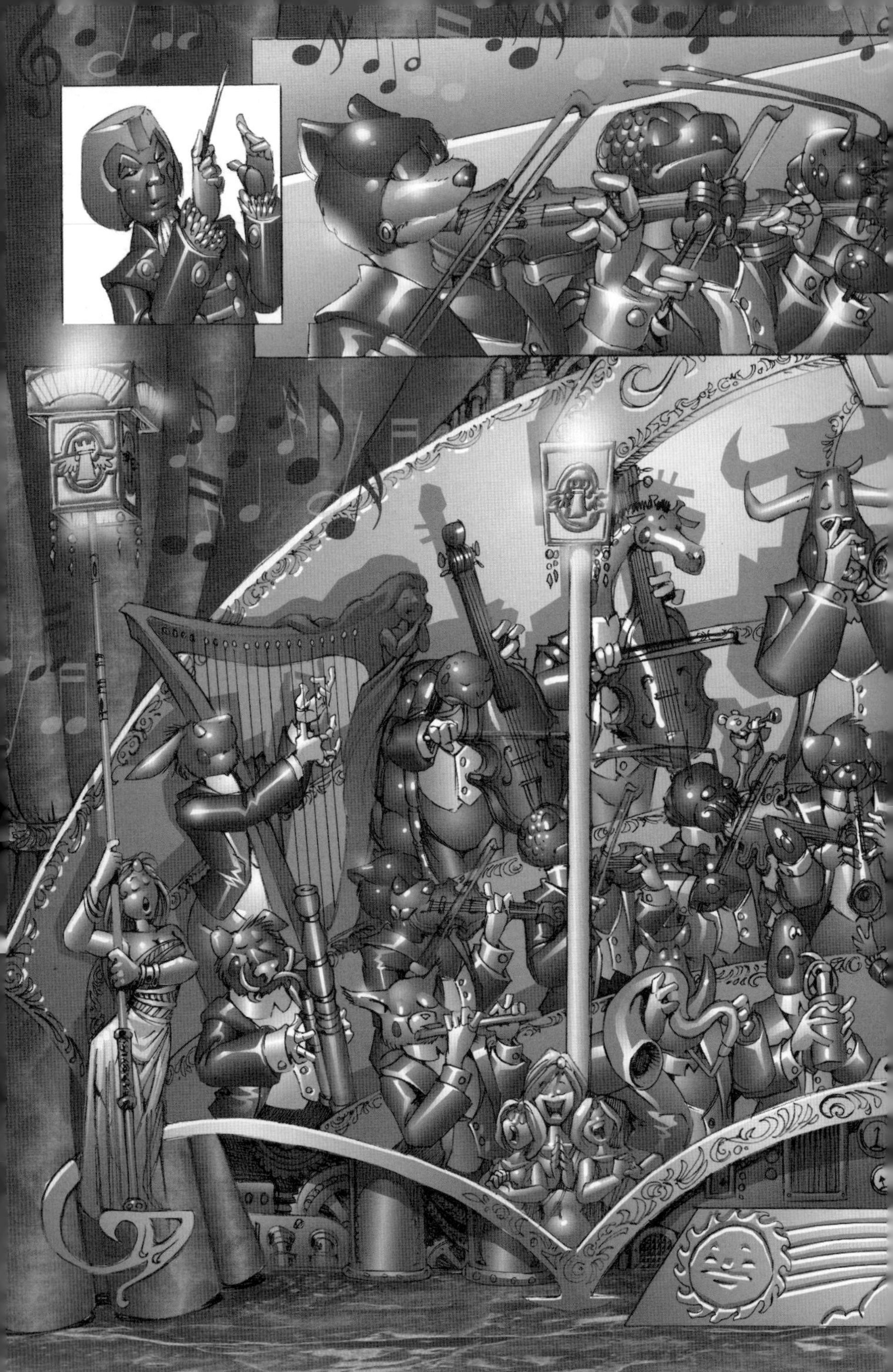

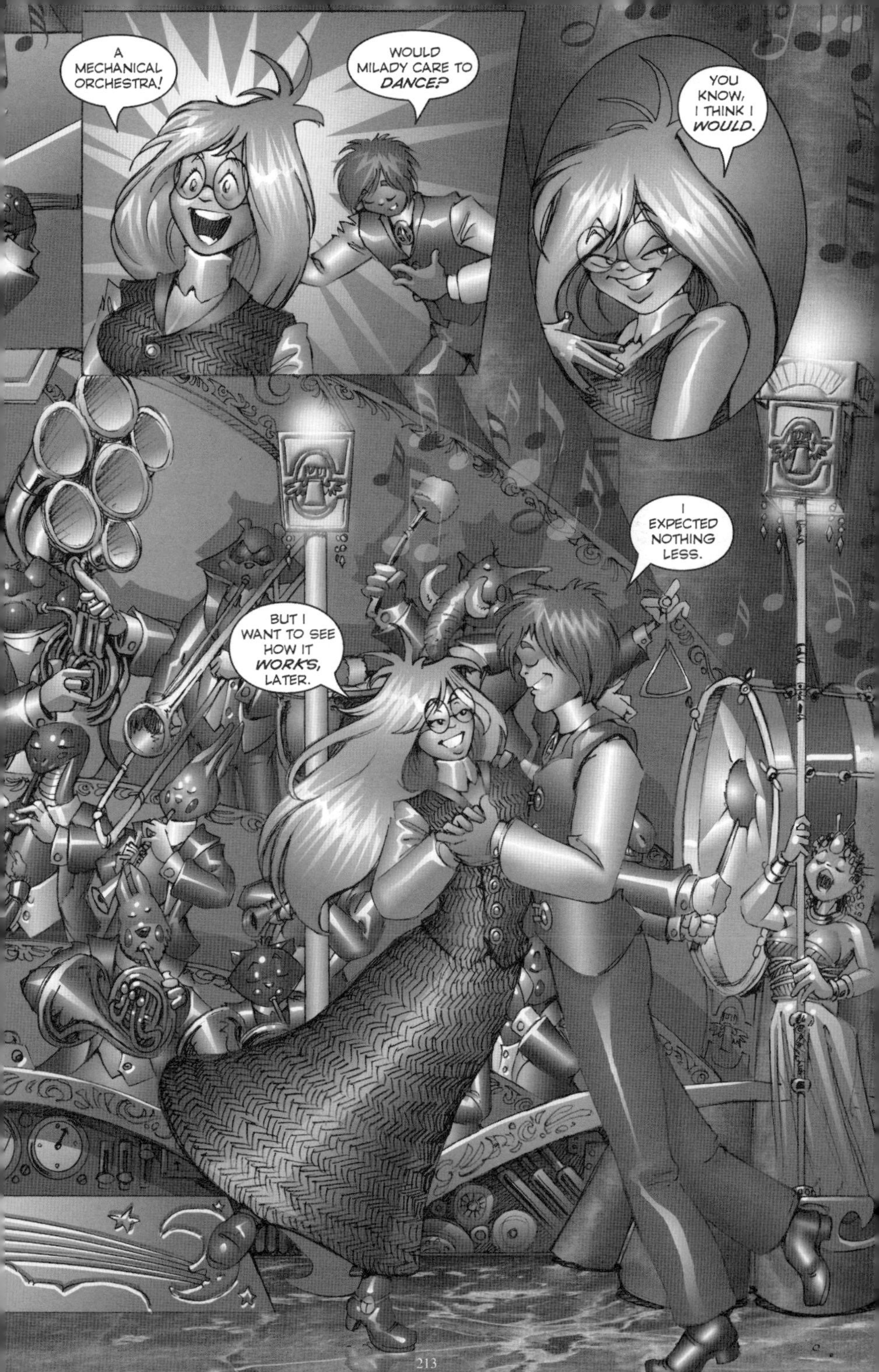
A MECHANICAL ORCHESTRA!
WOULD MILADY CARE TO DANCE?
YOU KNOW, I THINK I WOULD.
I EXPECTED NOTHING LESS.
BUT I WANT TO SEE HOW IT WORKS, LATER.

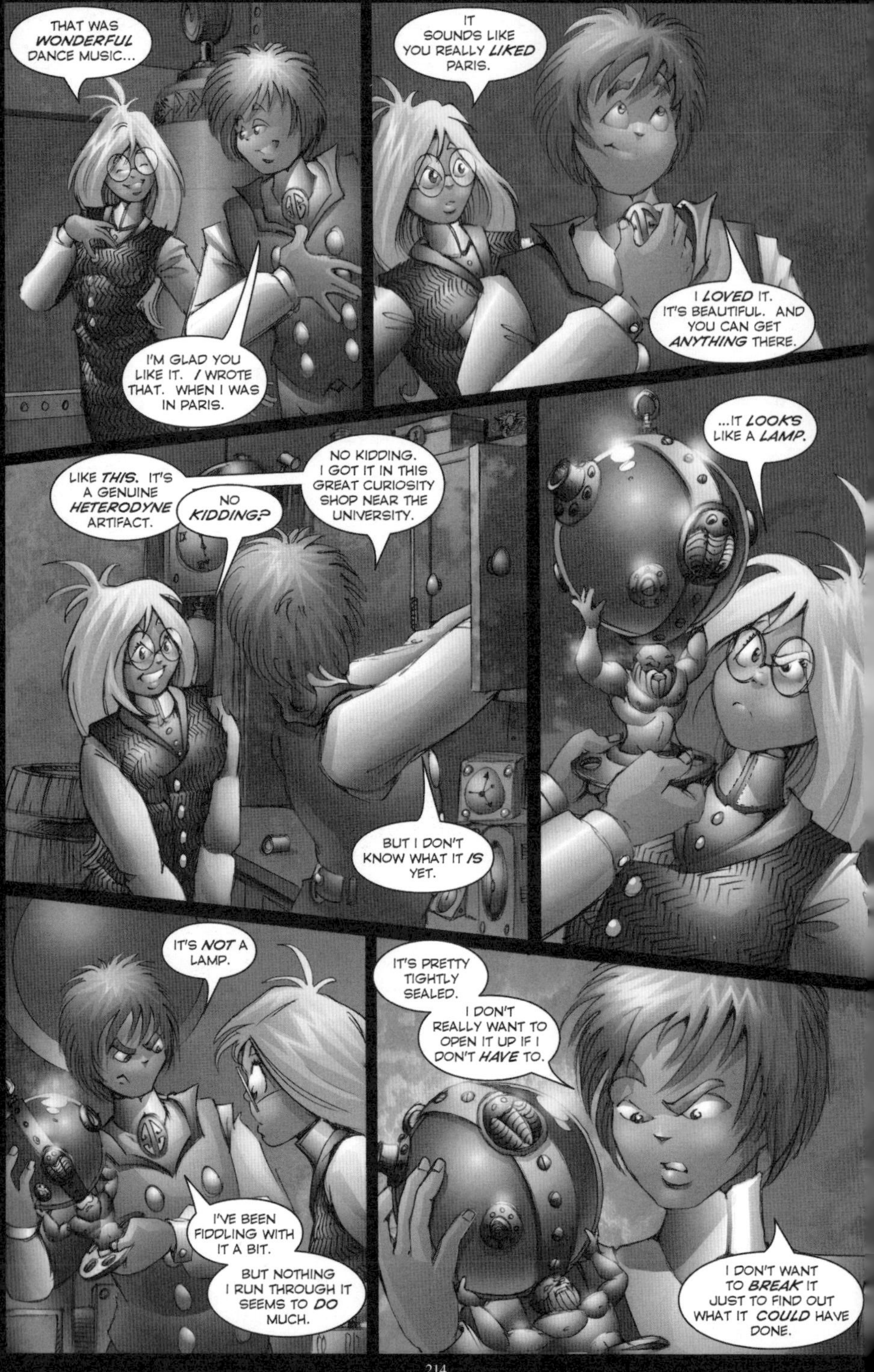
THAT WAS WONDERFUL DANCE MUSIC...
I'M GLAD YOU LIKE IT. I WROTE THAT. WHEN I WAS IN PARIS.
IT SOUNDS LIKE YOU REALLY LIKED PARIS.
I LOVED IT. IT'S BEAUTIFUL. AND YOU CAN GET ANYTHING THERE.
LIKE THIS. IT'S A GENUINE HETERODYNE ARTIFACT.
NO KIDDING?
NO KIDDING. I GOT IT IN THIS GREAT CURIOSITY SHOP NEAR THE UNIVERSITY.
BUT I DON'T KNOW WHAT IT IS YET.
...IT LOOKS LIKE A LAMP.
IT'S NOT A LAMP.
I'VE BEEN FIDDLING WITH IT A BIT.
BUT NOTHING I RUN THROUGH IT SEEMS TO DO MUCH.
IT'S PRETTY TIGHTLY SEALED.
I DON'T REALLY WANT TO OPEN IT UP IF I DON'T HAVE TO.
I DON'T WANT TO BREAK IT JUST TO FIND OUT WHAT IT COULD HAVE DONE.

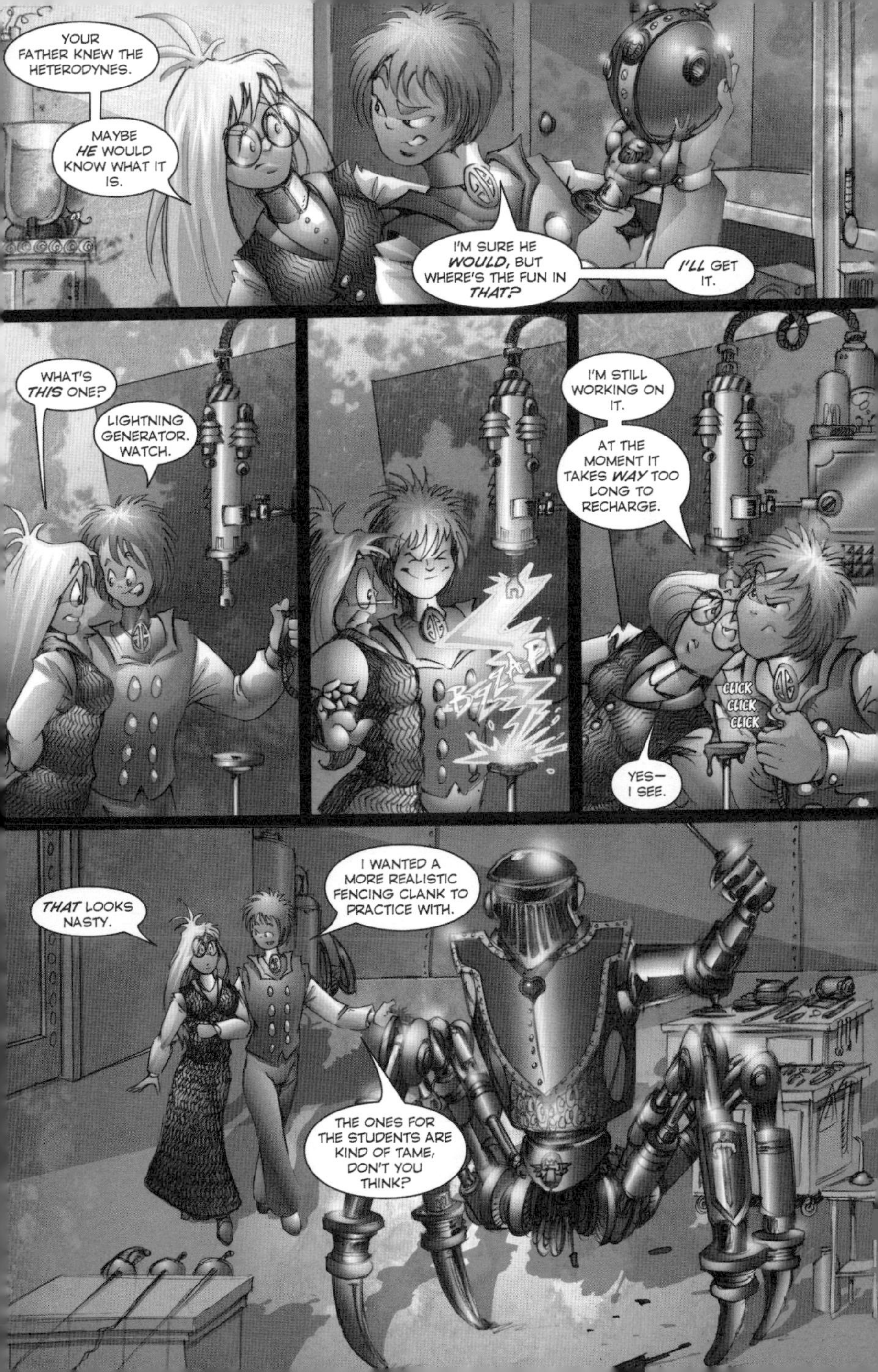
YOUR FATHER KNEW THE HETERODYNES.
MAYBE *HE* WOULD KNOW WHAT IT IS.
I'M SURE HE ***WOULD***, BUT WHERE'S THE FUN IN ***THAT?***
I'LL GET IT.
WHAT'S ***THIS*** ONE?
LIGHTNING GENERATOR. WATCH.
BZZAP!
I'M STILL WORKING ON IT.
AT THE MOMENT IT TAKES ***WAY*** TOO LONG TO RECHARGE.
CLICK CLICK CLICK
YES— I SEE.
THAT LOOKS NASTY.
I WANTED A MORE REALISTIC FENCING CLANK TO PRACTICE WITH.
THE ONES FOR THE STUDENTS ARE KIND OF TAME, DON'T YOU THINK?

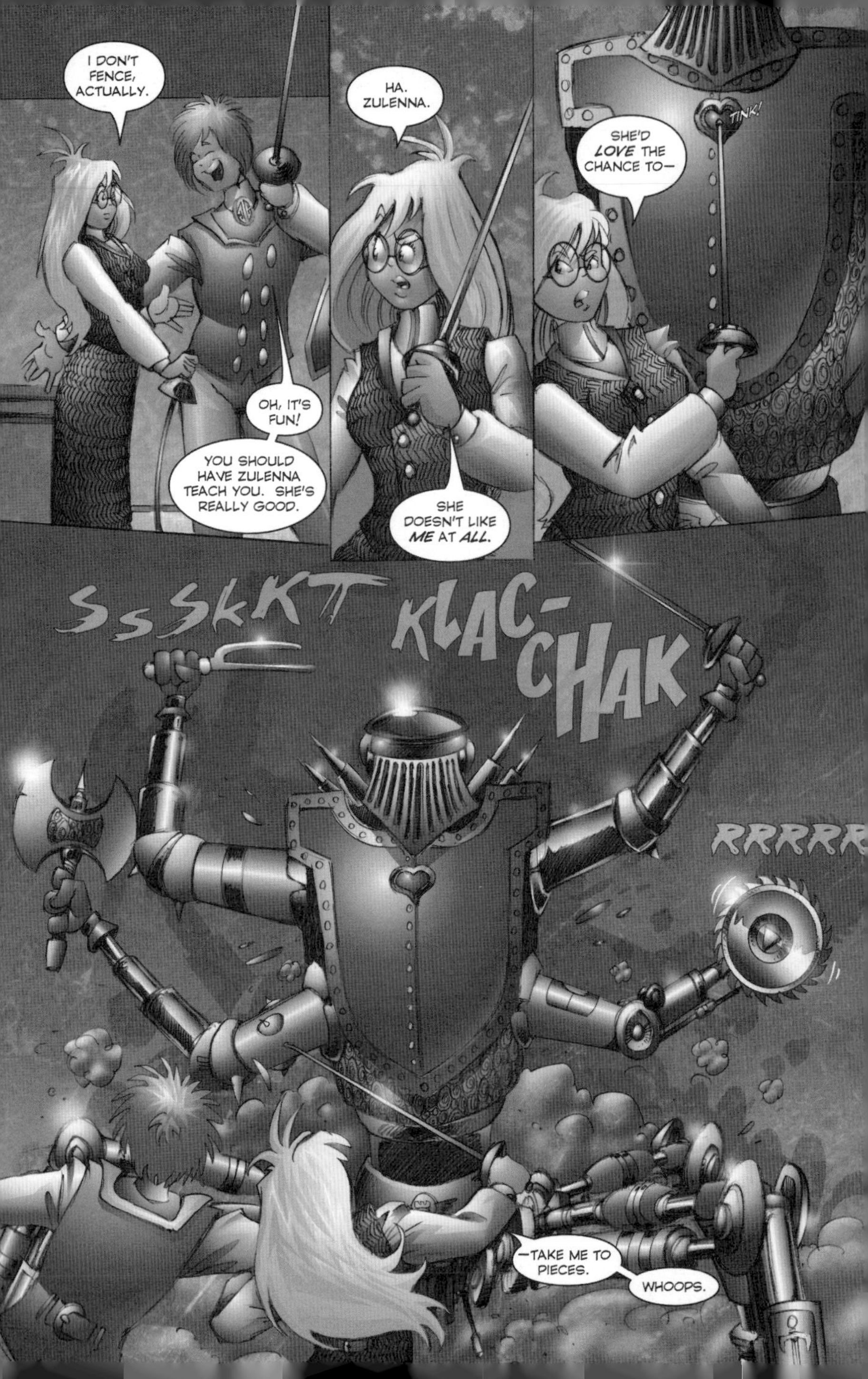

I DON'T FENCE, ACTUALLY.
OH, IT'S FUN!
YOU SHOULD HAVE ZULENNA TEACH YOU. SHE'S REALLY GOOD.
HA. ZULENNA.
SHE DOESN'T LIKE ME AT ALL.
TINK!
SHE'D LOVE THE CHANCE TO—
SSSKKT
KLAC-CHAK
RRRRR
—TAKE ME TO PIECES.
WHOOPS.

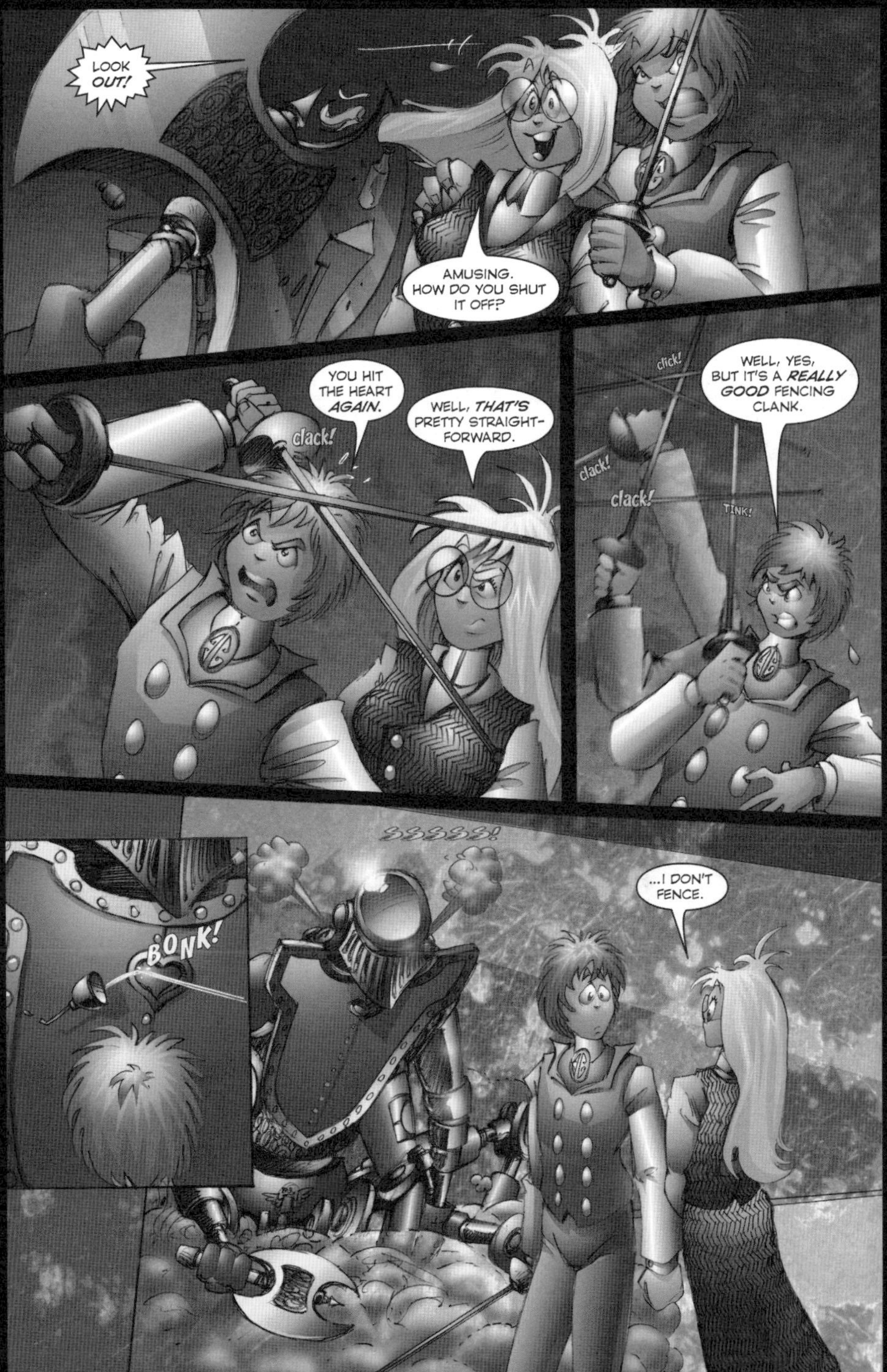

LOOK OUT!
AMUSING. HOW DO YOU SHUT IT OFF?
clack!
YOU HIT THE HEART AGAIN.
WELL, THAT'S PRETTY STRAIGHT-FORWARD.
click!
WELL, YES, BUT IT'S A REALLY GOOD FENCING CLANK.
clack!
clack!
TINK!
SSSSS!
BONK!
...I DON'T FENCE.

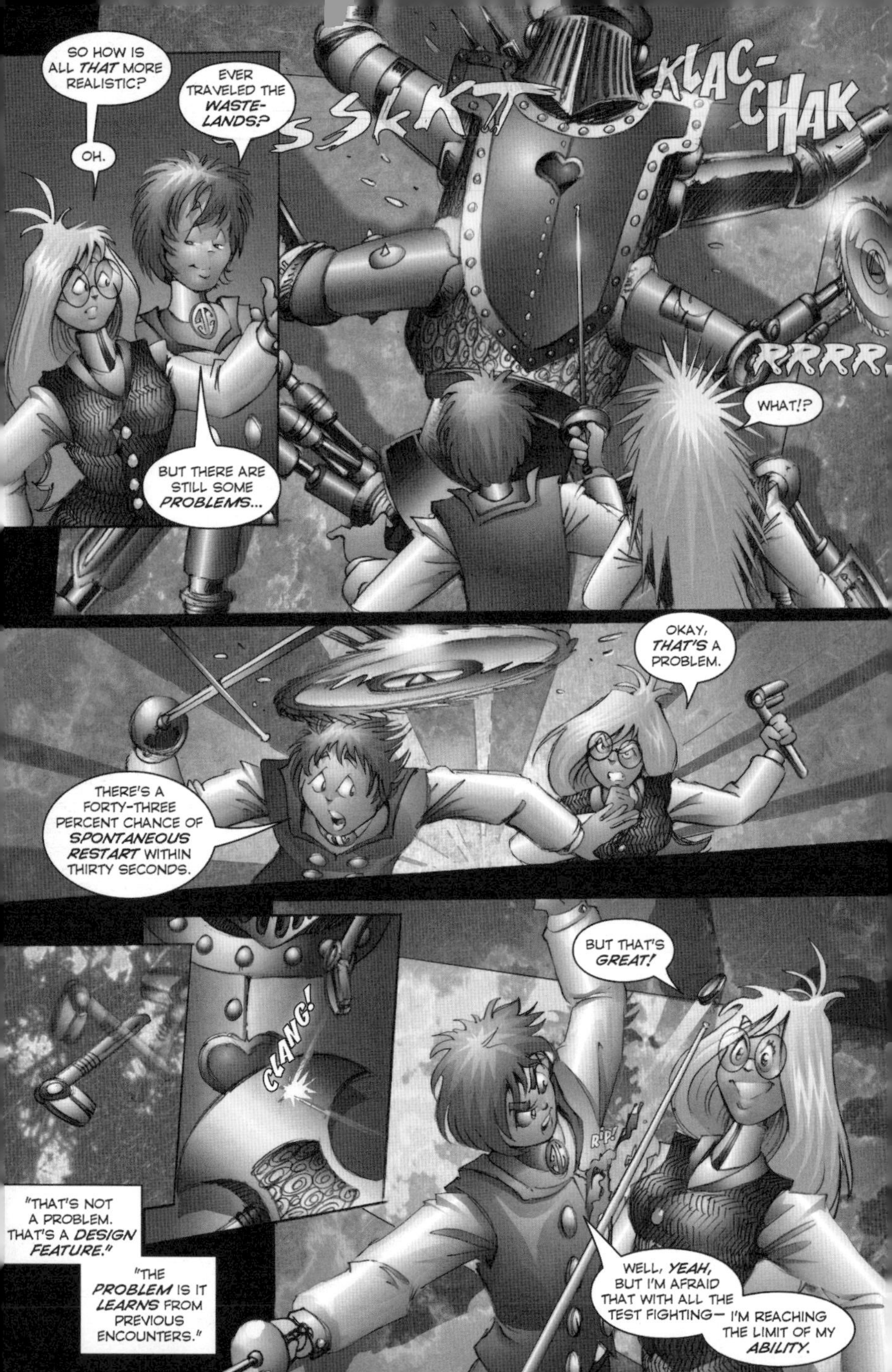

SO HOW IS ALL *THAT* MORE REALISTIC?
EVER TRAVELED THE *WASTE-LANDS?*
OH.
BUT THERE ARE STILL SOME *PROBLEMS...*
SSSKKT
KLAC-CHAK
RRRRR
WHAT!?
OKAY, *THAT'S* A PROBLEM.
THERE'S A FORTY-THREE PERCENT CHANCE OF *SPONTANEOUS RESTART* WITHIN THIRTY SECONDS.
BUT THAT'S *GREAT!*
CLANG!
RIP!
"THAT'S NOT A PROBLEM. THAT'S A *DESIGN FEATURE."*
"THE *PROBLEM* IS IT *LEARNS* FROM PREVIOUS ENCOUNTERS."
WELL, *YEAH,* BUT I'M AFRAID THAT WITH ALL THE TEST FIGHTING— I'M REACHING THE LIMIT OF MY *ABILITY.*

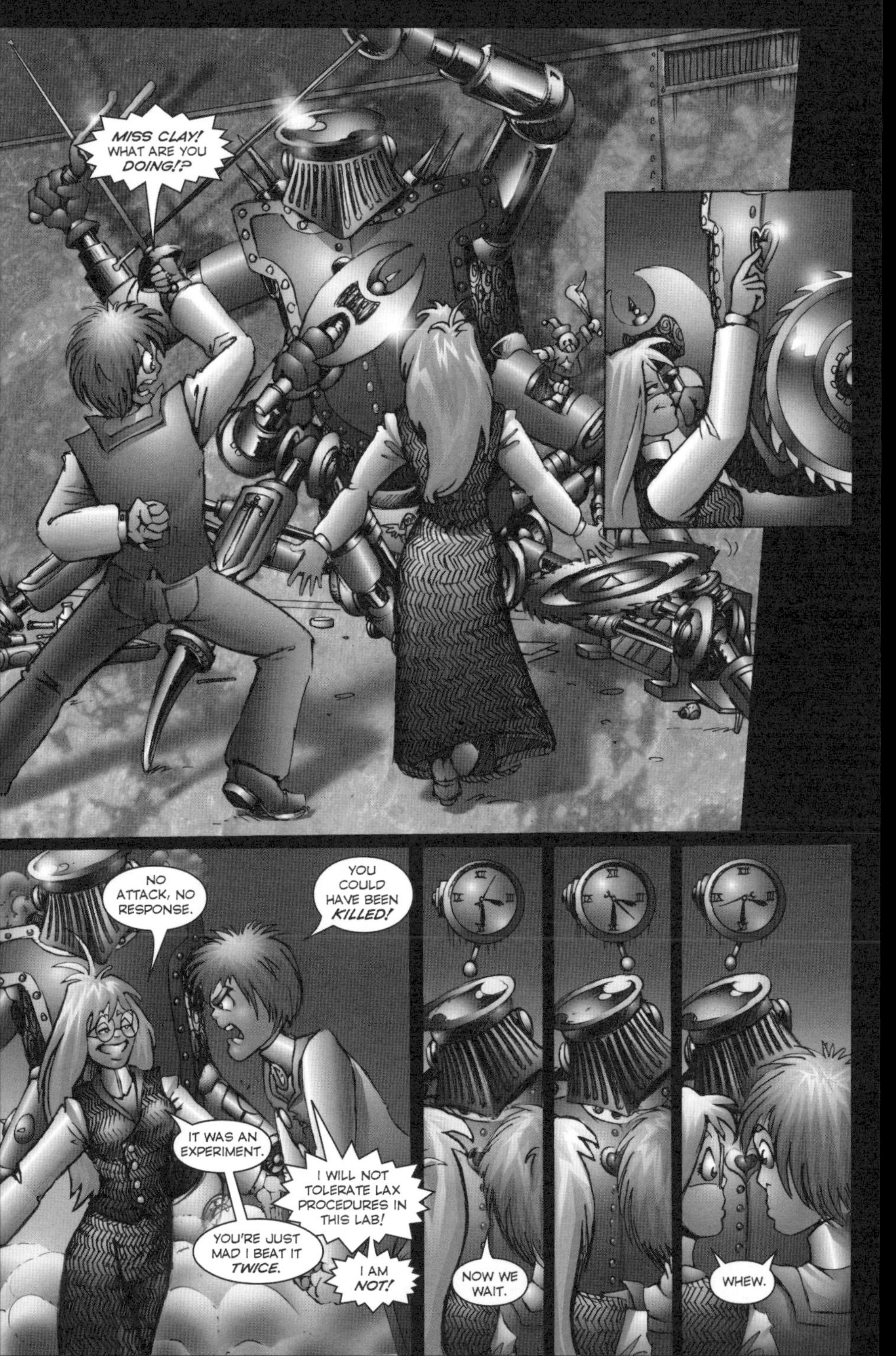
MISS CLAY! WHAT ARE YOU DOING!?
NO ATTACK, NO RESPONSE.
YOU COULD HAVE BEEN KILLED!
IT WAS AN EXPERIMENT.
I WILL NOT TOLERATE LAX PROCEDURES IN THIS LAB!
YOU'RE JUST MAD I BEAT IT TWICE.
I AM NOT!
NOW WE WAIT.
WHEW.

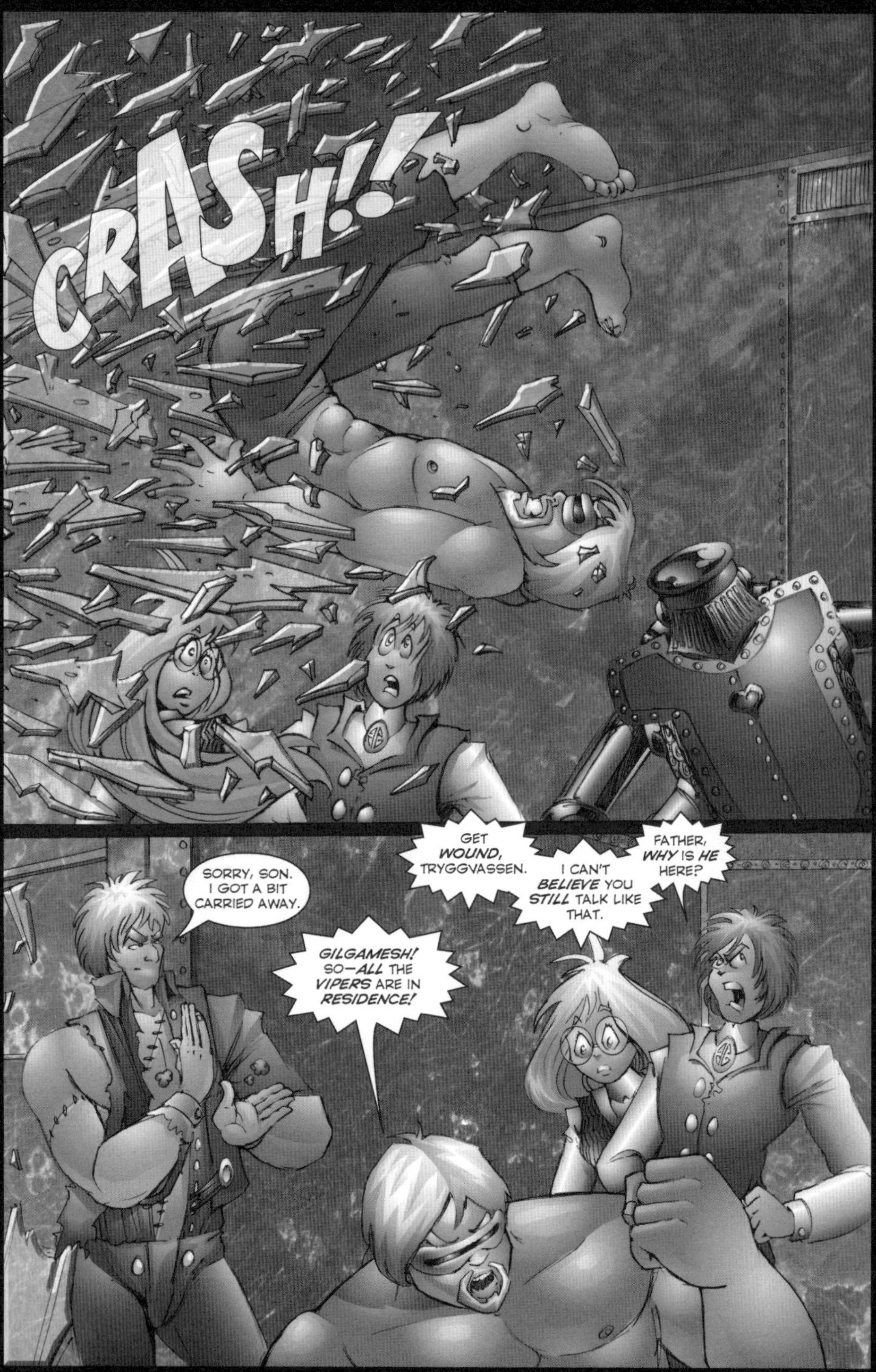
CRASH!!
SORRY, SON. I GOT A BIT CARRIED AWAY.
GET WOUND, TRYGGVASSEN.
I CAN'T BELIEVE YOU STILL TALK LIKE THAT.
FATHER, WHY IS HE HERE?
GILGAMESH! SO—ALL THE VIPERS ARE IN RESIDENCE!

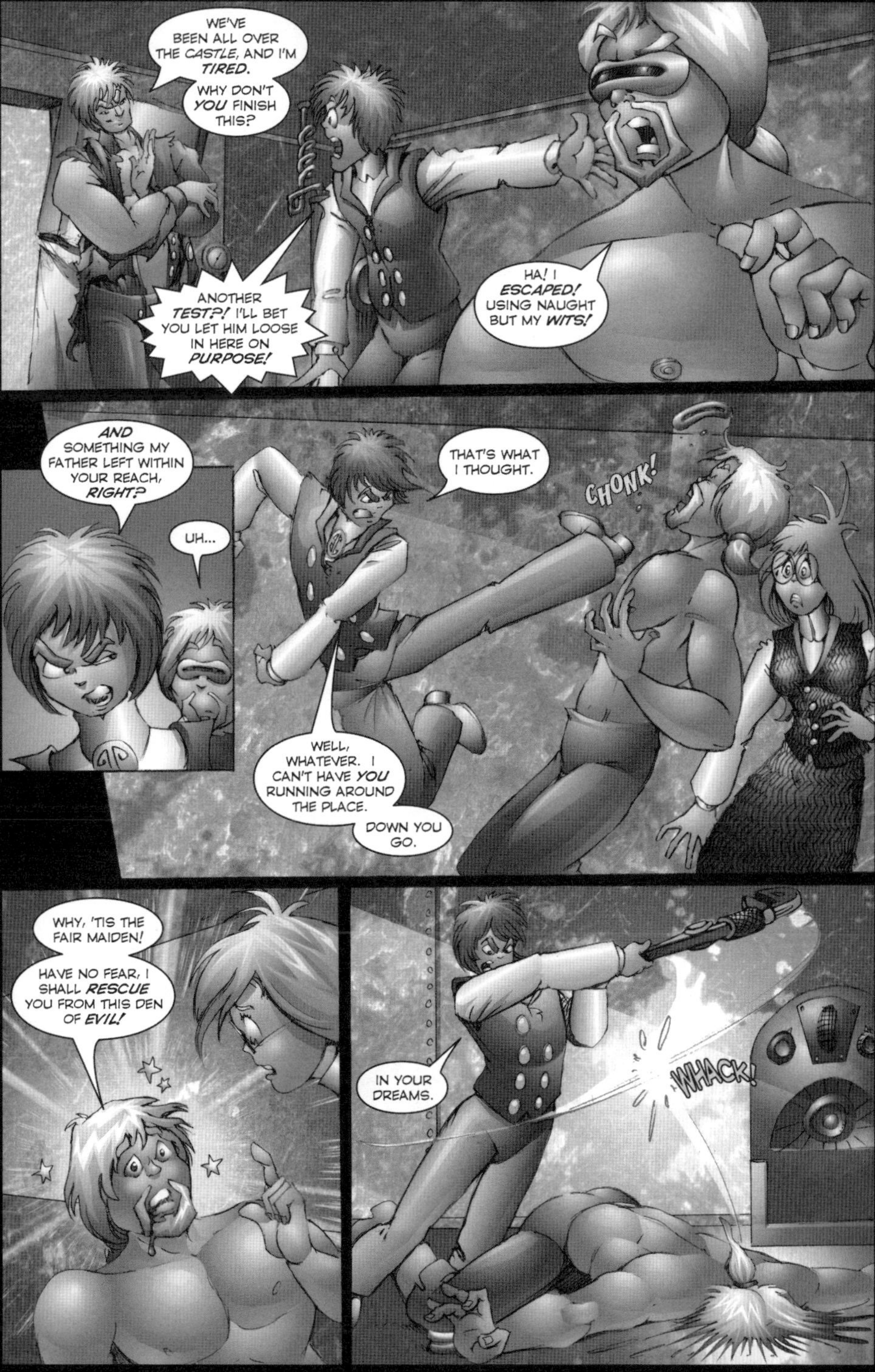

WE'VE BEEN ALL OVER THE CASTLE, AND I'M TIRED.
WHY DON'T YOU FINISH THIS?
ANOTHER TEST?! I'LL BET YOU LET HIM LOOSE IN HERE ON PURPOSE!
HA! I ESCAPED! USING NAUGHT BUT MY WITS!
AND SOMETHING MY FATHER LEFT WITHIN YOUR REACH, RIGHT?
UH...
THAT'S WHAT I THOUGHT.
CHONK!
WELL, WHATEVER. I CAN'T HAVE YOU RUNNING AROUND THE PLACE.
DOWN YOU GO.
WHY, 'TIS THE FAIR MAIDEN!
HAVE NO FEAR, I SHALL RESCUE YOU FROM THIS DEN OF EVIL!
IN YOUR DREAMS.
WHACK!

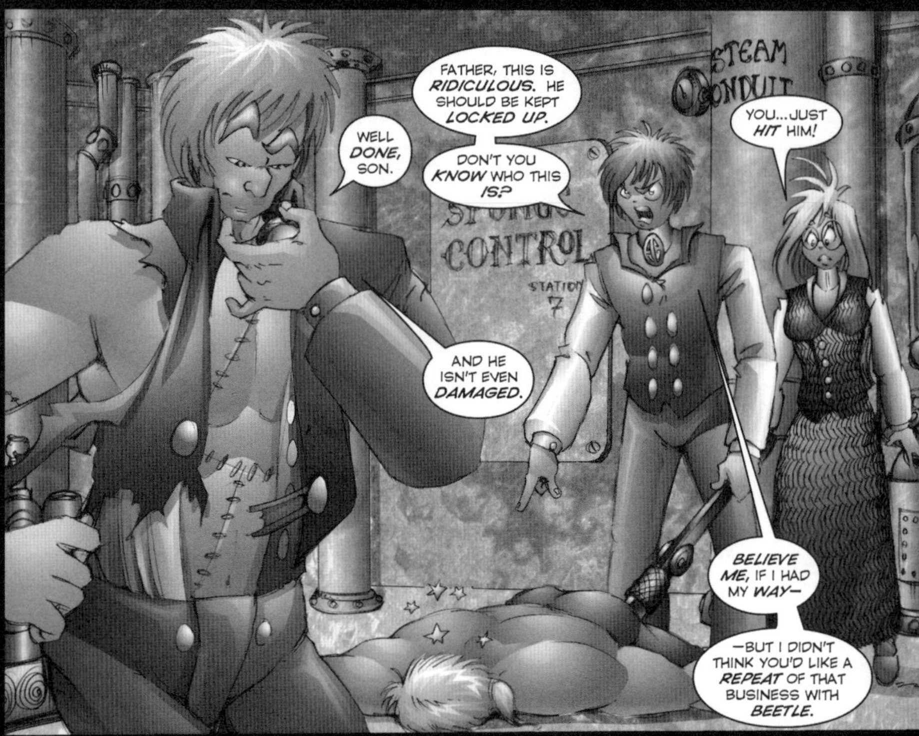
STEAM CONDUIT
SPONGE CONTROL STATION 7
WELL DONE, SON.
FATHER, THIS IS RIDICULOUS. HE SHOULD BE KEPT LOCKED UP.
DON'T YOU KNOW WHO THIS IS?
YOU...JUST HIT HIM!
AND HE ISN'T EVEN DAMAGED.
BELIEVE ME, IF I HAD MY WAY—
—BUT I DIDN'T THINK YOU'D LIKE A REPEAT OF THAT BUSINESS WITH BEETLE.

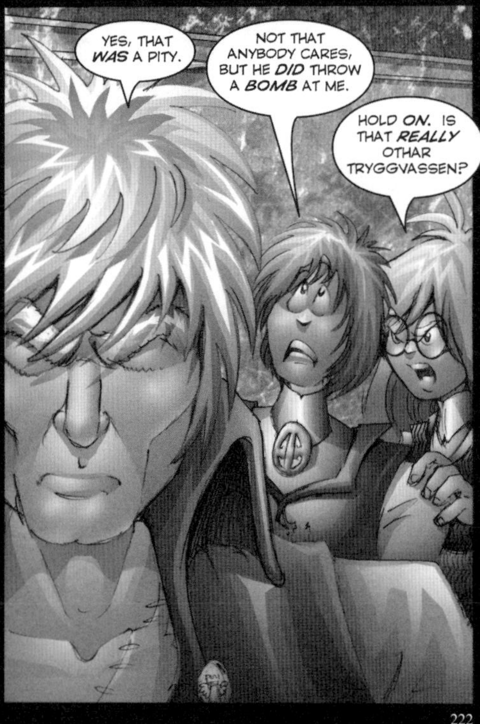
YES, THAT WAS A PITY.
NOT THAT ANYBODY CARES, BUT HE DID THROW A BOMB AT ME.
HOLD ON. IS THAT REALLY OTHAR TRYGGVASSEN?

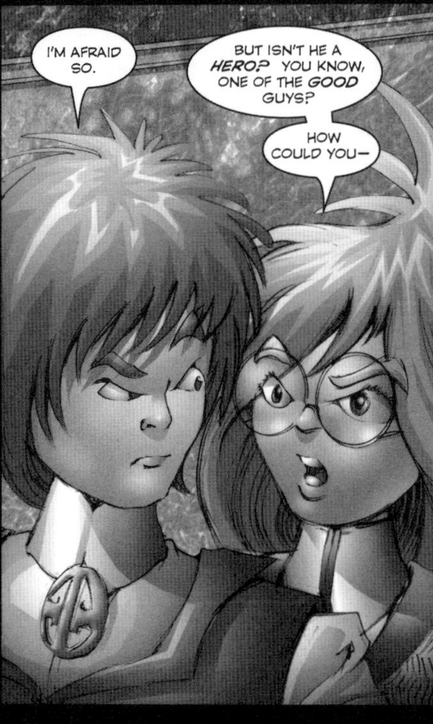
I'M AFRAID SO.
BUT ISN'T HE A HERO? YOU KNOW, ONE OF THE GOOD GUYS?
HOW COULD YOU—

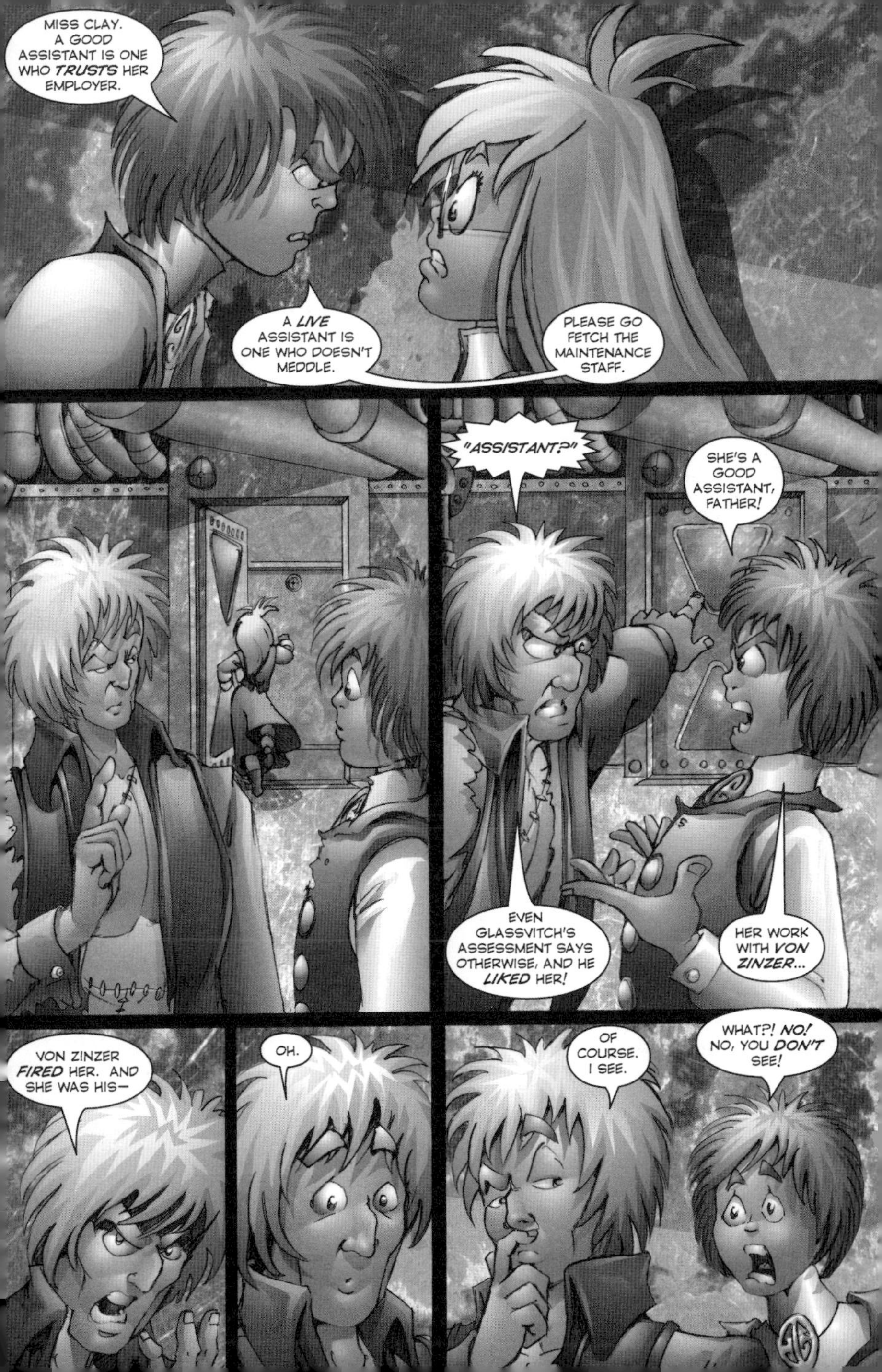
MISS CLAY. A GOOD ASSISTANT IS ONE WHO *TRUSTS* HER EMPLOYER.
A *LIVE* ASSISTANT IS ONE WHO DOESN'T MEDDLE.
PLEASE GO FETCH THE MAINTENANCE STAFF.
"ASSISTANT?"
SHE'S A GOOD ASSISTANT, FATHER!
EVEN GLASSVITCH'S ASSESSMENT SAYS OTHERWISE, AND HE *LIKED* HER!
HER WORK WITH *VON ZINZER*...
VON ZINZER *FIRED* HER. AND SHE WAS HIS—
OH.
OF COURSE. I SEE.
WHAT?! *NO!* NO, YOU *DON'T* SEE!

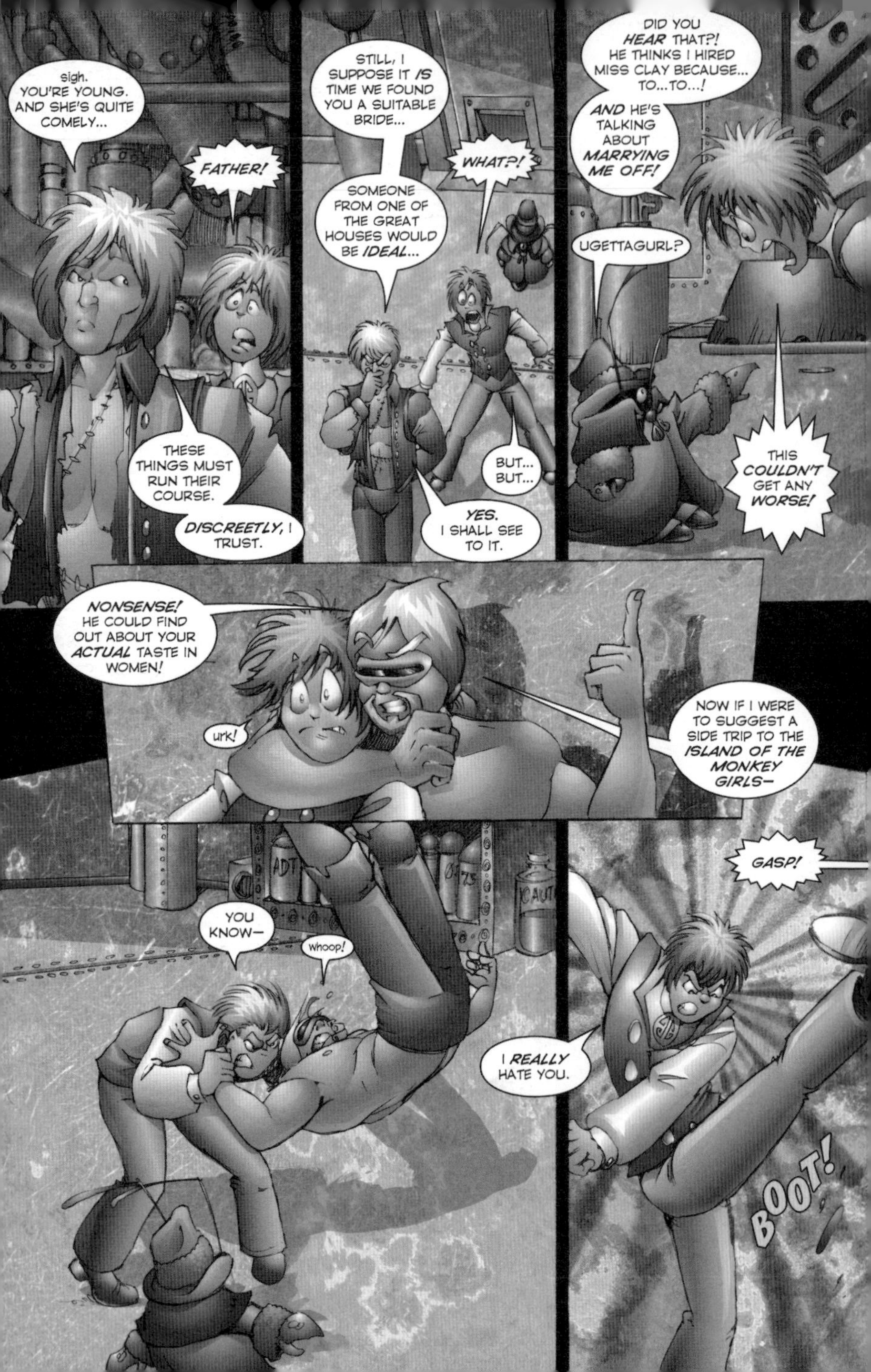
sigh. YOU'RE YOUNG. AND SHE'S QUITE COMELY...
FATHER!
THESE THINGS MUST RUN THEIR COURSE.
DISCREETLY, I TRUST.
STILL, I SUPPOSE IT IS TIME WE FOUND YOU A SUITABLE BRIDE...
SOMEONE FROM ONE OF THE GREAT HOUSES WOULD BE IDEAL...
WHAT?!
BUT... BUT...
YES. I SHALL SEE TO IT.
DID YOU HEAR THAT?! HE THINKS I HIRED MISS CLAY BECAUSE... TO...TO...!
AND HE'S TALKING ABOUT MARRYING ME OFF!
UGETTAGURL?
THIS COULDN'T GET ANY WORSE!
NONSENSE! HE COULD FIND OUT ABOUT YOUR ACTUAL TASTE IN WOMEN!
urk!
NOW IF I WERE TO SUGGEST A SIDE TRIP TO THE ISLAND OF THE MONKEY GIRLS—
YOU KNOW—
whoop!
GASP!
I REALLY HATE YOU.
BOOT!

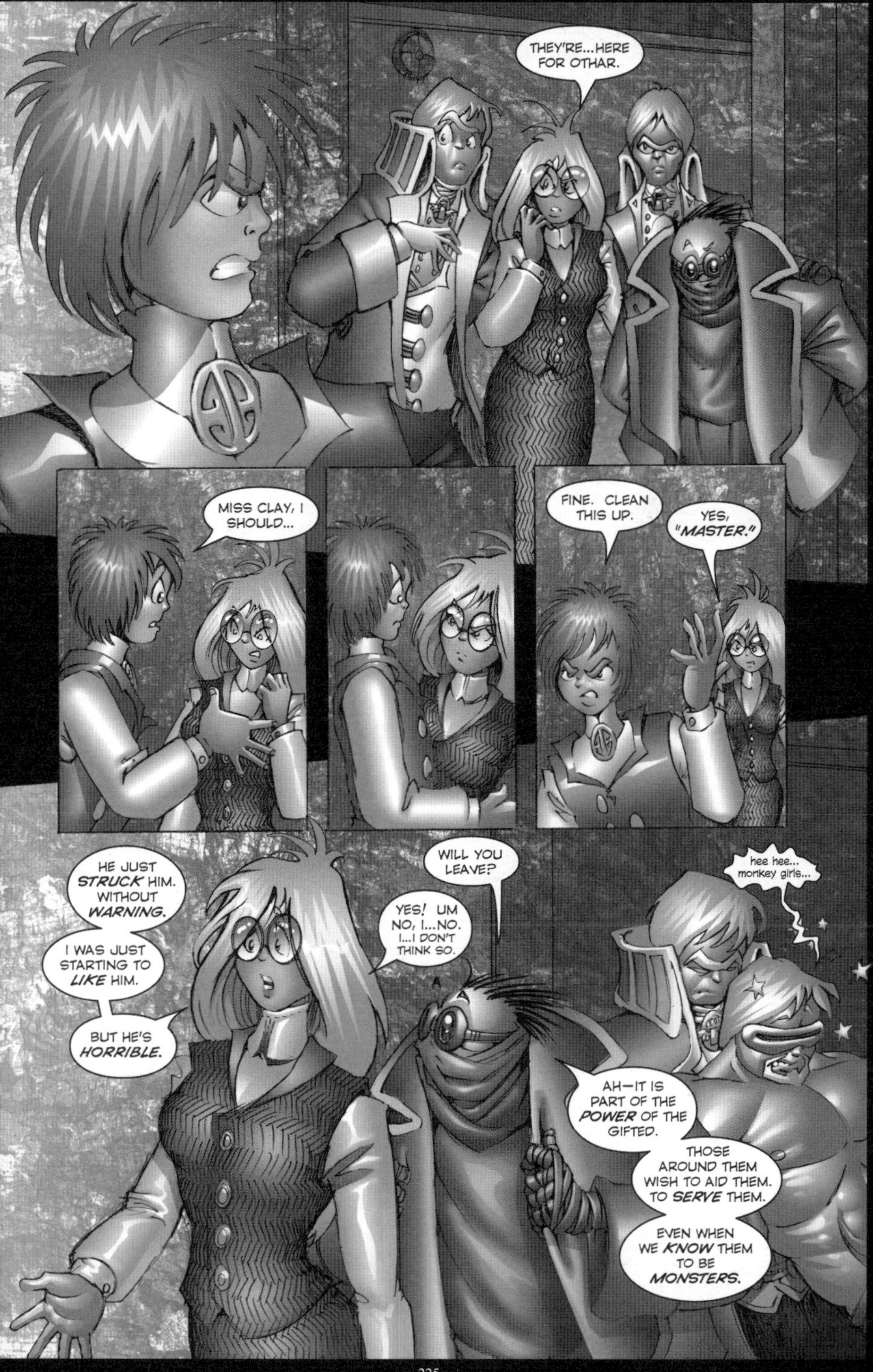
THEY'RE...HERE FOR OTHAR.
MISS CLAY, I SHOULD...
FINE. CLEAN THIS UP.
YES, "MASTER."
HE JUST STRUCK HIM. WITHOUT WARNING.
I WAS JUST STARTING TO LIKE HIM.
BUT HE'S HORRIBLE.
WILL YOU LEAVE?
YES! UM NO, I...NO. I...I DON'T THINK SO.
hee hee... monkey girls...
AH—IT IS PART OF THE POWER OF THE GIFTED.
THOSE AROUND THEM WISH TO AID THEM. TO SERVE THEM.
EVEN WHEN WE KNOW THEM TO BE MONSTERS.

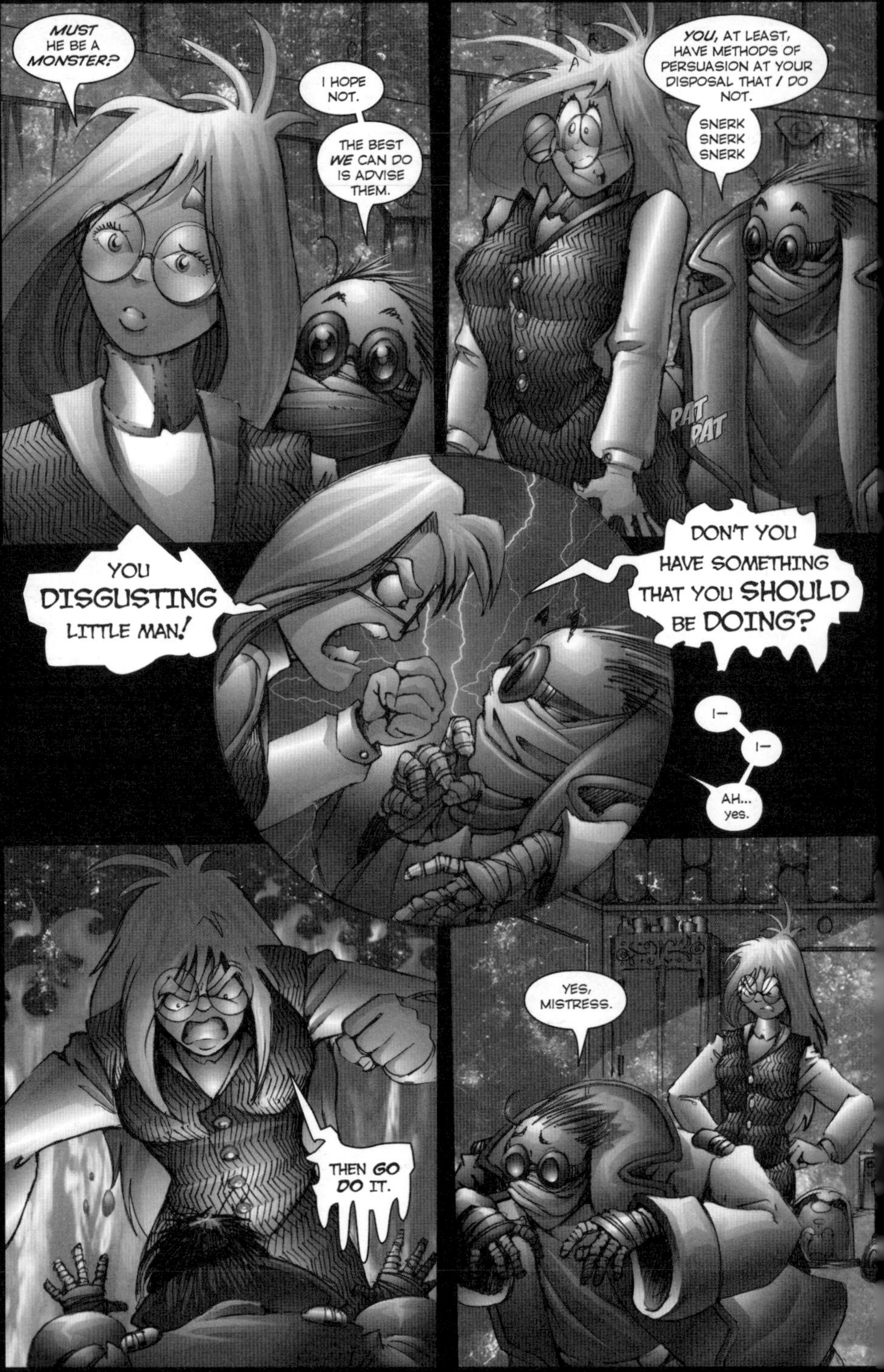
MUST HE BE A MONSTER?
I HOPE NOT.
THE BEST WE CAN DO IS ADVISE THEM.
YOU, AT LEAST, HAVE METHODS OF PERSUASION AT YOUR DISPOSAL THAT I DO NOT.
SNERK SNERK SNERK
PAT PAT
YOU DISGUSTING LITTLE MAN!
DON'T YOU HAVE SOMETHING THAT YOU SHOULD BE DOING?
I—
I—
AH... yes.
THEN GO DO IT.
YES, MISTRESS.

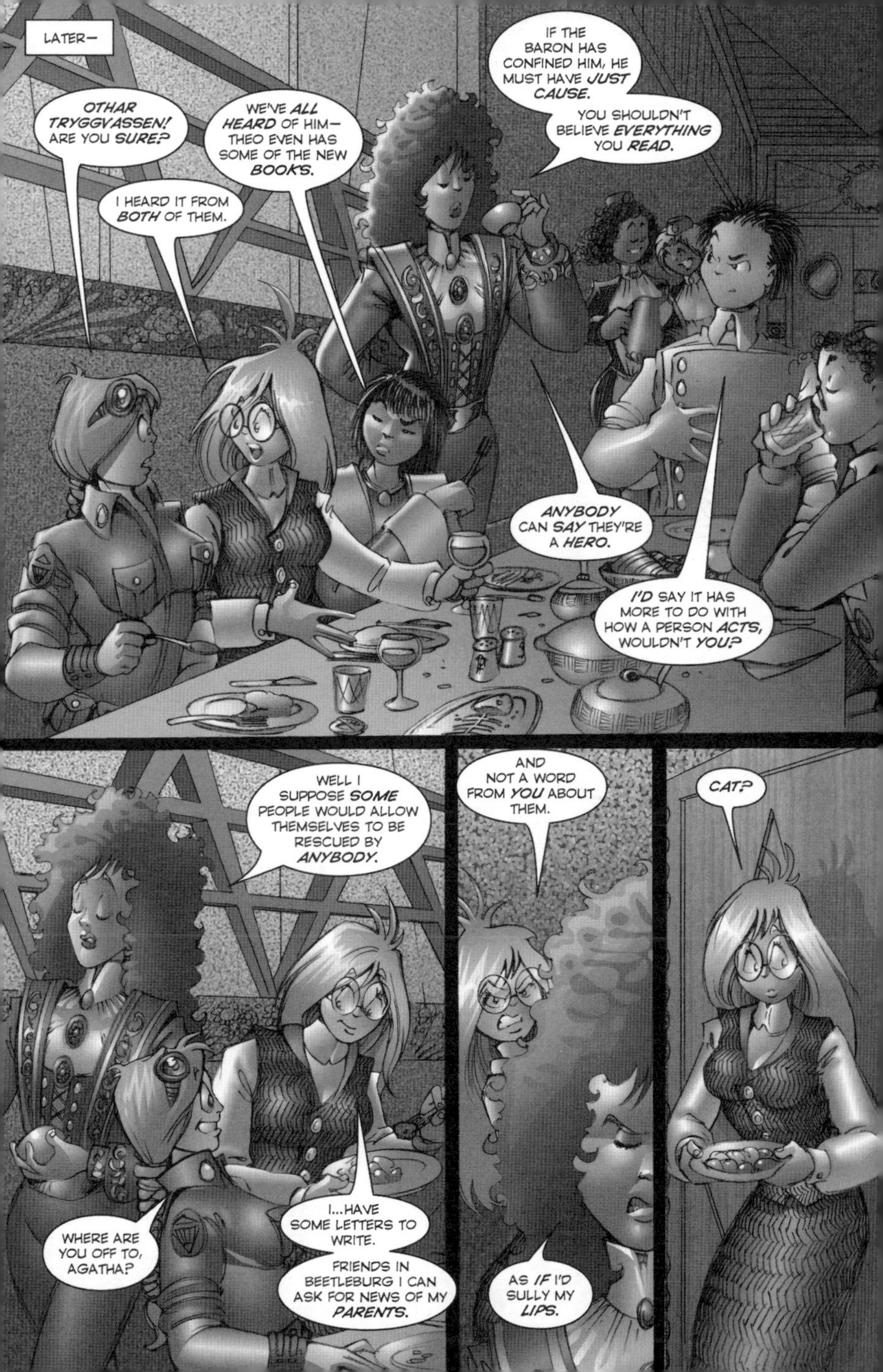
LATER—
OTHAR TRYGGVASSEN! ARE YOU SURE?
I HEARD IT FROM BOTH OF THEM.
WE'VE ALL HEARD OF HIM— THEO EVEN HAS SOME OF THE NEW BOOKS.
IF THE BARON HAS CONFINED HIM, HE MUST HAVE JUST CAUSE.
YOU SHOULDN'T BELIEVE EVERYTHING YOU READ.
ANYBODY CAN SAY THEY'RE A HERO.
I'D SAY IT HAS MORE TO DO WITH HOW A PERSON ACTS, WOULDN'T YOU?
WELL I SUPPOSE SOME PEOPLE WOULD ALLOW THEMSELVES TO BE RESCUED BY ANYBODY.
WHERE ARE YOU OFF TO, AGATHA?
I...HAVE SOME LETTERS TO WRITE.
FRIENDS IN BEETLEBURG I CAN ASK FOR NEWS OF MY PARENTS.
AND NOT A WORD FROM YOU ABOUT THEM.
AS IF I'D SULLY MY LIPS.
CAT?

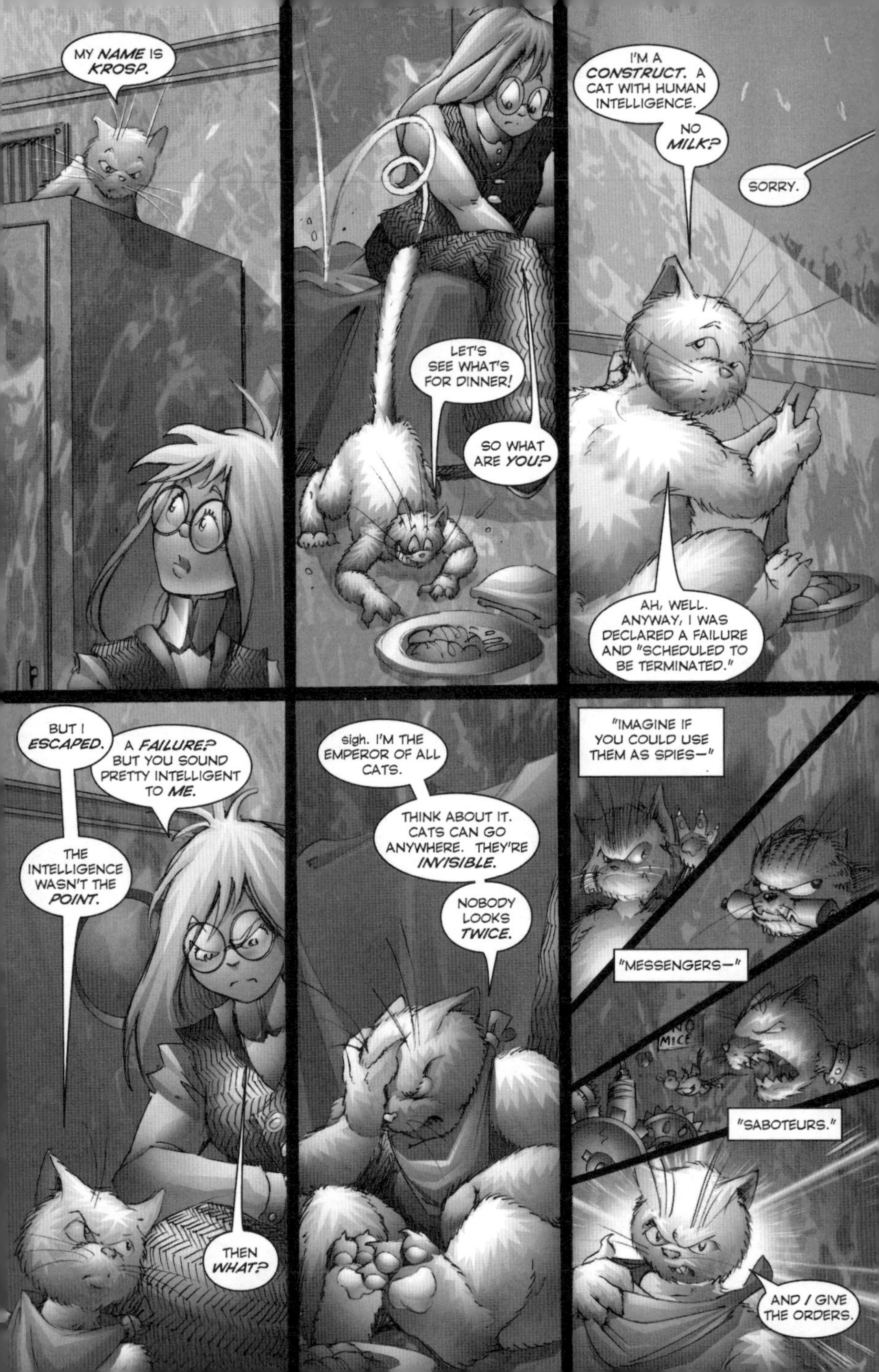

MY NAME IS KROSP.
LET'S SEE WHAT'S FOR DINNER!
SO WHAT ARE YOU?
I'M A CONSTRUCT. A CAT WITH HUMAN INTELLIGENCE.
NO MILK?
SORRY.
AH, WELL. ANYWAY, I WAS DECLARED A FAILURE AND "SCHEDULED TO BE TERMINATED."
BUT I ESCAPED.
A FAILURE? BUT YOU SOUND PRETTY INTELLIGENT TO ME.
THE INTELLIGENCE WASN'T THE POINT.
THEN WHAT?
sigh. I'M THE EMPEROR OF ALL CATS.
THINK ABOUT IT. CATS CAN GO ANYWHERE. THEY'RE INVISIBLE.
NOBODY LOOKS TWICE.
"IMAGINE IF YOU COULD USE THEM AS SPIES—"
"MESSENGERS—"
NO MICE
"SABOTEURS."
AND I GIVE THE ORDERS.

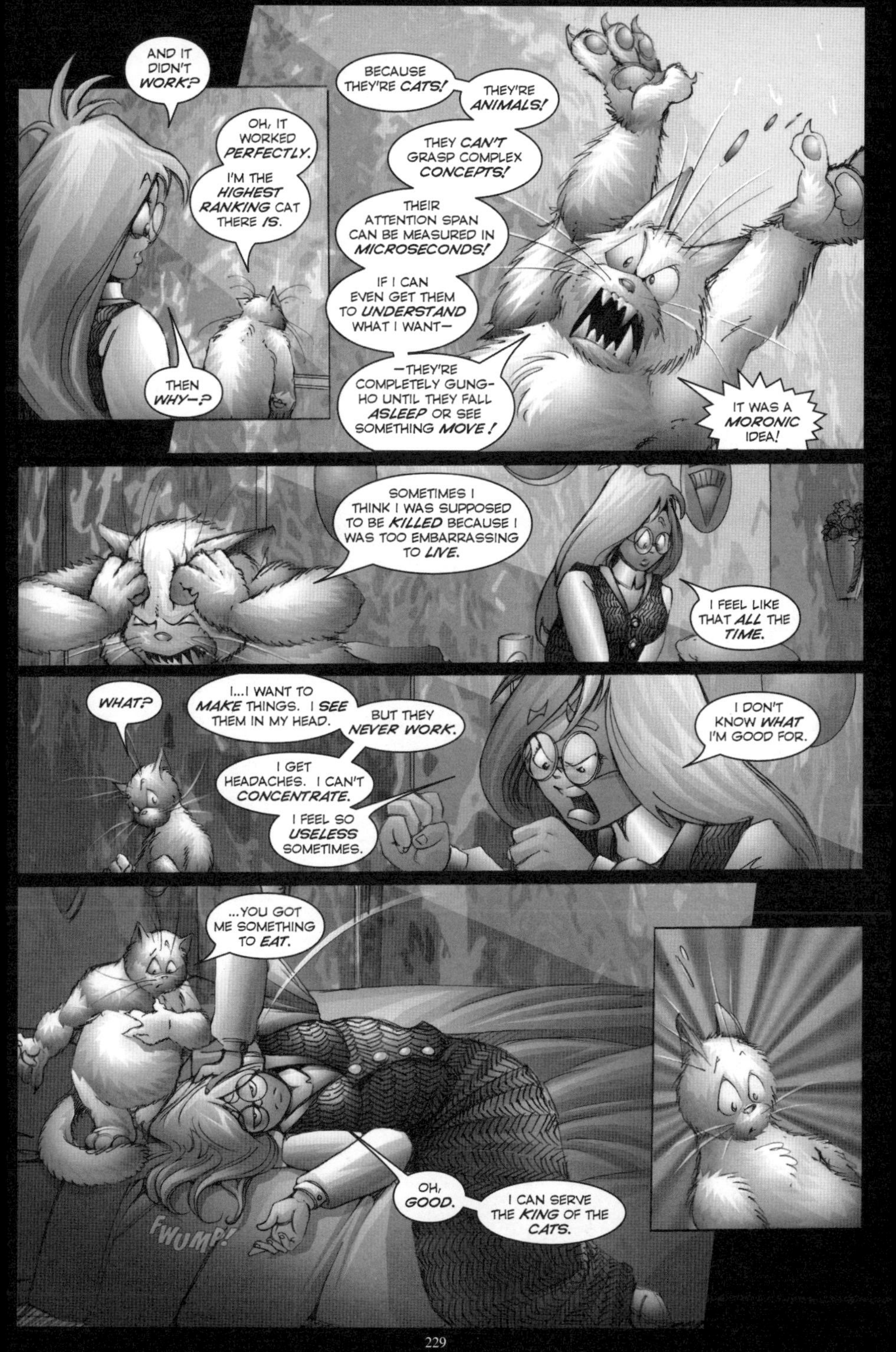
AND IT DIDN'T WORK?
OH, IT WORKED PERFECTLY.
I'M THE HIGHEST RANKING CAT THERE IS.
THEN WHY—?
BECAUSE THEY'RE CATS!
THEY'RE ANIMALS!
THEY CAN'T GRASP COMPLEX CONCEPTS!
THEIR ATTENTION SPAN CAN BE MEASURED IN MICROSECONDS!
IF I CAN EVEN GET THEM TO UNDERSTAND WHAT I WANT—
—THEY'RE COMPLETELY GUNG-HO UNTIL THEY FALL ASLEEP OR SEE SOMETHING MOVE!
IT WAS A MORONIC IDEA!
SOMETIMES I THINK I WAS SUPPOSED TO BE KILLED BECAUSE I WAS TOO EMBARRASSING TO LIVE.
I FEEL LIKE THAT ALL THE TIME.
WHAT?
I...I WANT TO MAKE THINGS. I SEE THEM IN MY HEAD.
BUT THEY NEVER WORK.
I GET HEADACHES. I CAN'T CONCENTRATE.
I FEEL SO USELESS SOMETIMES.
I DON'T KNOW WHAT I'M GOOD FOR.
...YOU GOT ME SOMETHING TO EAT.
OH, GOOD.
I CAN SERVE THE KING OF THE CATS.
FWUMP!

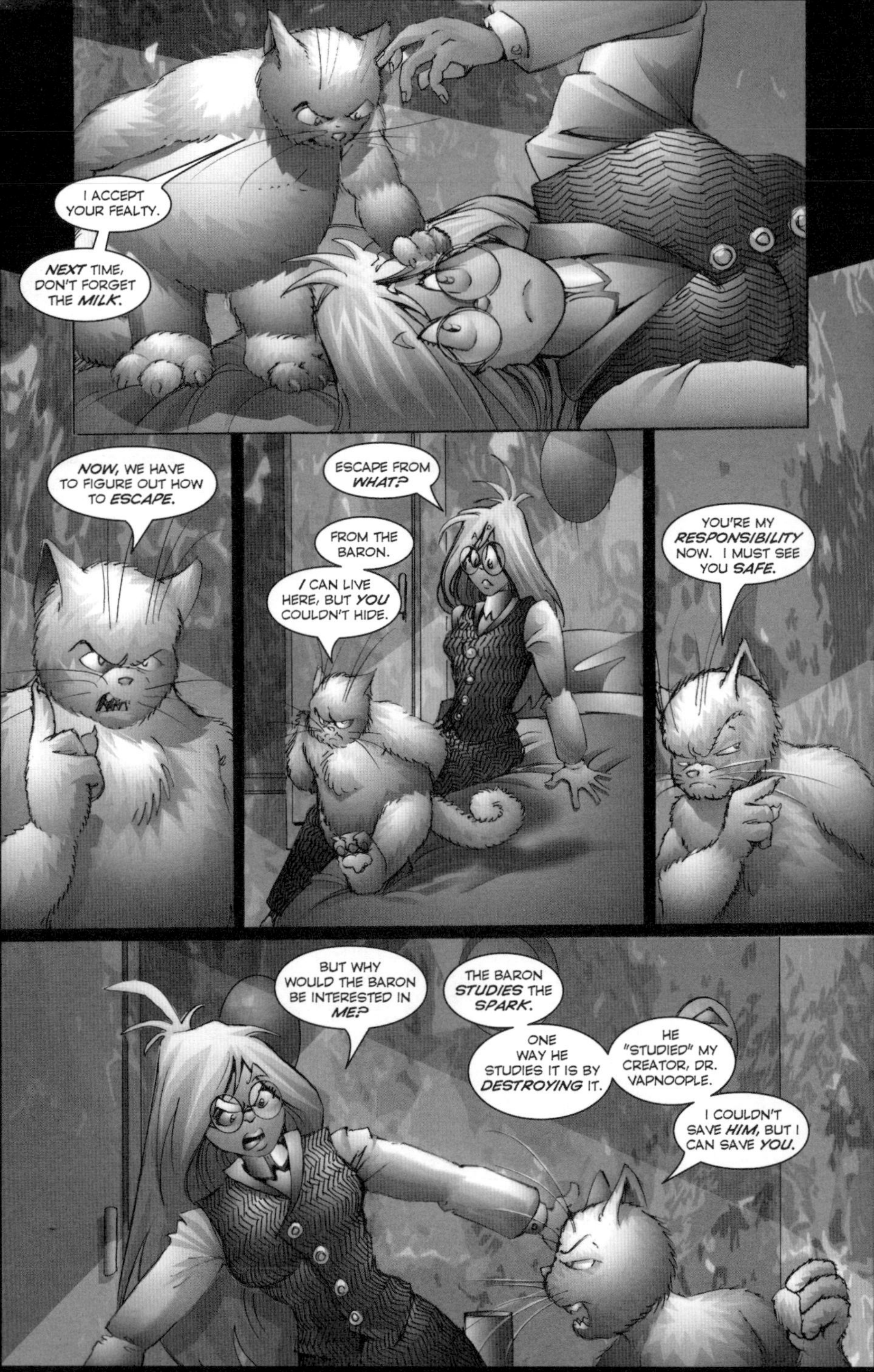
I ACCEPT YOUR FEALTY.
NEXT TIME, DON'T FORGET THE MILK.
NOW, WE HAVE TO FIGURE OUT HOW TO ESCAPE.
ESCAPE FROM WHAT?
FROM THE BARON.
I CAN LIVE HERE, BUT YOU COULDN'T HIDE.
YOU'RE MY RESPONSIBILITY NOW. I MUST SEE YOU SAFE.
BUT WHY WOULD THE BARON BE INTERESTED IN ME?
THE BARON STUDIES THE SPARK.
ONE WAY HE STUDIES IT IS BY DESTROYING IT.
HE "STUDIED" MY CREATOR, DR. VAPNOOPLE.
I COULDN'T SAVE HIM, BUT I CAN SAVE YOU.

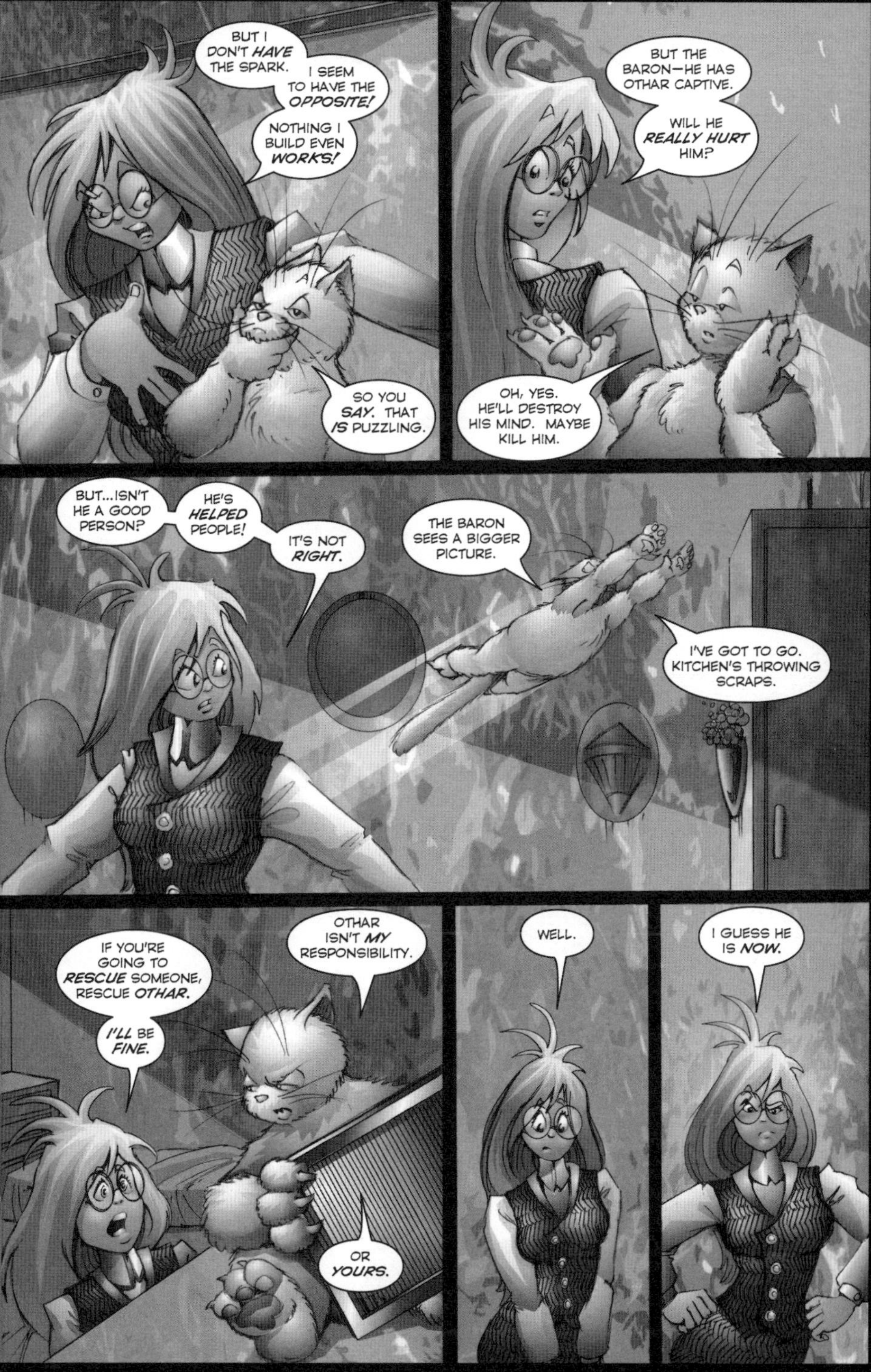
BUT I DON'T HAVE THE SPARK.
I SEEM TO HAVE THE OPPOSITE!
NOTHING I BUILD EVEN WORKS!
SO YOU SAY. THAT IS PUZZLING.
BUT THE BARON—HE HAS OTHAR CAPTIVE.
WILL HE REALLY HURT HIM?
OH, YES. HE'LL DESTROY HIS MIND. MAYBE KILL HIM.
BUT...ISN'T HE A GOOD PERSON?
HE'S HELPED PEOPLE!
IT'S NOT RIGHT.
THE BARON SEES A BIGGER PICTURE.
I'VE GOT TO GO. KITCHEN'S THROWING SCRAPS.
IF YOU'RE GOING TO RESCUE SOMEONE, RESCUE OTHAR.
I'LL BE FINE.
OTHAR ISN'T MY RESPONSIBILITY.
OR YOURS.
WELL.
I GUESS HE IS NOW.

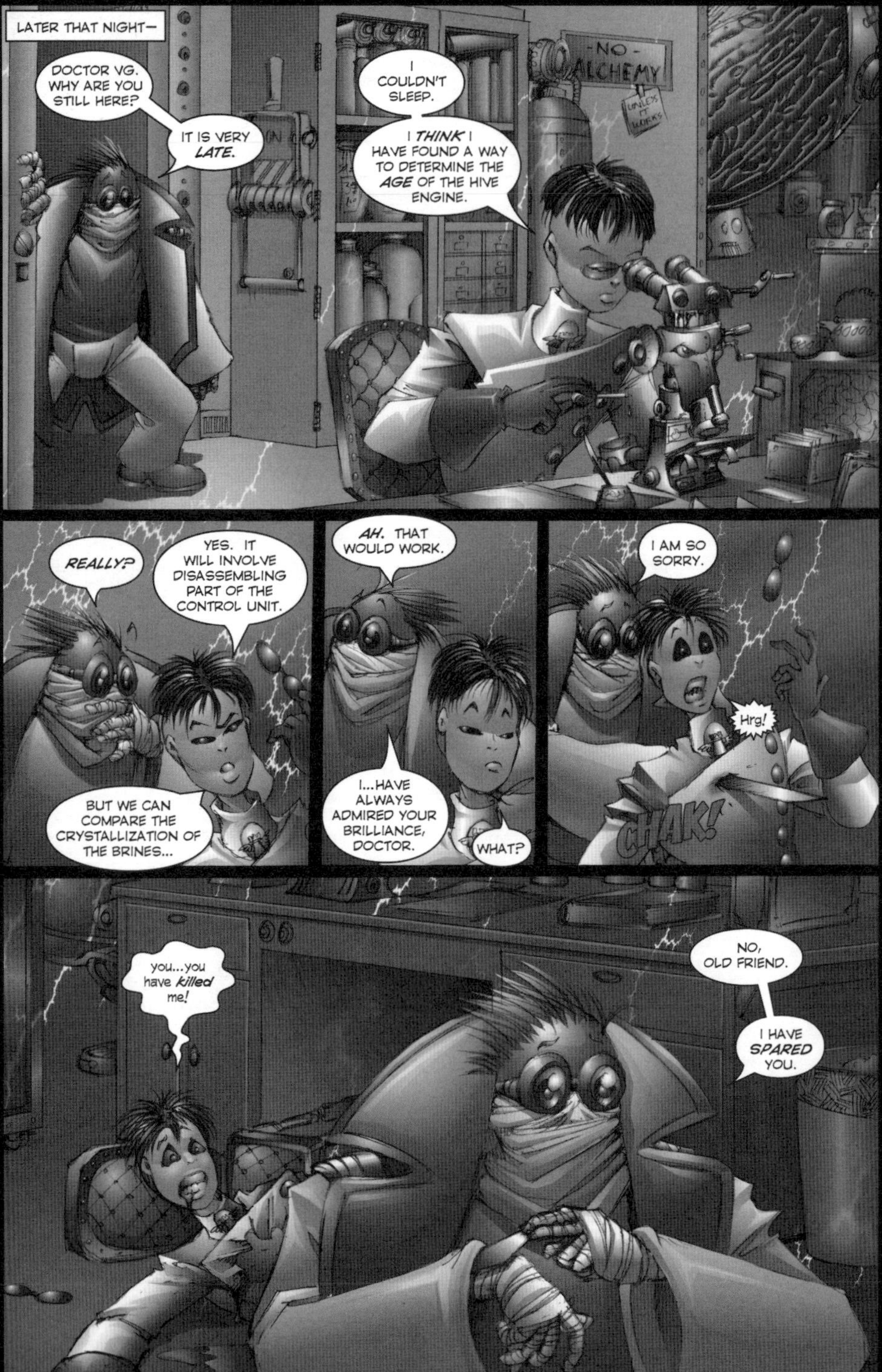
LATER THAT NIGHT—
DOCTOR VG. WHY ARE YOU STILL HERE?
IT IS VERY LATE.
I COULDN'T SLEEP.
I THINK I HAVE FOUND A WAY TO DETERMINE THE AGE OF THE HIVE ENGINE.
-NO- ALCHEMY
UNLESS IT WORKS
REALLY?
YES. IT WILL INVOLVE DISASSEMBLING PART OF THE CONTROL UNIT.
BUT WE CAN COMPARE THE CRYSTALLIZATION OF THE BRINES...
AH. THAT WOULD WORK.
I...HAVE ALWAYS ADMIRED YOUR BRILLIANCE, DOCTOR.
WHAT?
I AM SO SORRY.
Hrg!
CHAK!
you...you have killed me!
NO, OLD FRIEND.
I HAVE SPARED YOU.

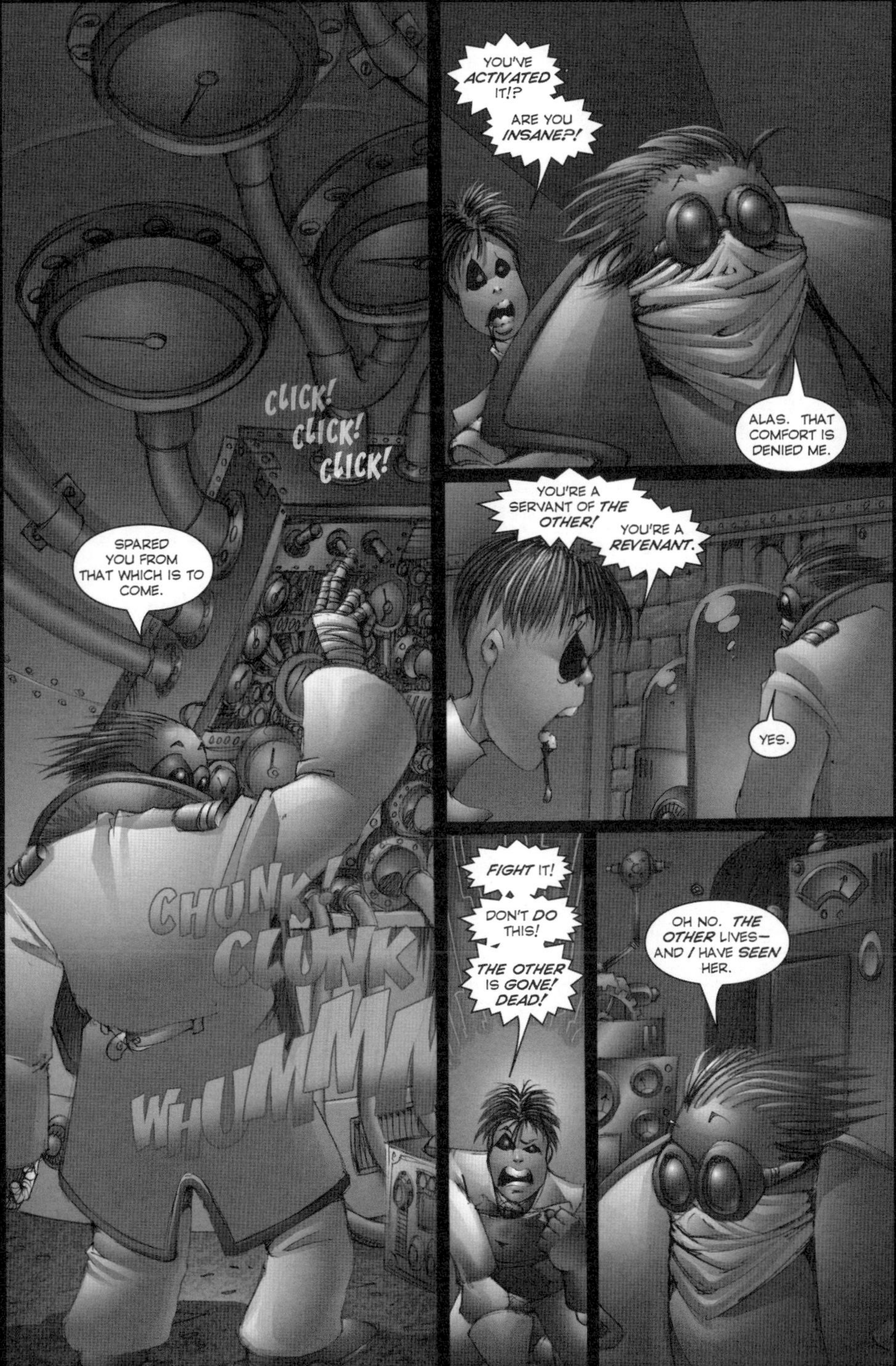
CLICK!
CLICK!
CLICK!
SPARED YOU FROM THAT WHICH IS TO COME.
CHUNK!
CLUNK!
WHUMM
YOU'VE ACTIVATED IT!?
ARE YOU INSANE?!
ALAS. THAT COMFORT IS DENIED ME.
YOU'RE A SERVANT OF THE OTHER!
YOU'RE A REVENANT.
YES.
FIGHT IT!
DON'T DO THIS!
THE OTHER IS GONE! DEAD!
OH NO. THE OTHER LIVES— AND I HAVE SEEN HER.

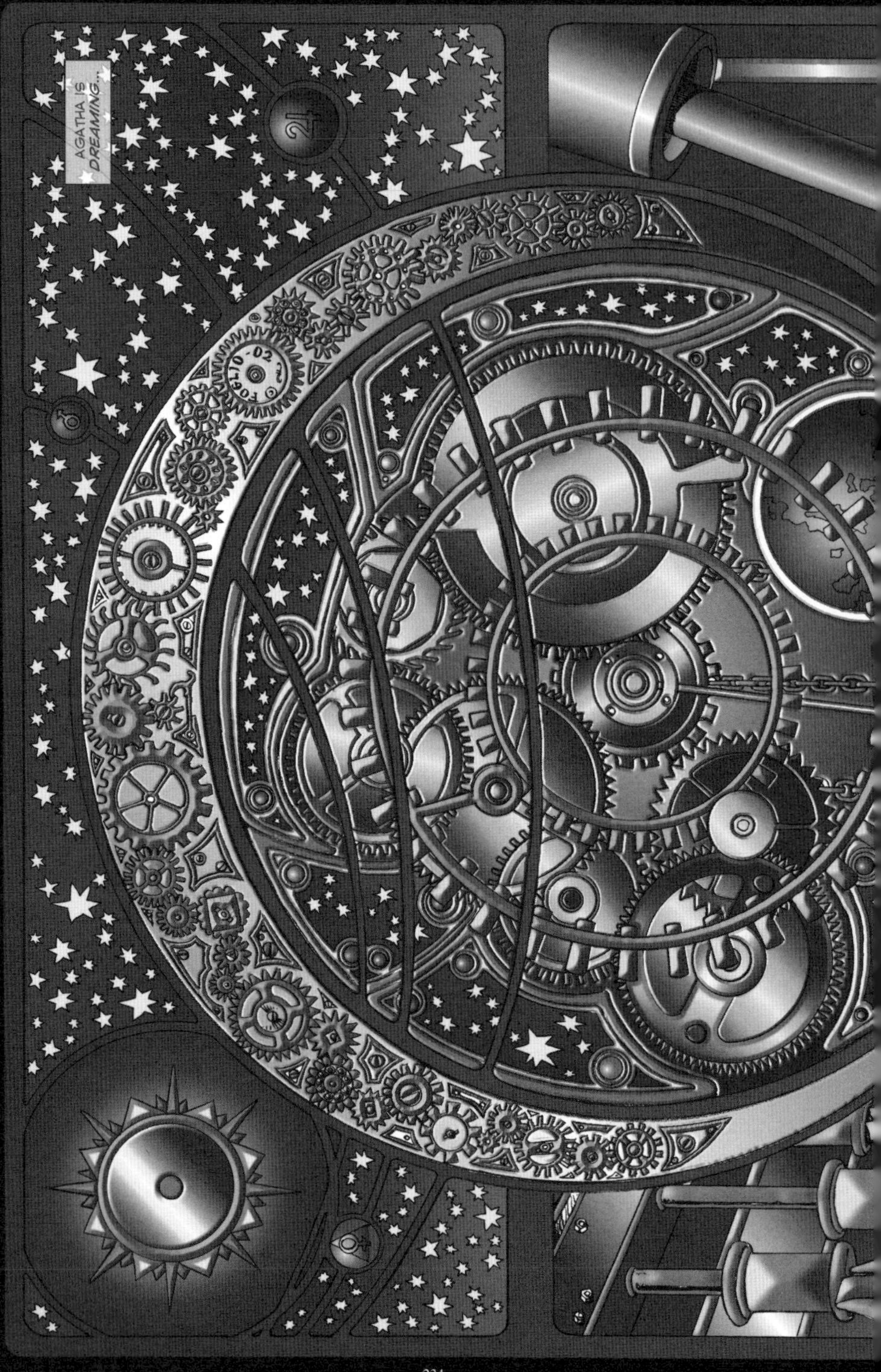
AGATHA IS DREAMING...
FOGLIO-02

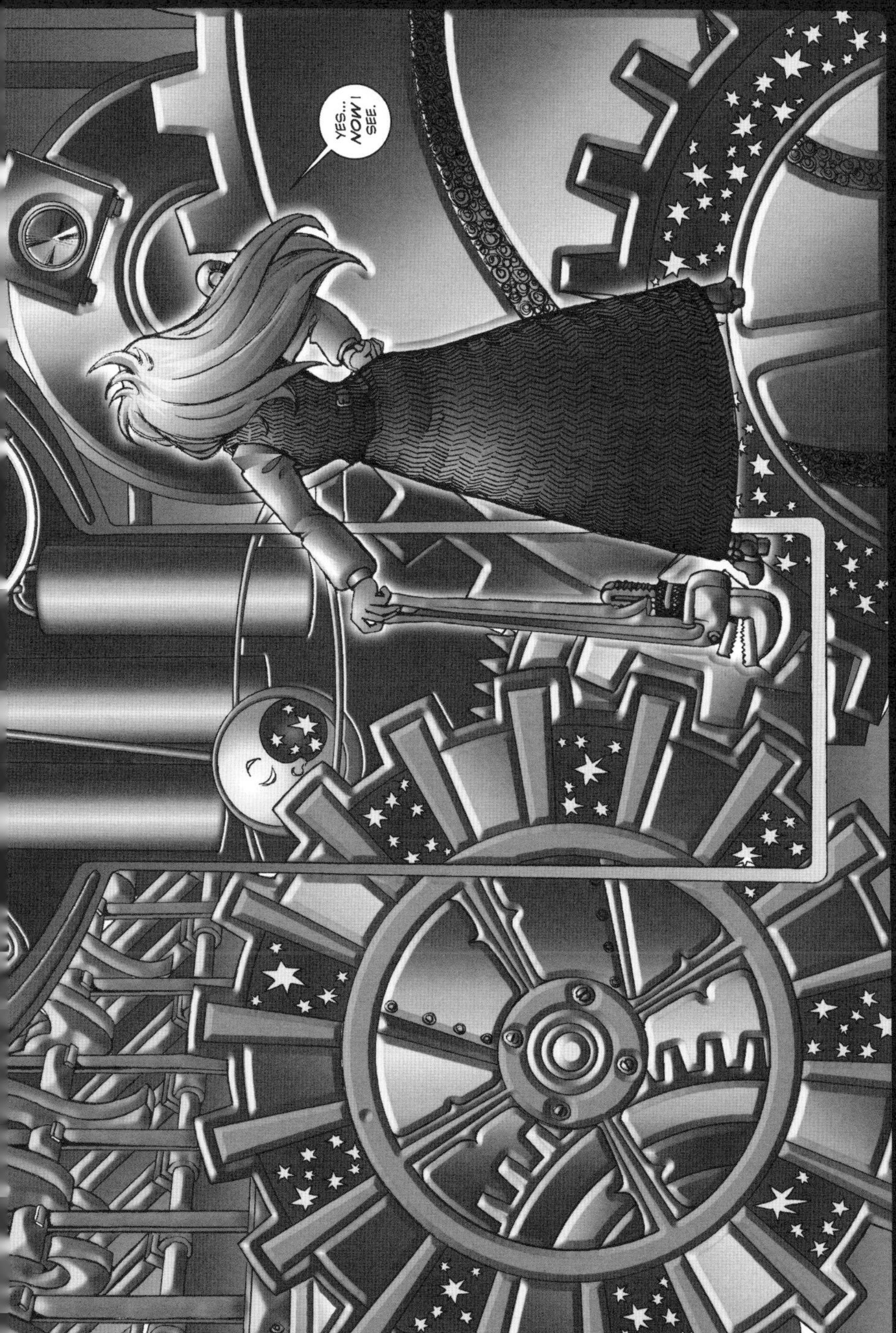
YES... NOW I SEE.

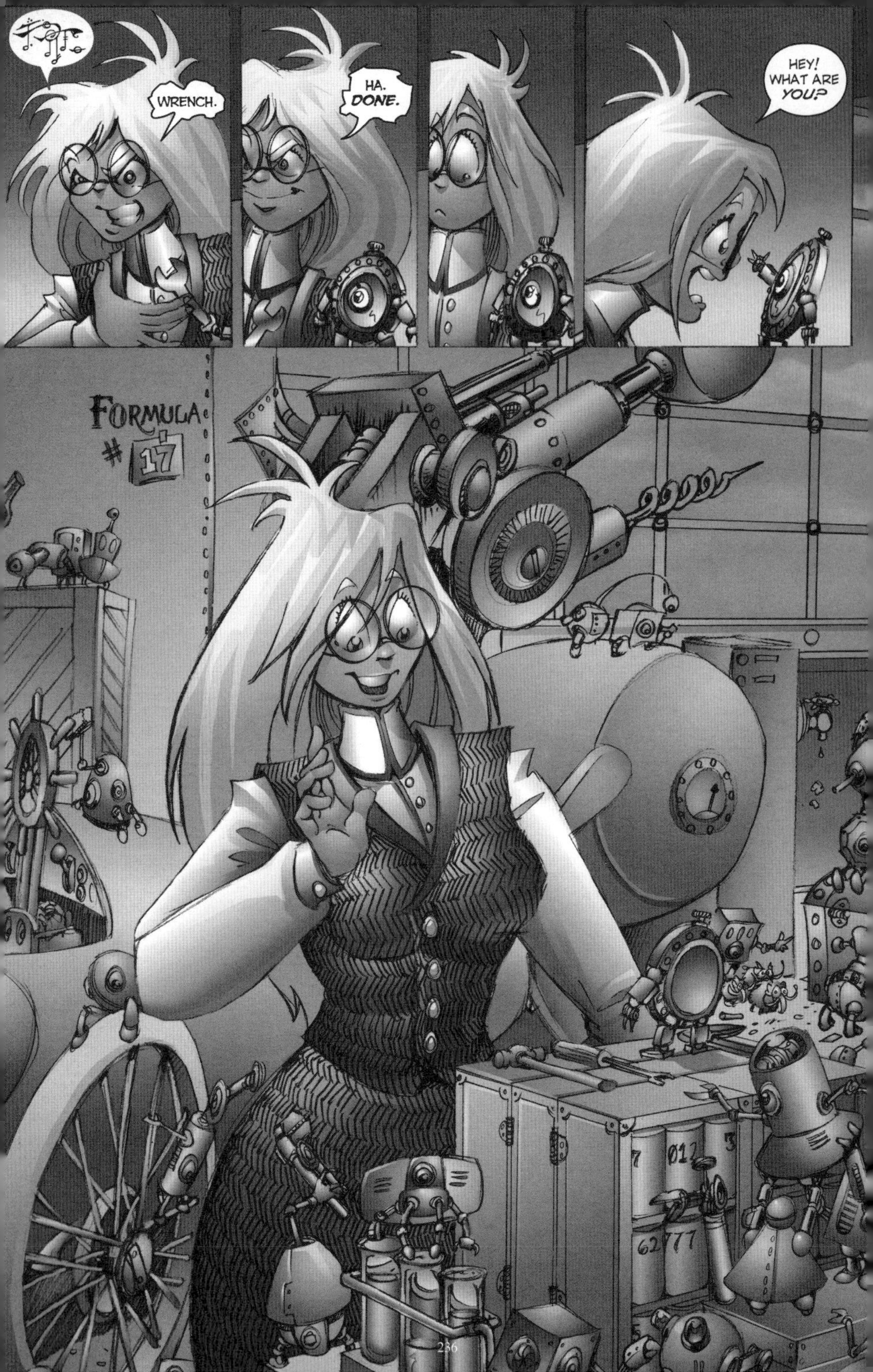
WRENCH.
HA. DONE.
HEY! WHAT ARE YOU?
FORMULA #17

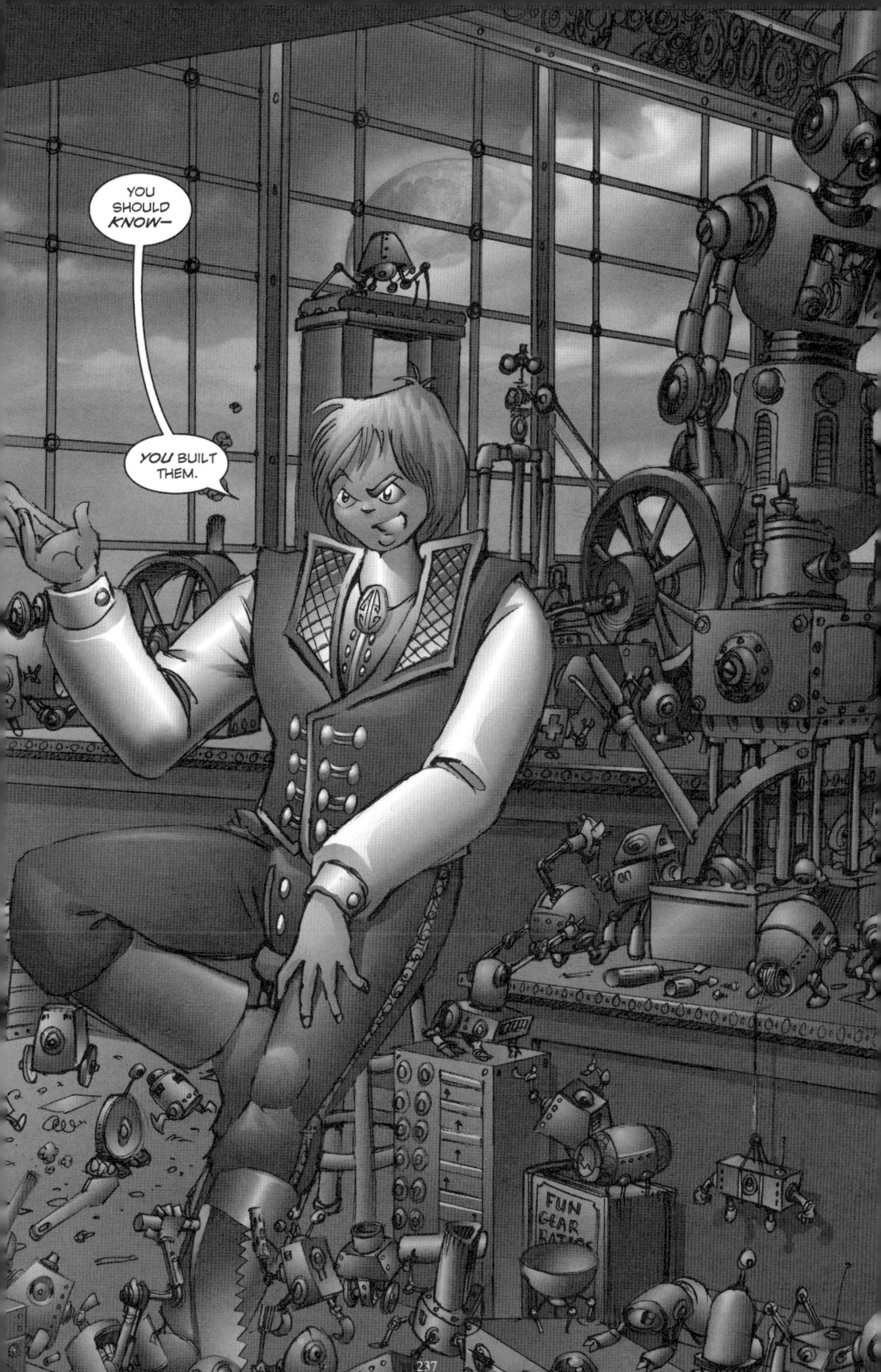
YOU SHOULD KNOW—
YOU BUILT THEM.
FUN GEAR RATIOS

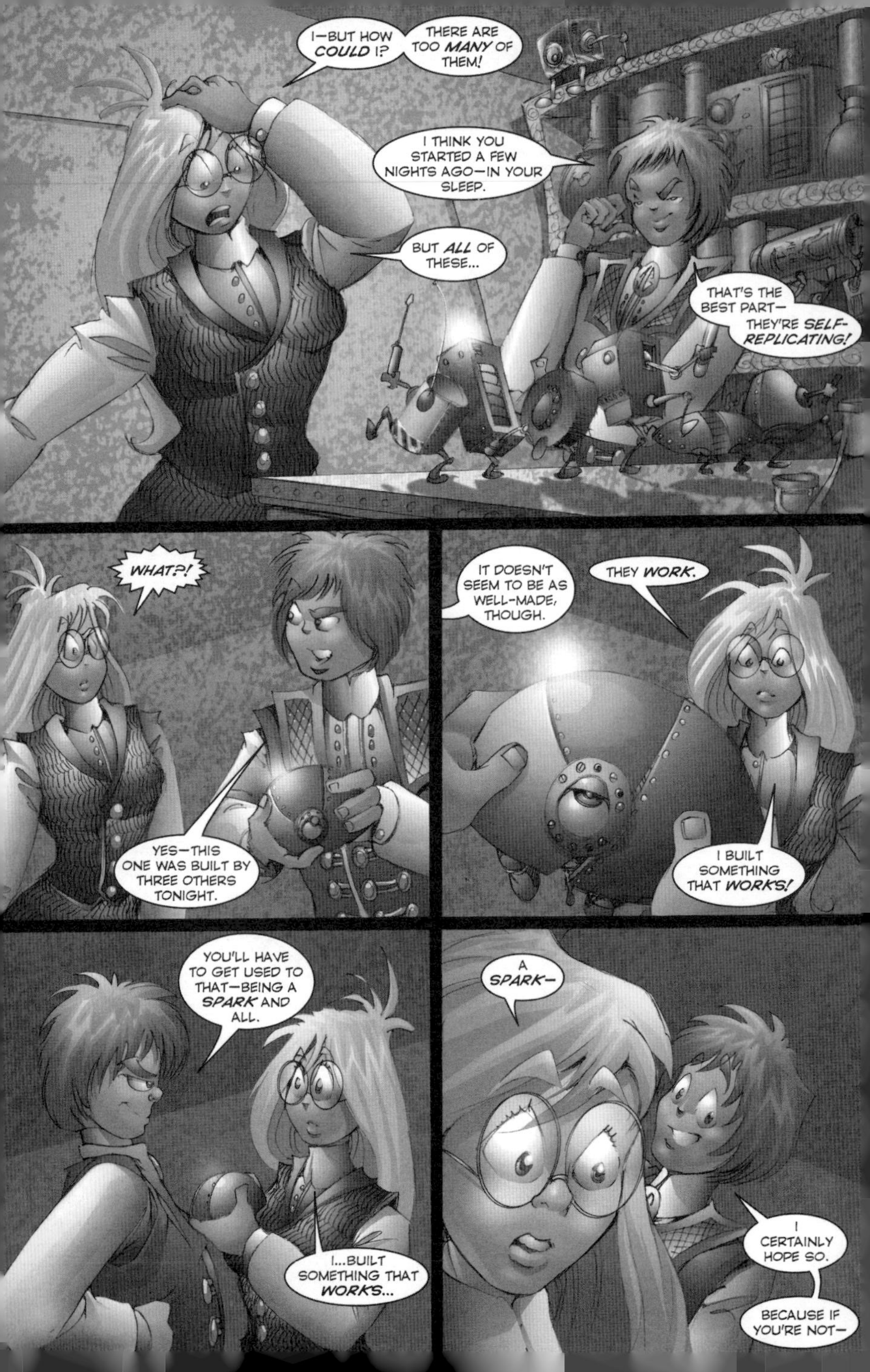
I—BUT HOW COULD I?
THERE ARE TOO MANY OF THEM!
I THINK YOU STARTED A FEW NIGHTS AGO—IN YOUR SLEEP.
BUT ALL OF THESE...
THAT'S THE BEST PART—
THEY'RE SELF-REPLICATING!
WHAT?!
YES—THIS ONE WAS BUILT BY THREE OTHERS TONIGHT.
IT DOESN'T SEEM TO BE AS WELL-MADE, THOUGH.
THEY WORK.
I BUILT SOMETHING THAT WORKS!
YOU'LL HAVE TO GET USED TO THAT—BEING A SPARK AND ALL.
I...BUILT SOMETHING THAT WORKS...
A SPARK—
I CERTAINLY HOPE SO.
BECAUSE IF YOU'RE NOT—

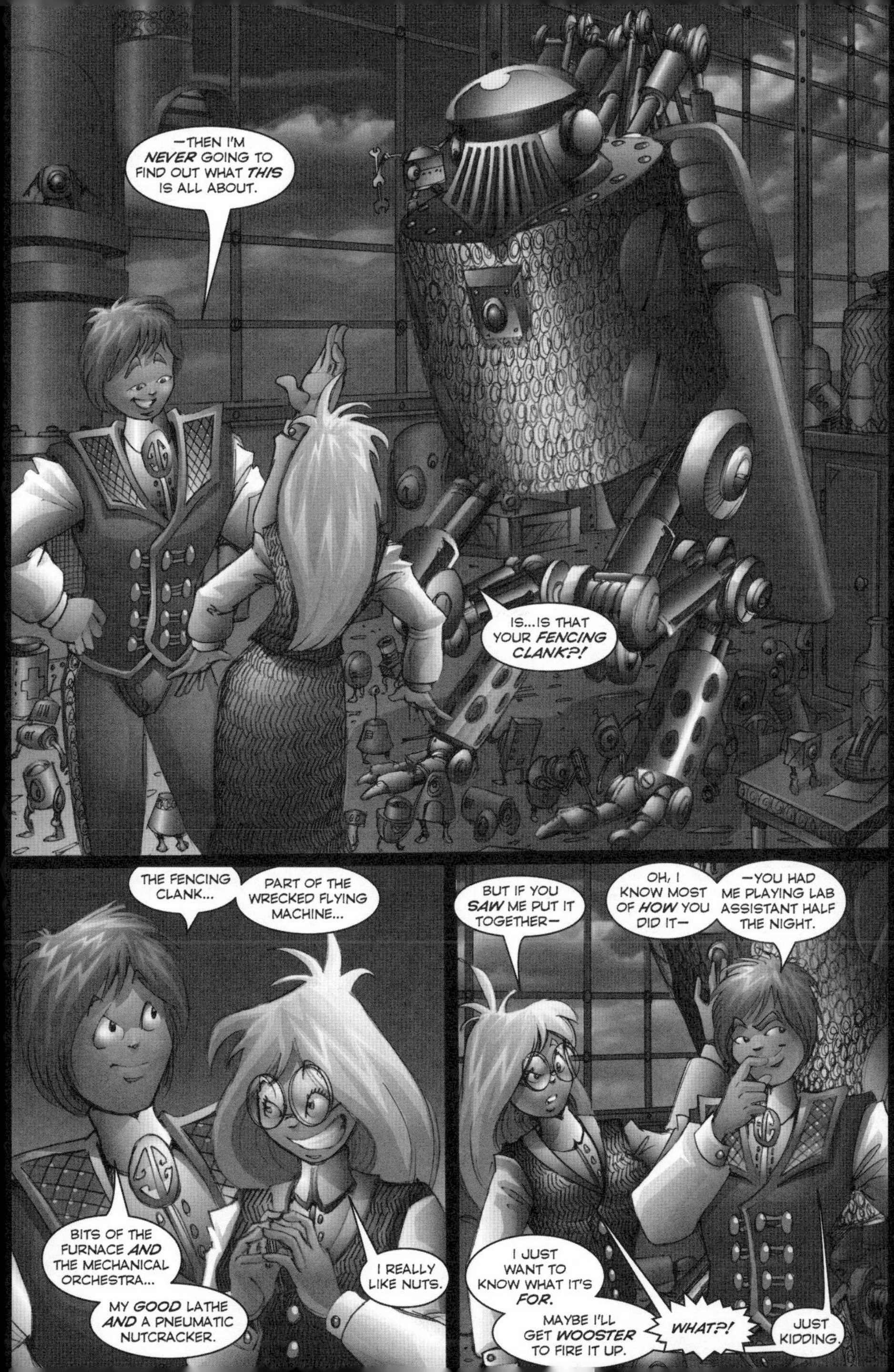
—THEN I'M NEVER GOING TO FIND OUT WHAT THIS IS ALL ABOUT.
IS...IS THAT YOUR FENCING CLANK?!
THE FENCING CLANK...
PART OF THE WRECKED FLYING MACHINE...
BITS OF THE FURNACE AND THE MECHANICAL ORCHESTRA...
MY GOOD LATHE AND A PNEUMATIC NUTCRACKER.
I REALLY LIKE NUTS.
BUT IF YOU SAW ME PUT IT TOGETHER—
OH, I KNOW MOST OF HOW YOU DID IT—
—YOU HAD ME PLAYING LAB ASSISTANT HALF THE NIGHT.
I JUST WANT TO KNOW WHAT IT'S FOR.
MAYBE I'LL GET WOOSTER TO FIRE IT UP.
WHAT?!
JUST KIDDING.

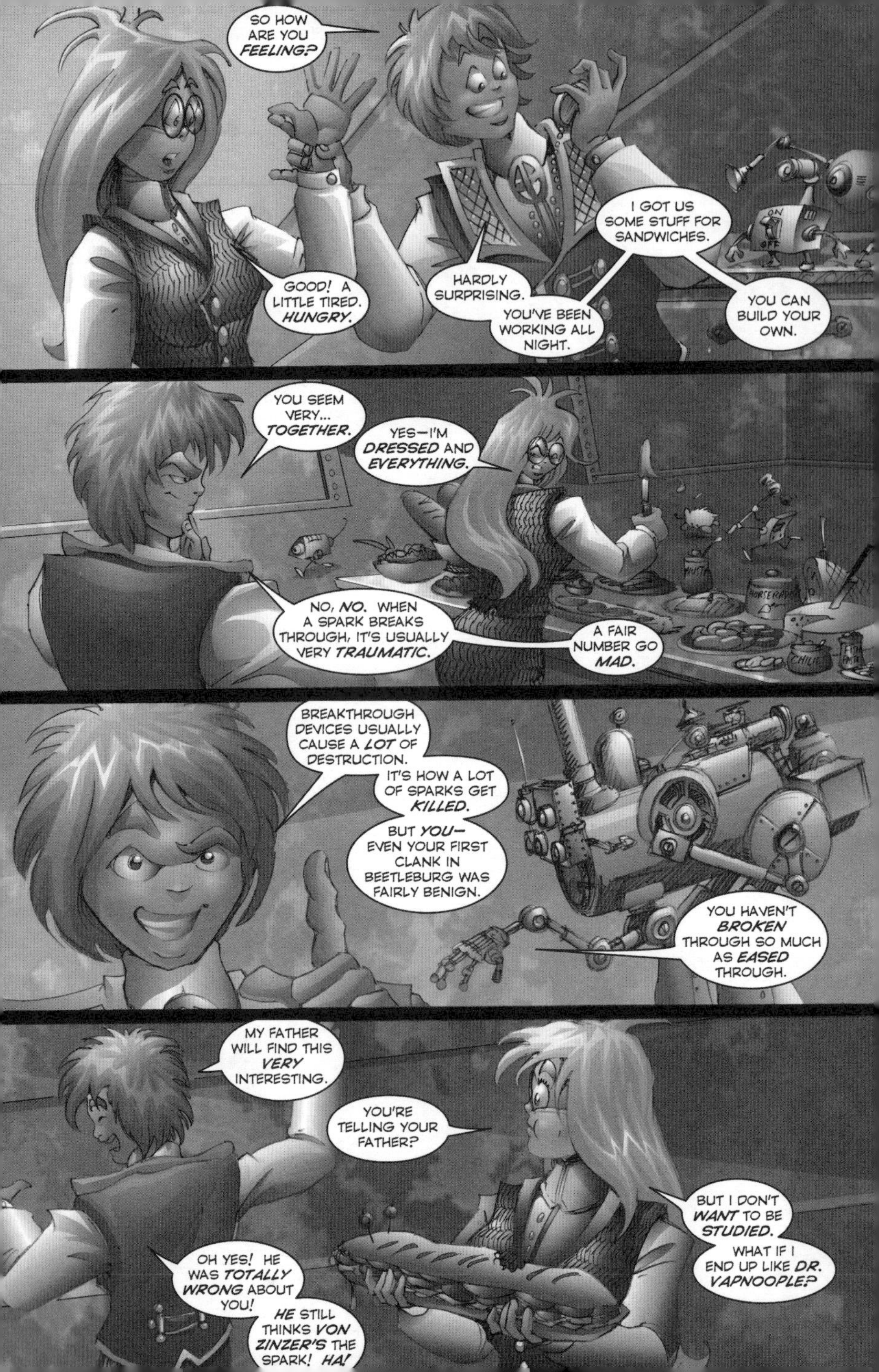
SO HOW ARE YOU *FEELING?*
GOOD! A LITTLE TIRED. *HUNGRY.*
HARDLY SURPRISING.
YOU'VE BEEN WORKING ALL NIGHT.
I GOT US SOME STUFF FOR SANDWICHES.
YOU CAN BUILD YOUR OWN.
YOU SEEM VERY... *TOGETHER.*
YES—I'M *DRESSED* AND *EVERYTHING.*
NO, *NO.* WHEN A SPARK BREAKS THROUGH, IT'S USUALLY VERY *TRAUMATIC.*
A FAIR NUMBER GO *MAD.*
BREAKTHROUGH DEVICES USUALLY CAUSE A *LOT* OF DESTRUCTION.
IT'S HOW A LOT OF SPARKS GET *KILLED.*
BUT *YOU*— EVEN YOUR FIRST CLANK IN BEETLEBURG WAS FAIRLY BENIGN.
YOU HAVEN'T *BROKEN* THROUGH SO MUCH AS *EASED* THROUGH.
MY FATHER WILL FIND THIS *VERY* INTERESTING.
YOU'RE TELLING YOUR FATHER?
OH YES! HE WAS *TOTALLY WRONG* ABOUT YOU!
HE STILL THINKS *VON ZINZER'S* THE SPARK! *HA!*
BUT I DON'T *WANT* TO BE *STUDIED.*
WHAT IF I END UP LIKE *DR. VAPNOOPLE?*

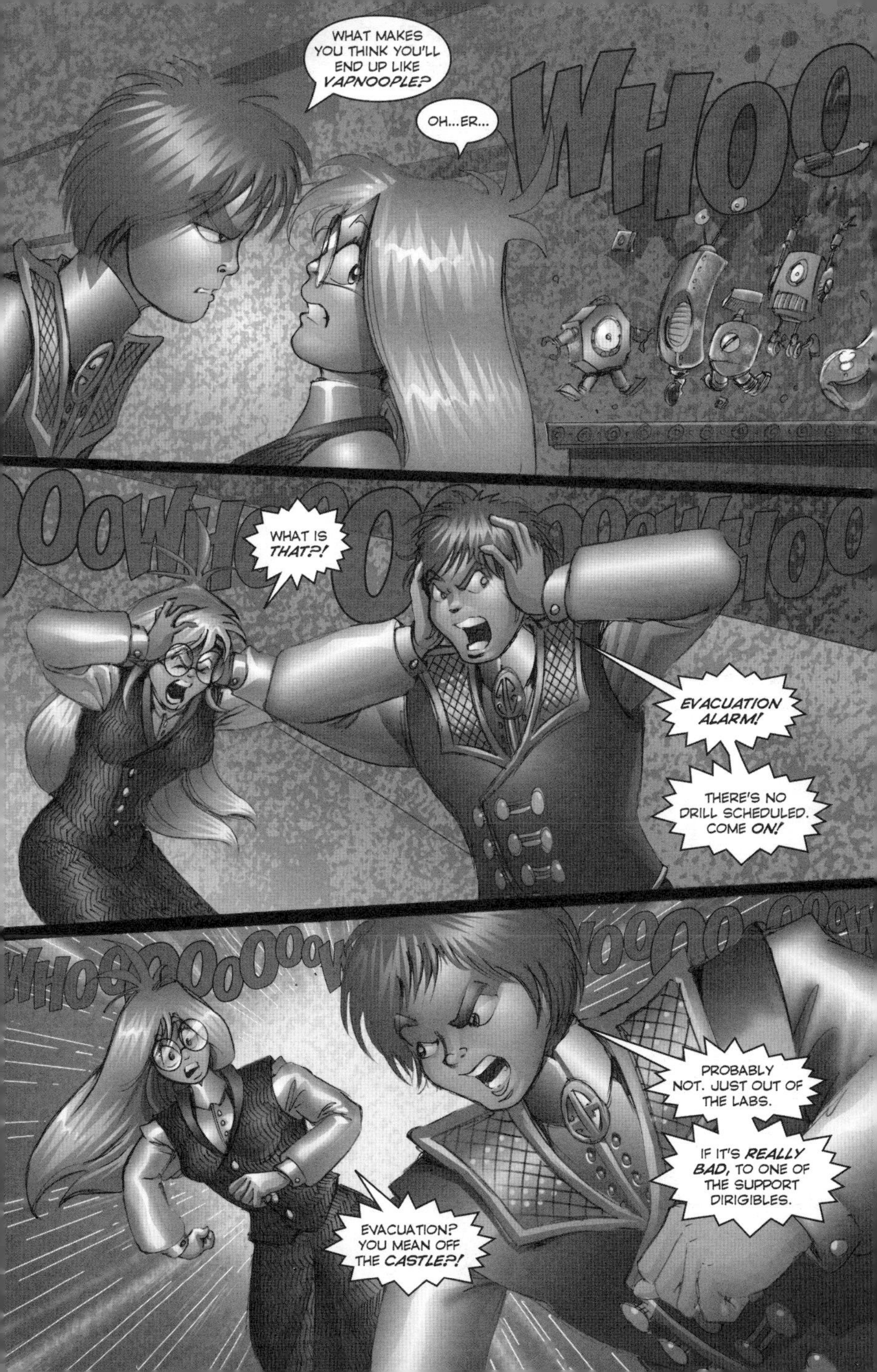
WHAT MAKES YOU THINK YOU'LL END UP LIKE VAPNOOPLE?
OH...ER...
WHOO
OOOWHOOOOOOOWHOO
WHAT IS THAT?!
EVACUATION ALARM!
THERE'S NO DRILL SCHEDULED. COME ON!
WHOOOOOOOOOW
WOOOOOOOOW
PROBABLY NOT. JUST OUT OF THE LABS.
IF IT'S REALLY BAD, TO ONE OF THE SUPPORT DIRIGIBLES.
EVACUATION? YOU MEAN OFF THE CASTLE?!

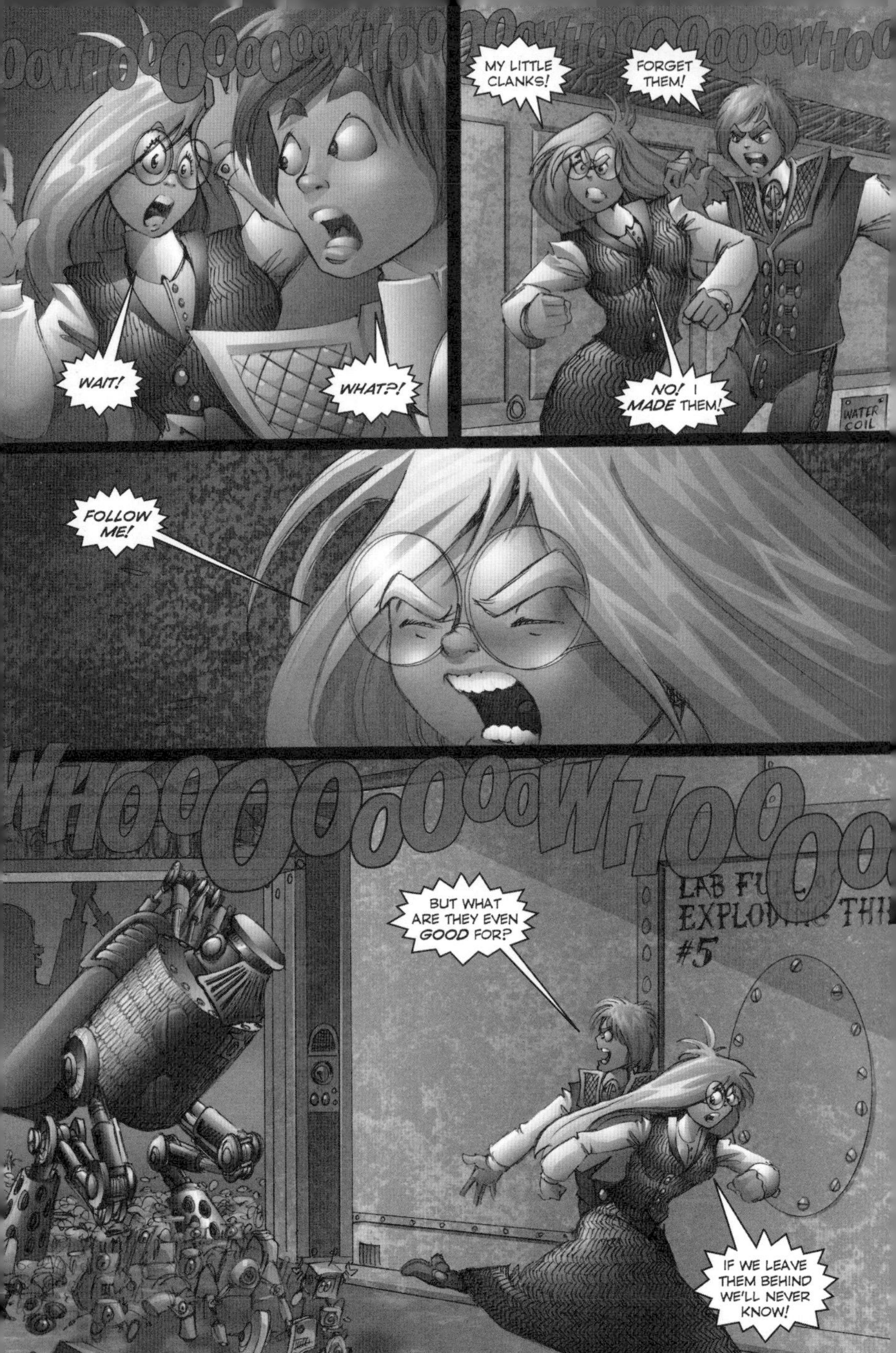
WAIT!
WHAT?!
MY LITTLE CLANKS!
FORGET THEM!
NO! I MADE THEM!
FOLLOW ME!
BUT WHAT ARE THEY EVEN GOOD FOR?
IF WE LEAVE THEM BEHIND WE'LL NEVER KNOW!
#5

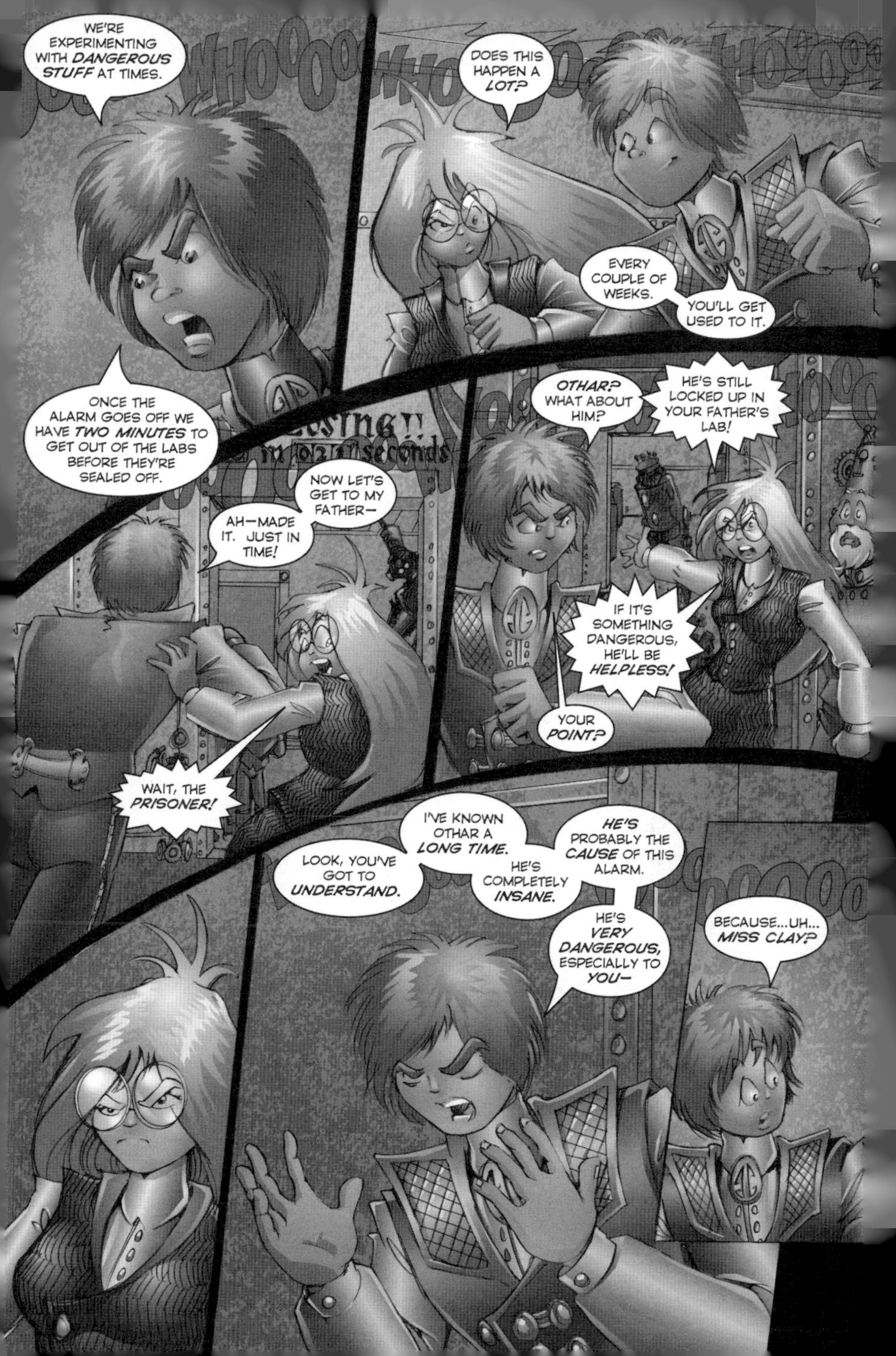
WE'RE EXPERIMENTING WITH DANGEROUS STUFF AT TIMES.
DOES THIS HAPPEN A LOT?
EVERY COUPLE OF WEEKS.
YOU'LL GET USED TO IT.
ONCE THE ALARM GOES OFF WE HAVE TWO MINUTES TO GET OUT OF THE LABS BEFORE THEY'RE SEALED OFF.
AH—MADE IT. JUST IN TIME!
NOW LET'S GET TO MY FATHER—
WAIT, THE PRISONER!
OTHAR? WHAT ABOUT HIM?
HE'S STILL LOCKED UP IN YOUR FATHER'S LAB!
IF IT'S SOMETHING DANGEROUS, HE'LL BE HELPLESS!
YOUR POINT?
LOOK, YOU'VE GOT TO UNDERSTAND.
I'VE KNOWN OTHAR A LONG TIME.
HE'S COMPLETELY INSANE.
HE'S PROBABLY THE CAUSE OF THIS ALARM.
HE'S VERY DANGEROUS, ESPECIALLY TO YOU—
BECAUSE...UH... MISS CLAY?

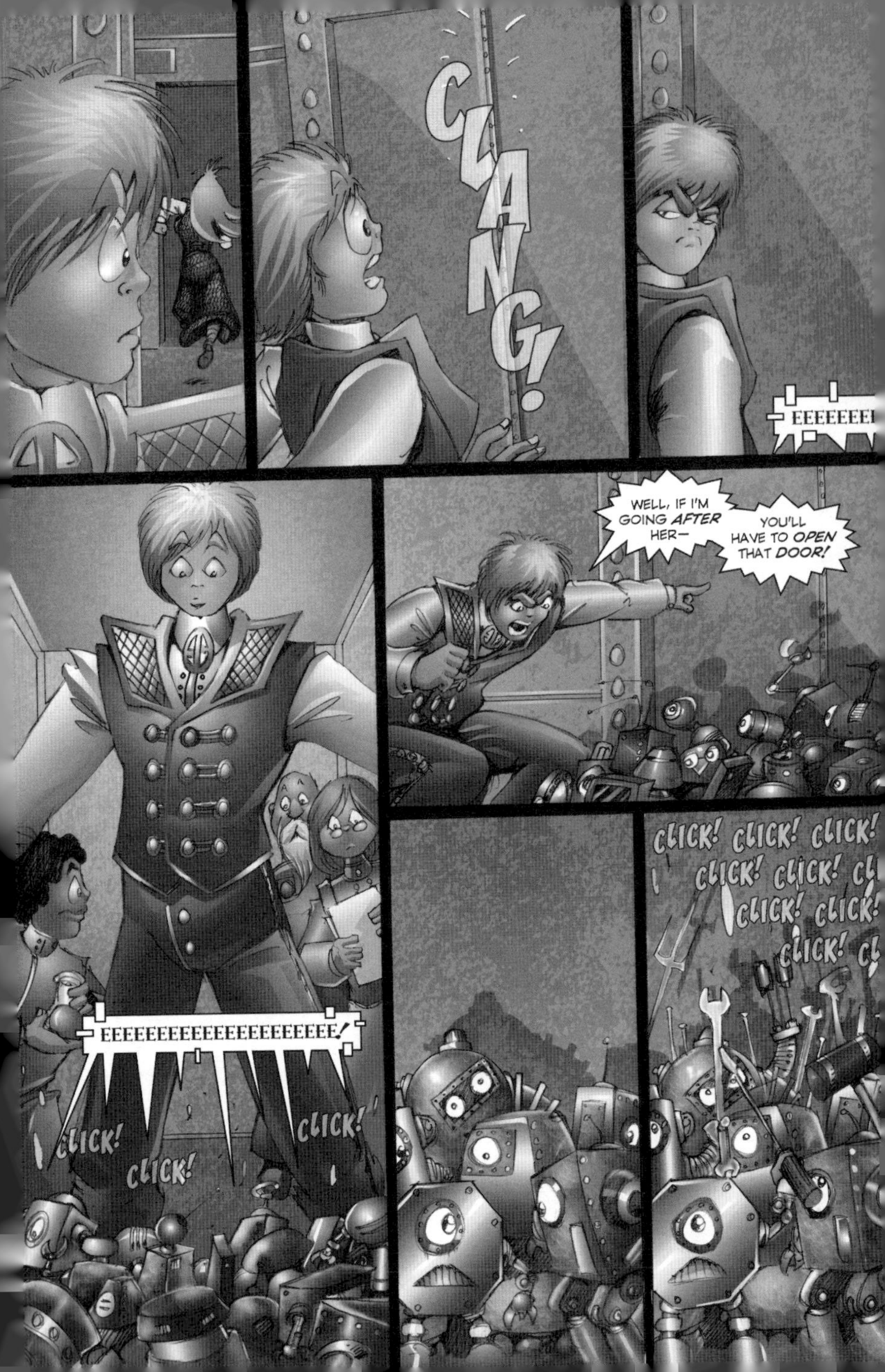
CLANG!
EEEEEEEE
EEEEEEEEEEEEEEEEEEEE!
CLICK!
CLICK!
CLICK!
WELL, IF I'M GOING AFTER HER—
YOU'LL HAVE TO OPEN THAT DOOR!
CLICK! CLICK! CLICK!
CLICK! CLICK!
CLICK! CLICK!
CLICK!

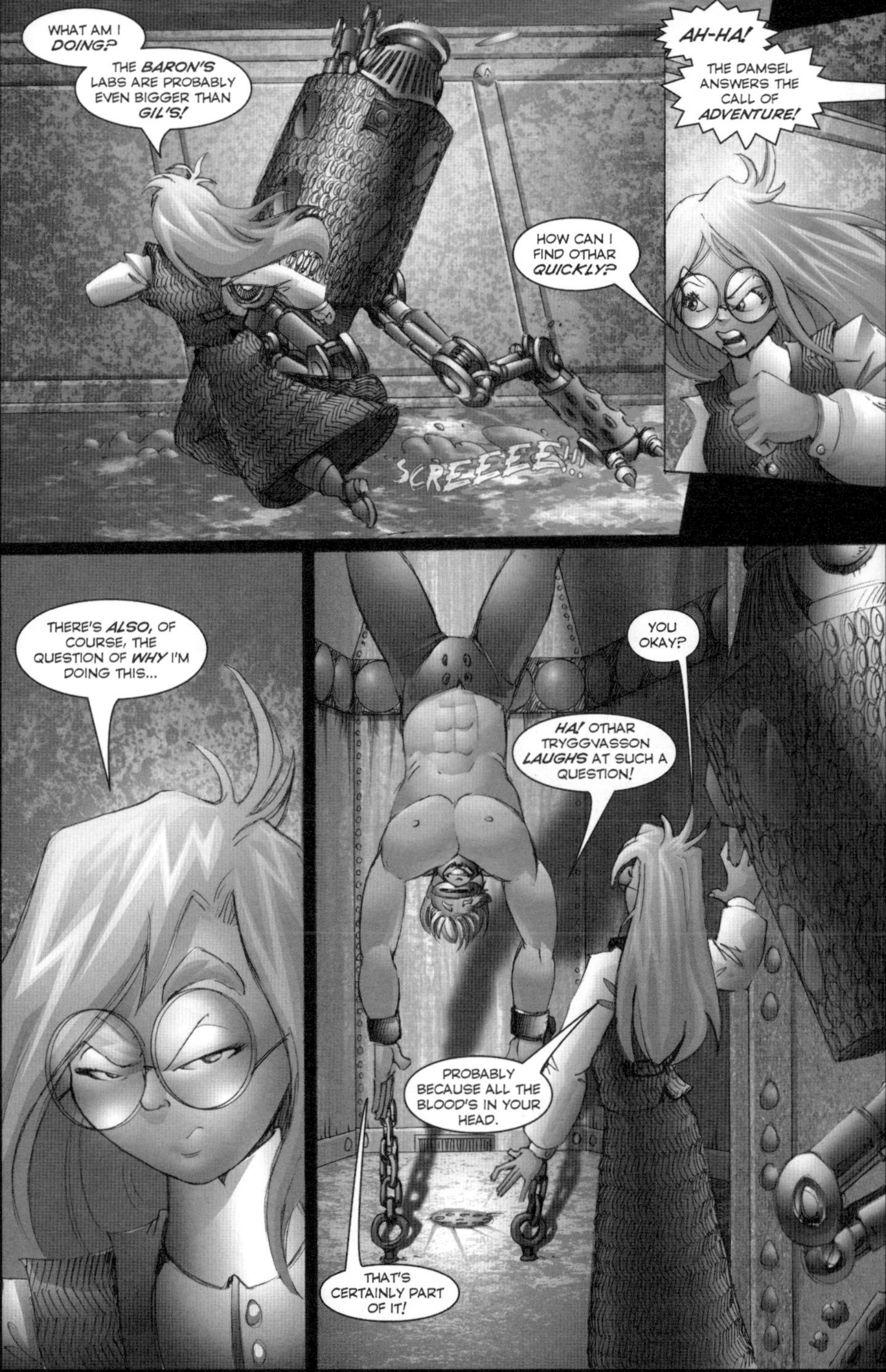
WHAT AM I DOING?
THE BARON'S LABS ARE PROBABLY EVEN BIGGER THAN GIL'S!
AH-HA!
THE DAMSEL ANSWERS THE CALL OF ADVENTURE!
HOW CAN I FIND OTHAR QUICKLY?
SCREEEEE!!!
THERE'S ALSO, OF COURSE, THE QUESTION OF WHY I'M DOING THIS...
YOU OKAY?
HA! OTHAR TRYGGVASSON LAUGHS AT SUCH A QUESTION!
PROBABLY BECAUSE ALL THE BLOOD'S IN YOUR HEAD.
THAT'S CERTAINLY PART OF IT!

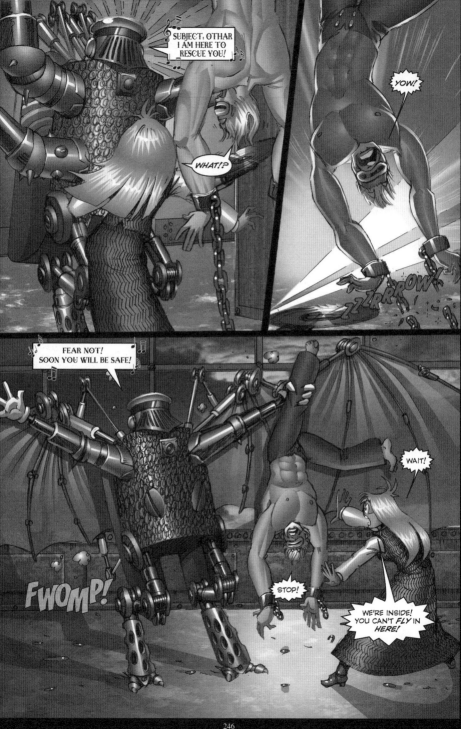

♪ SUBJECT, OTHAR I AM HERE TO RESCUE YOU! ♪

WHAT!?

YOW!

ZZRRROW!

♪ FEAR NOT! SOON YOU WILL BE SAFE! ♪

WAIT!

FWOMP!

STOP!

WE'RE INSIDE! YOU CAN'T *FLY* IN *HERE!*

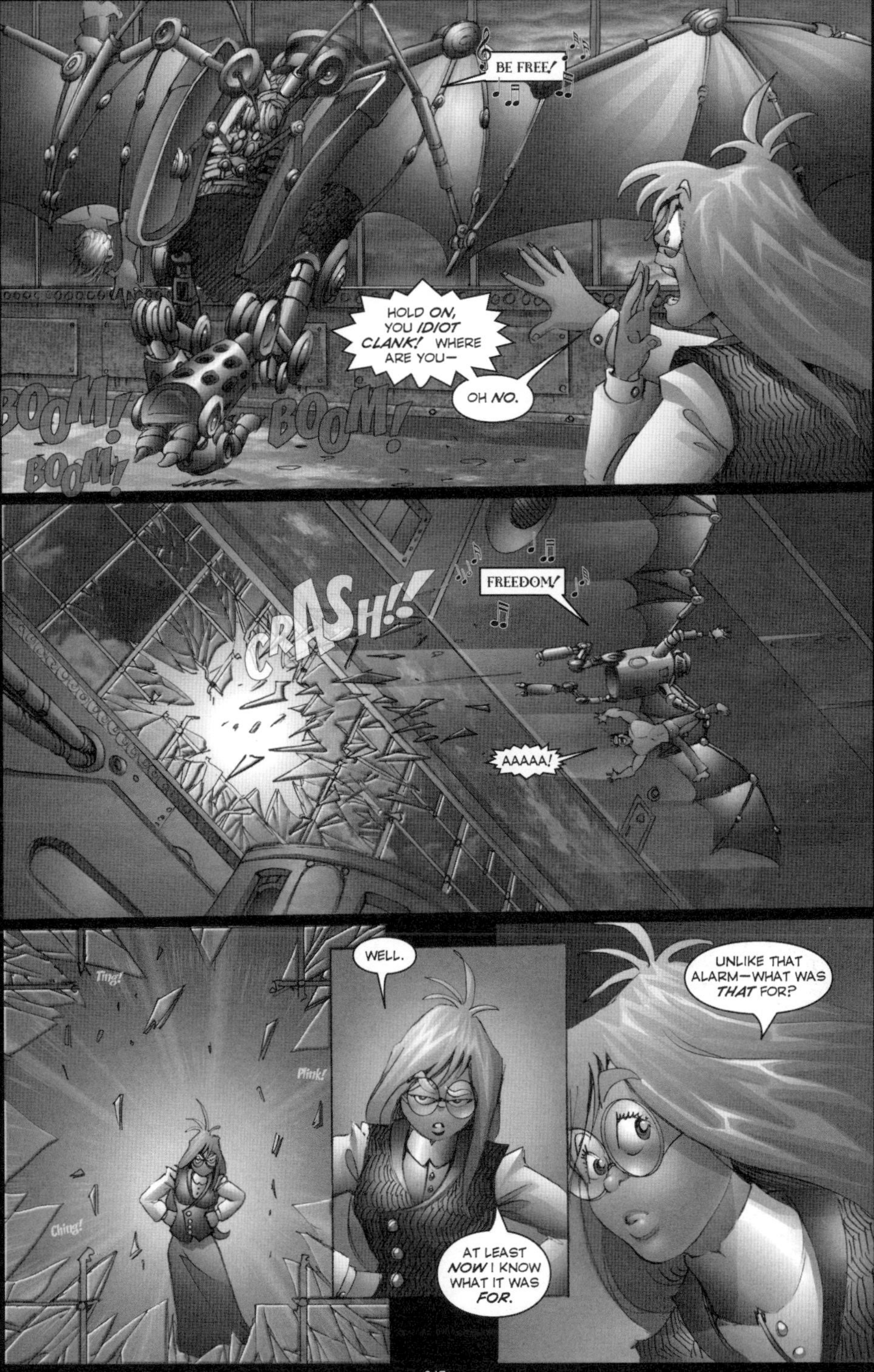

BE FREE!
HOLD ON, YOU IDIOT CLANK! WHERE ARE YOU—
OH NO.
BOOM! BOOM! BOOM!
FREEDOM!
CRASH!!
AAAAA!
Ting!
Plink!
Ching!
WELL.
AT LEAST NOW I KNOW WHAT IT WAS FOR.
UNLIKE THAT ALARM—WHAT WAS THAT FOR?

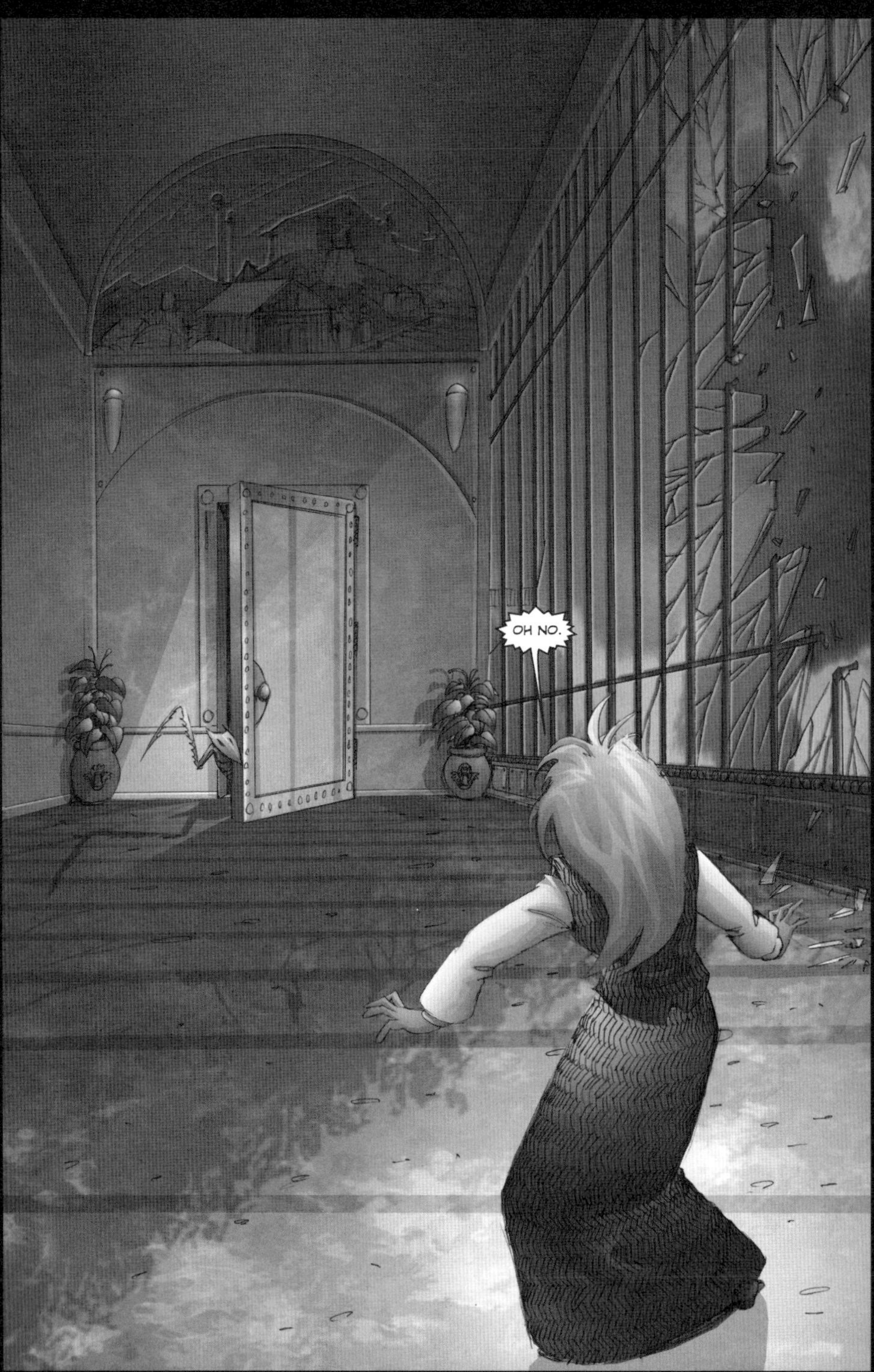
OH NO.

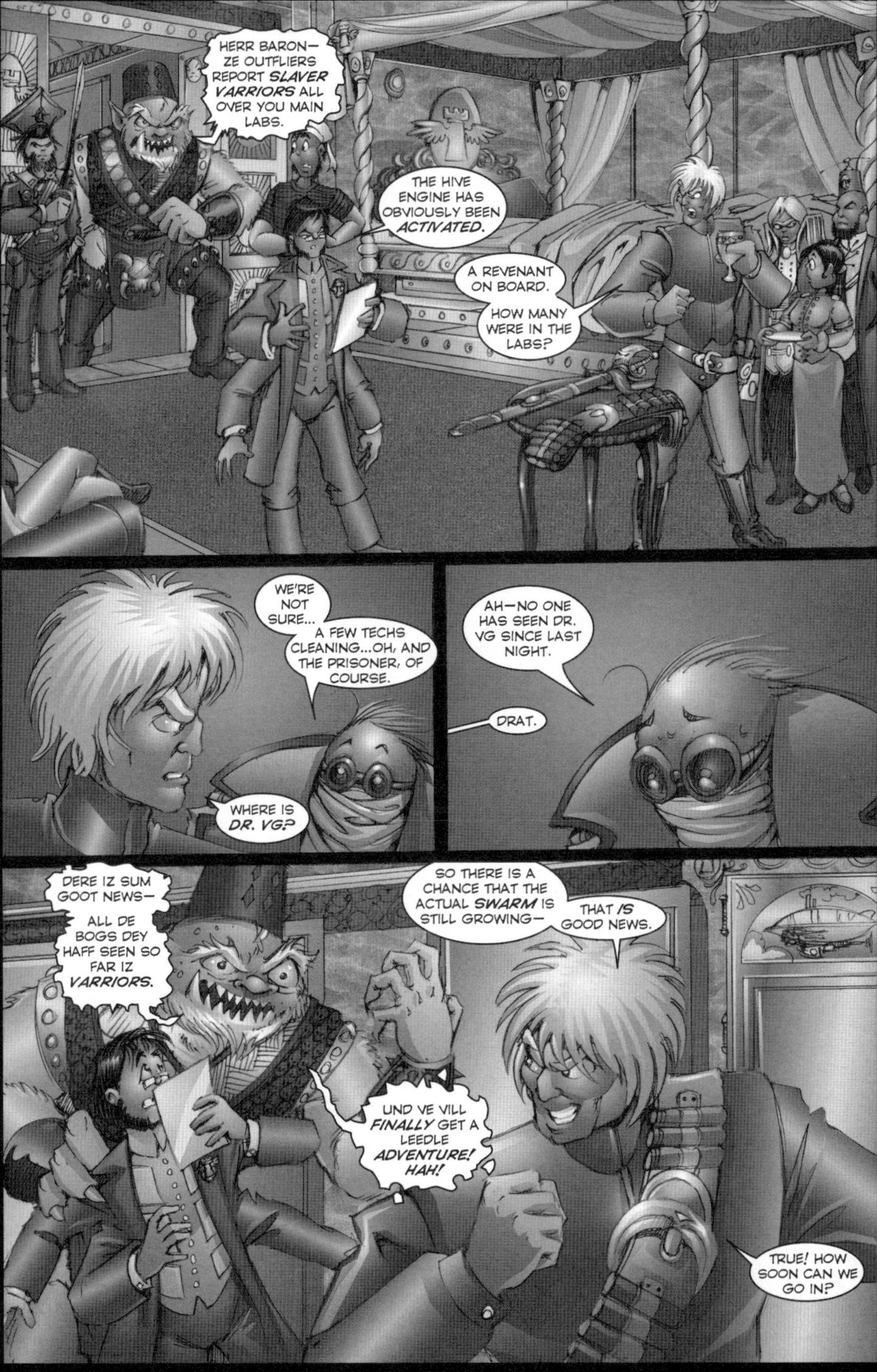
HERR BARON—ZE OUTFLIERS REPORT SLAVER VARRIORS ALL OVER YOU MAIN LABS.
THE HIVE ENGINE HAS OBVIOUSLY BEEN ACTIVATED.
A REVENANT ON BOARD.
HOW MANY WERE IN THE LABS?
WE'RE NOT SURE...
A FEW TECHS CLEANING...OH, AND THE PRISONER, OF COURSE.
WHERE IS DR. VG?
AH—NO ONE HAS SEEN DR. VG SINCE LAST NIGHT.
DRAT.
DERE IZ SUM GOOT NEWS—
ALL DE BOGS DEY HAFF SEEN SO FAR IZ VARRIORS.
SO THERE IS A CHANCE THAT THE ACTUAL SWARM IS STILL GROWING—
THAT IS GOOD NEWS.
UND VE VILL FINALLY GET A LEEDLE ADVENTURE! HAH!
TRUE! HOW SOON CAN WE GO IN?

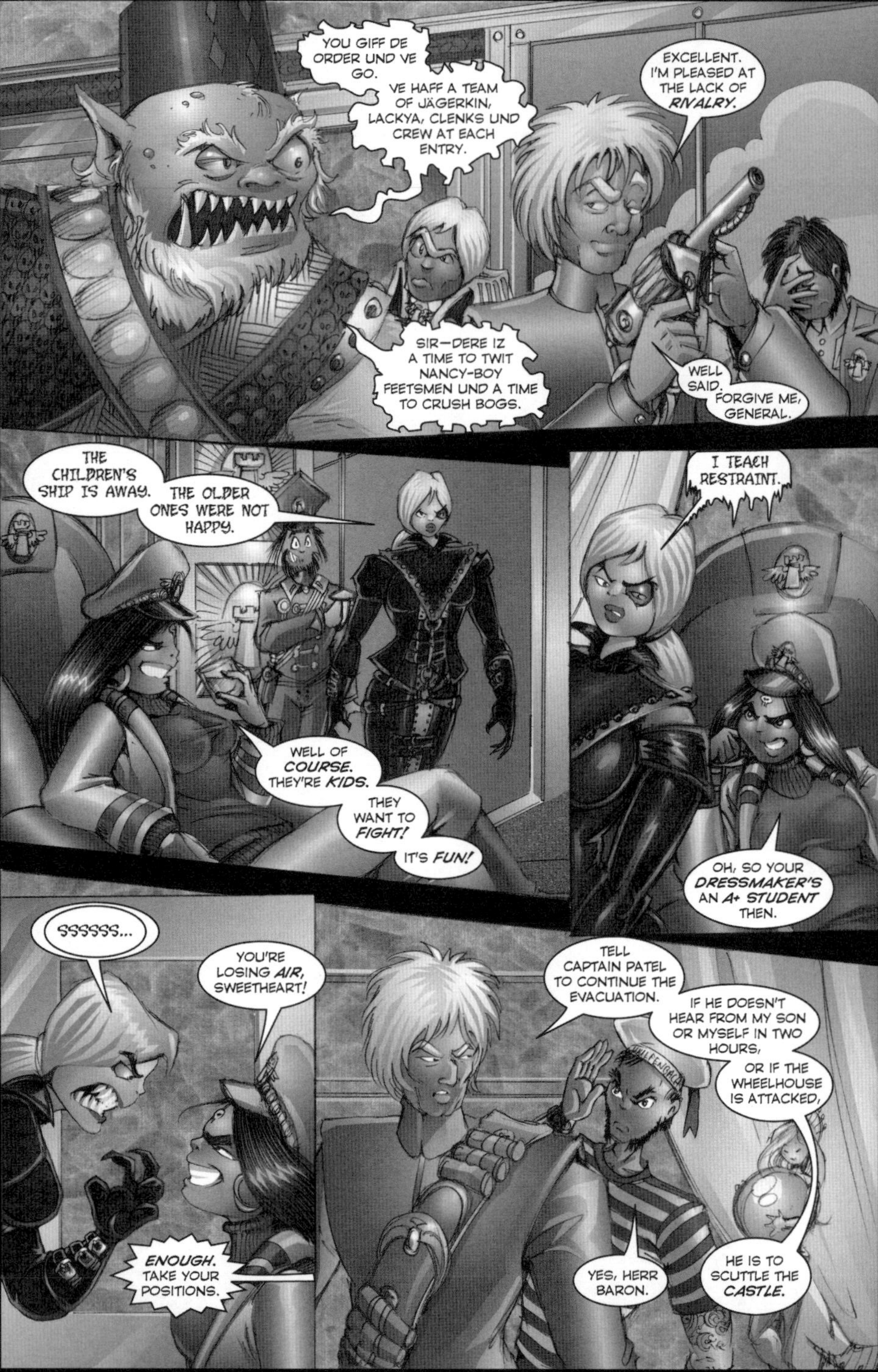
YOU GIFF DE ORDER UND VE GO.
VE HAFF A TEAM OF JÄGERKIN, LACKYA, CLENKS UND CREW AT EACH ENTRY.
EXCELLENT. I'M PLEASED AT THE LACK OF RIVALRY.
SIR—DERE IZ A TIME TO TWIT NANCY-BOY FEETSMEN UND A TIME TO CRUSH BOGS.
WELL SAID.
FORGIVE ME, GENERAL.
THE CHILDREN'S SHIP IS AWAY.
THE OLDER ONES WERE NOT HAPPY.
WELL OF COURSE. THEY'RE KIDS.
THEY WANT TO FIGHT!
IT'S FUN!
I TEACH RESTRAINT.
OH, SO YOUR DRESSMAKER'S AN A+ STUDENT THEN.
SSSSSS...
YOU'RE LOSING AIR, SWEETHEART!
ENOUGH. TAKE YOUR POSITIONS.
TELL CAPTAIN PATEL TO CONTINUE THE EVACUATION.
IF HE DOESN'T HEAR FROM MY SON OR MYSELF IN TWO HOURS,
OR IF THE WHEELHOUSE IS ATTACKED,
HE IS TO SCUTTLE THE CASTLE.
YES, HERR BARON.

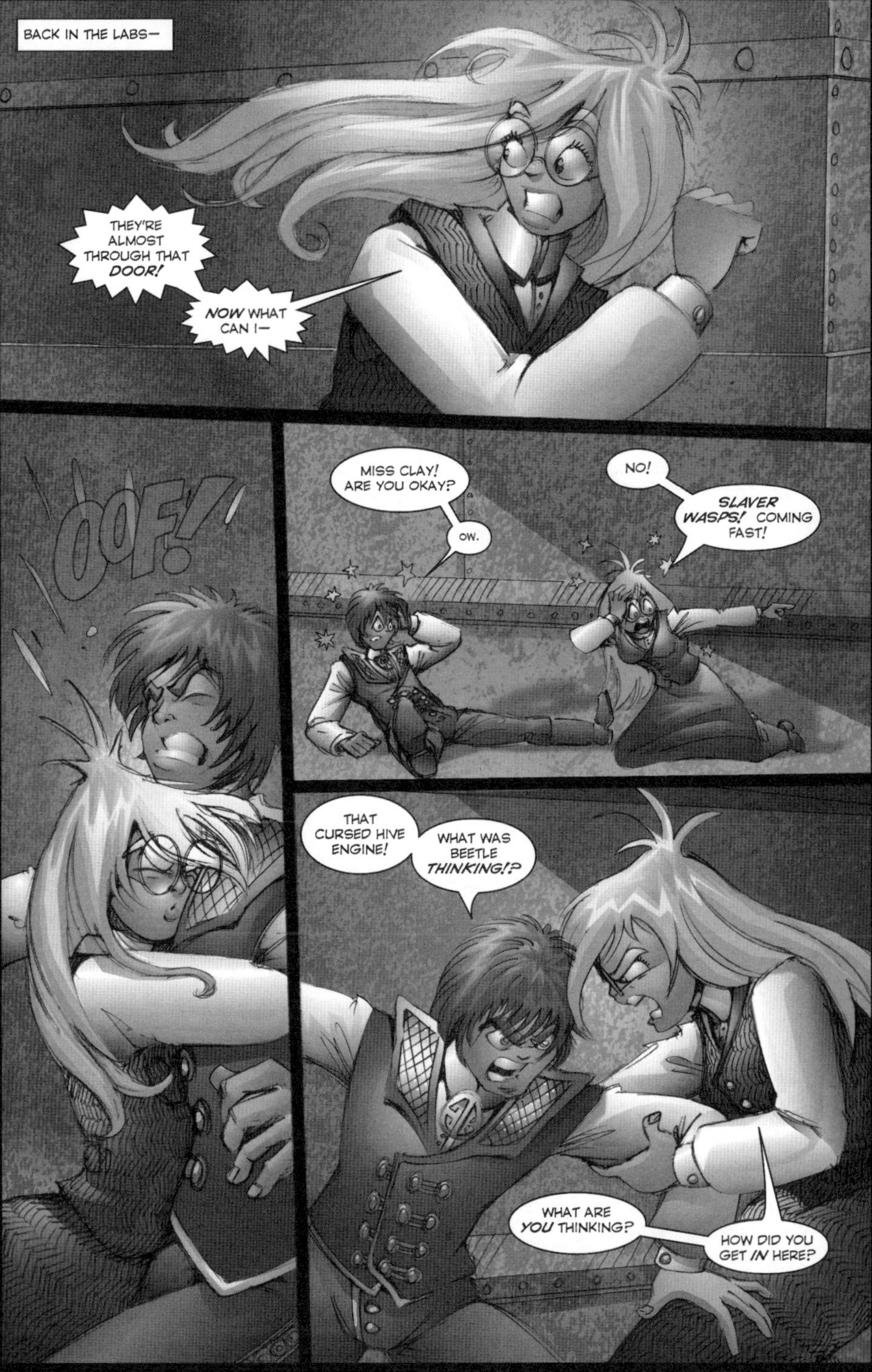

BACK IN THE LABS—
THEY'RE ALMOST THROUGH THAT *DOOR!*
NOW WHAT CAN I—
OOF!
MISS CLAY! ARE YOU OKAY?
OW.
NO!
SLAVER WASPS! COMING FAST!
THAT CURSED HIVE ENGINE!
WHAT WAS BEETLE *THINKING!?*
WHAT ARE *YOU* THINKING?
HOW DID YOU GET *IN* HERE?

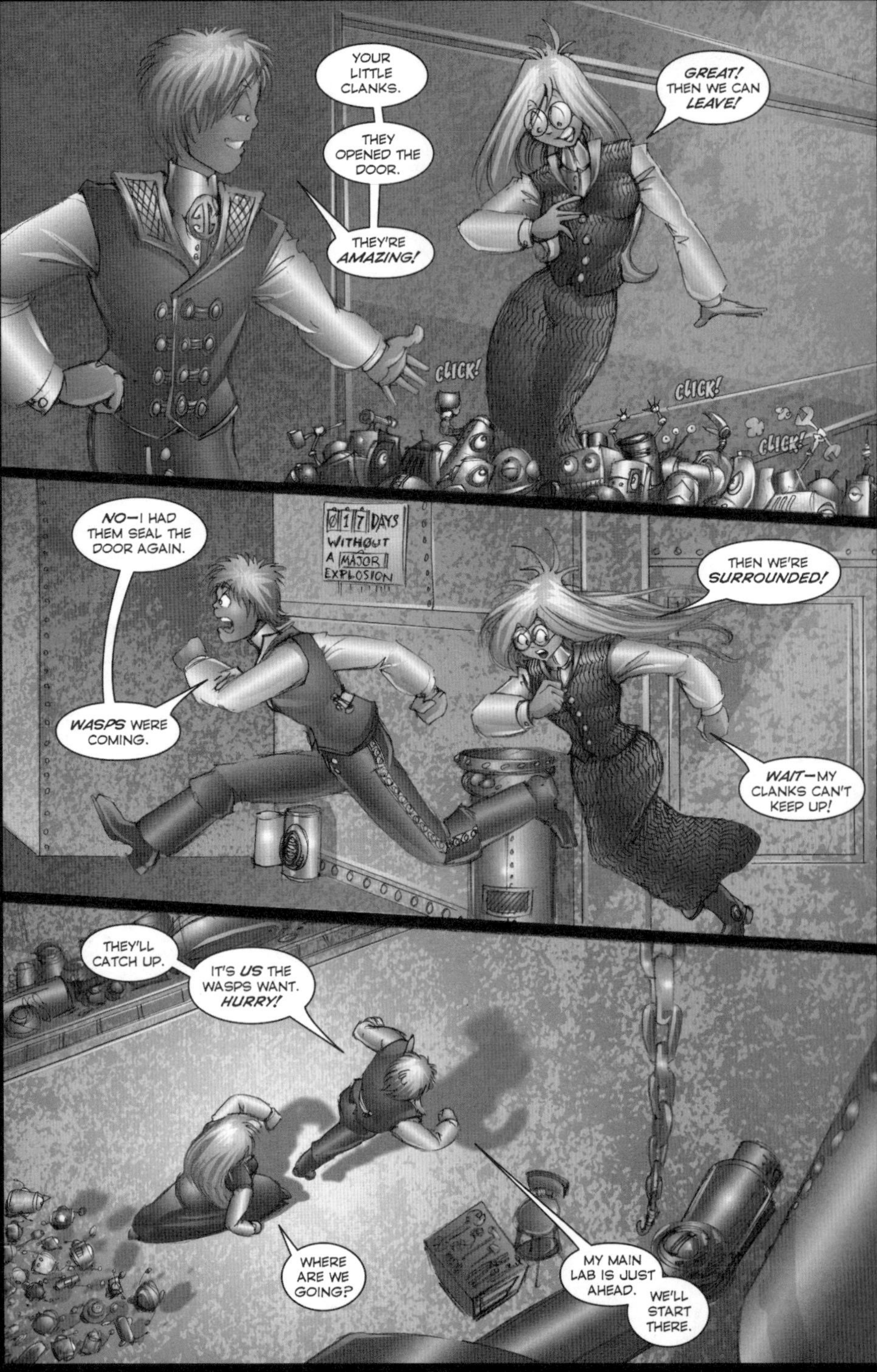
YOUR LITTLE CLANKS.
THEY OPENED THE DOOR.
THEY'RE *AMAZING!*
GREAT! THEN WE CAN *LEAVE!*
CLICK!
CLICK!
CLICK!
NO—I HAD THEM SEAL THE DOOR AGAIN.
WASPS WERE COMING.
017 DAYS WITHOUT A MAJOR EXPLOSION
THEN WE'RE *SURROUNDED!*
WAIT—MY CLANKS CAN'T KEEP UP!
THEY'LL CATCH UP.
IT'S *US* THE WASPS WANT. *HURRY!*
WHERE ARE WE GOING?
MY MAIN LAB IS JUST AHEAD.
WE'LL START THERE.

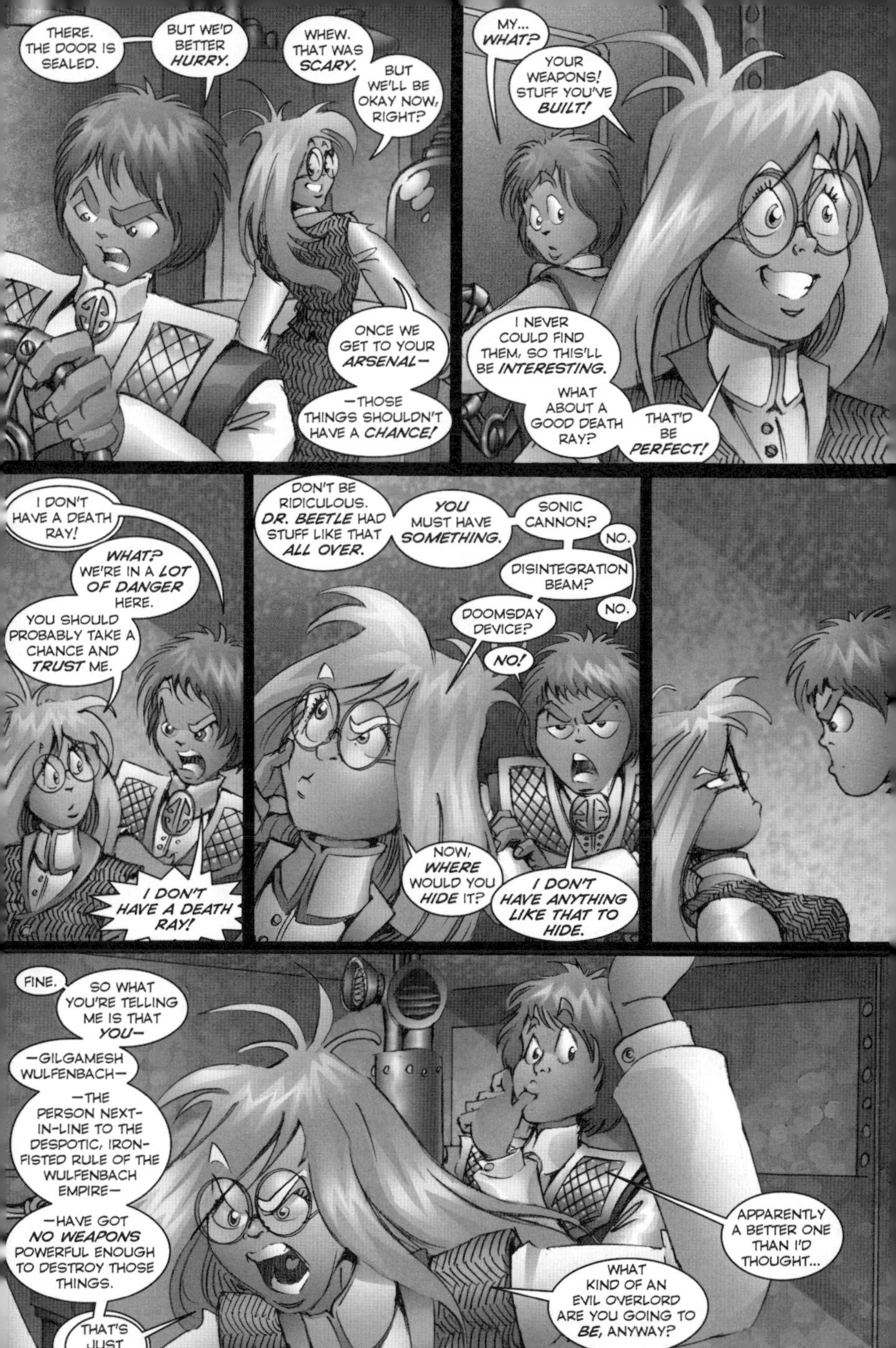
THERE. THE DOOR IS SEALED.
BUT WE'D BETTER HURRY.
WHEW. THAT WAS SCARY.
BUT WE'LL BE OKAY NOW, RIGHT?
ONCE WE GET TO YOUR ARSENAL—
—THOSE THINGS SHOULDN'T HAVE A CHANCE!
MY... WHAT?
YOUR WEAPONS! STUFF YOU'VE BUILT!
I NEVER COULD FIND THEM, SO THIS'LL BE INTERESTING.
WHAT ABOUT A GOOD DEATH RAY?
THAT'D BE PERFECT!
I DON'T HAVE A DEATH RAY!
WHAT? WE'RE IN A LOT OF DANGER HERE.
YOU SHOULD PROBABLY TAKE A CHANCE AND TRUST ME.
I DON'T HAVE A DEATH RAY!
DON'T BE RIDICULOUS. DR. BEETLE HAD STUFF LIKE THAT ALL OVER.
YOU MUST HAVE SOMETHING.
SONIC CANNON?
NO.
DISINTEGRATION BEAM?
NO.
DOOMSDAY DEVICE?
NO!
NOW, WHERE WOULD YOU HIDE IT?
I DON'T HAVE ANYTHING LIKE THAT TO HIDE.
FINE.
SO WHAT YOU'RE TELLING ME IS THAT YOU—
—GILGAMESH WULFENBACH—
—THE PERSON NEXT-IN-LINE TO THE DESPOTIC, IRON-FISTED RULE OF THE WULFENBACH EMPIRE—
—HAVE GOT NO WEAPONS POWERFUL ENOUGH TO DESTROY THOSE THINGS.
THAT'S JUST GREAT.
WHAT KIND OF AN EVIL OVERLORD ARE YOU GOING TO BE, ANYWAY?
APPARENTLY A BETTER ONE THAN I'D THOUGHT...

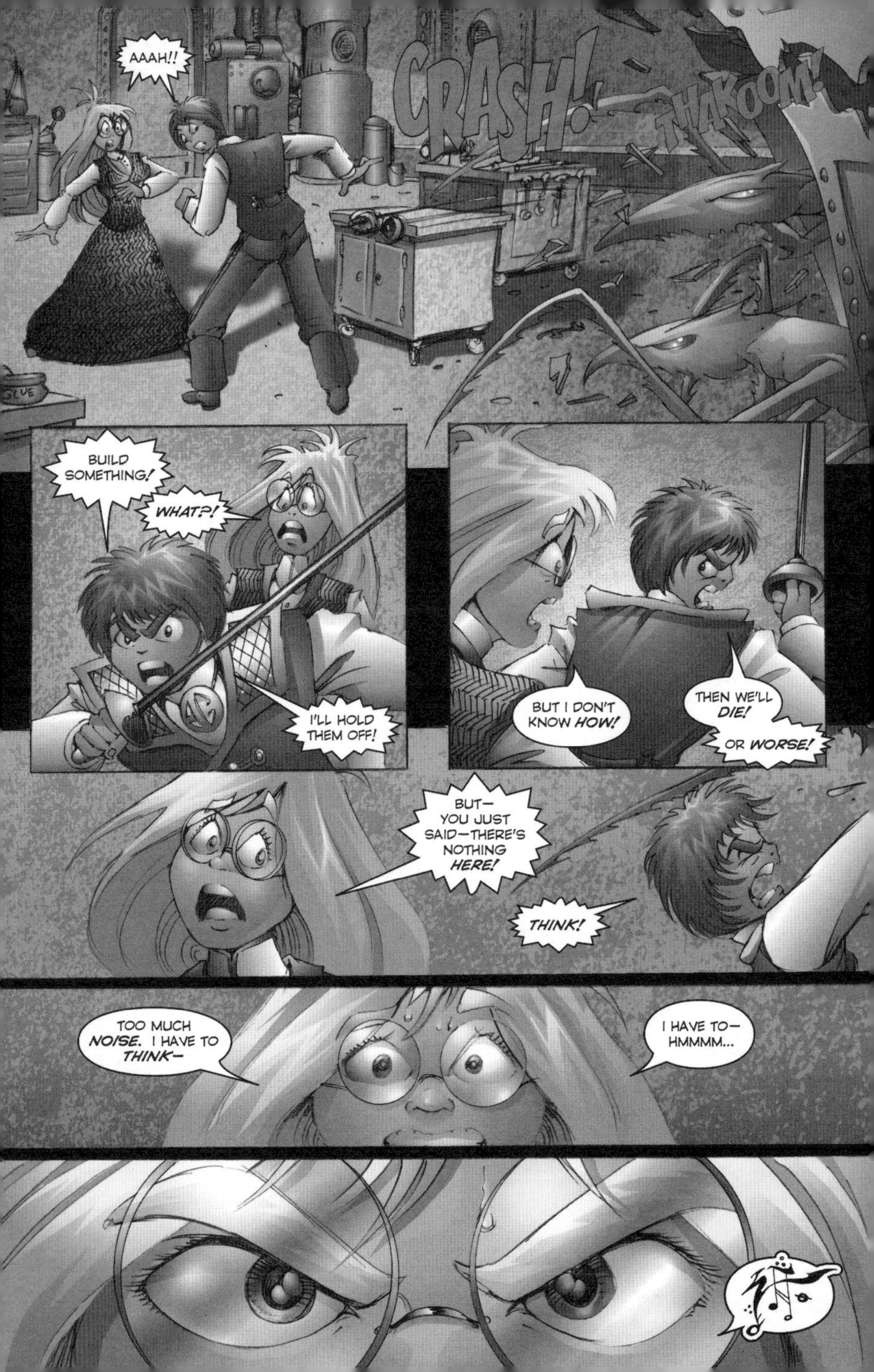
AAAH!!
CRASH!
THAKOOM!
GLUE
BUILD SOMETHING!
WHAT?!
I'LL HOLD THEM OFF!
BUT I DON'T KNOW HOW!
THEN WE'LL DIE!
OR WORSE!
BUT— YOU JUST SAID—THERE'S NOTHING HERE!
THINK!
TOO MUCH NOISE. I HAVE TO THINK—
I HAVE TO— HMMMM...

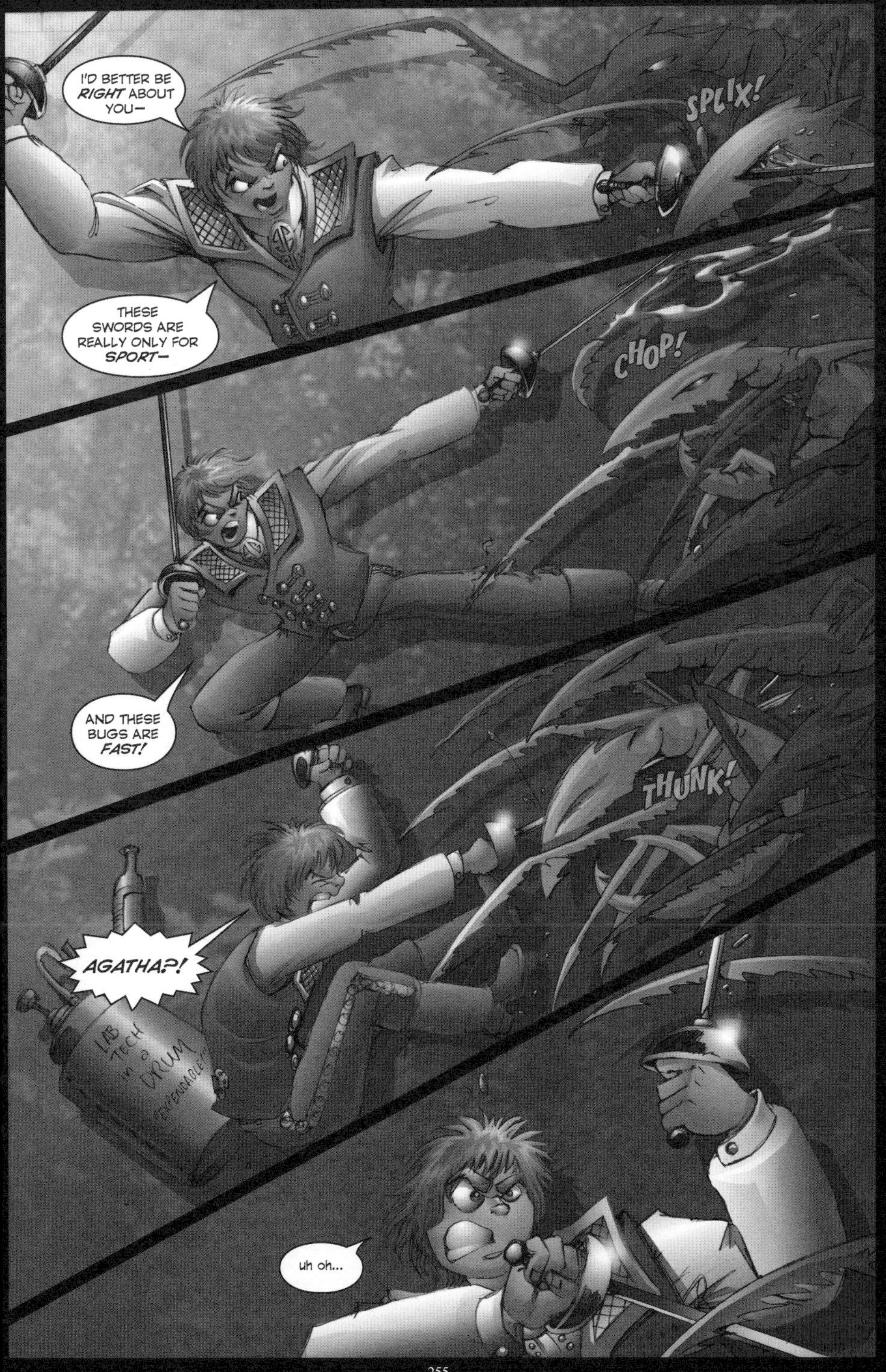
I'D BETTER BE RIGHT ABOUT YOU—
SPLIX!
THESE SWORDS ARE REALLY ONLY FOR SPORT—
CHOP!
AND THESE BUGS ARE FAST!
THUNK!
AGATHA?!
LAB TECH in a DRUM "EXPENDABLE!"
uh oh...

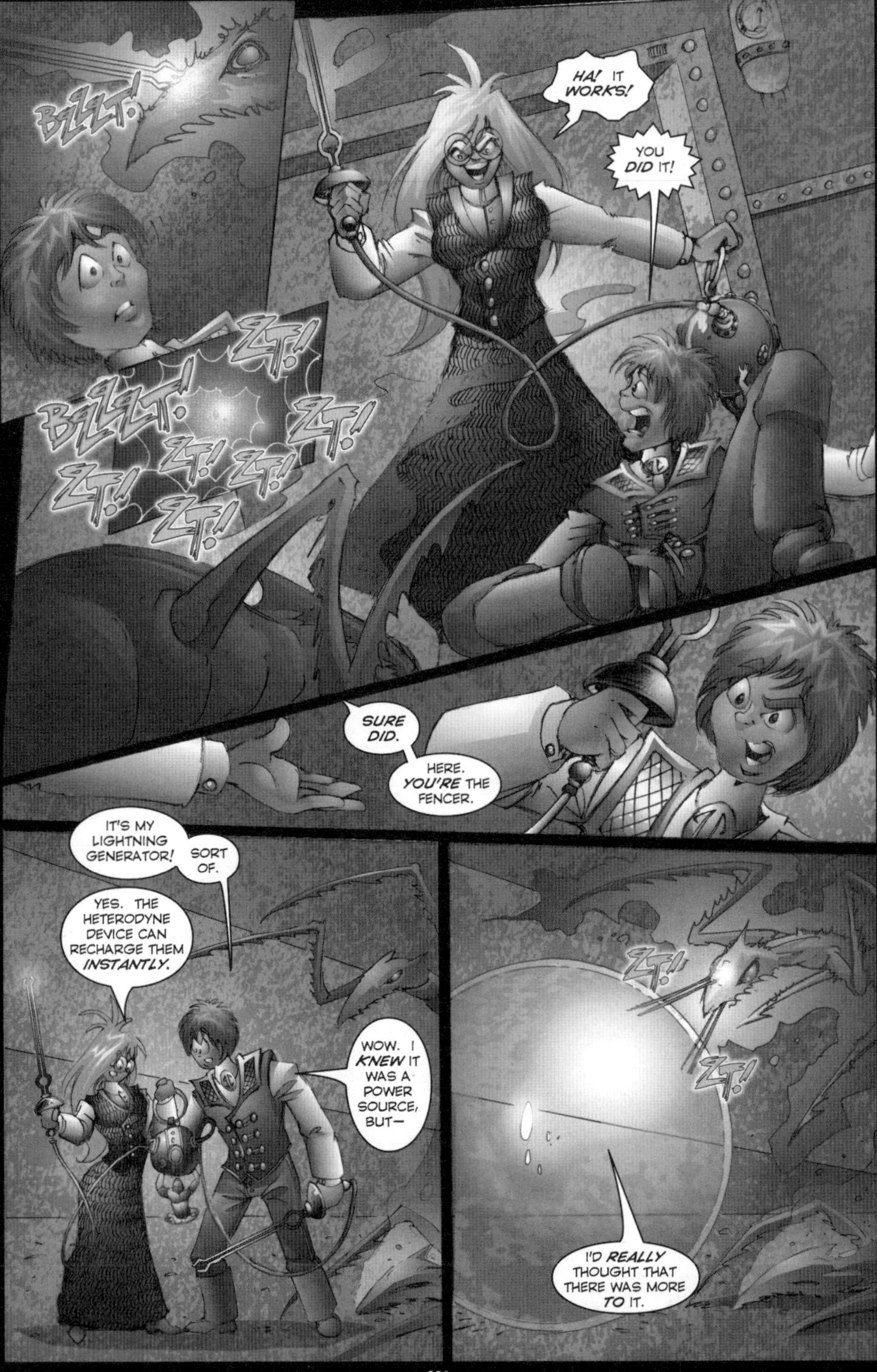
BZZZT!
HA! IT WORKS!
YOU DID IT!
BZZZT!
ZZT! ZZT! ZZT! ZZT! ZZT! ZZT!
SURE DID.
HERE. YOU'RE THE FENCER.
IT'S MY LIGHTNING GENERATOR!
SORT OF.
YES. THE HETERODYNE DEVICE CAN RECHARGE THEM INSTANTLY.
WOW. I KNEW IT WAS A POWER SOURCE, BUT—
ZZT!
ZZT!
I'D REALLY THOUGHT THAT THERE WAS MORE TO IT.

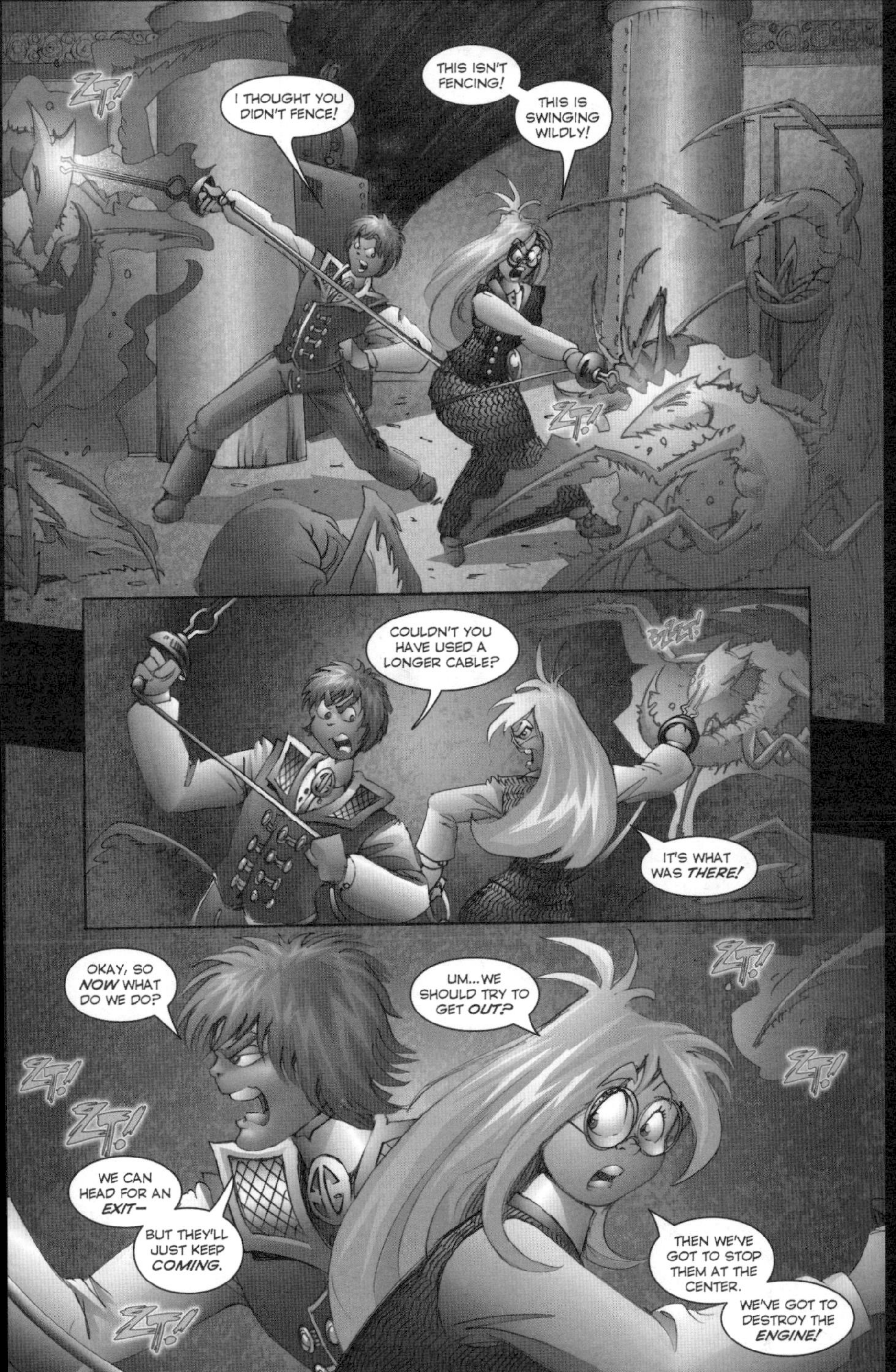
ZZT!
I THOUGHT YOU DIDN'T FENCE!
THIS ISN'T FENCING!
THIS IS SWINGING WILDLY!
ZZT!
COULDN'T YOU HAVE USED A LONGER CABLE?
BZZZT!
IT'S WHAT WAS *THERE!*
OKAY, SO *NOW* WHAT DO WE DO?
UM...WE SHOULD TRY TO GET *OUT?*
ZZT!
ZZT!
ZZT!
ZZT!
WE CAN HEAD FOR AN *EXIT—*
BUT THEY'LL JUST KEEP *COMING.*
THEN WE'VE GOT TO STOP THEM AT THE CENTER.
WE'VE GOT TO DESTROY THE *ENGINE!*
ZZT!

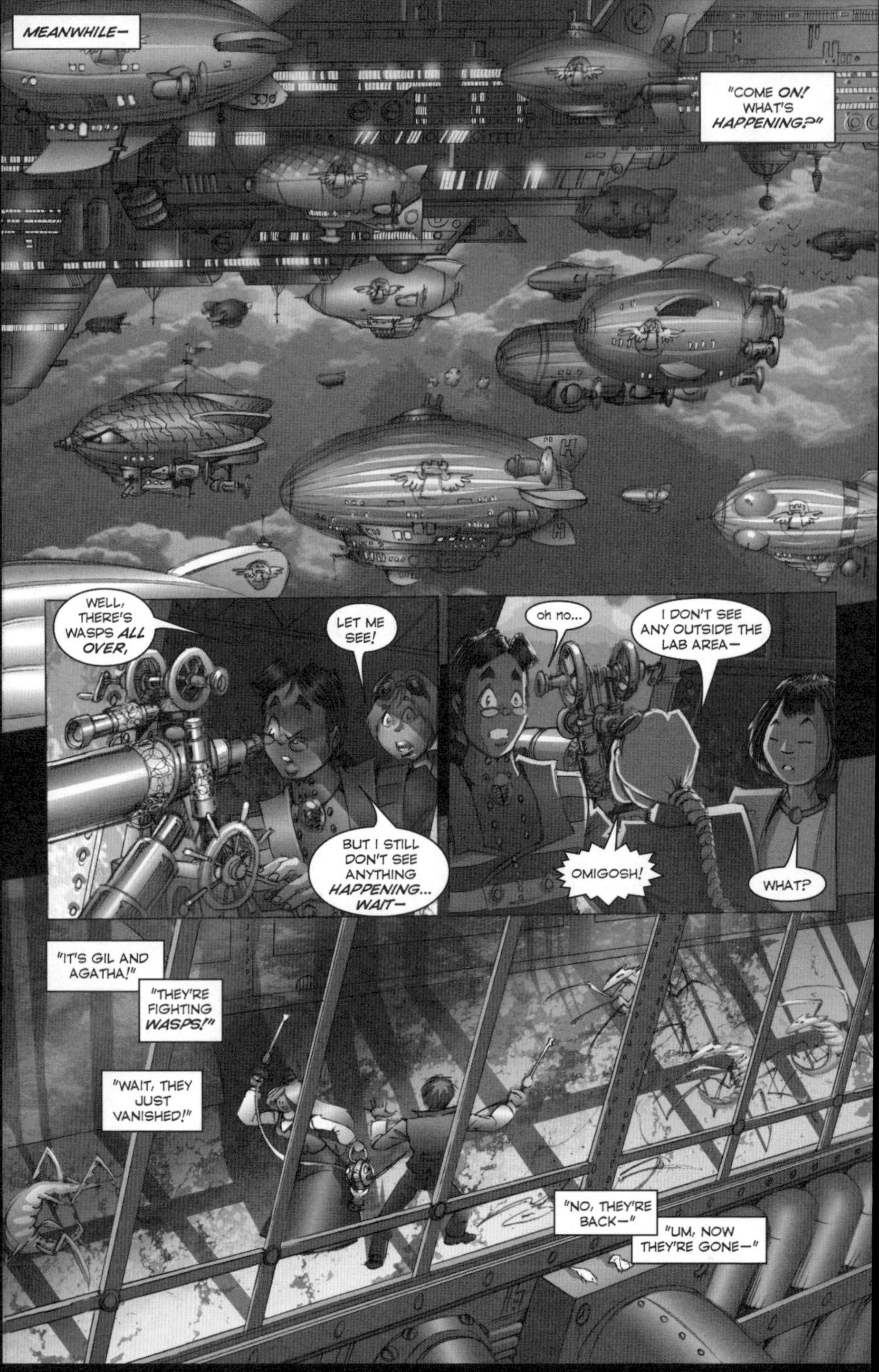
MEANWHILE—
"COME ON! WHAT'S HAPPENING?"
WELL, THERE'S WASPS ALL OVER,
LET ME SEE!
BUT I STILL DON'T SEE ANYTHING HAPPENING... WAIT—
oh no...
I DON'T SEE ANY OUTSIDE THE LAB AREA—
OMIGOSH!
WHAT?
"IT'S GIL AND AGATHA!"
"THEY'RE FIGHTING WASPS!"
"WAIT, THEY JUST VANISHED!"
"NO, THEY'RE BACK—"
"UM, NOW THEY'RE GONE—"

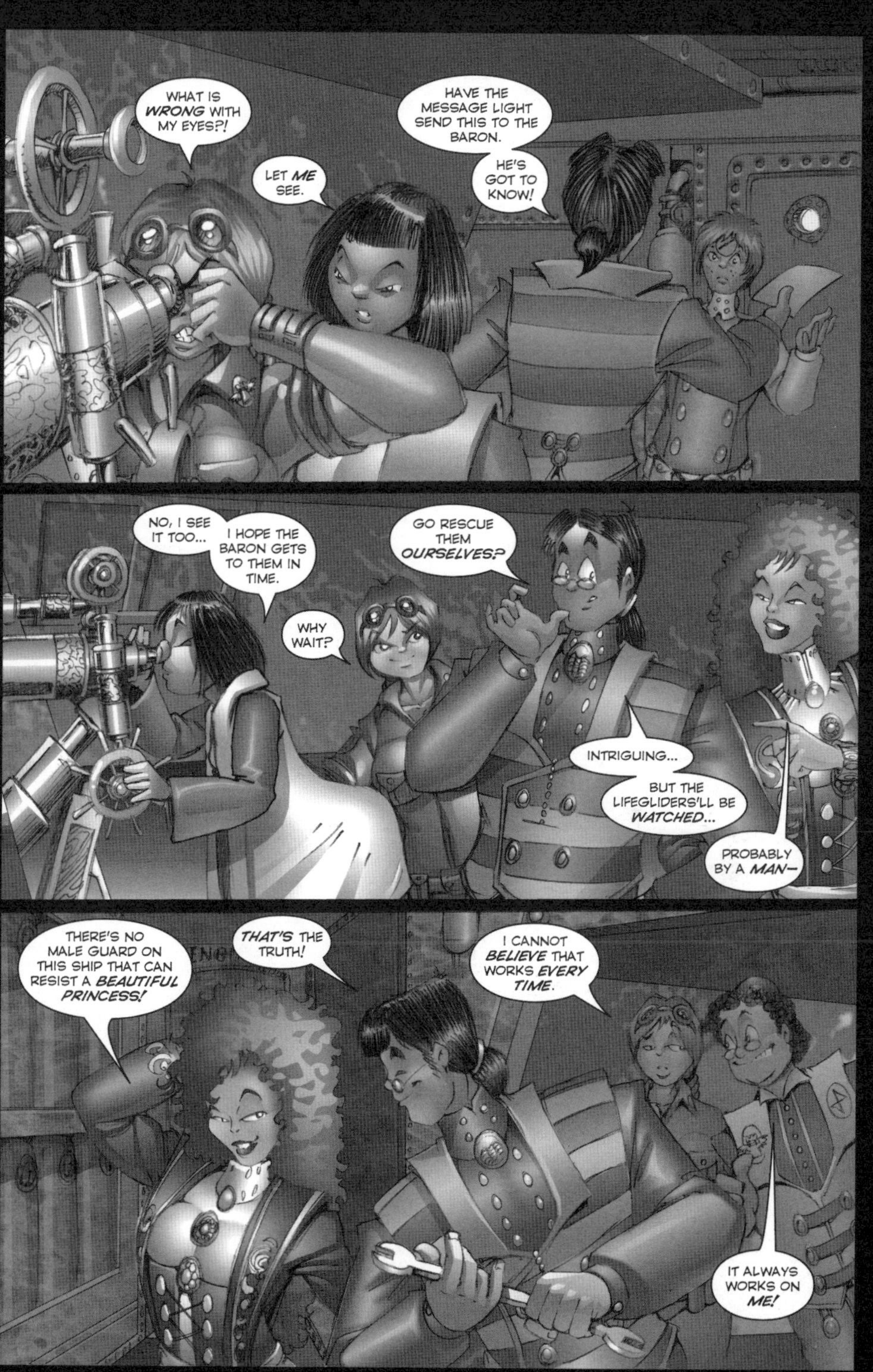
WHAT IS WRONG WITH MY EYES?!
LET ME SEE.
HAVE THE MESSAGE LIGHT SEND THIS TO THE BARON.
HE'S GOT TO KNOW!
NO, I SEE IT TOO...
I HOPE THE BARON GETS TO THEM IN TIME.
WHY WAIT?
GO RESCUE THEM OURSELVES?
INTRIGUING...
BUT THE LIFEGLIDERS'LL BE WATCHED...
PROBABLY BY A MAN—
THERE'S NO MALE GUARD ON THIS SHIP THAT CAN RESIST A BEAUTIFUL PRINCESS!
THAT'S THE TRUTH!
I CANNOT BELIEVE THAT WORKS EVERY TIME.
IT ALWAYS WORKS ON ME!

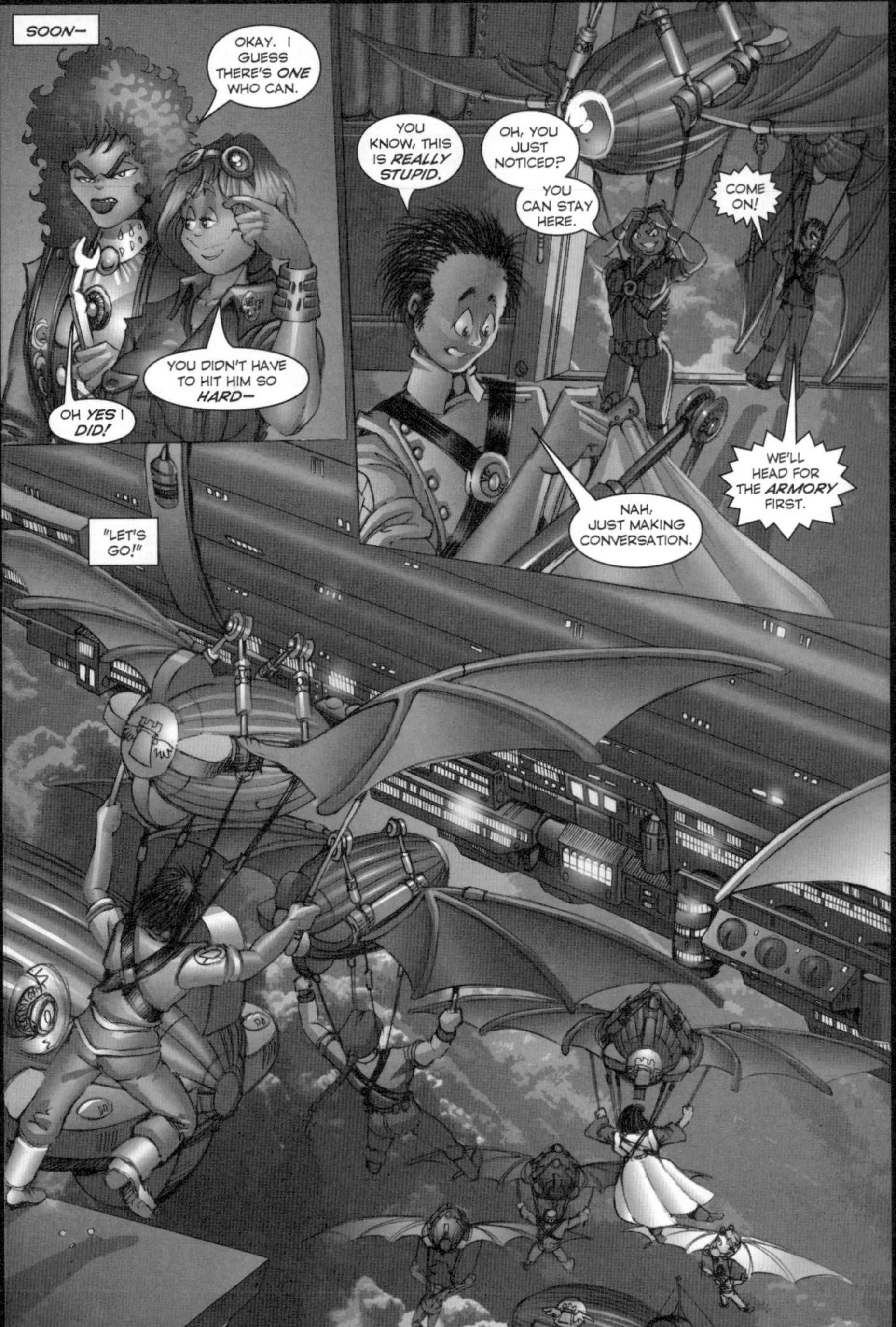
SOON—
OKAY. I GUESS THERE'S ONE WHO CAN.
YOU DIDN'T HAVE TO HIT HIM SO HARD—
OH YES I DID!
YOU KNOW, THIS IS REALLY STUPID.
OH, YOU JUST NOTICED?
YOU CAN STAY HERE.
NAH, JUST MAKING CONVERSATION.
COME ON!
WE'LL HEAD FOR THE ARMORY FIRST.
"LET'S GO!"

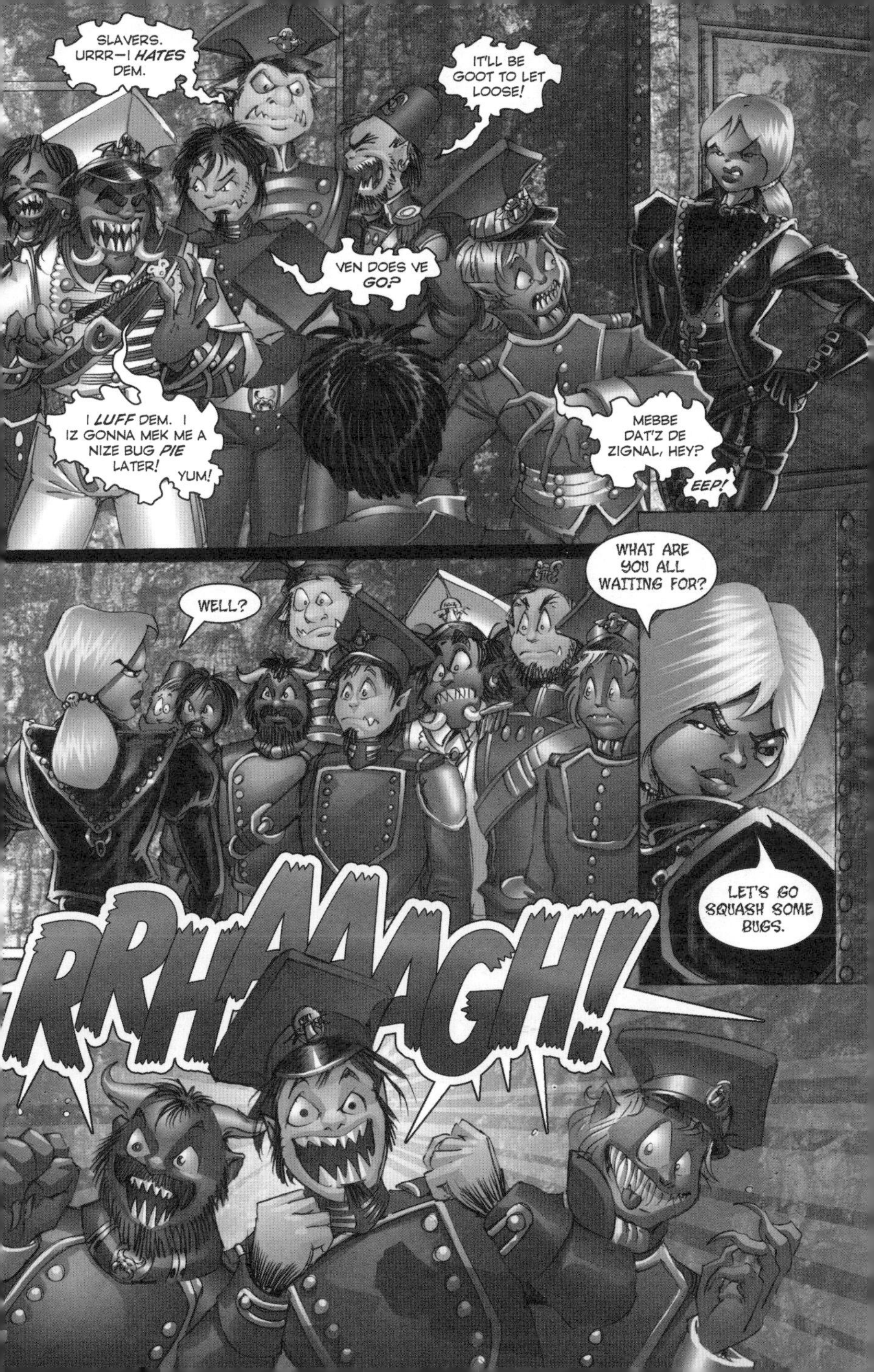
SLAVERS. URRR—I HATES DEM.
IT'LL BE GOOT TO LET LOOSE!
VEN DOES VE GO?
I LUFF DEM. I IZ GONNA MEK ME A NIZE BUG PIE LATER!
YUM!
MEBBE DAT'Z DE ZIGNAL, HEY?
EEP!
WELL?
WHAT ARE YOU ALL WAITING FOR?
LET'S GO SQUASH SOME BUGS.
RRHAAAAGH!

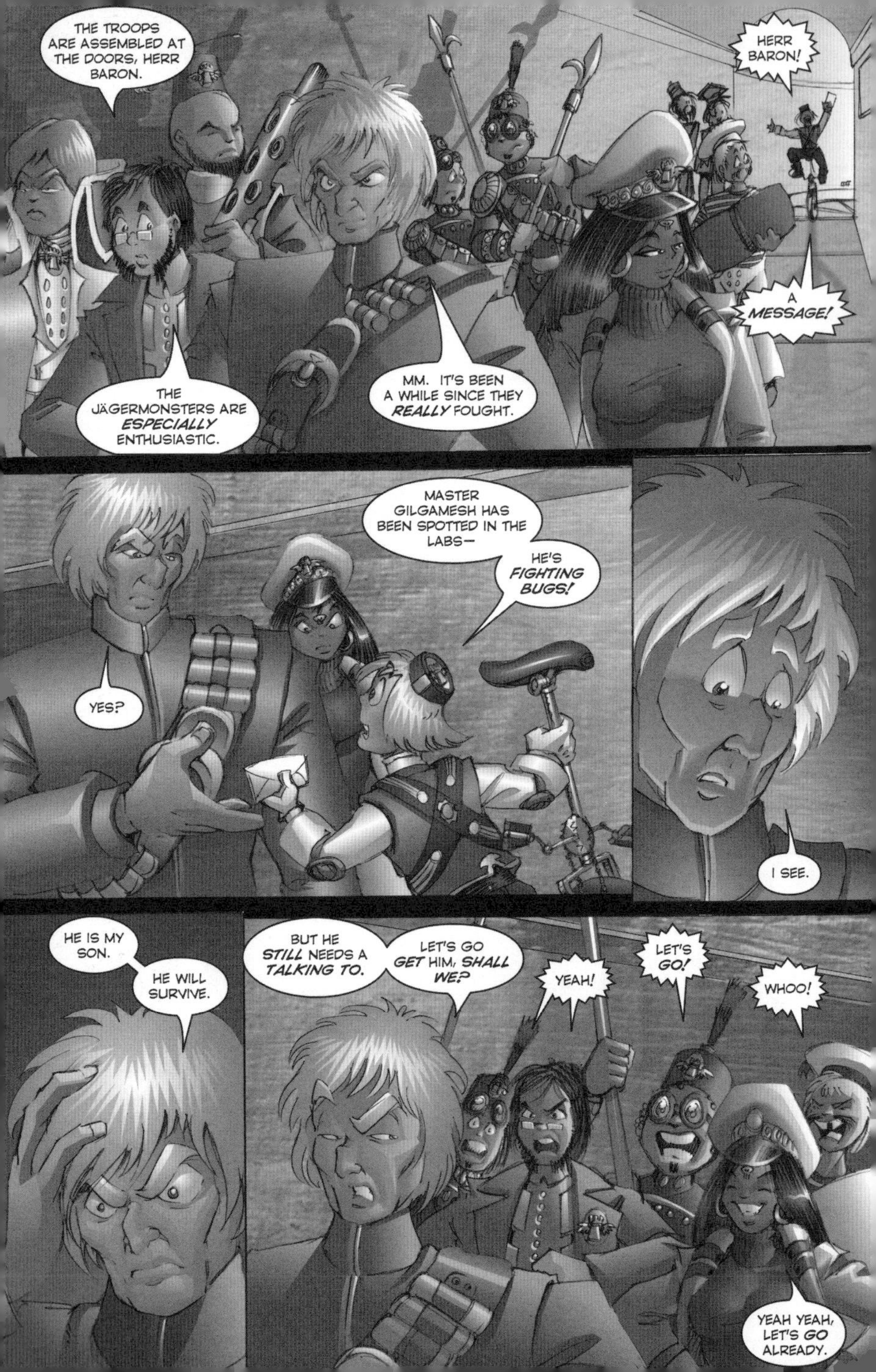
THE TROOPS ARE ASSEMBLED AT THE DOORS, HERR BARON.
THE JÄGERMONSTERS ARE *ESPECIALLY* ENTHUSIASTIC.
MM. IT'S BEEN A WHILE SINCE THEY *REALLY* FOUGHT.
HERR BARON!
A *MESSAGE!*
YES?
MASTER GILGAMESH HAS BEEN SPOTTED IN THE LABS—
HE'S *FIGHTING BUGS!*
I SEE.
HE IS MY SON.
HE WILL SURVIVE.
BUT HE *STILL* NEEDS A *TALKING TO.*
LET'S GO *GET* HIM, *SHALL WE?*
YEAH!
LET'S *GO!*
WHOO!
YEAH YEAH, LET'S *GO* ALREADY.

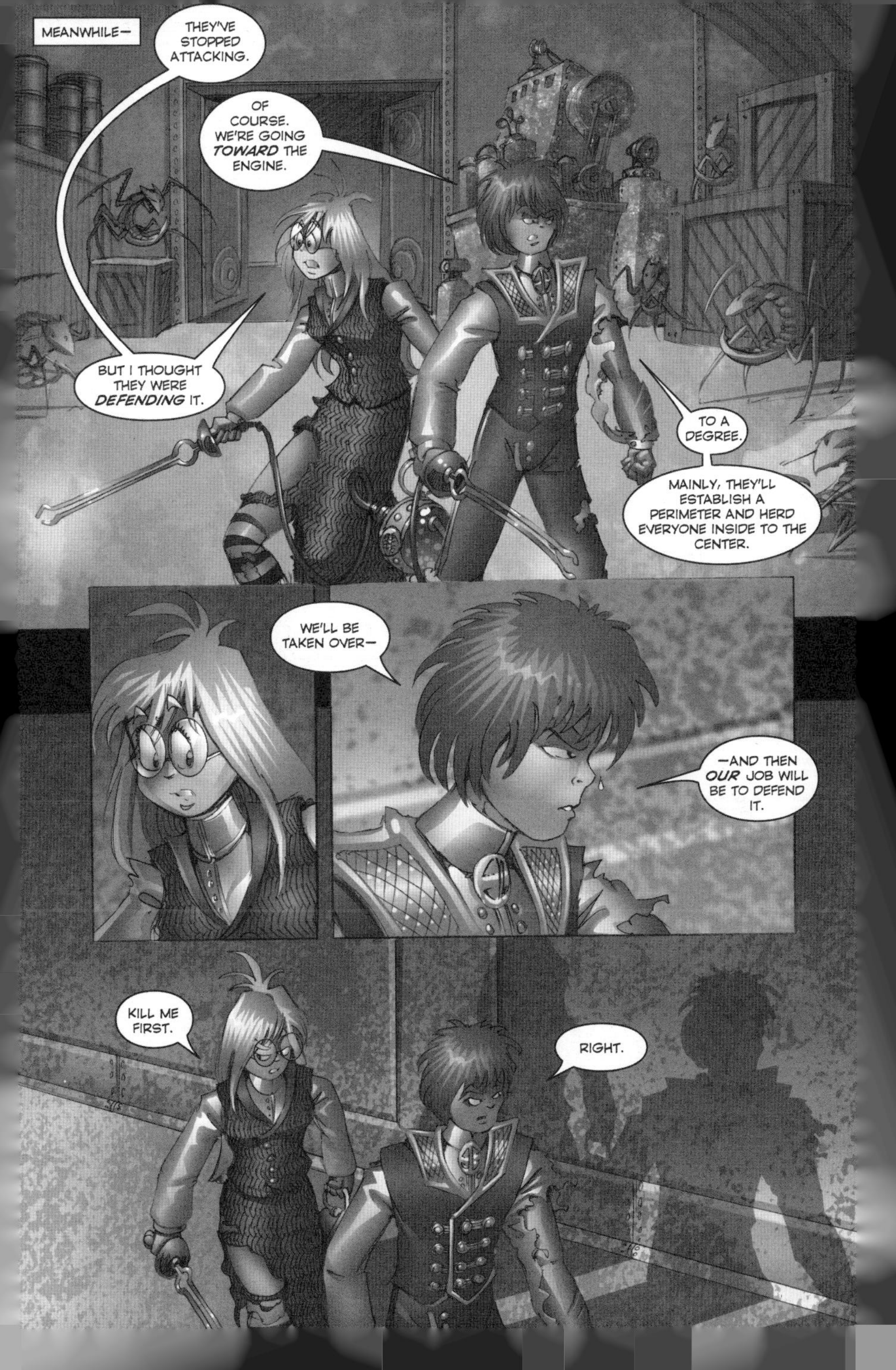
MEANWHILE—
THEY'VE STOPPED ATTACKING.
OF COURSE. WE'RE GOING *TOWARD* THE ENGINE.
BUT I THOUGHT THEY WERE *DEFENDING* IT.
TO A DEGREE.
MAINLY, THEY'LL ESTABLISH A PERIMETER AND HERD EVERYONE INSIDE TO THE CENTER.
WE'LL BE TAKEN OVER—
—AND THEN *OUR* JOB WILL BE TO DEFEND IT.
KILL ME FIRST.
RIGHT.

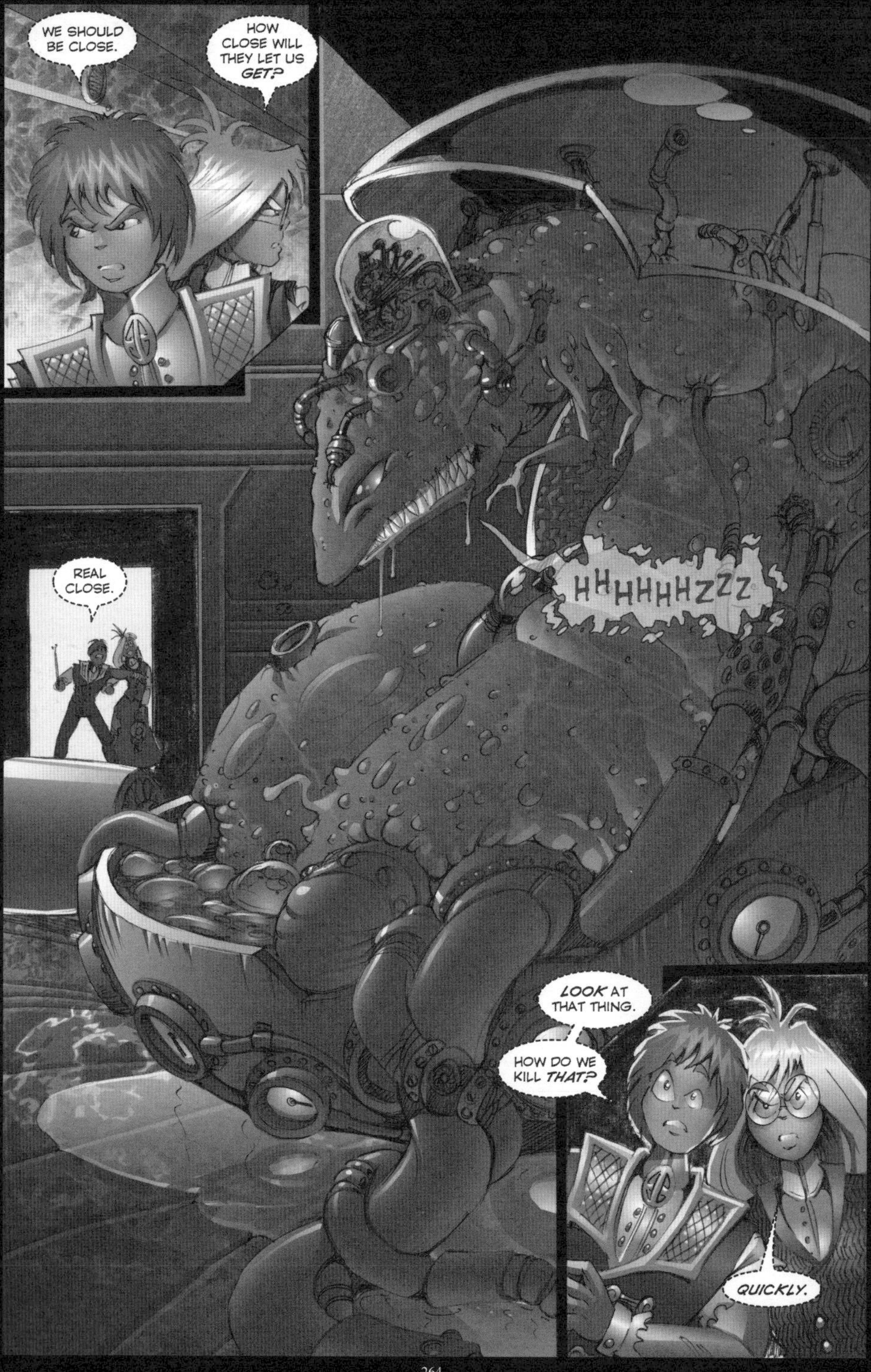
WE SHOULD BE CLOSE.
HOW CLOSE WILL THEY LET US GET?
REAL CLOSE.
HHHHHHZZZ
LOOK AT THAT THING.
HOW DO WE KILL THAT?
QUICKLY.

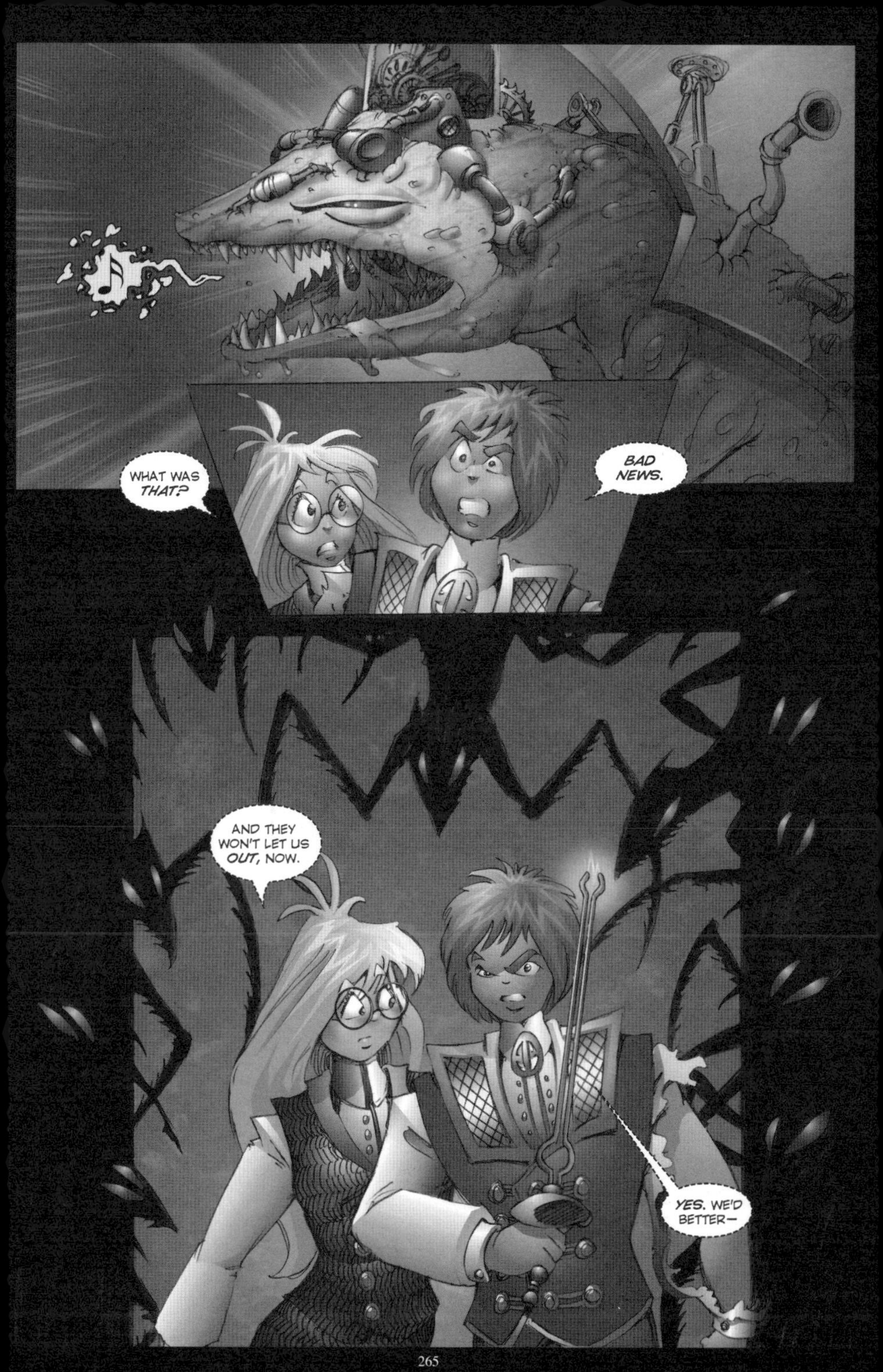
WHAT WAS *THAT?*
BAD NEWS.
AND THEY WON'T LET US *OUT,* NOW.
YES. WE'D BETTER—

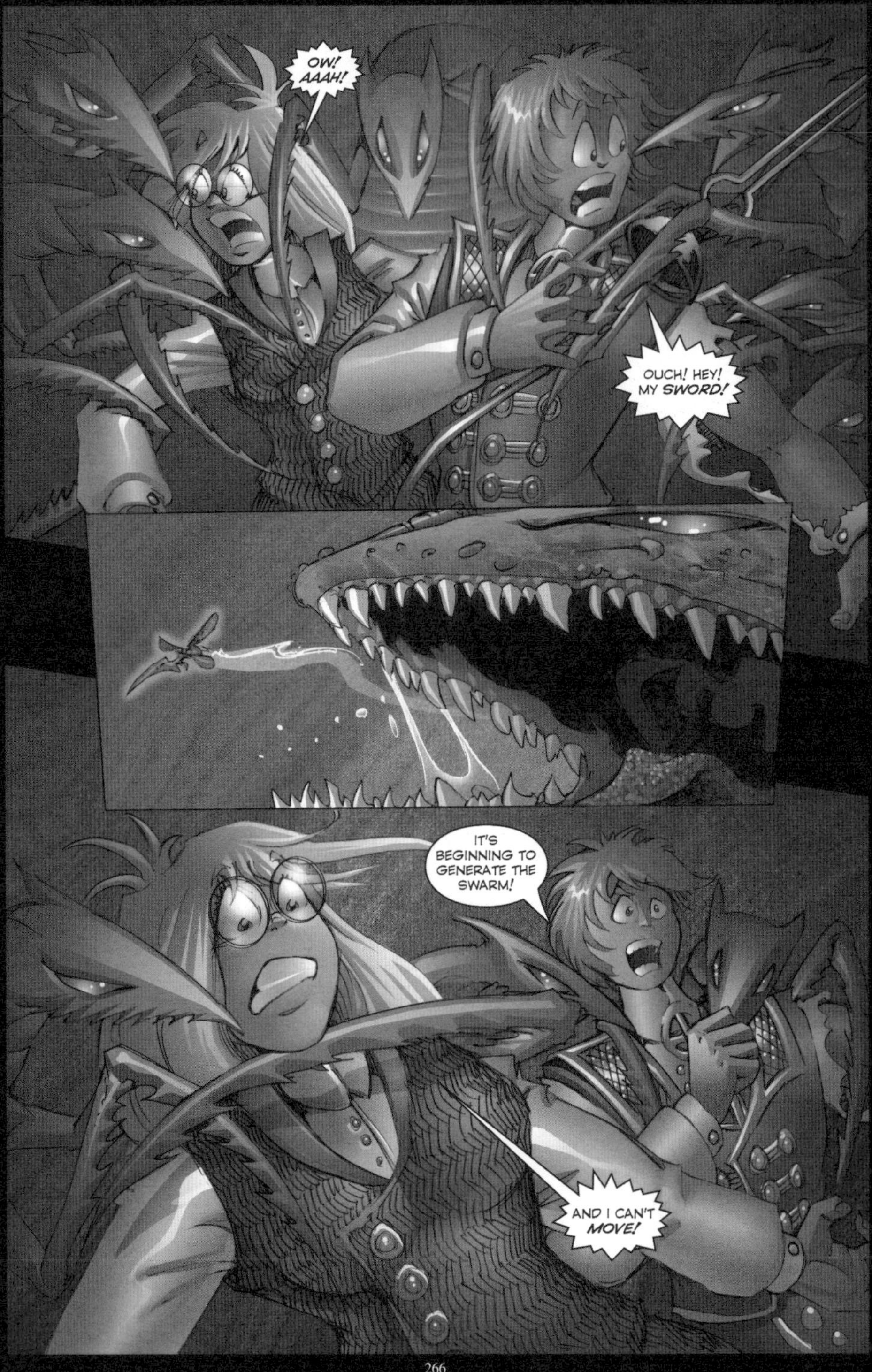
OW! AAAH!
OUCH! HEY! MY SWORD!
IT'S BEGINNING TO GENERATE THE SWARM!
AND I CAN'T MOVE!

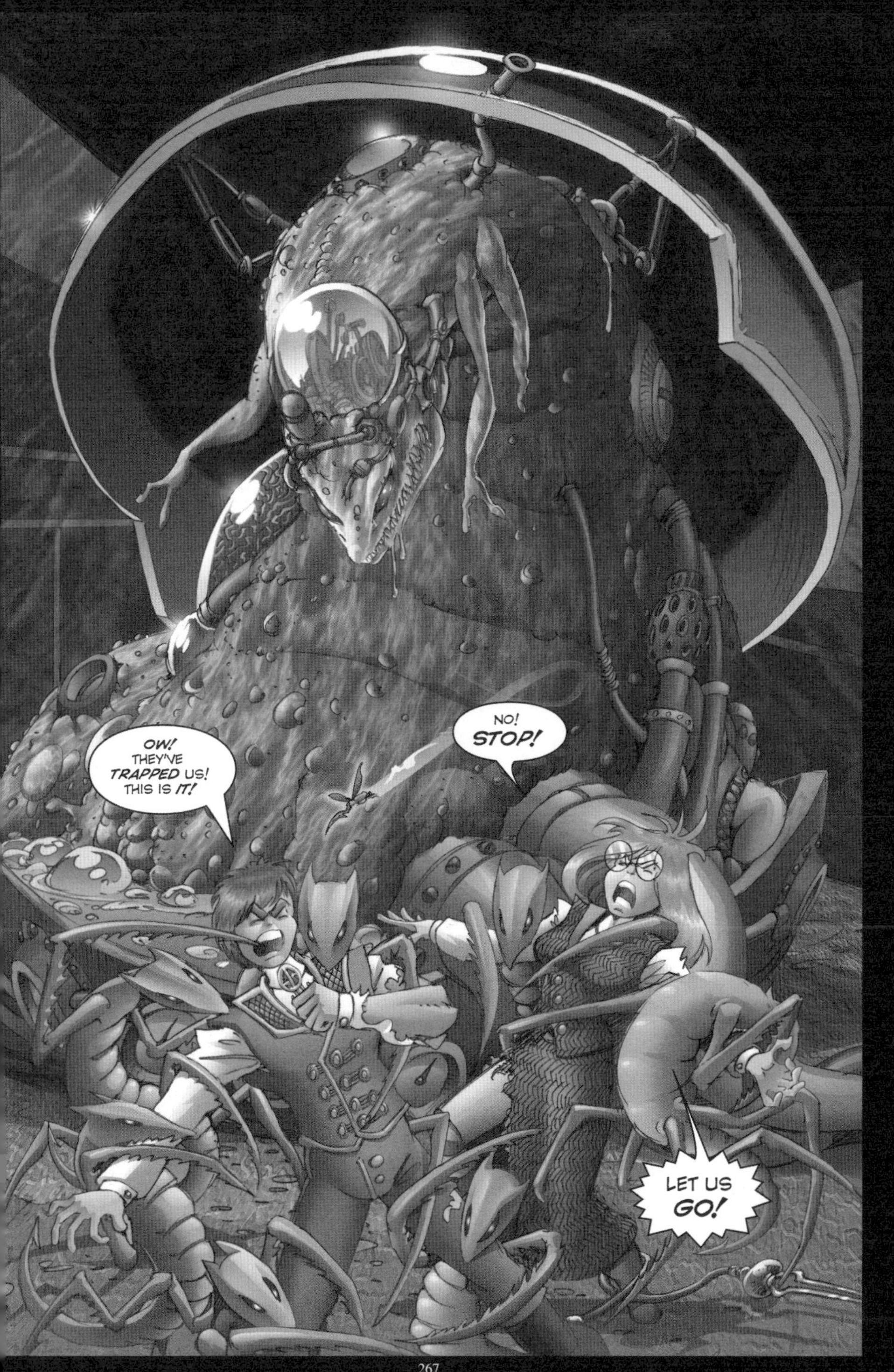
OW! THEY'VE TRAPPED US! THIS IS IT!
NO! STOP!
LET US GO!

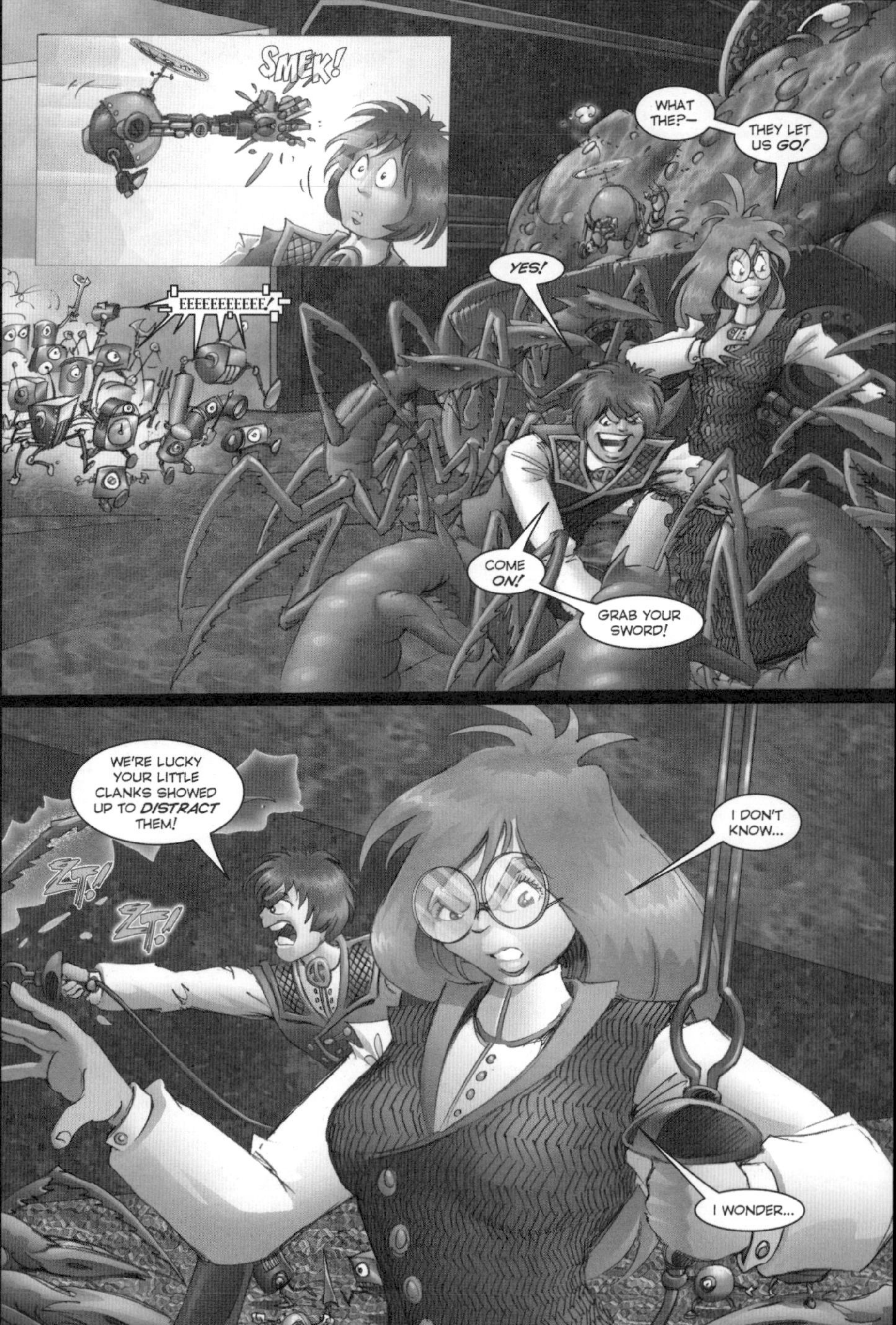
SMEK!
WHAT THE?—
THEY LET US GO!
EEEEEEEEEEE!
YES!
COME ON!
GRAB YOUR SWORD!
WE'RE LUCKY YOUR LITTLE CLANKS SHOWED UP TO DISTRACT THEM!
I DON'T KNOW...
ZZT!
ZZT!
I WONDER...

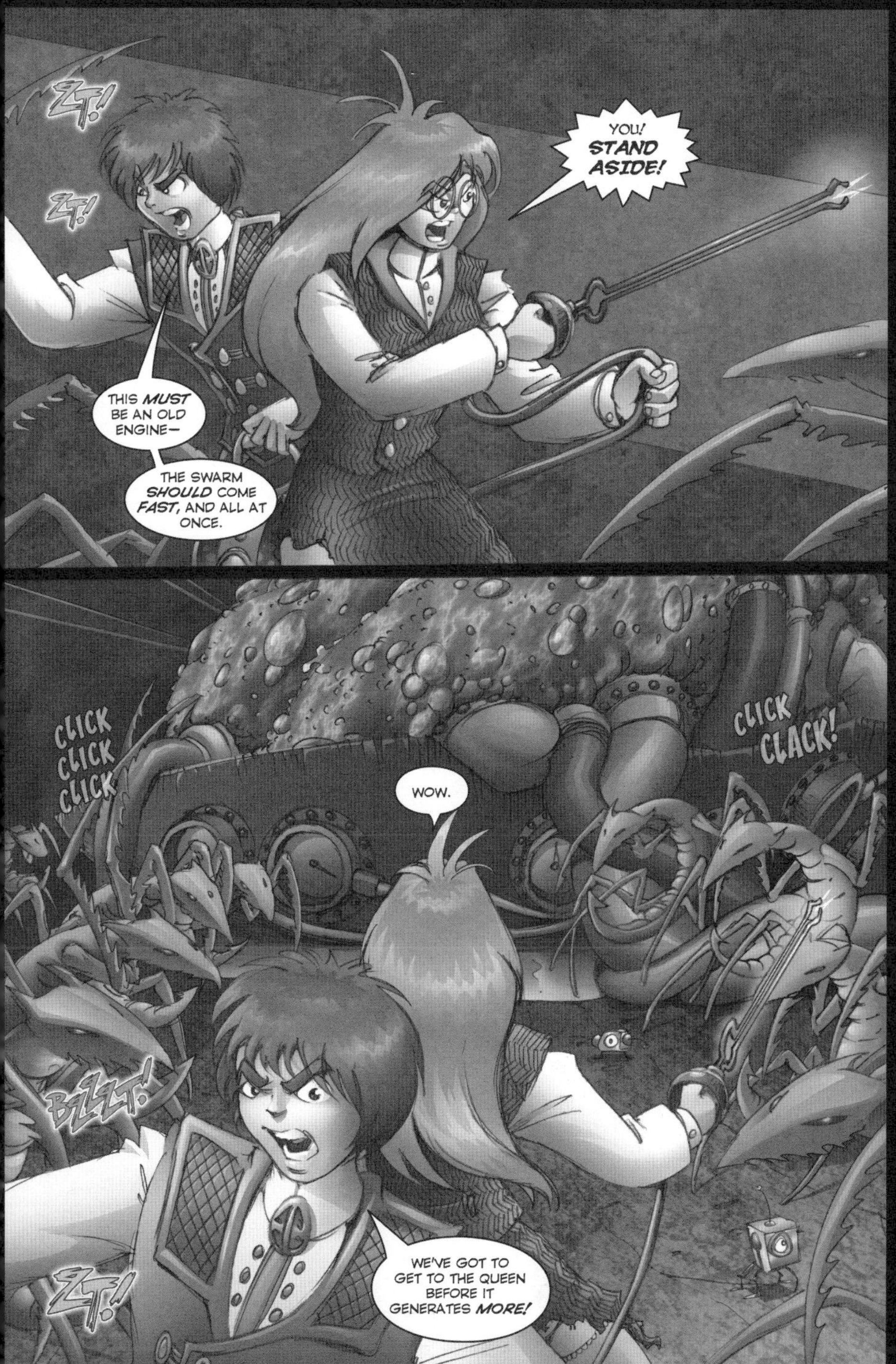
ZT!
ZT!
YOU! STAND ASIDE!
THIS MUST BE AN OLD ENGINE—
THE SWARM SHOULD COME FAST, AND ALL AT ONCE.
CLICK CLICK CLICK
CLICK CLACK!
WOW.
BZZZT!
ZT!
WE'VE GOT TO GET TO THE QUEEN BEFORE IT GENERATES MORE!

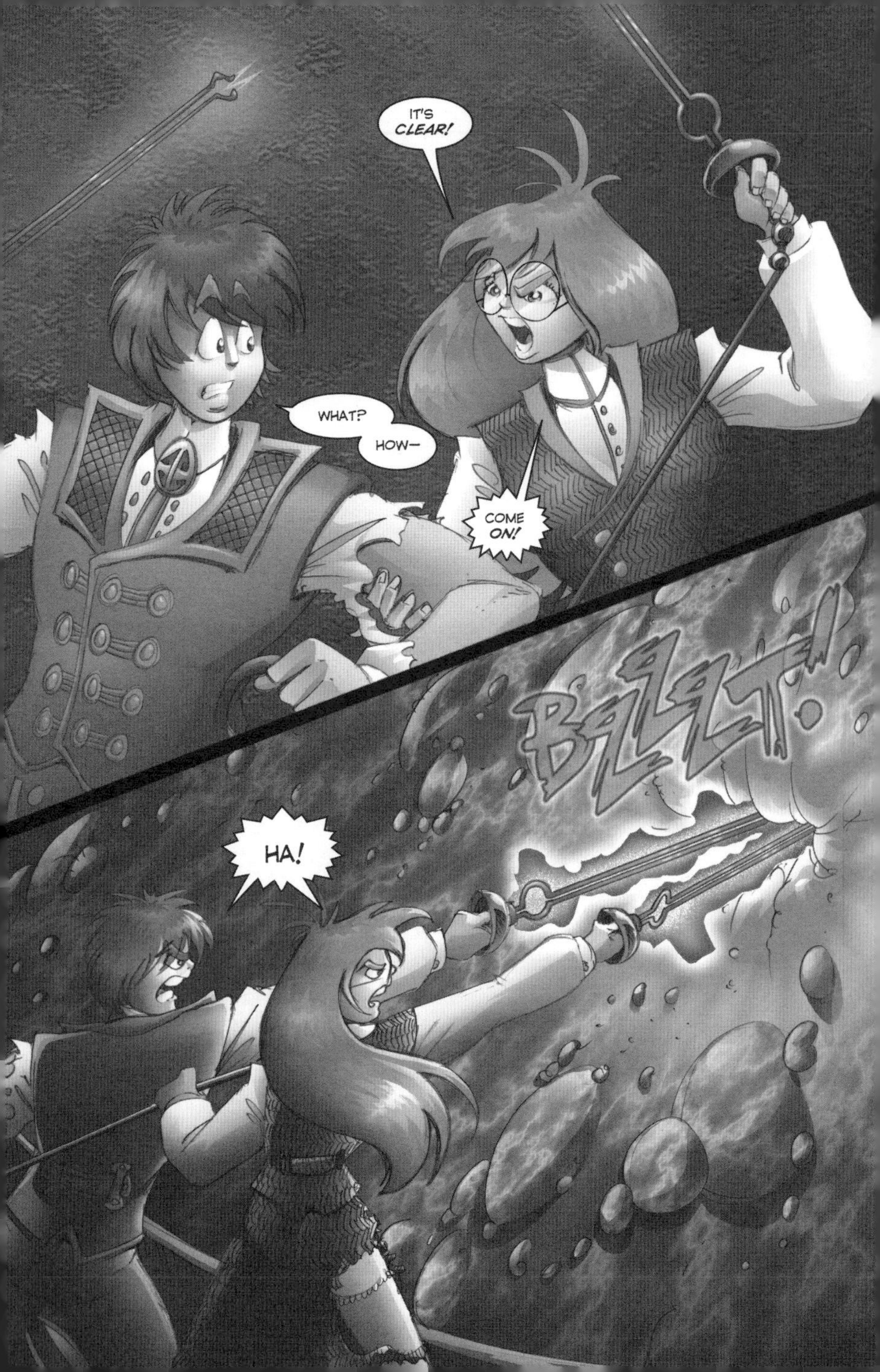
IT'S *CLEAR!*
WHAT?
HOW–
COME *ON!*
HA!

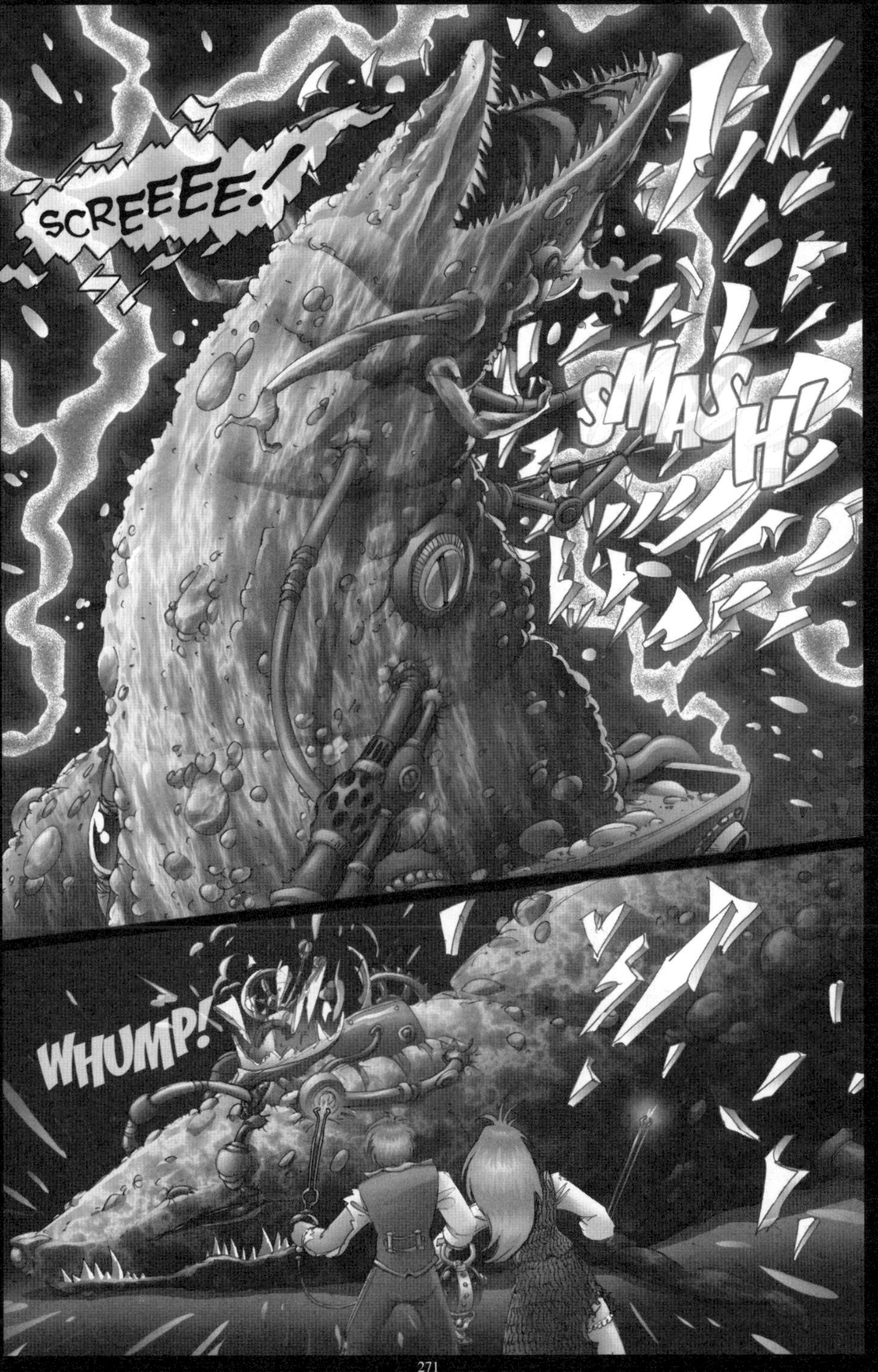
SCREEEEE!
SMASH!
WHUMP!

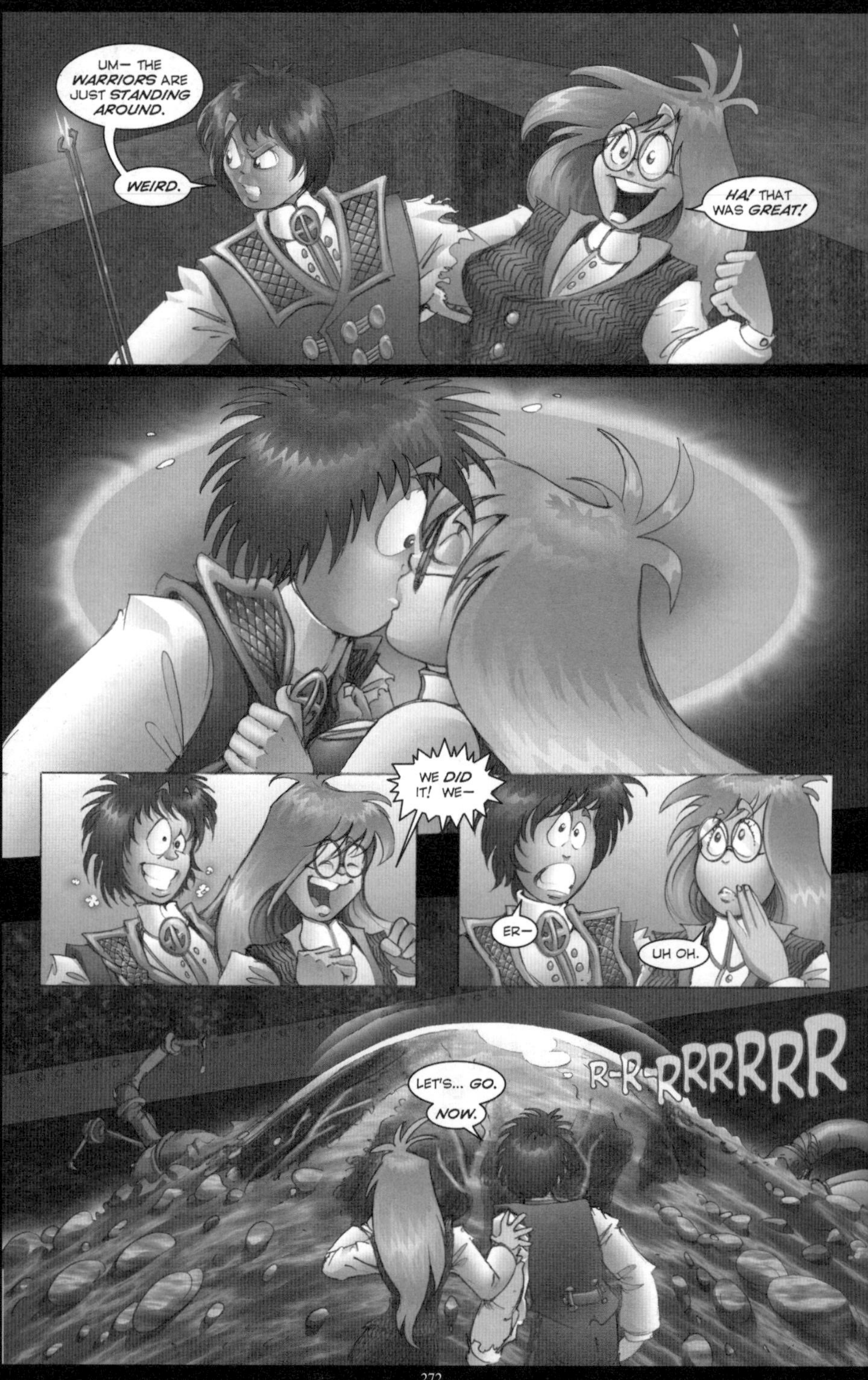
UM— THE WARRIORS ARE JUST STANDING AROUND.
WEIRD.
HA! THAT WAS GREAT!
WE DID IT! WE—
ER—
UH OH.
LET'S... GO. NOW.
R-R-RRRRRR

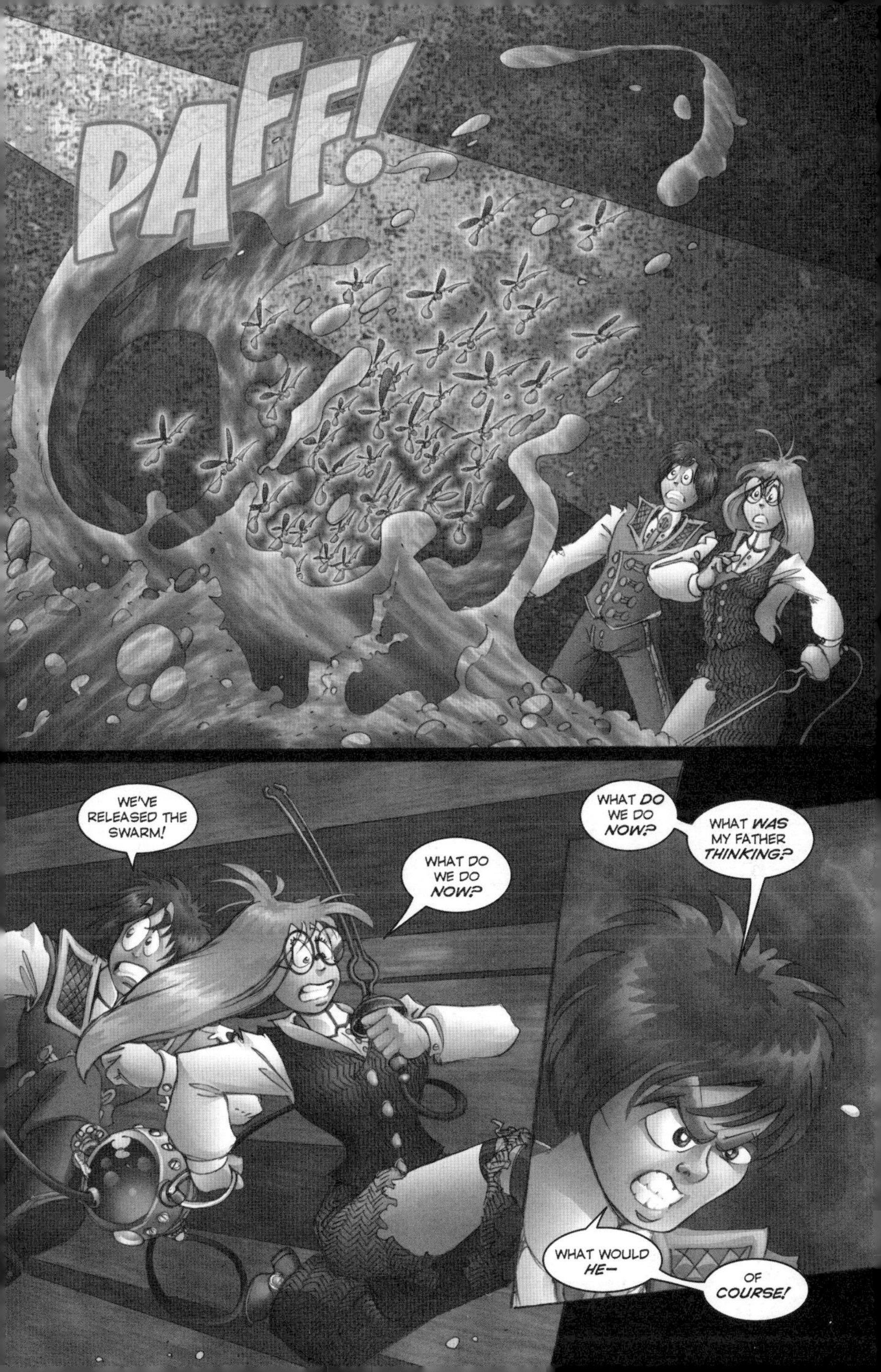
PAFF!
WE'VE RELEASED THE SWARM!
WHAT DO WE DO NOW?
WHAT DO WE DO NOW?
WHAT WAS MY FATHER THINKING?
WHAT WOULD HE—
OF COURSE!

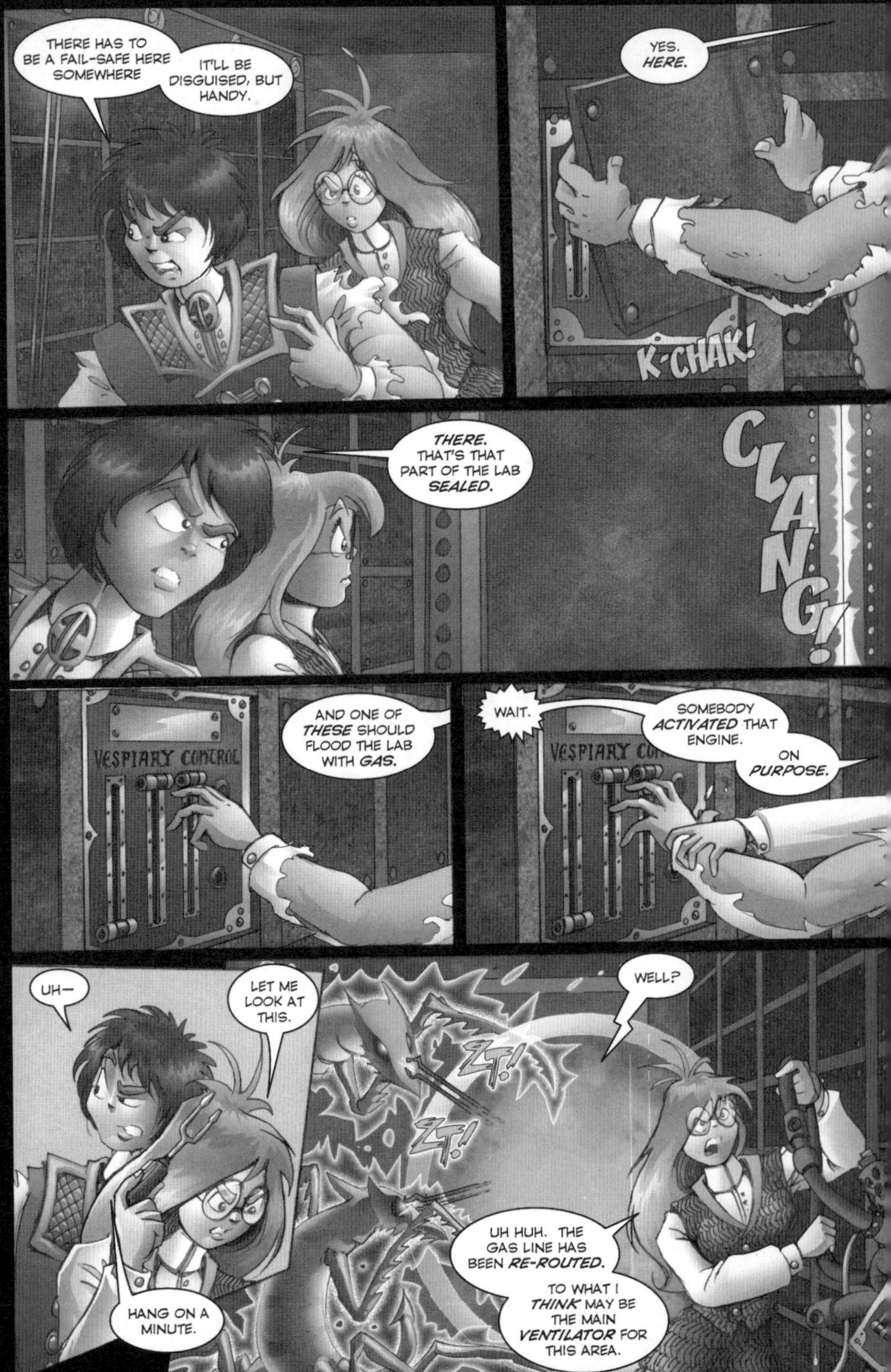
THERE HAS TO BE A FAIL-SAFE HERE SOMEWHERE
IT'LL BE DISGUISED, BUT HANDY.
YES. *HERE.*
K-CHAK!
THERE. THAT'S THAT PART OF THE LAB *SEALED.*
CLANG!
VESPIARY CONTROL
AND ONE OF *THESE* SHOULD FLOOD THE LAB WITH *GAS.*
WAIT.
SOMEBODY *ACTIVATED* THAT ENGINE.
ON *PURPOSE.*
UH—
LET ME LOOK AT THIS.
WELL?
ZT!
ZT!
UH HUH. THE GAS LINE HAS BEEN *RE-ROUTED.*
TO WHAT I *THINK* MAY BE THE MAIN *VENTILATOR* FOR THIS AREA.
HANG ON A MINUTE.

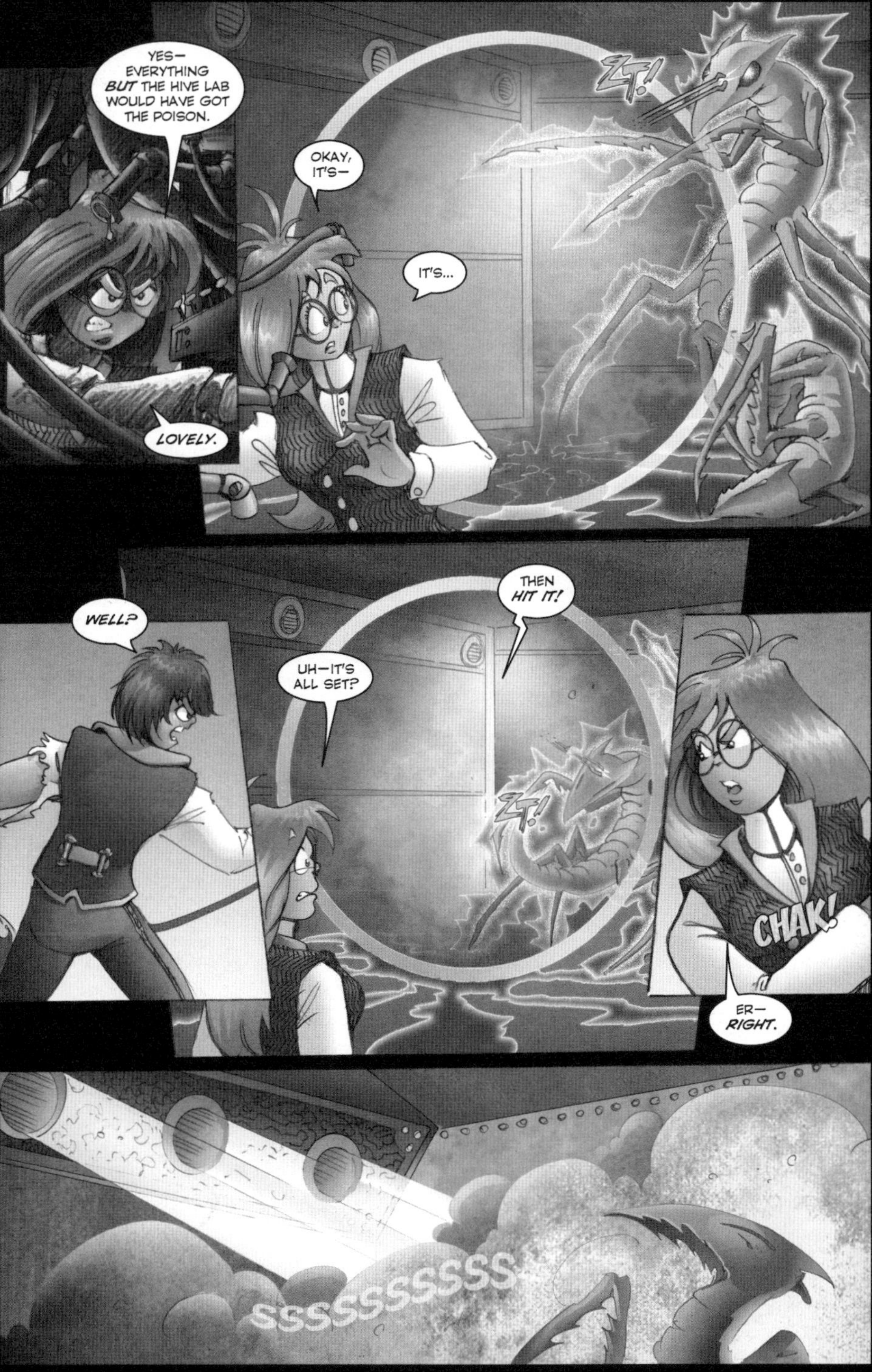
YES— EVERYTHING BUT THE HIVE LAB WOULD HAVE GOT THE POISON.
LOVELY.
OKAY, IT'S—
IT'S...
ZT!
WELL?
UH—IT'S ALL SET?
THEN HIT IT!
ZT!
CHAK!
ER— RIGHT.
SSSSSSSSSSSS

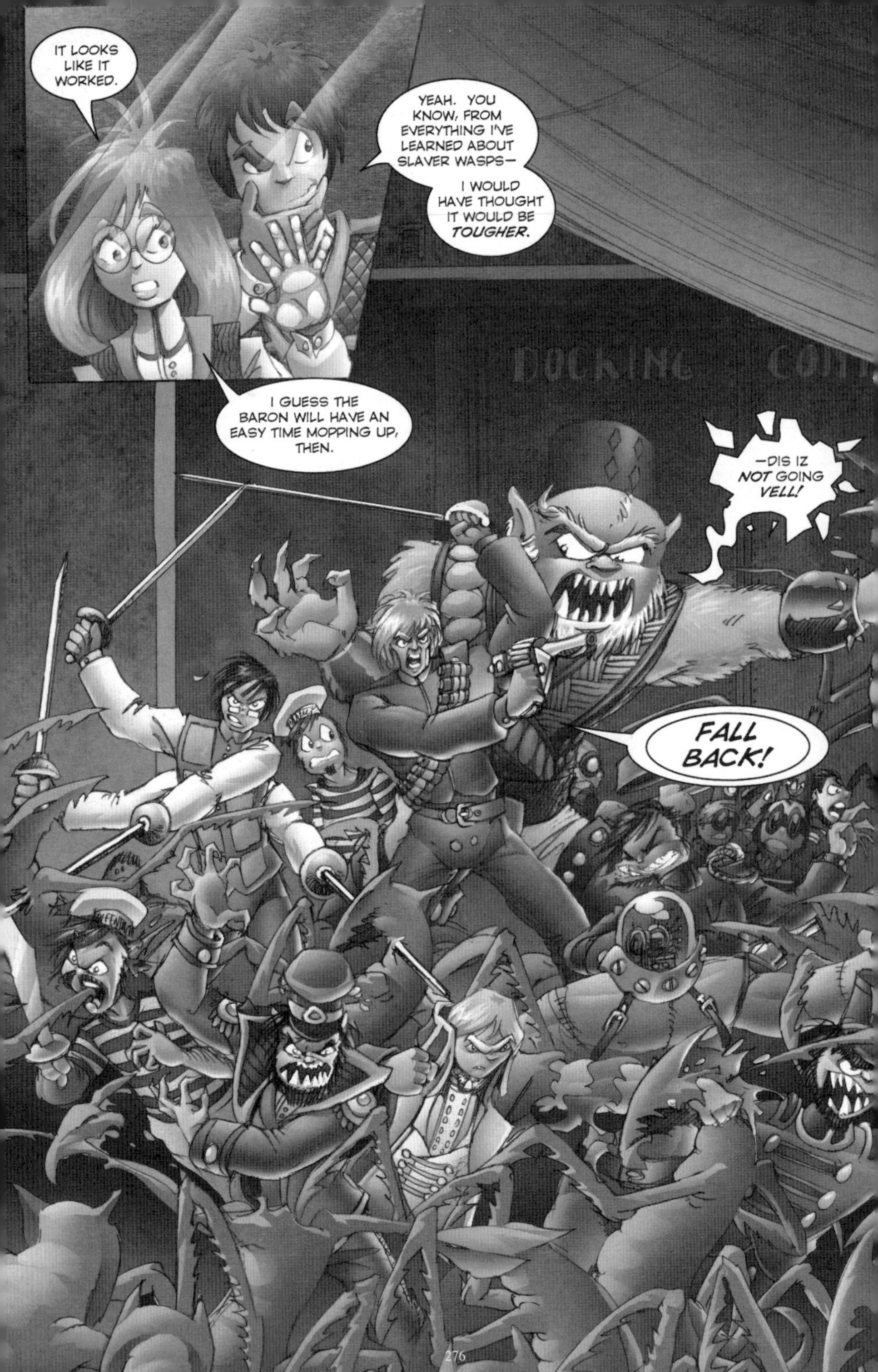

IT LOOKS LIKE IT WORKED.
YEAH. YOU KNOW, FROM EVERYTHING I'VE LEARNED ABOUT SLAVER WASPS—
I WOULD HAVE THOUGHT IT WOULD BE *TOUGHER*.
DOCKING
I GUESS THE BARON WILL HAVE AN EASY TIME MOPPING UP, THEN.
—DIS IZ *NOT* GOING *VELL!*
FALL BACK!

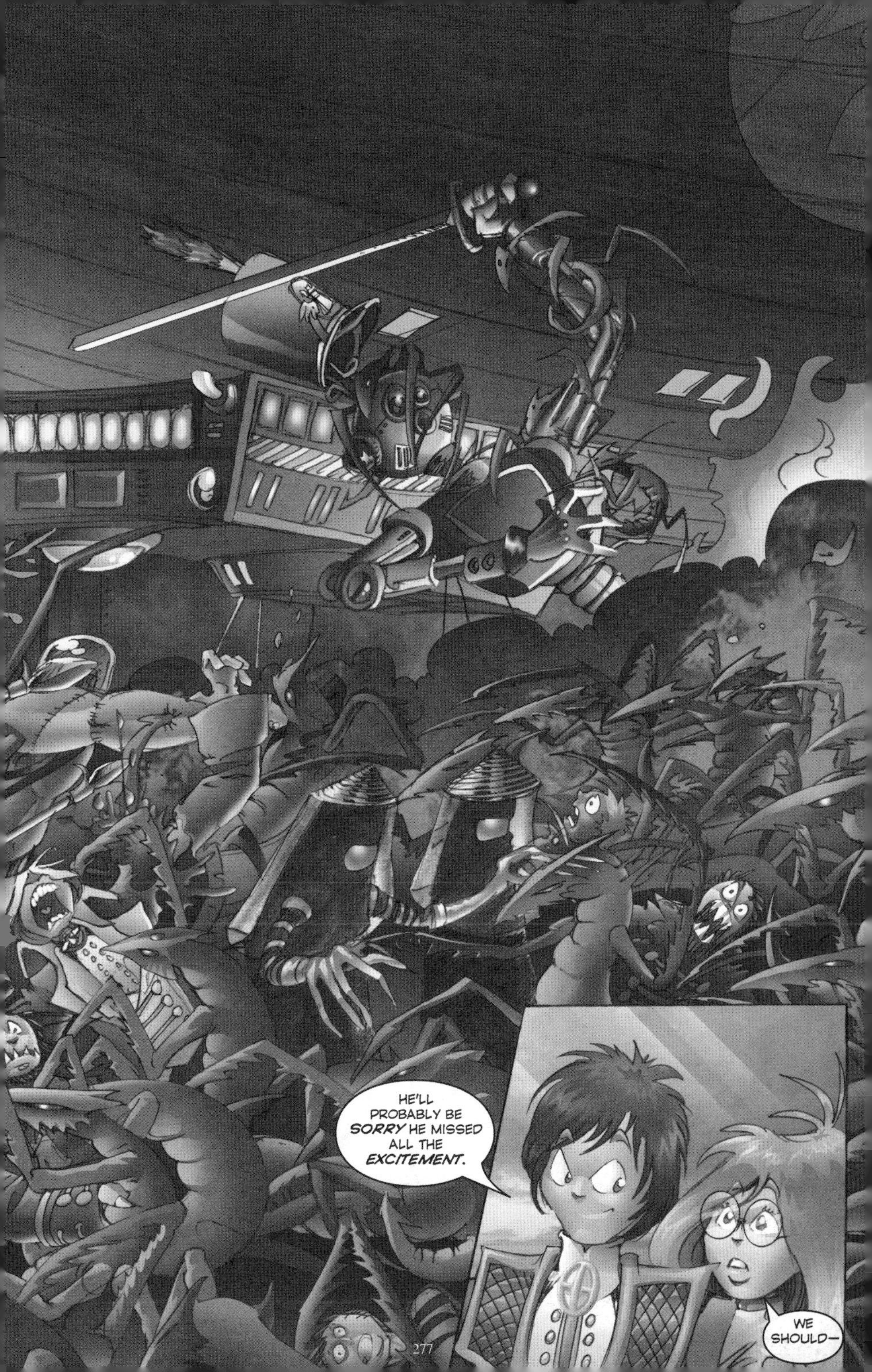
HE'LL PROBABLY BE SORRY HE MISSED ALL THE EXCITEMENT.
WE SHOULD—

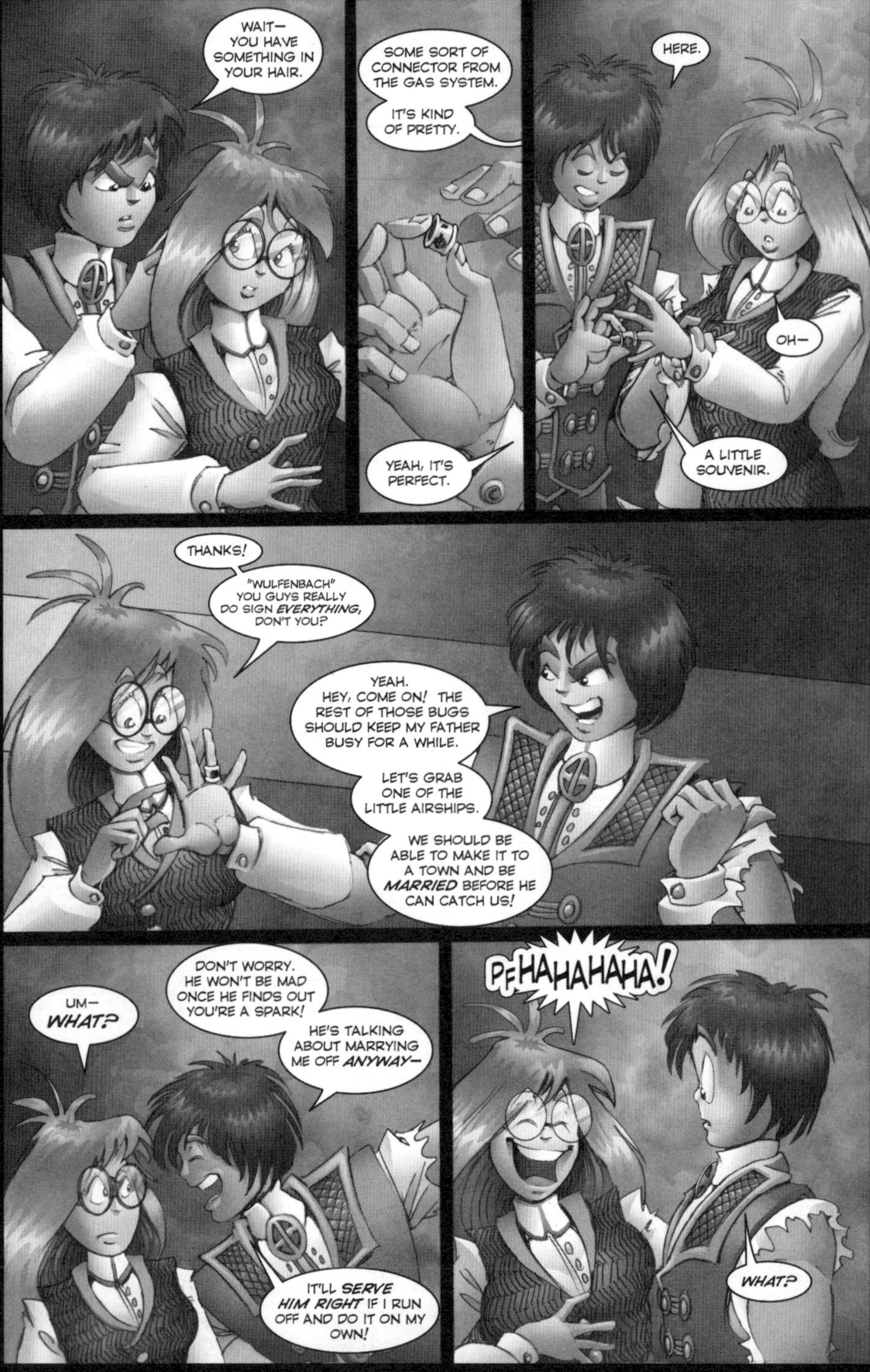
WAIT— YOU HAVE SOMETHING IN YOUR HAIR.
SOME SORT OF CONNECTOR FROM THE GAS SYSTEM.
IT'S KIND OF PRETTY.
YEAH, IT'S PERFECT.
HERE.
OH—
A LITTLE SOUVENIR.
THANKS!
"WULFENBACH" YOU GUYS REALLY DO SIGN *EVERYTHING*, DON'T YOU?
YEAH. HEY, COME ON! THE REST OF THOSE BUGS SHOULD KEEP MY FATHER BUSY FOR A WHILE.
LET'S GRAB ONE OF THE LITTLE AIRSHIPS.
WE SHOULD BE ABLE TO MAKE IT TO A TOWN AND BE *MARRIED* BEFORE HE CAN CATCH US!
UM— *WHAT?*
DON'T WORRY. HE WON'T BE MAD ONCE HE FINDS OUT YOU'RE A SPARK!
HE'S TALKING ABOUT MARRYING ME OFF *ANYWAY—*
IT'LL *SERVE HIM RIGHT* IF I RUN OFF AND DO IT ON MY OWN!
PFHAHAHAHA!
WHAT?

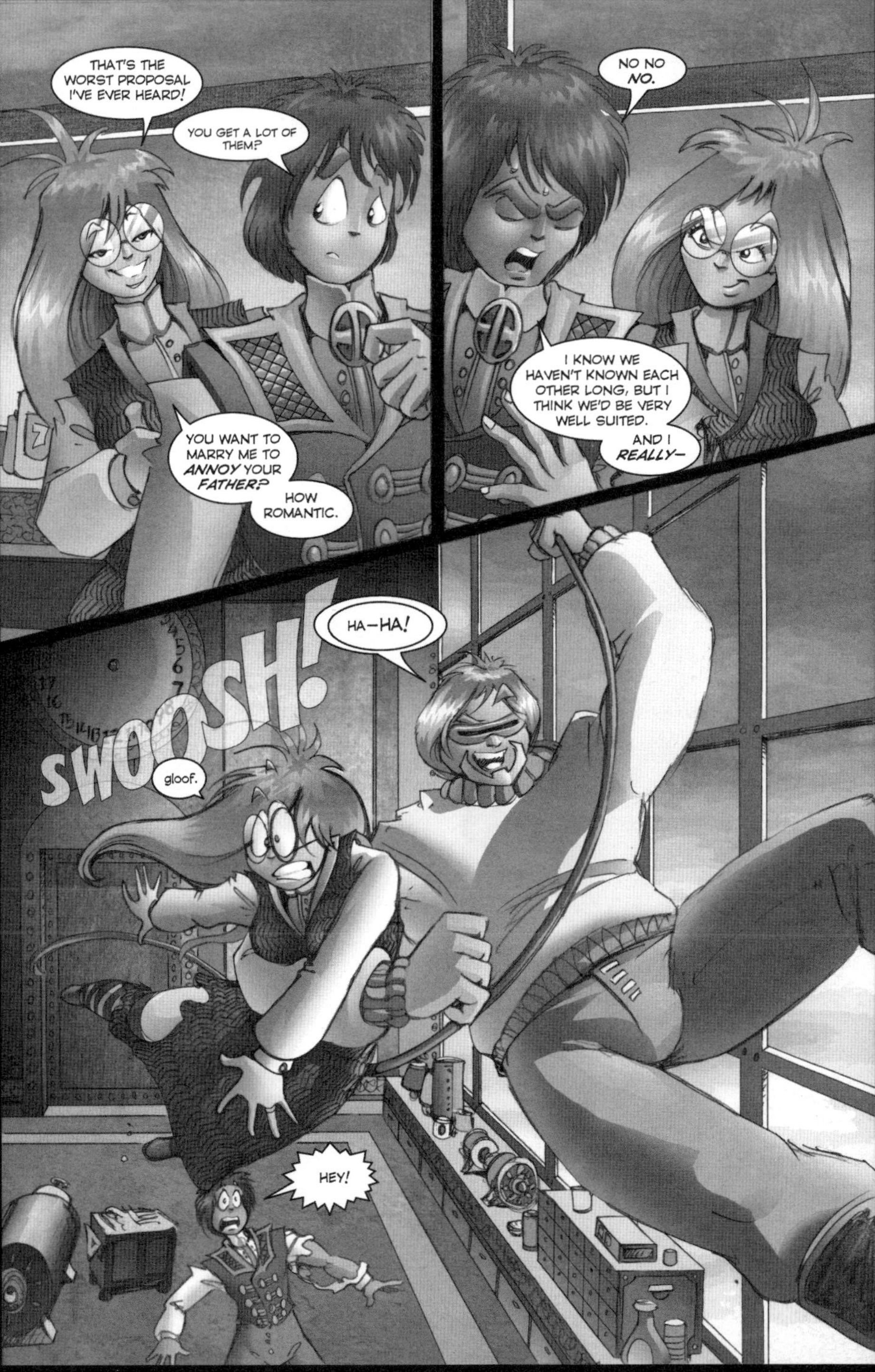

THAT'S THE WORST PROPOSAL I'VE EVER HEARD!
YOU GET A LOT OF THEM?
YOU WANT TO MARRY ME TO ANNOY YOUR FATHER?
HOW ROMANTIC.
NO NO NO.
I KNOW WE HAVEN'T KNOWN EACH OTHER LONG, BUT I THINK WE'D BE VERY WELL SUITED.
AND I REALLY—
HA-HA!
SWOOSH!
gloof.
HEY!

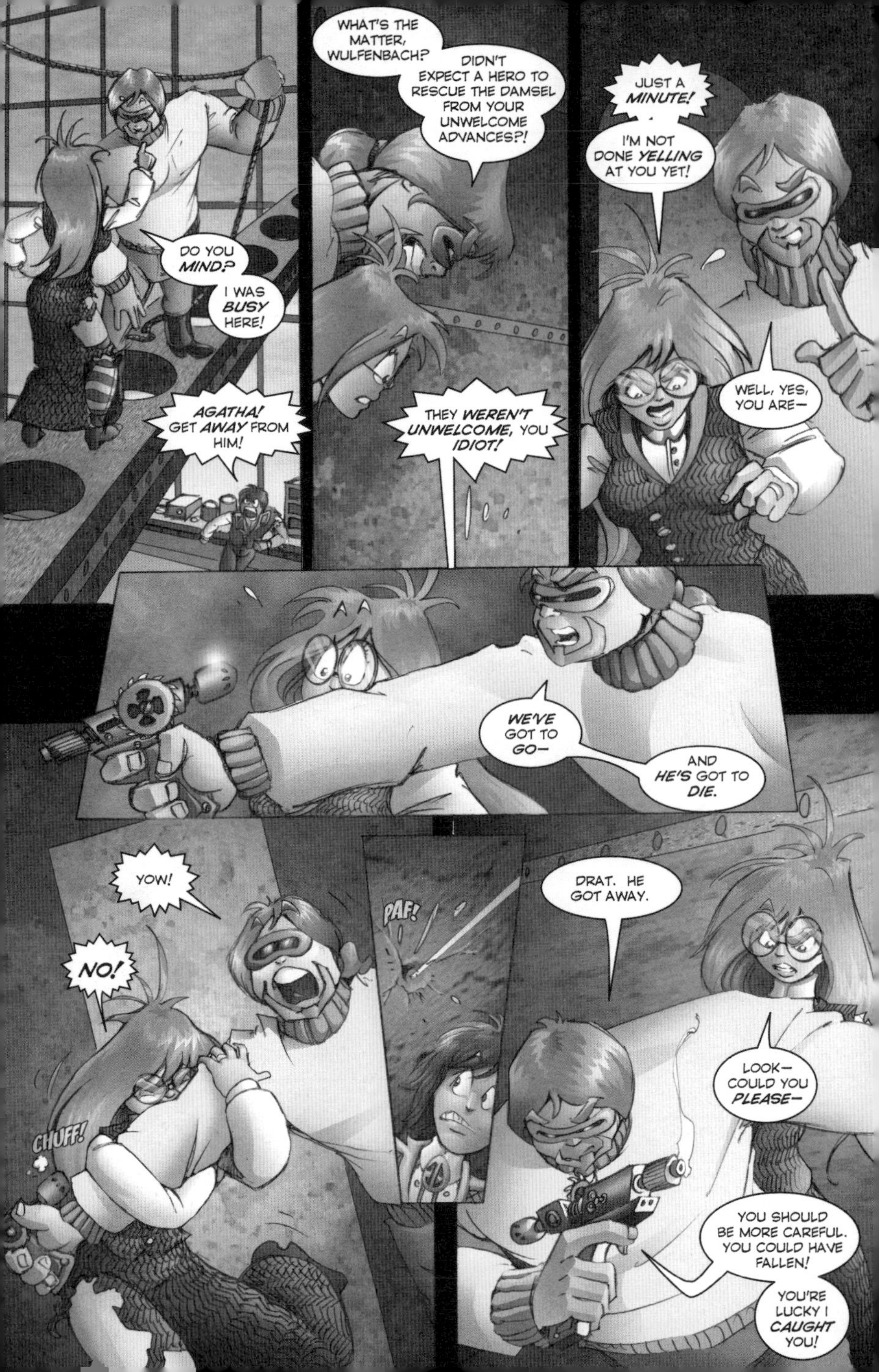
DO YOU MIND?
I WAS BUSY HERE!
AGATHA! GET AWAY FROM HIM!
WHAT'S THE MATTER, WULFENBACH?
DIDN'T EXPECT A HERO TO RESCUE THE DAMSEL FROM YOUR UNWELCOME ADVANCES?!
THEY WEREN'T UNWELCOME, YOU IDIOT!
JUST A MINUTE!
I'M NOT DONE YELLING AT YOU YET!
WELL, YES, YOU ARE—
WE'VE GOT TO GO—
AND HE'S GOT TO DIE.
YOW!
NO!
CHUFF!
PAF!
DRAT. HE GOT AWAY.
LOOK— COULD YOU PLEASE—
YOU SHOULD BE MORE CAREFUL. YOU COULD HAVE FALLEN!
YOU'RE LUCKY I CAUGHT YOU!

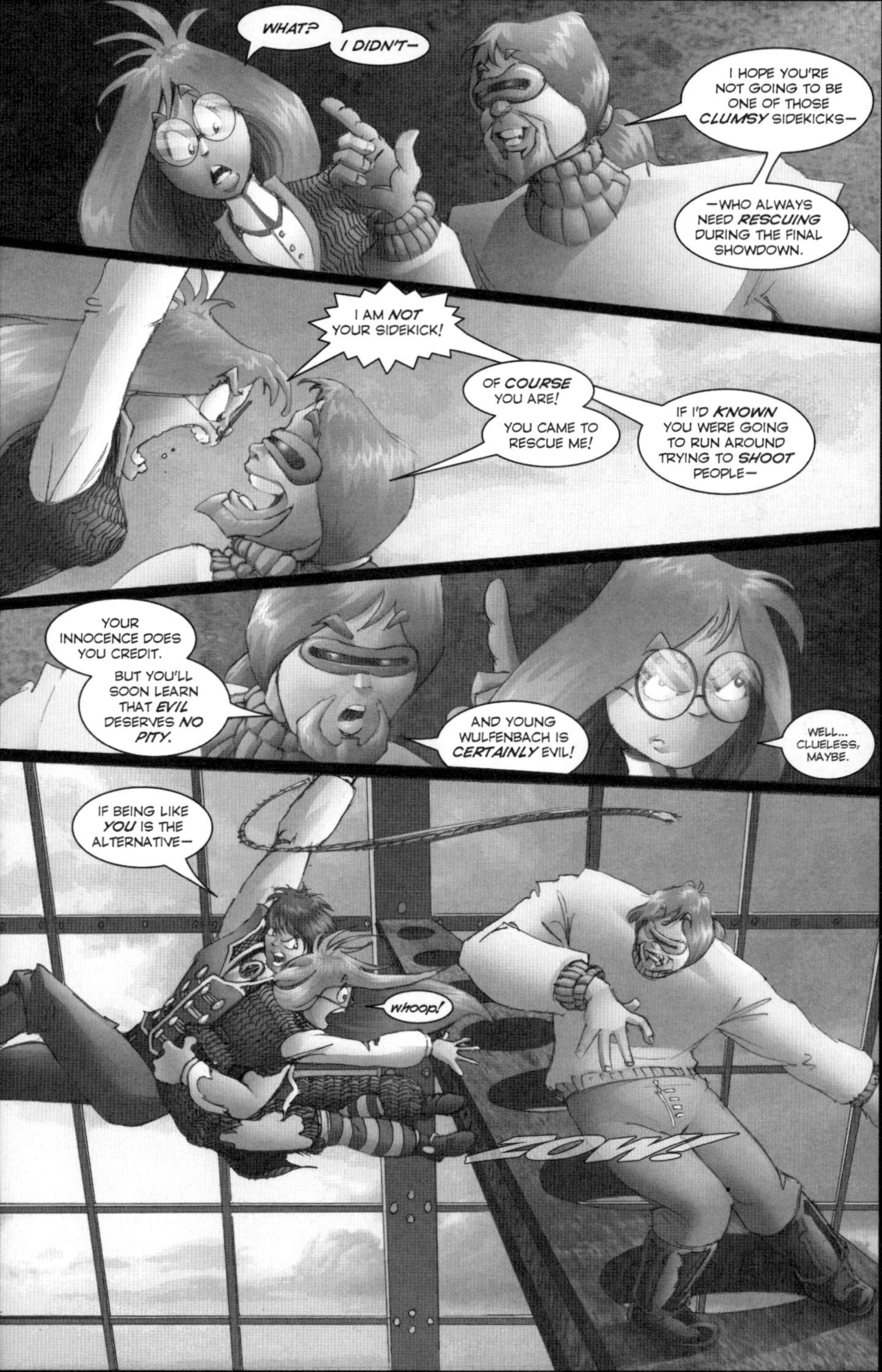

WHAT?
I DIDN'T—
I HOPE YOU'RE NOT GOING TO BE ONE OF THOSE CLUMSY SIDEKICKS—
—WHO ALWAYS NEED RESCUING DURING THE FINAL SHOWDOWN.
I AM NOT YOUR SIDEKICK!
OF COURSE YOU ARE!
YOU CAME TO RESCUE ME!
IF I'D KNOWN YOU WERE GOING TO RUN AROUND TRYING TO SHOOT PEOPLE—
YOUR INNOCENCE DOES YOU CREDIT.
BUT YOU'LL SOON LEARN THAT EVIL DESERVES NO PITY.
AND YOUNG WULFENBACH IS CERTAINLY EVIL!
WELL... CLUELESS, MAYBE.
IF BEING LIKE YOU IS THE ALTERNATIVE—
whoop!
ZOW!

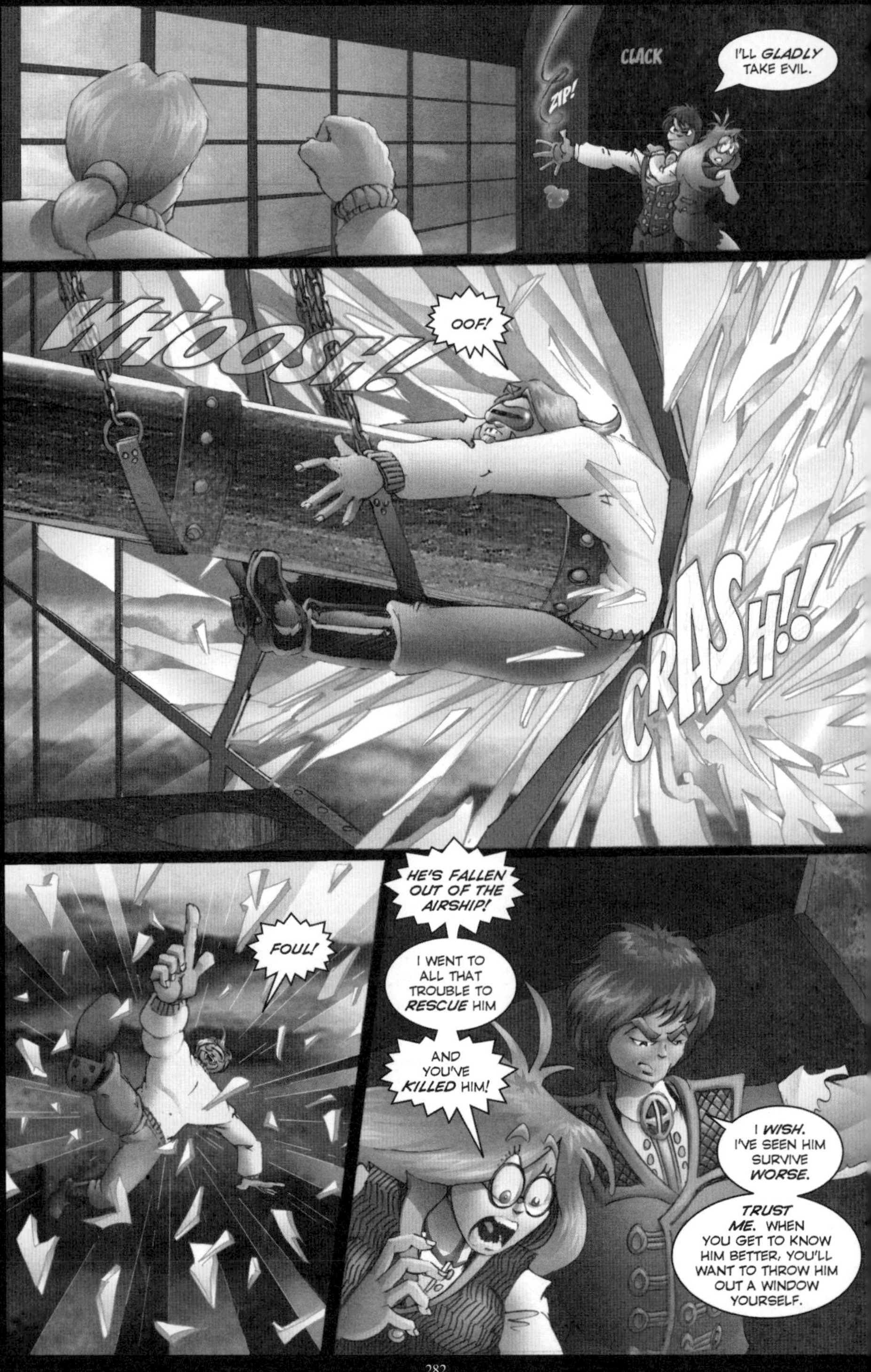
ZIP!
CLACK
I'LL GLADLY TAKE EVIL.
WHOOSH!
OOF!
CRASH!!
FOUL!
HE'S FALLEN OUT OF THE AIRSHIP!
I WENT TO ALL THAT TROUBLE TO RESCUE HIM
AND YOU'VE KILLED HIM!
I WISH. I'VE SEEN HIM SURVIVE WORSE.
TRUST ME. WHEN YOU GET TO KNOW HIM BETTER, YOU'LL WANT TO THROW HIM OUT A WINDOW YOURSELF.

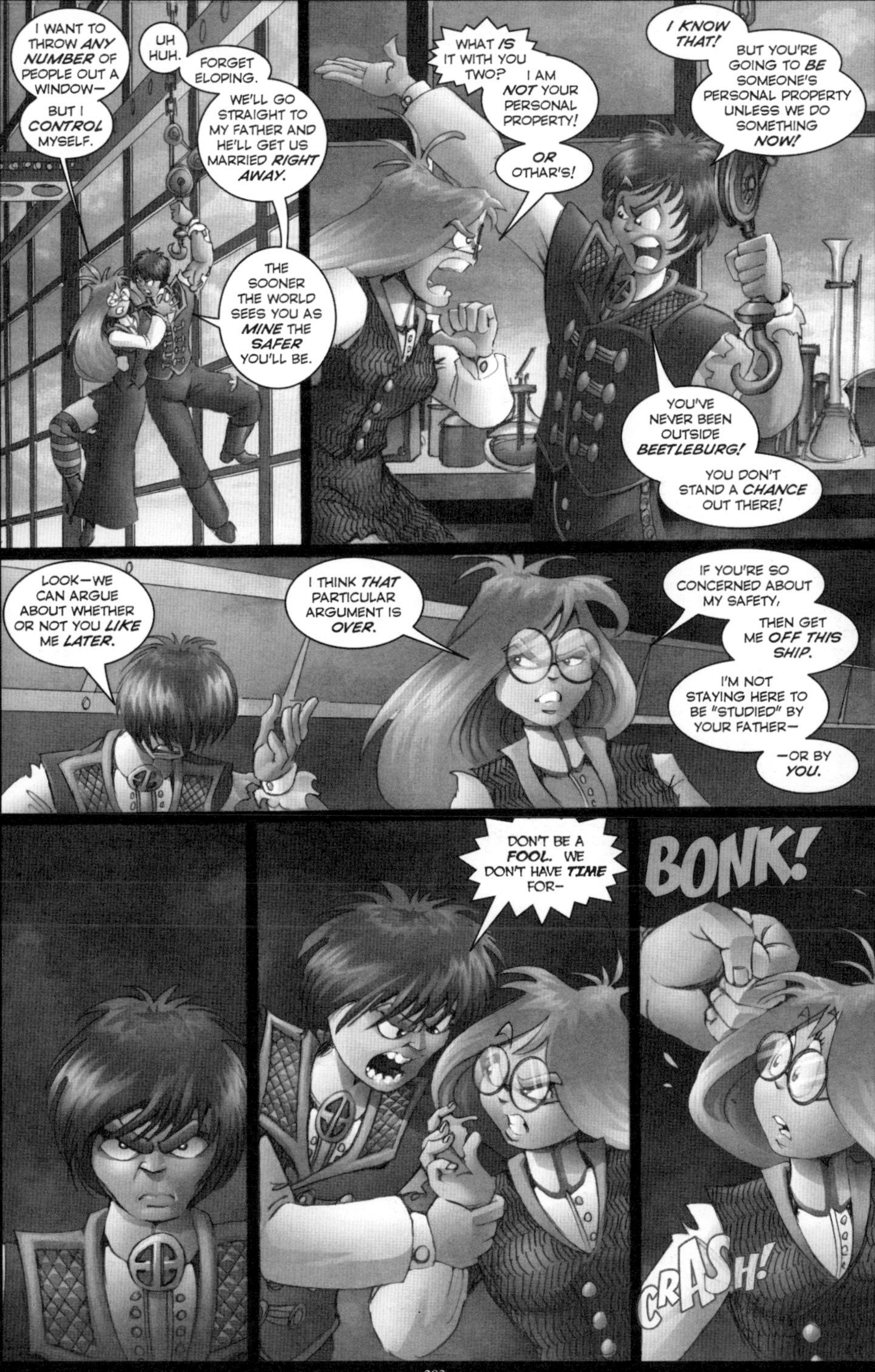

I WANT TO THROW ANY NUMBER OF PEOPLE OUT A WINDOW—
BUT I CONTROL MYSELF.
UH HUH.
FORGET ELOPING.
WE'LL GO STRAIGHT TO MY FATHER AND HE'LL GET US MARRIED RIGHT AWAY.
THE SOONER THE WORLD SEES YOU AS MINE THE SAFER YOU'LL BE.
WHAT IS IT WITH YOU TWO?
I AM NOT YOUR PERSONAL PROPERTY!
OR OTHAR'S!
I KNOW THAT!
BUT YOU'RE GOING TO BE SOMEONE'S PERSONAL PROPERTY UNLESS WE DO SOMETHING NOW!
YOU'VE NEVER BEEN OUTSIDE BEETLEBURG!
YOU DON'T STAND A CHANCE OUT THERE!
LOOK—WE CAN ARGUE ABOUT WHETHER OR NOT YOU LIKE ME LATER.
I THINK THAT PARTICULAR ARGUMENT IS OVER.
IF YOU'RE SO CONCERNED ABOUT MY SAFETY,
THEN GET ME OFF THIS SHIP.
I'M NOT STAYING HERE TO BE "STUDIED" BY YOUR FATHER—
—OR BY YOU.
DON'T BE A FOOL. WE DON'T HAVE TIME FOR-
BONK!
CRASH!

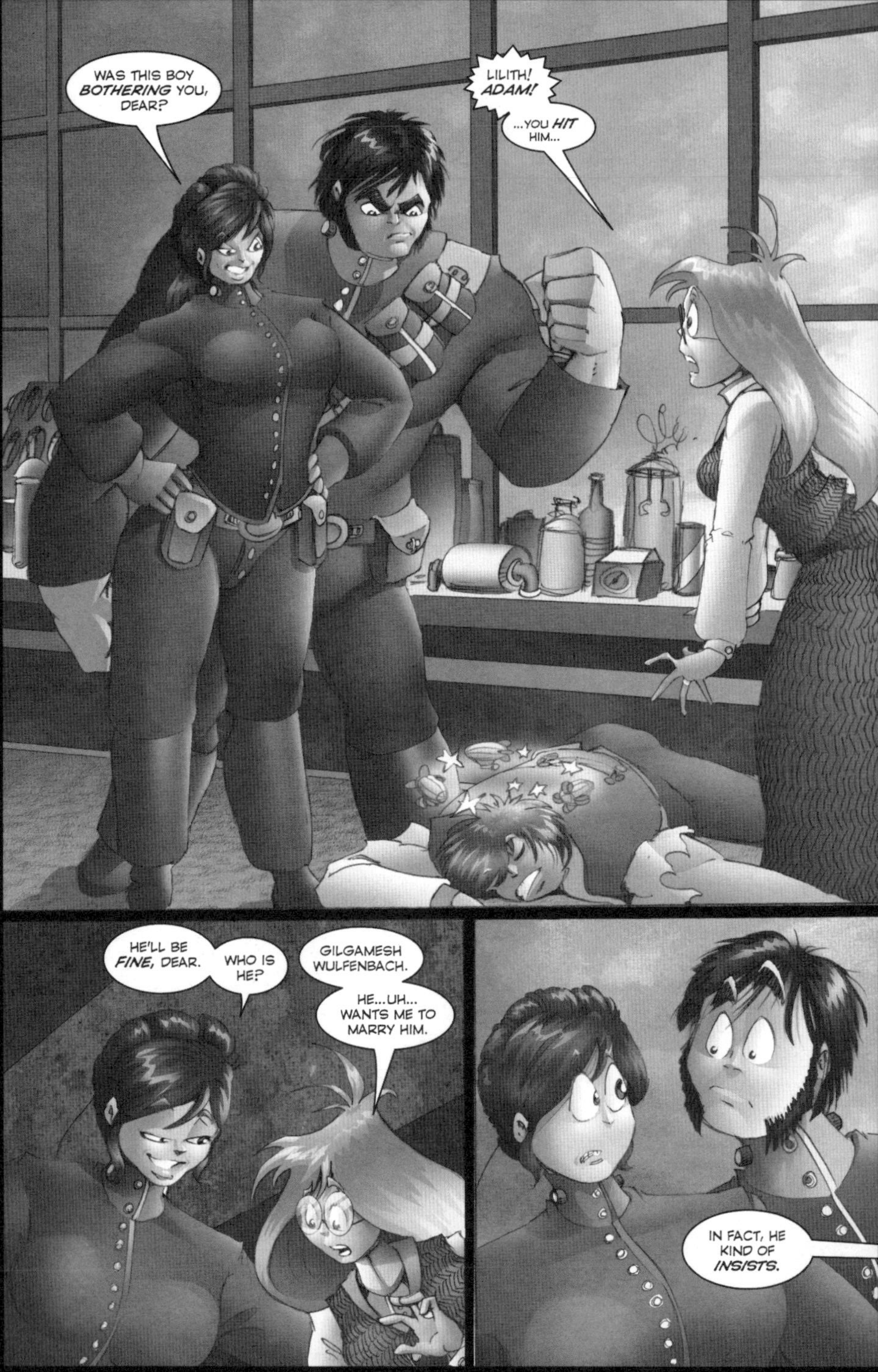
WAS THIS BOY BOTHERING YOU, DEAR?
LILITH! ADAM!
...YOU HIT HIM...
HE'LL BE FINE, DEAR.
WHO IS HE?
GILGAMESH WULFENBACH.
HE...UH... WANTS ME TO MARRY HIM.
IN FACT, HE KIND OF INSISTS.

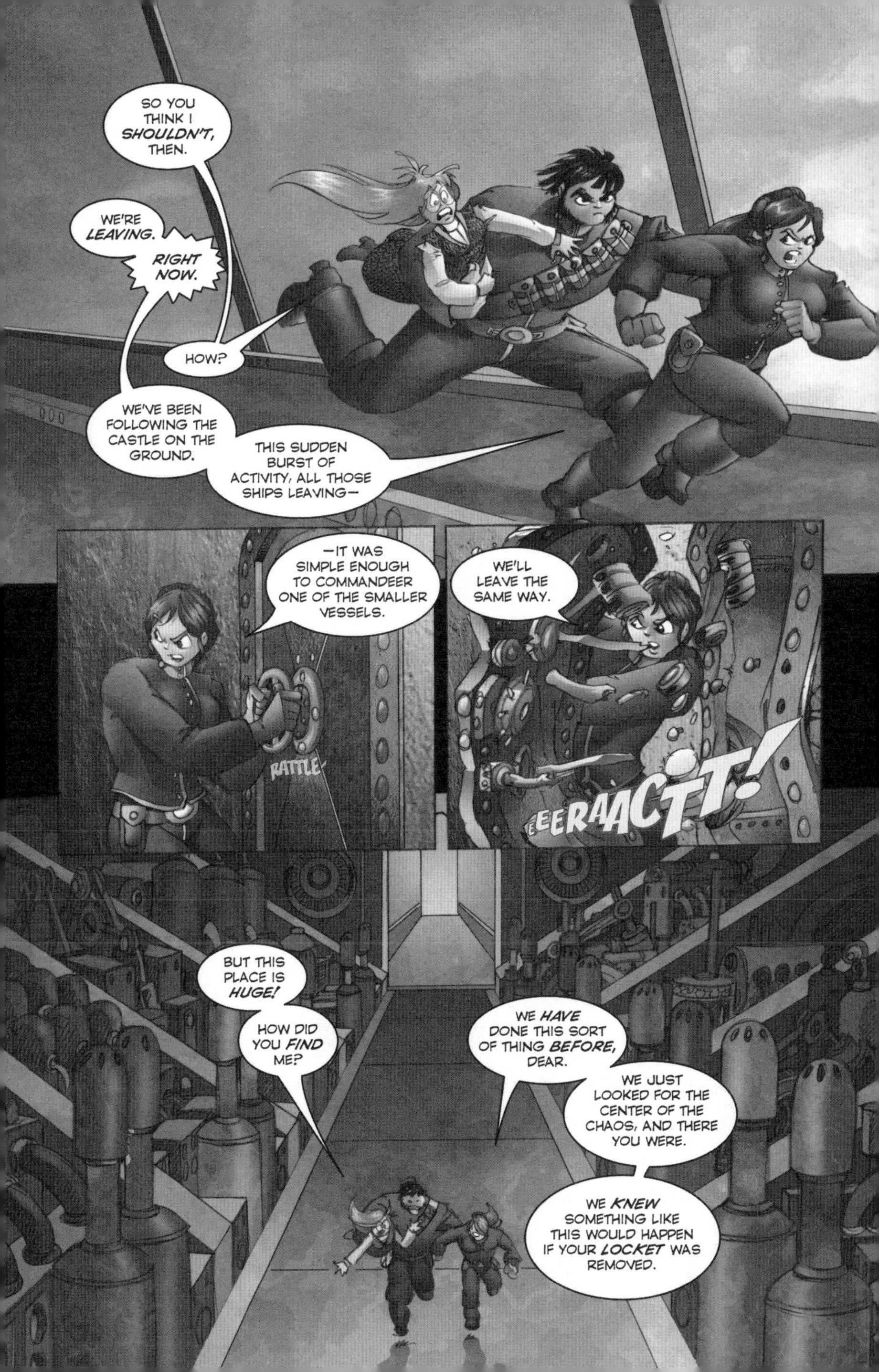
SO YOU THINK I *SHOULDN'T,* THEN.
WE'RE *LEAVING.*
RIGHT NOW.
HOW?
WE'VE BEEN FOLLOWING THE CASTLE ON THE GROUND.
THIS SUDDEN BURST OF ACTIVITY, ALL THOSE SHIPS LEAVING—
—IT WAS SIMPLE ENOUGH TO COMMANDEER ONE OF THE SMALLER VESSELS.
RATTLE
WE'LL LEAVE THE SAME WAY.
EEERAAACTT!
BUT THIS PLACE IS *HUGE!*
HOW DID YOU *FIND* ME?
WE *HAVE* DONE THIS SORT OF THING *BEFORE,* DEAR.
WE JUST LOOKED FOR THE CENTER OF THE CHAOS, AND THERE YOU WERE.
WE *KNEW* SOMETHING LIKE THIS WOULD HAPPEN IF YOUR *LOCKET* WAS REMOVED.

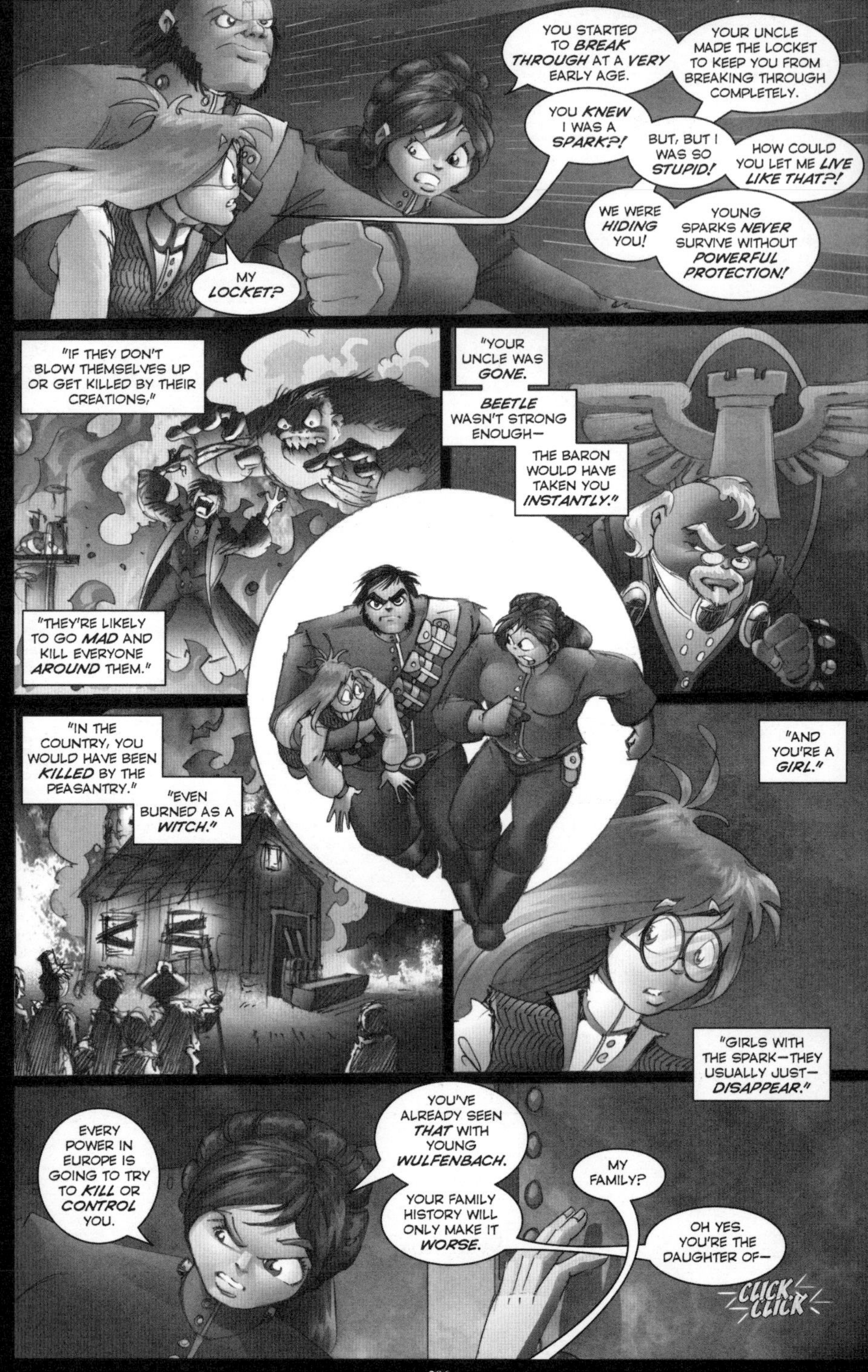

MY LOCKET?
YOU STARTED TO BREAK THROUGH AT A VERY EARLY AGE.
YOUR UNCLE MADE THE LOCKET TO KEEP YOU FROM BREAKING THROUGH COMPLETELY.
YOU KNEW I WAS A SPARK?!
BUT, BUT I WAS SO STUPID!
HOW COULD YOU LET ME LIVE LIKE THAT?!
WE WERE HIDING YOU!
YOUNG SPARKS NEVER SURVIVE WITHOUT POWERFUL PROTECTION!
"IF THEY DON'T BLOW THEMSELVES UP OR GET KILLED BY THEIR CREATIONS,"
"THEY'RE LIKELY TO GO MAD AND KILL EVERYONE AROUND THEM."
"YOUR UNCLE WAS GONE.
BEETLE WASN'T STRONG ENOUGH—
THE BARON WOULD HAVE TAKEN YOU INSTANTLY."
"IN THE COUNTRY, YOU WOULD HAVE BEEN KILLED BY THE PEASANTRY."
"EVEN BURNED AS A WITCH."
"AND YOU'RE A GIRL."
"GIRLS WITH THE SPARK—THEY USUALLY JUST—DISAPPEAR."
EVERY POWER IN EUROPE IS GOING TO TRY TO KILL OR CONTROL YOU.
YOU'VE ALREADY SEEN THAT WITH YOUNG WULFENBACH.
YOUR FAMILY HISTORY WILL ONLY MAKE IT WORSE.
MY FAMILY?
OH YES. YOU'RE THE DAUGHTER OF—
CLICK CLICK

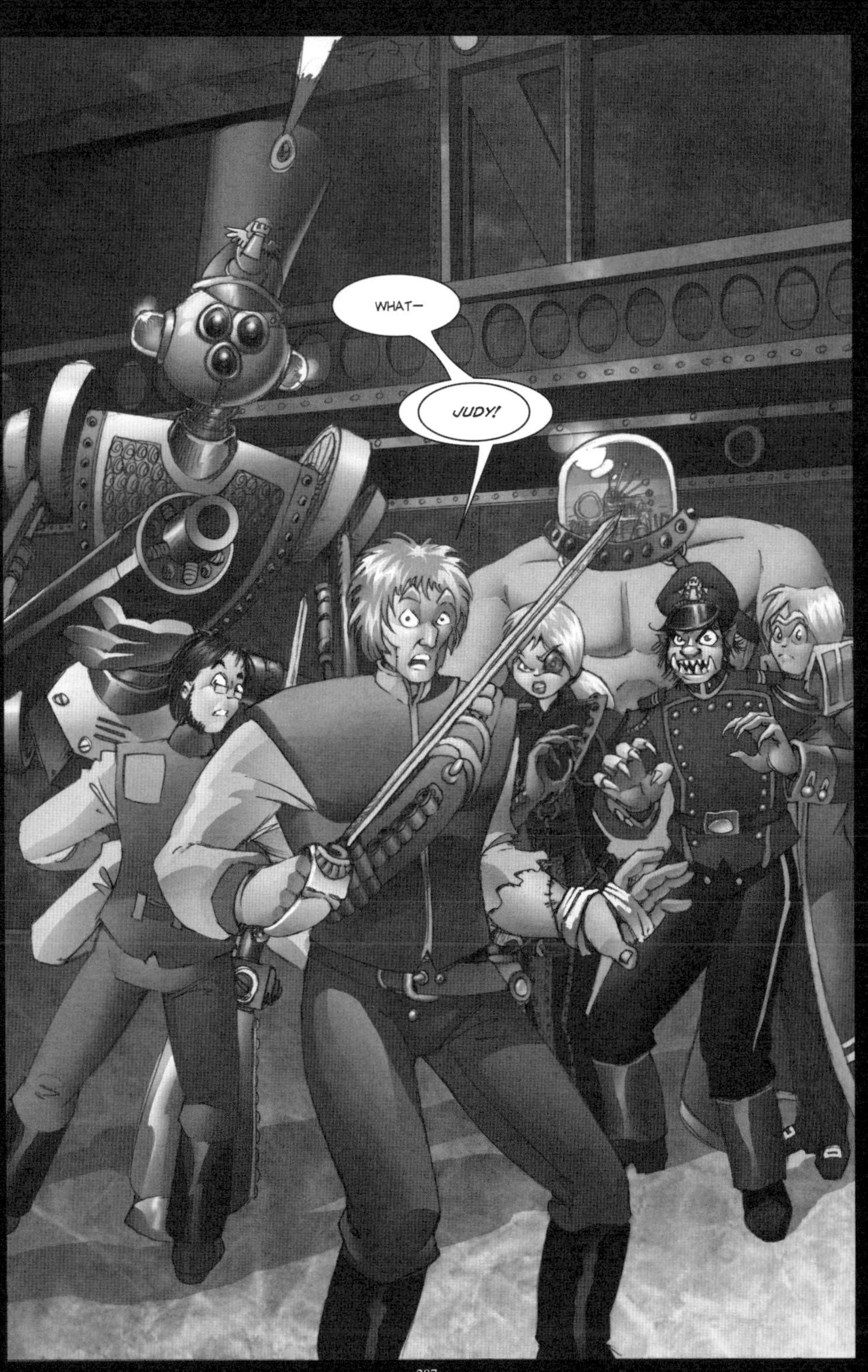
WHAT—
JUDY!

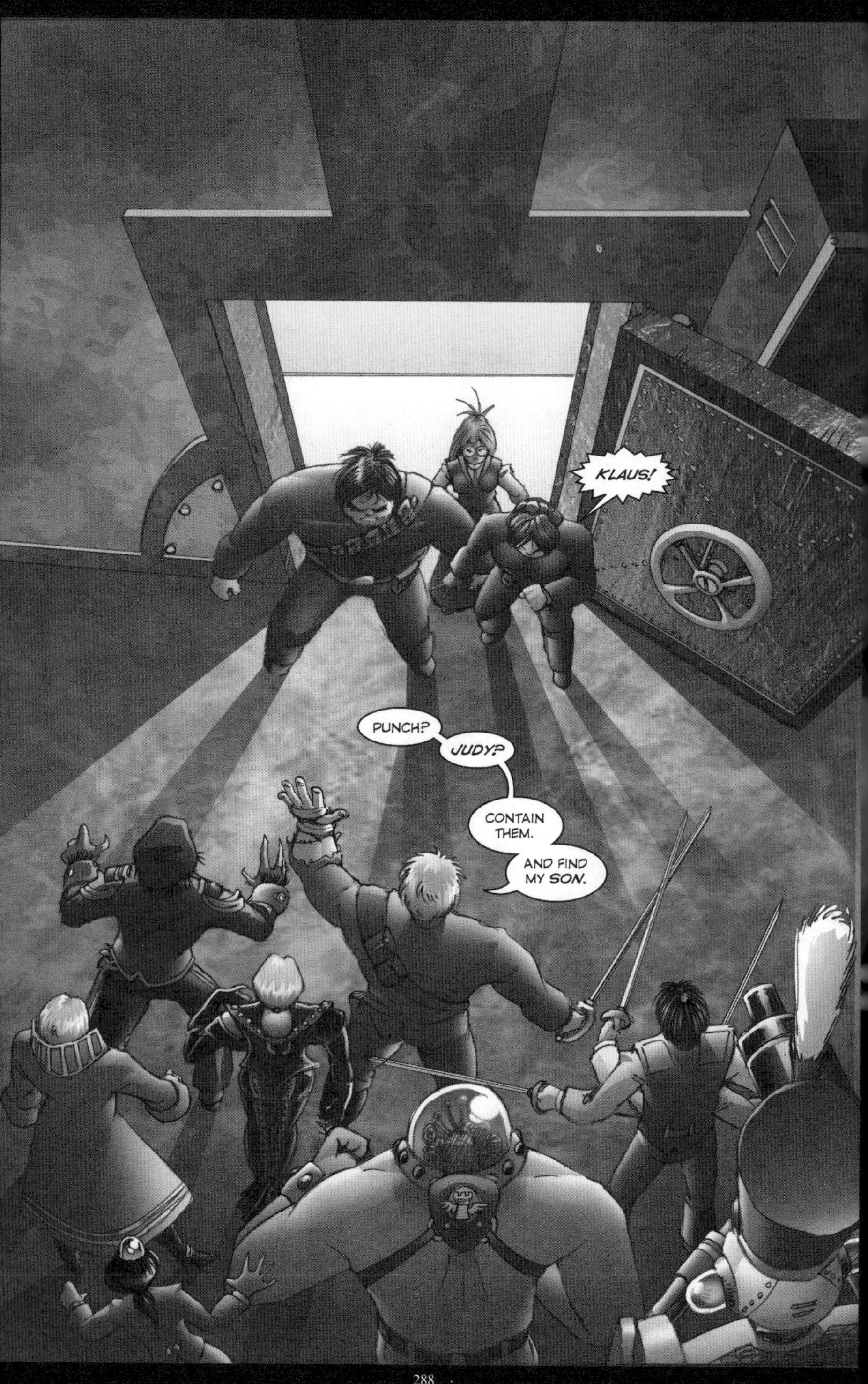
KLAUS!
PUNCH?
JUDY?
CONTAIN THEM.
AND FIND MY SON.

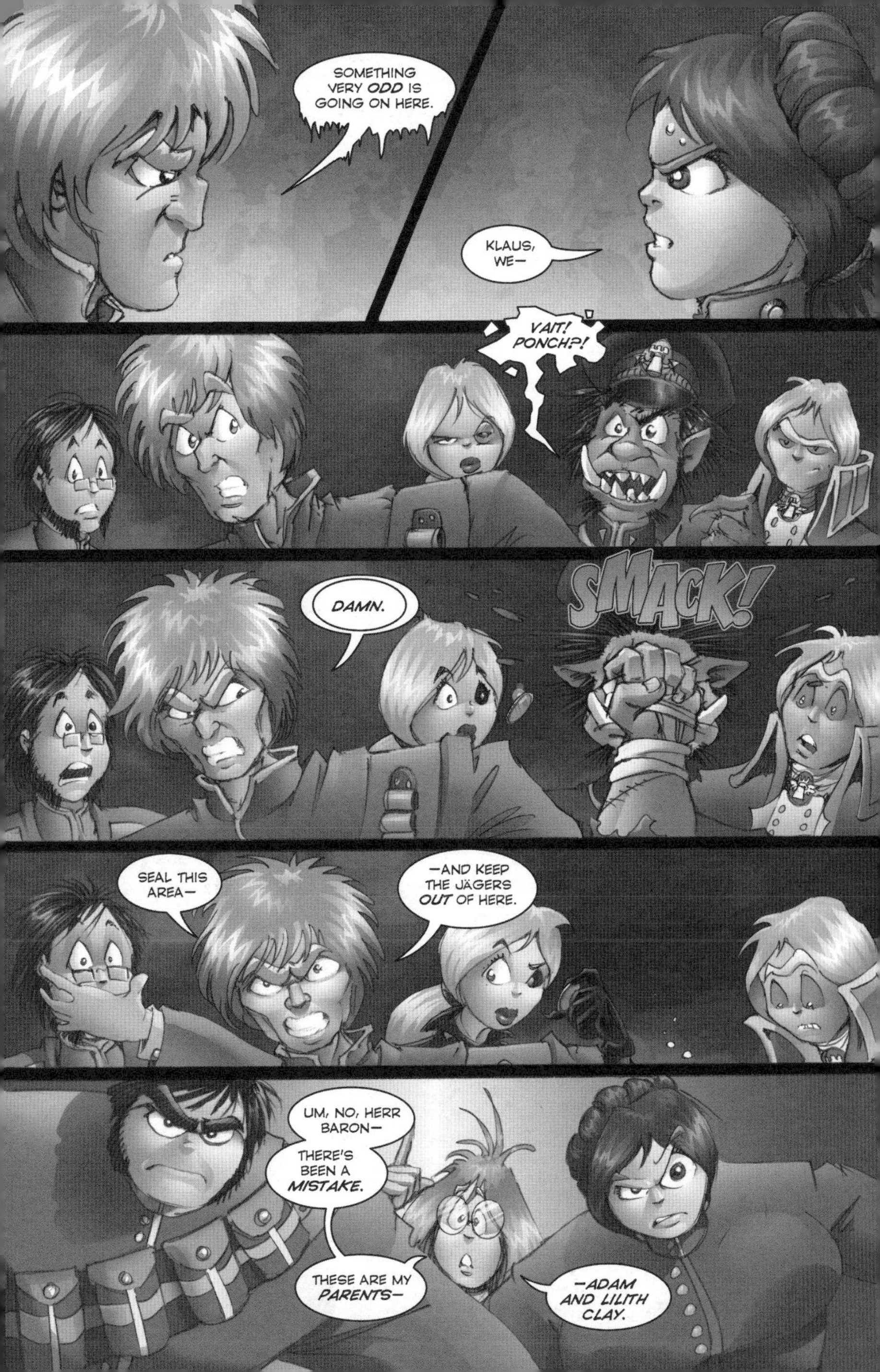
SOMETHING VERY ODD IS GOING ON HERE.
KLAUS, WE—
VAIT! PONCH?!
DAMN.
SMACK!
SEAL THIS AREA—
—AND KEEP THE JÄGERS OUT OF HERE.
UM, NO, HERR BARON—
THERE'S BEEN A MISTAKE.
THESE ARE MY PARENTS—
—ADAM AND LILITH CLAY.

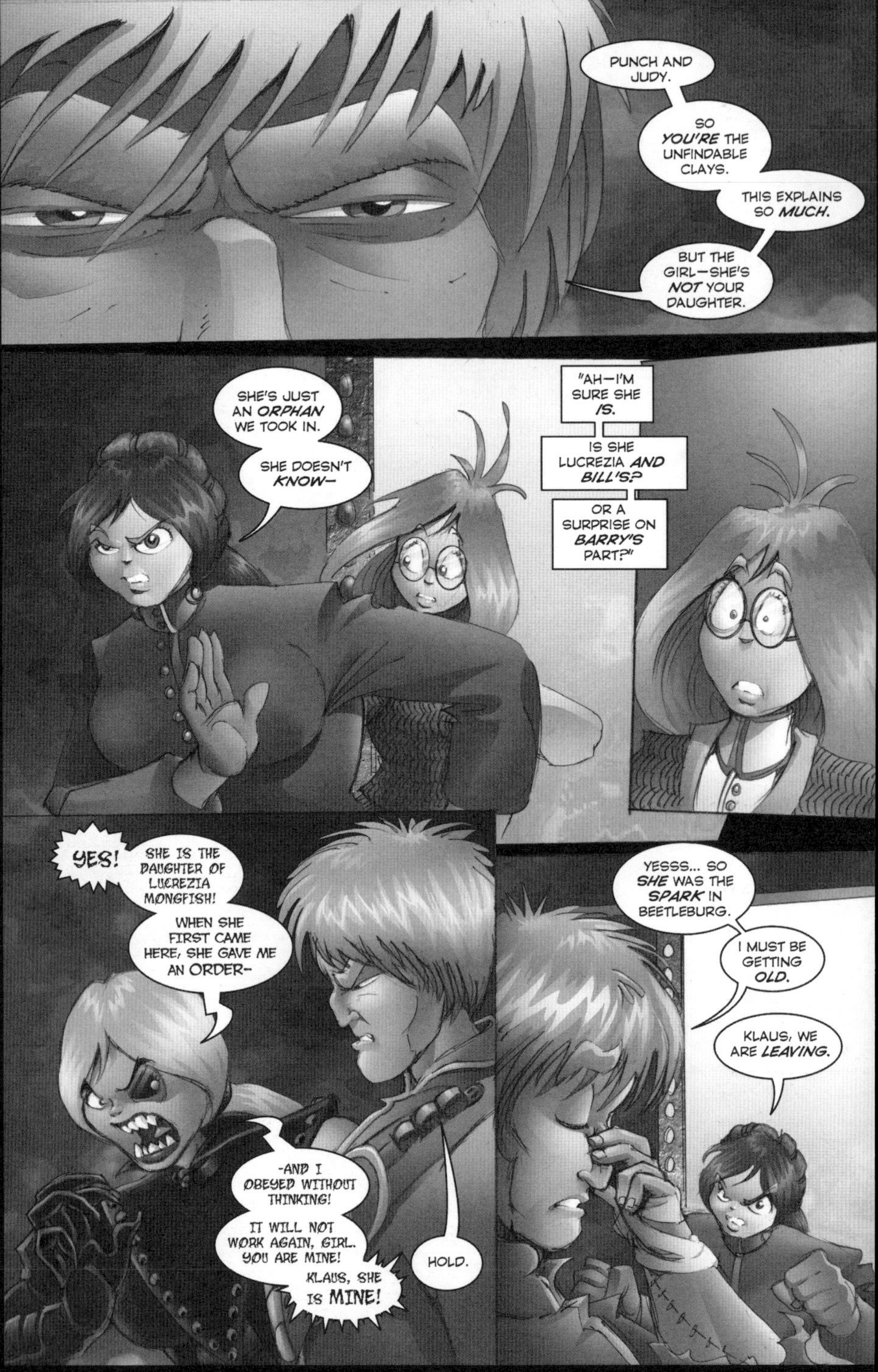
PUNCH AND JUDY.
SO *YOU'RE* THE UNFINDABLE CLAYS.
THIS EXPLAINS SO *MUCH*.
BUT THE GIRL—SHE'S *NOT* YOUR DAUGHTER.
SHE'S JUST AN *ORPHAN* WE TOOK IN.
SHE DOESN'T *KNOW*—
"AH—I'M SURE SHE *IS*.
IS SHE LUCREZIA *AND BILL'S?*
OR A SURPRISE ON *BARRY'S* PART?"
YES!
SHE IS THE DAUGHTER OF LUCREZIA MONGFISH!
WHEN SHE FIRST CAME HERE, SHE GAVE ME AN ORDER—
—AND I OBEYED WITHOUT THINKING!
IT WILL NOT WORK AGAIN, GIRL. YOU ARE MINE!
KLAUS, SHE IS MINE!
HOLD.
YESSS... SO *SHE* WAS THE *SPARK* IN BEETLEBURG.
I MUST BE GETTING *OLD*.
KLAUS, WE ARE *LEAVING*.

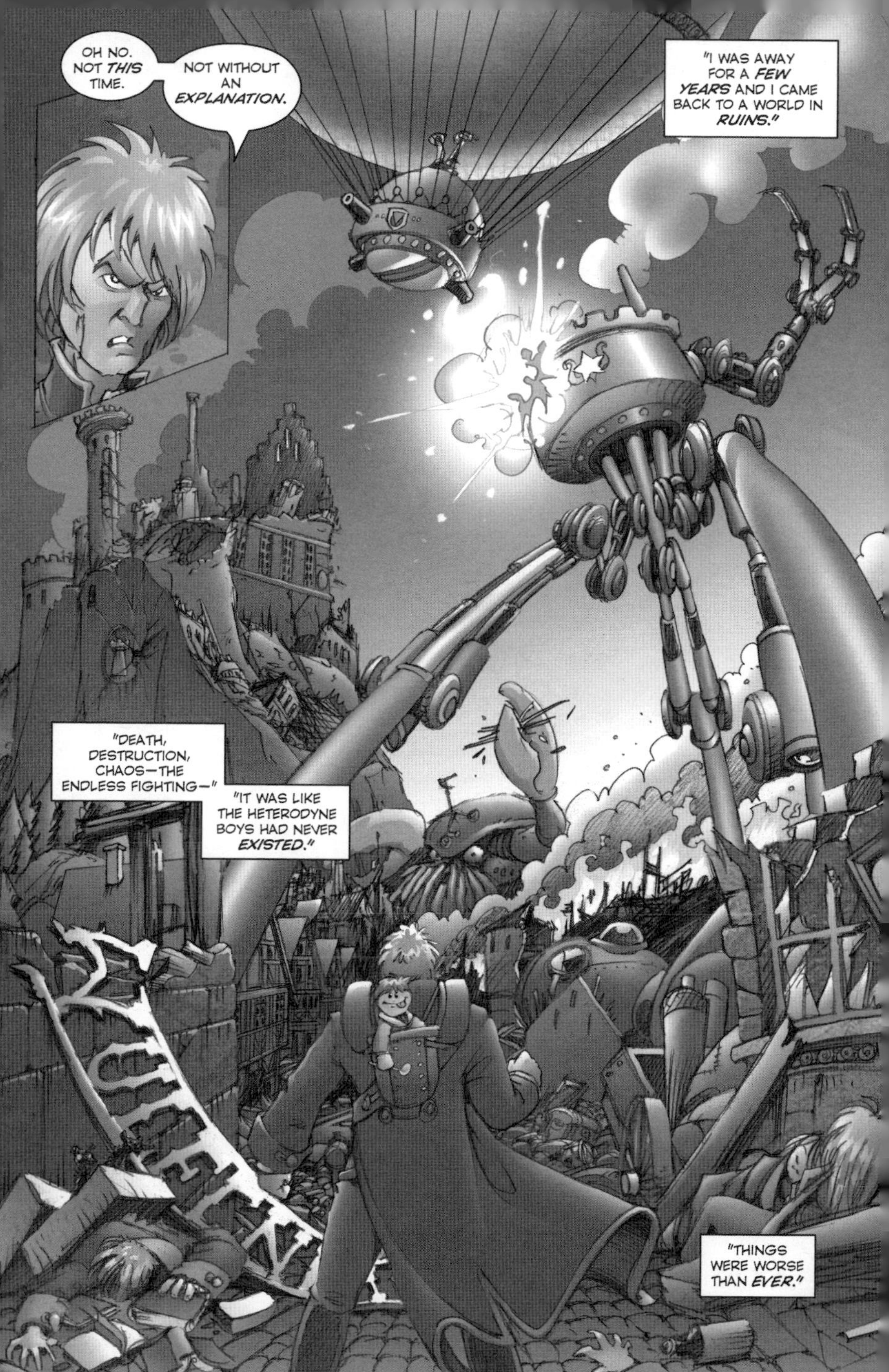

OH NO. NOT *THIS* TIME.
NOT WITHOUT AN *EXPLANATION.*
"I WAS AWAY FOR A *FEW YEARS* AND I CAME BACK TO A WORLD IN *RUINS.*"
"DEATH, DESTRUCTION, CHAOS—THE ENDLESS FIGHTING—"
"IT WAS LIKE THE HETERODYNE BOYS HAD NEVER *EXISTED.*"
"THINGS WERE WORSE THAN *EVER.*"

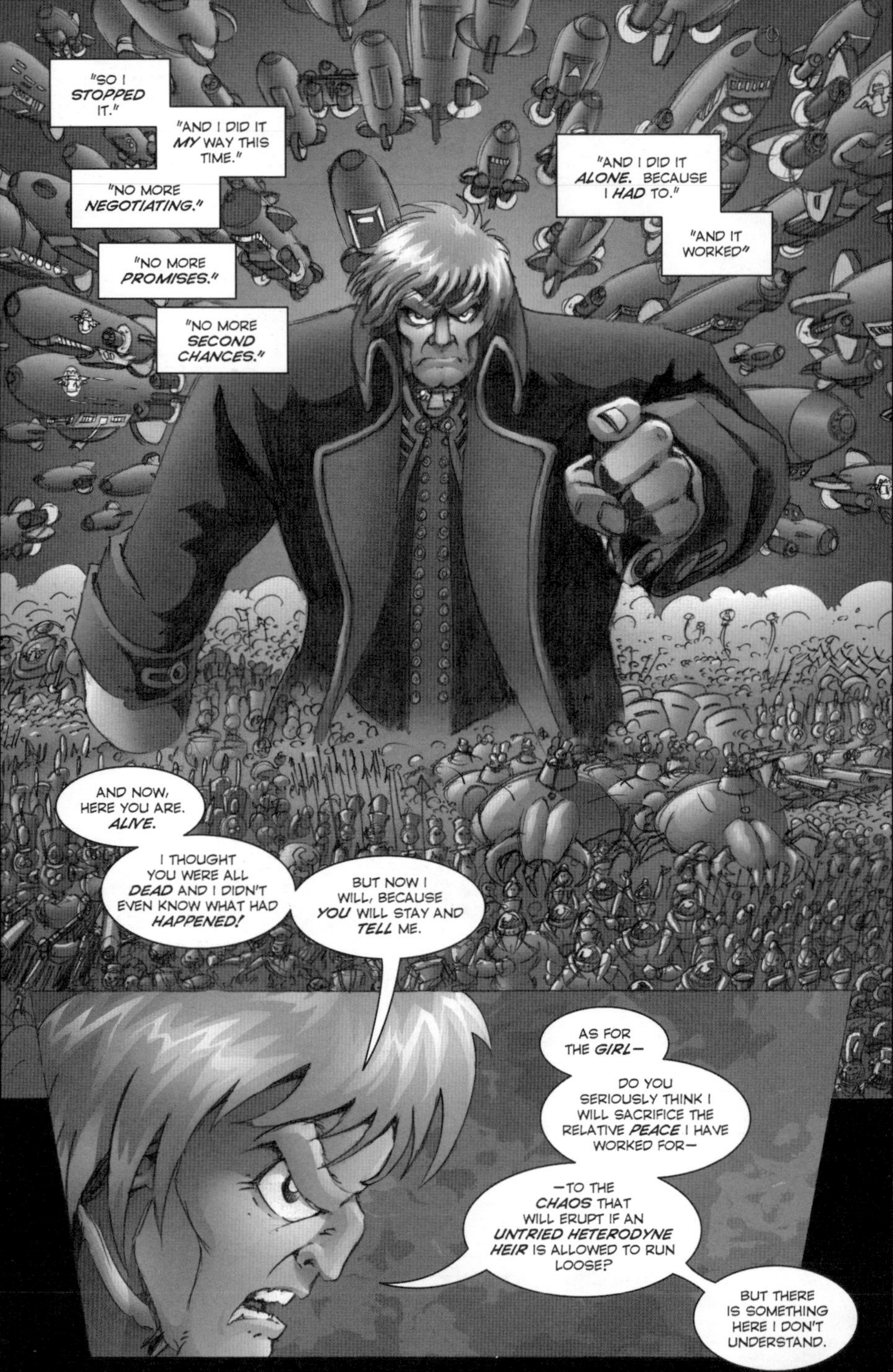
"SO I STOPPED IT."
"AND I DID IT MY WAY THIS TIME."
"NO MORE NEGOTIATING."
"NO MORE PROMISES."
"NO MORE SECOND CHANCES."
"AND I DID IT ALONE. BECAUSE I HAD TO."
"AND IT WORKED"
AND NOW, HERE YOU ARE. ALIVE.
I THOUGHT YOU WERE ALL DEAD AND I DIDN'T EVEN KNOW WHAT HAD HAPPENED!
BUT NOW I WILL, BECAUSE YOU WILL STAY AND TELL ME.
AS FOR THE GIRL—
DO YOU SERIOUSLY THINK I WILL SACRIFICE THE RELATIVE PEACE I HAVE WORKED FOR—
—TO THE CHAOS THAT WILL ERUPT IF AN UNTRIED HETERODYNE HEIR IS ALLOWED TO RUN LOOSE?
BUT THERE IS SOMETHING HERE I DON'T UNDERSTAND.

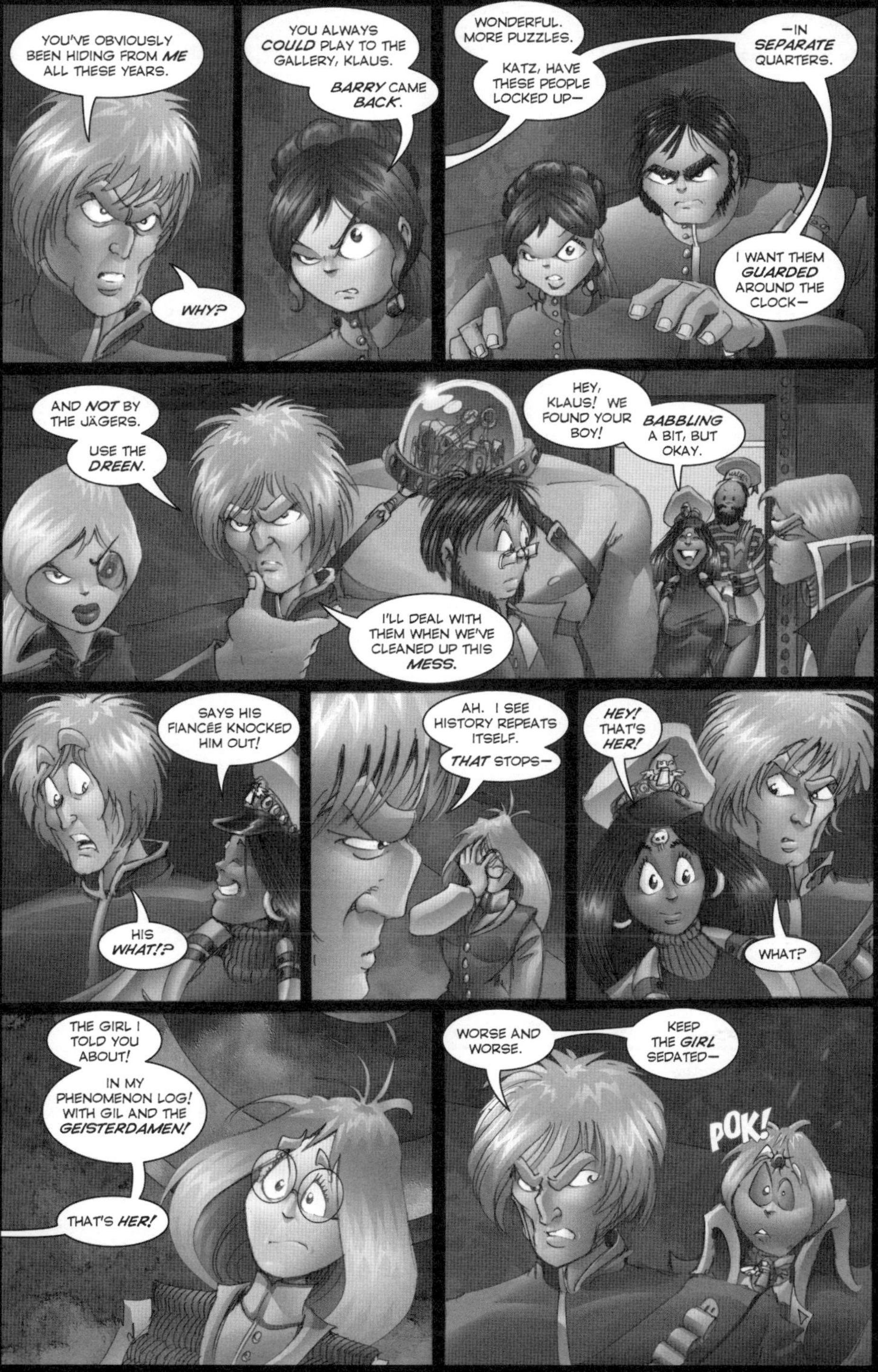
YOU'VE OBVIOUSLY BEEN HIDING FROM ME ALL THESE YEARS.
WHY?
YOU ALWAYS COULD PLAY TO THE GALLERY, KLAUS.
BARRY CAME BACK.
WONDERFUL. MORE PUZZLES.
KATZ, HAVE THESE PEOPLE LOCKED UP—
—IN SEPARATE QUARTERS.
I WANT THEM GUARDED AROUND THE CLOCK—
AND NOT BY THE JÄGERS.
USE THE DREEN.
I'LL DEAL WITH THEM WHEN WE'VE CLEANED UP THIS MESS.
HEY, KLAUS! WE FOUND YOUR BOY!
BABBLING A BIT, BUT OKAY.
SAYS HIS FIANCÉE KNOCKED HIM OUT!
HIS WHAT!?
AH. I SEE HISTORY REPEATS ITSELF.
THAT STOPS—
HEY! THAT'S HER!
WHAT?
THE GIRL I TOLD YOU ABOUT!
IN MY PHENOMENON LOG! WITH GIL AND THE GEISTERDAMEN!
THAT'S HER!
WORSE AND WORSE.
KEEP THE GIRL SEDATED—
POK!

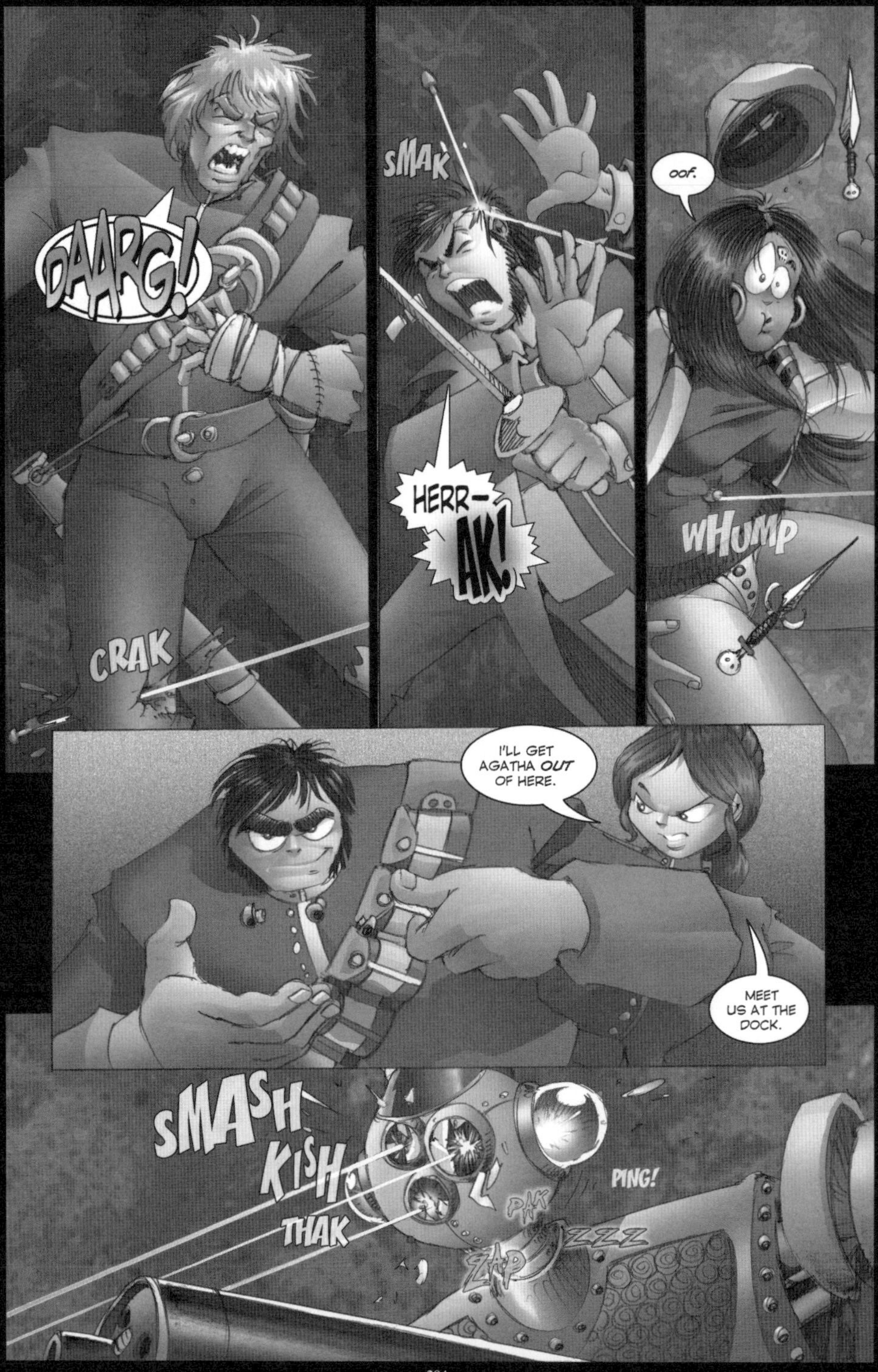
DAARG!
CRAK
SMAK
HERR-AK!
oof.
WHUMP
I'LL GET AGATHA OUT OF HERE.
MEET US AT THE DOCK.
SMASH
KISH
THAK
PING!
PAK
ZZZZ
ZAP

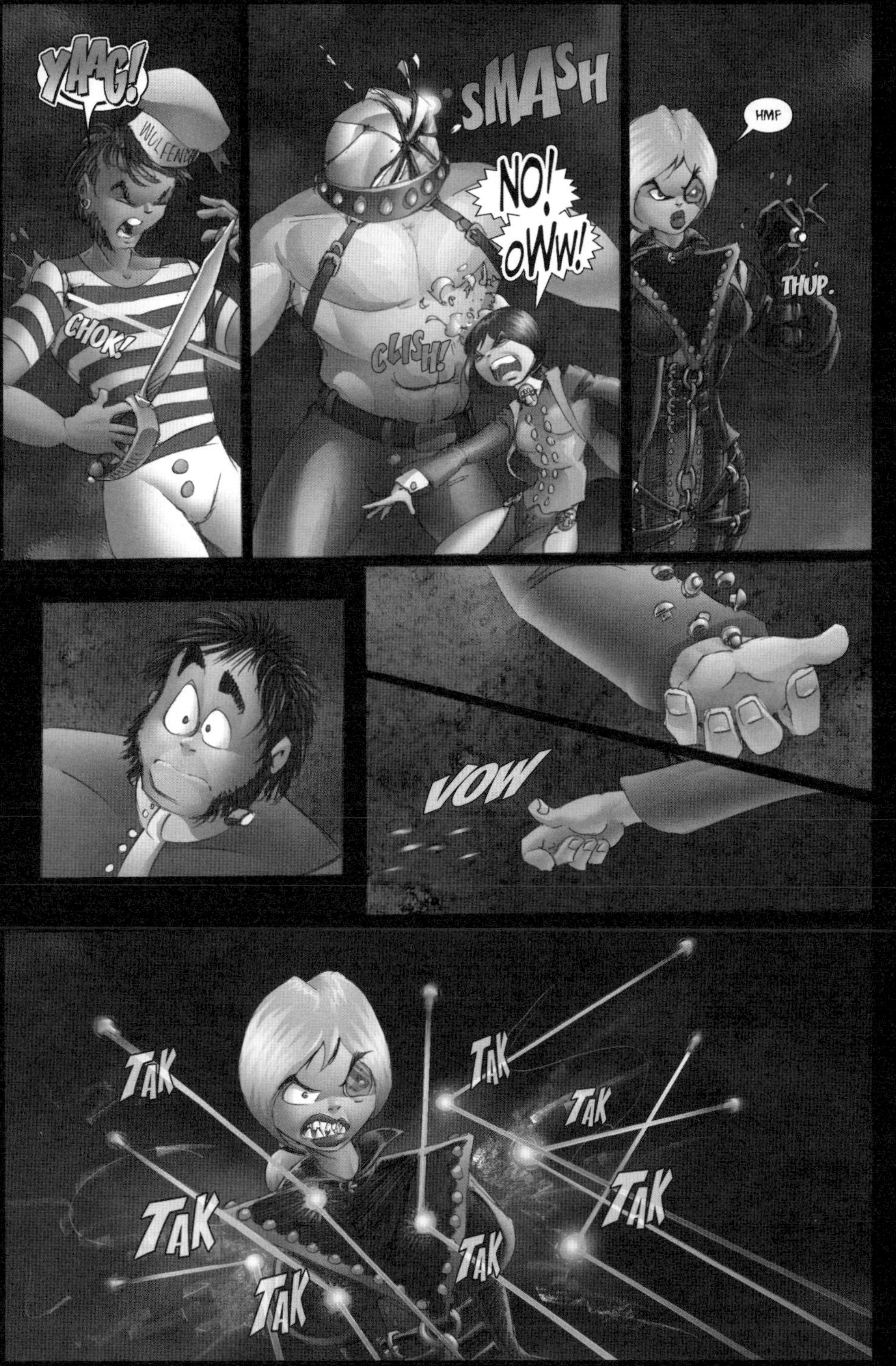
YAAG!
CHOK!
SMASH
NO! OWW!
CLISH!
HMF
THUP.
VOW
TAK
TAK
TAK
TAK
TAK
TAK
TAK

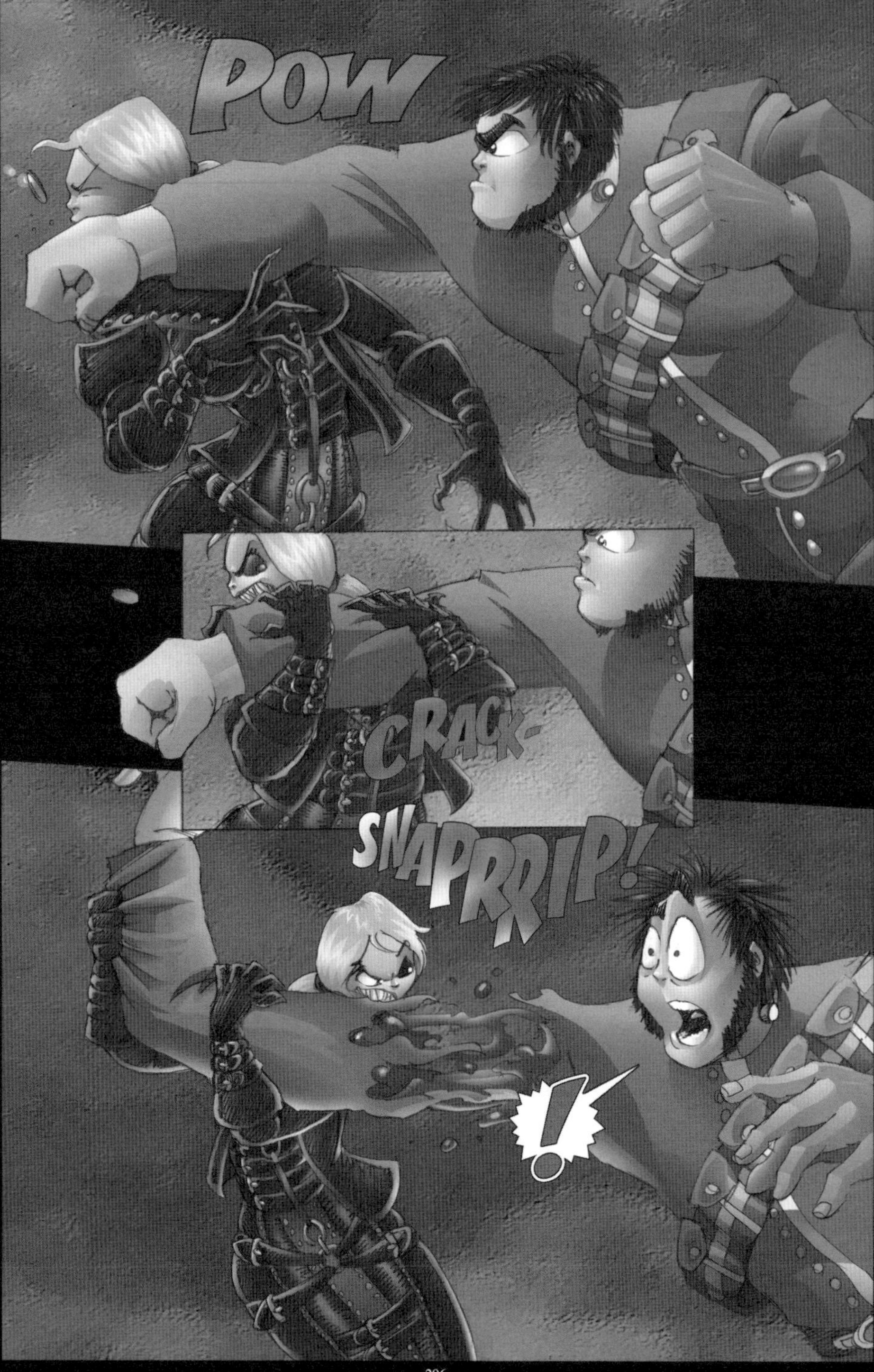
POW
CRACK-
SNAPRRRIP!
!

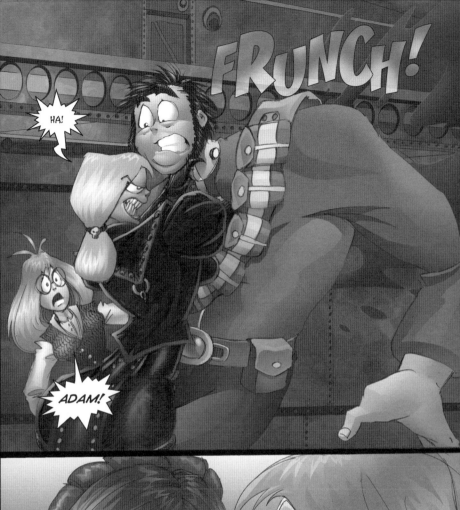

FRUNCH!

HA!

ADAM!

GO. GET TO *CASTLE HETERODYNE.* IT WILL *HELP* YOU.

WHAT?! BUT—

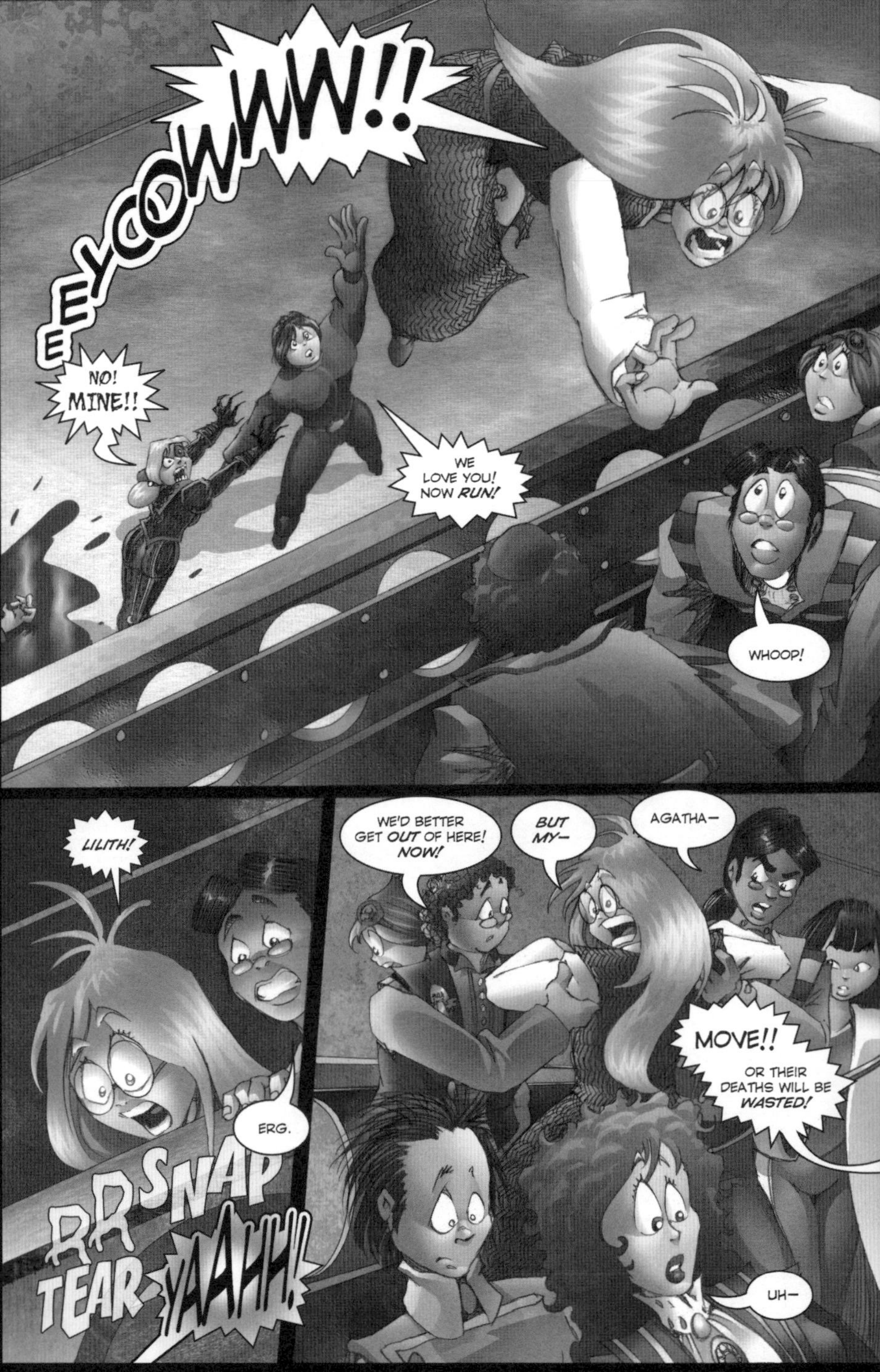
EEYOOWWW!!
NO! MINE!!
WE LOVE YOU! NOW RUN!
WHOOP!
LILITH!
ERG.
RRSNAP
TEAR
YAAHH!
WE'D BETTER GET OUT OF HERE! NOW!
BUT MY—
AGATHA—
MOVE!!
OR THEIR DEATHS WILL BE WASTED!
UH—

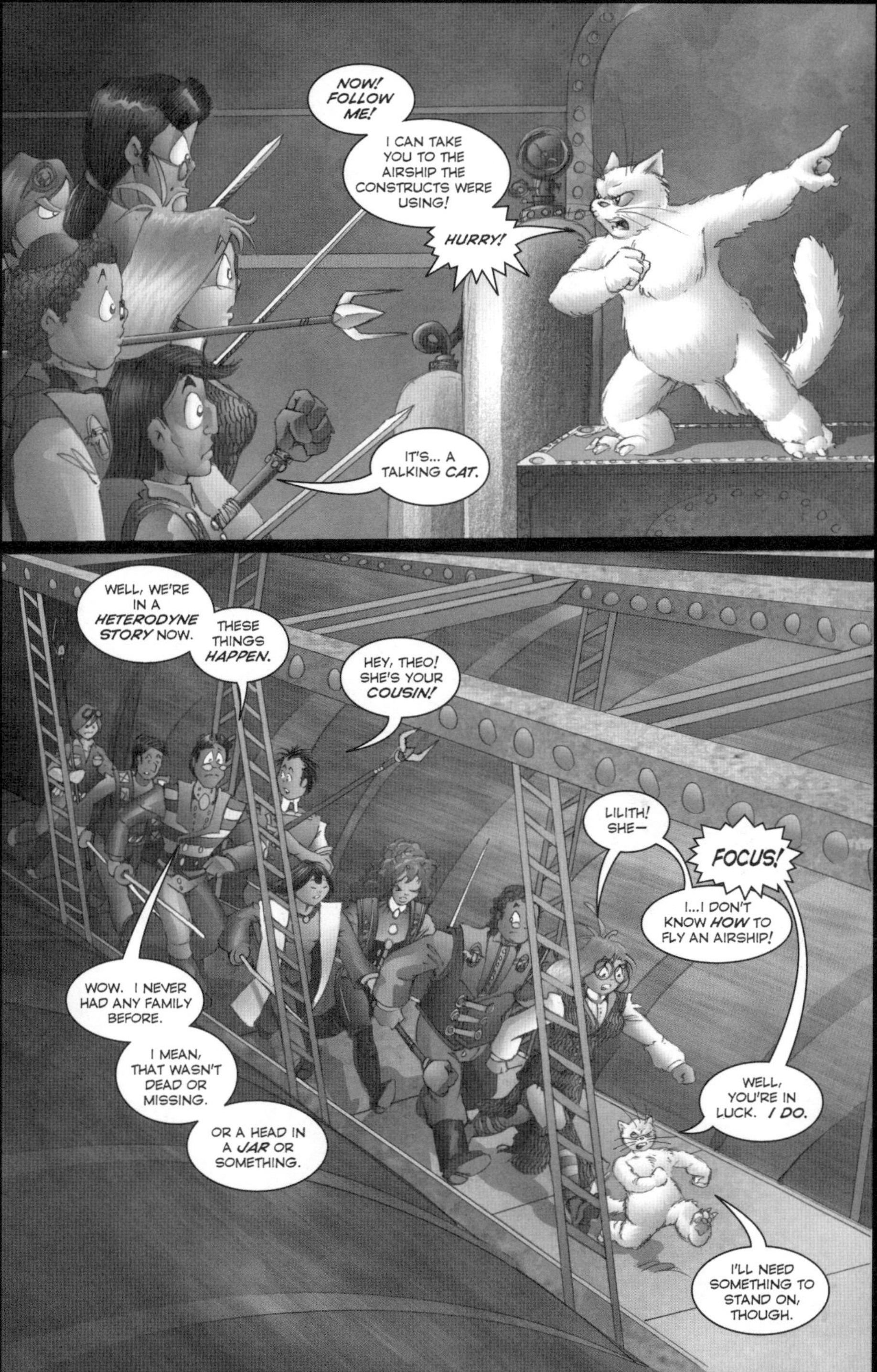

NOW! FOLLOW ME!
I CAN TAKE YOU TO THE AIRSHIP THE CONSTRUCTS WERE USING!
HURRY!
IT'S... A TALKING CAT.
WELL, WE'RE IN A HETERODYNE STORY NOW.
THESE THINGS HAPPEN.
HEY, THEO! SHE'S YOUR COUSIN!
WOW. I NEVER HAD ANY FAMILY BEFORE.
I MEAN, THAT WASN'T DEAD OR MISSING.
OR A HEAD IN A JAR OR SOMETHING.
LILITH! SHE—
FOCUS!
I...I DON'T KNOW HOW TO FLY AN AIRSHIP!
WELL, YOU'RE IN LUCK. I DO.
I'LL NEED SOMETHING TO STAND ON, THOUGH.

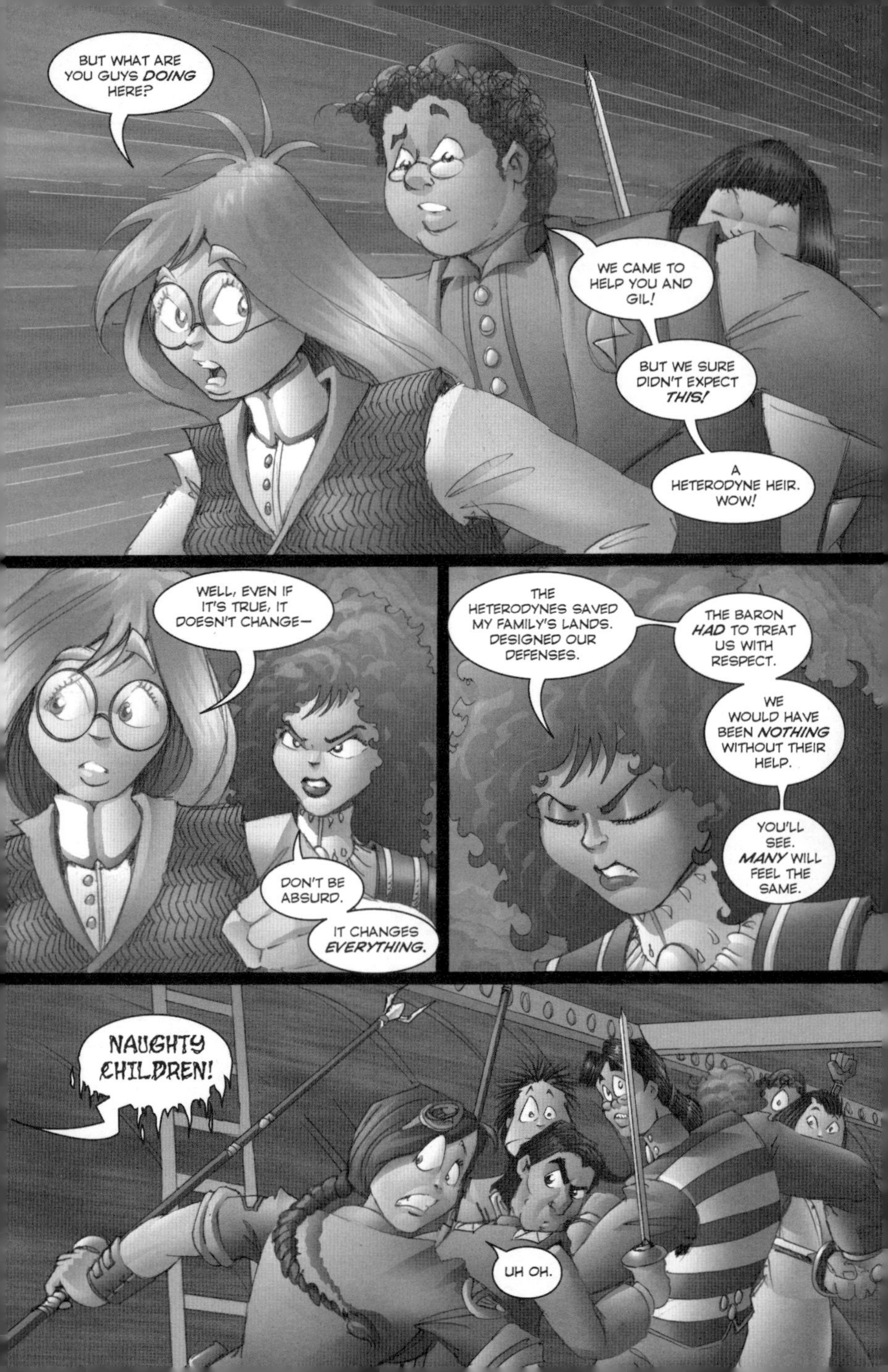

BUT WHAT ARE YOU GUYS DOING HERE?
WE CAME TO HELP YOU AND GIL!
BUT WE SURE DIDN'T EXPECT THIS!
A HETERODYNE HEIR. WOW!
WELL, EVEN IF IT'S TRUE, IT DOESN'T CHANGE—
DON'T BE ABSURD.
IT CHANGES EVERYTHING.
THE HETERODYNES SAVED MY FAMILY'S LANDS. DESIGNED OUR DEFENSES.
THE BARON HAD TO TREAT US WITH RESPECT.
WE WOULD HAVE BEEN NOTHING WITHOUT THEIR HELP.
YOU'LL SEE. MANY WILL FEEL THE SAME.
NAUGHTY CHILDREN!
UH OH.

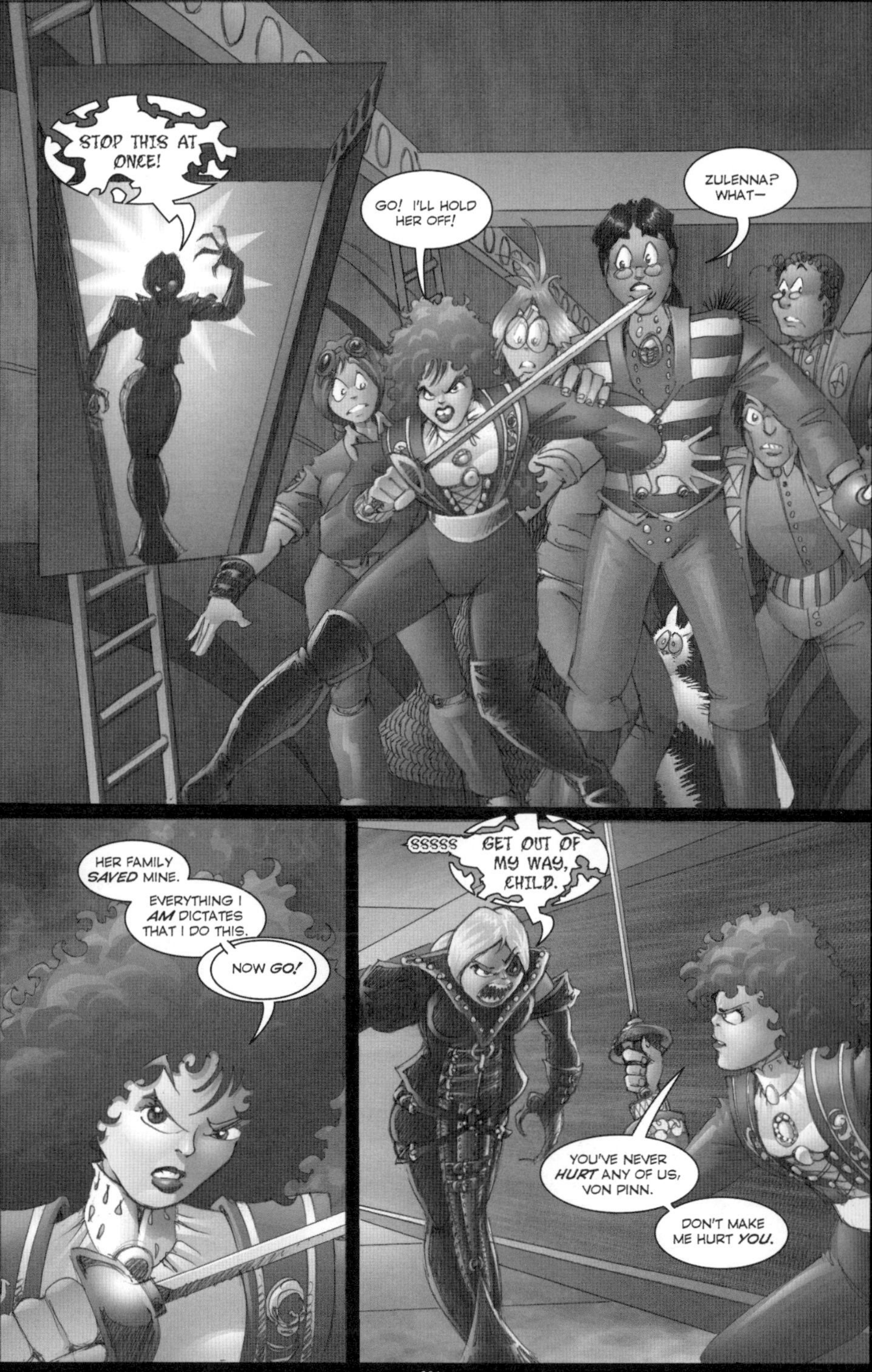

STOP THIS AT ONCE!
GO! I'LL HOLD HER OFF!
ZULENNA? WHAT—
HER FAMILY *SAVED* MINE.
EVERYTHING I *AM* DICTATES THAT I DO THIS.
NOW *GO!*
SSSSS
GET OUT OF MY WAY, CHILD.
YOU'VE NEVER *HURT* ANY OF US, VON PINN.
DON'T MAKE ME HURT *YOU.*

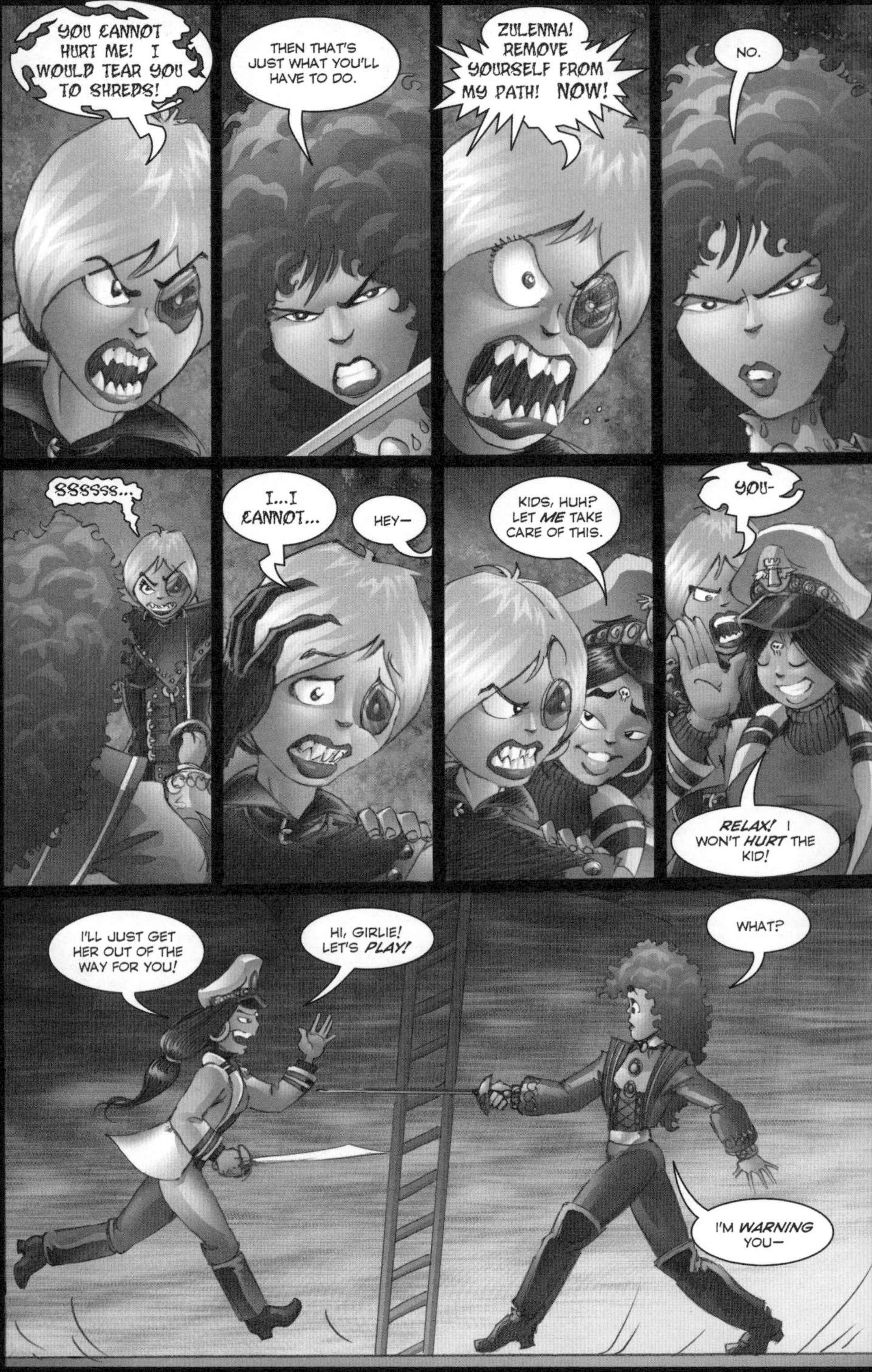
YOU CANNOT HURT ME! I WOULD TEAR YOU TO SHREDS!
THEN THAT'S JUST WHAT YOU'LL HAVE TO DO.
ZULENNA! REMOVE YOURSELF FROM MY PATH! NOW!
NO.
SSSSSS...
I...I CANNOT...
HEY—
KIDS, HUH? LET ME TAKE CARE OF THIS.
YOU-
RELAX! I WON'T HURT THE KID!
I'LL JUST GET HER OUT OF THE WAY FOR YOU!
HI, GIRLIE! LET'S PLAY!
WHAT?
I'M WARNING YOU—

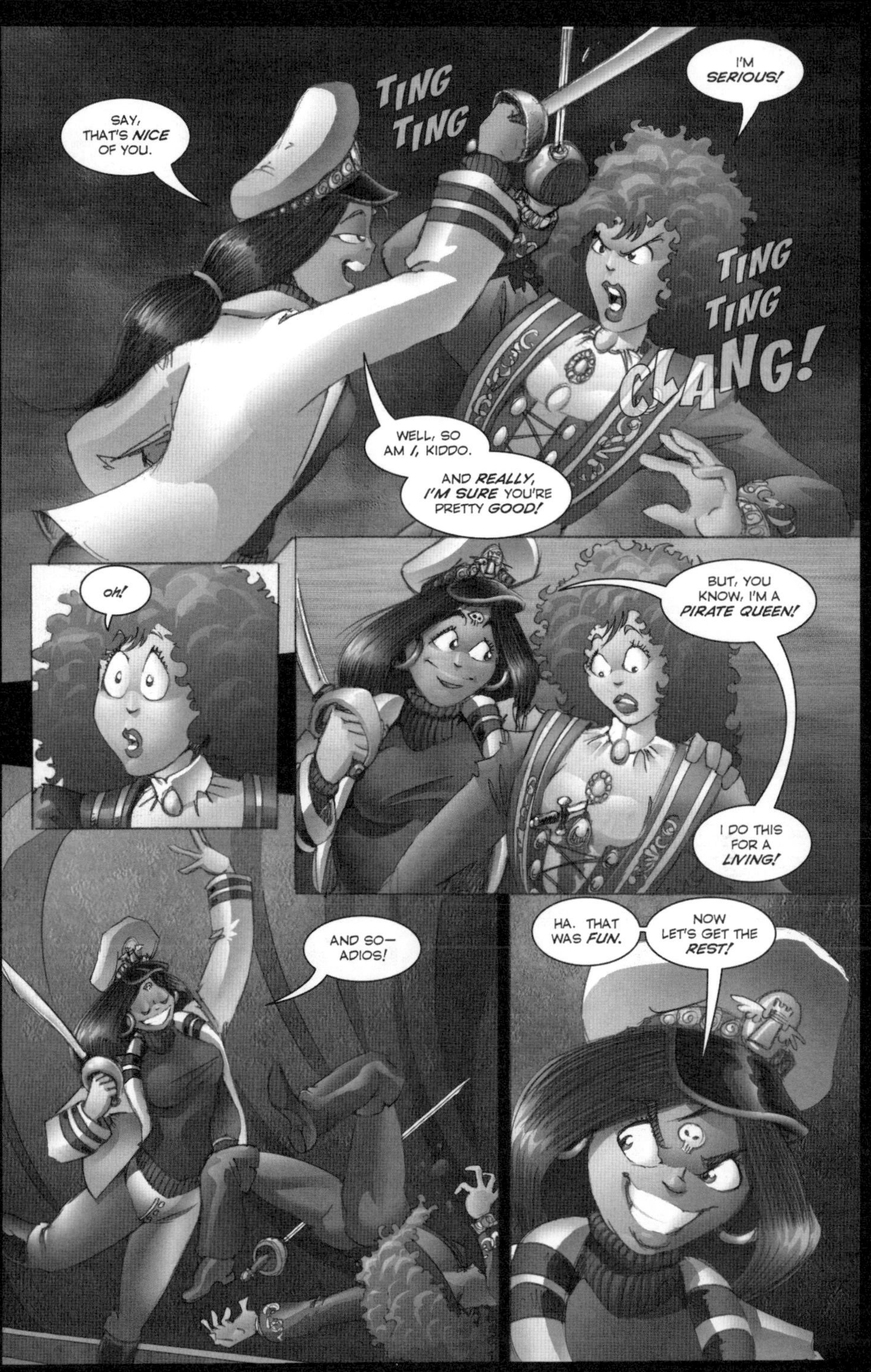
SAY, THAT'S *NICE* OF YOU.
TING TING
I'M *SERIOUS!*
TING TING CLANG!
WELL, SO AM *I*, KIDDO.
AND *REALLY, I'M SURE* YOU'RE PRETTY *GOOD!*
oh!
BUT, YOU KNOW, I'M A *PIRATE QUEEN!*
I DO THIS FOR A *LIVING!*
AND SO— ADIOS!
HA. THAT WAS *FUN*.
NOW LET'S GET THE *REST!*

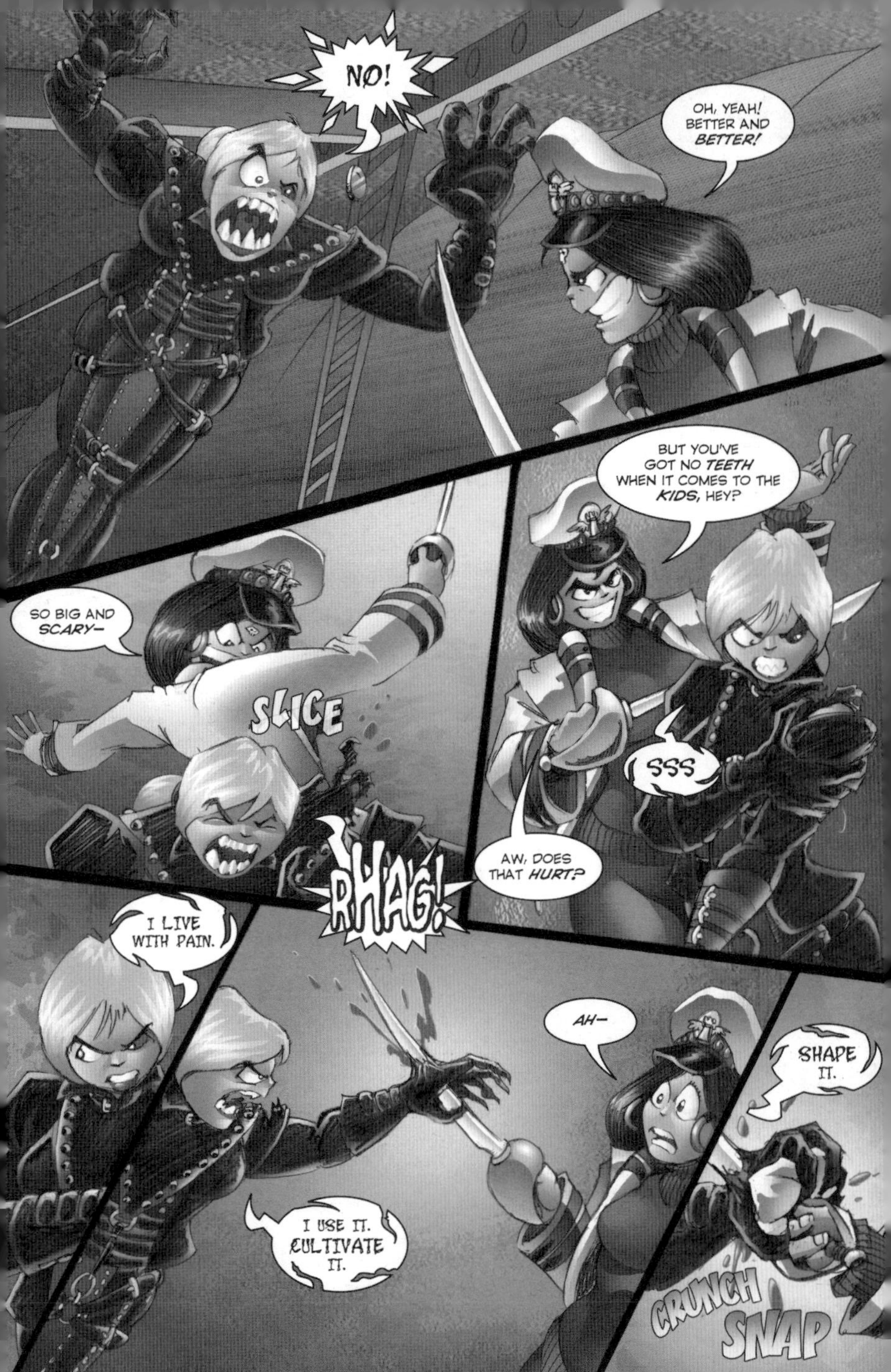
NØ!
OH, YEAH! BETTER AND BETTER!
BUT YOU'VE GOT NO TEETH WHEN IT COMES TO THE KIDS, HEY?
SO BIG AND SCARY—
SLICE
SSS
AW, DOES THAT HURT?
RHAG!
I LIVE WITH PAIN.
I USE IT. CULTIVATE IT.
AH—
SHAPE IT.
CRUNCH
SNAP

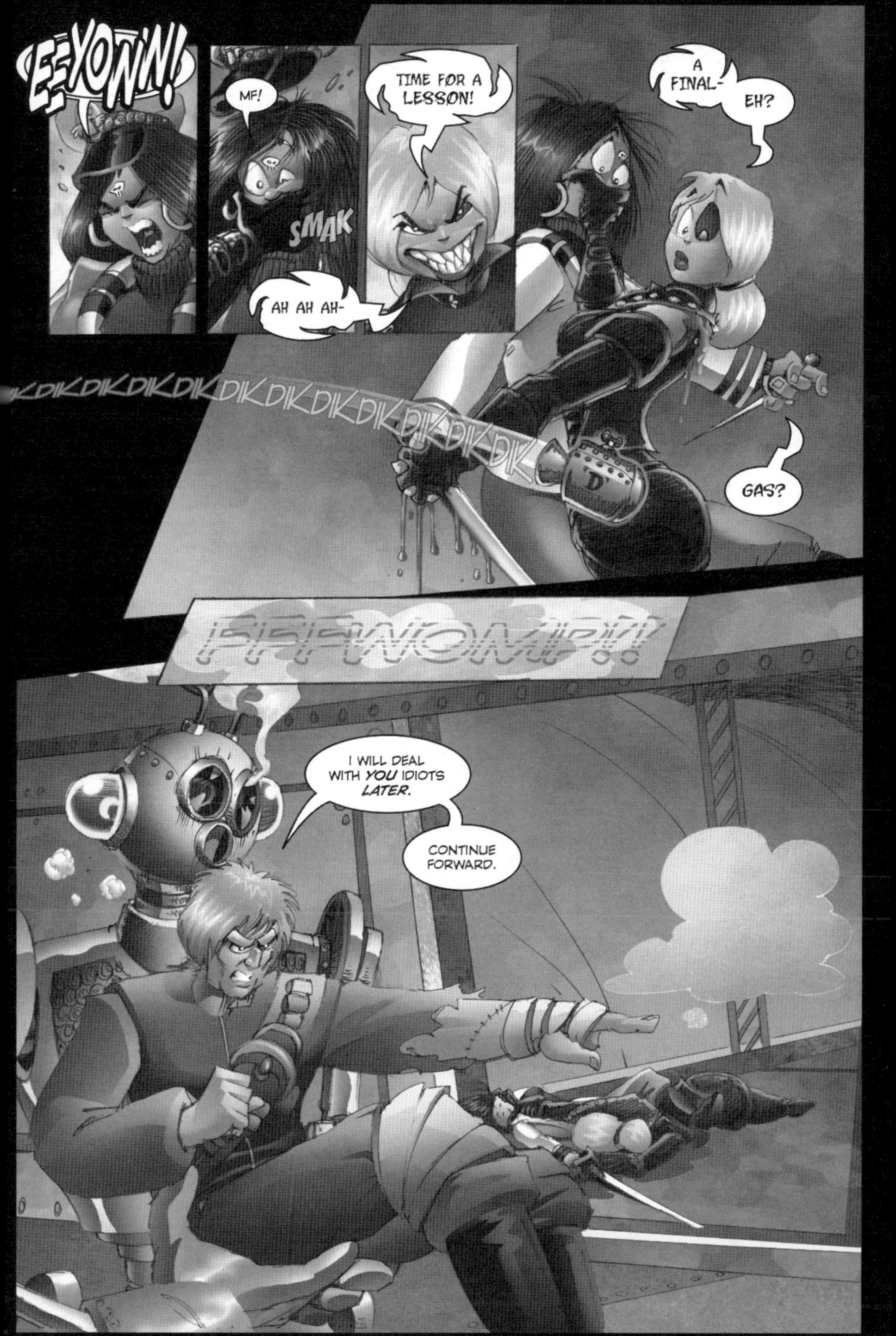
E-EYOWW!
MF!
SMAK
AH AH AH-
TIME FOR A LESSON!
A FINAL-
EH?
DIKDIKDIKDIKDIKDIKDIKDIKDIKDIKDIKDIKDIKDIK
GAS?
I WILL DEAL WITH YOU IDIOTS LATER.
CONTINUE FORWARD.

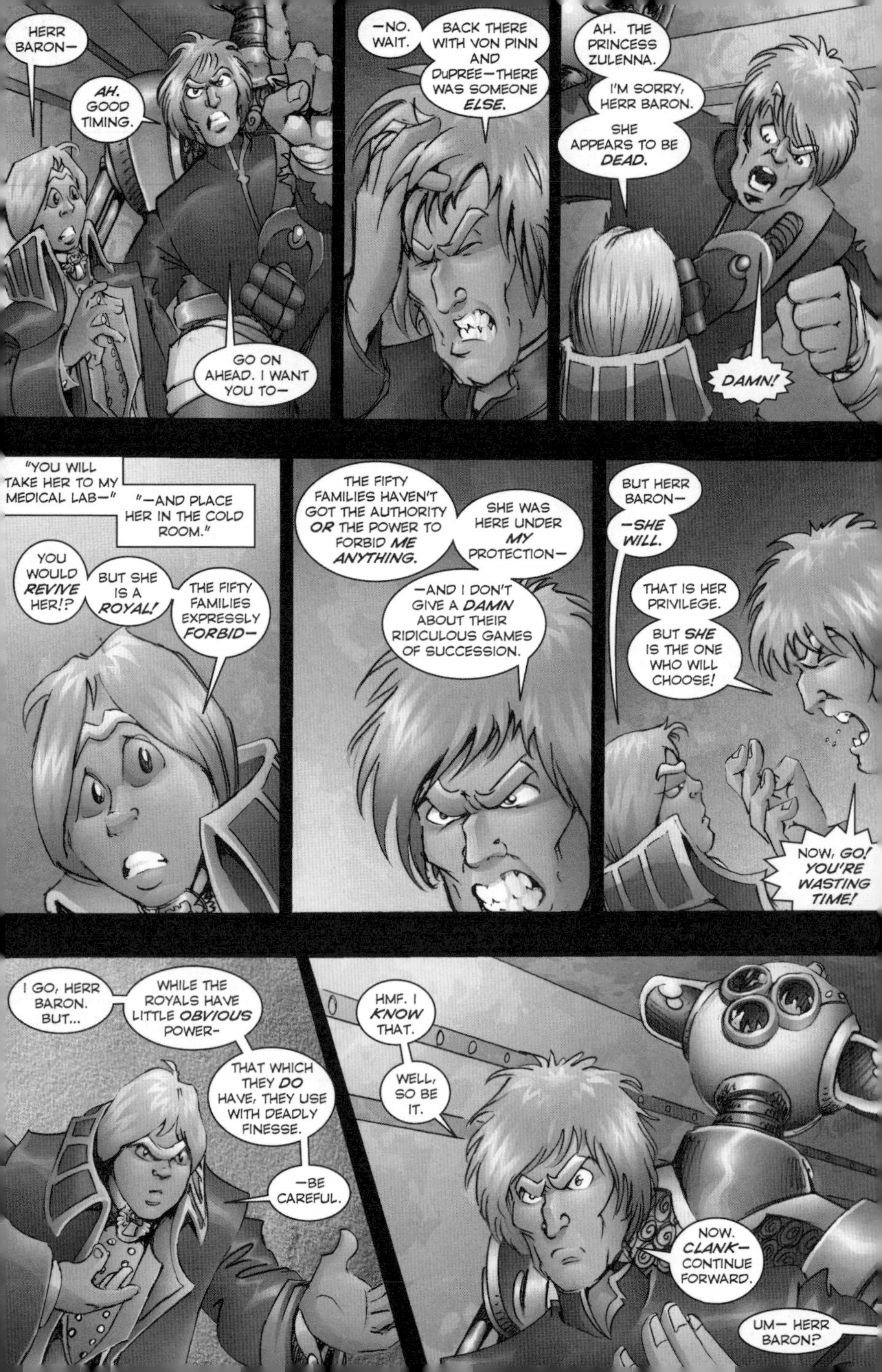
HERR BARON—
AH. GOOD TIMING.
GO ON AHEAD. I WANT YOU TO—
—NO. WAIT.
BACK THERE WITH VON PINN AND DuPREE—THERE WAS SOMEONE ELSE.
AH. THE PRINCESS ZULENNA.
I'M SORRY, HERR BARON.
SHE APPEARS TO BE DEAD.
DAMN!
"YOU WILL TAKE HER TO MY MEDICAL LAB—"
"—AND PLACE HER IN THE COLD ROOM."
YOU WOULD REVIVE HER!?
BUT SHE IS A ROYAL!
THE FIFTY FAMILIES EXPRESSLY FORBID—
THE FIFTY FAMILIES HAVEN'T GOT THE AUTHORITY OR THE POWER TO FORBID ME ANYTHING.
SHE WAS HERE UNDER MY PROTECTION—
—AND I DON'T GIVE A DAMN ABOUT THEIR RIDICULOUS GAMES OF SUCCESSION.
BUT HERR BARON—
—SHE WILL.
THAT IS HER PRIVILEGE.
BUT SHE IS THE ONE WHO WILL CHOOSE!
NOW, GO! YOU'RE WASTING TIME!
I GO, HERR BARON. BUT...
WHILE THE ROYALS HAVE LITTLE OBVIOUS POWER-
THAT WHICH THEY DO HAVE, THEY USE WITH DEADLY FINESSE.
—BE CAREFUL.
HMF. I KNOW THAT.
WELL, SO BE IT.
NOW. CLANK—CONTINUE FORWARD.
UM— HERR BARON?

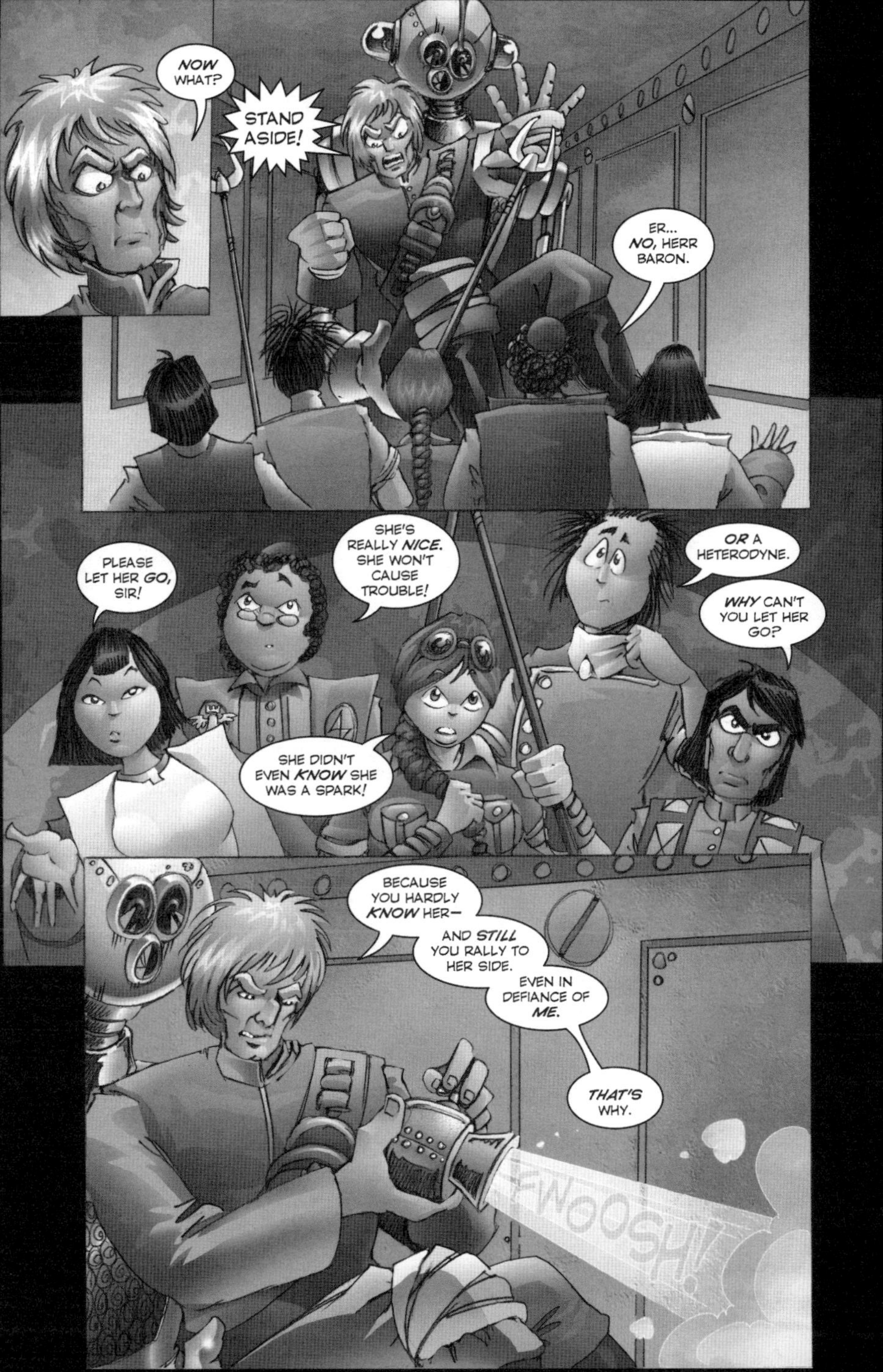
NOW WHAT?
STAND ASIDE!
ER... NO, HERR BARON.
PLEASE LET HER GO, SIR!
SHE'S REALLY NICE. SHE WON'T CAUSE TROUBLE!
OR A HETERODYNE.
WHY CAN'T YOU LET HER GO?
SHE DIDN'T EVEN KNOW SHE WAS A SPARK!
BECAUSE YOU HARDLY KNOW HER—
AND STILL YOU RALLY TO HER SIDE.
EVEN IN DEFIANCE OF ME.
THAT'S WHY.
FWOOSH!!

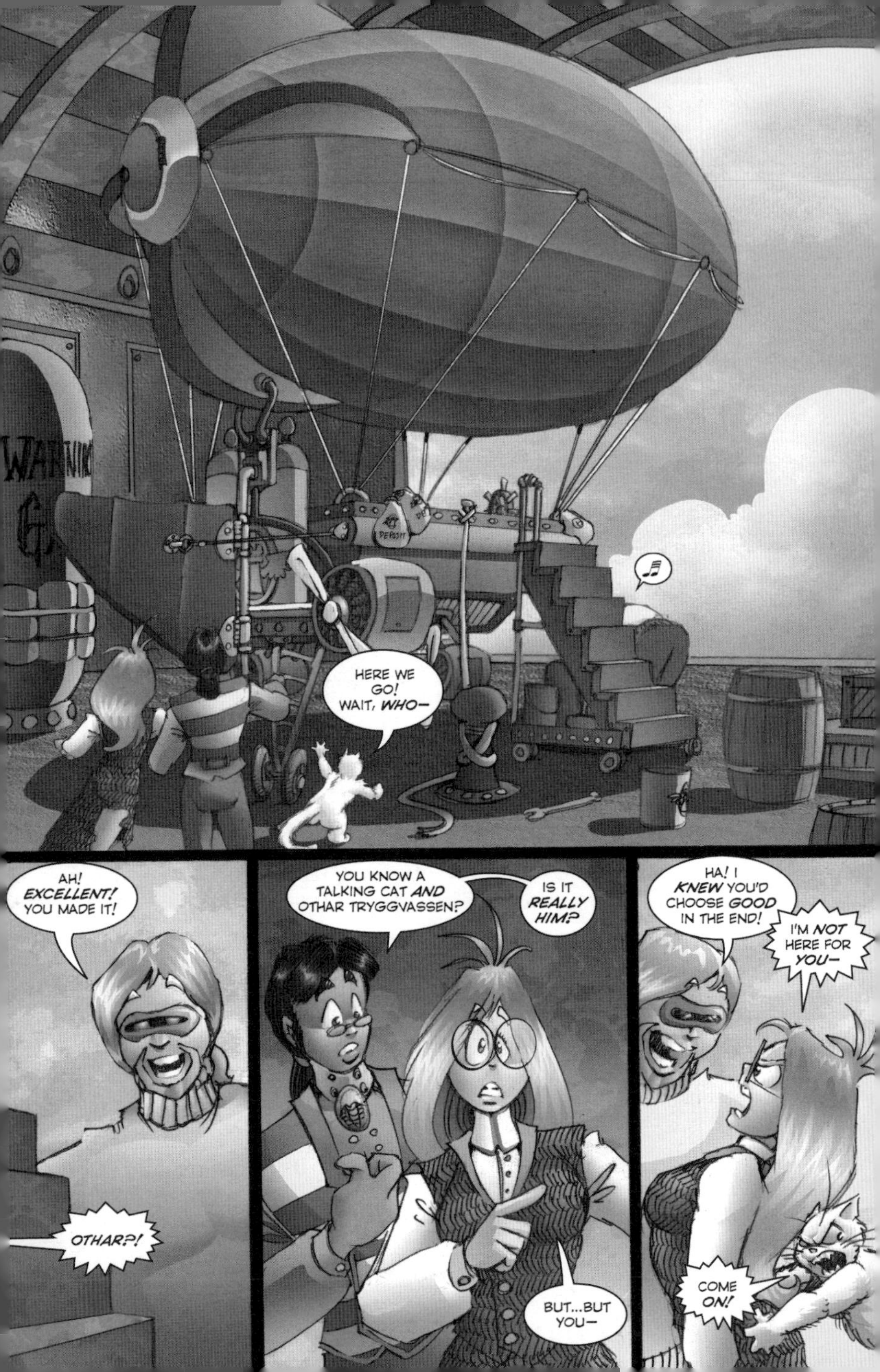
WARNIN
HERE WE GO! WAIT, WHO—
AH! EXCELLENT! YOU MADE IT!
OTHAR?!
YOU KNOW A TALKING CAT AND OTHAR TRYGGVASSEN?
IS IT REALLY HIM?
BUT...BUT YOU—
HA! I KNEW YOU'D CHOOSE GOOD IN THE END!
I'M NOT HERE FOR YOU—
COME ON!

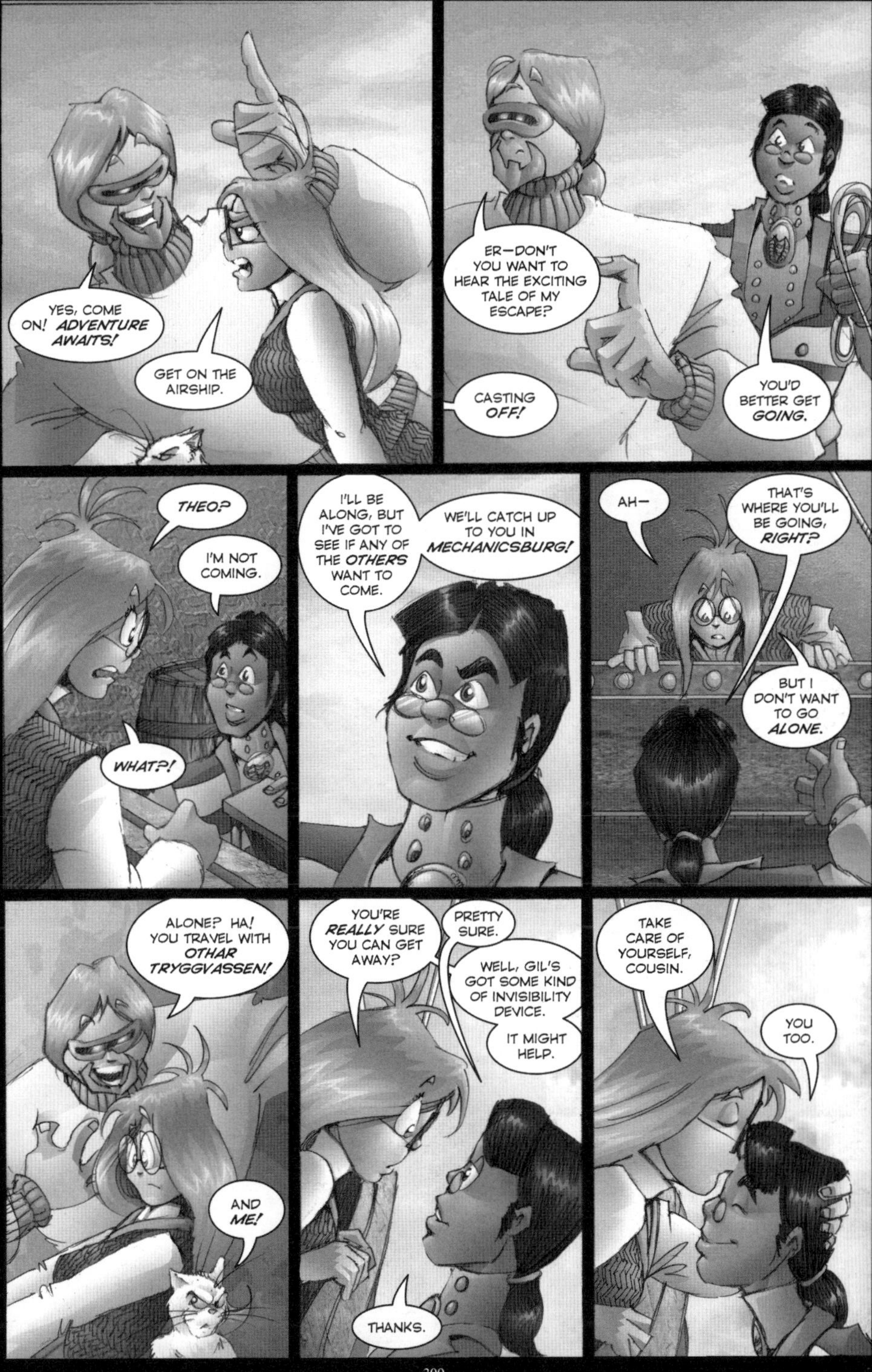

YES, COME ON! ADVENTURE AWAITS!
GET ON THE AIRSHIP.
ER—DON'T YOU WANT TO HEAR THE EXCITING TALE OF MY ESCAPE?
CASTING OFF!
YOU'D BETTER GET GOING.
THEO?
I'M NOT COMING.
WHAT?!
I'LL BE ALONG, BUT I'VE GOT TO SEE IF ANY OF THE OTHERS WANT TO COME.
WE'LL CATCH UP TO YOU IN MECHANICSBURG!
AH—
THAT'S WHERE YOU'LL BE GOING, RIGHT?
BUT I DON'T WANT TO GO ALONE.
ALONE? HA! YOU TRAVEL WITH OTHAR TRYGGVASSEN!
AND ME!
YOU'RE REALLY SURE YOU CAN GET AWAY?
PRETTY SURE.
WELL, GIL'S GOT SOME KIND OF INVISIBILITY DEVICE.
IT MIGHT HELP.
THANKS.
TAKE CARE OF YOURSELF, COUSIN.
YOU TOO.

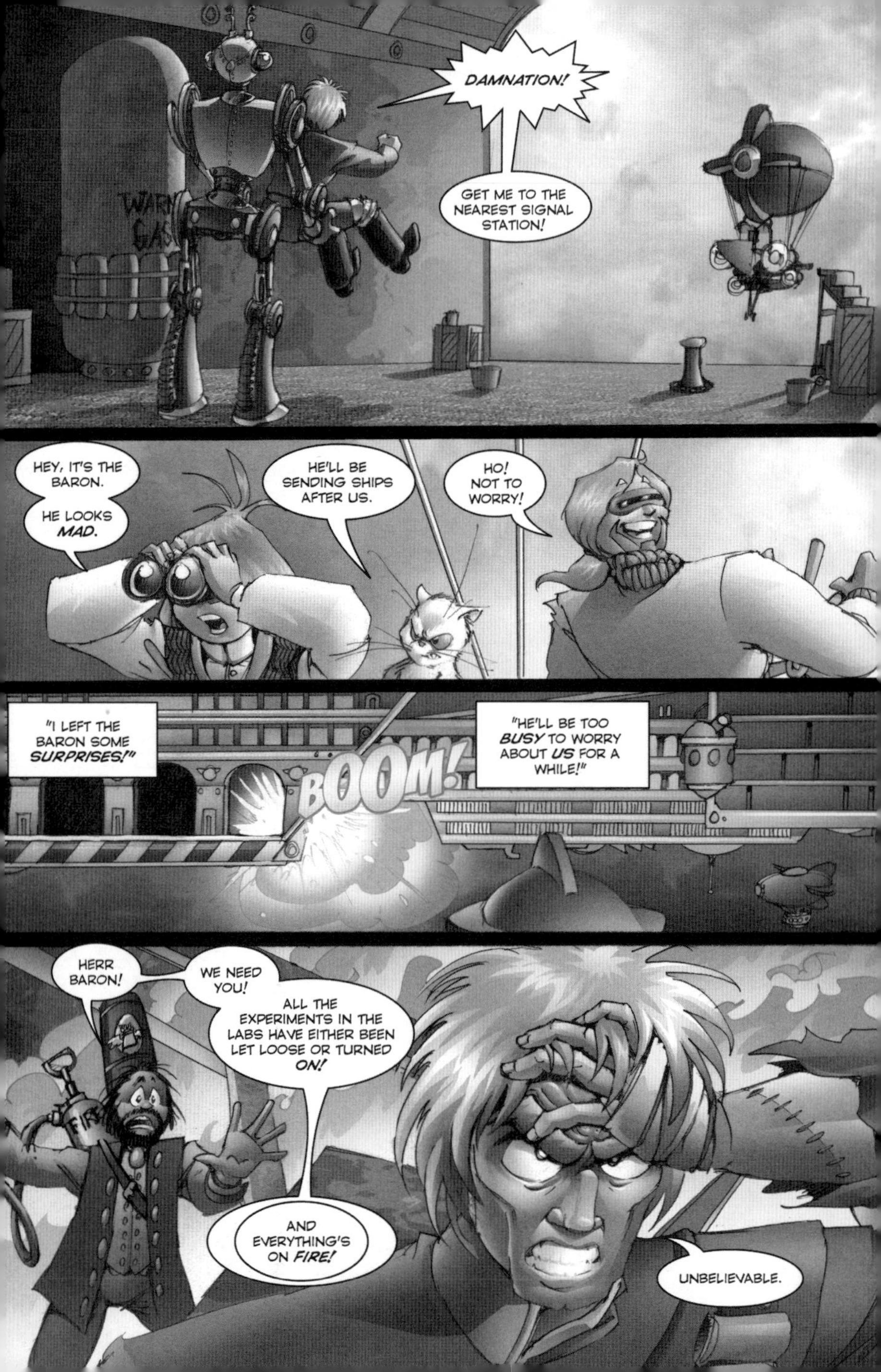
DAMNATION!
GET ME TO THE NEAREST SIGNAL STATION!
HEY, IT'S THE BARON.
HE LOOKS MAD.
HE'LL BE SENDING SHIPS AFTER US.
HO! NOT TO WORRY!
"I LEFT THE BARON SOME SURPRISES!"
BOOM!
"HE'LL BE TOO BUSY TO WORRY ABOUT US FOR A WHILE!"
HERR BARON!
WE NEED YOU!
ALL THE EXPERIMENTS IN THE LABS HAVE EITHER BEEN LET LOOSE OR TURNED ON!
AND EVERYTHING'S ON FIRE!
UNBELIEVABLE.

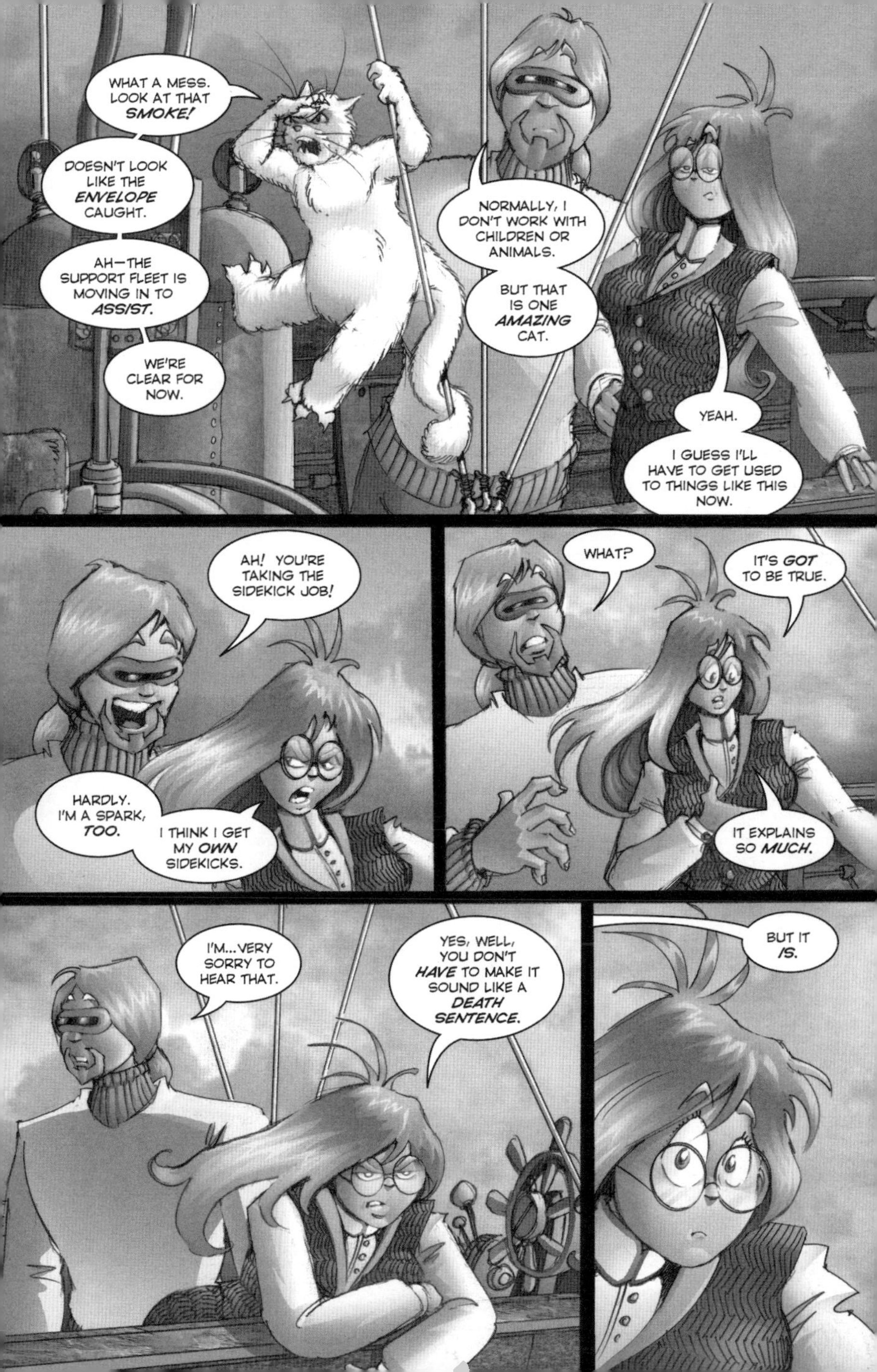
WHAT A MESS. LOOK AT THAT *SMOKE!*
DOESN'T LOOK LIKE THE *ENVELOPE* CAUGHT.
AH—THE SUPPORT FLEET IS MOVING IN TO *ASSIST*.
WE'RE CLEAR FOR NOW.
NORMALLY, I DON'T WORK WITH CHILDREN OR ANIMALS.
BUT THAT IS ONE *AMAZING* CAT.
YEAH.
I GUESS I'LL HAVE TO GET USED TO THINGS LIKE THIS NOW.
AH! YOU'RE TAKING THE SIDEKICK JOB!
HARDLY. I'M A SPARK, *TOO*.
I THINK I GET MY *OWN* SIDEKICKS.
WHAT?
IT'S *GOT* TO BE TRUE.
IT EXPLAINS SO *MUCH*.
I'M...VERY SORRY TO HEAR THAT.
YES, WELL, YOU DON'T *HAVE* TO MAKE IT SOUND LIKE A *DEATH SENTENCE*.
BUT IT *IS*.

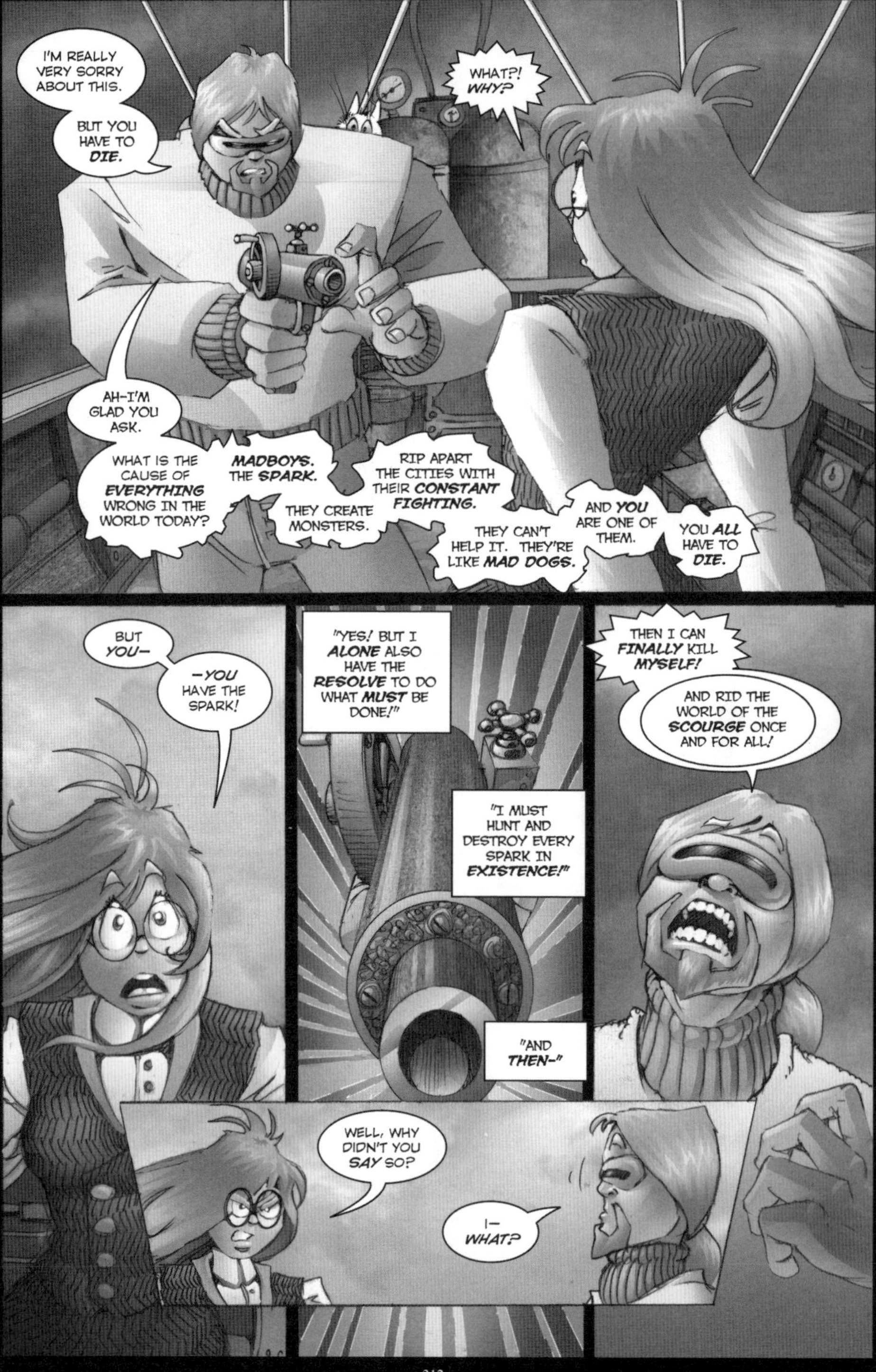
I'M REALLY VERY SORRY ABOUT THIS.
BUT YOU HAVE TO DIE.
WHAT?! WHY?
AH-I'M GLAD YOU ASK.
WHAT IS THE CAUSE OF EVERYTHING WRONG IN THE WORLD TODAY?
MADBOYS. THE SPARK.
THEY CREATE MONSTERS.
RIP APART THE CITIES WITH THEIR CONSTANT FIGHTING.
THEY CAN'T HELP IT. THEY'RE LIKE MAD DOGS.
AND YOU ARE ONE OF THEM.
YOU ALL HAVE TO DIE.
BUT YOU—
—YOU HAVE THE SPARK!
"YES! BUT I ALONE ALSO HAVE THE RESOLVE TO DO WHAT MUST BE DONE!"
"I MUST HUNT AND DESTROY EVERY SPARK IN EXISTENCE!"
"AND THEN-"
THEN I CAN FINALLY KILL MYSELF!
AND RID THE WORLD OF THE SCOURGE ONCE AND FOR ALL!
WELL, WHY DIDN'T YOU SAY SO?
I— WHAT?

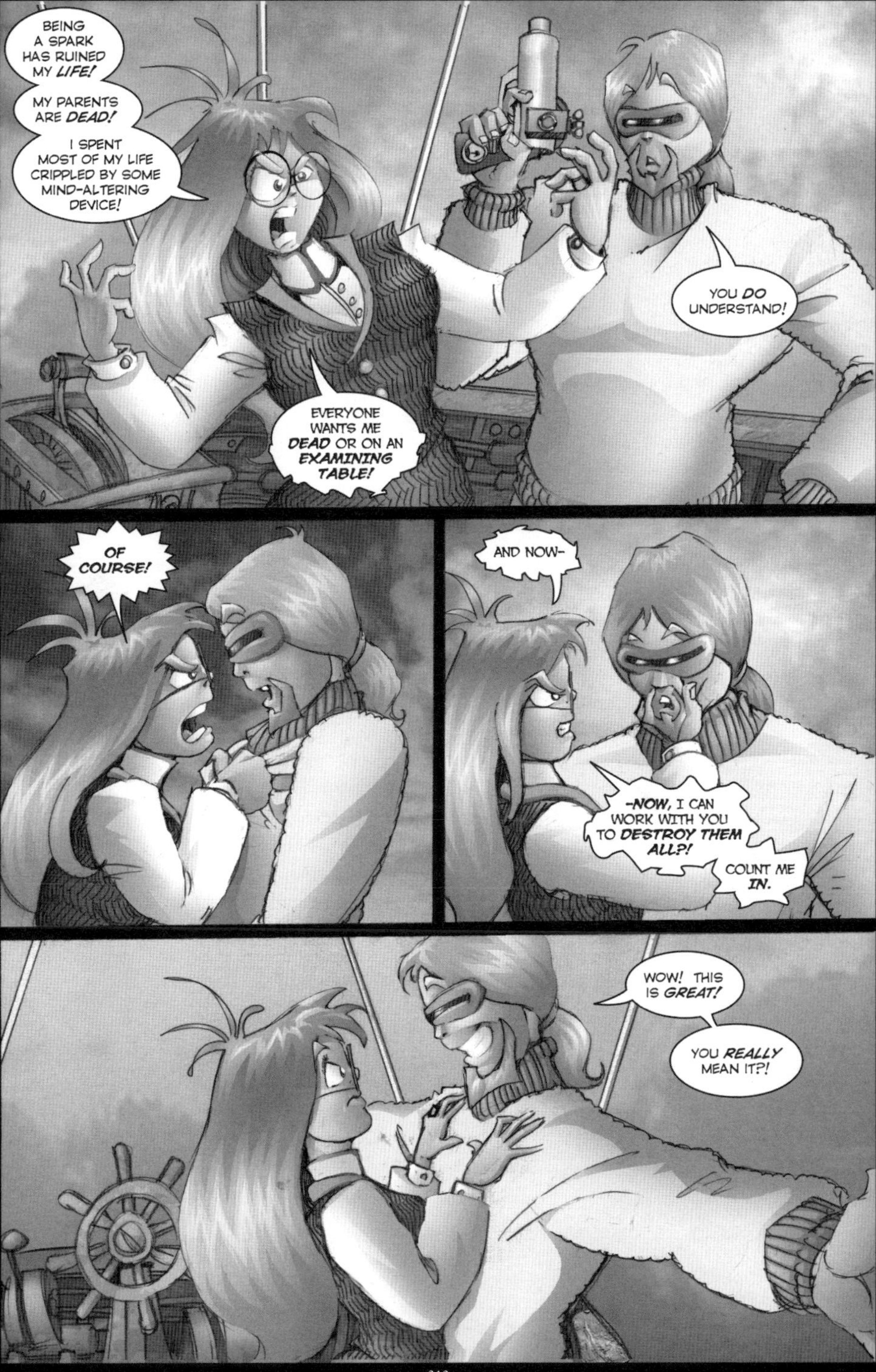
BEING A SPARK HAS RUINED MY *LIFE!*
MY PARENTS ARE *DEAD!*
I SPENT MOST OF MY LIFE CRIPPLED BY SOME MIND-ALTERING DEVICE!
EVERYONE WANTS ME *DEAD* OR ON AN *EXAMINING TABLE!*
YOU *DO* UNDERSTAND!
OF COURSE!
AND NOW-
-NOW, I CAN WORK WITH YOU TO *DESTROY THEM ALL?!*
COUNT ME *IN.*
WOW! THIS IS *GREAT!*
YOU *REALLY* MEAN IT?!

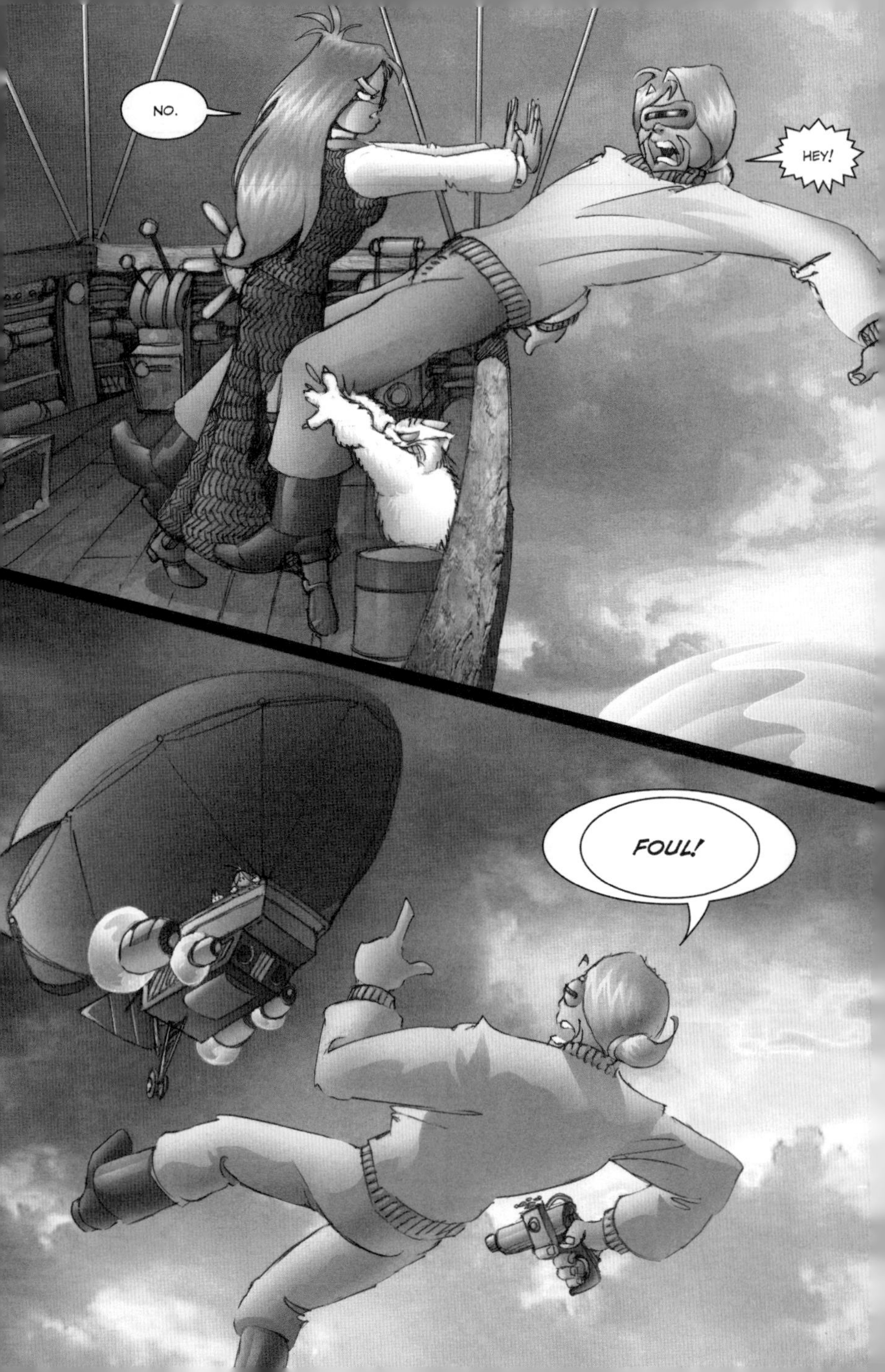
NO.
HEY!
FOUL!

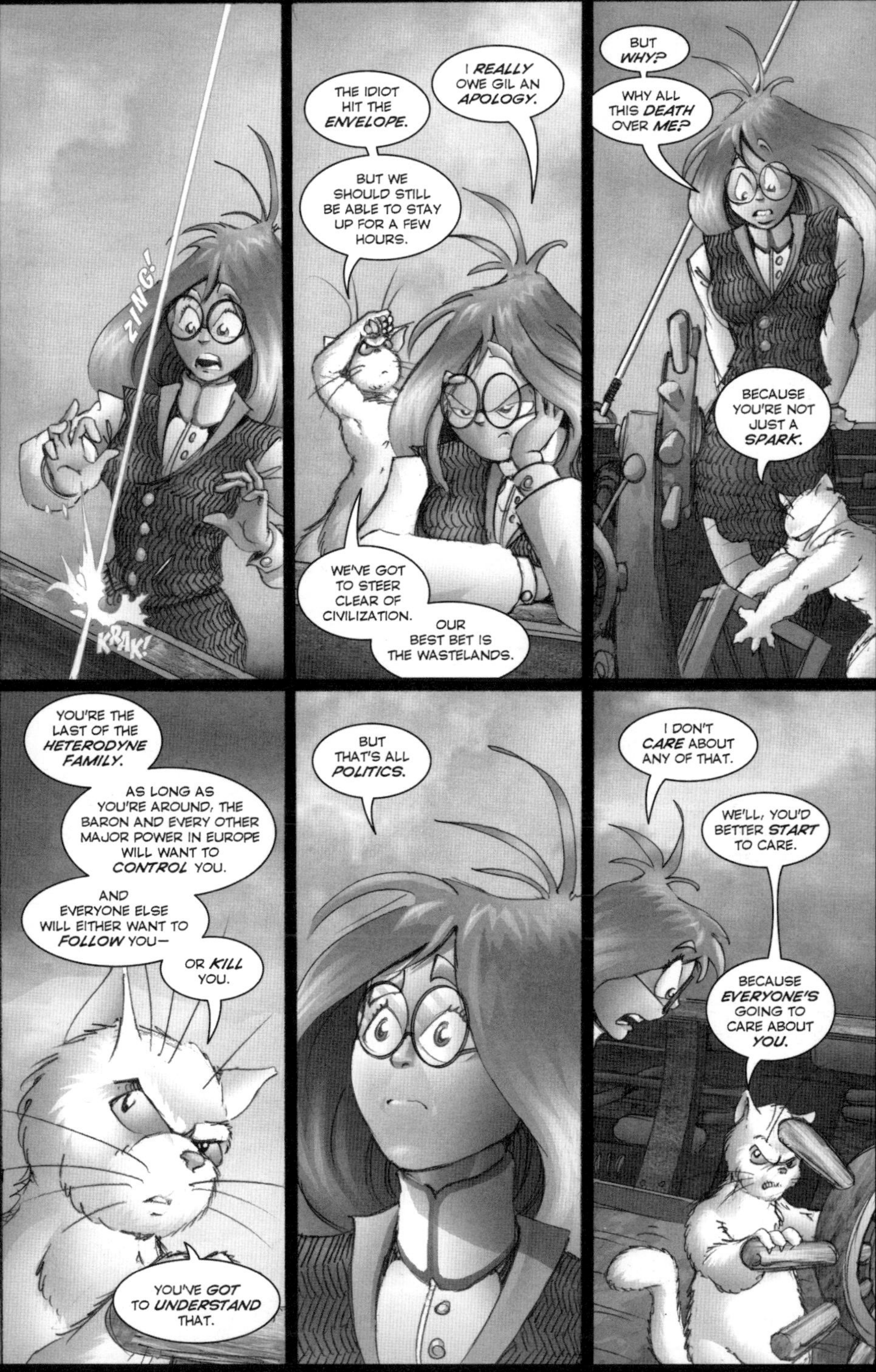
ZING!
KRAK!
THE IDIOT HIT THE ENVELOPE.
I REALLY OWE GIL AN APOLOGY.
BUT WE SHOULD STILL BE ABLE TO STAY UP FOR A FEW HOURS.
WE'VE GOT TO STEER CLEAR OF CIVILIZATION.
OUR BEST BET IS THE WASTELANDS.
BUT WHY?
WHY ALL THIS DEATH OVER ME?
BECAUSE YOU'RE NOT JUST A SPARK.
YOU'RE THE LAST OF THE HETERODYNE FAMILY.
AS LONG AS YOU'RE AROUND, THE BARON AND EVERY OTHER MAJOR POWER IN EUROPE WILL WANT TO CONTROL YOU.
AND EVERYONE ELSE WILL EITHER WANT TO FOLLOW YOU—
OR KILL YOU.
YOU'VE GOT TO UNDERSTAND THAT.
BUT THAT'S ALL POLITICS.
I DON'T CARE ABOUT ANY OF THAT.
WE'LL, YOU'D BETTER START TO CARE.
BECAUSE EVERYONE'S GOING TO CARE ABOUT YOU.

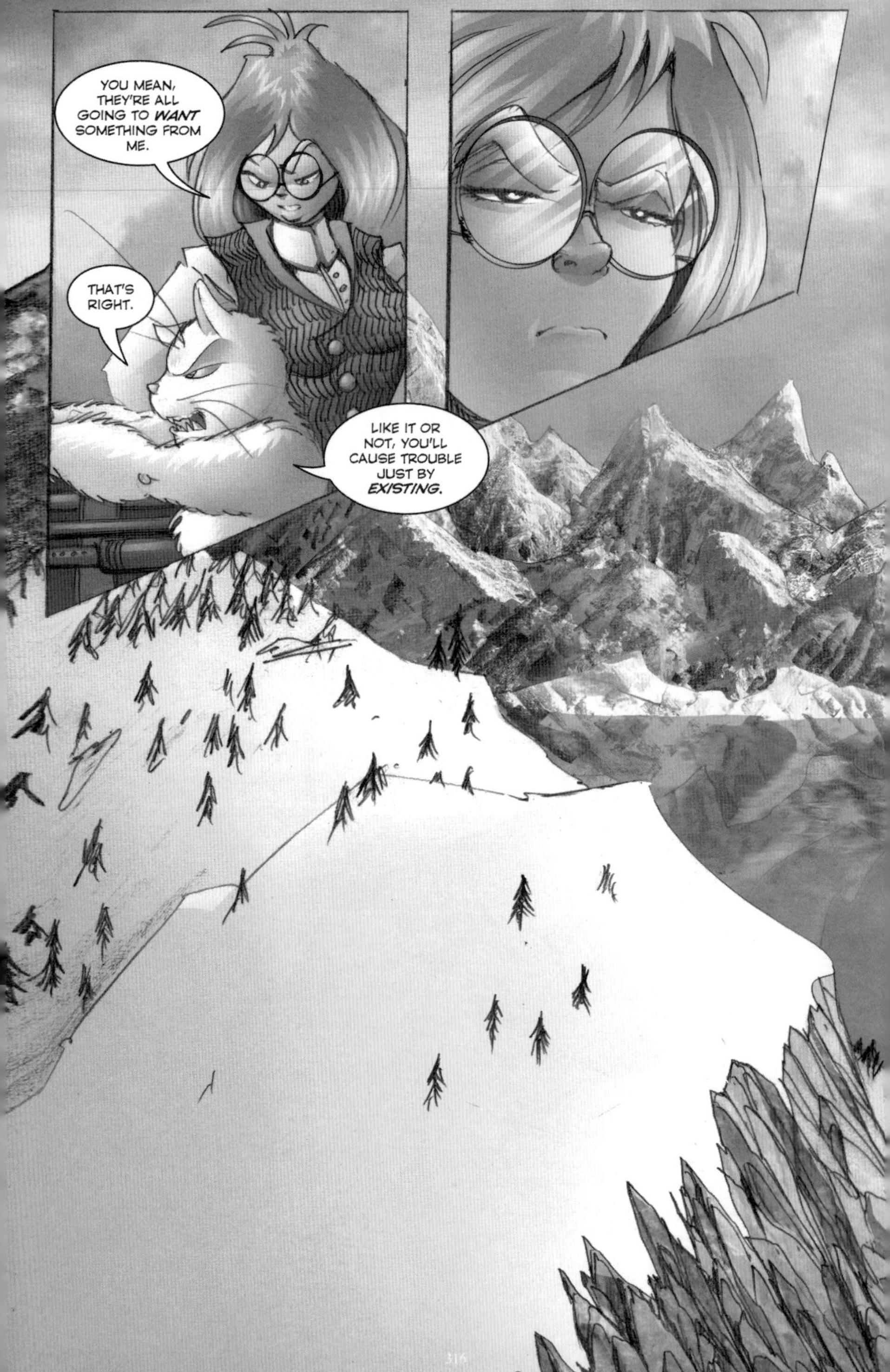
YOU MEAN, THEY'RE ALL GOING TO WANT SOMETHING FROM ME.
THAT'S RIGHT.
LIKE IT OR NOT, YOU'LL CAUSE TROUBLE JUST BY EXISTING.

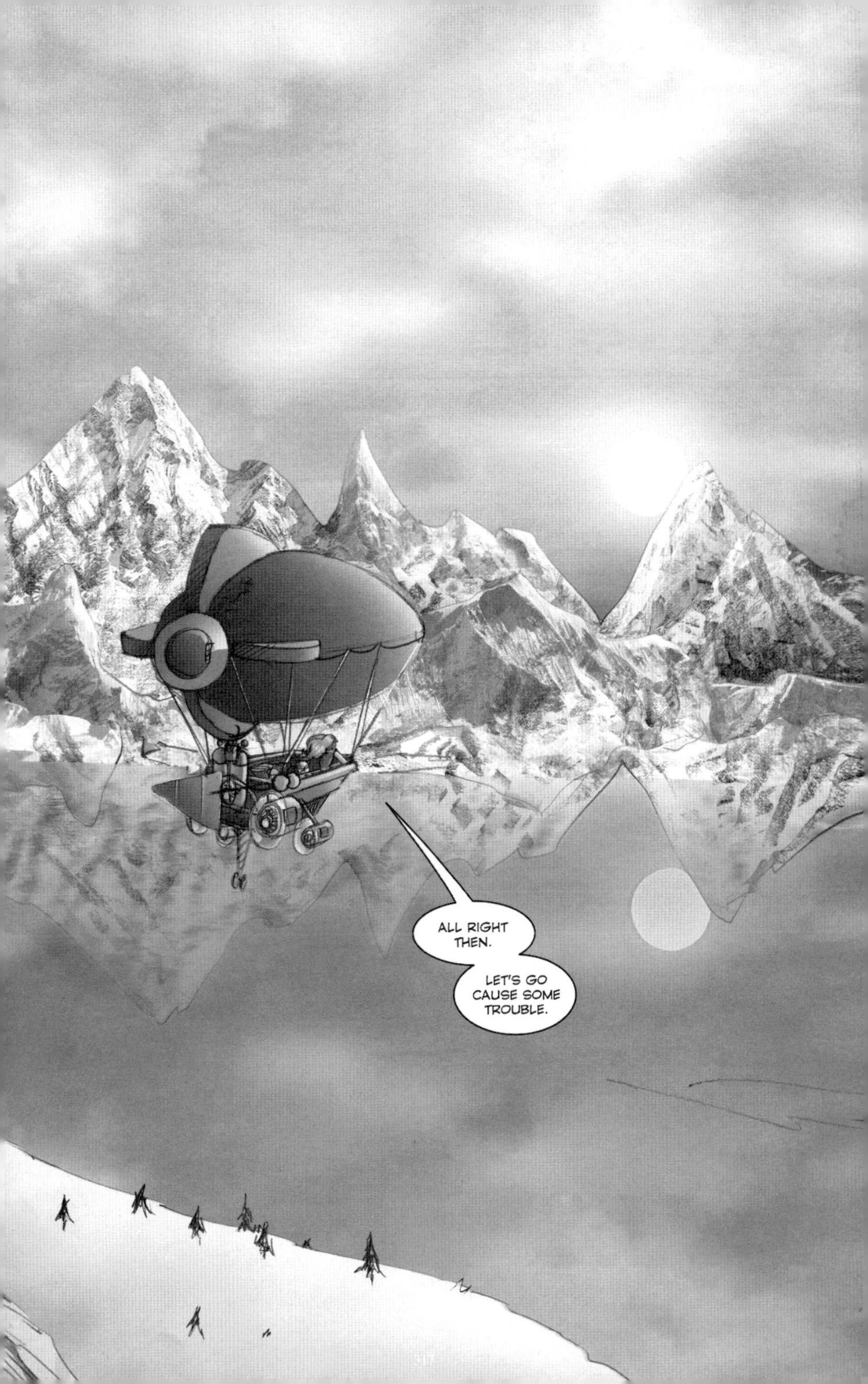
ALL RIGHT THEN.
LET'S GO CAUSE SOME TROUBLE.

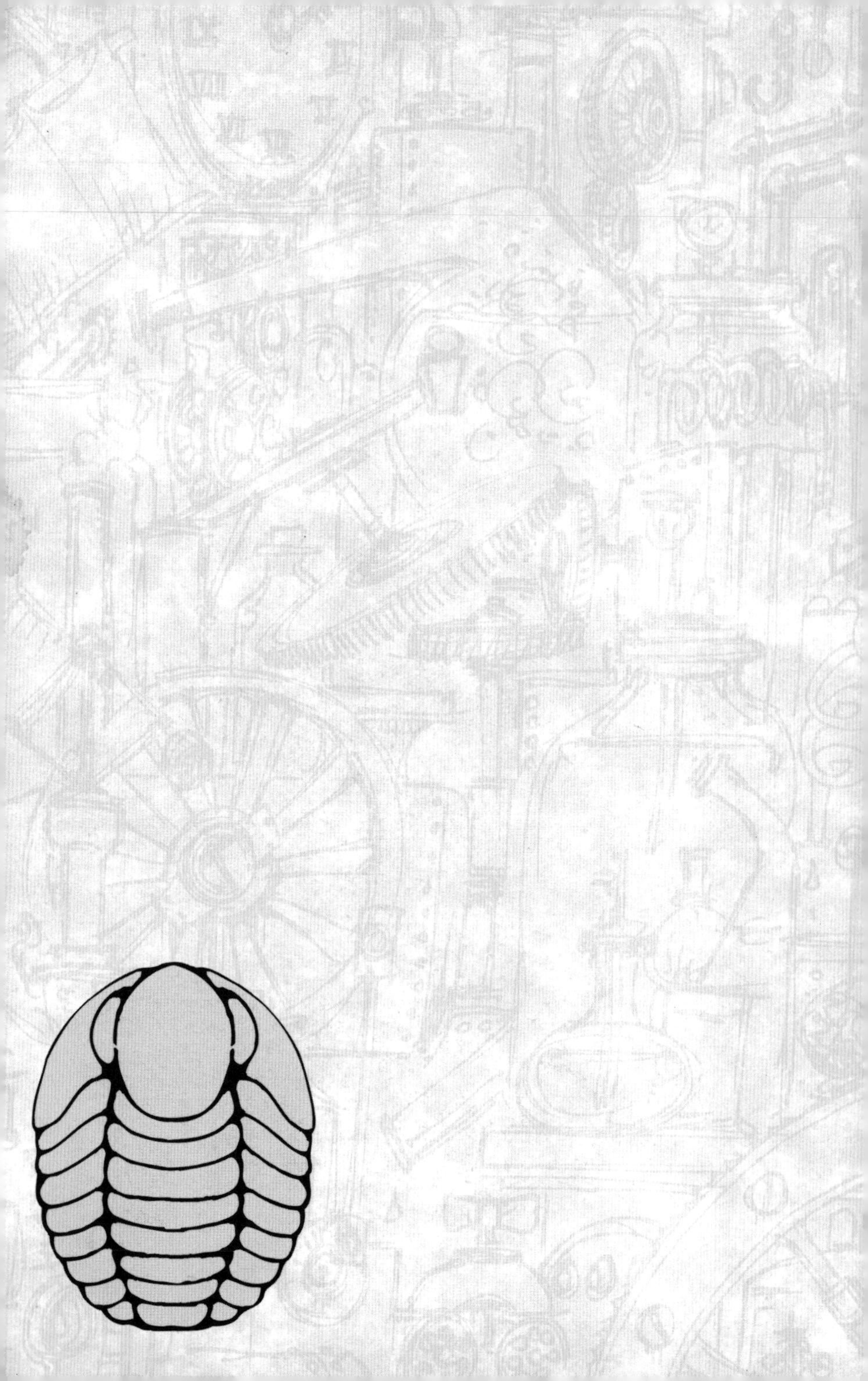

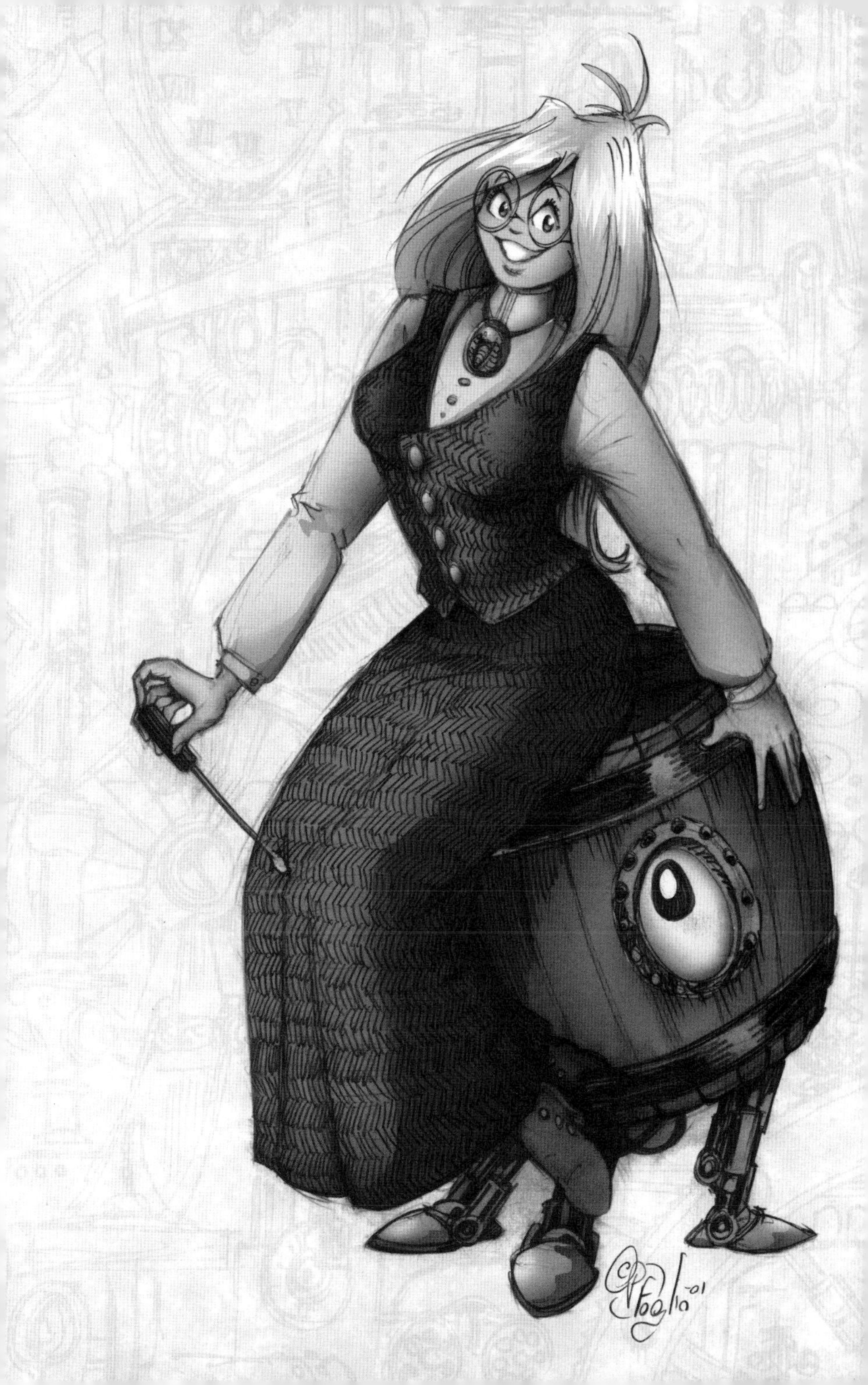

THE ADVENTURES CONTINUE AT:

WWW.GIRL·GENIUS.NET

MONDAY · WEDNESDAY · FRIDAY